Time Out

Toronto

timeout.com/toronto

D0778327

Penguin Books

PENGUIN BOOKS

Published by the Penguin Group
Penguin Books Ltd, 80 Strand, London WC2R ORL, England
Penguin Books USA Inc., 375 Hudson Street, New York, New York 10014, USA
Penguin Books Australia Ltd, 250 Camberwell Road, Camberwell, Victoria 3124, Australia
Penguin Books Canada Ltd, 10 Alcorn Avenue, Toronto, Ontario, Canada M4V 3B2
Penguin Books (NZ) Ltd, cnr Rosedale and Airborne Roads, Albany, Auckland, New Zealand

Penguin Books Ltd, Registered Offices: Harmondsworth, Middlesex, England

First published 2003
10 9 8 7 6 5 4 3 2 1

Colour reprographics by Icon, Crowne House, 56-58 Southwark Street, London SE1 1UN
Printed and bound by Cayfosa-Quebecor, Ctra. de Caldes, Km 3 08 130 Sta, Perpètua de Mogoda, Barcelona, Spain

Edited and designed by
Time Out Guides Limited
Universal House
251 Tottenham Court Road
London W1T 7AB
Tel + 44 (0)20 7813 3000
Fax + 44 (0)20 7813 6001
Email guides@timeout.com
www.timeout.com

Editorial

Editor Ruth Jarvis
Deputy Editor Ismay Atkins
Copy Editors Hugh Graham, Ronnie Haydon, Peter Watts
Consultant Editor Paul French
Listings Editor Bruce Gillespie
Proofreader Marion Moisy
Indexer Selena Cox

Editorial Director Peter Fiennes
Series Editor Ruth Jarvis
Deputy Series Editor Jonathan Cox
Guides Co-ordinator Anna Norman

Design

Group Art Director John Oakey
Art Director Mandy Martin
Art Editor Scott Moore
Senior Designer Lucy Grant
Designer Sarah Edwards
Digital Imaging Dan Conway
Ad Make-up Glen Impey
Picture Editor Kerri Littlefield
Deputy Picture Editor Kit Burnet
Picture Desk Trainee Bella Wood

Advertising

Group Commercial Director Lesley Gill
Sales Director Mark Phillips
International Sales Manager Ross Canadé
Advertisement Director, North American Guides Liz Howell
Advertsing in the US co-ordinated by Time Out New York
Alison Tocci (Publisher), Tom Oesau (Advertising
Production Manager), Maggie Puddu (Assistant to
the Publisher
Advertising Assistant Sabrina Ancilleri

Administration

Chairman Tony Elliott
Chief Operating Officer Kevin Ellis
Managing Director Mike Hardwick
Group Marketing Director Christine Cort
Marketing Manager Mandy Martinez
US Publicity & Marketing Associate Rosella Albanese
Group General Manager Nichola Coulthard
Group Financial Director Rick Waterlow
Guides Production Director Mark Lamond
Production Controller Samantha Furniss
Accountant Sarah Bostock

Contributors

Introduction Ruth Jarvis. **History** Hugh Graham (*Made in Toronto* Paul French). **Toronto Today** Paul French. **Hollywood North** Pamela Cuthbert. **Literary Toronto** Brent Ledger. **Accommodation** Patchen Barss. **Sightseeing: Introduction** Ruth Jarvis. **Downtown Toronto** Patchen Barss (Waterfront, *Walk on: Toronto Islands*, Entertainment District, Dundas Square, Chinatown, Cabbagetown, *Walk on: Cabbagetown*), Paul French (*Citytv*, *It's all a façade*, *Eco-worriers*), Ellen Himelfarb (*Nation states: China*), Steve Korver (*Bart was here*), Brent Ledger (Financial District, University, Church & Wellesley, *Molly Wood's Bush*), Steve Veale (St Lawrence). **Midtown** Patchen Barss (*Beaver tales* Steve Korver). **West End** Patchen Barss (*Nation states: Italy, Portugal & Poland* Ellen Himelfarb). **North Side** Patchen Barss (*Praise be to Bond* Paul French). **East Side** Steve Veale, Bruce Gillespie (*Nation states: Greece & India* Ellen Himelfarb). **Restaurants & Cafés** Ellen Himelfarb. **Bars** Patchen Barss (*Bloody Caesar!* Paul French, *Killing me softly with your song* Ellen Himelfarb, *Beer Haul* Steve Korver). **Shops & Services** Ellen Himelfarb. **Festivals & Events** Brent Ledger. **Children** Ellen Himelfarb. **Comedy** Patchen Barss (*Borderline funny* Steve Korver). **Film** Pamela Cuthbert. **Galleries** Sherri Hay. **Gay & Lesbian** Brent Ledger. **Music** Patchen Barss (*Local hero: Hawksley Workman* Will Fulford-Jones). **Nightlife** Ellen Himelfarb. **Sport & Fitness** Perry Stern. **Theatre** Kamal Al-Solaylee. **Trips Out of Town: Getting Started** Steve Veale. **Niagara Falls & Around** Steve Veale, Paul French, Ruth Jarvis. **Quick Trips** Steve Veale. **Further Afield** Steve Veale (*Northern desires* Steve Korver). **Directory** Bruce Gillespie (Media, *Local hero: Ted Rogers* Paul French).

Maps JS Graphics (john@jsgraphics.co.uk).

Photography Hannah Levy, except page 8 Ontario Archives; pages 9, 10, 11 Mike Filey; page 15 (left) Linda Fitzgerald; page 15 (right) Rex Features; page 20 Fraser Photos; page 21 John Bardwell; page 23 Martin Mordecai; page 25 Ken Woroner; page 245 Steven Elphick; page 245 the Bridgeman Art Library. The following images were provided by the featured establishments/artists: pages 166, 168, 169, 175, 180, 181, 211, 237, 240, 243, 247.

The Editor would like to thank Shane Armstrong, the Bartending School of Ontario, Cynthia Brouse, Sinead Canevin, Hugh Graham, Heather Jackson, Cathy Llmb, Aubrey Marshall, Marion Moisy, Sandy Pandya, Adam Sternbergh, Catherine Tunnacliffe, Lyne Wylie.

Contents

Introduction

No offence, but Toronto isn't the most visually impressive city you'll ever see. Its planning is somewhat arbitary, its past often overlaid, its lakefront potential largely wasted and, the needle of the CN Tower notwithstanding, its skyline modest. But we all know that (vertical) size is not important. It's a real, street-level city, in its vigorous youth, with none of the fin-de-siècle lassitude of a long history, and a future impatiently awaited.

You'll hear the bragadoccio so often, you might wonder if it's overcompensation. Toronto is the powerhouse of the Canadian economy, its media heart, the place to which people flock from all over Canada and the world, a city in a growth spurt. It has the world's third biggest Mardi Gras, second most important film festival, third biggest English-language theatre scene, great restaurants and so diverse a population that the UN deemed it the world's most multicultural city back in 1989. Perhaps the angst also comes from the fact that Toronto is confident, arrogant even, about its self-awarded status as Canada's greatest city, but insecure globally. The two go together to a degree. Canada itself has something of a branding problem, so city envy is intrinsic.

You will find your opinions of the city are frequently sought. The irony is that while Toronto is preoccupied by its global status, or perceived lack of it, visitors like it just the way it is. It's big, metropolitan and culturally abuzz, without being dirty, dangerous or terminally congested. Even in the centre, it is still entirely itself, a real non-identikit city with lots of small, individual shops and restaurants, working industry and a positive attitude. If visitors find it initially unimpressive, partly because of its urgent PR, they soon get into the swing: roll with the fact that Toronto has few obvious 'sights' as such, take the streetcar into its diverse neighbourhoods, eat out and go out, take time to let it grow on you – just pretend you live here and you'll understand why so many people actually do.

Recently, plans have been announced for some world-class (a frequently arising adjective here) cultural venues: a new opera house and revamps of the two main museums, the Royal Ontario Museum and the Art Gallery of Ontario by, respectively, Daniel Libeskind and native son Frank Gehry. So in the not-too-distant future, when a local asks you what you think of Toronto, you can answer positively, short-circuit your interlocuter's need for reassurance and get right back to enjoying the place.

ABOUT THE TIME OUT CITY GUIDES

The *Time Out Toronto Guide* is one of an expanding series of Time Out City Guides produced by the people behind London and New York's successful listings magazines. Our guides are all written and updated by resident experts who have striven to provide you with all the most up-to-date information you'll need to explore the city, whether you're a local or first-time visitor.

THE LOWDOWN ON THE LISTINGS

Above all, we've tried to make this book as useful as possible. Addresses, telephone numbers, website, transport information, opening times, admission prices and credit card details are all included in our listings, as are postal codes for anywhere you might want to write to. And, as far as possible, we've given details of facilities, services and events, all checked and correct at the time we went to press. However, owners and managers can change their arrangements at any time,

and many outdoor activities and venues in Toronto and southern Ontario operate to seasonal timetables and often close altogether in winter. Before you go out of your way, we'd strongly advise you to telephone and check opening times and other particulars. While every effort has been made to ensure the accuracy of the information contained in this guide, the publishers cannot accept responsibility for any errors it may contain.

PRICES AND PAYMENT

We have noted whether venues take credit cards but have only listed the major cards – American Express (**AmEx**), Diners Club (**DC**), Discover (**Disc**; seldom accepted in Toronto), MasterCard (**MC**) and Visa (**V**). Many business will also accept other cards, including **JCB**. Virtually all shops, restaurants and attractions will accept US dollar travellers' cheques issued by a major financial institution (such as American Express).

The prices we've supplied should be treated as guidelines, not gospel. Fluctuating exchange rates and inflation can cause charges, in shops and restaurants particularly, to change rapidly. If prices vary wildly from those we've quoted, ask whether there's a good reason. If not, go elsewhere. Then please write and let us know. We aim to give the best and most up-to-date advice, so we always want to know if you've been badly treated or overcharged.

THE LIE OF THE LAND

Toronto's geography is easy to grasp. To make it even easier, we have divided the city into areas, which are shown on the Toronto Transport & Areas map on page 284. Our area divisions are based on local usage but as there are no formal boundaries we have occasionally used arbitrary divisions. These areas are defined in our Sightseeing chapters and used through out the book, both in addresses and chapter subdivisions. We've included cross streets

There is an online version of this guide, as well as weekly events listings for over 35 international cities, at **www.timeout.com**.

in our addresses, so you can find your way about more easily. And there's a series of fully indexed street maps, along with Southern Ontario and Toronto Overview maps, at the back of the guide, starting on page 272. Venues listed in the book that fall into the area covered have a page and grid reference to take you directly to the right square.

TELEPHONE NUMBERS

Greater Toronto has three area codes: 416, 905 and 647, with 416 the most central. To dial from anywhere within the city to anywhere else, even within the same area code, you need to dial the code followed by the seven-digit number. To dial long-distance numbers, precede the area code with 1 (note that some 905 numbers are long distance). Numbers preceded by 1-800, 1-888, 1-877 and 1-866 can be called free of charge from Toronto (and usually the rest of Canada and the US) but incur an international charge from abroad. We have stipulated where phone numbers are charged at non-standard rates (though note that premium-rate lines are not generally available outside Canada and the US.

Canada shares the US's international code of 1 (so calling from the US is the same as making a long-distance national call). From abroad, dial your country's exit code (00 in the UK) followed by 1 and then the area code and number.

For more details of telephone use, *see p261*.

ESSENTIAL INFORMATION

For all the practical information you'll need for visiting the city – including visa and customs information, disabled access, emergency telephone numbers, a list of useful websites and the lowdown on the local transport network – turn to the **Directory** chapter at the back of this guide. It starts on page 250.

LET US KNOW WHAT YOU THINK

We hope you enjoy the *Time Out Toronto Guide*, and we'd like to know what you think of it. We welcome tips for places that you consider we should include in future editions and take notice of your criticism of our choices. There's a reader's reply card at the back of this book – or you can email us at guides@timeout.com.

Advertisers

We would like to stress that no establishment has been included in this guide because it has advertised in any of our publications and no payment of any kind has influenced any review. The opinions given in this book are those of Time Out writers and entirely independent.

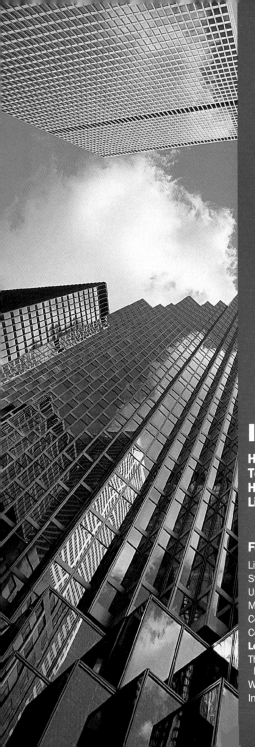

In Context

Once aimed at marauding Americans, a **Fort York** cannon. *See p7.*

History

Toronto's journey from hunting ground to concrete jungle.

The New World. That's what the British called North America. But Toronto had been populated for thousands of years. Hunters roamed the icy wilderness where the city now stands at least 13,000 years ago, pursuing caribou and bison with their stone-tipped spears. By 1000 BC, the ice had retreated and the nomadic types had been replaced by Toronto's first settlers: the ancestors of the Iroquois, who built villages along the lake and grew crops. By the 17th century, the Huron tribe had moved in. They christened the area Toronto, which means 'meeting place', because it was situated right at the southern end of their forest trails to the Upper Great Lakes. And it was these Native Canadians who brought the first white man to Toronto in 1615.

FRENCH TORONTO

Étienne Brûlé was a *coureur de bois* – an adventurous young Frenchman sent into the wilds by Samuel Champlain, his fur trader boss in New France (Quebec), to befriend the Indians. Facing frequent attacks from the fierce Iroquois, the French allied themselves to a rival tribe, the Huron, who showed Brûlé Toronto on

9 September, 1615. During the 17th and 18th centuries, French and English fur traders were engaged in a frenetic expansionist rivalry, building trading posts to gain control of the rich hunting grounds around the Great Lakes.

It wasn't until 1720 that the French established a permanent trading post in Toronto, by which time most of the Huron tribe had died from European diseases. Over the next 40 years, Toronto's population consisted of a mixture of Mississauga and Iroquois Indians, Jesuit missionaries and French fur traders who exchanged trinkets with the natives in return for pelts. To consolidate their supremacy, the French built Fort Rouillé (also known as Fort Toronto) in 1751, where the Canadian National Exhibition now stands. But in 1756 England and France went to war, and in 1759 the British took Toronto. Rather than surrender their fort, the French burned it to the ground in retreat.

While the 1763 Treaty of Paris brought an end to French rule in Toronto, the British took little interest in their new possession, leaving it undisturbed for 30 years. But when Britain lost the American Revolution in 1783, the city suddenly assumed strategic importance.

In Context

MUDDY YORK

After the American Revolution, thousands of United Empire Loyalists fled the US to settle in British North America. To handle the massive influx, the British government created a new province in 1791: Upper Canada, to the west of Quebec, was to have English systems of law, land tenure and politics.

The British appointed John Graves Simcoe, a decorated soldier who had fought in the American Revolution, as the province's lieutenant-governor. His mission was to carve a capital out of the wilderness and Toronto seemed perfect from a military and naval standpoint. It had a sheltered harbour and a good 20-mile stretch of water separating it from the US. Not only that, but Lord Dorchester, the governor of British North America, had already purchased the site from the Mississauga Indians in 1787 to secure the area for British trappers. For the mighty sum of £1,700, the British gained a portion of land 14 miles (22.5 kilometres) across and 28 (45 kilometres) deep.

On 30 July 1793, Simcoe arrived from England – after a brief stint at Niagara – in the forest that was Toronto, with his wife Elizabeth (*see p8* **Living the wildlife**). One of the first things he did was to change Toronto's name to York, in honour of Frederick, Duke of York, a son of King George III. Simcoe, after all, was on a mission to bring English civilisation to the New World. Moreover, he professed an 'abhorrence of Indian names'.

The second thing Simcoe did was to order his regiment, the Queen's Rangers, to construct a garrison, Fort York, for protection from a possible American invasion. He also had his men survey Yonge Street, which replaced the Indian trails to the Upper Great Lakes. Named after the British war secretary, Sir George Yonge, the street would eventually become the world's longest, starting at the lakeshore and running 1,178 miles (1,875 kilometres) to the north-west, ending at Rainy River, Minnesota. Yonge Street facilitated fur trade and allowed farmers a route to bring their goods to market. Other roads were also being laid – a very orderly, ten-block grid including King, Front, George, Adelaide and Berkeley Streets – which attracted merchants and craftsmen to the area. But Simcoe's main interest in Yonge Street was strategic: it could prove a useful escape route from marauding Americans.

Simcoe also ordered the construction of the first parliament buildings, which were erected in 1796. To placate grumpy colonial officials, resentful of being transferred to this marshy outpost, he granted them a series of free 100-acre 'park' lots north of Queen Street. The roads that ran between these farms were often given

family names, including Finch, Sheppard, Lawrence and Eglinton. This system of land concessions resulted in Toronto's very rectangular, evenly spaced layout. Despite Simcoe's generosity, the new residents were disparaging of the town, referring to it as 'Muddy York' because of its notoriously squishy streets. They were, after all, essentially living in the wilderness: packs of wolves attacked farmers' sheep, bears attacked horses, and deer were commonly seen on the streets.

THE WAR OF 1812

By 1812, York was positively civilised: it had a tailor, a baker, a brewer, a watchmaker and an apothecary to serve the population of 700. The ruling elite built dignified mansions along King Street, and a British-style landed gentry was firmly taking shape in York. York's leaders were all Church of England Tories, and fiercely Loyalist – they were horrified by American notions of democracy. And this anti-American sentiment was about to intensify.

On 18 June, 1812, America declared war on Britain. Former president Thomas Jefferson had said that 'the capture of Canada is a mere matter of marching'. President James Madison wanted to establish a trade monopoly on all of North America's natural resources. Americans were also furious at the devious British practices of kidnapping their sailors at sea and supplying hostile Indian tribes with guns.

> **'American immigrants, previously welcome additions to the town, were now banned by York's staunchly British, aristocratic leaders.'**

Within a year of declaring war, York's worst nightmare – an American invasion – became a grim reality. In April 1813, 14 ships carrying 1,700 American troops invaded the town, succeeded in blowing up Fort York and burning the parliament buildings to the ground. But although Americans won the Battle of York, the US army suffered devastating losses and failed to take the rest of Canada. By 1814, the British had negotiated an end to the war.

THE FAMILY COMPACT

In retaliation for the burning of Fort York, a group of angry local soldiers went down to Washington, DC, in 1814 and set fire to the president's residence. (It was painted white soon after to cover up the charred wood, and subsequently became known as the White

Living the wildlife

Elizabeth Posthuma Simcoe had an idyllic life in Devon – a pretty country estate, servants at her beck and call, and a lively social calendar consisting of balls, parties and more balls. Yet in 1793 this high-society wife traded her life of privilege for a humble canvas tent in the Canadian wilderness, joining her husband, Colonel John Simcoe, on his daunting colonial mission: to carve a new capital city, Toronto, out of a forest.

Remembered by historians as the first person to fall in love with Toronto, Simcoe adored the wildlife, spending her time riding, painting watercolours, observing nature and writing in her diary. She was particularly fond of the peninsula, now the island, where she whiled away happy days on horseback, picking wild grapes and lily of the valley and being dazzled by the delightful clarity of the water. A typical entry reads: 'Rode on the peninsula from one till four... saw Loons swimming... They make a noise like a Man hollowing in a tone of distress. The air on these Sands is peculiarly clear and fine. The Indians esteem this place so healthy that they... stay here when they are ill.' Indeed, the Indians provided a constant source of fascination for Simcoe, who thought them as dignified as figures painted by the Old Masters. 'They are extremely handsome and have a superior air... To see a Birch Canoe managed with that inexpressible ease... which is the characteristic of an Indian is the prettiest sight imaginable.'

Simcoe was also intrigued by the new foods she encountered: cranberries were a 'less bitter' version of elderberries, raccoon 'tasted like lamb if eaten with mint sauce', while the Canadian wild ducks were tastier than in England by virtue of feeding on wild rice. The wildlife was another revelation, particularly the seasonal migratory flights of pigeons, geese and ducks – 'the air is sometimes darkened by them' – and the thrilling presence of bears and wolves. Rattlesnakes are mentioned on more than one occasion in her diary, although Simcoe seems more curious than terrified. Her good-natured curiosity did not, however, extend to mosquitoes. One evening she observed, 'it is scarcely possible to write or use my hands, which are always occupied in killing them'.

While the winters were severe – 'weather so cold some water spilt near the Stove froze immediately' – she very rarely grumbled, despite spending much of her first year living in a tent. One of her favourite winter activities was to take her coterie of lady friends to the beach, where they would build a fire and toast venison. Back at York, the ladies would entertain themselves at night by holding dances – 'there are ten ladies here and as they dance reels we can make up a ball' – and playing games, although on one occasion, despite wearing three fur tippets, Simcoe 'was so cold I could hardly hold my cards... this is the first time we have felt want of a ceiling'. Come summer, she would often retreat deep into the forest to Castle Frank, the Simcoes' summer home in Rosedale, a wooden cottage built in the style of a Greek temple.

By the time her husband was ordered to return to England in 1796, Simcoe didn't want to leave. On their day of departure, her diary entry reads: 'Took leave of Mrs McGill and Miss Crookshank... could not eat... Cried all day'. Upon arriving back in England, she observes dolefully that the fields looked 'so damp, so cheerless, so uncomfortable from the want of our bright Canadian Sun'.

The junction of King and Yonge
Streets in the 1860s.

House.) American immigrants, who had
previously been welcome additions to the
town, were now banned by York's staunchly
British, aristocratic leaders.

Indeed, York's ruling political regime,
composed mainly of lawyers, doctors, judges
and Church officials, was so tight-knit, and
prone to intermarriage, that it became known
as the Family Compact. This elite group's
stranglehold on politics would come to be
resented as the population grew. And grow the
population did. In Britain, the demobilisation
of 400,000 soldiers following the Napoleonic
wars, coupled with a depression and the mass
evictions of Scottish crofters, prompted a
massive exodus to Canada. In the 20 years
following the war, the town's population
increased from 700 to 9,250.

The Old Guard suffered a blow in 1834, the
year the town became incorporated as a city,
when a bill was passed to change York's name
back to Toronto. Traditionalists were opposed
to the move – York sounded more British.
One politician offered the following analysis:
'Toronto for poets – York for men of business.'
On this occasion, poetry won the day, although
the likely reason for the change was growing
frustration at being referred to as 'Little York',
not the last time Torontonians would bristle at
comparisons to New York.

THE 1837 REBELLION

Around this time, resentment at the Family
Compact's political dominance reached fever
pitch. Even Charles Dickens, who visited the
city in 1842, was moved to comment on the
city's Conservative bent. 'The wild and rabid
Toryism of Toronto is, I speak seriously,
appalling'. Leading the resistance was William
Lyon Mackenzie, a Scottish firebrand who had
been publishing anti-Tory rants in his own
newspaper, the *Colonial Advocate*, since 1825.
Mackenzie called the ruling elite 'thieves',
arguing that too much money, land and power
was held by too few. The main target for his
scorn was Bishop John Strachan, whom he
dubbed 'the governor's jackal'. Mackenzie's
bilious columns became such a worry for the
Family Compact that Conservatives broke into
his office and threw his printing presses into
the lake. But it was too late: Mackenzie had
already amassed a devoted following of
farmers, merchants and new immigrants, and
was soon elected Toronto's first mayor in 1834.

Mackenzie hoped that a provincial election in
1836 would bring his party, the Reformers, to
power in the province of Upper Canada. But the
Tories won what was perceived to be a crooked
election – one of the Conservatives' ploys was to
offer free booze to anyone who voted for them –
and Mackenzie called for rebellion.

The **Great Fire** of 1904 destroyed 20 acres, including this stretch of Bay Street. *See p12.*

On 5 December 1837, Mackenzie and 700 rebels gathered outside the city, at what is now Yonge and Eglinton, outside Montgomery's Tavern. The plan was to march on the city, seize the 5,000 guns stored in City Hall, and capture the governor. But the sheriff, William B Jarvis, had been tipped off, and his militia crushed the rebellion. Mackenzie fled to America and lived there until 1849, when he was pardoned. He returned to Upper Canada and was elected to the Legislature, where he served until his death in 1858.

Despite the failure of the rebellion, a new era of more democratic government followed, coinciding with another wave of immigration. In addition to the British influx, scores of freed black slaves arrived from America. The British Empire officially outlawed slavery in 1834, and by the 1850s, blacks comprised three per cent of the city's 25,000-strong population.

Another group found refuge in York – the Irish. They arrived in droves, particularly in the 1840s, to escape the potato famine at home, and soon comprised a third of Toronto's population. Many were Catholic, which provoked sectarian tensions with the Irish Protestants. Riots on July 12, the day of the Orangemen parades, became an annual occurrence.

While immigrants flooded the city, Native Canadians disappeared from the area. Many died of European diseases, while some settled on nearby Indian reserves – such as the Six Nations Reserve near Brantford – established in treaties with the British throughout the period.

VICTORIAN TORONTO

As immigrants poured in, Toronto made the transition from rural backwater to bustling industrial city. The construction of a north–south railway line to America in the

1850s, followed by a coast-to-coast national line in the 1880s, further cemented Toronto's prosperity. In addition to the existing industries – sawmills, flour mills, tanneries, furniture, wagons, soap processing, leather goods, brewing, publishing – the city became a centre for ship manufacturing and a trading hub for timber imports and exports. Banks appeared everywhere, merchant empires were founded, railroad tycoons emerged and the Toronto Stock Exchange was opened in 1852.

If it was an age of industry, it was also an age of leisure. In 1858, Toronto's freakish weather for once provided the city with a blessing: the creation of Toronto Island. Formerly a peninsula, the island was formed when a storm destroyed the spit of land that joined it to the mainland. Taking a ferry across the harbour soon became a summertime tradition: holiday cottages went up, as did an amusement park, bicycle trails and the Royal Canadian Yacht Club.

In 1867, Canada gained independence from Britain, and Toronto was named the capital of the new province of Ontario. An accolade, but competition was hardly stiff, and locals were (and remain) more than miffed that Queen Victoria, apparently on the basis of a few paintings she'd seen, favoured Ottawa as the national capital. However, as a small compensation, Toronto finally got some decent shopping. In 1869, a young Irishman named Timothy Eaton opened a general store at the corner of Yonge and Queen. His new shop offered a revolutionary and exciting sales technique: satisfaction guaranteed or your money back. The successful shop quickly evolved into a bona fide department store, spawning a mail order catalogue that eventually reached all corners of Canada.

During this prosperous Victorian era, Toronto's architecture also became downright glamorous. The opening of the University of Toronto in 1843 was significant for more than just academic reasons: it yielded some of the city's most ornate buildings, most notably the spectacular Romanesque University College (King's College Circle, 1856). Throughout the city, the dignified colonial town of plain Georgian buildings gave way to a new craze for neo-Gothic. Jarvis and St George Streets and the neighbourhood of Rosedale became hotbeds of Romanticism in a flurry of gargoyles and turrets. American author John Updike called buildings 'lovingly erected brick valentines to a distant dowager queen'. Surviving examples include the Keg Mansion (515 Jarvis Street), the Flatiron building (49 Wellington Street East, 1892), the York Club (135 St George Street, 1892), the Ontario Legislature at Queen's Park (1892) and the Old City Hall.

Some of the most striking buildings of the period were Gothic churches, such as St James' Cathedral (65 Church Street, 1850). The city's

Stormy weather

Toronto is no stranger to freak storms; they usually originate somewhere near the Arctic Circle and send the city scrambling for shovels. But on 15 October 1954, Toronto's weather was more Caribbean-on-a-bad-day than Tuktoyaktuk. Hurricane Hazel had already crushed Haiti on 5 October, killing 200 with its 115mph (185kmph) winds. By some crazy twist of nature, Hazel made its way north to Canada, gathering strength over Lake Ontario, before wreaking havoc on an unsuspecting Toronto. Clueless weather forecasters predicted heavy rain. And the rest. The city got rained on all right – nine inches (20cm) fell over the course of a day – and wind gusts of up to 72mph (116kmph). Creeks spilled over banks, ravines flooded and many homes were swept away, particularly in the new suburb of Etobicoke. Eighty-three people died in the storm, Toronto's worst-ever natural disaster.

But from such tragedy, some positive elements emerged. In the aftermath of the storm, new laws forbade the construction of homes in flood plains, and the city bought up all undeveloped ravine properties and turned them into parks. Today, Toronto's network of romantic, wooded ravine parks is extensive, forming valuable green lungs for the city's population and a verdant backdrop to childhood games, dog walkers, joggers and summer picnics. As Toronto writer Robert Fulford put it: 'The ravines are to Toronto what canals are to Venice and hills are to San Francisco. They are the heart of the city's emotional geography.'

preponderance of spires, coupled with its puritanical mores, soon earned it the sobriquet 'Toronto the Good'. Anti-vice laws at various times in the city's history would include a ban on alcohol between 1916 and 1927, and Sunday bans on tobogganing, streetcars and films. Department stores drew curtains across their windows on Sundays, and public houses were closed on that day until 1971. Leopold Infeld, Einstein's collaborator, famously said that he hoped he would die on a Saturday 'so that I won't have to spend another Sunday in Toronto'.

The city's rather prissy outlook was coupled with a continued devotion to Queen and country. The Queen's Jubilee was celebrated in spectacular style in 1897, and on 25 October 1899, a massive parade sent off thousands of Toronto troops to fight in the Boer War, in a frenzy of Union Jacks and weeping mothers.

20TH-CENTURY TORONTO

If the 19th century ended in a surge of imperial fervour, then Toronto's 20th century started with a blaze of a different kind. On 19 April 1904, fire broke out at a downtown neckwear factory on Wellington Street West, and within eight hours, 122 buildings and 20 acres of downtown had been destroyed.

> **'When war came, citizens sang Rule Britannia in the streets, and thousands of volunteers poured into the armouries.'**

While the Great Fire devastated the city on one level – 6,000 people lost their jobs and the business district was destroyed – Toronto bounced back quickly. How could it not, with the wave of immigrants flooding in? In 1894, the population was 168,000; by 1924 it had risen to 542,000 and by 1934 it was 640,000. And they weren't all British. Jews from Russia and Poland settled in Kensington Market and opened textile businesses around King and Spadina, the garment district; Greeks worked on the railroads and settled in the Danforth. By 1921, more than 8,200 Torontonians were of Italian ancestry, many of whom built roads and bridges. The Chinese settled around Dundas Street West, opening laundries and restaurants.

The New World wasn't all bliss. Many Irish labourers settled in Cabbagetown, an area in the east of the city named for the vegetables they grew to feed themselves. Toronto writer Hugh Garner described Cabbagetown – now a gentrified neighbourhood – as 'North America's only Anglo-Saxon slum'.

WORLD WAR I

As is often perversely the case, war – in this case World War I – brought renewed prosperity to the city, not to mention another bout of imperial zeal. Citizens sang *Rule Britannia* in the streets, and thousands of volunteers poured into armouries. Seventy thousand men – one seventh of Toronto's population – left Toronto for Europe; 13,000 died.

The city played a major role in Britain's war effort, serving as a training ground for pilots. Toronto companies manufactured aeroplanes, including the famous Flying Jennies, and explosives and munitions. Jewish textile firms made blankets, tents and uniforms. Women went to work in large numbers, manufacturing weapons and volunteering for nursing duty with the Red Cross. In fact, a young Amelia Earhart was a nurse in Toronto during the war, and it was here, while watching pilots at Armour Heights, that she caught the flying bug.

THE ROARING '20S

The end of the war was followed by a mini economic slump, but by 1925, Toronto was roaring, spurred along by the age of the automobile. American firms such as General Motors and Ford set up plants in and around the city to avoid a 35 per cent Canadian tariff on car imports. Not everyone was cruising around in Buicks, however: the Toronto Transit Commission was founded in 1921, after the public voted to establish a publicly owned and operated mass transit system. Soon 575 electric streetcars cruised the streets.

The city was also reaping the benefits of a mining boom in Northern Ontario, triggered by the discovery there of gold, copper, nickel and silver. The price of wheat on the international market also sky-rocketed during this period, which meant that the agricultural machinery plants of Massey-Harris flourished.

Such a wealthy city required a spectacular hotel, and in 1929 the Royal York, with its 1,600 rooms, running water and a ballroom, opened. The largest hotel in the British Empire, it was built by the Canadian Pacific Railway for easy access to the similarly magnificent Union Station (1927), a Beaux Arts gem that epitomised the grandeur of the railway age.

Wealth provided riches for culture seekers, who flocked to the Art Gallery of Ontario to see the striking landscape paintings of The Group of Seven, Canada's most famous painters, or view Egyptian mummies at the Royal Ontario Museum. Acts such as Al Jolson entertained the masses at the Royal Alexandra Theatre, and hometown girl Mary Pickford, the world's biggest silent movie star, drew the hordes to the Shea's Hippodrome.

Urban legend

When Jane Jacobs moved from New York to Toronto in 1968, she was already a living legend. Her 1961 tome, *The Death and Life of Great American Cities*, was a merciless and eloquent critique of urban planning mistakes, a bible for urban activists the world over. Jacobs challenged the sterile modernist housing developments of the '50s, claiming such projects killed cities: in her eyes, Le Corbusier, with his utopian visions of high-rise living and motorways, was Satan. Healthy cities, said Jane Jacobs, were made up of densely populated, messy, bustling downtown neighbourhoods: a jumbled mix of residential and business, old and new buildings, bustling street life and public transport. She loved Toronto because, unlike so many American cities, there was still a heart to the place: it hadn't yet been bulldozed to make way for freeways and housing projects.

But when Jacobs arrived in Toronto, fleeing the oppression of Vietnam-era America, she discovered that a proposed highway, the Spadina Expressway, was set to rip through her downtown neighbourhood, the Annex. 'In the mind's eye, one could see the great trees and jolly Edwardian porches falling before the onslaught', she said. Jacobs led a furious campaign against the Expressway, which would have turned Toronto into another Detroit – a sad, hollow, crime-ridden core surrounded by a ring of suburbs. The defeat of the plan in 1971 was a defining moment in the city's history. Because despite its sleek downtown skyline, Toronto is arguably still a city defined by its great old neighbourhoods – the Annex, Little Italy, Kensington Market, Cabbagetown, Church and Wellesley, Chinatown, Forest Hill, the Beaches – and the city has Jane Jacobs to thank.

The good times came to an end with the stockmarket crash of 1929, and by the time the Great Depression hit in 1932, there was 30 per cent unemployment in the city. Queues formed around the block for soup kitchens. Poverty lead to bigotry, with signs that read: 'No Jews, Niggers or Dogs' appearing on the beaches. The scorching summer of 1936 compounded the misery, with temperatures reaching 41°C (106°F), coinciding with a polio epidemic.

WORLD WAR II

World War II brought the city back to life. As in the previous two wars, Toronto rushed to sign up for military duty – 3,300 would ultimately die in combat – but along with the exodus of soldiers, the city experienced its own European invasion: British children and Norwegian men. Eight thousand young Britons were shipped to Toronto to sit out the war safely, while Norway sent its airforce to the city to learn how to fly. Once again the city functioned as an aviation centre, with local companies manufacturing some 3,000 airplanes, including the Mosquito bombers that some experts believe won the air war. Women once again took up work in the factories, producing 100,000 machine guns. And in the tunnels of Casa Loma – the city's most eccentric architectural folly – anti-submarine weapons were developed. Behind this industriousness lay a continued fierce loyalty to the Mother Country, which helped Canadian citizens endure rationing on alcohol, sugar, meat and tea, and frequent 'dim-outs'.

In 1940, when the Toronto Squadron were killed in the skies above London, the Toronto Symphony Orchestra played 'There'll Always Be an England' at Massey Hall.

THE 1950S

Toronto's white-bread, Little England persona was about to receive a makeover. In 1920, 80 per cent of the city's population was of British origin. By 1960, only 50 per cent of the population could make that claim, and by the 90s, well, the UN had declared Toronto the most multicultural city on the Earth – Toronto had more Italians than Florence, more blacks than Kingston, Jamaica, and more Chinese than any other city in the world outside China. After the war, Canada had relaxed its immigration laws, and it seemed the world came to Toronto. Russians, Yugoslavs, Poles, Hungarians and other many other Eastern Europeans poured into the city, as did Portuguese, Greeks and West Indians, followed later by further waves of immigration from India, Africa, Central and South America, and Asia.

By 1953, the population of the Toronto urban area had mushroomed to 1.2 million. Disputes between the city and the suburbs were growing frequent, and the need for unified social services was so great that an effective administrative solution was required. The result was the establishment of a new, overarching city government: the Municipality of Metropolitan Toronto, which would be comprised of the city of Toronto, plus five other

Made in Toronto

Inventions, icons and institutions that call Toronto home.

● Edward Rogers Sr invented the world's first alternating current (AC) radio tube in 1925, which enabled radios to be powered by ordinary household current. The 'batteryless' radio became the key factor in popularising radio usage.

● The discovery of insulin by Frederick Banting and Charles Best at the University of Toronto in 1921 is the most famous Canadian medical achievement. Insulin remains the only effective treatment for diabetes today.

● The world's first fully electronic toll highway, Highway 407. A camera records licence plates and a bill in sent in the mail.

● Film firsts: IMAX, the jumbo-sized movie screen company is based here, and the world's first purpose-built multiplex cinema, the 18-screen Cineplex Eaton Centre (now closed).

● The Avro Jetliner, which was built in the early 1950s by AV Roe, was the world's first regional jet, but never went into production. UK-based Hawker Siddley, AV Roe's parent company, made sure its own commercial jet, the Comet, took to the skies one week before the Avro Jetliner.

● The Four Seasons Hotel chain began in Toronto and its first property, the Inn on the Park, is in the suburb of Don Mills

● Tractor maker to the world Massey-Ferguson began life as the Massey-Harris

Company in Toronto in 1891. After free trade opened up with the United States in 1989, the company changed its name and moved south of the border.

● M.A.C. Cosmetics was founded by Torontonians in the 1980s

● The world's first permanent AIDS memorial is in Cawthra Park, Church & Wellesley.

● The Canadian Opera Company invented 'surtitles', projecting the (often) translated text of opera on a screen above the stage, and licenses the technology to opera companies around the world.

● Canada's wealthiest individual – by a long shot – and 14th richest in the world, is Kenneth Thomson, of Toronto. Forbes.com picks his pockets to be worth $16.4 billion. Thomson Corp publishes financial and legal information and once owned the UK-based Thomson Travel organisation and Britannia Airways. Mr Thomson has a 30 per cent stake in Bell Globemedia, which owns the *Globe and Mail* newspaper and CTV, Canada's largest private broadcaster. He is an avid art collector and in 2002 paid the third highest price ever for a painting, the *Massacre of the Innocents* by Peter Paul Rubens, for UK£49.5 million. But that doesn't mean that Thomson doesn't know a bargain when he sees one: he has been known to ride Toronto's subways and load up on discounted toothpaste, just like a regular guy.

---

suburban boroughs: North York, East York, York, Scarborough and Etobicoke, each with its own mayor. This new government would be responsible for major infrastructure, while the individual municipalities would still retain control over local matters.

The mayor of this new super-city, Fred Gardiner, had grand visions of a great North American metropolis with major highways running through it: the first, the monstrous Gardiner Expressway, was laid down during the '50s along the lakeshore, effectively cutting the city off from the lake. The 401, a mega-highway to the north of the city, followed soon after, as did malls, malls, malls and utopian, post-war suburbs, perfect for baby-boomers. Don Mills, built in 1952, was a modernist's dream, designed to be a self-contained suburb where the car was king. Scarborough, a pretty farming community, became a nightmare of

strip malls, factories and bungalows. Yorkdale, a giant mall adjacent to the 401 highway in north Toronto, followed in 1962.

In the city centre, developers started ripping down old Victorian and Edwardian buildings – which were seen as fading relics of colonial Toronto and the Depression – and replacing them with high-rise apartment buildings and office blocks. Between 1955 and 1975, 28,000 buildings were torn down in the city.

THE NEW TORONTO

It wasn't a complete travesty. Many pretty, centrally located neighbourhoods – the Annex, Rosedale, Forest Hill and Cabbagetown included – managed to avoid the wrecking balls. And the first subway line, consisting of 12 stations and running for 4.6 kilometres) (7.4 miles) underneath Yonge Street, opened in 1954. This was to be followed by new lines and

Toronto gets hip with **Joni Mitchell** (left) and **Neil Young** in the 1960s.

extensions throughout the remainder of the century, resulting in today's sprawling underground and suburban rail network.

Moreover, some of the new buildings were stunning. The Toronto Dominion Centre (1967), a cluster of four black steel and glass skyscrapers, was hailed as the crowning glory in the career of Ludwig Mies van der Rohe, one of the gods of modernist architecture.

> **' In 1947, Toronto voted to go 'wet', and the city's first cocktail bar, the Silver Rail, opened on Yonge Street, spawning a thriving bar culture.'**

The New City Hall, built in 1965, was another modernist classic. Designed by Finnish architect Viljo Rewell, this *Star Trek*-style spectacle – two semi-circular office towers surrounding a UFO-esque council chamber – was adjoined by a public square, symbolising the birth of a more civic-spirited city. Other modern gems included the gold-coated Royal Bank Plaza (1976), the atrium-style Eaton Centre shopping mall (1977) and the Toronto Reference Library (1977). But of all the new

buildings, the CN Tower (1976) was the most important symbolically. The world's largest freestanding structure, this majestic television tower became Toronto's Big Ben or Empire State Building, lending the city an instantly recognisable skyline. 'As the tower was being planned, Torontonians were starting to consider, with shy pleasure, the novel idea that their city might be attractive, even enviable', wrote journalist Robert Fulford.

THE CITY SWINGS

Along with this great wave of construction and immigration, the once uptight city was at last outgrowing its Waspy, prudish image. In 1947, the people of Toronto voted to go 'wet', and the city's first cocktail bar, the Silver Rail, opened on Yonge Street, spawning a thriving bar culture. A British writer who returned to this relatively louche city in 1959 said 'it was like finding a Jaguar parked in front of a vicarage and the padre inside with a pitcher of vodka martinis reading *Lolita*'.

By the 1960s, Toronto was becoming positively hedonistic. Spliff-smoking flower children colonised Yorkville, playing acoustic music in coffeehouses and forming Toronto's answer to San Francisco's Haight-Ashbury district. Here, Joni Mitchell, Neil Young and Leonard Cohen all played the circuit. In 1972, Toronto got a hip television station, Citytv, which caused a stir by showing blue movies in the wee hours. Around this time, strip joints and adult movie theatres opened along downtown Yonge Street – even now US tourists flock to the city for its famously permissive nudity and lap-dancing laws – as did bars frequented by Toronto's burgeoning gay community. Jarvis Street, once home to Toronto's wealthiest families, became the city's unofficial red light district. It wasn't all salacious: amid the general buzz, the city became home to an increasing number of marvellous writers, including Robertson Davies and Margaret Atwood, and in 1966, it got its own version of *The New Yorker. Toronto Life* magazine. The highly respected Toronto Film Festival made its debut in 1975, and the local government poured money into the theatre.

The thriving cultural scene attracted, and was strengthened by, American draft dodgers protesting against the Vietnam War. Another protester with vision was Jane Jacobs, the famed urban planning critic (*see p13* **Urban legend**), who in 1971 led a successful fight against the proposed Spadina Expressway, which would have destroyed several downtown neighbourhoods. This victory spurred a civic reform movement in the '70s that emphasised preservation of historic neighbourhoods, public transport and smart development, including valuable, publicly funded projects designed to lure visitors to the city: Ontario Place (a waterfront park) in 1971, and the Metro Zoo and Ontario Science Centre in 1974.

'The glamorous living and conspicuous consumption of the 1980s continued apace in the 1990s.'

Tourists certainly discovered Toronto in the '70s, but so also did architects, urban planners and journalists. The US media was impressed that a city of its size had managed to avoid the mistakes of many a crime-ridden, dying American city. *Time* magazine devoted a cover story to 'the world's newest great city', *Harper's* dubbed it 'the city that works' and the actor Peter Ustinov called it 'New York run by the Swiss'. And the National Geographic announced that 'the drab step-sister of Montreal has become worldly, wealthy and relatively problem-free'. In fact, Toronto officially took over from Montreal as Canada's most populous city in 1976, when its population hit 2,303,206.

THE 'WORLD CITY'
The 'me decade' brought some badly needed glamour and decadence to the city. Yorkville, once beatnik central, became the city's most

exclusive shopping district, its old Edwardian houses transformed into chi-chi boutiques, while bond traders snorted lines in its embarrassingly flashy bars. Formerly poor immigrant areas like Cabbagetown, Greektown and Little Italy were discovered, and gentrified, by yuppies; great for the restaurant scene, bad for house prices. The gay community colonised the Church and Wellesley district during the 1980s, with the focus of the bar scene shifting away from seedy Yonge Street to the friendlier, neighbourhood atmosphere of Church Street. The old Victorian piles in the area were renovated in the best of taste, quadrupling in price over the course of ten years, as did real estate throughout the city. As the population mushroomed – 65,000 new immigrants arrived in Toronto every year – a development boom saw modest suburban bungalows demolished in favour of gigantic 'monster homes' crammed on to tiny lots. Architectural showpieces that were erected during the era included 'the glass hat box' (1982), aka the Roy Thomson Hall (the new home of the Toronto Symphony), and the SkyDome sports stadium, an engineering marvel with its retractable roof (1989). Three spectacularly ornate vaudeville theatres from the early 1900s were lovingly restored and reopened as commercial theatres: the Elgin, the Winter Garden and the Pantages (now the Canon), where *Phantom of the Opera* made its debut in 1985, kickstarting a thriving theatre scene which attracts busloads of American tourists. Toronto's cosmopolitan appeal began to attract US film producers, who discovered it was much cheaper to film movies set in New York in photogenic Toronto; with the result that these days you can't move for film crews.

The conspicuous consumption and glamorous living of the 1980s continued apace in the 1990s, but was accompanied by a loss of social conscience; indeed, the 'problem-free 1970s' seemed like a distant memory. Toronto experienced its very own Margaret Thatcher in the form of the right-wing, neo-conservative Ontario premier Mike Harris, who slashed funding for the city's social services, resulting in a severe housing shortage and a growing problem of homelessness. His conservative policies were designed to court the suburban vote, and indeed, during his reign public transport suffered, new highways were built, and urban sprawl became a serious problem. The city's six boroughs were centralised into one massive, 'megacity' government, which effectively took away self-government from neighbourhoods and resulted in further cuts to public services. In spite of this, the city consistently finishes near the top of the UN world survey of desirable places to live.

Toronto Today

What do you want to be when you grow up?
Toronto comes of age.

There was a time not long ago when Toronto was considered a great place to live but one that no one would ever want to visit. Clean streets, efficient public transport and law and order defined a kind of urban living where the sidewalks were practically rolled up at dusk and shop windows curtained on Sundays so as not to tempt the citizenry with dangerous thoughts of shopping.

'Toronto is a much more interesting place for the visitor than it was a generation ago.'

The city has come of age since then. It is now a thriving metropolis coping with the myriad pressures of modern life. There are more than a few Torontonians who lament the passing of more innocent times and who might even say – gasp – that Toronto isn't such a good place to live any more. That question is open for spirited debate, but one thing is certain:

Toronto is a much more interesting place for the visitor than it was a generation ago.

Balancing its success as 'the liveable city' with sustainable growth is a tricky tightrope act for such a popular place, especially when all signs point to a groundswell of new Canadians who plan on showing up on Toronto's doorstep wanting their piece of the action. Best bets put that figure at another one million inhabitants in the Greater Toronto Area (GTA) by 2030, up from the present four million or so.

AND STILL THEY COME

Toronto continues to be a magnet for successive waves of immigrants who have contributed hugely to the dynamic society that defines the city today. To Toronto's credit, this assimilation has occurred with an acceptance and celebration of diversity that impress many who come here. There are 80 substantial ethnic groups well established in the city.

A thriving downtown core where people actually choose to live rather than escape from at the end of the day has spared Toronto the blight of emptying out at 5pm that afflicts many

American cities. This has been reinforced by a strong sense of neighbourhoods and a collective understanding, a certain 'Toronto-ness' that has managed to keep the place on track.

Provincial government meddling, however, has undermined this civic cohesion and led to a systematic erosion of the local control and accountablility that kept the place well oiled. Recent cuts in housing, education, healthcare and transport in the name of giving taxpayers a break has tarnished the shine the city once had and filled its streets with the homeless.

Toronto still has a bad case of indigestion after amalgamating the five former cities that made up Metropolitan Toronto into one mega-city in 1998. The move was a cost-saving directive from the provincial government that has largely backfired and thrown the city's own planning initiatives off course while it tries to figure out how to address a larger constituency.

Another drawback of the merger was the ascent of suburban North York's long-standing mayor, Mel Lastman, to the throne of all Toronto. 'His Melness' has proven woefully inept at managing the task and keeps Torontonians in a state of embarrassment at his many gaffes. A fine example is his utterance of fears that natives might put him in a boiling pot on a visit to Africa. The mayor was embarking on a good-will mission to drum up support for

Condomania

Look no further than the condominium craze as proof of Toronto's wannabe status. Built for the most part on the bland and cheap, condos are sprouting like mushrooms throughout the GTA with an especially high concentration in the city's core. It's an easy way for people to get a toehold in a red-hot real estate market that has been surging since the early 1990s.

The average price for a new condo was $205,000 in 2002, and with only five per cent required as a down payment, Toronto's notoriously tight rental market is cooling off. People fed up with paying $900 a month for a basement apartment can buy into the glamorous world of condoland.

At least that's how developers pitch their goods. And here's where the wannabe part comes in. You too can live the high life in condos named Tribeca, SoHo, Radio City and Broadway, to name just a few. If those names sound more at home in another city – perhaps a larger and better-known one south of the border – you get an idea of the dearth of imagination and ersatz trappings that go with marketing Toronto's condominium lifestyle.

Christopher Hume writes a weekly colulmn for the *Toronto Star* reviewing new condos – there are enough of them to keep him busy for many years to come – and he rarely has kind things to say. It's a popular column, if you haven't bought a condo in the building he's

Toronto's ill-fated bid to host the 2008 Olympic games at a time when the city was closing public pools for lack of funding, leaving many to wonder just where Toronto's athletes might expect to get their training.

WORLD-CRASS

Failed Olympic bids (this was the second in recent memory) and other unrealised grandiose schemes for the city leave its more ardent boosters with the feeling that Toronto will ever be the bridesmaid and never the bride. In the face of such defeat, mayor Lastman rallies the discontent with his oft-repeated cry that the city is indeed 'world-class'. This tiresome moniker has taken on a life of its own and anyone you

trashing. Hume regularly notes the inappropriateness of many condo designs to their surroundings, how developers rely on fussy trappings to fake their lofty ideals. The result: a whole lot of condo kitsch.

There are, of course, exceptions, where living space is being created that is innovative, blends with the neighbourhood and reflects well on the urban design of the city. One of the most ambitious condo developments will change the skyline when it's completed in 2010. City Place will add 7,500 units in 21 towers – some as high as 60 storeys – in the old railway yards west of SkyDome. While construction proceeds, the developer has installed a nine-hole golf course and year-round driving range that will eventually be ploughed up to make room for more condos.

Keeping the inner city desirable as a place to live has always been one of Toronto's strengths and condos help fuel that notion of the liveable city. Toronto has led the way in converting office towers into condos for many years. The boom is reviving neglected districts and breathing new life into the cityscape. But many condo buyers have no intention of living in their property themselves. Condos are the most visible expression of a speculative real estate gambit. Investors are buying as much as 90 per cent of new condo projects downtown with the intent of renting them out or 'flipping' them (selling them on) once the building is finished. With 13,000 new units selling each year, developers have little incentive to invest in a longer-term vision for this liveable city.

encounter who says it should be avoided, or at least told that cities deserving such plaudits generally don't need the constant reminder.

Toronto can seem a petty place, from the moment at Pearson International Airport when new arrivals are forced to cough up a $1 loonie coin for the use of a baggage cart to the not-in-my-backyard agendas that have stymied attempts to map out a blueprint for the city's future. The amalgamated city finally got its first official planning legislation passed by council in late 2002; it protects many existing residential neighbourhoods from excessive vertical expansion while directing future population growth to dreary strip-mall thoroughfares in the hinterland that will be transformed into higher density, more user-friendly avenues.

GROWING PAINS

Key to the plan is keeping public transport alive as a realistic alternative to using the car. Cutbacks to the Toronto Transit Commission have made 'the better way' a less attractive alternative to cars and customer numbers are down. At the same time, Toronto risks being overwhelmed by cars and choked by their fumes unless improvements are made to meet the expected population boom. A new subway line running east to the suburbs from Yonge along Sheppard Street opened in November 2002, but critics reckon that it will end up underused since the area it serves is largely comprised of single-family dwellings. Still, Toronto has been well ahead of other North American cities in its public transport policy – it has the second largest system in North America after New York City – and a conservative habit of delaying big decisions has had its benefits. A case in point was resisting the urge to rip up the streetcar tracks at a time when many other cities were doing just that. The flip side of this is a city still waiting for a mass transit link to the airport.

If Toronto is looking for a world-class symbol it need look no further than its expansive suburbs. Frenetic growth outside the city proper in the past 20 years has produced truly world-class urban sprawl that's right up there with Los Angeles. Patterns of living have developed that are consistent with a generic North American suburban lifestyle and only serve to differentiate what are now two Torontos – the wide girth of the burbs and the island that is old Toronto downtown.

Many people speak of a lack of the vision, leadership and political will to make the city truly great. Toronto has always resisted grand plans and monumental structures – the two recent exceptions being the CN Tower and

Mayor **Mel Lastman**. *See p18.*

SkyDome, and earlier the new City Hall, which surfaced during rare moments when the city wanted its ego fully expressed. Putting the stadium in the downtown core had the bonus of spawning what is now the Entertainment District, turning old warehouses into a pulsating night scene that keeps the inner city active and safe and a place people want to be.

Still, Toronto can't rest on its laurels. Through the prosperous and excessive 1990s, few major initiatives were mooted to define the city for the 21st century. Particularly lacking were projects to support the cultural scene and those that would create landmark works of architecture. With no public money available, the affluent were shamed into coughing up big bucks to ensure their immortal legacies in the city that made them wealthy. One high-profile arts booster decried a 'philanthropy deficit'.

BUILDING FOR THE FUTURE

Consultants have seized on the power of culture to drive Toronto's economy into the future. Reports pumped out the statistics – 15 per cent of the city's workforce toil in the cultural sector, which includes everything from media and publishing to performing arts, film and museums. Suddenly, a city that was in search of

itself found a new purpose and the first decade of this century will see the addition of some shining new beacons that will shape the city's reputation. Among these are a new opera house, designed by local architect Jack Diamond. The Royal Ontario Museum is taking an 'if-you-build-it-they-will-come' approach by adding an immense glass enclosure designed by German architect Daniel Libeskind that screams, 'Look at Us! Here's your world-class architecture!'

The city that was said could not afford to hire its own native son, Frank Gehry, will indeed see him design an addition to the Art Gallery of Ontario to house a collection of Canadian art owned by one of the wealthiest men in the world, Ken Thomson. But this is Toronto, after all, and the wunderkind architect, who grew up in the shadow of the AGO, is not out to build a blockbuster. 'It's not gonna be Bilbao, OK?' he told onlookers when the expansion was unveiled late in 2002. British architect Norman Foster will spruce up the prominent intersection of College Street and Queen's Park Crescent with the new Pharmacy Building for the University of Toronto, while nearby the Ontario College of Art and Design gets a leg-up by adding a new wing on stilts designed by another Brit, Will Alsop, and the cherished Eaton Auditorium comes back to life in full deco splendour as the Carlu, named in honour of the original French architect.

'The final frontier is a large expanse of toxic industrial wasteland...'

All of these projects will contribute to making Toronto a more interesting place for residents and the millions who visit each year. Tourism Toronto harps on endlessly that the tourism inventory needs to be rejuvenated. It may finally get its wish. At the same time, the decidedly non-world-class budget of $8 million the agency has to promote the city lags well behind cities of comparable size. Toronto, it seems, gets good word of mouth.

A debate about the flyover that divides the city from the waterfront still fires the passionate civic heart. Problem is, it's a moot point now that a wall of concrete condos has risen beside the Gardiner Expressway. Developers ran roughshod over city council in seizing this prime real estate for themselves. However, a chance remains to get it right next time. The final frontier is a large expanse of toxic industrial wasteland called the docklands that extends east of the downtown core that schemers and dreamers hope will be Toronto's waterfront salvation. Watch that space: what happens here will be a true test of the city's character.

Hollywood North

Welcome to Toronto, California, where the camera always lies. Cue the credits.

Don't expect to find oversized letters on a hill spelling out Toronto's ties to the movie business. Hollywood North it might be, but Canadians are more discreet than that. There is no movie district as such, save a few street signs in South Riverdale and a couple of gated low-rise studios that stretch along a barren part of the eastern waterfront.

Hollywood North is not an area, or a state of mind. It's business. Sure, there are bragging rights, and some people take full advantage. *Chicago, Resident Evil, My Big Fat Greek Wedding, The Recruit*: the big-name Hollywood titles just keep on coming. And with them, the stars. You can sidle up to a bartender at plenty of watering holes (*see p22* **Celebrity stares**) and hear some of the urban legends: stories of

Mick getting down at Revival *sans* entourage; Rene Zellweger helping a homeless person; Colin Farrell partying into the night with local folk; Sam Shepard strolling across Bloor Street as if it were his ranch. Occasionally, you'll be stopped by an off-duty policeman and asked to wait. A man hollers 'Roll sound!' and Sharon Stone, or Al Pacino, or Richard Gere utters a few words and then disappears into the summer night.

On any given day, between 18 and 40 TV and film productions are shooting in Toronto, more than half of them American. It's no wonder that many locals, even those with no connection to the business, can talk the talk. Why not? They trip over the block-long cables that snake along kerbs and gutters. They sidestep the leather-jacketed camera crews that gather in scrums like pigeons around a pile of breadcrumbs. And they count the parked trailers in their long caravans, noting their relative size. These are the daily reminders of Hollywood North.

Toronto gets an apocalyptic makeover in **Resident Evil**. *See above.*

Celebrity stares

Unlike hockey or baseball, celebrity-spotting in Toronto is a year-round sport. It's always open season on the stars who wine and dine their way through the bars, cafés and restaurants whose proprietors are only too eager to boast that Pierce prefers his martini stirred, or that David Carradine likes to drink in the company of his little dog. So if your idea of a good souvenir is a first-hand account of whether Nicole prefers penne to spaghetti, or news that Al devours bottarga by the barrel, then this is your kind of town. Thanks to the number of films shot here, Toronto sparkeles with Hollywood's glitterati.

Most of the eat/drink action takes place in Yorkville (handy for the swank hotels). The popular restaurants, which usually offer good but not sensational food, have a few key things in common: Mediterranean cuisine, candlelight or dim lighting and discreet service.

Try a table at the back of **Sotto Sotto** (see p121), a cavernous Italian restaurant where sightings include Kate Hudson, Michael Imperioli (The Sopranos), Sharon Stone and director Mike Figgis. Robert De Niro, Greg Kinnear, Michael Douglas and Mary Louise Parker have all been seen at **Joso's** (202 Davenport Road, 416 925 1903), a well-established fish restaurant and hob-nob hang-out. Nearby, **JK at the ROM** attracts the stars as often as **Patriot** (for both, see p113) on Bloor Street (endorsed by Anthony Bourdain of Kitchen Confidential). **Spuntini** (116 Avenue Road, 416 962 1110) is another haunt for the smart set, as is **Bistro 990** (990 Bay Street, 416 921 9990), conveniently located across the road from the Sutton Place Hotel. Just about anyone who counts has munched frites and sipped Beaujolais here. In a local newspaper column, the sightings in one week included Peter Gallagher, George Lucas and Francis Ford Coppola with families in tow, John Corbett (My Big Fat Greek Wedding), Dianne Carroll and Ed Asner, Jason Alexander, Matthew Modine, Deborah Unger, James Spader... and the list goes on.

A word of caution to star-gazers: the big stars like Toronto in part for its polite citizens; people here might gawk, but they don't talk.

But look closer and you might notice something strange. Nowhere are the cameras turned towards anything distinctively Torontonian. Perhaps the city's biggest on-screen talent is its ability to disappear. Usually, it stands in for New York City (X-Men). Sometimes it's Chicago (Finding Forrester), Boston (Good Will Hunting) or urban America, or the occasional exotic destination (such as Morocco in Naked Lunch). The city benefits by about $1.5 billion each year from tarting itself up – or down – to look like SoHo or somewhere, but it almost never appears as itself. At the movies, locals can pinpoint familiar restaurants, street corners and parks, but they would mean nothing to outsiders. Actually, even the locals fail to pick out the city in most of its guises.

'Perhaps Toronto's biggest on-screen talent is its ability to disappear.'

A story – surely apocryphal – from the mid-1980s remains popular folklore, probably because it suggests that Toronto is inherently anonymous. A crew dressed a stretch of pavement to look like a dirty, American street, littering it with rubbish. Then everyone broke for lunch. When they returned, Toronto's sanitation department – no doubt alerted by an outraged citizen – had cleaned up the atrocity, and returned the city to its proper state of cleanliness.

Canada had invited America to dominate its movie scenes and screens from the outset. The Canadian Prime Minister in the second half of the 1930s – Mackenzie King – decided not to fund Canadian pictures when Hollywood came knocking with an offer to set American pictures in Canada. This agreement brought about such kitsch-flicks as Rose-Marie (1936), starring Nelson Eddy as a strapping Mountie. Filmmaking simply wasn't part of the city's cultural identity, unlike literature. Many of the biggest talents have left for America: Toronto was too small to hold Lorne Michaels, Eugene Levy, Jim Carrey, Mike Myers and many others. Nonetheless, the occasional local film talent emerged – and stayed home – against the odds, especially when a government agency (now Telefilm Canada) began handing out money for indigenous production in the 1980s.

Toronto made a splash in the 1960s when Don Shebib shot Goin' Down the Road, the classic tale of country boys who come to the big city: a kind of Midnight Cowboy, Canadian style. In the greasy 1970s, the city was hit by a wave of so-called 'dentist movies' – low-grade cash-grabs that were financed by teeth-pullers in exchange for whopping tax breaks. The flicks were made to look, sound, feel American.

Today, there is a small local movie industry, and occasionally it plays up the city's cultural identity. Most recently, Deepa Mehta celebrated the South Asian communities here in *Bollywood/ Hollywood*. David Cronenberg (*see* **Local hero**) excels at finding the twisted in the city's normalcy: think of the bland suburbs in *Crash*. Don McKellar used local colour to its fullest in *Last Night*: even the streetcars played a role.

And although the city is often secondary in Atom Egoyan's films, Toronto nightclubs did look downright dirty and local in *Exotica*. These are rare examples of an industry that is under-funded and little-loved by the locals. (In 2000, English-language Canadian movies accounted for 0.2 per cent of the national box office. The following year, the figure rose to an almighty 1.4 per cent.)

America – the real Hollywood – continues to dominate Toronto's screens, as well as its

Local hero David Cronenberg

scenario. *The Fly* carried Jeff Goldblum and Geena Davis into a land of insect erotica. And up went the ante. Jeremy Irons and his gynaecological instruments seduced Geneviève Bujold in the grisly *Dead Ringers*. There was nothing too slippery for *Naked Lunch*. *Crash*, which won a special prize 'for originality, daring and audacity' at the Cannes Film Festival, outraged censors in the UK and the US for its insistence that gory car accidents are sexy. The director is quoted as saying about *ExistenZ*: 'For a movie that has no sex in it, it has a lot of sex'. *Spider*, the latest Cronenberg creation, stars Ralph Fiennes in a bleak psychological tale of oedipal proportions.

The films might be loved or hated by Cronenberg's fellow Torontonians, but the man is genuinely admired. His manner is gentle. The weirdest thing about him seems to be his childhood love of insects. Not only is he a quiet family man who lives and works in his home town, but he accomplishes something unique in the world of Canadian cinema, over and over again: he makes mainstream-budget movies, usually at home, with American and foreign funds, and a mix of Canadian and foreign talent. He succeeds. And he does it his own peculiar way.

Honourable mentions: Atom Egoyan, born in Egypt, is a darling of the Toronto arts scene. Mostly known for his artistic films – *Exotica*, *The Sweet Hereafter*, *Ararat* – Egoyan has also proven himself as an opera director at home and in London.

Previous contenders: Oscar-winner Norman Jewison (*In the Heat of the Night*) made a brilliant career in Hollywood, and then gave his hometown of Toronto a unique gift: the Canadian Film Centre. The film school, now 16 years old, is developing a strong list of graduates, including Vincenzo Natali (*Cube*).

Kinky sex and Canadian movies make regular bedfellows, or so the cliché goes. The number of movies made in Canada without unusual sex scenes probably outweighs those with, but the bodice does seem to fit. Especially when it comes to film director David Cronenberg. Toronto's hometown king of intellectual creep and subversive sex has been called a pornographer, a sadist, a controversial visionary – and much, much more.

You'll know it when you've seen a Cronenberg film. *Stereo* featured the Canadian Academy for Erotic Enquiry. *Shivers* gave birth to parasite-infected sex maniacs. *Videodrome* intertwined Debbie Harry and James Wood in a snuff TV

production offices. The protests pour in daily – and the wounded party is not Canada. The country's ability to lure US production is so strong that a campaign, Blame Canada!, has been launched to discourage business (including timber and steel) from working across the border. Are the polite Canucks quietly stealing billions of dollars right out from under the noses of unsuspecting Americans? So it seems. New York's film office has claimed that movie production is down by ten per cent since Canada introduced its film-tax incentives in 1997. An American trade newspaper estimates that $1.8 billion (US) is flowing out of the movie business in the US and straight into Canada each year. Reports of so-called 'Runaway Productions',

American movies that shoot outside the country, are so common that Whoopi Goldberg, at the 2002 Academy Awards, joked about the 'actors, actresses, producers and directors who are no longer with us…the ones filming in Canada'. One of the latest incidents to stir the ire of America is that Canada, no less, is the chosen location for a biopic of former New York City mayor Rudolph Giuliani.

So why do they come? It helps that Toronto is either bland or flexible enough to look like so many other cities. And the crews are polite, talented and numerous. Over the past ten years, the city has developed a solid infrastructure for filmmakers and just about any request can be accommodated any day of the year. But the key

The Toronto International Film Festival

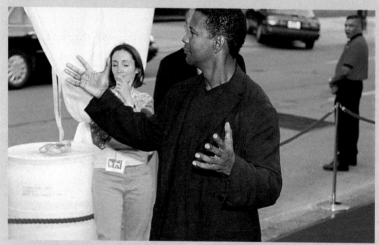

It's one of the city's prime boasting rights: the Toronto International Film Festival, which started out 27 years ago as a modest celebration of titles culled from other international festivals, is now established as the second most important film festival anywhere. (Cannes, with its unbeatably glamorous locale and its reputation for snooty French exclusivity, remains both the *grande dame* and the leading lady.)

Locals love the festival not only for its fame, but for the fact that it's an event geared to them. Unlike Cannes, Berlin, Sundance and Venice, Toronto focuses squarely on the public. It's precisely this devotion to the city's

movie-going fans that has made TIFF so important for buyers, sellers and the press. Here, the industry hears it straight from the ticket-buyers: what's hot and what's not. Oscar contenders, especially foreign-language winners such as *No Man's Land* (2002) and *Antonia's Line* (1995), are often premiered at the festival. And sometimes major hits are unearthed here, most famously *Diva*, *Shine* and *American Beauty*. There's something for everyone: splatter flicks at midnight, the latest from Burkina Faso, American indies, a strong documentary presence and a heavyweight selection of the best from Europe and Asia.

reason is the bottom line. It's cheap. There are major tax incentives for foreign productions that, combined with the weak Canadian dollar, can make shooting a multi-million-dollar film almost 25 per cent cheaper than it would be in the States. The business is important enough for the prime minister, the mayor and provincial premiers to travel to Los Angeles and New York to promote Hollywood North. In 2001, Toronto's film office registered over 10,000 shooting days (more than twice the tally ten years ago) and over 5,000 location permits.

But all is not Botox-beautiful in Canada's La-La Land. Toronto used to rate third in production levels after Los Angeles and New York, but no more. Increasingly, the shoots are

Lisa Ray in **Bollywood/Hollywood**. *See p23.*

going to Vancouver and Montreal. Why? There are whispers of 'attitude problems' and increased prices, but it really comes down to something that competing cities have that Toronto doesn't: a superstudio. The city has taken notice and there are plans to build not one, but two of these beasts. Great Lakes Studios, a local company headed by Paul Bronfman, has broken ground on its 600,000-square-foot (57,000 square-metre) soundstage and studio near the Leslie Street Spit. The Sequence project, which includes Pinewood Studios (of the Bond franchise) and promises to be the biggest sound-stage anywhere, was prematurely announced by mayor Mel Lastman before the necessary agreements had been made. It might pop up near Cherry Street, in the Port of Toronto. Either or both of these projects will likely create unsightly, sprawling boxes near the already bleak waterfront, but the city is determined to protect its treasure box of glam. A gamble, for America could fight back – and win. If good tax incentives were introduced at home, Toronto would hurt. And then there are the patriots. Arnold Schwarzenegger famously decided to shoot *Terminator 3*, a $200-million picture, in California. It was headed for production in Vancouver, but the actor wanted to make a statement and shoot it at home. 'Bring Hollywood Home!' is another rallying cry, another campaign aimed at keeping US movie and TV production south of the border. Time will tell where the chips will fall, but Toronto will continue to try and make Hollywood feel right at home when it comes north.

If anything, TIFF has been a victim of its own success. There aren't always enough tickets to go around, a situation exacerbated by the degradation of the circuit of cinemas around Bloor and Bay Streets that created the 'Festival Village' in Yorkville into a handful of multiplexes. The event has had to spread out, and gala screenings – generally Hollywood's latest with top stars parading on red carpets – take place at the Elgin Theatre (*see p218*) and at Roy Thomson Hall (*see p197*).

Over summer, the festival announces its 300-plus line-up of titles, and locals start making their lists. At the end of August, when the official programme book hits the streets and the box office opens, overnight campers zip into their sleeping bags to stake out a place in line. And then, for ten days starting on the Thursday after September's Labour Day holiday, the city is a inescapable frenzy of movie buzz. As the reels unspool, long queues crowd the pavements from morning to midnight, paparazzi gather outside hotel lobbies, increasingly punchy fans argue over lattes or lagers, comparing movie stories like old war wounds.

For tickets, contact the box office at 416 968 3456 from mid July, or go to www.bell.ca/filmfest. In 2002, tickets cost a reasonable $7-$12; a variety of passes are also available, including the good-value Daytime pass (for movies before 6pm) and the all-glitz Gala pass. 'Rush Tickets' are available on the day, particularly for lesser-known and international titles.

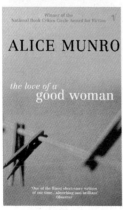

Literary Toronto

Read all about it...

As the media capital of Canada, Toronto draws writers like flies. Indeed, more than one sourpuss has accused Canadian publishers of ignoring writers who live anywhere else, and this despite the fact that some of biggest stars in CanLit are firmly identified with other parts of the country, and the world: **Mavis Gallant** with her adopted city of Paris, and **Alice Munro**, who is oft cited as Canada's greatest living writer, with the West Coast and small-town Ontario.

Still, Toronto hasn't always been a literary lodestar. Prominent early travellers and settlers such as **Anna Jameson**, **Susanna Moodie** and **Ernest Thompson Seton** left their sometimes acidic impressions of 19th-century Toronto. Seton's childhood adventures in Toronto's Don Valley, then a wilderness area, inspired parts of the classic books, *Two Little*

Savages and *Wild Animals I Have Known*. And Moodie, who wrote *Roughing It in the Bush*, inspired Margaret Atwood's 1970 poetry collection *The Journals of Susanna Moodie*. But TO Lit didn't really come into its own until the 1960s, when a wave of Canadian nationalism buoyed artistic ambition. Some academics might disagree with this thesis, but then academics are probably the only people still reading most of the stuff created pre-1960s.

The major exception to this rule is **Morley Callaghan**. Born in Toronto in 1903, Callaghan went on to become one of the giants of early 20th-century Canadian literature (along with Hugh MacLennan). He met Hemingway during the latter's time as a reporter at the *Toronto Star* and the American writer encouraged his writing. Views of Callaghan's achievement vary. American critic Edmund

Wilson called him 'perhaps the most unjustly neglected novelist in the English-speaking world'. Others find his style earnest, clunky and oddly Sunday school-ish. But there's no denying Callaghan's importance on the Toronto scene. He was the first major Canadian writer to use the city extensively in his fiction (though owing to the pressures of the US market, it's seldom directly identified), and he went on to win a Governor General's award in 1951 (for *The Loved and the Lost*) and the highly remunerative Royal Bank Award in 1970. Despite a famous visit to Paris in the 1920s (chronicled in his memoir, *That Summer in Paris*), Callaghan spent most of his long life in Toronto. He lived at 20 Dale Avenue in Rosedale from 1951 until his death in 1990. By the time he arrived there, Callaghan had already written the three novels for which he will probably be remembered – *Such Is My Beloved*, *For They Shall Inherit the Earth* and *More Joy in Heaven*. But it was on Dale Avenue that he wrote such books as *The Many Colored Coat*, *A Passion in Rome*, *A Fine and Private Place*, *Close to the Sun Again*, *The Enchanted Pimp*, *A Time for Judas*, *Our Lady of the Snows* and *A Wild Old Man on the Road*.

THE 1960S AND AFTER

Like many Canadian writers of the period, Callaghan was initially published abroad. It wasn't until the 1960s that literary Canadians started to feel at home in their own land. Buoyed by a surge of government support and nationalist ambition, local literati started their own small presses and magazines.

> **'Michael Ondaatje's greatest gift to Toronto may well have been his gilding of this city's seemingly quiet past.'**

Descriptions of the period can be found in **Douglas Fetherling**'s vivid memoirs, *Travels By Night* and *Way Down Deep in the Belly of the Beast*. But the products of that seminal time are everywhere to be seen. Some of the most influential small presses (Anansi, Coach House) are still going today and many of the authors who came of age in that period are now almost synonymous with CanLit.

Of these, the most famous is undoubtedly **Margaret Atwood**. Known as a feminist abroad and a nationalist at home, Atwood is in fact the poet laureate of modern Toronto. A winner of both the Booker Prize and Canada's most prestigious literary award, the Governor General's Award, Atwood lives in downtown Toronto with her partner Graeme Gibson and has set many of her novels in the city. *Life*

Before Man, her 1979 novel about a tense love triangle, is a terrific portrait of 1970s Toronto, complete with a truly startling description of the normally staid Royal Ontario Museum. *The Robber Bride* dissects female rivalry while providing an alluring portrait of hippy-dippy life on the Toronto Islands. Both *Lady Oracle* and *Cat's Eye* draw on middle-class life in the 1940s and 1950s, and *Cat's Eye* ranges forward to the artsy world of Queen Street West, the nearby 'fashion district' and the ravines that some critics have identified as Toronto's most distinctive imaginative and geographic feature.

Atwood worked as an editor at Toronto's House of Anansi in the early 1970s. Another veteran of the small-press scene, novelist Matt Cohen, is usually associated with the area north of Kingston, Ontario, about 160 miles (255 kilometres) east of Toronto. Both his so-called Salem quartet and the novel for which he belatedly received the Governor General's award just weeks before his death in 1999, the superb *Elizabeth and After*, are set there. But Cohen was very much a part of the Toronto scene and set various stories and the 1993 *roman à clef*, *The Bookseller*, in the city. A park

International Festival of Authors

When Greg Gatenby founded the International Festival of Authors in 1980, he couldn't have known how big it would become. There was already a regular reading series at Harbourfront (*see p27* **Where to find it**), but the idea of inviting foreign authors was relatively new. That first festival featured a mere 18 authors over six days. But Gatenby, a witty, erudite man with the air of a born *bon vivant*, was determined to promote a cosmopolitan literary culture. A poet and former book editor, he went on to write a literary guide to Toronto and edit two books collecting foreign literary views of Canada. And so the festival grew. Two decades later, it's one of the most prestigious literary events in the world, with more than 100 of the world's best novelists, poets, biographers and dramatists participating every fall in readings, talks and on-stage interviews. It's really only the climax of a weekly reading series that runs from September to June at Harbourfront. But it's quite a climax, with an astonishing range of award-winning writers (from Booker to Nobel) routinely gracing the stage.

International Festival of Authors

Various venues at the Harbourfront Centre, Waterfront (416 973 3000/ www.readings.org). Streetcar 509, 510/subway Union Station. **Date** late Oct-early Nov.

named in his honour can be found at the corner of Bloor Street West and Spadina Avenue, a street he once called the 'centre of the universe'.

Atwood's near contemporary, **Timothy Findley**, was born in Toronto's Rosedale and set some of his stories (see especially the Stones collection) and part of his best-known work, the GG-winning *The Wars*, in that affluent enclave. He's not always a fan, though. 'Them as live in Rosedale,' says a character in one of the Stones stories, 'are them as keep their shit in jars'.

Robertson Davies belongs to an earlier generation, having launched his fiction-writing career in the 1950s, but he didn't receive widespread public recognition until 1970 when he published *Fifth Business*, a novel of saints, fate and the theatre set partly in Toronto. Like Atwood and Findley, Davies could be cutting about his adopted home. (He was born in Thamesville, Ontario.) 'I always think of Toronto as a big fat rich girl who has lots of money, but no idea how to make herself attractive,' says his fictional alter ego, Samuel Marchbanks. But Davies went on to become the long-time master of Massey College, the pseudo-Oxbridge outpost at the University of Toronto, and he used the city in novels like *What's Bred in the Bone*, *The Rebel Angel*s and *The Manticore*, for which he won the Governor General's award.

Other glimpses of the city can be gleaned from books such as *Lunatic Villas*, the last novel from **Marian Engel**, better known for *Bear*, an inter-species love story which won her the Governor General's Award; and the poetry of **Raymond Souster**, a Torontonian who spent most of his life in the High Park area and named some of his poems for different parts of the city, including 'Kensington Market' and 'Yonge Street Bar'.

A CHANGING CITY

Anglo-Saxon Toronto died sometime around 1956 when the first wave of Hungarian refugees arrived, and the city has been growing more multicultural ever since, to the point where some of the most prominent voices on the local literary scene are immigrants'.

> **'Gowdy has a gently weird take on sex, women and the body.'**

Of these, the most famous is almost certainly the Booker Prize-winning author of *The English Patient*, **Michael Ondaatje**. Born in Sri Lanka, Ondaatje has written about everything from his family's Sri Lankan past (*Running in the Family*) to New Orleans jazz (*Coming Through Slaughter*). But his greatest gift to Toronto may well have been his gilding of this city's seemingly quiet past. In his second novel, *In the Skin of a Lion*, Ondaatje turned his eye on Toronto in the 1920s and morphed local landmarks such as the Bloor Street Viaduct, the RC Harris Filtration Plant and Union Station into places of magic, depth and consequence. Entering Union Station, a character says: 'This train station was a palace, its niches and caverns an intimate city… He spoke out his name… No one turned. They were in the belly of a whale.'

Toronto boasts fewer major Jewish writers than Montreal, which of course claims Leonard Cohen and the late Irving Layton and Mordecai Richler, but glimpses of local Jewish life can be found in the writings of **Shirley Faessler** (*A Basket of Apples, Everything in the Window*), and a 1988 novel by journalist and playwright Rick Salutin called *A Man of Little Faith*.

For years, African-Canadian writing boiled down to one name, the Barbados-born **Austin Clarke**. The author of nine novels, including *The Polished Hoe*, Clarke set the stage for a younger generation led locally by **Dionne Brand** (*In Another Place, Not Here*).

Local gay lit might be said to have started with **Scott Symons**, a curator of Canadiana at the Royal Ontario Museum, who was very much a part of the Toronto WASP establishment until he drew attention to his sexuality. Symons published the homoerotic *Place d'Armes* in 1967 and ran off to Mexico with a younger male lover a few years later. He eventually settled in Morocco. Much lionised, but seldom read, Symons set the stage for contemporary gay writers such as RM Vaughan, Sky Gilbert, Greg Kramer (who names some of his characters after Toronto streets), Camilla Gibb, Marnie Woodrow, Derek McCormack and the late Peter McPhee, who portrayed the Church Street ghetto in a trilogy beginning with *Boys Like Us*.

Oprah-fave **Ann-Marie MacDonald** set her bestselling debut novel, *Fall On Your Knees*, in the Maritimes and elsewhere, but is very much a part of the Toronto scene both as an actor and an award-winning playwright (*Goodnight Desdemona (Good Morning Juliet)*).

ATWOOD AND BEYOND

Of the post-Atwood generation, **Barbara Gowdy** is probably the most interesting. Born in Windsor but educated in Toronto and active in Toronto publishing before the appearance of her first book in 1982, Gowdy has a gently weird take on sex, women and the body. Her short stories, one of which inspired the film *Kissed*, concern (among other things) necrophilia and transvestism, while novels such as *Falling Angels* and *Mister Sandman* are set in a sexual suburbia far odder than anything John Updike could imagine. Still, it's identifiably Toronto. You can tell by the references to the subway, at least in *Mister Sandman*.

Despite the fact that Canada is a nation of city dwellers, CanLit is often tagged as a dour chronicle of dusty rural life. The writer who's done the most to put that notion to rest is Toronto columnist **Russell Smith**, whose novels (*How Insensitive*, *Noise*) and short stories (*Young Men*) celebrate Toronto's club, restaurant and media scene. *Much of Young Men* was reportedly written in the trendy College Street bar/restaurant, Bar Italia.

Other local writers of note include: **Katherine Govier**, who chronicled the city's hip Annex district in her popular story collection *Fables of Brunswick Avenue*; **Sarah Dearing**, who set her latest novel, *Courage My Love*, in the raffishly bohemian neighbourhood of Kensington Market; and novelist **Susan Swan**, who gives a terrific description of Toronto's 'Cottage Country' vacationland paradise in *The Last of the Golden Girls*.

Genre writing has also prospered in the last few decades. What Ian Rankin is to Edinburgh and Sue Grafton to Santa Barbara, **Eric Wright** is to Toronto. His most popular hero, Charlie Salter, is an inspector with the Metropolitan Toronto Police. Award-winning **Peter Robinson** sets his Inspector Banks mysteries in Yorkshire but their author lives in Toronto. Other popular local writers include kids' writer **Kenneth Oppel** (the Silverwing series) and sci-fi guru **Robert Sawyer** (*Frameshift*), who lives just a short distance north of the city.

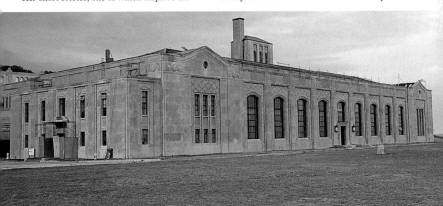

The **RC Harris Filtration Plant**, which features in Michael Ondaatje's *The Skin of a Lion*.

Hotel Services at Hostel Rates

Neill-Wycik College Hotel

- We've been hosting groups & individuals for over 30 years.
- Open from early May to late August each year.
- Located in the heart of the city, close to public transportation, major attractions, shopping, theatres, and night life.
- Rooms are arranged in residence-style units with 5 private bedrooms sharing 2 bathrooms, a kitchen and common area.
- Breakfast is included in our very affordable rates. We provide 24 hour guest services and security, as well as on-site laundry and tourist information

"The Travellers' Community"

96 Gerrard St. East, Toronto, ON M5B 1G7 Canada
(416) 977-2320 • 1-800-268-4358 •
Fax: (416) 977-2809 • hotel@neill-wycik.com
www.neill-wycik.com

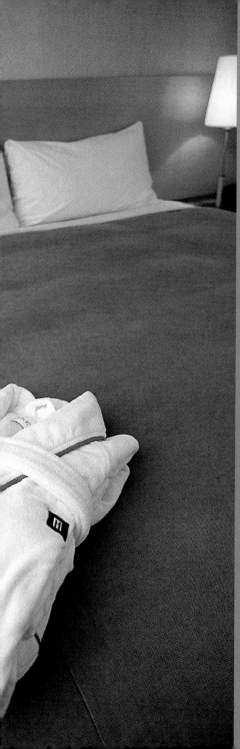

Accommodation

Accommodation 32

Features

Accommodation

Thousands of functional rooms do the trick, while a flurry of new boutique hotels deliver the trend factor.

If you were to spend one night in each of the Greater Toronto's 35,000 hotel rooms, it would take you 95 years to get through them all. Furthermore, much of the time you'd hardly notice when you changed rooms. Toronto has an excess of modern, clean rooms that are almost devoid of character. There are, however, many notable deviations from the cookie-cutter norm and things are beginning to trend toward greater individuality in design and services.

The change is partly due to the weak Canadian dollar, which means that Americans and Brits can get a night in a luxury room in Toronto for the price of a ham sandwich back home. (Well, almost.) That means many tourists can afford to be fussy and demanding, which puts pressure on Toronto hoteliers to offer up something extraordinary. New boutique hotels – small, luxury hotels that place an emphasis on interior design and individualised service – have been popping up with increasing frequency, redressing a noticeable dearth. Of the most recent are the **SoHo Metropolitan** (see p34) and the **Hotel Le Germain** (see p33), both due to open in February 2003.

One hotel Toronto won't be getting is the Donald Trump-financed Ritz-Carlton, which had been slated to occupy part of a 65-storey tower in the Financial District. Alas, after much boasting and lofty aspirations, plans came back down to earth and Trump pulled out.

At the other end of the spectrum, watch out for the re-emergence of the **Drake**, a flophouse in down-at-heel Parkdale turned art hotel. Ex-dot.commer Jeff Stober draws on varied inspirations with touches like a juice bar, live music venue, vegetarian restaurant and yoga studio. He describes the 20-room hotel as 'cheap chic' and the 'anti-Four Seasons'. The Drake is scheduled to open in summer 2003 (115 Queen Street W, 416 531 5042).

Toronto has accommodation to suit a wide range of budgets. We have divided our listings according to the price of a mid-range, mid-season double room into **Budget** (up to $90) and **Moderate** hotels and inns ($100 to $140), which while sometimes basic get the job done, providing a comfortable bed in a clean, safe, quiet room, **Expensive** ($150 to $250) and **Luxury** ($260 to your life savings). Hotels in the latter two categories vary in character and

services, so it's worth shopping around. During slow periods, a luxury hotel might discount itself down into the expensive bracket (ditto expensive into moderate), and during special events like the Film Festival or the Molson Indy, everyone's prices shoot through the roof.

For most hotels, high season runs from April to October, when deals are hard to come by. But some places that are heavily oriented toward corporate customers get very quiet in the summer. Hit them while they're down, and ask for a reduced rate. Also, inquire about deals for students, seniors, CAA, AAA or AA members, teachers, or other groups to which you belong, and it's always worth asking if a hotel has any special offers or upgrades. Remember that, unless otherwise stated, you must add seven per cent federal tax (though you can claim this back: see p12).

BOOKING AGENCIES

Bear in mind that most booking agencies will only hook you up with their own members, so you still need to do a little shopping around. The **Toronto Convention & Visitors Association** (416 203 2600/

The best Hotels

For travelling with children
Delta Chelsea. See p35.

For the first night of your honeymoon
Old Mill Inn. See p43.

To share an elevator with a movie star
Four Seasons Hotel. See p44.

To imagine you're a king
Le Royal Meridien King Edward. See p40.

If you actually are a king
The Royal Suite at the Fairmont Royal York Hotel. See p33.

If you're on a road trip
Executive Motor Hotel. See p39.

www.torontotourism.com) is the city's official booking service, while **CanadaTravel.ca** (1-800 603 3837/www.canadatravel.ca) is a private company that also arranges car rentals and package tours. The **Travellers' Aid Society of Toronto** (416 366 7788) provides shelter and information for emergencies. This society also has booths at many rail and bus stations, as well as the airport.

The **Bed & Breakfast Homes of Toronto Association** (416 363 6362/www.bbcanada.com/toronto2.html) comprises a handful of independent B&Bs in the Greater Toronto Area. Though basic information and photos are given online, booking should be done direct with the B&B. The **Downtown Toronto Association of Bed & Breakfast Guest Houses** (416 410 3938/www.bnbinfo.com) will be able to match your accommodation preferences, via a detailed online form or by phone, to B&Bs in central Toronto. **Toronto Bed & Breakfast** (877 922 6522 or 705 738 9449/www.torontobandb.com) helpfully brings together a handful of B&Bs mainly in downtown areas.

Downtown West

Luxury

Fairmont Royal York Hotel

100 Front Street W, at University Avenue, Entertainment District, ON M5J 1E3 (1-800 257 7544/416 368 2511/fax 416 3689040/www.royalyorkhotel.com). Subway St Andrew or Union. **Rates** $199-$289 single/double; $379-$469 Fairmont gold rooms. **Credit** AmEx, DC, MC, V. **Map** p277/p278 E8.

When it opened in 1929, it was the largest and tallest building in the British Empire. Although it's now dwarfed by the banking towers of Toronto's Financial District, the hotel's castle-like exterior still merits its royal name. Among the 40 million guests who have stayed here over the years are three generations of Britain's royal family, along with Cary Grant, Steven Seagal and N'Sync. The owners have invested more than $100 million in renovations over the past decade, merging historical magnificence with modernity. Chandeliers and a hand-painted ceiling in the sumptuous lobby set a tone of regal awe, while the design of the new EPIC restaurant and lounge show grudging acknowledgement that the world has grown hipper. The informal Pipers Bar and Eatz on the lower level of the hotel features waiting staff who also sing for your entertainment. Don't say we didn't warn you.

Hotel services *Air-conditioning. Babysitting (on call). Bars (4). Beauty salon. Business services. Concierge. Disabled: adapted rooms. Gym. Limousine service. No-smoking rooms. Parking (valet $27) Restaurants (5). Swimming pool (indoor).* **Room**

services *Bathrobe. Dataport (high-speed). Iron. Minibar. Newspaper. Room service (24hrs). Turndown. TV: cable/pay movies/VCR (on request).*

Hilton Toronto

145 Richmond Street W, at University Avenue, Financial District, ON M5H 2L2 (1-800 445 8667/416 869 3456/fax 416 869 3187/www.toronto.hilton.com). Streetcar 501/subway Osgoode. **Rates** $219-$389 single/double. **Credit** AmEx, DC, MC, V. **Map** p277/p278 E7.

This is a rarity: a modern hotel (built in 1975, with a major redesign completed in 2000) with character. The lobby, with its raised wooden floor and hanging curtain, looks as though it was created by stage designers, which it was. Exit stage left for the Canadian-themed (both in terms of design and food) Tundra restaurant, and exit stage right for chunky glass elevators that carry you to hallways designed to mimic the flow and activity of a river (note the abstract fish, stones and ripples in the carpet patterns). The rooms have asymmetrical furniture and sleek fixtures that are modern, but comfortable and warm. The Hilton shares its polygonal pool with a nearby health club and in return guests get access to the club's squash courts and aerobics classes. It's also worth a trip to the basement conference centre where dozens of photographs of Lake Ontario hang.

Hotel services *Air-conditioning. Babysitting (on call). Bars (2). Beauty salon. Business services. Concierge. Disabled: adapted rooms. Gym. Internet point. Laundry. Limousine service. No-smoking floors. Parking ($22 Mon-Fri; $12 Sat, Sun). Restaurants (3). Swimming pool (indoor/outdoor).* **Room services** *Bathrobe. Dataport (high-speed; limited). Iron. Minibar. Room service (24hrs). Turndown. TV: cable/pay movies.*

Hotel Le Germain Toronto

30 Mercer Street, at Windsor Street, Entertainment District, ON M5V 1H3 (1-866 345 9501/416 345 9500/fax 416 345 9501/www.hotelboutique.com). Streetcar 504. **Rates** $225-$275. **Map** p277 D8.

To add to its outposts of swank in Montreal and Quebec City, the Germain Group was at press time set to open the doors of its fourth boutique hotel in February 2003. Call to check details before visiting.

Renaissance Toronto Hotel at SkyDome

1 Blue Jays Way, at Front Street W, Entertainment District, ON M5V 1J4 (1-800 237 1512/416 341 7100/fax 416 341 5091/www.marriott.com). Streetcar 504/subway St Andrew or Union. **Rates** *Summer* $249-$579. *Winter* $169-$249 single/double. **Credit** AmEx, DC, MC, V. **Map** p277 D8.

The Renaissance is built into the fabric of the SkyDome, the stadium that is home to the Blue Jays baseball team and sundry other events. However, in the wake of the BJ's fall from grace from its early '90s heyday, and after a complete refit in 2001, it is cutting its jock roots and presenting itself, successfully, as a more sophisticated all-rounder. Gone are the baseball memorabilia and concrete decor; in are muted reds, golds and greens, business facilities and all round comfort. There's no getting away from the fact that 80 of the rooms overlook the ballpark (with opening windows), along with the bar and restaurant – a bonus if you're a sports fan and compelling even if you're not. They're split level (protecting the bedroom from the camera angles – *see p34* **Score!**), with a comfortable lounge and marbled bathroom. Classy. We hope they're working on internet access, though. The lack of a minibar irritates too.

Hotel services *Air-conditioning. Babysitting. Bar. Business services. Concierge. Disabled: adapted rooms. Gym. Internet point. No-smoking rooms. Parking ($18; valet $25). Restaurant. Swimming pool (indoor).* **Room services** *Bathrobe. Dataport. Iron. Minibar (some rooms only). Newspaper (Mon-Fri only). Room service (6am-1am). TV: cable/satellite.*

Soho Metropolitan

328 Wellington Street, at Blue Jays Way, Entertainment District (416 597 6316). Streetcar 504. **Rates** *$295-$435.* **Map** *p277 D8.*
This spanking new 86-room boutique hotel – due to open in March 2003 at press time – looks set to be an upscale affair. Sister to the Metropolitan Hotel Toronto (*see p37*), the Soho Met is promising the earth – enormous rooms (averaging 600 square feet), top of the range facilities and windows that open. Call to check details before visiting.

Windsor Arms

18 St Thomas Street, at Bloor Street E, University, ON M5S 3E7 (1-877 999 2767/416 971 9666/fax 416 921 9121/www.windsorarmshotel.com). Bus 4/subway Bay. **Rates** *$275-$375 single/double; $425-$1,800 suite.* **Credit** *AmEx, DC, MC, V.* **Map** *p280 E4.*
In 1927, this tiny hotel first opened its doors to the world's celebrities and millionaires. Business decayed along with the building and, in 1991, the Arms folded. But in 1995 developer-about-town George Friedmann bought the property and oversaw a painstaking reconstruction, wrestling the Arms back to its original neo-Gothic stateliness. (Only the stained-glass windows and the stone portico of the entrance are original. Everything else is a reproduction.) It proudly (bordering on haughtily) reopened in 1999, with only 28 rooms and suites. Many rooms have fireplaces and 'private butlers' cupboards' through which one can receive room service without having to interact with another human being. Discretion is the better part of service here. The regal Courtyard Café has 50-foot ceilings and the two-floor spa features skin care products from the Darphin company of Paris.

Hotel services *Air-conditioning. Babysitting (on call). Bars (2). Beauty salon. Concierge. Garden. Gym. Laundry. Limousine service (Bentleys). No-smoking rooms. Parking (valet $16). Restaurants (3). Swimming pool (indoor).* **Room services** *Bathrobe. Dataport (high-speed). Iron. Newspaper. Room service (24hrs). Turndown. TV: cable/DVD/VCR. Video/DVD library.*

Score!

Some days, it's just not easy for the batting team at SkyDome. They're knocking themselves out just trying to get to first base, while a couple in a hotel room above are already scoring. About 70 rooms at the **Renaissance Toronto Hotel at SkyDome** (*see p33*) come with a view of the stadium and some guests apparently like to do the same. It's debatable whether a mid-game tryst is a testament to baseball's sexiness or its dreariness, but it certainly captures the audience's attention.

The case that has become legend was an incident on 12 May 1996, when the Blue Jays were hosting the Boston Red Sox in front of 31,188 fans. Toronto won the game 8–7, but many spectators were more interested in the amorous action taking place in plain view in room 42 of the hotel. In addition to many pairs of binoculars, a TV camera was also trained on the coupling couple. Naturally, the tape was never broadcast, but the cameraman did give the Jays an instant replay in the video room after the game. Hotel security interrupted the pair after half an hour. Jays coach Alfredo Griffin told reporters at the time, 'It's a good thing they finished before the game ended or I don't think anyone would have seen the game'.

Expensive

Colony Hotel Toronto

89 Chestnut Street, at Dundas Street W, Chinatown, ON M5G 1R1 (1-800 387 8687/416 977 0707/ fax 416 585 3164/www.colonyhoteltoronto.com). Streetcar 505/subway St Patrick. **Rates** *$149-$179 single/double.* **Credit** *AmEx, DC, MC, V.* **Map** *p277/p278 E6.*
At the high end of the mid-range (actually, the two-level suites go far into the expensive category), the Colony has a nice touch of elegance, with dark wood and brass accents in the rooms and the lobby. Some of the meeting rooms open on to the outdoor pool and large sundeck. (The second, indoor pool is handy in poor weather.) The restaurants in the hotel are informal and the atmosphere is relaxed and friendly. If you're looking for an unusual place to hold a function like a wedding reception, try the Lakeview Room on the hotel's 27th floor – it rotates.

Hotel services *Air-conditioning. Bars (2). Beauty salon. Business services. Concierge. Disabled: adapted rooms. Gym. Internet point. Laundry. Limousine service. No-smoking floors. Parking ($20).*

Many people don't realise that the SkyDome bonking legend is not a one-off. There have been reports of at least two other such public trysts since the hotel opened. And in July 2000 – on Family Day no less – a local strip club pulled a promotional stunt, placing a gaggle of topless women in front of a hotel window for an inning to cheer the Jays on. Many people have suggested that SkyDome should be renamed 'Exhibition Stadium'.

Historically, the hotel has been grudgingly good-natured about such incidents after the event, but they'd be happier if they never happened in the first place. While the stories have given the hotel international publicity, it's not quite the image they'd like to project. New management took over the hotel in 2000, and they are strictly enforcing a clause in the room contract, which bans any form of lewdness or exhibitionism. One strike and you're out. Even so, stadium employees say they still catch plenty of frisky behaviour, so it seems only a matter of time before baseball fans are subjected to more off-field swinging.

Restaurants (2). Swimming pools (indoor/outdoor). **Room services** *Bathrobe (some rooms). Dataport (high-speed). Iron. Kitchenette (some suites). Minibar (some rooms). Room service (6am-1am). Turndown (on request). TV: cable/pay movies.*

Crowne Plaza Toronto Centre

225 Front Street W, at Simcoe Street, Entertainment District, ON M5V 2X3 (1-800 227 6963/416 597 1400/fax 416 597 8128/www.torontocentre. crowneplaza.com). Subway St Andrew or Union. **Rates** $200-$250 single/double. **Credit** AmEx, DC, MC, V. **Map** p277/p278 E8.

Because it is built at an angle to Toronto's grid system, few of the rooms in the Crowne Plaza have obstructed views (although the harbour is slowly disappearing from sight behind new waterfront condo towers). Attached as it is to the Toronto Convention Centre, the hotel attracts a lot of business traffic, but it has made better steps than many toward attracting leisure travellers. Its Accolade restaurant is rated one of the best in the city and the Victoria Spa (operated in the hotel by a separate company) is beautifully done up in printed floor tiles and bamboo. Services vary according to the room:

touches such as high-speed internet, bathrobes and kitchenettes only come with more expensive rooms. **Hotel services** *Air-conditioning. Babysitting. Bars (2). Beauty salon. Business services. Concierge. Disabled: adapted rooms. Gym. Internet point. Laundry. Limousine service. No-smoking. Swimming pool (indoor).* **Room services** *Bathrobe. Dataport (high-speed & dial-up). Iron. Kitchenette. Minibar. Newspaper. Room service (6am-2am). Turndown. TV: cable/pay movies/satellite/VCR/web TV.*

Delta Chelsea

33 Gerrard Street W, at Bay Street, Chinatown, ON M6G 1Z4 (1-877 814 7706/416 595 1975/fax 416 585 4375/www.deltachelsea.com). Bus 6/subway College or Dundas. **Rates** $139-$239 single/double. **Credit** AmEx, DC, MC, V. **Map** p277/p278 E6.

With 1,590 rooms, this is the largest hotel in the British Commonwealth. It feels as though an entire village is housed in this one-building complex at the corner of Bay and Gerrard Streets. The restaurants run the gamut from food court to fine dining and the hotel has an affiliation with a spa around the corner. The Chelsea is kid-friendly to the extreme, with a well-equipped child care centre (with live bunnies),

a video arcade, specialised family suites with bunkbeds and child-compatible fixtures, plus plans for a hundred-foot waterslide dropping into the all-ages pool. But it's also grown-up friendly, with a second, less frenetic, adults-only pool, which adjoins a fitness centre and a drinks lounge.
Hotel services *Air-conditioning. Babysitting. Bars (3). Business services. Concierge. Disabled: adapted rooms. Garden. Gym. Internet point. Laundry (self-service & valet). No-smoking floors. Parking ($23; valet $29). Restaurants (3). Swimming pools (indoor; 2).* **Room services** *Bathrobe. Dataport. Iron. Kitchenette (some rooms). Newspaper. Room service (24hrs). Turndown. TV: cable/pay movies/videogames.*

Holiday Inn on King

370 King Street W, at University Avenue, Entertainment District, ON M5V 1J9 (1-800 263 6364/416 599 4000/fax 416 599 7394/www.hiok. com). Streetcar 504/subway St Andrew. **Rates** $159-$289 single/double. **Credit** AmEx, DC, MC, V. **Map** p277/p278 E7.

The hotel rises like a white mountain, looming over the nearby Entertainment District. The art deco lobby harks back to a time before this building was built in 1990; a $2 million renovation programme in late 2002 has decked out the rooms in rich browns and dark greens. Wraparound windows provide many of the rooms with abundant natural light and great views of the city. About 65 of the 425 rooms have balconies and the west-facing rooftop pool on the 17th floor is the perfect place to float above the city. Do check out the totem pole in the Canadian Bar & Grill in the basement. The hotel paid $25,000 for it, so the least you can do is go have a look.
Hotel services *Air-conditioning. Babysitting. Bars (2). Business services. Concierge. Disabled: adapted rooms. Gym. Internet point. Laundry. Limousine service. No-smoking floors. Parking ($18; valet $24). Restaurants (2). Swimming pool (outdoor).* **Room services** *Bathrobe. Dataport. Internet. Iron. Minibar. Newspaper. Room service (6.30am-2am). Turndown. TV: cable/pay movies.*

Metropolitan Hotel Toronto

108 Chestnut Street, at Dundas Street W, Chinatown, ON M5G 1R3 (1-800 668 6600/416 977 5000/fax 416 977 9513/www.metropolitan.com/ toronto). Streetcar 505/subway St Patrick. **Rates** $170-$215 single/double; $295-$455 suite. **Credit** AmEx, DC, MC, V. **Map** p277/p278 F8.

This Asian-owned Metropolitan is probably a little less stylish than it likes to think itself, but nonetheless it has tasteful and comfortable rooms with narry a floral in sight: think beige and beech, with intelligent touches such as double decker desks, good lighting, large bath towels and your radio tuned to French *chansons* at turndown time. The rooms aren't huge, but they are lovely. The restaurants are distinctly smart (gourmet Chinese Lai Wah Heen is highly thought of) and room service meals of a high standard. It's a little let down by its ordinary public areas, though the nearby city hall dictates that there

are a lot of business visitors who probably don't mind it that way. A good, central location.
Hotel services *Air-conditioning. Bar. Business services. Concierge. Disabled: adapted rooms. Gym. Laundry. Limousine service. No-smoking floors. Parking ($19; valet $24). Restaurants (2). Swimming pool (indoor).* **Room services** *Bathrobe. Dataport. Ethernet (executive suites only). Iron (on request). Minibar. Newspaper. Room service. Turndown (luxury rooms & executive suites). TV: cable/pay movies/VCR (executive suites).*

The Sutton Place Hotel

955 Bay Street, at Wellesley Street, University, ON M5S 2A2 (1-800 268 3790/416 924 9221/fax 416 924 1778/www.suttonplace.com). Bus 6, 94/subway Wellesley. **Rates** $129-$159 single/double; $299-$329 suite. **Credit** AmEx, DC, MC, V. **Map** p277/p280 E5.

A local newspaper once referred to it as the 'cereal box on Bay', but the blocky, International Style exterior hides some of the most luxurious rooms in the city. The hotel shoots for a European feel with a ballroom lit by stunning Venetian-style chandeliers and suites named after great operas. The intersection of Bay and Wellesley is no oil painting, but the hotel is located across the street from Bistro 990, the host restaurant for the Toronto Film Festival (*see p24*). Sutton Place graciously receives celebrity traffic year-round, especially in its penthouse suites. But even the ordinary rooms are furnished with fine antiques and east-facing rooms have balconies. The hotel opened in 1967, and they're still getting return visitors from the first year.
Hotel services *Air-conditioning. Babysitting. Bar. Beauty salon. Business services. Concierge. Disabled: adapted rooms. Gym. Internet point. Laundry. Limousine service. No-smoking floors. Parking ($20; valet $28). Restaurant. Swimming pool (indoor).* **Room services** *Bathrobe. Dataport. Iron. Kitchenette (in luxury suites). Minibar. Newspaper. Room service (24hrs). Turndown. TV: cable/pay movies/VCR (in suites)/web TV.*

Toronto Marriott Eaton Centre

525 Bay Street, at Dundas Street W, Dundas Square, ON M5G 2L2 (1-800 905 0667/416 597 9200/fax 416 597 9211/www.marriotteaton centre.com). Bus 6/streetcar 505/subway Dundas. **Rates** $169-$299 single/double. **Credit** AmEx, DC, MC, V. **Map** p277/p278 E6.

Love to shop but hate fresh air? There is no better place to stay in Toronto if you want never to go outside. But although the attached shopping mall is a big selling point, many rooms overlook Trinity Church and the small but peaceful Labyrinth Park, which beckon you to set aside any agoraphobic tendencies. The lobby of the hotel has lots of natural light and plenty of greenery, and skylights illuminate the pool on the 18th floor. Expect to be greeted when you arrive – the hotel front desk is overstaffed just so there's always someone to welcome you.
Hotel services *Air-conditioning. Babysitting (referral). Bars (2). Beauty salon. Business services. Concierge. Disabled: adapted rooms. Gym. Internet*

Light touches at the **Metropolitan Hotel Toronto**. *See p37.*

point. Laundry. Limousine service (on call).
No-smoking floors. Parking ($16; valet $20).
Restaurants (3). Swimming pool (indoor). **Room**
services *Bathrobe (some rooms). Dataport (high-*
speed). Iron. Newspaper. Room service (24hrs).
Turndown (on request). TV: cable/videogames.

Moderate

Bond Place Hotel

65 Dundas Street E, at Bond Street, Dundas Square,
ON M5B 2G8 (1 800 268 9390/416 362 6061/fax
416 362 6046/www.bondplacehoteltoronto.com).
Streetcar 505/subway Dundas. **Rates** $95-$130
single/double. **Credit** AmEx, DC, MC, V.
Map p277/p278 F6.
The hotel staff here are a collective polyglot, able to
serve travellers in, amongst other languages,
Cantonese, Tamil, most of the Romance languages
and, of course, English. The independently run hotel
is far enough from Yonge Street to keep the rent
down, but close enough to still be considered central. While prices can shoot upward during special
events such as Caribana and the Molson Indy, most
of the time this hotel is great value, especially if your
gang can fill a triple or quadruple occupancy, which
cost only a little more than a standard double.
Hotel services *Air-conditioning. Babysitting*
(on call). Bar. Concierge. Disabled: adapted rooms.
Internet point. Laundry. Limousine service.
No-smoking floors. Parking ($12). Restaurant.
Room services *Dataport. Iron (on request).*
Room service (7am-11pm). TV: cable/pay movies.

Hotel Victoria

56 Yonge Street, at Wellington Street, Financial
District, ON M5E 1G5 (1-800 363 8228/416 363
1666/fax 416 363 7327). Streetcar 504/subway
King or Union. **Rates** $90-$170 single/double.
Credit AmEx, DC, MC, V. **Map** p277/p278 E8.
Old and small are good things when it comes to
hotels, and this one is both. Built in 1908, Hotel

Victoria is one of the oldest continuously operating
hotels in the city. Recently, the second floor was converted from meeting areas into new bedrooms,
bringing the total up to 56. The rooms are on the
small side and some have vastly better views than
others, but this venerable institution has more character than many nearby behemoths. At press time,
the hotel plans to contract in a restaurant.
Hotel services *Air-conditioning. Laundry.*
No-smoking floors. **Room services** *Dataport.*
Iron. TV: cable.

The Strathcona Hotel

60 York Street, at Wellington Street, Financial
District, ON M5J 1S8 (1-800 268 8304/fax 416
363 4679). Streetcar 504/subway King or Union.
Rates $75-$129 single/double. **Credit** AmEx, DC,
MC, V. **Map** p277/p278 E8.
Some of the rooms are quite small, but a recent
redesign makes the most of the space, with furniture
that is both cosy and functional. The hotel gets a fair
bit of overflow business from the Fairmont Royal
York Hotel across the street, so it can fill up when
there's a big conference in town. But it's a logical
choice if you need to be right downtown and don't
want to blow your entire holiday budget on the hotel.
The Strathcona has a deal with a nearby fitness club
that gives guests cheap access to hot tubs, squash
courts and a full gym.
Hotel services *Air-conditioning. Babysitting (on*
request). Bar. Concierge. Laundry. Limousine service.
No-smoking floors. Parking ($12). Restaurants (2).
Room services *Bathrobe (corporate only). Dataport*
(corporate only). Iron. Newspaper (corporate only).
Room service (6.30am-9pm). TV: cable/pay movies/
videogames.

Budget

The Bay Hotel

650 Bay Street, at Elm Street, Chinatown, ON
M5G 1M8 (416 971 8383/fax 416 971 8527/

www.baystreethotel.com). Bus 6/streetcar 505/subway College, Dundas. **Rates** $55 single; $70 double. **Credit** AmEx, MC, V. **Map** p277/p278 E6.

There are nicer budget hotels in town, but none with a lobby painted quite so vibrant a shade of pink. Its main selling points are that it's central (close to the bus station), the staff are surprisingly friendly, and it's cheap, especially for longer stays – commit to a week and cut your room rate by more than a third; a month brings it down by more than two thirds. Look at your room before you settle in to check the varying ameneties. Bathrooms are shared.

Hotel services *Air-conditioning (some rooms). Cooking facilities. Internet point. Laundry (self-service). No-smoking floors.* **Room services** *TV: cable.*

Executive Motor Hotel

621 King Street W, at Bathurst Street, Entertainment District, ON M5V 1M5 (416 504 7441/fax 416 504 4722). Streetcar 504, 511. **Rates** $65-$99. **Credit** AmEx, MC, V. **Map** p276 C8.

All the retro with none of the irony. Built in 1983, and the beneficiary of $1.5 million in renovations in 2002, this classic motor inn still feels like something from the 1950s. The rooms have been gutted and outfitted with new furniture, linens and fixtures, the balconies spruced up, and the parking lot smartly re-landscaped. There are many decent restaurants nearby, though be warned that most close pretty early. Rates include breakfast and parking, the latter being particularly valuable this close to downtown. It's basic, but cool.

Hotel services *Air-conditioning. No-smoking rooms. Parking (free).* **Room services** *Dataport (dial-up). Iron. TV: cable/pay movies.*

Victoria's Mansion Guest House

68 Gloucester Street, at Church Street, Church & Wellesley, ON M4Y 1L5 (416 921 4625/fax 416 944 1092/www.victoriasmansion.com). Subway Wellesley. **Rates** $65-$130 single/double. **Credit** MC, V. **Map** p281 F4.

In the calm garden in front of this old Victorian house, four lions spit water eternally into a small fountain. The inn's human-friendly grey cat (named China) can often be seen prowling nearby. The brick mansion, built as a residence in the 1890s, sits on a wide, shady street very close to the Church Street Village. It opened as a tourist hotel in 2000, with 23 highly individual rooms. All rooms have been refurbished and have a fridge and microwave. Some are set up with kitchen facilities to suit longer stays.

Hotel services *Air-conditioning. No-smoking rooms. Parking ($10).* **Room services** *Dataport. Iron. Kitchenette (some rooms). TV: cable.*

Downtown East

Expensive

Days Inn & Conference Centre Downtown

30 Carlton Street, at Church Street, Church & Wellesley, ON M5B 2E9 (416 977 6655/fax 416 977 0502/www.daysinn.com). Streetcar 506/ subway College. **Rates** $119-$199 single/double. **Credit** AmEx, DC, MC, V. **Map** p277/p278/p281 F5.

Another of Toronto's many buildings that are nicer on the inside than on the outside, this outwardly drab building has a surprisingly lofty lobby, with marble floors and art deco fixtures. Strongly reliant

Your car will thank you for choosing the **Executive Motor Hotel**.

on the a hockey-oriented clientele, the largest Days Inn in Canada has been forced to reposition itself, after Toronto's hockey team moved from Maple Leaf Gardens next door, to the Air Canada Centre across town a few years ago. The ground floor sports bar is slated to move upmarket and a hot tub is going in next to the pool. The rooms are still small and cheery, and the services are good value for money. **Hotel services** *Air-conditioning. Babysitting (on-call). Bar. Barber. Concierge. Disabled: adapted rooms. Gym. Laundry. Limousine service. No-smoking floors. Parking ($15). Restaurant. Swimming pool (indoor).* **Room services** *Dataport (high-speed). Iron. Newspaper (corporate rooms). Turndown (on request). TV: cable/pay movies.*

The Grand Hotel & Suites Toronto

225 Jarvis Street, at Dundas Street E, Moss Park, ON M5B 2C1 (1-877 324 7263/416 863 9000/ fax 416 863 1100/www.grandhoteltoronto.com). Streetcar 505. **Rates** $149-$269 junior/deluxe suites; $399-$599 ambassador suites. **Credit** AmEx, DC, MC, V. **Map** p277/p278 F6.

Opened in 2000, this boutique hotel caters largely for the film industry and other business travellers who require longer stays. Its large, luxurious suites, complimentary breakfasts, softly lit pool and unparalleled views of the lake and the city from two rooftop hot tubs – not to mention the understated beauty of the neo-classical limestone lobby – allow stars such as Gabriel Byrne and Shaquille O'Neal to feel right at home here. (You'd never know, incidentally, that this building was fomerly the headquarters of the Royal Canadian Mounted Police.) **Hotel services** *Air-conditioning. Babysitting. Bar. Boutique (24hrs). Business services. Cooking facilities. Disabled: adapted rooms. Gym. Internet point. Laundry (self-service). No-smoking rooms. Parking ($12). Patio (covered). Restaurant. Swimming pool (indoor).* **Room services** *Bathrobe. CD player. Dataport (high-speed). Iron. Kitchenette. Newspaper. Room service (24hrs). Turndown. TV: pay movies/satellite/DVD/VCR.*

Marriott Courtyard

475 Yonge Street, at College Street, Church & Wellesley, ON M4Y 1X7 (1-800 487 5075/416 924 0611/fax 416 924 8692/www.courtyard.com). Streetcar 506/subway College. **Rates** $199-$299 single/double. **Credit** AmEx, DC, MC, V. **Map** p277/p278/p281 F5.

This tower has changed custody many times over the years. When its latest foster parent, Marriott, took over in 1999, it was a shell of a hotel. So, all the fixtures and furniture are modern and the rooms are spacious if somewhat soulless. Despite its address, the hotel entrance faces away from Yonge Street, so it's central but quiet. Although the hotel occupies a 17-storey building, the views aren't great, even from the top. The casual restaurant and pool make this a good place for families. **Hotel services** *Air-conditioning. Babysitting. Bar. Business services. Concierge. Disabled: adapted rooms. Gym. Laundry (valet & self-service).*

Limousine service. No-smoking floors. Parking ($15; valet $20). Restaurant. Swimming pool (indoor). **Room services** *Dataport (high-speed). Iron. Newspaper. Room service (5-10pm). TV: cable/pay movies/videogames.*

Novotel Toronto Centre

45 The Esplanade, at Scott Street, St Lawrence, ON M5E 1W2 (416 367 8900/fax 416 360 8285/ www.novotel.com). Subway Union. **Rates** $170-$310 single/double. **Credit** AmEx, DC, MC, V. **Map** p277/p278 F8.

The absence of any porters (and wheeling your own brass luggage cart makes supermarket trolleys seem like Porsches) flags a non-sycophantic level of service, but the unpretentious, solid Novotel offers good facilities and a decent location for the money. A well-kept traditional lobby complete with gift shop, bar and liveried concierge hustling theatre tickets belies rooms that are simple (though well kitted out) and with maybe one pastel colour too many. The breakfast buffet cuts no corners and the gym, though ill-advisedly muralled with people of a sickly cast, does the job well, with four types of cardio machines, a multi gym and free weights. Not luxury, then, nor stylish, but reliable, well run and good value (particularly the room service and minibar). **Hotel services** *Air-conditioning. Bar. Disabled: adapted rooms. Gym. No-smoking rooms. Parking ($15.50). Restaurant. Swimming pool (indoor).* **Room services** *Dataport. Iron (on request). Minibar. Room service. TV: cable/pay movies.*

Le Royal Meridien King Edward

39 King Street E, at Victoria Street, St Lawrence, ON M5C 1E9 (416 863 0888/fax 416 863 4102/www.lemeridien-kingedward.com). Streetcar 504/subway King. **Rates** $179-$200 single/double; $300-$500 suites. **Credit** AmEx, DC, MC, V. **Map** p277/p278 F8.

Architect E J Lennox, who also built Casa Loma and Old City Hall, sure knew how to show off with his work. Even regular guests look up in awe as they pass through the soaring marble columns of the four-storey lobby, overseen by a portrait of King Edward VII himself. The King Eddy, which celebrates its centenary in 2003, is a designated historic building and retains all of its grandeur, from the original chandeliers in public areas, to the high ceilings in the 294 gloriously spacious rooms and suites. But the hotel is also keeping up with the times. They have plans to add 165 'Art & Tech' rooms, featuring wide-screen plasma televisions, beds stuffed with the latest comfort-producing technology and sci-fi inspired bathroom and lighting fixtures. The hotel's Café Victoria is a favourite breakfast spot for Toronto's power elite. **Hotel services** *Air-conditioning. Babysitting. Bar. Business services. Concierge. Disabled: adapted rooms. Gym (24hr). Laundry. Limousine service.*

Luxuriate in a bucolic setting at the **Old Mill Inn**. *See p43.*

No-smoking floors. Parking (valet $26). Restaurant.
Room services *Bathrobe. Dataport (high-speed).*
Iron. Minibar. Newspaper. Room service (24hr).
Turndown. TV: cable/pay movies/satellite/web TV.

Moderate

The Aberdeen Guest House

52 Aberdeen Avenue, at Parliament Street,
Cabbagetown, ON M4X 1A2 (416 922 8697/fax
416 922 5011/www.aberdeenguesthouse.com). Bus
65/streetcar 506. **Rates** $110-$130 single/double.
Credit AmEx, MC, V. **Map** p281 G5.
This beautifully decorated bed and breakfast is in a
Victorian house on a quiet street in Cabbagetown.
A low iron gate opens into a small front flower
garden and each guest room is named after a flower.
During good weather, breakfast is served in a lush
and blooming backyard. But owners Gary and
Richard aren't just resting on their florals. They
work hard to make guests feel welcome and
comfortable, but they are also adamant about
giving people their own space. No children under 16.
Hotel services *Air-conditioning. Garden. Gym.*
Laundry. No-smoking hotel. Parking ($5; limited).
Room services *Bathrobe. TV: cable.*

Au Beauregard Bed & Breakfast

12 Prospect Street, at Parliament Street,
Cabbagetown, ON M4X 1C6 (416 960 5682/fax
416 960 9249/www.aubeauregardbandb.com). Bus
65/streetcar 506. **Rates** $85-$115 single/double.
Credit AmEx, MC, V. **Map** p278/p281 G5.
This new-ish B&B gets a lot of the Aberdeen's (*see
above*) overflow business and it's a good second
choice. In a slight variation on Toronto's ubiquitous
Victorian architecture, the house, constructed
in 1902, is Edwardian, and therefore a little less
ornate. Each room is different, but the handsome one
with a private jacuzzi is very popular, as is another
with a large, private balcony.
Hotel services *Air-conditioning. No-smoking hotel.*
Room services *TV: cable.*

Howard Johnson
Selby Hotel & Suites

592 Sherbourne Street, at Bloor Street E, Church
& Wellesley, ON M4X 1L4 (1-800 446 4656/416
921 3142/fax 416 923 3177/www.hojo-canada.com).
Bus 75/subway Sherbourne. **Rates** $119-$199
single/double/suites. **Credit** AmEx, DC, MC, V.
Map p281 G4.
In the 1920s, Ernest Hemingway pitched up here,
while making his name as an intrepid newspaper
reporter. Today, this historic building has a suite
named in his honour. The red brick hotel was
builtas a private home in 1880, then served as a
girls' school until 1915. Today, its 82 clean, basic
rooms provide travellers with an attractive alternative to the downtown high-rises. It's a little out of
the centre, but handy for the subway, and close
enough to walk to Yonge Street. You'd be wise to
studiously avoid the home office rooms in the

Fourth Street Bed & Breakfast. See p44.

basement: the windows in them are so small, you
might not be able to tell when the sun rises.
Hotel services *Air-conditioning. Laundry (self-*
service). No-smoking rooms. Parking ($10). **Room**
services *Dataport (some rooms). TV: cable.*

Ramada Hotel & Suites Downtown

300 Jarvis Street, at Carlton Street, Church &
Wellesley, ON M5B 2C5 (1-888 298 2054/416 977
4823/fax 416 977 4830/www.ramada.ca). Streetcar
506/subway College. **Rates** $99-$159 single/double;
$175-$239 1-bed suites; $199-$299 2-bed suites.
Credit AmEx, DC, MC, V. **Map** p277/p278/p281 F5.
Right across the street from Allen Gardens and the
greenhouses of the Toronto Horticultural Society
(*see p76*), this 1929 designated historic building was
originally an apartment complex. Some legacies
from the early days remain: the elevator shafts are
smaller than average, and old (refinished) cast-iron
bathtubs are larger than average, and look even bigger in the small bathrooms. The hotel shares its pool,
fitness room, squash court and billiards table with
an adjacent condo complex.
Hotel services *Air-conditioning. Babysitting. Bar.*
Beauty salon. Disabled: adapted rooms. Gym. Internet
point. Laundry. Limousine service (on call). No-
smoking floors. Parking ($15). Restaurant.
Swimming pool (indoor). **Room services** *Dataport*
(high-speed). Iron. Newspaper. Room service (7am-
2pm, 5-9pm). TV: cable/pay movies.

Budget

Neill-Wycik College Hotel

96 Gerrard Street E, at Church Street, Church &
Wellesley, ON M5B 1G7 (1-800 268 4358/416 977
2320/fax 416 977 2809/www.neill-wycik.com).

Streetcar 506/subway College or Dundas.
Rates $38 single; $55 double; $76 triple/suite.
Credit AmEx, MC, V. **Map** p277/p278 F6.
During the academic year, this is a co-operative students' residence, but from May to October, it becomes a tourist hotel, which offers some of Toronto's best value rooms in terms of location. Rooms are grouped in clusters of four or five, with each cluster sharing two common bathrooms, a kitchen and a living area. Unfortunately, there's no bar on the premises, but the Love at First Bite restaurant on the ground floor is licensed and provides a place to drink and socialise with other travellers. The hotel gives discounts to students, seniors and hostel members.
Hotel services *Concierge. Cooking facilities. Garden (on roof). Internet point. Laundry. Parking ($10). Restaurant. TV room.*

West End

Expensive

Old Mill Inn

21 Old Mill Road, at Bloor Street W, ON M8X 1G5 (1-866 653 6455/416 236 2641/fax 416 236 2749/www.oldmilltoronto.com). Subway Old Mill. **Rates** $195-$375 single/double; $395-$595 suite. **Credit** AmEx, DC, MC, V.
The original mill was built on this site next to the Humber River in 1793, the year Toronto was founded. Today the wooded valley feels almost as secluded as it would have been then. The Tudor-style hotel incorporates the stone ruins of a later mill and it exudes history and luxury. The Tea Room restaurant has been operating on this site since 1914. The inn itself opened in 2001, a boutique hotel with only 47 rooms and 13 large suites. The individually designed rooms encircle a wild, multi-level garden with water flowing every which way. Dining and dancing, tennis courts, a spa and easy access to trails and parks make you forget you're even in a city (should you want to). And if you like your fluffy bathrobe, duvet, or even your bed, remember that they're all for sale.
Hotel services *Air-conditioning. Babysitting. Bars (2). Beauty salon. Business services. Concierge. Disabled: adapted rooms. Garden. Gym. Laundry. Limousine service (on call). No-smoking hotel. Parking (free). Restaurants (2). Spa.* **Room services** *Bathrobe. CD player. Dataport (high-speed). Iron. Minibar. Newspaper. Room service (24hrs). Turndown. TV: cable/pay movies/VCR (on request).*

East Side

Moderate

Beaches Bed & Breakfast

174 Waverley Road, at Queen Street E, ON M4L 3T3 (416 699 0818/fax 416 699 2246). Streetcar 501. **Rates** $85-$170. **Credit** AmEx, MC, V.

The character of this longstanding B&B is a direct result of the character who runs the place. Enid Evans, who used to own a lingerie shop called Enid's Underworld, has decked out each of the four guest rooms in this century-old house with eclectic themes, including a jungle room (and jungle bathroom) and a romantic, curtain-shrouded loft bed. The location is great, just off Queen Street East, and a block and a half from the boardwalk. Allergy sufferers beware: Enid shares the property with three cats – Silky, Fluffy and the White Fang.
Hotel services *Air-conditioning. Garden. Internet point. No-smoking hotel. Parking ($5).* **Room services** *Kitchenette (some rooms). TV: cable.*

Waterfront & Islands

Expensive

Radisson Plaza Hotel Admiral

249 Queen's Quay W, at Rees Street, Waterfront, ON M5J 2N5 (1-800 333 3333/416 203 3333/fax 416 203 3100/www.radisson.com). Streetcar 509, 510. **Rates** $169-$349 single/double. **Credit** AmEx, DC, MC, V. **Map** p277 D7.
This nautically themed hotel offers great views of the harbour from the Promenade deck and outdoor pool, as well as from Commodore's Restaurant. The lobby is all lacquered wood and brass, with a smattering of interesting marine art and artefacts. Nearby activities abound during the day – golf, tennis, cycling and sailing – but at night, the surrounding area is a bit of a wasteland. To compensate, there's a complimentary limousine service into downtown.
Hotel services *Air-conditioning. Bar. Business services. Concierge. Disabled: adapted rooms. Gym. Internet point. Laundry. Limousine service. No-smoking floors. Parking ($18) Restaurants (3). Swimming pool (outdoor).* **Room services** *Bathrobe (on request). Dataport. Iron. Minibar. Newspaper. Room service (24hrs). Turndown. TV: cable/pay movies.*

The Westin Harbour Castle

1 Harbour Square, at Bay Street, Waterfront, ON M5J 1A6 (1-888 625 5144/416 869 1600/fax 416 869 0573/www.starwood.com/westin/index.html). Bus 6/streecar 509, 510. **Rates** $128-$394 single/double. **Credit** AmEx, DC, MC, V. **Map** p277/p278 F9.
Light, spacious rooms, and unobstructed harbour views (request accommodation on the south side of the building) are the big draws here. Sunshine glints off the glassed-in pool and bakes the large rooftop terrace. A day spa opened in autumn 2002 with a two-storey waterfall and views of Lake Ontario from each treatment room. With its recently renovated meeting spaces, the hotel draws a lot of convention business, but it also has better than average services for families with children, who appreciate all the leisure facilities. The waterfront area ceases to bustle in the evening but the hotel operates a shuttle

service to downtown in compensation. Some rooms are showing their age, with the rather noisy air conditioning and wallpaper in need of a touch-up. **Hotel services** *Air-conditioning. Babysitting. Bars (2). Business services. Concierge. Disabled: adapted rooms. Gym. Internet point. Limousine service. No-smoking floors. Parking ($15; valet $26). Restaurants (3). Swimming pool (indoor).* **Room services** *Bathrobe. Dataport. Iron. Minibar. Newspaper. Room service (24hrs). Turndown. TV: cable/pay movies/DVD (on request)/VCR.*

Budget

Fourth Street Bed & Breakfast

10 and 22 Fourth Street, The Islands, ON M8V 2Y3 (416 203 7551). Ferry to Ward's Island. **Rates** $80-$100 single/double. **No credit cards.**
Sisters Ronni and Julie Bates rent out a total of three rooms in their two homes in the heart of the village on Ward's Island. The setting is so idyllic, it's no surprise that almost half their business comes from Torontonians looking for an escape from the city. The upstairs rooms are mostly windows and have private bathrooms. Breakfast is served hot and to order. Rates also include the use of bicycles. **Hotel services** *Garden. Internet point. No-smoking hotel.*

Midtown

Luxury

Hotel InterContinental Toronto

220 Bloor Street W, at Admiral Avenue, the Annex, ON M5S 1T8 (1-800 327 0200/416 960 5200/fax 416 960 8269/http://toronto.canada.intercontinental. com/). Subway Museum. **Rates** $226-$410 single/double. **Credit** AmEx, DC, MC, V. **Map** p280 D4.
Über-company Six Continents is in the process of rebranding its InterContinental chain, to dissociate it from its poorer siblings, Holiday Inn and Crowne Plaza. They recently dropped more than $400,000 on refurbishing the private and public spaces at the Toronto location. (Oddly, the dark, heavy wooden doors and rich carpet make the hallways the area that feels the most sumptuous.) With fax machines, computer printers, wireless keyboards for TV web access and extensive meeting space, the hotel is clearly courting business traffic. The narrow lap pool in the fitness centre is fine for executive stress-busting yet unsuitable for child's play. But the rooftop deck, courtyard café and proximity to the shops of Yorkvilleall attract holidaymakers as well. **Hotel services** *Air-conditioning. Babysitting. Bar. Business services. Concierge. Disabled: adapted rooms. Garden. Gym. Laundry. Limousine service. No-smoking floors. Parking (valet $30). Restaurant. Swimming pool (indoor).* **Room services** *Bathrobe. Dataport (high-speed). Iron. Minibar. Newspaper. Room service (24hrs). Turndown (on request). TV: cable/pay movies/video games/web TV.*

Four Seasons Hotel

21 Avenue Road, at Cumberland Street, the Annex, ON M5R 2G1(1-800 819 5053/416 964 0411/fax 416 964 2301/www.fourseasons.com/toronto). *Subway Museum.* **Rates** $285-$570 single/double. **Credit** AmEx, DC, MC, V. **Map** p280 E4.
A staff of 600 serve a hotel that can hold a maximum of 764 guests. So if the hotel is only three quarters full, you can have your own servant. OK, so that's not quite true, but the Four Seasons prides itself on its attentive service, which has made it a preferred resting spot for countless A-list movie and rock stars. (It was here, also, that Jean Chrétien, whilst dining on a hamburger in his suite, decided to step down as prime minister.) A swanky anchor of this sophisticated area's moneybags scene, the hotel's four restaurants, include multi-award-winning Truffles. In 2001, the Four Seasons spent $1.5 million to reinvent their ground floor bar, formerly known as La Serre, into Avenue Bar & Lounge (*see p135*), in what has proven to be a highly successful attempt to maintain its youthful image. The mostly outdoor pool is kept at 95°F (35°C) in winter, so you can swim when it's snowing. **Hotel services** *Air-conditioning. Babysitting. Bars (2). Business services. Concierge. Disabled: adapted rooms. Garden. Gym. Internet point. Laundry. Limousine service. No-smoking floors. Parking ($8; valet $26). Restaurants (4). Spa. Swimming pool (indoor/outdoor).* **Room services** *Bathrobe. Dataport (high-speed). Kitchenette (some suites). Minibar. Newspaper. Pressing service. Room service (24hrs). Turndown. TV: cable/paymovies/videogames.*

Park Hyatt

4 Avenue Road, at Bloor Street, the Annex, ON M5R 2E8 (416 925 1234/fax 416 924 4933/http://park toronto.hyatt.com/property/index.html). Subway Museum. **Rates** $249-$419 single/double. **Credit** AmEx, DC, MC, V. **Map** p280 E4.
Classy as you'd expect: marbled halls, be-capped bellboys, soft carpets and seamless service. Not a style leader – that would be far too vulgar – but a provider of international top-end comforts taste-fully rendered. Among them are an own-renowned top floor bar with terrace, a coffee shop with the standards of a upmarket restaurant and a very beautiful spa, though guests have to pay to use anything other than the fitness room, including, rather inconveniently, the changing rooms. Though it's probably worth the 20 bucks to luxuriate on your own private TV couch while you get over the exertions of the sauna. Rooms vary in size but share pleasant, if rather safe decor with good-quality wooden furniture, marble-topped desks and photos hung under their own lights. Here's a tip: if you can't figure out the tap, pull it towards you. **Hotel services** *Air-conditioning. Bars (2). Beauty salon. Business services. Disabled: adapted rooms. Gym. No-smoking rooms. Parking ($27 valet). Restaurants (2).* **Room services** *Bathrobe. Dataport. Iron. Minibar. Newspaper. Turndown (on request). TV: cable/pay movies.*

Park Hyatt: clean and classy. *See p44.*

Moderate

The Casa Loma Inn

21 Walmer Road, at St Clair Avenue W, Forest Hill, ON M5R 2W7 (416 924 4540/fax 416 975 5485). Subway Dupont. **Rates** *$90-$140 single/double.* **No credit cards. Map** p280 C1.

If you come by taxi to this strategically named inn, make the address clear to the cabby. Sometimes guests get dropped off at the tourist attraction of the same name, which is several blocks away. Many of the carved ash pillars and crown mouldings in this 1885 house are original and more character has been preserved than in many Victorian hotels. The high ceilings and arches of the foyer are, unfortunately, not duplicated in the rooms, but the tall windows are. Every room has a fridge and microwave. **Hotel services** *Air-conditioning. Laundry (self-service). Parking ($10-$15).* **Room services** *Bathrobe. TV: cable.*

Howard Johnson Downtown

89 Avenue Road, at Yorkville Avenue, Yorkville, ON M5R 2G3 (1-800 446 4656/416 964 1220/fax 416

964 8692/www.hojo-canada.com). Subway Museum. **Rates** *$105-$159 single/double.* **Credit** AmEx, DC, MC, V. **Map** p280 E4.

This is the best bet for staying in Yorkville on a budget. Located right next door to Hazelton Lanes, this chain hotel has homely rooms with wooden furniture and exposed brick walls. (The down side is that some rooms have windows that look out on to other brick walls). It's not cramped exactly but in the halls, lifts, rooms and bathrooms you'll always wish you had just a little more space. Although there's no restaurant, your room fee includes a free breakfast, and round-the-clock coffee and tea. **Hotel services** *Air-conditioning. No-smoking floors. Parking ($10).* **Room services** *Dataport. Iron. TV: cable/pay movies.*

Madison Manor Boutique Hotel

20 Madison Avenue, at Bloor Street W, the Annex, ON M5R 2S1 (1-877 561 7048/416 922 5579/ fax 416 963 4325/www.madisonavenuepub.com/ madisonmanor). Subway St George or Spadina. **Rates** *$89-$194 single/double; $194 suite.* **Credit** AmEx, DC, MC, V. **Map** p280 D4.

This historic Victorian mansion on a quiet road just off Bloor Street W has 23 rooms, each individually decorated by co-owner Isabel Manore. (She and her husband David also own the adjoining Madison Avenue Pub, *see p136.*) Furnished with antiques found in Queen Street boutiques, the rooms vary in size, price and amenities. Four rooms have balconies, and three have fireplaces. (A word to the wise: the hotel says it has never had a complaint about it, but some of the rooms appear disturbingly close to the patios of the bar next door.) The hotel gives discounts to U of T students' parents, but children under 13 years of age are not allowed. Rooms include continental breakfast. **Hotel services** *Air-conditioning. Bar. No-smoking hotel. Parking ($10; limited). Restaurant.* **Room services** *Dataport. Iron (on request). Kitchenette (some rooms). TV: cable.*

Budget

Ainsley House Bed & Breakfast

19 Elm Avenue, at Sherbourne Street, Rosedale, ON M4W 1M9 (1-888 423 3337/416 972 0533/fax 416 925 1853/www.interlog.com/~hannigan). Subway Sherbourne. **Rates** *$49-$100 single/double.* **Credit** MC, V. **Map** p281 G3.

Staying at this European-style guesthouse gives you rare access to a Rosedale mansion, though that access is limited. Guests are steered away from the living room, which is used by the Hannigan family who run the B&B (Ruth Hannigan named the business after her university residence). The rooms in this century-old English cottage-style house have high ceilings and iron beds, plus en suite bathrooms. Hot breakfast is served every day. **Hotel services** *Air-conditioning. Babysitting. Internet point. No-smoking hotel. Parking (free).* **Room services** *TV: cable.*

The friendly **Global Village Backpackers**.

Global Guest House

*9 Spadina Road, at Bloor Street W, the Annex,
ON M5R 2S9 (416 923 4004/fax 416 923 1208/
www.inforamp.net/~singer). Streetcar 510/subway
Spadina.* **Rates** *$56-$66 single; $66-$76 double.*
Credit MC, V. **Map** p280 C4.

Norman and Rhona Singer run this renovated 1889
house, next door to Spadina subway station. Rhona's
paintings decorate each room and Norman has been
known to play ragtime on the old piano in the office.
With only ten rooms, the hotel is intimate, but it's
by no means a hostel, nor is it a B&B. It doesn't serve
breakfast, but there are free hot and cold beverages
in the common room – the Singers call it a 'Bed and
Tea'. Not all rooms have an en suite bathroom. The
backyard is available for use on request.
Hotel services *Air-conditioning. Cooking facilities.
Garden. Internet point. Laundry (self-service). No-
smoking hotel.* **Room services** *TV: cable.*

Hostels

College Hostel

*280 Augusta Avenue, at College Street, Chinatown,
ON M5T 2L9 (416 929 4777/fax 416 925 5495/
www.affordacom.com). Streetcar 506, 510.*
Rates *$55-$65 single; $70-$80 double; $25 dormitory.*
Credit AmEx, DC, MC, V. **Map** p276 C5.

Just off College Street on the edge of Kensington
Market, this popular hostel is pretty well equipped.
The single and double rooms have cable TV and
phones, and the games room has a pool table and
pinball machine. The restaurant, Oishi Kada, is a
fast and friendly sushi bar.
Hotel services *Cooking facilities. Internet point.
No-smoking hotel. Parking (free). Restaurant.*
Room services *TV: cable.*

Global Village Backpackers

*460 King Street W, at Spadina Avenue,
Entertainment District, ON M5V 1L7 (1-888
844 7875/416 703 8540/fax 416 703 3887/
www.globalbackpackers.com/toronto/tor.htm).
Streetcar 504, 510.* **Rates** *$50-$56 single; $19-$25
dormitory.* **Credit** MC, V. **Map** p276 C7.

Jack Nicholson slept here. Of course, it was a hotel
then, not a hostel. Now it's a bright and friendly rest
spot offering dormitories, quads and a few private
rooms. The busy bar is a good place to meet fellow
travellers, and the hostel organises many events,
including memorable tours of Niagara Falls in their
rainbow-painted 'Magic Buses'.
Hotel services *Bar. Cooking facilities. Garden.
Internet Point. Laundry (self-service). No-smoking
rooms. Payphone. TV room: cable/VCR.*

Hostelling International Toronto

*76 Church Street, at Adelaide Street E, St Lawrence,
ON M5C 2G1 (1-877 848 8737/416 971 4440/
fax 416 971 4088/www.hostellingint-gl.on.ca/
toronto.htm). Streetcar 504, 501/subway King.*
Rates *$64 single/double; $23 dormitory.* **Credit** MC,
V. **Map** p277/p278 F7.

This is a basic hostel whose 188 beds are mostly
found in dorms, though the few private rooms do
have en suite bathrooms. There is a rooftop patio.
It's a social place, with organised walking tours of
the city and a pub crawl every Wednesday.
Hotel services *Air-conditioning. Cooking facilities.
Internet point. Laundry (self-service). No-smoking
hotel. TV room: cable/VCR.*

The Planet Traveler's Hostel

*175 Augusta Avenue, at Dundas Street W,
Chinatown, ON M5T 2L4 (416 599 6789/
www.theplanettraveler.com). Streetcar 505,
510.* **Rates** *$50-$65 single; $20 dormitory.*
Credit AmEx, MC, V. **Map** p274 C6.

There's no sign, so look for the garden planted in a
vaguely planetary pattern, and the stained-glass
Earth above the door. It's a small hostel with a big,
friendly attitude. Staff throw barbecue and blender
drinks parties each Saturday on the back patio,
which also has a popular one-hole mini-golf course.
Bathrooms are shared and there's a complimentary
breakfast of pastries and fruit.
Hotel services *Cooking facilities. Internet point.
No-smoking hotel. TV room: cable/VCR.*

Camping

Indian Line Campground

*Near highways 427 and 407; 5 Shoreman Drive,
Downsview ON M3N 1S4 (1-800 304 9728/905 678
1233/fax 416 667 6271/email iline@trca.on.ca).*
Rates *Serviced site $26/night; $156/week. Unserviced
site $21/night; $126/week.* **Credit** AmEx, MC, V.

From May to October, you can camp at the 234
serviced and unserviced sites on the Humber River.
Facilities include a swimming pool, a laundry, hot
showers and a campground store. They have some
sites for RVs as well as tents.

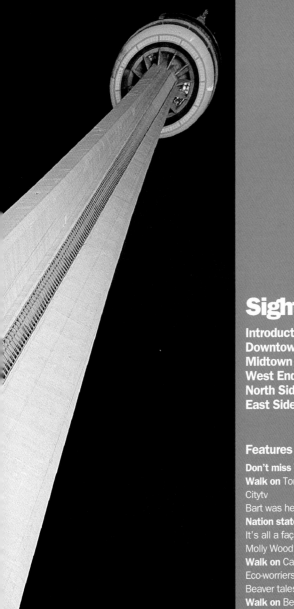

Sightseeing

Features

Introduction

Welcome to Toronto. Now get out and explore.

Sightseeing

Toronto has a clutch of big-hitting sights: the CN Tower, obviously, and, depending on your cultural orientation, the Hockey Hall of Fame, SkyDome, Royal Ontario Museum and Art Gallery of Ontario. But compared to some other cities, it has few must-see attractions or major museums to commit an indoors afternoon to. Much of the pleasure of experiencing Toronto during the day comes from being out on the streets exploring its diverse neighbourhoods, dipping in to whatever you find along the way: riding the streetcars, wandering around markets, stopping for a patio lunch or walking in a historic district or parkland artery (we've included three guided walks in this section, along with boxes on Toronto's ethnic neighbourhoods, another quintessential element of the city). For tourist information, *see p262*.

ORIENTATION

It is therefore particularly handy that Toronto is exceptionally easy to find your way around. First, it borders a lake, so if you sense a slight slope downwards, then that's south. Second, it has the world's tallest freestanding building – by definition almost ubiquitously visible – acting as a handy marker near the lakefront, just west of centre. Third, it's built largely on a grid system, with just enough variation to keep it interesting but not so much that getting lost is particularly easy.

Point zero for east–west street designation and numbering is Yonge (pronounced 'Young') Street, famously if tenuously the longest street in the world. (This is one piece of trivia you will never forget, so often is it brought to your attention during your stay.) Yonge starts on the central lakefront and heads north – yes, yes, all the way to the state line. So King Street, for example, which runs east–west, is called King Street West to the west of Yonge, and King Street East to the east, with numbers starting from zero at Yonge and running upwards and outwards along each arm. (North–south numbering starts at zero at the south end of roads and goes up as the road heads north.) On an east–west street, even numbers are on the north side, odd numbers on the south; on a north–south street, even numbers are to the west and odd to the east. Armed with this information, you (or your taxi driver) should seldom get lost. The only mildly confusing factor is that numbers on

either side of a street don't necessarily match up, or realign in any predictable way at intersections.

Some major thoroughfares have two names, notably Bloor Street, which turns into Danforth Avenue once you cross the Don River, and College Street, which becomes Carlton Street east of Yonge Street. Spadina (Spad-eye-na) Avenue is arbitrarily downgraded to a mere Road in midtown, despite the presence of the august Spadina (Spad-ee-na) House Museum.

Wandering at will is helped by the fact that you're unlikely to inadvertently find yourself in a dangerous area: there really aren't that many. As usual, keep your wits around you at transport terminals, and don't be tempted to short-cut from Cabbagetown to St Lawrence through the slightly ropy Regent Park/Moss Park area. For more on safety, *see p260*.

OVERVIEW

When Metropolitan Toronto amalgamated its five internal cities into one, it officially dropped the 'Metropolitan' moniker. That was in 1998. Now the whole shebang is simply known as the City of Toronto, or the 'mega-city', and stretches some 32 kilometres (20 miles) across and from the lakeshore to Steeles Avenue in the north. The population is 2.4 million and growing by the second, if you believe the statisticians. But there's another world on the Toronto's doorstep with a population that threatens to exceed the city's own: the vast expanse of suburbs, which go by the names of Mississauga, Brampton, Richmond Hill, Markham and Pickering, to name a few, strung out on a concrete necklace of freeways and malls. Torontonians dismiss hinterland residents as '905-ers', referring to the telephone area code that surrounds the city proper. (Add the appropriate adjectival expletive when you're caught in a traffic jam during rush hour.) Taken together, the city and its 'burbs are now called the GTA, or Greater Toronto Area, which is not a political entity as such and even less of a unified mindset.

This book focuses principally on the area defined by the original city of Toronto, roughly bounded by Eglinton Avenue on the north side, Victoria Park Avenue to the east, the waterfront and Islington Ave on the west, though we have extended those boundaries where an attraction warrants it.

Toronto has relatively few defined, named areas; often neighbourhoods are marked by a strip of businesses and called after their main artery – Queen West, the Danforth, Yonge & Eglington, for example – or their character: Entertainment District, Little Italy and so on. Our Sightseeing chapters, and the rest of the book, follow an area schema that sticks closely to local use but as there are no formal boundaries we have sometimes used arbitrary divisions.

Downtown Toronto, south of Bloor Street and between Bathurst and the Don Valley Parkway, is the business and civic heart of the city. Almost all the main 'sights' are here, along with the University of Toronto and the major arts and entertainment venues. People very much still live here, so although Toronto seldom bustles, it is seldom dead, either, day or night (Chinatown and the Entertainment District particularly). Next up is culturally diverse **Midtown**, where the money lives, plays and spends itself in tasteful fashion. Casa Loma and Spadina Historic House are here. The **West End** is the hipper side of town, with independent, individual shops, bars and restaurants and a boho lifestyle mainlining down Queen Street West and, to a lesser degree, College Street (Little Italy). If you go out at night and like to eschew the obvious for the characterful, you'll find yourself here often. The **East Side** is a little more unreconstructed, with traditional residential areas, the Greek-influenced Danforth, Little India and The Beach: exactly what it sounds like, with pleasant eating and drinking and some interesting residential roads to wander. Finally, the **North Side** has the civic amenities of North York, prior to amalgamation one of Canada's largest cities, and a lot of suburbia.

KEEP IT CHEAP

Toronto is a relatively cheap city to spend time in. The fact that Americans and Brits usually get a favourable exchange rate helps, of course, but so does the fact that lots of city facilities are free, including swimming pools and ice rinks. If you're planning on doing a lot of sightseeing, the **Museum Passport** ($25 adults, $20 concessions, $15 children), available from the Royal Ontario Museum (*see p73*) or TicketKing (416 872 1212/1-800 461 3333/www.ticketking), allows you in free to ten worthwhile museums and historic sites, though some are a way out.

Tours

Toronto is somewhere you can enjoyably explore independently, on foot or by public transport (the reliable, characterful streetcars particularly). If you prefer to be guided, **Gray Line** (416 594 3310/www.grayline.ca) and **Toronto Tours** (416 868 0400/www.toronto tours.com) both run standard tour rosters; Gray Line also offers a hop-on, hop-off bus.

In summer uniformed touts around the Harbourfront jetties hawk boat tours of the harbour. **Mariposa Tours** (416 203 0178) offers one-hour cruises; the **Great Lakes Schooner Company** (416 203 2322) will take you out on a three-masted tall ship. **Toronto Hippo Tours** (*see p171*) is a lot of fun; the bus turns into a raft and plunges into the harbour.

A Taste of the World

416 923 6813/www.torontowalksbikes.com.
Cost *Short walks* $25; $13 concessions; $9-$13 children. *Longer walks* $35; $30 concessions; $22 children. **No credit cards.**
Off-beat, culturally oriented walks, all with a prominent edible element, and some actively foodie. The First Chinatown, for example, kicks off with Chinese pastries, looks at cooking ingredients and utensils and ends with dim sum. Food is included in the cost. Literary and ghost walks are also offered, and bike tours may return to the schedule in future.

Sightseeing

Don't miss Toronto

Mainstream sights

CN Tower (*see p59*); **SkyDome** (*p59*); **Kensington Market** (*p69*); **Chinatown** (*p66*); **The Beach** (*p98*); **Queen Street West** (*p60*); **Royal Ontario Museum** (*p73*); **Art Gallery of Toronto** (*p55*); **Casa Loma** (*p84*).

Lesser-known sights

Hudson's Bay Company Gallery (*see p63*); **Bata Shoe Museum** (*p74*); **RC Harris Filtration Plant** (*p98*); **Elgin/Winter Garden Theatre Centre** (*p65*); **Toronto Islands** (*p52*); **Little India** (*p100*); **'West Queen West'** (*p89*).

Quintessential Toronto experiences

A peameal bacon sandwich at St Lawrence Market (*p71*); watching hockey in a bar; taking a streetcar; a dim sum lunch (*p112*); strolling a lakeside boardwalk; skating at Nathan Phillips Square (*p212*).

Viewpoints

CN Tower (*p59*); **Canoe Restaurant & Bar** (*p109*); looking back at the Waterfront from a Toronto Islands ferry (*p52*); the **Roof Lounge** (*p136*); **Panorama Lounge** (*p134*).

Downtown Toronto

From skyscraping modernity to collegiate tranquillity, Toronto's thriving downtown packs it in.

Waterfront

Maps p276, p277, p278 & p279

Useful transport: streetcar 509, 510/subway Queens Quay or Union

You'd never know it today, but Toronto owes its very existence to its natural harbour, a safe haven from tempestuous Lake Ontario. Long before the city was founded, this sheltered bay served aboriginal peoples as a centre for trade and commerce. In the 18th century the French and English found the inland port to be an ideal place to transfer animal pelts from shore to ship and send them back to satisfy Europe's huge market for beaver hats and muskrat stoles.

Through the 19th and 20th centuries, the harbour remained a centre for business and pleasure. In the early 1900s, these waters were filled with steamboats, which used Toronto as a base for tours of the Great Lakes. The opening of the Saint Lawrence Seaway in 1959 meant that huge ocean-going freighters could use the port. But in the years that followed, road transport took over much of the aquatic shipping business. The waterfront fell into decline, and the city turned its back on it. It's a pleasant place to wander but compared (as it inevitably is) to Chicago's, it's hardly a compelling urban focus.

These days, there is much huzzahing and ballyhoo about the rejuvenation of Toronto's harbour, a project that has essentially been ongoing since the 1970s. The waterfront has indeed improved greatly and it's easy to fill a day or two exploring the shops, galleries, theatres, museums and outdoor art installations. But Toronto's urban planners have yet to find a way to fix one major flaw: the harbour remains cut off from the rest of the city. You could spend weeks in Toronto without ever realising you were next to one of the world's largest bodies of fresh water.

Three barriers stand between the city and its harbour: first, a series of raised railway tracks create cavernous, echoing underpasses that pedestrians must share with speeding traffic. Then, the soaring, roaring ramps of the Gardiner Expressway block passage to the water. (Planners still bat around the idea of sinking the Gardiner into a tunnel, à la Boston's Big Dig, but

the project would be too costly and disruptive for it ever to become a reality.) Finally, you have to negotiate a concrete and glass fortress of condominium towers. By the time you can see the water, you're close enough to touch it.

Though the harbourfront attractions theoretically span the entire length of Queens Quay from the mouth of the Don River in the east to Ontario Place in the west, most of the good stuff is clustered around a series of quays between Cooper Street and Lower Portland Street. The best place to begin exploring is at the terminus of Yonge Street. (If you arrive by subway to Queens Quay, you will emerge one street further west, at Bay.) Here, a wave motif bridge overhangs the water and provides a decent first view of Lake Ontario. You'll also find the names of increasingly distant cities and towns inscribed in the pavement. This is a nod to Yonge Street's claim to fame: it is the world's longest street. (Or alternatively, the world's longest cul-de-sac. It depends on your opinion of Rainy River, the city at the far end, 1,896 kilometres/1185 miles away). Just across Queens Quay, you can see the office tower at the seminal address, 1 Yonge Street, home of the *Toronto Star*, Canada's largest newspaper.

A little to the east, on Queens Quay, in the complex of storage towers and giant machinery of the Redpath sugar refinery, is the **Redpath Sugar Museum** (*see p56*). The warehouses, bus garages and highway ramps just to the east of the museum are of little interest unless you happen to be a fan of urban infrastructure. But a bicycle path that runs along the waterfront will eventually take you further out to the Port of Toronto, where all the shipping takes place now, and on to the Beaches area, or north into the Don Valley park system.

Where Bay Street joins Queens Quay, there is a path that leads behind the Westin Harbour Castle to the Island ferry docks (*see p52* **Walk on Toronto Islands**) and to **Harbour Square Park**. If you're looking for quiet green space in which to escape the crowds and the hustle of the city, this is not the place. City towers loom over the busy strip of grass, squeezing it against the water. If you follow the park around Harbour Square back to the main road, you'll find **Pier 6** (145 Queens Quay W, at the foot of York Street), the oldest building

Walk on Toronto Islands

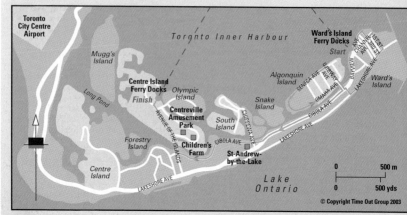

Handwritten (vertical, left margin): Matt 203 8605
Handwritten (vertical, left margin): Bcb 2030935 /3rd st

Start: Ward's Island Ferry Terminal
Finish: Centre Island Ferry Terminal
Distance: About 6km (4 miles)
Time: 60-90 minutes, not including stops
General information: 416 392 8195
Ferry timetable: 416 392 8193 ($5; $3 concessions; $2 under-15s)

Even in Toronto's big parks, you are rarely free from the sounds of sirens, horns and traffic. But the Toronto Islands are a remarkable exception, providing a complete escape from the worst aspects of the city, while giving some of the best views of the Toronto skyline. Ferries run year-round but the Islands are at their best during the dog days of summer, when they also provide relief from the withering heat and smog of the city. This walk takes in the community, beaches and park facilities of the islands. It can easily be done in two hours but leave yourself extra time to get sidetracked.

Take the Ward's Island Ferry from the terminal behind Westin Harbour Castle Hotel at Bay Street and Queen's Quay Boulevard. Walk begins from the ferry dock on Ward's Island.
'Ah.' That's the first feeling as you disembark into the clean air of the Toronto Islands. The second feeling is that you've woken up in The Village and will hereafter be known as 'Number Six'. There are almost no motor vehicles. Instead, you're greeted by bicycles, tandems, quadricycles and other weird velocipede variations swishing along asphalt paths.

Bear to the left along the waterside concrete path that turns into Bayview Avenue. Turn right on to Third Street.
Although the street signs look like those on the mainland, the streets are interconnected paths, barely wide enough for two people to walk abreast. (You can bike through here, but it's better for everyone if you walk.) The houses in this village comprise dozens of variations on the theme of twee serenity. The paths are hemmed by flower gardens, picket fences, spreading trees and cottages. In the 1950s the city tried to chase the locals off the islands to make way for a park. Walking through this quiet paradise, it's easy to see why people fought so hard to keep their island community.
Turn left at Channel Avenue and walk to First Street.
In 1858, a massive storm washed out the land bridge that connected the islands to the mainland. The Eastern Gap has since been dredged and deepened. It is now an important shipping route, as well as a backdrop for a spectacular garden of lilies, primroses and daisies.
Follow First Street to Lakeshore Avenue, where you turn right.
Lakeshore Avenue, the major east–west thoroughfare, runs like a spine along the south side of the islands. It becomes a boardwalk for a stretch, from which you have a view across the water of a migratory bird sanctuary. Several paths to the right lead back through an imposing wall of greenery to

the gardens, picnic tables and playgrounds in the interior of the island. A few hundred metres along, take the one that leads to the **Rectory Café** (416 203 2152). This is the nicest spot to eat on the islands. An escape from the omnipresent burgers and fries, it offers home-made soups, sandwiches and other tasty treats. The Rectory is also a cultural centre with gallery shows and music performances. Check the bulletin board near the entrance to find out what's on.

Continue along the path to Cibola Avenue. Turn left and then quickly turn right on to Algonquin Bridge, which turns into Ojibway Avenue after it crosses Omaha Avenue. Keep following it north to the shore.

Swans, ducks, geese and kayakers are all commonly seen paddling through these still waters, while the city rises up behind them. This is the best view there is of the Toronto skyline.

Turn left on Seneca Avenue. At Wyandot Avenue, a secluded trail leads off the path. This trail loops around and rejoins Omaha Avenue. Recross Algonquin Bridge and continue west on Cibola Avenue. When the path forks, stay to the right.

Just after it crosses Chippewa Avenue, the path runs by **St Andrew-by-the-Lake Church** (416 203 0873). This small Anglican Church, built in 1884, still offers regular Sunday services, as well as weddings and baptisms. The humble clapboard exterior forms a contrast with the gothic arches of its stained-glass windows. The shady setting and nearby picnic tables make this a good resting spot on your walk.

The path continues west to Avenue of the Islands. Turn right.

A small hedge maze just east of the avenue is light on dead ends and provides a shady diversion if you like to turn 90 degrees every few footsteps.

Follow Avenue of the Islands north over a white and pastel-green bridge, peaking over a quiet canal.

If you have children, turn right just after the Iroquois Coffee Shop to enter the **Centreville Amusement Park** (416 203 0405). (If you don't have children, flee this area.) This noisy, crowded amusement park has enough sugar shops, carny games, fast-food joints and rides, to keep any kid fat and amused indefinitely. Attractions include swan, pedal and bumper boats, plus a miniature train, a petting farm, a video arcade and a bare-bones miniature golf course.

The main path continues on to the Centre Island Ferry dock, where you can make the journey back to the smoke and noise of civilisation.

THE BATA SHOE MUSEUM

TORONTO'S MOST UNIQUE MUSEUM IN THE HEART OF THE CITY.

The Bata Shoe Museum
327 Bloor St. West (at St. George subway)
www.batashoemuseum.ca 416.979.7799

on the waterfront. Built in 1907, the former freight shed has had many incarnations, including a stint as the shore station for the Royal Canadian Yacht Club. It now houses a coffeeshop franchise and souvenir shop. On warm days, the former cargo doors are opened up, allowing you to sip your latte while enjoying the sights, sounds and smells of boats to-ing and fro-ing.

A quarter of a century ago, the **Queens Quay Terminal** (207 Queens Quay W), just to the west, was a disused food warehouse, a casualty of hard times at the harbour. Today, it's an affluent office/shopping mall complex with about 30 boutiques that cater to the discriminating – in other words, wealthy – souvenir hunter. The restaurants in the mall have large terraces, perfect for a harbourside meal. The terminal also houses the **Premier Dance Theatre** (416 973 4000; see p222).

Next door, the **Power Plant** gallery (416 973 4949, 231 Queens Quay W) is easy to spot thanks to its distinctive smokestack, a vestige from its days as a generating plant. Built in 1926, the Power Plant and its conjoined sibling, the Ice House (now the **Du Maurier Theatre Centre**), provided heating and cooling for the Toronto Terminal Warehouse (which later became Queens Quay Terminal). Its conversion to a gallery began in 1980 but the doors didn't open to the public until 1987. The Power Plant features contemporary works and installations by Canadian and international artists. A word to the credulous: the Du Maurier Theatre is reputed to be haunted by as many as three different ghosts. When Para-Researchers of Ontario (www.pararesearchers.org) investigated a few years ago, 'several members of the team experienced identical sensations of difficulty in breathing' and there were reports of an 'apparition' running with supernatural silence down a hallway. Employees at the theatre have heard the rumours but none has actually confirmed any ghostly presences.

Next door, in yet another converted terminal building, the **York Quay Centre** (235 Queens Quay W) is home to a complex of exhibition and performance spaces administered by a not-for-profit cultural organisation called the **Harbourfront Centre** (416 973 3000). The Brigantine Room is where the Harbourfront Reading Series (see p27 **Where to find it**) takes place, featuring writers as diverse as Ethan Hawke and Salman Rushdie. The **Craft Studio** (416 973 4963) gives visitors the opportunity to see real live craftspeople making blown glass, textile and ceramic knick-knacks. These products are for sale at the Bounty Contemporary Canadian Craft Shop (416 973 4993). The studio also offers classes and it

occasionally features guest artists. The York Quay complex also includes indoor and outdoor performance spaces, and four art galleries.

Just outside, in the summer, hobbyists skipper remote-controlled model boats around a wee pond. In the winter, this knee-deep water becomes a public skating rink. Also facing the lake, the outdoor **Harbourfront Centre Concert Stage** features multicultural music festivals each weekend from Canada Day (1 July) to Labour Day (first Monday in September). Along this stretch of pier, you'll also find many uniformed touts shilling boat tours of the harbour. You can also take sailing lessons and rent kayaks at the waterfront.

From here, the attractions peter out somewhat, particularly since the Pier Waterfront Museum closed in the summer of 2002. It is, however, worth visiting the charming **Toronto Music Garden** a few blocks further west at Spadina Avenue and Queens Quay Boulevard W, with areas landscaped and planted to reflect various musical forms (there's no actual music). This is a peaceful place to wind down, with a pleasing view of a small marina. Across the boulevard, the **Harbourfront Antique Market** (390 Queens Quay Boulevard W, 416 260 2626) is Canada's largest.

At the foot of Bathurst Street, behind the last standing grain elevator on the Waterfront, is a public boat service that crosses the Western Channel to Toronto City Centre Airport. Dubbed 'the shortest ferry ride in the world', the trip takes less than 60 seconds. The city has approved a plan to replace the ferry with a bridge if a controversial expansion of the airport proceeds. A half-hour walk further along the shore through a dead space of condominiums and benign parks takes you to **Ontario Place** (see p56) and **Exhibition Place** (see below).

Exhibition Place

Lakeshore Boulevard W, between Strachan Avenue & Dufferin Street (416 263 3600/www.explace.on.ca). Bus 29/GO Exhibition/streetcar 509, 511/subway Union. **Open** call for details. **Admission** varies. **Map** p276 A9.

The imposing Princes' Gates that rise up to meet you as you approach the grounds from the east promise much pomp and circumstance. But don't let them fool you. The 100 or more major events that take place each year on these vast grounds range from the homey to the holy, such as the Canadian National Exhibition, which celebrated its 130th anniversary in 2002, the Royal Agricultural Winter Fair, the Molson Indy car race and the Canadian Hardware & Home Improvements Show (*see also chapter* **Festivals & Events**). Exhibition Place also hosted the Pope and several hundred thousand Catholic whippersnappers at the 2002 World Youth Day.

Ontario Place

955 Lake Shore Boulevard W, between Aquatic Drive & Newfoundland Drive (416 314 9900/www.ontario place.com). Bus 29/GO Exhibition/streetcar 509, 511/subway Union. **Open** *Summer only; dates and times vary; call for details.* **Admission** $10-$25.50; $12-$15 concessions; free under-4s. *IMAX tickets* $6. **Credit** AmEx, MC, V. **Map** p276 A9.

This amusement park makes the most of its lakeside location. The walkways, cafés and even the IMAX theatre are built out over the water and many of the rides – from waterslides to an oddly likeable faux-log boat ride – involve getting at least a little wet. The pedal boats, normally the runt of the amusement park litter, are quite a lot of fun here, as you can chug over a large distance, in and out of the futuristic structures that criss-cross the water. Amid the usual grease and sugar confections, you can actually find some non-toxic food at the park, including submarine sandwiches and freshly squeezed lemonade. The park has several stages, including the Molson Amphitheatre, and hosts concerts, readings and other special events.

Redpath Sugar Museum

95 Queens Quay E, between Yonge Street & Lower Jarvis Street (416 366 3561). Bus 6, 75/streetcar 509. **Open** 10am-noon, 1-3.30pm Mon-Fri. **Admission** free. **Map** p277/p278 F9.

Although its hours don't lend themselves to the weekend tourist trade, free admission makes this unusual museum one sweet deal. The entrance is poorly marked but when you sign in the gate attendant will point you in the right direction. The museum, housed in a converted sugar bag warehouse, was opened in 1979, and underwent a major revamp in 1996. In addition to generic exhibits on the history of the Redpath dynasty and of the sugar industry in general, there are also special programmes for groups. To the museum's credit, these programmes have often delved into meaty, controversial issues of the sugar trade, including the role of child and slave labour in the sugar business, the introduction of women into the workforce and the role of immigrant labour in Ontario's beet sugar industry.

Downtown West

Maps p276, p277 & p278

Useful transport: streetcar 501, 504, 510/subway Osgoode, St Andrew & Union.

This area is not misnamed. Its southern stretch does it monolithically and the northern grid on a more human scale, but this is where Toronto comes to have fun, as do busloads of visitors.

A triumvirate of major atttractions are plonked between the tracks running in to Union Station and the Gardiner Expressway:

Citytv

As brash and self-promoting as the medium itself, the home of Citytv on Queen Street W is something of a pilgrimage point for media junkies. The wedding -cake Victorian Gothic edifice at the corner of Queen and John Streets is a study in contrasts. Look for one of the station's original news vehicles smashing through the outer wall, three storeys up.

It's Citytv, the brainchild of Moses Znaimer, a broadcast executive who champions local coverage and likes to see his name on the small screen; his is the first credit to appear after every in-house production. Nobody said TV wasn't about ego and his has propelled the station to pioneer many techniques that are now industry standards the world over. The whole building acts as a set for roving hosts and announcers: rigid talking heads are anathema to the station's high-energy, quick-cutting style.

The station has spawned a number of programmes that are sold internationally – *Fashion Television*, *The New Music* and *Media Television* among them. Even the format of its from-the-hip style of news reporting – where just one person operates the camera, does the interviewing as well as the stand-ups to camera – has been licensed, along with the Citytv name, to stations around the globe.

the **Air Canada Centre** arena, the thrusting needle of the **CN Tower** and **SkyDome** stadium (for all *see p59*) with its famous retractable roof. All are accessible via indoor walkways from Union Station, and if you're on foot they are best approached from there or the walkway's other street junction at Front and opposite John Streets – this is otherwise not a pedestrian-friendly area. Still, damned conveniently, the walkway has another exit on to Bremner Boulevard right opposite **Steam Whistle Brewing** (*see p60*), a microbrewery that offers frequent tours and tastings of its fine pilsner lager.

Moving north, many of Toronto's media and fashion elite work in the more user--friendly area Queen Street West roughly between Bathurst and University Avenue, and accordingly it is densely populated with nightclubs, theatres, too-cool-for-school cafés, designer clothing shops and plenty of good-looking people.

A cult following has grown around a late-night talk show on Fridays, hosted by a puppet with a bad attitude named Ed the Sock. In a nod to the station's groundbreaking early days, Citytv has brought back the 'Baby Blue Movie' after the stuffed sock has had his say, titillating midnight viewers with soft-core porn.

The Chumcity Building – so called because the station is part of the Chum radio broadcasting empire – also houses MuchMusic, the country's music video station. Pavements outside the street-level studio are packed with gawking teens eager to catch a glimpse of the veejays and the music stars they interview. Studio concerts by pop acts like the Backstreet Boys and Alanis Morissette routinely shut down traffic on Queen Street. A weekly dance programme called *Electric Circus* turns the building into a disco-lit rave.

At the other end of the TV spectrum – and the building – is the Bravo! channel studio where Phillip Glass, Diana Krall and internationally known authors stop by for an impromptu performance or reading.

But it's perhaps the little booth on the corner that best identifies the unconventional approach to television that has defined City from the start. Drop a loonie in the slot and have your say on *Speaker's Corner*. Znaimer says it's all about democratising the medium. The media

savvy know it as the cheapest – and most ingenious – form of programming out there. On this station, everyone can have his or her 15 minutes of fame.

A guided tour of the **Canadian Broadcasting Corporation's** Toronto headquarters (250 Front Street W, at John Street, live tapings 416 205 3700, guided tours & museum 416 205 8605) is the perfect way to get to know a great Canadian institution and to get a sense of Canadian culture. The CBC, Canada's publicly owned radio and television broadcaster, has a tendency to produce on-air personalities who, while not celebrities in the Hollywood sense, are well-known and much beloved across the country. Interviewers such as Peter Mansbridge and the late Peter Gzowski come to feel like friends of the family. If that sounds hokey, well, that's part of the CBC too. The small, free museum generally has engaging exhibits combining the history of Canadian public broadcasting with the history of Canadian arts and culture. Many shows are recorded in front of a live studio audience, so check if something is being taped during your stay. The **Glenn Gould Studio** (*see p196*) is also in this building.

A few blocks north, on Richmond Street, at the corner of John Street, is the **Paramount Cinema** (259 Richmond Street W, 416 368 5600). If you can stand the sensory overload, you will find an out-of-place and often-overlooked display at the top of the long staircase that leads from the lobby to the cinemas. This, the Paramount Historic Railing, includes sections of the bronze railing from the lobby of the original Paramount Theatre in Times Square, New York. A small collection of old photographs and a continuous video presentation help recapture the grandeur of the 1920s movie experience.

The **MZTV Museum of Television** (277 Queen Street W, 416 591 7400 ext 2870) offers regular guided tours. Founded by Moses Znaimer (*see p56* **Citytv**), the museum features what it claims is the world's largest collection of television sets and memorabilia. The exhibition includes about 200 tellies, including a 1928 General Electric 'Octagon',

Albrecht Dürer *Adam and Eve* (detail), 1504, engraving on laid paper. © 2003 Art Gallery of Ontario

Can we tempt you?

Discover a world of delights at the AGO!

Enjoy special exhibitions and tours, one-of-a-kind shopping at the Gallery Shop, or lunch or weekend brunch at AGORA.

The Art Gallery of Ontario is one of North America's largest art museums, with a permanent collection of 36,000 works representing 1,000 years of European, Inuit, modern, Canadian and contemporary art, plus the world's largest public collection of works by renowned British sculptor Henry Moore.

Art Gallery of Ontario

317 Dundas Street West, Toronto, Canada   416-979-6648
Tue, Thu, Fri: 11-6; Wed: 11-8:30; Sat & Sun: 10-5:30   www.ago.net

an experimental model never sold to the public, and the 1939 Phantom Teleceiver, which launched the television age in North America.

In the heart of the fashion district, at Richmond and Spadina, a century-old warehouse known by its address – **401 Richmond** (416 595 5900) – has been converted into a centre for all things creative. Grab a snack at the airy café on the ground floor and you may well be solicited to watch a performance installation at one of the building's many art galleries. Or you can transport your food up to the large rooftop garden, though the tables fill up quickly during fine weather. Among more than 130 tenants, you'll find sculptors, architects, animators and environmental groups, as well as the headquarters of two of Canada's more interesting publications, the politically left-wing *THIS Magazine* and *FUSE Magazine*, which covers alternative arts and culture.

Air Canada Centre

40 Bay Street, S of Front Street W (416 815 5500/ www.theaircanadacentre.com). Subway Union. **Tours** *May-Aug hourly 10am-4pm daily* (dependent on events; call to check). Closed Sept-Apr. **Admission** $12; $8-$10 concessions. **Credit** AmEx, MC, V. **Map** p277 E8.

The 21,000-seat arena offers regular 'behind the scenes' tours that, schedule permitting, include a glimpse inside the dressing rooms of home teams the Raptors (basketball) and the Leafs (ice hockey), as well as a chance to try on a goalie outfit. This tour is definitely for fans of sport, not fans of architectural megastructures.

CN Tower

301 Front Street W (416 868 6937/www.cntower.ca). Subway Union. **Open** *Tower* Summer 8am-11pm daily; winter 9am-11pm daily. *Other attractions* call for details. **Admission** $16-$30; $11-$20.50 concessions; free under-4s. **Credit** AmEx, MC, V. **Map** p277 D8.

A comedian once said that the best thing about the CN Tower is that it's the only place you can be in Toronto where you don't have to look at the CN Tower. Love it or hate it, there's one thing everybody agrees on: it's very, very tall. Completed in 1976 by the Canadian National company, it's the world's tallest freestanding structure (there's ongoing debate about whether it qualifies as a building, given that most of it is just an unoccupied pillar of reinforced concrete). It stands 553 metres (1,815 feet) high and is basically a big radio antenna (and tourist attraction). Visitors are awed by its height and locals are pleased to have such clear TV reception. The tower is about twice as high as its closest competitor in the city and it is astounding to watch the surrounding 40- and 50-storey buildings fall away below you from the glass elevator. The basic ticket takes you up to the 346-metre (1,136-foot) Lookout Level, where there are indoor and outdoor

CN Tower's glass floor: *do* look down.

observation decks plus a nerve-jangling section of glass floor. The Horizons Café is cheaper and more casual than the tower's swanky and improved rotating restaurant called 360. From here, you can pay to reach the Sky Pod another (notional) 30 floors further up. The experience is truly breathtaking and, at busy times, can also be mildly claustrophic. Vertigo sufferers can head to the basement to find a short documentary on the construction of the tower, as well as some underwhelming simulator rides and video games. Oh, and a vast gift store.

SkyDome

1 Blue Jays Way (416 341 2770/www.skydome.com). Streetcar 504/subway Union. **Tours** *hourly 10am-3pm daily* (dependent on events; call to check). **Admission** $12.50; $7-$8.50 concessions; free under-5s. *Roof tours* 10.30am & 1pm daily (dependent on events; call to check). **Admission** $25. **Credit** AmEx, Disc, MC, V. **Map** p277 D8.

Looking like a giant, white beetle, the SkyDome is a more interesting building than the Air Canada Centre and has a more interesting tour. It begins with a 15-minute film about the construction. The walking tour varies according to what's happening in the stadium but, in addition to the boxes, media centre and memorabilia room, it can include a walk on the field, or even a tour of the amazing roof. When the stadium opened in 1989, the fully retractable roof was the only one of its kind in the world. An efficient, quiet rail system allows it to open or close in only 20 minutes, expending about $6's worth of electricity. The stadium holds up to 70,000 people, though few events actually draw that many fans especially since the fall from success of resident ball team the Blue Jays. One thing the tour does not cover is Toronto artist Michael Snow's sculpture, *The Audience*, on the outside of the stadium. You can find this frieze of 14 agog spectators high on the northeast corner of the SkyDome.

Steam Whistle Brewing

255 Bremner Boulevard, at Spadina Avenue (416 362 2337/www.steamwhistle.ca). Streetcar 509, 510. **Open** *Winter* noon-6pm Mon-Thur; noon-7pm Fri, Sat. *Summer* noon-8pm daily. **Tours** (every hr from 1pm) $4. **Map** p277 D9.

Of the many microbreweries in Toronto, this recent addition gets top marks for location, sandwiched betwen the ACC and the CN Tower in a railway roundhouse (turntable) building. The brewery tour informs about combining hops and malt as well as offering a glimpse into Toronto's railroading past. Rail buffs hope to convert the other portion of the roundhouse into a railway museum. For now, Steam Whistle pours sizeable samples and hosts art exhibits.

Queen Street West

Home to the cutting edge arty set in the 1970s and early 1980s, Queen Street West, from University Avenue to Bathurst Street, looks more like a mall with every passing day. Well-known retailers have moved in to cash in on the area's cachet, leaving the funkier galleries, restaurants and bookshops to emigrate further west in search of cheaper rent. Famous clubs like the Beverly and the Cameron remain, not to mention the Peter Pan, a refurbished diner that launched the 1970s renaissance, and the **Horseshoe Tavern** (*see p200*), a club that's played host to everyone from Stompin' Tom Connors to the Rolling Stones. But the new Queen West is elsewhere, further west on Queen Street towards Parkdale, and north-west on the newly groovy College Street strip.

Financial District

Maps p277 & p278

Useful transport: streetcar 501, 504/subway King, Osgoode, Queen, St Andrew & Union.

Bay Street is both a very real street that runs north to south through the middle of the Financial District, and a synonym for Canadian financial power. Four of the five major Canadian banks scrape the sky at the corner of King and Bay Streets and the twin golden towers of the fifth, Royal Bank, maintain an iconic presence a block south. Dozens of loan, trust, insurance, brokerage and legal firms surround them.

Bart was here

It finally happened! In a recent Simpsons' episode called *The Bart Wants What it Wants*, television's first family visits Toronto. It doesn't come easy: Homer asks the very reasonable question 'Why should we leave America to visit America Junior?'. But in the end, the family joins Bart to chase down his love interest, Greta, who has accompanied her father, the Arnie-like action movie star, to 'Hollywood North' for the filming of his latest McBain movie. In short, this is must-see TV for those still preparing their visit to Hogtown (even though it was a pretty dismal episode all told).

Such a 'tribute' should come as no surprise to fans of the show. Rarely does an episode go by without such snide Canuck asides as a 'Nuke Canada' arcade machine, immigrants groaning when told they have been refused entry to the US and have to go to Canada, a French-Canadian circus called *Cirque de Purée*, a Japanese game show combining Canadians and scorpions called *Sting Those Canadians*, a National Film Board of Canada production of a very nasty Zorro film, and the list goes on and on. Of course, this constant barrage of Canuck references has been obsessively documented on the internet – along with the speculation that Springfield is in fact in Canada since the town is located on Highway 401, the name of Ontario's main traffic artery, and since Homer expresses an inordinate amount of love for Canada's three basic food groups: doughnuts, bacon and a breakfast glass of maple syrup.

This obsession with Canada is also mirrored in *Seinfeld* (which is peppered with hints that perhaps Kramer is in fact a closet Canadian) and *South Park* (which features the fictional comedy sphincter duo of Terrance and Phillip, 'Canada's hottest stars'). Why? Well, of course natural jealousy does play a role here but the real reason is that there's always a Canadian in any self-respecting American comedy writing team (*see p175* **Borderline funny**). And when Canadians get tired of taking the piss out of Americans, they start taking the piss out of themselves...

Steam Whistle Brewing: vat's life. *See p60.*

Banks have clustered in the neighbourhood of King, Bay and Yonge Streets since at least the mid 19th century but the first wave of 'skyscrapers' didn't arrive until the early 20th century and the first biggies didn't appear until the 1920s and 1930s, a period that produced the still stunning **Canadian Imperial Bank of Commerce** building at 25 King Street W. Built 1929-31 and 34 storeys tall, it has a 20-metre (65-foot) high banking hall modelled on the Baths of Caracella in Rome and was once the tallest building in the British Commonwealth.

It retained its command of the neighbourhood until the mid 1960s, when the three original towers of the **Toronto-Dominion Centre** arose on the south-west corner of King and Bay Streets. Designed by the giant of modernism Ludwig Mies van der Rohe, the austere black-steel and bronzed-glass towers quickly became a Toronto landmark.

Other, taller structures quickly followed as rival banks sought to catch the public's eye. But none of them equals the TD Centre's austere pzazz and today the neighbouring banks are mostly notable for their helpful colour coding: the shiny steel of the 57-storey tower of the **Canadian Imperial Bank of Commerce** (designed by IM Pei); the white marble of the Bank of Montreal's **First Canadian Place** with its 72-storey tower; and the red granite of the **Bank of Nova Scotia**'s 66-storey tower. A more nondescript tower west of the Bank of Montreal tower, at York Street, houses

the Toronto Stock Exchange, while the TSE's former home round the corner at 234 Bay Street is now the **Design Exchange** (*see p62*).

Further south on Bay Street, the triangular towers of **Royal Bank Plaza** at 200 Bay Street are shorter (41 and 26 storeys) but more resonant of the Bay Street ethic, their mirrored golden windows an apt metaphor for Bay Street's driving materialism. Built in the mid 1970s, their opulent reflections have enriched the pages of many a corporate calendar.

Across the street, the massive towers of **BCE Place** look like a series of tin cans stacked haphazardly one atop the other. The complex incorporates the façades of several historic buildings on its Yonge Street side and houses the remains of Toronto's oldest surviving stone building, the former Commercial Bank of the Midland District (1845), within its bulk. The bank was designed by William Thomas who is also responsible for two other important structures in old Toronto – St Lawrence Hall and the old Don Jail. But the overall effect is one of kitschy Disneyfication. The centre's best feature, in fact, is its astonishing galleria. Designed by the Spanish architect Santiago Calatrava (who also designed a pedestrian bridge for the Etobicoke waterfront), the high white arches of the galleria resemble the ribs of a giant whale or the vaulted roof of an old cathedral.

An underground mall leads to the **Hockey Hall of Fame** (*see p63*), part of which occupies a rococo bank building on the north-west corner of Front and Yonge Streets. Once the main Toronto office for the Bank of Montreal, it dates from 1886 and boasts a 14-metre (45-foot) high banking hall and a stained-glass dome. Too bad that the architecture is now overshadowed by hockey memorabilia.

West on Front Street, the **Fairmont Royal York Hotel** (*see p33*) bestrides the street like a massive Stalinist chateau. One of a string of railway hotels that spans the country, the Royal York has been one of Toronto's signature hotels since it opened in 1929.

Across the street lies the massive colonnade of **Union Station**, a gateway to the city and a landmark in the struggle to preserve its past. Built between 1915 and 1927 in Classical Revival style, the railway hub was slated for redevelopment in the 1970s but was saved by angry preservationists. Today, it's both the intersection point of subway, rail and commuter lines and an architectural landmark. It's almost 259 metres (850 feet) long and its celebrated Great Hall is considered to be one of the finest public rooms in Canada.

At the other, northern end, of the Financial District, the **Hudson's Bay Company**'s handsome department store anchors the south-west corner of Queen and Yonge Streets. Built 1895-6 (with later additions), the former Simpsons store houses both contemporary

fashions and part of Ken Thomson's famous collection of Canadian art (*see p63*), the latter in a quiet gallery that often gives you the chance to savour the works in solitude. West on Queen Street, Toronto's first real opera house rises from the corner of Queen Street and University Avenue, just opposite Osgoode Hall. Despite its reputation as an arts centre, Toronto has never had a designated opera house before. Designed by Diamond and Schmitt (the folks who did the Metro-Central YMCA), the **Four Seasons Centre for the Performing Arts** opens in 2005 with seats for about 2,000 people.

PATH, a much ballyhooed system of underground pathways, connects most of the major buildings in the downtown core, protecting you from the winter cold and summer heat. But it's not to be recommended unless: a) you really like mid-market shopping malls and b) you have an especially keen sense of direction. Signage is not especially clear and it's easy to get lost.

Design Exchange

234 Bay Street, at King Street W (416 216 2160/ www.dx.org). Streetcar 504/subway King. **Open** 10am-6pm Mon-Fri; noon-5pm Sat, Sun. **Admission** $8; $5 concessions. **Credit** AmEx, MC, V. **Map** p277/p278 E8.

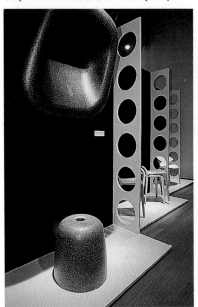
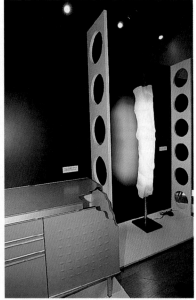

Design Exchange: throwing shapes.

The plaza of the **Toronto-Dominion Centre**: ruminating on a bull market.

The former home of the Toronto Stock Exchange, this art deco structure now houses a design museum with a permanent collection devoted to post-war Canadian design. Students and emerging designers are promoted on the first floor, other exhibits on the third. The 1930s structure is surrounded and surmounted by a late addition to the Toronto-Dominion Centre but many of the building's original features are still intact, including the two-storey former trading floor with its eight murals by Canadian artist Charles Comfort, and the stone frieze on the exterior, also by Comfort.

Hockey Hall of Fame

BCE Place, 30 Yonge Street, at Front Street W (416 360 7765/www.hhof.com). Streetcar 504/subway King or Union. **Open** *June-Aug* 9.30am-6pm Mon-Sat; 10am-6pm Sun. *Sept-May* 10am-5pm Mon-Fri; 9.30am-6pm Sat; 10.30am-5pm Sun. **Admission** $12; $5 concessions; free under-4s. **Credit** AmEx, MC, V. **Map** p277/p278 F8.

A tribute to Canada's national game, this sports shrine features more than 5,110 square metres (50,000 square feet) of games, displays and memorabilia, including Olympic artefacts and information on the hall's 300-odd inductees. Most people come to get their photo taken with the Stanley Cup and other hockey trophies but you can also test your skills against a couple of virtual greats.

Hudson's Bay Company Gallery

9th Floor, the Bay, 176 Yonge Street, at Queen Street W (416 861 4571). Streetcar 501/subway Queen. **Open** 11am-5pm Tue-Sat. **Admission** $4. **Credit** AmEx, MC, V. **Map** p277/p278 F7.

Tucked away at the top of a downtown department store, this private collection is hard to find but a must for fans of Canadian iconography. Drawn from the massive private collection of Canadian newspaper magnate Ken Thomson, it features some 400-odd Canadian paintings, mostly by Group of Seven artists (famous for their depiction of the Canadian north) and their contemporaries from the early years of the 20th century, including Emily Carr, David Milne, Tom Thompson and James Wilson Morrice, plus a large number of works by the 19th-century landscape artist Cornelius Krieghoff, perhaps the world's busiest painter of snow.

Toronto-Dominion Centre

66 Wellington Street W, at Bay Street (416 869 1144/www.tdretail.ca). Streetcar 504/subway King or Union. **Open** 10am-6pm Mon-Fri. **Admission** free. **Map** p277/p278 E8.

Mies van der Rohe's late modernist masterpiece is a close cousin to his famous Seagram Building in New York, but the black steel and bronze glass towers are now very much a part of Toronto's self-image. Together with City Hall, it set the pace for the rejuvenation of Toronto in the 1960s. Later additions to the complex, one of them towering over the former Toronto Stock Exchange, now the Design Exchange, have unbalanced the plaza in which the towers are set but the complex remains one of the few architectural masterpieces in modern Toronto. Most of the centre is of course off limits to the public, including the banking boardroom on the 54th floor of the main tower with its original Mies-designed furniture. But two large outdoor sculptures are worthy of remark: Al McWilliams' eerie circle-and-chairs (officially known as *Wall and Chairs*) on the King Street side and Joe Fafard's exceedingly popular bronze cows in the central plaza. The seven life-size bovines ruminate on a tiny patch of grass indifferent to the urban activity all around them. Directly south of the cows is the celebrated Toronto Dominion Gallery of Inuit Art (Ground Level, Maritime Life Tower, 416 982 8473). Housed in the southernmost tower of the T-D complex, this gallery is part of the bank's vast worldwide collection of art that consists mainly of sculptures from the 1950s and 1960s.

Toronto Stock Exchange

130 King Street W, at York Street (416 947 4723/ www.tsx.ca). Streetcar 504/subway St Andrew. **Open** 8.30am-5pm Mon-Fri. **Admission** free. **Map** p277/p278 E7.

Canada's largest stock exchange has no trading floor – it closed when the exchange was computerised – but you can experience the whiz-bang thrill of high-tech trading by visiting the organisation's interactive visitor centre, Stock Market Place, and taking a self-guided tour.

Dundas Square

Map p277 & p278

Useful transport: streetcar 501, 505/subway Dundas, Osgoode, Queen & St Patrick.

This neighbourhood is, in many ways, the heart of the city. Saints and sinners cram into these few city blocks, bounded by Gerrard, Jarvis, Queen and Bay Streets. Here you'll find some of Toronto's oldest and largest churches, rubbing shoulders with a string of porn cinemas, discount electronics shops and music megastores that line this stretch of Yonge Street. The busy Yonge/Dundas intersection, with its neon signs, constant crowds, burned-out buskers and evangelical kooks, is a good place to begin exploring. It's here that you truly feel you've arrived in Toronto.

The latest addition to the area is a granite park that basks in the neon glare of billboards above the intersection of Yonge and Dundas. Many had hoped that grass and trees would replace the tacky low-rise shops that were expropriated in this effort to create a converging point for the city's throngs, but at least yahoos and hosers now have a new civic square in which they can let loose over the triumphs and defeats that mark the daily rhythms of the city.

Over Yonge Street, just outside **Toronto Eaton Centre** shopping mall (*see p65*), the pavement is inscribed with a map of the meandering route traced out by Yonge Street, the longest street in the world. In this open area, souvenir shills unload cheap baubles, while vigilant Bible-thumpers foretell the apocalypse.

Escape to tranquil Trinity Square Park behind the mall, where the groovily progressive Anglican **Church of the Holy Trinity** (10 Trinity Square, beside the Eaton Centre, 416 598 4521/www.holytrinitytoronto.org) offers a less intrusive version of Christianity. The activist church makes a point of welcoming marginalised groups, including lesbian, gay, bisexual and transgendered people, uprooted people and non-traditional families. The south entrance of the church opens on to a small grassy copy of the 13th-century stone labyrinth at Chartres Cathedral in France. Walking the circuitous path is meant to be meditative, not puzzling – the turf grass walls are only a few inches high, meaning that the only way you'll get lost here is in your own thoughts.

South from here, nothing beats Toronto's **Old City Hall** (60 Queen Street W, at Bay Street, City of Toronto info line 416 338 0338) for making you feel awed and puny. Designed by architect Edward James Lennox, who also created Casa Loma (*see p87*) and the King Edward Hotel (*see p40*), the castle-like hall opened in 1899 and is now a National Historic Site. The massive stone building features a 104-metre (341-foot) clock tower and highly ornamented Romanesque façades. It costs nothing to visit the grand entrance hall and it's a worthwhile stop to see its mosaic floor, wrought-iron grotesques, stained-glass windows and scagliola columns. Since 1965, when the new City Hall was built across Bay Street, this building is now used as a courthouse, so if you want to see more of the place, try getting arrested. You're welcome, of course, to sit in on court proceedings and listen to the many excuses for speeding, parking illegally or otherwise disturbing the peace.

Back on Yonge Street, you'll find two of Toronto's best-known theatres, the **Canon Theatre** (*see p218*) and the **Elgin & Winter Garden Theatre Centre** (*see p65*). Just north-east, at the corner of Shuter and Victoria Streets, is **Massey Hall** (*see p196*); heading north along Victoria (passing the lovely **Senator** diner; *see p119*) will take you to Ryerson Polytechnic University, home of **Ryerson Theatre** (44 Gerrard Street E, near Church Street, 416 979 5086). The university's grassy quad, accessible from Gerrard Street between Yonge and Church Streets, can provide quiet respite from the main streets.

East of Yonge is worship central. This area puts the 'church' in Church Street (although most of the entrances are in fact on Bond Street). **St George's Greek Orthodox Church** (115 Bond Street, near Gould Street, 416 977 3342) is recognisable by its semi-circular mosaic of the fabled George slaying the dragon and by its hemispherical domes capped with distinctive orthodox crosses. Across the road at No.116, the **First Evangelical Lutheran Church** (416 977 4786), erected in 1898 by German immigrants to the Toronto area, still offers services in both English and German.

The Gothic **St Michael's Cathedral** (65 Bond Street, at Shuter Street, 416 364 0234) is the principal church of Canada's largest English-speaking Catholic archdiocese. Reverend Michael Power, Toronto's first Catholic bishop, laid the first cornerstone of the cathedral in 1845. The building was completed three years later. The design is adapted from 14th-century English Gothic style by William Thomas, an English architect who designed many other landmark buildings in Toronto and throughout southern Ontario. St Michael's has a traditional cathedral shape, with a floor plan that resembles a crucifix. The cathedral does not stage concerts but from September to June many masses at the cathedral are graced by the world-renowned choirs of **St Michael's Choir School** (66 Bond Street, at Shuter Street, 416 393 5518) – these boys really know how to sing praise unto the Lord. If you don't catch them at mass, their many CDs are available at the cathedral's shop.

Metropolitan United Church (56 Queen Street E, 416 363 0331, www.metunited.org) places a strong emphasis on spreading the word through music and has done so for decades. The first building on this site was constructed by Methodists and opened its doors in 1872. In 1925, the Methodists merged with the Congregational Union of Canada and most of the Presbyterian Church of Canada to form the United Church. Three years later, this church was devastated by fire. Undaunted, the congregation rebuilt on the same foundation, resulting in the cathedral-style church that stands here today. The building was dedicated in 1929, and in 1930 'Met United' installed Canada's largest pipe organ, with about 8,000 pipes, the largest of which is 10 metres (32 feet) high. In addition to their house (of God) performers, there are regular guest musicians, often with a new-agey, multicultural bent.

Wedged in among these sacred institutions, **Mackenzie House** (82 Bond Street, 416 392 6915) is a densely packed museum devoted to the building's former tenant, William Lyon Mackenzie (1795-1861). Mackenzie was the first mayor of Toronto, a radical journalist and political reformer, but he's best known for leading the 1837 Upper Canada Rebellion (*see p10*). The rebellion failed and Mackenzie fled to the United States. Eventually, though, he was pardoned, and in 1850 he returned to Canadian politics and publishing. His humble home was converted into a museum in 1950, which today is administered by the city's Culture Division. Take the guided tour to see demonstrations of contemporaneous technology such as the gaslight and a printing press similar to the one Mackenzie used.

Elgin & Winter Garden Theatre Centre

189 Yonge Street, between Dundas Street E & Queen Street (416 314 2871). Streetcar 501, 505/subway Dundas or Queen. **Tours** 5pm Thur; 11am Sun. **Admission** $7; $6 concessions. **No credit cards**. **Map** p277/p278 F7.
It's touted as the last operating double-decker theatre in the world but that wouldn't mean much if both theatres weren't so insanely beautiful. They have been painstakingly restored to their original luxury: the Elgin was re-covered in ruby fabric and gilt, while the botanical fantasy of the Winter Garden's hand-painted walls was enhanced by thousands of leafy beech branches hung from the ceiling. A tour covers both theatres, the lobbies, as well as an exhibit of vaudeville era scenery. *See also p218.*

Toronto Eaton Centre

1 Dundas Street W, at Yonge Street (416 598 8560/ www.torontoeatoncentre.com). Streetcar 501, 505/ subway Dundas or Queen. **Open** 10am-9pm Mon-Fri; 9.30am-7pm Sat; noon-6pm Sun. **Admission** free. **Map** p277/p278 E6.

Toronto's catch-all **Eaton Centre**.

While Dundas Square contains some of Toronto's most important places of worship, the biggest shrine here is devoted to consumerism. The Eaton Centre opened its doors in 1979, transforming Yonge Street from a tavern-lined, seedy street, into a tavern-lined, seedy street with a gigantic shopping mall. Actually, the mall paved the way for many other commercial enterprises in the area and also served as a model for a new breed of upmarket shopping centres across North America. Its offspring have outpaced it: it has to be said that the Eaton is looking a little dated these days.

The complex stretches a full block from Dundas to Queen Street. At the north end (near Dundas subway station), on Level One, is the Ontario Tourism Travel Information Centre (*see p262*). At the south end, on upper floors, check out the sculpture *Flight Stop* by Toronto afrtist Michael Snow. This flock of life-sized Canada geese, swooping down through the upper five storeys of the atrium, was created by affixing hand-tinted photographs on to fibreglass sculptures. In between, you'll find about 300 stores, restaurants and services. Unfortunately, Eatons – the mall's flagship store – no longer exists. The Eaton Company declared bankruptcy in 1999. Sears Canada Inc bought out the major stores and tried to resurrect the historic Eaton name but that attempt failed and, in 2002, the last Eatons outlets were converted into Sears stores. *See also p141.*

Chinatown

Maps p276 & p277

Useful transport: streetcar 501, 505, 510/ subway Osgoode, Queens Park & St Patrick.

There are at least five Chinatowns in the Greater Toronto Area but this is the oldest. Many second and third generation Asian-Canadians have moved off and formed new communities in affluent suburbs but the area around Spadina and Dundas retains an exotic, just-off-the-durian-truck feel. The presence of Chinatown can be felt up to College Street, down to Queen Street, along Dundas Street and almost as far west as Bathurst Street, with a real strip running up Spadina. The hub used to be further east but in the 1960s, it was displaced by the construction of Toronto's fourth and current **City Hall** (*see p68*) on Nathan Phillips Square, whose futuristic spaceship council chambers and arcing office towers made the perfect symbol for a burgeoning, confident city on the move.

There are a few other non-Asian attractions in this enclave. **Osgoode Hall** (130 Queen Street W, at University Avenue, 416 947 3300) was built in 1932 and held Canada's first law school (which has since moved to become a part of York University). The iron entry gates on

Nation states China

Population: 500,000
Home base: Spadina Avenue and Dundas Street W; Gerrard Street E and Broadview Avenue

The Gold Rush brought the first Chinese up from California to Canada (mainly Vancouver) but the construction of the Canadian Pacific Railway transported them to Toronto. After the last track was laid, a good portion set themselves up as laundrymen, a fact that still haunts the city's Chinese, who have suffered 'wannee washee' stereotypes for the last century. When, at the turn of the last century, they began to evolve into restaurant owners and shopkeepers, they found the cheap housing of Spadina Avenue to their liking. After an exclusion act was repealed following World War II, immigration began to surge, and what is now known as Chinatown proper took its shape as a bustling marketplace blasting Mandarin pop, reeking of rotten bok choy and hoisin duck, and offering everything from imported bamboo furnishings to ground bull's penis.

As the city's focus shifted westward in the 1960s and '70s and Spadina Avenue was redesignated as an important artery, cheaper rents lured immigrants to the east side. The intersection of Broadview Avenue and Gerrard Street E is an alternative Chinatown favoured for its superlative restaurants, bakeries and supermarkets. Meanwhile, the second and third generations, and those who came from Cantonese parts to invest in Toronto's future, built up suburbs in the north-east of the city like Mississauga, Scarborough and Markham. It's in Markham that one can find those more cleansed traces of Hong Kong: designer knock-offs, dim sum to die for, and as much Hello Kitty as the Shenzen factories can turn out.
Trading places: The poor relation of the Pacific Mall (*see p149*) is Times Square (550 Highway 7 E, at Leslie Street), a chaotic plaza flush with plastic rubbish, club clothes and trendy cosmetics, along with fast food of a most exotic nature. (If you can't fit a visit into your city sojourn, hit it during an excursion north or east.) Imports from the mainland please more

Queen Street were built in 1868, when the city looked somewhat different: their unusual design ensures that no cows make it on to the grounds. Across University Avenue at 160 Queen Street W, **Campbell House** (*see p68*) sits in the shadow of the **Canada Life Building** (330 University Avenue, 416 597 1456), on top of which there is a small tower covered in lights. This isn't just another pretty ornament – the tower is a weather beacon, broadcasting coded forecasts from Environment Canada to weather-wise citizens. The **Canada Life Beacon** emitted its first signal on 9 August 1951, when the lights could be seen by boaters far out on the lake. A light in the shape of a cube flashes red for rain, white for snow, shines a steady green for clear conditions and steady red for clouds. If the 19 rows of white lights on the tower flash upward, it means hotter weather is on the way. Sinking or steady lights mean sinking or steady temperatures. The forecast is updated four times a day. Worth a look is the nearby **Textile Museum of Toronto** (55 Centre Avenue, at Dundas Street W, 416 599 5321, www.museumfortextiles.on.ca), dedicated to over 10,000 textile artefacts from all over the world, including carpets, garments and quilts.

A little west, you'll find the **Ontario College of Art & Design** (100 McCaul Street, 416 977 6000) and the **Art Gallery of Ontario** (*see p68*), due to get a Frank Gehry-designed addition for Ken Thomson's Canadian art collection (*see also p20*). On the other side of Grange Park, ivy-covered **St George the Martyr Anglican Church** (197 John Street, entrance on Stephanie Street, 416 598 4366) is one of Toronto's oldest places of worship, dating from 1844. A fire in 1955 destroyed all of the church except the tower, which still, well, towers over the area today. The congregation meets in the original parish hall, which also holds some objects saved from the fire.

A couple of blocks north of here, **Baldwin Street**, between Beverley and MacCaul Streets, with its health food shop, upscale Chinese restaurants and vaguely boho cafés, has a backwater neighbourhood feel that makes it a good spot to dive out for lunch or a reality check on a day's sightseeing.

Travelling west along Dundas Street, English quickly wanes, and Cantonese, Vietnamese and Thai dominate. On Chinese New Year, the traditional dragon parade comes straight along this street. The livid green sign of **Ten Ren Tea** (454 Dundas Street W, at Huron Street, 416 598 7872) marks the site of the local outlet for Ten Ren, one of the world's

discriminating types at Re:Oriented Interiors (1177 Yonge Street, 416 920 9094), where dowry cabinets are set off by dainty etchings and embroidered silk cushions.

A taste of: The most succulent (Chinese) buns in town – barbecue pork, shredded beef, chicken curry – are to be found by the streetcar junction at Gerrard Street E and Broadview Avenue (Miao Ke Hong Bakery, 345 Broadview Avenue, 416 463 6388, has the tastiest, though there are others on the block).

Join in: The city's largest Chinese New Year celebration (typically the first week in February) features pop music, drum and dragon performances, parades, markets, feng shui predictions, a food extravaganza and fashion shows. Hop on a streetcar (or the provided shuttle) to the Canadian National Exhibition fairgrounds to partake.

Local luminary: *Globe and Mail* reporter and author Jan Wong, a native Torontonian, embraced Maoism as a teen and travelled to China to join the communist party. She wrote *Red China Blues* about her experience.

Sightseeing

largest tea producers. It's an oft and justly recommended place to buy black, white, green, oolong, pouchong and jasmine teas, along with the cutest little pots and cups. The store is also riding the recent wave of popularity for bubble tea, although you still can't get a haircut there. That makes no sense until you hit the brightly coloured and friendly **ezone** (170 Spadina Avenue, at Queen Street W, 416 603 1700), a bubble tea café and hair salon. (Bubble tea originated in Taiwan in the early 1980s. The bubbles are pearl-sized balls of tapioca, which are served lurking at the bottom of sweetened, flavoured milk or tea. Torontonians appear to love sucking up wet, gooey balls through fat straws, and Bubble Tea is now everywhere in the city; *see p109* **Bubble tea**). You can design your own drink here, while browsing the hair products and waiting for a stylist to become available.

Spadina Avenue is one of the widest streets in the city but on the weekends the sidewalks are packed with diminutive women picking through the exotic fruit at the market stalls, and young Asian teens gabbing away on cellphones and showing off the fashions of tomorrow. Dead ducks hang in the windows, market vendors scream out impossible-to-understand bargain prices and the whole place smells like the forgotten contents of a Tupperware container lodged in the back of a fridge. You will find many storeowners here who practise the ancient Chinese art of selling cheap plastic trinkets but the **Tap Phong Trading Company** (360 Spadina Avenue, at Baldwin Street, 416 977 6364) has souvenirs you can use, like inexpensive woks and saké sets.

If progress along the avenue is getting you down, duck into the slightly less chaotic **Dragon City** shopping centre (280 Spadina Avenue, at Dundas Street W, 416 596 8885) where you can pick up deer antler and ginseng, alongside the latest Hello Kitty products. (There are also public washrooms, air-conditioning and a food court.)

Art Gallery of Ontario

317 Dundas Street W, at Beverley Street (416 979 6648/www.ago.net). Streetcar 505/subway St Patrick. **Open** 11am-6pm Tue, Thur, Fri; 11am-8.30pm Wed; 10am-5.30pm Sat, Sun; opens 11am-6pm Mon for selected exhibitions. **Admission** $12; $6-$9 concessions; $25 family; free under-6. **Credit** MC, V. **Map** p274 D6.

The modern, low-slung AGO is a pleasure to visit: airy, beautifully designed, well-curated and not overwhelming. It doesn't aim to be comprehensive but combines Toronto, Canadian and international art from various periods in interesting and

varied presentations in no fixed order, which means you never get bored. And it's very non-preachy. Highlights are the Henry Moore and Barbara Hepworth room, where thoughtful displays encourage you to really 'see' the work, the Group of Seven section (though the interactive element could use a millennial boost) and the conservatory-style restaurant, Agora, along with the major international exhibitions that visit (Paul Gaugin and Yoko Ono recently). Though a new highlight could blow all these all out of the water: in 2002 patron Ken Thomson bought the most expensive piece of art ever, Peter Paul Rubens' *Massacre of the Innocents*, for £49.5 million. It remains to be seen whether it will be hung here, but Thomson is definitely part-financing a major addition to the AGO, designed by Frank Gehry, to house his sizeable collection. Work begins in 2005 with a scheduled 2007 opening date.

Campbell House

160 Queen Street W, at Simcoe Street (416 597 0227/www.campbellhousemuseum.ca). Streetcar 501/subway Osgoode. **Open** May-Oct 9.30am-4.30pm Mon-Fri; noon-4.30pm Sat, Sun. Closed Nov-Apr. **Admission** $4.50; $2-$3 concessions; $10 family (2 adults & 2 children). **No credit cards**. **Map** p277/p278 E7.

This is one of the oldest buildings in the city, a survivor from the original city of York and a prime example of Georgian architecture. Sir William Campbell, a judge who would later become Chief Justice of Upper Canada, built this house in 1822. It passed through many hands over the ensuing years, until finally, in 1973, the 300-ton house was moved from its original location on Adelaide Street to its current location. The operation was massive, but it saved the building from demolition. In 1974 it opened as a museum, although parts of the building are used as offices and are off limits to the public. In addition to guided tours, the museum features a herb garden with explanations of how herbs were used for food and medicine.

City Hall & Nathan Phillips Square

100 Queen Street W, at York Street (416 338 0338/ www.city.toronto.on.ca). Bus 6/streetcar 501/subway Osgoode or Queen. **Open** 8.30am-4.30pm Mon-Fri. **Admission** free. **Map** p277/p278 E7.

When it was completed in 1965, Toronto's fourth City Hall was one of the city's few modernist buildings. Then-mayor Nathan Phillips held an international architectural competition, won by Finnish architect Viljo Revell. Revell designed the council chamber as a low, round building, embraced by two concave office towers of differing heights. The dramatic design has aged well, remaining bold and futuristic 40 years on. The ground floor is open to the public (check out the scale model of the city) and tours can be arranged by appointment.

City Hall faces south on to the concrete expanse of Nathan Phillips Square. Phillips' successor as mayor, Phil Givens, fought hard for the Henry Moore bronze

Sightseeing

Kensington Market.

Kensington Market

Tucked behind Chinatown on a few narrow streets (Baldwin Street is the gateway between Chinatown and the market. Augusta Avenue, Nassau Street and Kensington Avenue are the other major streets.), Kensington Market (an area rather than a single market) reflects Toronto's multicultural past, not to mention its multicultural present. For the past 200 years, it has been the landing point for many immigrants beginning their lives in the city. The British were the first, but in the 1920s most of Toronto's Jewish population lived in this area. The 'Jewish Market', as it was called then, began when merchants decided to put the cart before the house and sell their wares right on their own front lawns. Through successive waves of European, Chinese and Caribbean immigrants, the market has grown and evolved. But you still get the sense that many of the stores and restaurants were just set up on a whim, with clothing racks and cardboard signs pitched up in the frontyard. Reggae wafting from a Caribbean market blends – or clashes, depending on your sensibility – with strumming Italian mandolins emanating from a cheese store and the discordant twang of Asian pop music from a greengrocer. Shops come and go in the market but along one crowded stretch of brightly painted brick storefronts, **Courage My Love** (*see p147*) is an old stand-by for vintage clothing and accessories.

Kensington Market's cultural mix means that it has some of the city's best – and cheapest – fruit and veg markets, not to mention numerous bulk food stores and an eclectic mix of vintage and discount clothing and snack foods from every continent. The market is open to traffic but cyclists and pedestrians rule the road, weaving around slow-moving delivery trucks. For more tips on shopping here, *see p150*.

The **Kiever Synagogue** (25 Bellevue Avenue, 416 593 9702) is one of Canada's oldest Jewish landmarks. Designed by an architect named Benjamin Swartz, the synagogue (or 'shul') served a small congregation of Jewish immigrants from Kiever, Ukraine. The formal name of the congregation is the 'First Russian Congregation of Rodfei Sholem Anshei Kiev', but for entirely understandable reasons is generally known simply as 'the Kiever'.

The Kiever overlooks **Bellevue Square**, a small but pleasant community park at the corner of Wales and Augusta Avenues. Near the wading pool and swings, keep an eye out for a life-sized statue of a smiling Al Waxman. The Canadian actor and humanitarian, who died in 2001, is best remembered for playing Al King, the lead character in *King of Kensington*, a

on the hall's forecourt, believing high status art conferred a high status world image, but this vision proved his undoing. He won his battle against the philistines but lost the next election due in large part to the outrage of the electorate at what was seen as a waste of public funds. History vindicates him: *The Archer*, as the sculpture is known, is far and away the most popular public sculpture in the city. The square succeeds as a genuine gathering place. During the summer, it's busy with concerts, dance performances, outdoor exhibitions and a weekly Wednesday farmers' market; in winter, the reflecting pool becomes a popular ice rink and skaters whisk under the huge cement arches that span it. Skates are available to hire (*see p212*), and the snack bar specialises in powdery cocoa in Styro cups.

Sightseeing

1970s TV show set here in the market. Quote the first two lines of the show's theme song ('When he walks down the street/he smiles at everyone…') to any Torontonian over the age of 25 and they will likely burst into song with the next two lines ('Everyone that he meets/He's King of Kensington'). **King's Café** (192 Augusta Avenue, 416 591 1340) doesn't have anything to do with the show but it does offer a book-length menu of Chinese-influenced vegetarian dishes that can take more time to read than you'll actually spend eating there.

University

Map p280

Useful transport: bus 94/streetcar 506, 510/subway Bay, Bloor-Yonge, Museum, Spadina & Wellesley.

If Yonge Street is Toronto's libido and Bay Street its wallet, then the area in and around the University of Toronto's downtown campus is its soul. The St Lawrence district has an equal claim to historical significance but the university has the lock on beauty, reflection and tranquillity. A stream once ran through the middle of the university and while the famous Taddle Creek is long gone, confined to underground sewers, the bucolic atmosphere remains. Thanks to the university's many courtyards, quandrangles and large open spaces, the area feels like a park interrupted by chapels of learning. And thanks to the innate conservatism of the academic character, the area is a treasure trove of historic architecture.

Until preservationist instincts took hold in the 1960s and 1970s, Toronto had a nasty habit of eating its own history. (Historian William Dendy devoted an entire book, *Lost Toronto*, to buildings that have been destroyed or substantially altered.) The university, which was founded in 1827 as King's College, is one of the few local institutions that has done a decent job of conserving its heritage – turrets and all.

Bordered on the north by the expensive shops of Bloor Street and on the east by the bars and clubs of Yonge Street, the St George campus is divided into three almost equal sections by two imposing north–south avenues, Queen's Park and St George Street. Together with two suburban campuses – Erindale and Scarborough – the University of Toronto is the third largest public university in North America.

Central

The university's oldest and most iconic buildings lie smack in the middle of the two streets, directly west of Queen's Park and the provincial legislature.

It's all a façade

Love it or hate it, façadism is Toronto's attempt at architectural compromise, a way of responding to a sense of collective guilt at the demolition of many fine buildings in a rush to keep up with the times. Down at street level, below the shining beacons of prosperity, you'll find remnants of what has passed this way before. But the integration of fragments or façades from old and architecturally important structures into the fabric of modern buildings has proved to be a hit-and-miss proposition.

Queens Quay Terminal (1972, architect Ed Zeidler) started it all, transforming a waterside warehouse into a successful experiment in living by the lake. High-end condos and a shopping concourse happily coexist within the shell of a terminal that has taken on new grace.

In the stunning atrium of **BCE Place** (*see p61*; pictured), designed by Spanish architect Santiago Calatrava, façadism broke one of its cardinal rules by moving a bank façade from the 1840s just a few hundred feet from where it once stood. Isolated from its context, it sits like a displaced stone set amid a whirling current of glass and steel. At the other end of this complex, some of the few remaining façades to escape the Great Fire of 1904 blend in harmoniously and provide a rare glimpse of what the streetscape must have looked like a century ago.

Hart House was a gift from the wealthy Massey family and named after its chief patriarch, Hart. With its Gothic arches, bay windows and Great Hall, it has a terribly English, terribly Oxbridge feel and is comfortingly old Toronto. Formerly an undergraduate men's centre, it's now open to women too. There's a small gallery, the Justina M Barnicke, in its west wing (*see p71*).

University College is one of the oldest buildings on campus and still very much a landmark. You can see its lone, asymetrical spire and central tower from as far away as Yonge Street and the interior woodwork is worth a visit in itself. In the Laidlaw Wing is the **University of Toronto Art Centre** (*see p72*), housing the eclectic and enjoyable art collection of New York psychoanalyst Dr Lillian Malcove Ormos, who donated it in 1982.

The **Design Exchange** (*see p62*) on Bay Street preserves one of the best-known façades in Canada, that of the Toronto Stock Exchange, built in 1937. The bas-relief frieze on a theme of the working man famously depicts, four figures in from the right, a businessman with his hand reaching into the pocket of the labourer in front of him. The interior has been kept as an exhibition space for the museum but the art deco granite and limestone building now squats under the imposing heft of a later addition to the Mies van der Rohe-designed **Toronto-Dominion Centre** (*see p63*), looking like a squashed bug.

It's all part of the tussle between preservation and expansion. Façadism risks being skin-deep and insincere, adding nothing more than a two-dimensional Hollywood sensibility. The ceramic brick surface of a bank façade on the north-east corner of Queen and Yonge Streets does little, for example, to mask the incongruous block tower that now sits on top.

The latest addition to Toronto's façadism can be found at 100 Bloor Street W, where the **University Theatre**'s sleek and minimalist front and curvy marquee now usher in shoppers rather than those in search of escapism.

The **Air Canada Centre** (*see p59*) tastefully incorporates the remarkable stone etchings that surround this former postal sorting station. Bas-relief images of maple leaves

and beavers gnawing away at tree stumps are proof that even the rampant commercialism of professional sport must bow at the altar of such iconic Canadian imagery. One wonders what fate awaits the empty hulk of **Maple Leaf Gardens** (33 Carlton Street; *see p75*) and how façadism will express itself in a building that was, in its day, one of the most revered in the land.

Cross the playing field in front of the college and you'll find **Convocation Hall**, a vast domed building from the 1920s that has seen its fair share of graduation exercises.

Travel further south to College Street and you'll hit the newly renovated **Faculty of Architecture** with its sleek modernist gallery and the very different **Lillian H Smith Public Library** (*see below*) with its distinctly postmodern design. Two even flashier buildings are slated to rise near the corner of College Street and University Avenue: the Centre for Cellular Biomolecular Research by a Stuttgart firm, and a new pharmacy building by well-known British architect Norman Foster.

Justina M Barnicke Gallery

Hart House, 7 Hart House Circle (416 978 8398). Subway St George. **Open** *Sept-June* 11am-7pm Mon-Fri; 1-4pm Sat, Sun. *July, Aug* 11am-6pm Mon-Fri; 1-4pm Sat. **Admission** free. **Map** p280 D5. Great Canadian art hangs in all corners of Hart House, in reading rooms, restaurants and even stairwells but this is the official gallery and, though it's tiny, it often features intriguing exhibitions. (It's also free.)

Lillian H Smith Public Library

239 College Street, at Huron Street (416 393 7746/ www.tpl.toronto.on.ca). Streetcar 506, 510. **Open** 10am-8pm Mon-Thur; 10am-6pm Fri; 9am-5pm Sat. (also open 1.30-5pm Sun Sept-June). **Admission** free. **Map** p274 D6.
A PoMo chateau with a dungeon-like basement and giant bronze griffins flanking the central doorway, this public library is a fanciful piece of architecture but it's also a must for fans of science fiction and/or children's literature, as it houses famous collections of both.

Hart House: kick back on campus. *See p70.*

University of Toronto Art Centre

Laidlaw Wing, University College, 15 King's College Circle (416 978 1838/www.utoronto.ca/artcentre). **Bus** *94/streetcar 506/subway Queen's Park.* **Open** *Sept-June noon-5pm Tue-Fri; noon-4pm Sat. July, Aug noon-5pm Tue-Fri.* **Admission** free. **Map** p280 D5.
This little-known museum in the quiet quad of University College houses the private collection of New York city psychoanalyst Dr Lillian Malcove Ormos, whose passions were more Byzantine than oedipal. Medieval icons and a stunning 1538 panel painting of Adam and Eve by Lucas Cranach are on view, as are drawings by Picasso, Matisse and Henry Moore.

Queen's Park & east

The provincial parliament building sits in the middle of Queen's Park and the government is often referred to as Queen's Park. A Toronto novelist once likened the massive pinky-brown building, built 1886-92 with later additions, to a giant wedding cake, but it's too dignified for that. A fine example of Richardsonian Romanesque, it's built in the same style as Old City Hall.

Another fine example of the genre lies north-east of Queen's Park in the middle of the Victoria College quadrangle. Built in 1892, the turreted baronial structure known as **Old Vic** looks out on a men's residence, a theological college and a couple of elegant 1960s structures to the south. Named after a prominent Canadian poet, the **EJ Pratt Library** at the quad's south-east apex was

built in 1961 and recently refurbished in a lighter, more playful style. Check out the polka dot walls and the famous portrait of literary guru Northrop Frye. The eminent critic appears to be sitting on air.

To the north lies Charles Street and two of the city's more interesting new buildings – the **McKinsey & Company** building and the **Isabel Bader Theatre**, a gift from Alfred Bader to the college in the name of his theatre-loving wife. The limestone-clad building echoes the scale and colour of Burwash Hall to the east and Emmanuel College to the west. Across Charles Street, on the north side, the rather West Coast-looking **Wymilwood Student Centre** is the creation of Eric Arthur, the influential Toronto architect who helped save such early Toronto landmarks as St Lawrence Hall and Old City Hall, and who gave his name to the Faculty of Architecture's new gallery (*see p73*). Arthur died in 1982 but his posthumously revised *Toronto: No Mean City* remains the bible of Toronto historical architecture.

North of Charles Street, two of Toronto's most important museums face each other across the broad lanes of Queen's Park. The **Gardiner Museum of Ceramic Art** (*see p73*) was founded by a local philanthropist and his wife in 1984; a big revamp is planned for 2004-5. Its older cousin across the street, the **Royal Ontario Museum** (*see p73*) explores both natural history and human cultures and is the largest museum in Canada, the fifth largest in North America.

While you're in the neighbourhood, take a glance at the **Royal Conservatory of Music** (273 Bloor Street W). Originally the Toronto Baptist College, the hulking building does indeed look as if it could rain down hail and brimstone. Walk through the ornate iron gates to the east of the conservatory and down Philosopher's Walk and you can usually hear the sound of dozens of piano students practising.

Eric Arthur Gallery

230 College Street, at St George Street (416 978 5038/www.ald.utoronto.ca). Streetcar 506/subway Queen's Park. **Open** 9am-5pm Mon-Fri; noon-5pm Sun. **Admission** free. **Map** p280 D5.

It looks like an ice cube stuck in a brick block, but if you're into architecture and design this tiny gallery is the place to be. It's located within the Faculty of Architecture at U of T.

Gardiner Museum of Ceramic Art

111 Queen's Park, at Avenue Road (416 586 8080/ www.gardinermuseum.on.ca). Subway Museum. **Open** 10am-6pm Mon, Wed, Fri; 10am-8pm Tue, Thur; 10am-5pm Sat, Sun. **Admission** $10; $6 concessions; free under-5s. **Credit** AmEx, MC, V. **Map** p280 E4.

The first specialised museum of ceramic art in North America, the Gardiner holds ceramics from Europe, Asia and the Americas, including Italian maiolica, English delftware and a large collection of pre-Columbian artifacts. The Gardiner is set to expand by 929 square metres (10,000 square feet), thanks to hefty public and private donations. It will gain three new galleries and a glass-covered atrium with views of the area. Construction is due to start in March 2004 and the reopening celebrations are slated for autumn 2005. Though the gallery will be closed to the public between these dates, some off-site exhibitions and activities are planned.

Royal Ontario Museum

100 Queen's Park (416 586 8000/www.rom.on.ca). Subway Museum. **Open** 10am-6pm Mon-Thur, Sat; 10am-9.30pm Fri; 11am-6pm Sun. **Admission** $18; $10-$14 concessions; free under-5s. Free to all 4.30-9.30pm Fri. **Credit** AmEx, MC, V. **Map** p280 E4.

The grand old lady of Toronto museums is set to get a frisky facelift, due to be completed in 2006, courtesy of Berlin-based designer Daniel Libeskind, the architect behind Berlin's Jewish Museum and Manchester's Imperial War Museum North. In the meantime, there's much to enjoy both inside and out. Known for its enormous Chinese collection, Canada's largest museum surveys everything from natural history to human culture. Kids will love the bat cave, dinosaurs and mummies. Adults may prefer the Canadian and indigenous peoples' collections (and the respected restaurant JK at the ROM; *see p112*). Check out the totem poles inside the main entrance.

St George Street & west

A recently re-landscaped St George Street is now the principal north–south axis of the western campus. Walk north from College Street and you'll pass everything from the beaux arts splendour of the **Koffler Student Services Centre** (originally a public reference library, now the home of the university's main bookstore) to the brand new **Bahen Centre for Information Technology**; from the very '60s **Sidney Smith Hall** to the very '70s **Robarts Library**. The latter, sometimes known as Fort Book, is a bulky concrete structure that looks like a overloaded spacecraft attempting lift-off, but it has a serious purpose and is the largest of the U of T's 30 libraries. The beaked tower at the south end is home to the Thomas Fisher Rare Book Library. Where St George joins Bloor Street is a collection of somewhat less academic interest, the Bata Shoe Museum (*see p74*).

North of Robarts lies **Innis College**, named after the academic who inspired the communications theorist Marshall McLuhan. East of the library, at the corner of Hoskin and Devonshire Place, lies a celebrated re-imagining of the monastic ideal – **Massey College**. Conceived by the former governor-

Boo! The **Royal Ontario Museum**.

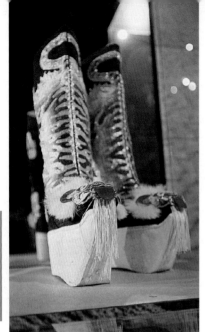

Get your kicks at the **Bata Shoe Museum**.

general, Vincent Massey, it was designed by Canadian architect Ron Thom.

Spadina Avenue marks the western edge of the university and here, near the junction of Harbord Street, lies the athletics centre and one of the most controversial buildings in the city, **Graduate House**. Built in a brutal, almost industrial style, by a team of Toronto and Los Angeles architects, the residence offends and attracts people to almost equal degrees. The pivotal point in any discussion is usually the sign-cum-cornice that overhangs Harbord Street and welcomes you to the university.

Bata Shoe Museum

327 Bloor Street W, at St George Street (416 979 7799/www.batashoemuseum.com). Subway St George. **Open** 10am-5pm Tue, Wed, Fri, Sat; 10am-8pm Thur; noon-5pm Sun. **Admission** $6; $2-$4 concessions; free 1st Tue of mth. **Credit** AmEx, MC, V. **Map** p280 D4.
A playful pun on a shoe box, Raymond Moriyama's odd-angled design houses everything from native footwear to celebrity footwear – Marilyn Monroe's red pumps to Elton John's platforms. A permanent exhibition follows the history of western footwear.

Harbord

Map p280

Bus 94/streetcar 510, 511/subway Bathurst, Spadina.

Situated at the western edge of the university, Harbord Street is a bastion of upscale leftish liberalism. The street houses everything from

the **Toronto Women's Bookstore** (73 Harbord Street, 416 922 8744) to a women-friendly sex shop **Good For Her** (*see p193*), not to mention some of the city's better restaurants and patios.

Downtown East

Church & Wellesley
Map p281
Useful transport: streetcar 75, 94, 506/ subway Bloor-Yonge, College, Wellesley.

Church & Wellesley is best known as the home of the local gay village or 'the ghetto', as it's most commonly called. And Church Street, which was named after St James's Church (now a cathedral) is today almost synonymous with secular gay life. But the area from Bloor Street to Gerrard Street and Yonge Street to Sherbourne Street is also home to several Toronto landmarks and historic homes.

Church Street has sheltered unmarried men for decades and in substantial numbers since at least the opening of the Yonge Street subway in 1954 and the construction of massive apartment complexes in the 1950s and 1960s. Buildings like the **City Park** apartments (now co-op housing) at No.484 and the Village Green complex a block north encouraged the arrival of many a confirmed 'bachelor' (*see p75*).

But the area only took off in 1984 when the **Second Cup** (*see p190*) opened near the corner of Church and Wellesley. Fortuitously equipped with a broad set of steps suitable for lounging, chatting and cruising, the tiny coffeeshop attracted a dedicated gay following and 'the Steps' became a local landmark, mythologised by frequent references on the TV series *Kids in the Hall*. Five years later, **Woody's** (*see p188*) opened a block further south at Church and Maitland in a Queen Anne rowhouse originally built in 1893, and the gay gold rush was on. Today, it's almost impossible to run a gay business without a Church Street connection.

The city has acknowledged at least some of this history with the dedication of a tiny park that runs parallel to Yonge Street between Charles and Isabella Streets. Marked with a sign but no explanatory information, **George Hislop Park** is named after the businessman and longtime gay activist.

The names of many more gay men are incised on the upright steel markers of the AIDS Memorial, erected in 1993, in **Cawthra Park**, which is located behind the **519 Church Street Community Centre** (*see p255*) at Church and Wellesley Streets. The

Molly Wood's Bush

The modern gay village dates only from the mid 1980s but the area has a long history as a homo hangout. In 1810, a rich local merchant, magistrate and bachelor named Alexander Wood earned the opprobrium of his peers when he got a little too close to another man. He left town for Scotland but returned two years later and in 1826 bought 25 acres north-east of what is now Yonge and Carlton Streets. The area quickly became known as 'Molly Wood's Bush'. Today it forms the nucleus of the modern gay ghetto and two of the area's key streets, Alexander and Wood, bear the name of the wealthy bachelor who developed the area.

In a further twist on the legend, two of the largest and gayest apartment complexes in the area are situated on Wood's namesake streets: the three **City Park** towers straddle the block between Wood and Alexander Streets. Built in 1954, their extra-large apartments encouraged the arrival of interested singles and quickly became known as 'the Queens' Palaces'; a block north, two boxy buildings and a very tall circular tower form a particularly phallic arrangement formally known as the **Village Green** apartments but better known as 'Vaseline Towers'. There have been efforts to rename it K-Y Towers have been thwarted.

Wood's life inspired a 1994 play called *Molly Wood, A Naughty Gothic Romp* but modern attempts to resurrect the area's old name and rename it 'Molly Wood's Bush' have failed.

original home of the ritzy Granite Club, 'the 519' is now home to innumerable support groups, community meetings and legal clinics, not to mention a popular beer garden on Pride Day and a phone line for reporting anti-gay violence.

At its southern end, the ghetto encircles one of Canada's premier jock palaces, **Maple Leaf Gardens**, at Church and Wood Streets. Built in 1931, the lovely building, mostly deco with Art Moderne details, was long home to the Toronto Maple Leafs hockey team, not to mention dozens of concerts by everyone from the Beatles and the Rolling Stones to touring circuses and occasional opera. But the Leafs moved to the **Air Canada Centre** (*see p59*) in the late 1990s, and the gardens await redevelopment.

A century ago, this area, and especially Jarvis and Sherbourne Streets, was home to some of the city's more eminent movers and shakers. Today it's home to an oddball collection of historic homes, high-rise condos and hard-working hookers. The **Massey Mansions** at Nos.515 and 519 Jarvis Street, north of Wellesley Street, are good examples of the old order. Originally designed for a dry goods merchant, the house at No.515, now a Keg Mansion restaurant, was later home to the Masseys, the influential Canadian family that made its money in farm machinery and gave its name to several Toronto landmarks, including **Massey Hall** (*see p196*) and Massey College (at U of T). Hart Massey, the 19th-century Methodist patriarch who moved the family firm into the front ranks, lived at No.515. Two of his most famous grandsons lived next door at No.519, a baronial home designed by E J Lennox, the architect of Old City Hall. Vincent

Massey grew up to become Canada's first native-born governor-general, while his younger brother Raymond became an actor famous for his portrayal of Abraham Lincoln.

The **National Ballet School** owns several historic buildings south of the Massey mansions, near the corner of Jarvis and Maitland Streets, including the classically inspired Quaker Meeting House at 111 Maitland Street (currently a dance studio) and the Victorian home at 404 Jarvis Street. As part of a partnership with a condo developer, the ballet school is also expanding south, taking over historic Northfield House at 372 Jarvis Street, an early home of Oliver Mowat, later a Father of Confederation and a long-serving premier of Ontario, and the wonderfully Jacobethan pile at 354 Jarvis. With its forbidding stone exterior, the latter looks like a set for *Jane Eyre* (and a proper perch for a madwoman in an attic), but it was actually once home to the Havergal Ladies College (now located on Avenue Road near St Clair Avenue) and later the Canadian Broadcasting Corporation from from where Canada's first television broadcast was transmitted in 1952. Like so many other historic buildings in the city, this one is in the process of being divided up into condominiums.

Sherbourne Street houses many excellent 19th-century buildings but the most interesting is probably the **Howard Johnson** hotel (*see 42*), at No.592. It's almost certainly the only residence that can boast of having housed both Ernest Hemingway *and* a gay backroom bar – at different times, of course. The original macho man stayed here in September 1923, when the building was the Selby Hotel and Hemingway

No.515 Jarvis Street, historic seat of Massey family money and influence. *See p75.*

was a reporter for the *Toronto Star*. The bar flourished during the building's long stint as a gay bar-and-hotel complex in the 1980s and 1990s. The mansion at the centre of the complex was built in 1883 and originally belonged to a member of the Gooderham liquor dynasty.

At the junction of Sherbourne and Gerrard Streets, **Allen Gardens** contains a complex of conservatories dating back to 1909, beautifully planted with flora from various climatic zones.

Cabbagetown

Map p281

Useful transport: bus 75/streetcar 506/subway Sherbourne.

In the 1840s, many Irish families flocked to Toronto, fleeing the potato famine that was devastating their ancestral home. They settled in a working-class district of Toronto and so as not to be done in by a spud shortage a second time, they filled their frontyards with cabbage plants, hence the name. New waves of immigrants brought wealthier residents to the area, creating an unusually diverse economic mix that continues into modern times.

During a post-World War II push for urban renewal, Cabbagetown became both a proving ground for low-income public housing projects and a stomping ground for more affluent Torontonians, who were drawn by the plenitude of beautiful fixer-upper homes.

Today, the vast majority of houses have been modernised on the inside but their historic façades remain. Toronto's most neighbourly of neighbourhoods is full of hushed, leafy streets lined with red- and yellow-brick houses. Parks and cemeteries bound much of the northern and eastern borders, creating many cosy cul-de-sacs. And while you'd be hard pressed to single out one particular architectural masterpiece, the neighbourhood as a whole comprises one of the best collections of 19th-century residences in North America. For a sampling, *see p78* **Walk on Cabbagetown**).

The borders of Cabbagetown are particularly fluid and disputed, and they have crept north over the decades. Originally extending down to Queen Street E, Cabbagetown is now bounded by Bloor, Sherbourne and Gerrard Streets. To the east, the neighbourhood spills down a wooded hill into the Don Valley.

Cabbagetown's main commercial artery, **Parliament Street**, was so named after Upper Canada's original parliament buildings, which were built at the base of the street in 1793. Recent efforts to develop the site where the building stood have been stymied by archaeological interest in the area.

Parliament Street retains an independent character, with many unusual cafés, shops and services. The community loves its preserved neighbourhood and even new condo developments such as the one at the corner of Parliament Street and Aberdeen

Avenue have bowed to local pressure to blend in with the surrounding Victorian and Edwardian houses.

The area is thick with historic buildings, but most of them are private residences. One exception is the recently renovated theatre at 509 Parliament Street, home to, among others, the **Canadian Children's Dance Theatre** (416 924 5657, www.ccdt.org).

If you prefer to get your architecture hit during prayer rather than performance, **Saint Luke's United Church** (353 Sherbourne Street, 416 924 9619) makes all the buildings around it seem plain in comparison. Originally known as Sherbourne Street Methodist, the church threw open its huge wooden doors to worshippers on 5 June 1887. Its castle-like stonework exterior and stained-glass panels are among the best in the city.

The church stands at the corner of Carlton Street, which is the neighbourhood's secondary commercial artery. Though the street's beauty has faded, it still boasts many fine examples of Second Empire and Gothic Revival buildings dating from the 1880s and 1890s.

Carlton Street becomes residential east of Parliament Street, culminating in **Riverdale Park**. The park is full of trees (and usually equally full of dogs peeing on them). Trails lead from the park down to a footbridge that gives access to the Don Valley park system.

Just to the north of Riverdale Park is **Riverdale Farm** (*see below*), a combination of a kid-friendly farm and an environmentally friendly project. Cows, sheep and pigs occupy the upper part of the farm, while re-created wetlands in the lower areas are a haven for ducks and help mitigate the savage industrial damage that has been suffered by the Don River. The farm sponsors community events, from pottery lessons via cow milking to Old Farm Equipment Clean-Up Day.

Within mooing distance of the farm is the **Toronto Necropolis** (200 Winchester Street, 416 923 7911, www.mountpleasantgroupof cemeteries.ca). A cemetery and crematorium in the late 1800s, this majestic cemetery replaced Potter's Field, Toronto's first non-sectarian cemetery, which was located at Bloor and Yonge Streets. Many former Potter's Field denizens now sleep eternally in the Necropolis, including William Lyon Mackenzie (Toronto's first mayor), Thomas D Morrison (Toronto's third mayor), and world champion sculler Edward Hanlan. Also interred here is Henry Langley, a Toronto architect noted for Gothic Revival style churches. He designed the Necropolis Chapel at the entrance to the cemetery, as well as the attached lodge and *porte-cochère*, which were all built in 1872.

The chapel is considered to be one of the finest examples of Gothic Revival in Canada. The nave and sanctuary of the small chapel are lit by disproportionately large arched stained-glass windows. The innovative design allowed funeral processions to enter through the porch, pass through the nave to the chancel and exit through the sacristy to the cemetery grounds.

On the north side of the Necropolis is **Wellesley Park**, which was once the site of the area's sole industry, an animal crematorium run by Peter R Lamb & Company. In addition to glue, lime and animal charcoal, the factory also produced a stench that slowed development for several decades. A fire destroyed the main building in 1888, and the factory that lived by incineration died by it on that day. Now a row of tidy little homes sits precisely two steps from the park, and a paddling pool and small playground make this a popular place for local families.

To its north, **St James Cemetery** (635 Parliament Street, 416 964 9194, www.stjamescathedral.on.ca) completes Cabbagetown's collection of peaceful green spaces. Impressive crypts with historic Ontario names such as Brock and Jarvis cast shadows on broken tombstones whose names have eroded away. Many original Irish immigrants are buried here along with such luminaries as Sir William Pearce Howland, one of the Fathers of Confederation. At the entrance to the cemetery stands the Gothic yellow-brick Chapel of Saint James-the-Less, built in 1858.

Between Cabbagetown and St Lawrence is Moss Park. This is one of downtown Toronto's few slightly sketchy districts – the kind of area that nice kids from the suburbs visit to buy dope, with little to interest the visitor.

Riverdale Farm

201 Winchester Street (416 392 6794/www. city.toronto.on.ca/parks/riverdalefarm.htm). Bus 65/streetcar 506. **Open** *Nov-Jan* 9am-5pm daily. *May-Oct* 9am-6pm. **Admission** free. **Map** p281 H5.

St Lawrence

Maps p277, p278 & p279
Useful transport: bus 75/streetcar 501, 504/ subway King, Queen.

This rectangle of foreshore east of Yonge Street was the original city market and warehouse area of Toronto, or York as it was then called. The shoreline of Lake Ontario came right up to the back of huge warehouses that lined Front Street, where ships would unload their merchandise. (The land between Front Street and the current waterfront is landfill from the excavations of downtown buildings over the

Walk on Cabbagetown

Begin: Castle Frank Station
Finish: Castle Frank Station
Length: 6km (4 miles)
Time: 2 hours, not including distractions

This walk takes in many of the highlights of Cabbagetown's 19th-century construction, and provides ample opportunity for further exploration of side-streets and alleys. It also takes you into two of Toronto's most beautiful cemeteries.

Turn left out of Castle Frank Station (away from Bloor Street E). Find the steep unpaved trail leading down and to the west, passing under the subway bridge.
This short trail, leading from one busy street to another, is unexpectedly tranquil but at the bottom the traffic moves quickly.
Cross Rosedale Valley Drive and turn left on the paved path.
The path takes you deep into a wooded ravine, past St James Cemetery. Unfortunately, the graveyard's lower gates are locked and there is no way out of the valley until you reach a flight of stairs where Rosedale Valley meets Bayview Avenue. (Note: Just across Bayview Avenue is a tent village of homeless people. They sometimes congregate around the base of the stairs. They can be pretty outgoing so it's best to do this walk with a friend if such things make you uncomfortable.) The top of the stairs are in Wellesley Park (*see p77*).
Take Wellesley Street from the north-west corner of the park and turn south on Sumach Street.
Let the architecture fest begin: many fine 19th-century homes can be found on Sumach Street. The double house at 420-2 is a well regarded Second Empire building, recognisable by its mansard roof and dormers whose wooden ornaments are painted a soft, creamy white.
Turn left on Winchester Street, to find the entrance to the Toronto Necropolis cemetery (see p77). Public washrooms across the road.
Cross Riverdale Park to Carlton Street.

years.) The area along Front Street between Church and Sherbourne Streets has been gentrified over the past two decades. Condos, apartments and Crombie Park, a successful example of public housing that has been studied by urban planners the world over, have transformed the original market district into one of the liveliest neighbourhoods in the city. Few experiences in Toronto can match a fossick around **St Lawrence Market** at its heart. Enliven your senses – they will most certainly be stirred – any day of the week except Sunday and Monday (Saturday is probably best) by strolling through this vast two-storey complex. This is where the crowds jostle for supplies and load up for the coming week or a Sunday dinner, continuing a Toronto tradition that began near this location 200 years ago in 1803. You can get a sense of its past at the city-run **Market Gallery** (*see p81*) on the second level. You can easily miss it, so ask how to get there if you don't see the elevator. Changing exhibits feature old photos, documents and historical artefacts about the art and cultural history of Toronto.

The gallery is also a good place to look down on the bustle of a typical Saturday shopping spree. Permanent vendors including butchers, fishmongers and seafood stands, plus stalls selling fresh breads, spices and cheeses, attract the mall-weary from all over town. Keep your elbows up and your bags at your side as you make your way from stand to stand, sampling as you go. On the lower level, cooking supplies,

The park abuts Riverdale Farm (*see p77*), which you'll smell on your left, but is not part of this tour.

The easternmost block of Carlton Street, approaching the lip of the lower Don Valley, is paved with red brick that matches the row of townhouses that line its southern side. One of the oldest houses on the street, at No.397, was built for a barrister named James Reeve in 1883, when the area was still essentially rural. White brick highlights and large decks on both storeys make this house as enviable now as it was then. *Follow the path south between the houses and the Don Valley to Spruce Street. Walk west on Spruce.*

The rowhouses at Nos.74-86 are drab, but they still comprise one of the area's most successful public housing projects. Designed by Eden, Smith & Sons, they have communal courtyards, and plenty of space and light. Turn North on Parliament Street. You emerge in the heart of Cabbagetown's commercial district. **Jet Fuel** (519 Parliament Street, 416 968 9982; *see p115*) is a favourite among bicycle couriers and trendies and, as the name suggests, it's the best place on the street to get fired up for the rest of the walk. To pick up a terrific lunch to go, head for Daniel et Daniel, just around the corner at 248 Carlton Street. This French patisserie has filling sandwiches on crusty breads, quiches, salads and heavenly desserts. *Continue north and turn right on Winchester Street.*

The former Presbyterian church at 80 Winchester Street now houses the **Toronto**

Dance Theatre (416 967 1365; *see p222*) and school. The Romanesque Revival church was built in 1891, and its unpretentious red brick motif makes it look like the mother of all the houses around it.

No.156 was originally owned by Daniel Lamb, the founder of Riverdale Zoo, and the son of crematorium founder Peter Lamb (*see p77*). The wonky porch speaks to the hard times the house has seen, but now the trim is freshly painted blue and the large front garden is well kept and there's not a cabbage in sight. *Turn left back on to Sumach Street and left again on to Wellesley Street.*

Wellesley Street has the quintessential mix of Cabbagetown styles, including bay-and-gable, and cottage style, among others. It is quite simply one of the nicest streets in the city. Briefly detour north on Sackville Street to Alpha Avenue. This tiny dead-end street is lined with mansard roofed rowhouses that date from the 1880s. They are so tiny and festive, you half expect to see a hobbit emerge and invite you to tea.

Back on Wellesley Street, No.314 is a number indeed. Completed in 1890, the front façade is crammed with carved stone ornaments that must have been great publicity for the original owner, Thomas Harris, who owned a stone cutting company. *Turn right on to Parliament Street.*

On this side, you have access to St James Cemetery (*see p77*). *Turning right on Bloor Street E, takes you over the bridge you passed under at the beginning, and back to Castle Frank Station.*

pastries and more greengrocers are found as well as many handmade crafts, often sold by the artist. At **Domino's Foods Ltd** (95 Front Street E, 416 366 2178), the closest thing to a grocery store in the market, stock up on candies of your youth, sold in bulk from large bins.

St Lawrence Market is not just about stocking the larder. Many people drop in during the week for a breakfast speciality that tastes good any time of day – peameal bacon on a kaiser bun, that famous Canadian delicacy. This is more like a thick slice of ham, salt-and-sugar cured and then rolled in cornmeal and fried on the grill. Bite into a warm peameal at **Carousel Bakery** (95 Front Street E, 416 363 4247) or **Paddington's Pump** (95 Front Street E, 416 368 6955).

Crowds also gather at the little hole-in-the-wall **Churrasco of St Lawrence** (95 Front Street E, 416 862 2867) for slow roasted, specially seasoned, mouthwatering Portuguese chicken on a bun, usually accompanied by a bag of French fries, a soft drink and a couple of rich custard tarts. For many, this treat is close to an addiction.

On Saturdays, the **North Market**, an annex on the opposite side of Front Street, features a farmer's market selling fresh goods brought in straight from the countryside. It opens at an ungodly hour – many farmers are setting up at 5am. Cured and fresh meats, farm-raised trout, fruit and vegetables, herbs and even Ontario-grown peanuts are sold. But the vendors like to call it a day by 1pm so don't arrive too late.

Eco-worriers

Sightseeing

It's easy being green in Toronto, at least during the warmer months. Parkland arteries extend deep into the heart of the city, bringing a hint of the vast woodland expanse that lies to the north, as well as the odd coyote. Forests touch the psyche of city dwellers who long for pine-scented air. Perhaps that's why the city is mad about trees and goes to extraordinary lengths to preserve the unusually dense green canopy.

Woe to anyone who cuts down a tree on city property. The fine for a first offence is $10,000, and it's double that for delinquents who do it again. And as the city has control over a good portion of private front yards, you're stuck with the tree that grows there. You can even get another one free. Of course, if it falls or clogs drains, the city is responsible for the damage. When thunderstorms rip across the city, trees have a habit of crushing parked cars, knocking down power lines and disrupting traffic. Remember to look up when you're out in a storm on a tree-lined street.

With nature comes an abundance of man's furry friends. Tourists have been known to turn away from landmark edifices and chase after the ubiquitous squirrel for a photo op. They come in many different colours – black, brown, grey, tawny and the odd albino. But one thing you'll rarely see is a baby squirrel.

Mamma keeps them in their lofty tree nests until maturity. Squirrels are so inured to the presence of humans that they will boldly approach, looking for handouts. In Queen's Park, it's not unusual to be accosted by a gang of roving squirrels who surround the unsuspecting stroller, defying passage without some form of compensation, preferably peanuts or bits of bread. So intertwined is the life of the bushy-tailed one with Toronto that the city invented a squirrel mascot for its sesqui-centennial celebrations (150 years). Strange, then, that Sesqui the Squirrel was not a big seller in the plush toy category that year.

Torontonians generally accept the presence of animals as part of the deal for keeping things green. But tolerance is tested when it comes to the larger critters. Toronto's racoons make squirrels look like wallflowers when it comes to human interaction. These furry, masked rodents upend garbage cans and dig up gardens, hiss back when confronted and yield ground only when the odds get seriously stacked against them. The Humane Society has a phone hotline that provides elaborate instructions on how to rid attics and rooftops of racoons. One method involves installing a portable radio and keeping it tuned to an all-talk station.

On Sundays, the building is transformed into an antiques market. For more shopping tips for both markets, *see p154*.

One of the city's most photographed vantage points lies between the north and south markets. Looking west, the skyscrapers are symmetrically lined up behind the **Gooderham Building** (49 Wellington Street E), or as most people know it, the Flatiron. It was built in 1891, ten years before its more famous and much larger cousin in New York City. On the opposite side of the building is a clever *trompe-l'oeil* by artist Derek Besant that fills the 'flat' side of the Flatiron Building. And if you want to get inside, drop into the basement bar known as **Flatiron & Firkin** (49 Wellington Street E, 416 362 3444, www.firkinpubs.com).

Two important theatres are across Berczy Park behind the Flatiron. The 2,000-seat **Hummingbird Centre for the Performing Arts** (*see p219*) is home to both the National Ballet of Canada and Canadian Opera

Company). The future of this slab-like venue built in the 1960s is uncertain as both companies will be moving out some time in the middle of the decade. The **St Lawrence Centre for the Arts** (27 Front Street E, 416 366 7723) presents Canadian Stage Theatre Company and music performances in two smaller, more intimate venues – the Jane Mallet and Bluma Appel theatres (*see p217*).

While on Front Street E, look for the **Dixon Building** (No.45-49), with the city's only remaining cast-iron façade. The 1872 structure is a tribute to architectural illusion: what appears to be painted wood and stone is actually units of cast iron. Also note the 1877 warehouse at 67-69 Front Street E that underwent a meticulous restoration of its ornate Renaissance Revival style.

To get a real feel for St Lawrence's history head to **Toronto's First Post Office** (*see p81*). The last four digits of its phone number – 1833 – correspond with the year the post office opened. Step across the threshold – and the centuries – into this fascinating and perfectly restored working post office. Sit by the fireplace and dip a quill in an ink well to write a letter home on old-fashioned paper. You can learn about the role the first post office played in the Rebellion of 1837 (*see p9*). The postmaster, James Scott Howard, was dismissed for refusing to open the mail to see who was planning the uprising. There's also a scale model of York from that era that closely corresponds to the St Lawrence district today.

Another building not to be missed in this district is the Edwardian classic structure of the King Edward Hotel at 39 King Street E. The 'King Eddie' was the city's most fashionable hotel for some 60 years. Now known as **Le Royal Meridien King Edward** (*see p40*) the original property was developed in 1901 with an 18-storey addition in 1920. This grand old dame slowly fell into decades of decline, which mirrored the seedy slide of the neighbourhood. However with the downtown revival of the late '70s and '80s, the hotel returned to its former glory with new owners and a multi-million dollar facelift. This

is the spot for an elegant afternoon tea or drink in the stately street-level bar with its leather chairs and oak panelling. A favourite game is to guess which of the massive faux marble columns in the lobby isn't original.

Market Gallery

95 Front Street E, at Jarvis Street (416 392 7604/ http://gvanv.com/SLM/gallery/gallery.html). Streetcar 504/subway Union. **Open** 10am-4pm Wed-Fri; 9am-4pm Sat; noon-4pm Sun. **Admission** free. **Map** p277/p278 F8.

St Lawrence Market

92 Front Street E, at Jarvis Street (416 392 7120/http://gvanv.com/SLM/index.html). Streetcar 504/subway Union. **Open** *South Market* 8am-6pm Tue-Thur; 8am-7pm Fri; 5am-5pm Sat. *North Market* 7am-6pm Mon-Sat. *Farmers' Market* 5am-close (usually around 1pm) Sat. **Admission** free. **Map** p277/p278 F8.

Toronto's First Post Office

260 Adelaide Street E, at George Street (416 865 1833/www.townofyork.com). Streetcar 504. **Open** 9am-4pm Mon-Fri; 10am-4pm Sat, Sun. **Admission** free. **Map** p277/p278 F7/F8.

Sightseeing

Gooderham Building: the 'Flatiron' holds its own against the 'scrapers. *See p80.*

Midtown

Style boutiques, students and Canada's oldest sex shop: suburbia this ain't.
Well, not all of it...

Delving into the area north of Bloor Street,
you start to get a sense of Toronto's voracity.
Today, the area between Bathurst Street and
the Don Valley is a seamless stretch of urban
sprawl, just another chunk of the Greater
Toronto Area. But most of the neighbourhoods
that make up Midtown were originally small
villages or family estates, located deliberately
far from the hustle and bustle of the urban
centre. One by one, these areas were
swallowed up by the omnivorous blob of
the expanding city. Yorkville was the first
down Toronto's gullet, while Forest Hill was
one of the last. Each neighbourhood retains
a distinctive flavour, from the culturally
diverse, student-heavy Annex, to the stately
homes of Rosedale.

Note that this guide takes Bloor Street as
the dividing line between Central Toronto and
Midtown: venues on the north of Bloor are
covered here but those on its south side (such
as the Bata Shoe and Royal Ontario Museums)
are in the relevant section of Central Toronto.

Yorkville

Map p280
Subway Bay.

Incorporated as a village in 1853, Yorkville
existed as its own entity for only 30 years
before it became part of Toronto. This tiny
wedge of an area, bounded by Bloor Street,
Avenue Road and Davenport Road, contains
some of Toronto's most exclusive and
expensive hotels and shops. Cumberland Street
and Yorkville Avenue are the major commercial
thoroughfares. The pedestrian lanes that
connect these parallel streets give the area a
peaceful, slightly European feeling. It's easy
to spend an afternoon meandering round here,
though you could blow your entire holiday
budget at any one of the jewellery, antiques
or art stores. But it hasn't always been this way.
In the 1960s, this was Austin Powers territory,
a hotbed of swinging hippie counterculture
spawning Joni Mitchell and Gordon Lightfoot.
The area aged with the baby boomers, and now

You're booked: the striking **Toronto Reference Library**. *See p83.*

the hedonism is mostly left to the musicians and movie stars who stay in Yorkville's five-star hotels. This is a reasonable place to spot celebrities, although you're much more likely to see rich matrons and hotshot lawyers prowling the streets than your favourite rock star.

At the east end of Cumberland Street is the **Toronto Reference Library** (789 Yonge Street, 416 395 5577). It's the largest reference library in Canada, but even if you have no research to do, the building is well worth a visit. The sculptural fountain near the entrance leads to a soaring space lit with natural light. There are often sales here, where you can pick up good reference books for next to nothing. There is a small café on the ground floor, though you can't take food into the stacks. Among he library's holdings are an extensive map collection, genealogical source materials for Canada, Great Britain, Ireland and the US, plus an entire section devoted to the works of Sir Arthur Conan Doyle.

Around the corner, **Yorkville Library** (22 Yorkville Avenue, 416 393 7660) is heavily involved in the community, and it's a good place to find out about local events. Just across the street at No.27, is another Toronto landmark, **Lovecraft** (416 923 7331), the oldest sex store in Canada. Opened by two Toronto women in 1971, Lovecraft's brightly lit, comfortable atmosphere was inspired by European sex stores. Now, as then, it's aimed at couples and well-adjusted enthusiasts, rather than creepy men in trenchcoats.

At the west end of the neighbourhood, **Alliance Atlantis Cumberland 4 Cinemas** (159 Cumberland Street, 416 646 0444; *see p179*) gets good non-Hollywood films. It's located near **Hazelton Lanes** (55 Avenue Road, 416 968 8600), a 'lifestyle' shopping mall that recently became home to the first Canadian branch of the Texas-based trendy organic supermarket chain Whole Foods (*see p156*), where Toronto's elite meet to buy food and browse through the vast choice of designer bottled water.

The Annex

Map p280

Bus 26/Subway Bathurst, Bay, St George or Spadina.

Unlike Yorkville, this area was designed to be a suburb of Toronto. In one fell swoop, 259 lots went up for sale in 1886, which sparked the first of two waves of construction in the area. Many Victorian houses went up before 1910, followed by a second building spurt of Georgian and Tudor residences. But by 1930, the popularisation of the automobile meant that the smart money (well, all the money, really)

Beaver tales

● Canada's national symbol is a monogamous 20-kilogram (44-pound) water rat with a distinctive flat tail.
● The European lust for beaver hats largely motivated the settling of Canada after the European beaver was hunted to near extinction. At the height of demand, Canada provided 200,000 pelts per year.
● A large beaver pelt can make 18 hats.
● In the Toronto area, fossils have been found of the beaver's Ice Age ancestor that measured three metres (9.9 feet) in length and weighed a whopping 360 kilogrammes (57 stone). And the teeth were... OK, let's not think about the teeth...
● The University of Toronto Police has a heraldic beaver on its uniform patch.
● The substantial beaver is the largest rodent in North America and the second largest in the world.
● An industrious beaver can cut down 216 trees a year if he puts his mind to it.
● The first toilet seen on television was on an episode of *Leave it to Beaver*.
● Food purveyors advertising 'Beaver Tails for Sale' are lying: they are actually selling deep-fried flattened blobs of dough.
● Beavers are damn good dam builders.

was moving further out to Rosedale and Forest Hill. Today, the Annex is one of Toronto's most diverse communities, mixing up Yorkville's fabulous wealth and the University of Toronto's exuberant student culture. As well as being the southern boundary of the neighbourhood, Bloor Street is the commercial hub, where most of the Annex's famous shopping, restaurants, and nightlife can be found. The northern boundary, Davenport Road, was originally a Native American path that connected the Don and Humber river valleys.

Going north from Bloor on Spadina takes you past two important cultural organisations – the **Native Canadian Centre of Toronto** (16 Spadina Road, 416 964 9087), which organises public gatherings and events to promote First Nations culture, and the **Alliance Française de Toronto** (24 Spadina Road, 416 922 2014) which stages events related to French culture throughout the year, including art and photography exhibitions, concerts, plays, films and lectures. The **Italian Cultural Institute**, also housed in an Annex manse (496 Huron Street, 416 921 3802), features rotating exhibits and seminars on contemporary Italian art.

On the far side of the railway tracks, you'll find the large warehouse and exhibition hall of the **City of Toronto Archives** (255 Spadina Road, 416 397 5000). The downstairs of this clean, modern building has rotating exhibits on Toronto's urban history and geography. Old maps and blueprints, photographs, and artefacts are accompanied by texts that provide both information and narrative context. From subways to subdivisions, from highways to high society, the archives have lore galore on Toronto's land and landmarks. Of course, it can't all be on display at once – but follow the sign that says 'View our "miles of files" ' for a window on the true magnitude of the information stored here. To find out more about a particular topic, head upstairs to the research hall. Registration is quick and free, and the knowledgeable staff can help you find books, clippings, photographs and historical documents concerning any aspect of the city.

Casa Loma

Map p280

Streetcar 512/Subway Bay, Rosedale, St Clair, St Clair W or Summerhill.

Toronto's grid system suddenly goes all twisty through this hilly neighbourhood, which stretches north from Davenport Road to St Clair Avenue between Yonge and Bathurst Streets. Early on in the city's history, the outstanding view from this hilly summit led many of Toronto's wealthiest citizens to settle here. Of course at that time this was wooded land, and the city was merely part of a pleasing but distant view. Two remnants from those heady days, **Casa Loma** and **Spadina Historic House** (for both, *see below*) are now open to the public, and are conveniently located next door to one another. The former is the more famous venue, and it's certainly more spectacular from the outside, but if you only have time to tour one of these museums, take a quick photo of Casa Loma and head into Spadina House: it's actually the more interesting museum. Between the two attractions, a small parkette leads to **Baldwin Steps**. Named after the family that originally owned the land on which Casa Loma House now stands, these 110 stairs span a section of hillside that is too steep for a road. They offer a great (and free) view of downtown. North along Spadina Road takes you to **Sir Winston Churchill Park**, at the corner of St Clair Avenue. This park has floodlit tennis courts and a playground, and it's also popular with joggers. You can also get access to **Nordheimer Ravine** from the park, which has many good picnic spots, as well as a long tree-shaded trail that you can follow for miles.

Casa Loma

1 Austin Terrace (416 923 1171/www.casaloma. org). Bus 127/streetcar 512/subway Dupont. **Open** 9.30am-5pm daily. **Admission** $10; $6-$6.50 concessions; free under-4s. **Credit** AmEx, MC, V. **Map** p280 C2.

In a recent local newspaper survey, Casa Loma was voted Toronto's most beautiful building, while some consider it a triumphant monument to kitsch. And truly, its corbelled towers and battlements are a wonder to behold. Turn-of-the-century magnate Sir Henry Pellatt enlisted architect EJ Lennox to build this medieval-style castle with a stunning view of the city below. It was completed in 1914, but Pellatt hit hard times a decade later and had to move out. Casa Loma opened as a tourist attraction in 1937. Inside, the high ceilings and wide-open rooms feel oddly empty, despite the many displays from the heyday of the 'House on the Hill'. Seek out the dome in the conservatory, which is made with Italian glass, cut and stained into images of grapes and trellises. Pendulous lights hang down from the dome, resembling bunches of grapes. The house also has a bona fide secret passage to the stables, which were done on an equally grand scale and are included in the price of admission.

The six acres of gardens at the back of the building are lovely, dark, and steep, with fountains, waterfalls and woodsy pools. Ring the bells on the dragon sculpture in the so-called Secret Garden. If you're pure of heart, the dragons are supposed to come to life. (Odds are, neither you nor the marketing manager who promotes that little legend is going to be animating firebreathers any time soon.) In place of guided tours, the museum offers multilingual mobile phone-like devices that play explanatory recordings upon request. Not only does this mean you can't ask questions, it also results in hundreds of people shuffling around the museum in silence, phones clamped to their ears.

Spadina Historic House & Gardens

285 Spadina Road (416 392 6910/spadina@city. toronto.on.ca). Streetcar 512/bus 127/subway Dupont. **Open** May-Aug noon-5pm Tue-Sun. Sept-Dec noon-4pm Tue-Fri, noon-5pm Sat, Sun. **Admission** $5; $3.50-$5 concessions. **No credit cards. Map** p280 D2.

This 50-room mansion was built for Toronto financier James Austin in 1866. His son Albert expanded and renovated the family home in the early 20th century, so that it now has elements of both Victorian and Edwardian architecture. When they sold the family home to Ontario Heritage Foundation in 1984, Austin's descendants donated the contents of the house to the new museum, meaning that each exhibit contains furniture, appliances, crockery, and books that were actually used by the people who lived there. In addition to providing guided tours, the enthusiastic staff regularly tweak the exhibits to suit a particular theme or season. The extensive historic gardens (free, if you don't enter the museum) are filled with the flowers, vegetables and herbs of

Austin's day. Don't miss the archaeological display on the lower level, which contains items from an even earlier house built on the same foundation by the Baldwin family. Occasionally, contemporaneous dishes are cooked up for visitors in the mansion's working kitchen. All this means the museum gives an especially good sense of what high-society life was like a century ago.

Rosedale

Map p281

Bus 32/subway Davisville, Eglinton, St Clair or St Clair W.

Whether you enter Rosedale from Bloor Street, Yonge Street, or Saint Clair Avenue, you immediately feel that you've entered a magical land, where every citizen is a king or a queen. Aside from Mount Pleasant Road, a multi-lane extension of Jarvis Street, Rosedale's streets are quiet, shady, and lined with stone and brick mansions. In the 1820s, Sheriff William Botsford Jarvis (after whom Jarvis Street is named) settled here with his wife Mary. William is credited with founding Rosedale, but Mary named it, giving a nod to the wild roses that grew on the hills of their large estate. Mary spent many a day wandering these hills on foot and on horseback, and the trails she made are reputed to form the template for modern Rosedale's roads. Visitors get lost here more than anywhere in the city, and most of the locals like it that way.

Many of Toronto's wealthiest and most prominent citizens live in Rosedale. Rosedale's Victorian, Georgian, Tudor and Edwardian mansions were built between 1860 and 1930 and many are listed in the Toronto Historical Board's Inventory of Heritage Properties. Rosedale has a row of gourmet shops and restaurants along Yonge Street north of Church and south of the railway tracks, where you can shop and eat alongside Toronto's idle rich.

A series of ravines forms a horseshoe shape through Rosedale, cutting it off nicely from the rest of the city. These woody crevasses bear names that further evoke a fairytale atmosphere: the Vale of Avoca, Moore Park, and Rosedale Valley. These ravines also lead into the Don Valley, which forms the eastern boundary of the neighbourhood.

Well manicured **Rosedale Park** has tennis courts, a playing field and a skating rink. This was also the location of Canada's first Grey Cup game in 1909, between the University of Toronto and the Parkdale Canoe Club. Given the more watery bent of their rivals, it's perhaps it's not surprising that U of T took the cup, which has ever since been the top trophy of Canadian football.

Classy or kitschy? **Casa Loma**. *See p84.*

Walk on Better homes & gardens

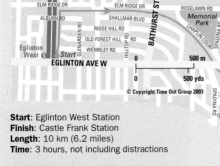

Start: Eglinton West Station
Finish: Castle Frank Station
Length: 10 km (6.2 miles)
Time: 3 hours, not including distractions

In Rosedale and Forest Hill, a walk in the park means more than smelling the flowers and watching the birds. It's a chance to see how the other half lives, or rather the other two per cent. This walk takes in some of the city's most peaceful trails, and the quiet, mansion-lined streets that make the area famous.

*Just to the east of the subway station, a path leads north between a soundproofing wall, and a series of dead-end streets. After Aldburn Road, turn right on to the **Belt Line Trail**.* Ravines, river valleys and railway beds shape Toronto's major green spaces, meaning that parks tend to be long and narrow. The doomed Belt Line Railway served Forest Hill commuters for two glorious years between 1892 and 1894. The tracks were still used for freight until the early 1960s. Kay Gardner, a community activist and later a City Councillor, persuaded the city to buy the Belt Line lands and convert them into a 4.5-kilometre (2.8-mile) walking and biking trail. It was renamed the **Kay Gardner Belt Line Park** in 2000.

The trail does not get beautiful until it bends south under Eglinton Avenue. (A set of stairs lead to street level here. At the top, there's a coffeeshop if you need refuelling.) Trees and shrubs arch over the well-groomed trail, while gaps in the greenery afford glimpses into the backyards of the massive houses of Forest Hill Road and Chaplin Crescent. The trail has several access points to both streets, so you can slip out to look at the house fronts. *Double back through Forest Hill Park to reach Forest Hill Road. Turn left up the hill toward Lonsdale Road.*

The neo-Georgian mansions – note the arches, round windows, and overall symmetry of many of the houses – give way to the grassy campus and brick tower of **Upper Canada College** (*see p87*).
Turn left on to Lonsdale Road, and the make a right on to Lawton Boulevard. Cross Yonge Street.
The narrative stained-glass windows are a highlight of **Yorkminster Park Baptist Church** (1585 Yonge Street, 416 922 1167), scenes depict events as recorded in the Gospels. A few steps north of the church stand the Gothic gates of **Mount Pleasant Cemetery** (*see p89*).
Follow the first southbound path, which takes you down a hill to a cul-de-sac. A trail leads from here through a gate to a path by a stream. The path branches almost immediately. Stay on the your side of the stream.

The path climbs over steep hills in a real forest. This dirt path is slippery when wet, but wooden stairs climb the steepest parts. St Clair Avenue passes far overhead, crossing the ravine. Down on the trail, the giant concrete and metal feet of the bridge form a stark contrast with the wooded surroundings in a way that is eerie but strangely beautiful. *The path merges with a larger trail. Continue south across the stream. Smaller trails lead off the path. Stick to the straight, wide path.* Just before Mount Pleasant Road, the trail passes through David A Balfour Park, whose grass and picnic tables make it a good place to take a break. *Cross Mount Pleasant Road and follow the Park Line Reservation Trail, which runs south-east just below Roxborough Drive. Continue until you see a sign for Milkmen's Road, which leads up to South Drive. A sharp left on to South Drive takes you to the gates of Craigleigh Gardens. Follow the park's only path to the far exit, which comes out on Castle Frank Road.* The contrast between the streets of Rosedale and Forest Hill is immediately apparent. Although the lots in Rosedale are smaller, the houses are older and classier. Craigleigh Gardens is named after Craigleigh, a 25-room Victorian mansion that used to stand on this site. When Craigleigh's owner, a wealthy businessman by the name of Sir Edmund Osler, died in 1924, the house was torn down and the land presented to the city. Today the well-manicured park is a leash-free area where locals take their pedigrees for a spot of exercise. The exit to Castle Frank Road is a beautiful brick path lined with vine-covered iron fences. *Turn right on to Castle Frank Road and follow the trail of houses to Castle Frank subway station.*

Forest Hill

Bus 32B, 32C/subway Davisville, Eglinton, St Clair or St Clair W.

You won't see a forest, but you will see trees. Forest Hill was incorporated as a village in 1923, succeeding the former community of Spadina Heights. Its snooty status was assured in 1929, when **Upper Canada College** (200 Lonsdale Road, 416 488 1125), one of Canada's most respected private schools, opened its doors to young men. Today, the non-denominational school draws students from across Canada and the world to its spacious campus, where they are educated, trained and prepared to become the rich young men of tomorrow.

This area developed as a result of the wealthy buying cars and so being able to live further from the centre. In an effort to keep the place classy, building codes were enacted in 1936 that required a tree be planted at the front of each property. From little bylaws, mighty oak trees grew, and Forest Hill, especially its lower part, still feels like an exclusive town in the middle of the country. That said, Forest Hill has had many more homes torn down and rebuilt than Rosedale, which gives it a more modern feel. Neo-Georgian, neo-Victorian and other 'neo-traditional' forms are common along Forest Hill Road and Old Forest Hill Road. A cluster of pleasant shops and restaurants just north of St Clair on Spadina is a good place to take a break from the flaunting of wealth. Even better, escape to the **Nordheimer Ravine**, which runs along the southwest section of Forest Hill, with access at **Relmer Gardens**. The Belt Line Trail (*see p86* **Walk on**) cuts across the northeast corner.

Davisville

Bus 32B, 32C/subway Davisville, Eglinton or St Clair.

Things start to calm down again east of Yonge Street and north of St Clair Avenue. The eastern boundary of Bayview Avenue is a major north–south thoroughfare, but along this stretch, traffic slows down along a stretch of trendy cafés, bars, patisseries and kidswear shops. This largely residential area was named after John Davis, who immigrated to Canada from Staffordshire, England, in 1840. He was Davisville's first postmaster.

The neighbourhood is architecturally less interesting than those to its west and south, and is home to yuppies rather than millionaires. The centre of the community, geographically and metaphorically, is Davisville Park, which has popular tennis courts, a wading pool and a

Mount Pleasant Cemetery: dead pretty.

playground built for the area's copious yuppie toddlers. But the only real reason for visitors to come to Davisville is to visit **Mount Pleasant Cemetery** (375 Mount Pleasant Road, 416 485 9129). The mile-long graveyard has been an outing destination for everyone from Toronto's unicyclists to its Goth community. (In Toronto, even the Goths have a slogan: 'Making Toronto a darker place.') Almost the entire property, extending all the way from Yonge Street to Bayview Avenue, was purchased in 1873 in what was then the village of Deer Park. The cemetery was developed for three years before its first burial on 13 March 1876. By 3 December 1945, more than 117,000 interments had taken place, which is about twice the population of Toronto when the cemetery first opened. Many notable Canadians have found their final resting place here, including **William Lyon Mackenzie King**, Canada's tenth and longest-serving prime minister. World-renowned pianist **Glenn Gould** lies here, as do **Frederick Banting** and **Charles Best**, whose experiments in the early 20th century led to the discovery of insulin.

Yonge & Eglington

The intersection of Yonge and Eglinton has become a focus for the bars and restaurants patronised by the new suburbanites who've moved north into Davisville and Forest Hill.

Several of these are worth travelling up here for, though there's not a lot else round other than their houses and a neighbourhood feel.

Leaside

Bus 51, 56, 100/subway Davisville, Eglinton or St Clair.

This neighbourhood is named after a farming family headed by John and Mary Lea, who emigrated here from Lancashire, England, in 1819. As so often happens, it was the second generation that rose to prominence: their son William Lea opened a tomato cannery, became township counselor for seven years, and built an octagonal house that he called Leaside.

Part residential and part industrial, the streets of Leaside proper don't have much to offer, but this is a gateway into the Don Valley park system. Just north of Eglinton, a bike path leads from Broadway Avenue down into **Serena Gundy Park**. If you cross back south under Eglinton, you'll end up in **Ernest Thompson Seton Park**. Ernest Thompson Seton was an eccentric naturalist, and author of *Wild Animals I Have Known*, reputedly one of the inspirations for Rudyard Kipling's *Jungle Book*. When Seton moved to Toronto in 1870, this part of the Don Valley was still wilderness, and it became a natural research laboratory for his zoological studies. Today, it's tamer, with picnic tables dotting grassy areas along the West Don River, but science remains a part of the area. Where the park meets Taylor Creek, and where the Don Valley Parkway meets Don Mills Road, sits a series of sculptures that look like giant exposed molars, roots and all, rising from the ground. Filled with soil and plants, they actually make up an experimental water purification system. Further north is the **Ontario Science Centre**.

Ontario Science Centre

770 Don Mills Road, at Eglinton Avenue (416 696 1000/www.ontariosciencecentre.ca). **Open** *Sept-June* 10am-5pm daily. *July, Aug* 10am-6pm daily. **Admission** $13; $7-9 concessions; free under-5s. **Credit** AmEx, MC, V.
Sprawling from a suburban boulevard and tumbling down into the lush Don Valley, the multi-level centre houses 800 or so permanent science exhibits, plus Toronto's only planetarium, and an Omnimax movie theatre. The centre opened in 1969, and some exhibits now have a distinctly retro feel. But the interactive Science Arcade at the far end of the complex is well worth the trip, and the temporary shows are consistently engaging and topical. The excellent gift shop will please any science junkie, but the food services are disappointing. If weather permits, pack a lunchbox and picnic in the park behind the museum.

West End

From Italian delis to Polish revolutionaries, ethnic influences dominate this trendy part of town.

Useful transport: Bloor-Danforth subway line (Bloor Street); 506 streetcar (College Street); 505 streetcar (Dundas Street); 501 streetcar (Queen Street & Martin Goodman Trail); 504 streetcar (King Street & Roncesvalles Avenue).

In Toronto's West End, an urban vibe continues into residential areas that, near-in, at least, are far too buzzy to call suburbs. Though there are few sights here as such, visitors will frequently find themselves hopping a streetcar to eat, drink, listen to music or just generally hang out here, particularly along the corridors of College Street and Queen Street West.

Heading west from Bathurst Street and still in the heart of the city, downtown starts to take on the characteristics of distinct neighbourhoods, each shaped in a large part by their ethnic make-up. Along Bloor Street, under which runs the subway, Koreatown has taken hold, as became clear during the 2002 World Cup, when South Korea reached the quarter finals. This community extends to Christie Street and Christie Pits Park and is not the only immigrant culture to make the West End its home.

College Street is home to the oldest of the city's Italian neighbourhoods (far more Italo-Canadians now live north of the city in Woodbridge). As the *macellerias* and *frutta* and *verdura* shops closed up, cafés, nightclubs and restaurants took their place, giving Little Italy a no less distinctive feel though one that at times seems far removed from anything Italian, save for the gloriously tacky illuminated outlines of the boot-shaped country hanging from every lamp-post. The neighbourhood, however, has managed to retain a village quality – and a very hip one at that – that spills into the streets on warm summer nights. The corner of College and Clinton Streets was named one of the ten coolest neighbourhoods in North America by the US publication *Utne Reader*. More places to nosh and sip per square foot than probably any other in the city keep this patch of Little Italy buzzing on an espresso-induced high.

Quiet, tree-lined residential streets run north and south from College Street. The entrance to **Palmerston Boulevard** is framed by an old stone gate and is lined with century-old trees and old-fashioned light stands that make it one of the most scenic in Toronto. Dundas Street, west of Bathurst, is stirring from a long slumber while College Street to the north and Queen Street to the south made huge inroads in capturing the zeitgeist. But that's changing, partly from the encroaching pressures from either side. New cafés and galleries are opening along a stretch that is more Portuguese-influenced than anything else, but also Vietnamese and Spanish influences can be seen before you come to the Brazilian quarter near Dufferin Street.

In the past few years a build-up of coolness on **Queen Street West** burst the former barrier of Bathurst and forced trendy restaurants and vintage clothing stores many more blocks into the West End. Sometimes referred to by the amusing name of West Queen West, this stretch takes you past **Trinity Bellwoods Park**. This spacious expanse was originally the site of Trinity College, which opened in 1852. Today only the gates of the college remain at Queen and

Gone fishin': **High Park**. *See p90.*

Sightseeing

Strachan Avenue. The undulating park has good sports facilities, and it's a popular hangout for hip young locals.

Developers are cultivating the ecosystem of West End **King Street** into an ideal habitat for young, condo-dwelling urbanites. The conversion from a warehouse/studio district is going slowly, though, and the area can still feel deserted, especially at night.

Further west, **Parkdale** is still recovering from the intrusion of the Gardiner Expressway, which cut this former beach town off from the water in the 1950s. As poor areas go, it's more sad than scary, but the commercial district on Roncesvalles Avenue is experiencing a renaissance, and the Polish influence makes it a fun place to shop and eat. If you come down Queen Street to get here, you'll pass the iconic **Gladstone Hotel** pub, a cult karaoke venue (*see p132*), and, inexplicably, a string of used fridge and cooker stores.

West of Roncesvalles is **High Park**, one of Toronto's few major green spaces that is neither long nor skinny. This is an excellent strolling and lolling park, but it's also an easy place to keep busy. The small zoo will only be interesting if you've never seen a zoo before, but the flower gardens are elaborate, and when the Japanese cherry trees blossom in the spring, you can't take two steps without being in someone's wedding photos. The park's amphitheatre, home to the long-running Dream in High Park outdoor theatre series, is to the north of the **Colborne Lodge** museum (*see p93*).

Bloor West Village, to the west of High Park, is the oldest and one of the city's most successful Business Improvement Areas, a scheme in which local merchants band together and pay a levy to promote and improve their area. Once a run-down retail strip, it's now a fashionable shopping district. Trendy cafés, upscale markets and classy clothes shops make this the perfect place for a post-park wind down. Nearby, Riverside Drive runs through the neighbourhood of Swansea, and is a trove of Tudor-style houses. Keep an eye out for 210 Riverside, identifiable by the spreading oak tree on the front lawn. The home's first owner was **Lucy Maud Montgomery**, the Canadian author most famous for her *Anne of Green Gables* books. Montgomery nicknamed her house 'Journey's End'. (Parenthetically, Riverside is, in fact, beside a river.) Swansea itself was one of the last independent villages to be assimilated by the city of Toronto, and the hilly, affluent neighbourhood retains its character. Its individuality is aided by its being bounded on three sides by water – Grenadier Pond, Lake Ontario and the Humber River. You can walk – or better yet bike – along the Humber through an almost unbroken chain of parks all the way to the northern limits of the city.

To explore the western lakefront, walk or bike the **Martin Goodman Trail**, which follows the shoreline and is a good conduit for walkers, bikers and bladers going further west. The trail is part of the **Waterfront Trail**, which extends 300 kilometres (186 miles) from

Spit and Polish: eastern Europe meets the West End on **Roncesvalles Avenue**.

Nation states Italy

Population: 500,000
Home base: College Street and Bathurst Street, St Clair Avenue W and Dufferin Street.

That Toronto's Italians come from humble beginnings is an understatement. Yet, as one of the first ethnic groups to settle in the city en masse, they've become so successful that Little Italy has become too lowbrow for them. The community (mostly southern Italians from the Calabrese region) first came to the neighbourhood via the Ward – a shanty town of railway workers that grew north from Union station – when, in the early 1900s, accomplishments in railway building were parlayed into constructing the streetcar lines and sewers, which branched out from the city centre (the junction of College and Bathurst Streets is a well-used streetcar hub). In Little Italy, builders merged with fruit merchants, barbers and shopkeepers, whose strong work ethic had allowed them to escape the Ward and establish a *gentile e civile* enclave.

After World War II, Canada opened up its borders, and Italians already in Toronto sponsored the entrance of family members. At the same time, a building boom attracted huge numbers to the construction trade. Another zone consisting of mostly northern Italians formed at St Clair Avenue W and Dufferin Street and is now even richer in Italian flavour than its downtown counterpart. Migration continued north-west into the suburbs of Woodbridge and Erindale, where many of the city's construction royalty have built their estates. Today, the community supports a radio station (CHIN) and a newspaper (*Corriere Canadese*), and Italian conglomerates such as Parmalat and Pirelli have established headquarters in the city.
Trading places: Smack in the heart of Little Italy proper, Motoretta (554 College Street, 416 925 1818) sells enough retro ice-cream coloured Vespas to furnish an entire library of Fellini films. Venture to Faema (*see p123*) for slick imported cappuccino machines (and the best Italian coffee known to Toronto).

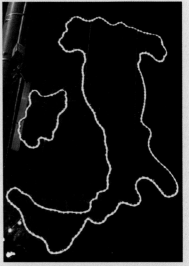

A taste of: Find yourself a crusty Italian bun at one of College Street W's strip of bakeries and fill it with slivers of *prosciutto* and *provolone* from Fratelli Porco/La Gustosa Meat Market (692 College Street, 416 531 3911); for better, you'd have to trek north to Woodbridge. The stretch of St Clair Avenue W between Dufferin Street and Lansdowne Avenue is bliss for those who like it sweet; go further west for a *canoli* climax at Messina Bakery (19 Scarlett Road, 416 762 2496).
Join in: A smile will get you everywhere in the sociable parks south of College Street towards Ossington Avenue. Hang out on a quiet afternoon and cross your fingers that the area's elders spark up a friendly *bocci* match and let you join in. If that fails, grab a seat on the patio at Café Diplomatico (*see p123*) and watch what remains of Old World Italian life.
Local luminary: Italian-Canadian Nino Ricci, author of *Lives of the Saints*, has lived in the city for years.

Trenton to Hamilton. It begins at the foot of Spadina but you might want to start at Bathurst after visiting **Historic Fort York** (*see p93*), which crouches in the shadow of the Gardiner Expressway. A little further on, the path passes **Exhibition Place** (*see p55*); then, as it rounds Humber Bay, it is dotted

with pavilions, picnic tables and public art. At the bay's midpoint, you can cut under the Gardiner on Colborne Lodge Drive for an excursion into High Park (*see p90*).

Look out for two monuments: in **Sir Casimir Gzowski Park** three or so miles along from Bathurst you'll find a bust of Sir Casimir

Nation states Portugal

Population: 350,000

Home base: College Street and Dundas Street W, between Ossington Avenue and Dufferin Street.

Mass Portuguese immigration didn't hit Toronto until the mid-1960s and '70s, yet today the group is the third largest in the city by mother tongue (there's well over a page of Pereiras in the phone book). Originally roosting in Kensington Market, where they opened rice, bean and fruit stands similar to those in Madiera, the Azores, Macau and Portugal proper, the community soon shifted south to the area around St Mary's Church (589 Adelaide Street W, 416 703 2326), the city's largest Portuguese parish, and westward to the inexpensive village surrounding Trinity Bellwoods Park at Dundas Street W. Difficult though it was to find employment in a city teeming with immigrants, the Portuguese eventually rose above their station as cleaners and construction workers and absorbed themselves in the hospitals, schools and restaurants in their community, taking the place of Italians heading to the suburbs.

If there were a Portuguese word for barrio, it would describe the area around Dundas Street W and Dovercourt Road. Here you'll find plenty of mom-and-pop groceries, imported banks, tiny travel outfits and used-car dealerships. Gangs of boys in football kits kick dusty balls or cluster around restaurant TVs to watch the real thing, while elders in poor-boy caps stoop over chess sets on outdoor tables.

The local churches reflect the local population. The Santa Cruz Parish Church (142 Argyle Street, 416 533 8425) rivals the Church of St Patrick (at Dundas and Grace Streets) as the neighbourhood's spiritual nucleus: both conduct mass in Portuguese.

Trading places: For those unafraid of slimy sea beasts, the Mira Mar Fish Store (225 Ossington Avenue, 416 533 5900) keeps iced crates of fresh shellfish and other seafood for authentic soups and stews. The shop busies itself with just about any other import it can cart in, from pottery, tiles and religious artefacts to olive oil, canned goods and cheeses.

himself, along with biographical information. Casimir Stanslaus Gzowski, a Polish revolutionary who arrived here in 1841, was an entrepreneur, a soldier, a railway builder, a politician, and the great-great-great-grandfather of the late Peter Gzowski, a beloved broadcaster (*see p94* **Nation states**).

Half a mile further along the trail, the **Queen Elizabeth Monument** commemorates a visit by King George VI and his wife Elizabeth (later the Queen Mother) to Canada in 1939 when they officially opened the Queen Elizabeth Way highway. As highway dedications go, this one is strangely moving, having been chiselled 'in the face of imminent war' during 'the Empire's darkest hour'. It's almost enough to make you forget that the monument itself, a column of stone with a regal crown on top, looks, shall we say, circumcised. The path continues through many neighbourhoods, including Mimico (a Mississauga Indian name meaning 'The home of wild pigeons'), the former industrial centre of New Toronto, and Long Branch. Even this far out, you can cut inland and jump the 501 or 508 streetcar back along Lake Shore Boulevard.

On the western limits of the Greater Toronto Area (GTA), you'll find another (unrelated) historic Montgomery, the **Montgomery's Inn**

Museum (*see p94*). And far distant from all of these attractions, the **Black Creek Pioneer Village** (*see below*) is a day trip unto itself.

Black Creek Pioneer Village

1000 Murray Ross Parkway, Jane Street at Steeles Avenue (416 736 1733/bcpvinfo@trca.on.ca). Bus 35, 60. **Open** *May-June* 9.30am-4.30pm Mon-Fri; 10am-5pm Sat, Sun. *July-Sept* 10am-5pm daily. *Oct-Dec* 9.30am-4.30pm Mon-Fri; 10am-4.30pm Sat, Sun. **Admission** $10; $6-$9 concessions; free under-5s. **Credit** AmEx, MC, V.

This catch-all re-creation of 19th-century village life could easily have become 'Ye Olde Disneyesque Embarrassment', but the low-key staff and the attention to historic detail make it a kind of cool place to spend an afternoon. And with special events like 'Meet the pigs', and 'Seven uses for a goose', how could you go wrong? The village is at the end of the long and bleak Jane Street, on the fringe of the GTA. The property was a farm that belonged to Daniel Stong and his family in the 1800s (there never was a village of Black Creek).

Five of the buildings, including two homes and a grain barn, were built by Stong and his family. The rest of the 40 or so buildings on the site date from the same era, but were moved here from the surrounding area. There's a working mill, a blacksmith, a printing house and a weaver's shop. The barns, workshops and other restored village buildings are

A taste of: For a carnivore, there's no more exciting strip than Dundas Street W, with its motley *churrasqueiras* and butchers (trendier chicken grills are on College Street). At snack time, drop in at Caldense Bakery & Pastries (1209 Dundas Street W, 416 534 3847), or Nova Era Bakery (1172 Bloor Street W, 416 538 7700/www.bridal.ca/novaera) across the street, to procure store-baked breads and sweet treats.

Join in: In the second weekend of June Dundas Street W and Trinity Bellwoods Park are clogged with Portuguese Day revellers participating in football tournaments, barbecuing chicken and fish, folk dancing, watching live music and moving to Brazilian beats. The Azorean festival of Senhor Santo Cristo dos Milagres takes place in April at St Mary's. If you fancy watching footie with a cool Brazilian beer, case the area of College Street west of Ossington Avenue.

Local luminary: Nelly Furtado moved here from her native Victoria, BC, after launching her singing career.

Nelly Furtado. She's like a bird, you know.

staffed by costumed animators who practise traditional trades and crafts. The Halfway House, one of the village's restaurants, was an actual inn that used to trade on one of the major thoroughfares leading in to Toronto. (There is also ample picnic space if you're brown-bagging it.) In the entry building the McNair Gallery has a good collection of pressed glass, along with many other household items from the Victorian era. With all those craftspeople at work, the gift shops in the village are well stocked with tin lanterns, woven textiles, straw brooms and many other functional souvenirs that you won't find anywhere else.

Colborne Lodge

Colborne Lodge Drive & The Queensway (416 392 6916/clodge@city.toronto.on.ca). Streetcar 501/subway High Park. **Open** *Jan-Apr* noon-4pm Sat Sun. *May-Oct* noon-5pm Tue-Sun. *Nov, Dec* noon-4pm Tue-Sun. **Admission** $3.50; $2.50-$2.75 concessions. **No credit cards**.

Architect John G Howard knew a thing or two about making a house a home. Shortly after becoming Toronto's first surveyor, he designed a villa for himself and his wife Jemima on the highest point of land overlooking the Humber Bay (prompting Jemima to dub the area 'High Park'). Howard made several additions to the house, including installation of the city's first indoor toilet. Other nice touches such as the extra-large windows that allow light into the

basement rooms and a large greenhouse for seedlings make the house feel cosy and snug. The Howards donated most of their land to the city to create a new park. When John died in 1890, the remainder of his land, plus the lodge, became part of the park. It's now a museum, chock full of the Howards' furniture, kitchen gadgets and other possessions, arranged as they would have been in the 1860s. John and Jemima are buried nearby, their grave marked by a stone monument that overlooks Grenadier Pond.

Historic Fort York

100 Garrison Road (416 392 6907/fortyork@ city.toronto.on.ca). Streetcar 511. **Open** *Jan-May, Sept-mid Dec* 10am-4pm Mon-Fri; 10am-5pm Sat, Sun. *May-Sept* 10am-5pm daily. Closed last 2wks Dec. **Admission** $5; $3-$3.25 concessions; free under-5s. **No credit cards**. **Map** p276 B8.

This is where it all began. Lt-Governor John Graves Simcoe founded the fort in 1793 to protect the town of York, which was incorporated the same year. The fort only saw real military action once, at the Battle of York in 1813 (which took place during the War of 1812). It was sacked by the Americans, but was rebuilt shortly thereafter. Modern refurbishment began in the 1930s, but the fort then fell victim to a different kind of attack. This one was led by urban planners, who laid waste to many old buildings to make way for the Gardiner Expressway. But the buildings that remain, including a magazine, barracks and officers' quarters, still comprise the largest collection of buildings in Canada that date from the War of 1812. The museum offers guided tours and historical re-enactments, plus performances of period music and dance.

Montgomery's Inn Museum

4709 Dundas Street W (416 394 8113). Subway Islington, then 10min walk. **Open** 1.30-4.30pm Tue-Fri; 1-5pm Sat, Sun. **Admission** $3; $1-$2 concessions. **No credit cards**.

It's a shame that this inn, the main part of which dates back to 1830, is so far from anywhere else. But if you are in the area the small museum is well worth

a visit. Thomas Montgomery operated the inn and tavern for 25 years. When Thomas's wife Margaret died in 1855, he took down the sign and closed up shop. The late Georgian stone house fell into disrepair until it was rescued, restored and reopened as a museum in 1975.

The old sign, emblazoned with a picture of a plough, is one of the few artefacts that have survived from Montgomery's day, and it now hangs in the museum. Cutbacks mean there are fewer demonstrations at the museum than there used to be, with the emphasis shifting to guided and self-guided tours. Don't miss the Briarly room in the basement, which has a good history display on many of western Toronto's neighbourhoods.

Nation states Poland

Population: 150,000
Home base: Roncesvalles Avenue, between the Lake Shore Boulevard W and Bloor Street W.

The first Polish émigrés settled in the city in the 18th century, but it was 1850 before peasants began to arrive in large numbers, attracted by advertisements for railway and land development (a number headed westward toward Saskatchewan to take up beet farming). Determined to express themselves religiously and culturally, they established a community of churches, bakeries and butchers, just a few blocks north of the railway yards.

A lull in immigration between the world wars was followed by an influx of political refugees; defecting athletes and performers – along with accredited doctors, engineers and professors – chose this fastest-growing Canadian city as their harbour from communist rule. Today, Toronto's Polish community supports two daily newspapers and several TV and radio timeslots, and has grown far beyond the confines of Roncesvalles Avenue to the West End (Bloor West Village, Etobicoke) and Mississauga. And though the Roncesvalles neighbourhood, between the churches of St Casimir (156 Roncesvalles Avenue) and St Vincent de Paul (263 Roncesvalles Avenue), continues to trade heavily in Polish delicacies, books and videos, the focus has shifted to suburban strip malls, where merchants need not cater their approach to the assimilated population downtown.

A taste of: The city's largest Polish population now resides – not surprisingly – outside the city, in adjacent Mississauga, home to Plaza

Wisla (named after the longest river in Poland), at Dundas Street W and Dixie Road, and the cheapest baked goods this side of Warsaw. The downtown pedestrian can find his mecca at Dundas Street W and Roncesvalles Avenue, where 80 per cent of businesses are run by Polish Canadians and residential streets are flooded with the sounds of Polish pop by the group Ich Troje and rocker Kayah. Threatened by mass gentrification (a trendy antiques strip flourishes at Queen Street W), the strip still remains sausage central. Copernicus Delicatessen (79 Roncesvalles Avenue, 416 536 4054) is the best link to superlative spicy *kielbasa*, as evidenced by the babushkas making pleasant conversation with burly butchers who stink of garlic and pickled herring. If you're keen, Czechowski Polish Sausage (935 The Queensway, 416 252 4567), an Eastern European grocer and sausage vendor, is worth the hike along a deserted stretch of Lakeshore Boulevard W to Etobicoke for fancy varieties stuffed with foreign cheeses.
Join in: Off-season for the majority of travellers, save for a few hardy northern Europeans, is the Feniks Polish Film Festival. Two theatres – one on Bloor Street W at the Kingsway, the other in Mississauga – promote the films of the two Krzysztofs (Kieslowski and Zanussi).
Local luminary: Late radio and TV broadcaster Peter Gzowski is the great-great-great-grandson of one of Canada's first Polish immigrants, Sir Casimir Gzowski, a military and civil engineer who oversaw the building of bridges, canals and railways across Ontario, and once served as the province's deputy Lieutenant-Governor and honourary aide-de-camp to Queen Victoria.

North Side

Parks, museums and galleries; there's more to the suburbs than meets the eye – at least Prince thinks so.

For many Torontonians, the area north of Eglinton Avenue might as well be marked 'Here there be dragons'. Other than zipping through on their way to their summer cottages, many urban dwellers rarely find a reason to leave their centre of the universe to explore these distant suburbs. But before it was amalgamated into the City of Toronto in 1998, North York was one of Canada's largest cities, and the North Side has a full complement of theatres, galleries and other cultural institutions. There's lots of space up this way, which means the attractions are more spread out – you should consider a bicycle, if not a car, if you're serious about exploring. But all that space also means that the parks get huge and wild.

Many of the best places to visit are clustered around North York Centre subway station, near the intersection of Yonge Street and Park Home Avenue. The fountain at **Mel Lastman Square** (5100 Yonge Street), which was named for and by his Melness before he took on the bigger job of steering the amalgamated city on a wobbly course to integration, is topped with a similarly wobbly wind-powered kinetic sculpture, whose rotating metallic disks are covered with silhouettes of horses, cars and trolleys. The fountain water flows under a burbling boardwalk to a reflecting pool/skating rink in the square below. Many civic celebrations and free concerts are held at the small stage in the paved park. The square is just in front of **North York Civic Centre** (5100 Yonge Street, 416 338 0338), which before amalgamation was North York's City Hall. To the south, the **Toronto Centre for the Arts** (5040 Yonge Street, 416 733 9388) houses three theatres, including the acoustically superlative **George Weston Recital Hall** (*see p196*), plus the **Museum of Contemporary Canadian Art** (*see p96*). North of the square, **Gibson House** (*see p96*) stands in sharp contrast to the landscaped modern high-rises that surround it. Just to the west of all of these sites, **York Cemetery** (101 Senlac Avenue, 416 221 3404), opened in 1948, is a peaceful place to walk. The section of Bathurst Street at the far end of the cemetery is where to find all things related to Toronto's Jewish culture. The **Holocaust Centre of Toronto** (4600 Bathurst Street, 416 635 2883) has a small

museum, plus audio-visual presentations, and live speakers. Just down the road at 4588 Bathurst Street, the **Bathurst Jewish Community Centre** (416 636 1880) is a well-equipped complex that houses the respected **Koffler Gallery**, the **Leah Posluns Theatre** and **My Jewish Discovery Place Children's Museum**. The museum has regularly changing displays and special events that promote Jewish culture and values. South of Sheppard Avenue in **Earl Bales Park**, stands a **Holocaust Memorial** monument created by Toronto sculptor and Holocaust survivor Ernest Raab. Another monument, also by Raab, commemorates Raoul Wallenberg, a Swedish diplomat who saved the lives of thousands of Jews in Budapest, Hungary.

Earl Bales Park connects to the **Don River West**, a series of parks and golf courses that follow the river south-east into the city (and north-west into the wilderness of extra-Urbia).

Holocaust Memorial by Ernest Raab.

But it's much faster to travel by road to get to **The Bridle Path**, a must-see for fans of nouveau riche excess. The homes on this street in the neighbourhood of York Mills might not be as monstrously ostentatious as many people have made them out to be, but they are still plenty ostentatious. A home on this cul-de-sac can cost anywhere from $1.7 million to $20 million. With that kind of money most people would buy privacy, but on The Bridle Path, residents might as well stand on their massive front lawns and scream their bank balance to passers-by. Most owners have bought a lot, torn down the existing house, and custom-built their dream home in its place. The resulting pastiche of building styles makes you feel that you've entered a tour of architectural history designed by Disneyland. Maybe that's what attracted the Artist Now Known Again As Prince to pick up a palatial pad here in 2002 after he married a local girl. The exact address is a well-kept secret but you might want to look for shades of purple on Post Road. Otherwise, the Colonial brick monster at No.24 looks like it houses an exiled dictator who can't give up the presidential lifestyle. No.18 is a three-storey neo-Georgian goliath, while No.19 looks suspiciously like a 1970s subway station.

If you don't feel you've travelled far enough from the city centre, consider taking a public tour of the **David Dunlap Observatory** (123 Hillsview Drive, 905 884 9562 ext 232) in Richmond Hill. Tours include a presentation by a member of the Royal Astronomical Society of Canada, and a chance to look at the night sky through the largest optical telescope in Canada. The multi-domed observatory is located in a large and airy park north of the GTA, a property the astronomers share with a small population of white-tailed deer. This is a serious research facility, and children under seven are not allowed on tours.

Gibson House

5172 Yonge Street (416 395 7432). Subway North York Centre. **Open** noon-5pm Tue-Sun. **Admission** $2.75; $1.75-$2.25 concessions; free under-2s. **No credit cards.**
Tucked behind the North York Rose Garden, Gibson House commemorates one of the major figures from the Rebellion of 1837, David Gibson. Gibson was a Scottish immigrant to Upper Canada (as Ontario was known) who built his first family home here in 1826. The neighbouring shopping mall hadn't yet been built on what was then a large area of farmland. His involvement in local politics led him to join William Lyon Mackenzie's 1837 rebellion against the 'family compact', a cabal of wealthy men who held a death grip on political and economic power. The rebellion failed, Gibson was exiled, and troops burned his house to the ground. Gibson was later pardoned, and returned with his wife and seven children. He then built the 1851 farmhouse that stands here today. Supplementing the exhibits in the museum, costumed tour guides demonstrate such 19th-century skills as spinning yarn, churning butter and making ice-cream by hand.

The Museum of Contemporary Canadian Art

5040 Yonge Street (416 395 0067/www.mocca. toronto.on.ca). Subway North York Centre. **Open** noon-5pm Tue-Sun. **Admission** free.
What's in an acronym? This curvaceous building used to be known as the Art Gallery of North York, but went through a public-relations motivated name change so that its short form would be MOCCA, rather than AGONY. It's the third largest of Toronto's visual arts museums (though not huge), with a permanent collection and changing exhibitions, running hard to keep up with Toronto's buzzing art scene. The oak floors and natural light provide an excellent showcase for contemporary art. The museum focuses on works produced after 1985, and many group shows feature international artists alongside their Canadian contemporaries.

Praise be to Bond

'Open your books now to hymn 007 as we join the choir in singing the praises of his Holiness, St James Bond'. All right, you won't hear the minister say that, but the St James-Bond United Church (1066 Avenue Road) is indeed an oddity nestled in north Toronto, wrapped in an enigma.

The real story is that two churches came together in 1925 – St James Presbyterian and Bond Street Methodist. But, in true Ian Fleming style, there is a twist. The British author was seconded to Canada during World War II for some hush-hush intelligence duty, probably with the Department of Defense, which was based up the road from this church with the head-turning title. Fleming possibly passed by on a regular basis. And all this time he led people to believe the inspiration for his sinful spy was the American ornithologist whose seminal text, *Checklist of the Birds of the West Indies*, he happened upon at his Jamaican home, Goldeneye. Torontonians would like to think otherwise.

East Side

Live in this residential area and you'll never need a holiday – beaches and samples of Greece and Asia are right on your doorstep.

We've used the term East Side to mean everything east of the Don Valley Parkway, but strictly speaking it refers to the area south of O'Connor Drive as far east as Scarborough. (The Don Valley Parkway is named after the **Don River**, which, in and of itself, is no great attraction in this urban stretch. While it was once a major waterway, years of urbanisation and pollution have turned the once-mighty river into a sickly stream much of the year. Still, recent years have seen increased efforts to 'bring back the Don', and a pleasant walking and cycling path now runs along the river.)

Locals love the East Side because they get to live in an old-fashioned, small-town neighbourhood – quiet, canopy-tree-lined streets, sprawling parks, mom-and-pop cornerstores – just a 10- or 15-minute subway ride from downtown. And locals' Toronto this is: there are no major attractions to draw you here, just an eclectic mix of neighbourhoods, of which **the Beach** (*see p98*), **the Danforth** (*see p98*) and **Little India** (*see p100*) are the most obviously visitable. But don't neglect

Riverdale, facing Cabbagetown across the DVP. Favoured by the city's liberal chattering classes, it stretches from Broadview Avenue to Pape Avenue, and Mortimer Avenue to the lake, although its eastern boundary is constantly expanding. As affordable property in Riverdale proper becomes scarce, more families are buying less expensive homes further east in largely immigrant neighbourhoods as far as Coxwell Avenue. If you like to house-browse, take a stroll down any of the streets surrounding the impressive **Withrow Park**, located between Logan and Carlaw Avenues, south of Danforth Avenue (Riverdale Avenue, Langley Avenue, Sparkhall Avenue).

Another nice walk is through **Leslieville** (Queen Street E, between Logan and Connaught Avenues). As well as having a range of funky antiques shops strong on 1950s and '60s kitsch, it's also the based of a number of the city's film production houses. And **Maple Cottage** (62 Laing Street, 416 392 1376), was home of Alexander Muir, the first principal of Leslieville Public School and creator of the classic

Pull on your shorts and join the strollers along **The Beach**. *See p98.*

Canadian song (though not anthem) 'The Maple Leaf Forever'. Legend has it Muir was inspired to write it after being struck by a falling maple leaf from the ancient tree that grows there still.

The Beach

Streetcar 501.

This community was created during the 19th century when the landed gentry decided they needed homes 'outside' the city and built small mansions by the lake. In summer they would close up their downtown Rosedale homes and relocate here. Since then the city has sprawled out to swallow them, and it's a direct 30-minute trolley ride from Yonge Street straight along Queen Street E. But the Beach remains a world unto itself, still a little like a resort town. Though people visit all year round – as if there weren't enough residents to begin with – in summer swarms of downtowners escape the heat by packing on to the beaches and filling every outdoor patio along Queen Street.

The Beach occupies the stretch of Queen Street between Woodbine Avenue and Victoria Park Avenue, after which you will find yourself in Scarborough (a mainly residential district that turns into a land of fast food outlets and strip malls). For years the debate raged over the name. Some called it the Beach, others the Beaches. So confusing! What to do? Eventually this silliness made it to the floor of Toronto Council and these officials in all their wisdom decided that the singular was fine, thank-you.

Whatever its name, it remains the same gentri-fashionable area, filled with chic shops, cafés and bars, casual restaurants serving wings and beer and more well-heeled dining that begs a credit card. And then there is the beach itself. Miles of white sand on the shores of Lake Ontario, ringed by a well-maintained wooden boardwalk almost four kilometres (two and a half miles) long. From Balmy Beach in the east to Ashbridges Bay Park in the west, the beach is filled with strollers, joggers and dog walkers meandering through perfectly manicured parkland with paths for cyclists and Rollerbladers, tennis and volleyball courts, children's playgrounds and parks with bandstands and gazebos.

As unlikely as it may seem, fans of art deco will want to pay a visit to the **RC Harris Filtration Plant** (2701 Queen Street E, at the foot of Victoria Park Avenue), the monolithic building prominent at the eastern end of the beach. Designed by English architet Thomas Pomphrey in the 1930s, this operational water treatment plant, all towers and arched doorways, sits atop a grassy knoll and affords one of the best views the city has to offer (as

evidenced by the many films and TV shows that have been shot there). Tours are offered haphazardly, so it's best to call the city (416 338 0338) to find out times. The south-eastern tip of the property also offers one the best views of the **Scarborough Bluffs**, dramatic limestone cliffs that plunge into the lake, taking a few houses with them every now and again as erosion undermines their grand yet fragile facades, so eerily out of place in the city.

Off the beach, there are pleasant walks along the roads that connect it to Queen Street (and on further north), where houses range from cute and quaint to massive and stunning, with massive and stunning prices to match. For refreshment, **Boardwalk BBQ Pub** (1681 Lakeshore Boulevard E, at Coxwell Avenue, 416 694 8844) sitting all by itself just off the boardwalk near Ashbridges Bay is one of the few licensed spots close to the beach. Queen Street has several local joints with patios including **Legends Restaurant & Bar** (1943 Queen Street E, 416 693 9337) and the **Lion on the Beach** (1958 Queen Street E, 416 690 1984). The **Sunset Grill** diner (2006 Queen Street E, 416 690 9985) is unmissable for breakfast.

You'll find all kinds of shops along Queen Street E – think small-town staples combined with chi-chi tourist resort. Don't miss the bins outside **Ends** (1930 Queen Street E, 416 699 2271), which are crammed with drastically discounted and sometimes designer clothing.

The Danforth

Subway Chester or Pape.

Opa! Once you cross the Don River on the Bloor Street Viaduct (Price Edward Viaduct on the map, but no one says that) and pass Broadview Avenue, you have entered Greektown, known by locals as the Danforth. (Bloor Street E changes its name to Danforth Avenue when you cross the bridge). Settled by Greeks over much of the last century, and peppered with shops, restaurants and cafés in the style of the homeland, this is not as yet a cute ethnic tourist trap, though as the forces of gentrification have their inevitable effect and some of the original inhabitants move out it does risk becoming a second Little Italy. It already has a similarly fashionable bar and restaurant scene.

The Danforth is a pleasant place to amble at any time, but you do have to be hungry to get the most out of the area. Greeks like to feed you and the aroma of succulent souvlaki, pungent feta, and mouthwatering moussaka waft from storefronts all along the street. Most of the restaurants stay open late so you can always get a plate piled with chicken or beef kebabs, roast potatoes, savoury rice and Village Salad

Nation states Greece

Population: 150,000
Home base: Danforth Avenue toward East York; Scarborough

It would hardly be mistaken for the motherland, but the Danforth, aka Greektown, has that unmistakable southern Mediterranean feel, especially in the summer, when patios with no concept of last orders spill on to the street and chiming Hellenic music (not just 'Zorba the Greek') can be heard from open kitchens, private homes and passing cars. The neighbourhood of modest homes and shops was settled by Greek immigrants who had escaped Turkish occupation in the early 20th century to toil away – not unlike other ethnic groups – on the Canadian National Railway, and as miners or farmers. Successive waves in the mid-century brought over women sponsored by their husbands and fathers, who worked as domestics to the city's establishment. Whereas in 1907 only two dozen Greek names appeared in city telephone directories, today the Greek population on the Danforth and beyond is the second largest outside Greece (Queens, New York, is the first). Consequently, the local flavour is unique in its authenticity, with its Greek-language signage, blue-and-white flying flags and Mediterranean banks and manufacturers. Restaurants – the favoured business of first-generation emigrés in the latter half of the century – are considered to be among the best reviewed in the city.

In the 1990s this social scene, along with low house prices, made the area attractive to Toronto's upward mobility, who gutted and reno'ed to yuppie standards. More Greeks have moved eastward than remain. According to the archbishop of the Greek Orthodox Metropolis (86 Overlea Boulevard), 'Nobody lives on the Danforth anymore. Thousands of families have gone on to Scarborough, Markham, Mississauga'.

Trading places: Those who have forsaken the quarter have nonetheless remained faithful to Mister Greek Meat Market (801 Danforth Avenue, 469 0733), purveyor of lamb and pig for backyard spits and wedding banquets.

A taste of: Hub though Danforth is (Myth remains a hangout par excellence; see p127), the strip is in danger of becoming a wax museum of Greek life, its souvlaki joints and pastry shops mere kitsch amid new-era coffee dens and health food houses. A few high points remain: Sun Valley Fine Foods (583 Danforth Avenue, 469 5227) is a modest fruit shop-cum-produce bazaar in the thick of Danforth's hectic heart, catering to the grandchildren of the old 'yayas' it once served.

Join in: Early each August, stone ovens and grills are towed on to the pavement for the week-long Taste of the Danforth festival (see p168). St George's Greek Orthodox Church (see p65) in Downtown West, established in the 1930s, is the pre-eminent venue for experiencing Greek Easter celebrations and St George's Day, both in April.

Local luminary: Greek Prime Minister Andreaous Papendreaou resided in the Danforth while in exile in the early 1970s. Papendreaou also taught economics at Toronto's York University.

(the 'real' Greek salad of onions, tomatoes, cucumber and feta cheese – no lettuce) after the bars close at 2am. The classic, if institutional, experience, is **Mr Greek** (568 Danforth Avenue, 416 461 5470/www.mrgreek.com), serving heaped platters at low prices; $8.95 for chicken souvlaki, potatoes, rice, salad, and bread. For more culinary finesse, check our Restaurants & Cafés chapter, on page 129.

The Danforth is also known throughout the city for a little shopping complex known as **Carrot Common** (348 Danforth Avenue, 416 361 3803), anchored by **The Big Carrot** (see p155), which is the original – and still the most extensive – site for health food shopping and natural products in Toronto.

Gerrard Street East

Streetcar 506.

When you start to notice signs with the titles Mo Pa, Hoi Tan and Wing Kee, you know you have wandered into another of the city's authentic ethnic sections.

This area east on Gerrard Street was an offshoot of Chinatown but many other cultures including Vietnamese and Cambodian have since joined the neighbourhood. And since it is still not considered as trendy as the central Dundas–Spadina district, the bargains are better in the restaurants, groceries and little specialty shops, especially those dispensing Chinese herbs and medicines, such as **Dai**

Kuang Wah Herb Market (595 Gerrard Street E, 416 466 9207). At the **Grand Sea Food House** (615 Gerrard Street E, 416 778 8888) you can order a fresh lobster dinner for a positively meagre $12.95.

You will be at a real advantage if you can decipher the menu, however. Most of these restaurants feature Chinese symbols, which is no problem for the vast majority of their customers. In other words, you know you are getting authentic Chinese cuisine as opposed to pre-frozen egg rolls.

Little India

Streetcar 506.

A few blocks further east along Gerrard Street, between Greenwood and Coxwell Avenues, is Little India with its slightly garish and colourful advertisement signs. This neighbourhood is famous for its Indian Bazaar where you can purchase saris, fine silks and brightly coloured scarves, and special spices and foods. Both professional and weekend chefs peruse these markets on a regular basis.

Nation states India

Sightseeing

Population: 200,000
Home base: Gerrard Street E, west from Coxwell Avenue

In Toronto, as in cities throughout the world, immigrants tend to flock downtown, settle, prosper, then shift their focus to spacious suburbs while the next displaced culture takes its place. Toronto's Indian community, however, colonised a remote patch of the east end, off the radar of some long-time residents, who managed eventually to detect its presence only once the numbers had exploded and vast tracts of this hitherto ignored suburbia had been developed in the name of Indian progress.

Indian immigration began, largely, in the 1960s and '70s, mostly in the form of young men who drove taxis, took over convenience stores, opened restaurants and laboured in construction while upgrading professional studies that didn't translate from the old country. Families followed – parents, grandparents, cousins, children – and soon the population that still occupies a two-kilometre stretch around Gerrard Street E and Coxwell Avenue had fragmented into developments further east in Scarborough, and west by the airport and in the suburb of Bramalea. 'Many first-generation Indians still adhere to a caste system,' says Narain Subramanian, a community worker who has served at the Indian consulate as a labour minister. 'And that is the generation that aspires to a higher place in the community. They seek better education and become accountants, doctors, dentists.'

Of course, the community itself is fragmented into Sikhs, Tamils and the Hindu majority, the traditional Southern Indians (who adorn their temples with black granite icons) and the more liberal northerners (who prefer lighter marble). In all, there are 45 Hindu temples in the city, the neighbourhood of Richmond Hill claiming the largest – the Hindu Temple Society of Canada (10865 Bayview Avenue, 905 883 9109) – where nary a week goes by without some fête.

Trading places: Though more of Toronto's Indians make their home outside the Gerrard/Coxwell community than within it, business there is overwhelmingly Indian, with silks and saris attracting seamstresses and fashionistas taken with the Bollywood trend. Subramanian recommends silk importer Nalli International (1447 Gerrard Street E, 778 4542/www.nallisilk.com), though there are a dozen such sari players on Gerrard Street E (most in the 1400s).

A taste of: On Gerrard Street, you're best at the simplest end: stalls sell authentic street treats and there are good takeaways and caffs but some of the restaurants proper compare poorly to those in the world's other Indian communities. For palak paneer, barfi, halwa, jelabi and other pastries and sweets, comb Gerrard Street E or the Albion and Islington area in Etobicoke, the only other Indian-predominant community in Toronto. Madras Palace (1249 Ellesmere Road, 759 5400) is a South Indian hotspot in faraway Scarborough, whose thali is worth the dreary drive eastwards.

Join in: Meditate with true gurus at the Vedanta Society of Toronto (120 Emmett Avenue, 240 7262/www.total.net/~vedanta) in Etobicoke, Mondays through Thursdays from 6pm to 7pm. In mid-May, for 15 days, Hindus celebrate Rathotsawam (the Chariot Festival), during which processions of lotus-shaped wood chariots can be seen circling the neighbourhood.

Local luminary: The novelist Rohinton Mistry emigrated from Bombay in 1975.

Eat, Drink, Shop

Restaurants & Cafés

Hogtown no more: variety and quality come in equally large portions in Toronto's restaurants. Though they still do a great bacon sarnie...

That the city has endured the nicknames Hogtown and Muddy York says nothing of the quality of food to be found in Toronto. For a town that is by and large forgotten in the discussion of 'world-class' cities (even though it's the fifth largest in North America), Toronto enjoys a standard of eating that quietly rivals that of the gastronomic capitals of the world. Moreover, if you head to the city armed with a world-class currency, you're likely to be pleased with the low impact that dining out will have on your wallet.

Yet, despite its epicurean tendencies, Toronto has no culinary traditions as such. Prior to World War II, the city's palate was as bland as that of a Midwestern farming community –

Hogtown indeed. It has taken more than 50 years of increasing prosperity and the gradual influence and acceptance of uncompromised immigrant cuisines for Toronto to get past naked pork chops and soggy spaghetti.

The theme, when it comes to dining out in Toronto, is neighbourhoods – the neighbourhood defines the food. The ethnic and cultural patchwork means that you can count on finding Chinese in Chinatown, Greek in the Danforth, funky cafés on West Queen – choosing where to go for what is a no-brainer. But gentrification of the downtown core has begun to muddle the distinct essence of each pocket, so that you can now find Belgian bistro on the Danforth, French in Little Italy and Mexican on Korean-dominated Bloor Street, though the dominant cultural flavour in each area still remains potent.

Dressing for dinner in Toronto is easy: be casual. You'll spot denim and trainers even in top haunts. You might want to smarten up for places like **Centro Grill & Wine Bar** (*see p119*). *Streetcar. 506*. **Open** 11.30am-10pm Tue; 11.30am-11pm Wed-Thur; 11.30am-midnight Fri; 11am-midnight Sat; 11am-10pm Sun. **Main courses** $8-$20. **Credit** MC, V. **Map** p276 C7.

It's easy to forget this fishbowl off the hectic intersection of Bathurst and Queen Streets. But that's precisely its allure: Azul is quiet, soothing even, with muted bluey green walls and pop artwork that can only be described as cute. This is not a juice bar, though it smells and often acts like one: lunches are fruit-filled and veggie-friendly with juices and

Don't miss Cuisine

Café Societa
Where the Italian-style service warms you up for the French bistro fare. *See p124*.

Canoe Restaurant & Bar
Proves that form and function can exist together in upscale dining. *See p109*.

Centro Grill & Wine Bar
The uptown stalwart that hasn't let its age hinder its quest for production value. *See p119*.

The Fifth
Where the food is as exclusive as the guest list: just try to get a table on a Saturday night and you'll see what we mean. *See p104*.

JOV Bistro
A neighbourhood favourite that defines fusion cooking for the city. *See p120*.

Sushi Kaji
Offers the definitive seafood adventure. *See p125*.

Susur
For complex concoctions that taste simply divine. *See p105*.

Smoking is generally forbidden in Toronto restaurants, though some choose to classify themselves as bars in order to evade the law. Beware: anyone under 19 is restricted from entering restaurants that declare bar status.

Entertainment District

Cafés & coffeehouses

Azul
181 Bathurst Street, at Queen Street (416 703 9360). Streetcar 511, 506. **Open** 11.30am-10pm Tue; 11.30am-11pm Wed-Thur; 11.30am-midnight Fri; 11am-midnight Sat; 11am-10pm Sun. **Main courses** $8-$20. **Credit** MC, V. **Map** p276 C7.
It's easy to forget this fishbowl off the hectic intersection of Bathurst and Queen Streets. But that's precisely its allure: Azul is quiet, soothing even, with muted bluey green walls and pop artwork that can only be described as cute. This is not a juice bar, though it smells and often acts like one: lunches are fruit-filled and veggie-friendly with juices and

Pizzas, panini and pop after the shops at **Lettieri**.

sprouty sandwiches in the spotlight. Dinners are more sophisticated, featuring selections that share Asian and Mexican sensibilities with starch figuring in most of the entrées, be it rice, noodles or tortillas. Nights often end with the house DJ coaxing guests towards the fruity cocktails on offer.

La Hacienda

640 Queen Street W, at Bathurst Street (416 703 3377). Streetcar 501, 511. **Open** noon-11pm Mon-Fri; 11am-11pm Sat. **Main courses** $6-$14. **Credit** MC, V. **Map** p276 C7.
Queen West dwellers are not as discriminating with their decor as you might imagine. Case in point: La Hacienda offers wobbly tables and scruffy chairs in a dingy, cramped space; the lack of illumination is mitigated only by its patio and two tiny bistro tables by the front windows. Yet you'll never be alone here. LaHa caters to an army of pink-haired, vintage-clad hipsters looking for a good cheap meal. Vegetarians are particularly pleased with hearty salads, quesadillas, chilli and burritos with fresh veg, beans and cheese. Sides of corn chips with spicy salsa or salad are an experiencce in themselves. Brunch is as gourmet as any of the designer diners in the area.

Lost Camel

559 Queen Street W, at Denison Avenue (416 703 5275). Streetcar 501, 510. **Open** 7am-11pm daily. **Main courses** $6-$7. **Credit** AmEx, MC, V. **Map** p276 C7.
Starbucks did not forget Toronto when planning its takeover of the universe and urbanites appalled at its penetration of the city avoid it at all costs in favour of the Lost Camel, one of the few independent coffeehouses that still manage to survive. The food could maybe be fresher, but it's cheap, and the portions charitable. The real joy is in the java, adequate for Monday morning jolts and late-night road trips. New (but still non-corporate) owners are gradually retitling the joint as the Caffeine Bean Bar.

Lettieri

441 Queen Street W, at Spadina Avenue (416 592 1360). Streetcar 510, 501. **Open** 7am-10pm Mon-Wed, Sun; 7am-midnight Thur-Sat. **Main courses** $4-$6. **No credit cards**. **Map** p276 D7.
Bridging the divide between coffeehouse and trattoria, Lettieri has conceived a brilliant alternative: high-end coffees, nectars and sodas served alongside grilled panini, mixed salads and pizza. It's as close as you'll get to an Italian caffè with its exuberant staff (many right off the boat from the old country) and scone-free baked goods.

The Rivoli

332 Queen Street W, at Spadina Avenue (416 597 0794/http://rivoli.ca). Streetcar 501/subway Osgoode. **Open** 11.30am-1am daily. **Main courses** $8-$18. **Credit** AmEx, MC, V. **Map** p276 D7.
The Rivoli was ever-present during the formative years of the now legendary stretch of Queen West between University and Spadina, and is still a central meeting place for hipsters of all generations. The functions of the space are severalfold: diners gather on the east side of the building, drinkers on the west, and the two mingle on the patio out front. Upstairs is a pool hall, and the back room serves as a venue for up-and-coming bands and DJs. Nourishment is bistro style, with some Asian fusion thrown into the mix. Soups and salads are run of the mill, noodle dishes fare better; burgers and pad Thai are the best bet. This is no gourmet fantasy but the (fair) price you pay for food includes scenery and music.

Tequila Bookworm

490 Queen Street W, at Denison Avenue (416 504 7335). Streetcar 501, 510. **Open** 8am-11pm Mon-Thur; 10am-midnight Fri, Sat; 11am-10pm Sun. **Main courses** $3-$9. **Credit** AmEx, MC, V. **Map** p276 C7.
You can visit the mega-bookstores for a latte and the latest pulp, but a much better option is to curl up with an ancient copy of *Wuthering Heights* at the

loft-like reading lounge at Tequila Bookworm. One of the last bastions of Queen West bohemia (even though it's only been around for a decade), the café offers more relaxation on a ratty selection of Chesterfields (as Canadians are prone to call sofas) than the trendy coffee spas further east. And there's no pressure to buy: as long as you have a coffee in hand, you're free to browse. There's also a decent selection of sandwiches for those who want more substance with their *InStyle*.

Continental

Crush

455 King Street W, at Spadina Avenue (416 977 1234). Streetcar 504, 510. **Open** 11.30am-11pm Mon-Sat (drinks only 2.30-5.30pm). **Main courses** $19-$29. **Credit** AmEx, MC, V. **Map** p276 C8.
Recommending this industrial-sized bar-resto requires a caveat. Today, it might be the coolest thing to have moved into this fast-gentrifying neighbourhood of film houses and architecture firms since Susur opened its doors in the late '90s. But tomorrow, who knows? A restaurant cannot survive on waves of fickle hipsters alone. Still, Crush aspires to be more than just passing fancy, wowing newcomers with all things French (curious since the chef Masayuki Tamaru is Japanese). You'll come across magret of duck, hearty Breton pork and boudin blanc among other famously French delicacies, and the bar pours more than 30 wines by the glass. Informal, and naturally very popular, evening wine tastings are a weekly event, usually taking place on Wednesdays. Well worth a visit.

The Fifth

5th floor, 225 Richmond Street W, at Duncan Street (416 979 3005/www.easyandthefifth.com). Streetcar 501/subway Osgoode. **Open** 6-11pm Thur-Sat. **Set menu** $80; terrace $50. **Credit** AmEx, DC, MC, V. **Map** p276 D6.
Widely considered to be one of the city's best and most stylish dining rooms, the Fifth nevertheless had the odds stacked against it, the tenant below being one of the area's less classy nightclubs. Fortunately, the pop music is muted by soft piano jazz. Expect the utmost in French delicacy from chef Marc Thuet, formerly of Centro Grill & Wine Bar (*see p119*): filet mignon, foie gras and a wide selection of cheeses. In warm weather, the patio extends the capacity. The Fifth is open only Thursday to Saturday, so reservations are highly recommended.

Le Sélect Bistro

328 Queen Street W, at Spadina Avenue (416 596 6406/www.leselect.com). Streetcar 501, 510. **Open** 11.30am-11pm daily. **Main courses** $17-$29; set menu $26. **Credit** AmEx, DC, MC, V. **Map** p276 D7.
This series of nooks and crannies suits romantics who crave a bouillabaisse with a well-aged red. The bistro sits atop one of the most plentiful wine cellars in town. Sit down at a table to ponder the book-like list or take advice at the zinc bar if you just want a casual sip and a bite, backed by a jazz playlist that extends beyond Ella and Louis (Le Select is often a venue on the jazz festival circuit). On summer evenings, the front patio – protected from Queen West riff raff by a trellised enclosure – is the quaintest place to nibble and savour the vintage.

Crush: it's hip, it's slick but will it stick?

Cool and refreshing: that's **Rain**.

YYZ Restaurant & Wine Bar
345 Adelaide Street W, at Spadina Avenue (416 599 3399). Streetcar 510, 504. **Open** 4.30-10pm Mon-Wed, Sun; 4.30-11pm Thur-Sat. **Main courses** $25-$29. **Credit** AmEx, DC, MC, V. **Map** p276 D7.
The acronym refers to Pearson International Airport's call letters, but this is more catwalk than runway and the food more jet set than airport lounge. In the epicentre of Downtown, it attracts fabulous people from business and media, darling. It's hard to imagine why, though, when you inspect your bill and wonder what you've spent so much on. Best to come in a group and try a bit of everything: you're bound to find something to your liking (food spans western Europe, and is heavy on the seafood). Smokers share a tiny lounge.

Fusion

Rain
19 Mercer Street, at John Street (416 599 7246/ www.rainlounge.ca). Streetcar 504/subway St Andrew. **Open** 5.30-10.30pm Tue, Wed; 5.30-11pm Thur-Sat. **Main courses** $18-$36. **Credit** AmEx, DC, MC, V. **Map** p276 D8.
Toronto might not have shed its conventional image if it weren't for entrepreneurs like Michael and Guy Rubino, who also own the post-work mecca Zoom. Here, they've chosen a Barbarella-meets-Tarzan decor scheme that favours Lucite along with jungle bamboo. Though doormen can be ridiculously brazen, Rain is worth braving just for the experience: nibble for hours on appetisers over expensive drinks (a sake martini is $12), or watch your (Asian fusion) main be marched to your table on a steaming serving stone. They've also – to the surprise of the old guard – successfully integrated communal dining into the environment.

Susur
601 King Street W, at Bathurst Street (416 603 2205). Streetcar 504, 511. **Open** 6-9.30pm Mon-Sat. **Dinner** $100 approx. **Credit** AmEx, MC, V. **Map** p276 D8.

Eating at this minimalist haven (behind the stucco façade of the old world Italian eaterie it replaced) is like opening Pandora's box: the sum of the taste is so much more than the complex blend of ingredients involved. Main courses are standard haute cuisine fare – lamb and pork tenderloin, lobster, roasted quail – though chef Susur Lee's (*see also p122* **Local hero**) influence on them is decidedly Asian. When the Hong Kong native works in maple syrup, plum, raisin or olive, you'll know it, because Lee is remark-

Eat, Drink, Shop

The best Dining

Brunch spots
Agora Restaurant (*see p112*); **Bar One** (*p124*); **Bonjour Brioche** (*p127*); **By the Way Café** (*p117*); **Courtyard Café** (*p113*); **Curiosity** (*p119*); **Verveine** (*p128*).

Late-night filling stations
Café Diplomatico (*see p123*); **Gypsy** (*p124*); **Lee Garden** (*p111*); **Ouzeri** (*p129*); **7 West** (*p115*); **Swatow** (*p111*).

Pre-theatre
Biff's (*see p108*); **Bravi** (*p117*); **Esplanade Bier Markt** (*p115*); **La Maquette** (*p117*); **Rain** (*p105*); **Torch Bistro** (*p109*).

Patios
Allen's (*see p129*); **The Boulevard Café** (*p114*); **The Fifth** (*p104*); **The Rivoli** (*p103*); **Le Sélect Bistro** (*p104*); **7 Numbers** (*p121*); **Utopia** (*p124*); **Wish** (*p115*).

Trendy restos
Amber (*see p118*); **Brasserie Aix** (*p124*); **Crush** (*p104*); **Lolita's Lust** (*p129*); **Rain** (*p105*); **Rouge** (*p114*); **Teatro** (*p126*); **YYZ Restaurant & Wine Bar** (*p105*).

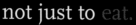

ably light on salt and other clashing ingredients. Susur's famous dozen-course tasting menu – a $100 affair that can last hours – has its mains at the outset followed by appetisers, soup and dessert. (The less adventurous can dine the traditional way, but they have to pay more for it.) Either way, the foie gras terrine and foie gras mousse with soy aspic and mustard sauce should not be missed.

Indian

Babur

273 Queen Street W, at Duncan Street (416 599 7720). Streetcar 501/subway Osgoode. **Open** 11.45am-2.30pm, 5-10.30pm daily. **Main courses** $8-$11. **Credit** AmEx, MC, V. **Map** p276 D7.

A more economical lunch buffet you won't find at this quality: Babur's is a mere $11 and offers all the standards along with bottomless rice and tender naan. The location is also unparalleled – arty types working along Queen and King enjoy easy access, as do the suits across University Avenue. The butter chicken is the way to go for those who go easy on the spice – heavy on the sauce, without masking tender chicken. Goan fish curry is the fish eater's favourite, and shashlik paneer will please the veggie in your party.

Italian

Amato

534 Queen Street W, at Bathurst Street (416 703 8989). Streetcar 501, 510. **Open** 11am-4am daily. **Pizza slices** $3-$4. **Credit** AmEx, MC, V. **Map** p276 C7.

The jury is still out on this by-the-slice pizzeria. Those who prefer their dough less laden will think these wedges over-adorned, and those who dislike garlic will be offended by their pungency. Still, it's several cuts above Pizza Pizza and other big chains. An Amato pizza is like a meal on a crust, no longer a means to shun your broccoli. Kids like all the variety too. Locations – five in all – are open past clubbing hours for combating the munchies. **Branches**: throughout the city.

La Fenice

319 King Street W, at John Street (416 585 2377). Streetcar 504/subway St Andrew. **Open** 11.30am-2.30pm, 5.30-10.30pm Mon-Fri; 5.30-10.30pm Sat. **Main courses** $10-$15. **Credit** AmEx, DC, MC, V. **Map** p276 D8.

Old-world service in a sleek, modern setting. Diners slide into comfy leather chairs and tuck into hearty pastas and Flintstonesque chops and ribs. Antipasti include seafood classics such as calamari and shrimp doused in olive oil from the family grove in Italy. A staggering selection of 350 wines got La Fenice the nod from *Wine Spectator* in 2002. A pre-theatre fave.

Japanese

Sushi Bistro

204 Queen Street W, at St Patrick Street (416 971 5315). Streetcar 501/subway Osgoode. **Open** 11.45am-10.30pm Mon-Sat; 4-10.30pm Sun. **Main courses** $7-$15. **Credit** AmEx, MC, V. **Map** p276 D7.

You may not reckon you're in a local institution, but this is the restaurant that whetted the city's now insatiable appetite for (cheap) sushi. Justifying its longevity, the Bistro offers the cleanest, most pleasant experience of all bars of its calibre. The sushi slips down a dream and the chicken teriyaki arrives completely skinned – visit the competition and you'll see just how wonderful that is.

Wah Sing blares its wares. *See p111.*

North American

Rodney's Oyster House

469 King Street W, at Spadina Avenue (416 363 8105). Streetcar 504, 510. **Open** 11.30am-1am Mon-Sat. **Main courses** $16-$50. **Credit** AmEx, DC, MC, V. **Map** p276 C8.

A transplant from the East Coast, Rodney Clark imported his dad's oysters before a backer helped him open his own joint. Rodney's is one of the city's first, and still most traditional, oyster bars; its no-frills offerings include Dungeness crab, lobster and other seafood alongside oysters, and the atmosphere is merry. As Rodney is his own middle man, you won't find fish this fresh elsewhere. Just add a drop of lemon and slurp away.

Thai

Queen Mother Café

206 Queen Street W, at Duncan Street (416 598 4719). Streetcar 501. **Open** 11.30am-midnight Mon-Sat; noon-midnight Sun. **Main courses** $10-$15. **Credit** AmEx, MC, V. **Map** p277 D7.

People who have been shopping this strip of Queen West since Elizabeth Bowes-Lyon was a sprightly 85 will tell you they learned the words pad Thai over candlelight at a banquette here. The Queen Mother is an icon in this community, a symbol of the city's royal past and its multicultural future. Dishes haven't lost their shape or size over the years: bowls of noodle soup are still deep, skewers fat and friendly and rice dishes heaped with chunks of chicken, lemongrass and spice. The back patio comes alive over summer lunches.

Never a bum note. **La Palette**. *See p112.*

Financial District

Cafés & coffeehouses

Mövenpick Marché

42 Yonge Street, at King Street (416 366 8986/www.movenpickcanada.com). Streetcar 504/subway King. **Open** 7.30am-midnight daily. **Main courses** $9-$15. **Credit** AmEx, DC, MC, V. **Map** p277/p278 F8.

Mövenpick loves Toronto, and in the past few decades several incarnations have sprung up, from Yorkville and the Eaton Centre to trendified Loblaws grocery outlets. Mövenpick Marché is the esteemed occupant of the award-winning BCE Place, whose atrium encompasses the historic façade of the Chamber of Commerce and the grandest skylight in town. Tables beneath the glass on the 'patio' offer alfresco eating. In the restaurant proper, things are more hectic. The protocol here is to wander with an undersized tray from kiosk to kiosk, and wait for the chef to prepare your meal from scratch – not very relaxing. That said, the mostly Swiss delicacies are above par and the desserts are scrummy. **Branches**: throughout the city.

Continental

Biff's

4 Front Street E, at Yonge Street (416 860 0086/ www.biffsrestaurant.com). Streetcar 504/subway King or Union. **Open** 11.30am-2.30pm, 5-10pm Mon-Thur; 11.30am-2.30pm, 5-10.30pm Fri; 5-10.30pm Sat; 5-9.30pm Sun. **Main courses** $19-$28. **Credit** AmEx, DC, MC, V. **Map** p277/p278 F8.

Peter Oliver and Michael Bonacini are the Hepburn and Tracy of Toronto's restaurant scene, back every few years with a new spectacle whose decidedly unbranded vision strikes a chord with the foodie public. After scoring successes with TD Tower's Canoe (*see below*) and Steakfrites (*see p120*) they surprised cynical foodies by doing it again with Biff's, a sleekly assured bistro that raises the bar for the neighbourhood's dire pre-theatre scene. Start with divine French onion soup (flavoured with unlikely oxtail), or chicken liver parfait. Then move on to bigger and better entrecôte steak or salmon fillet with baby potatoes and winter vegetables, served by particularly tuned-in staff. A front patio generously extends the restaurant's size, though passing buses may make the experience unbearable.

North American

Canoe Restaurant & Bar

*54th Floor, Toronto Dominion Bank Tower,
66 Wellington Street W, at Bay Street (416 364
0054/www.canoerestaurant.com). Bus 6/subway
King or St Andrew.* **Open** 11.30am-2.30pm,
5-10.30pm Mon-Fri. **Main courses** $25-$42.
Credit AmEx, DC, MC, V. **Map** p277/p278 E8.

It appeals, in large part, to the CEOs and aspiring
CEOs who toil away in the Toronto Dominion complex and habitually hit the bar here between
marathon meetings. Even if you're weak of wallet,
you too can enjoy the panoramic view and a glass of
Niagara chardonnay without committing yourself to
a meal (the free nibble selection will fill you up in any
case). Should you seek further fulfilment – and you
should – we recommend the six-course tasting menu.

Canoe is Canadian only – that means beef is from
Alberta, salmon from Newfoundland, lobster from
Nova Scotia, Yukon Gold potatoes from Prince
Edward Island, cheese from Quebec and greens are
locally grown. As if to hammer home the point,
designers of the bright, wood-panelled space have
employed a curling stone as a door stopper.

Dundas Square

Continental

Torch Bistro

*253 Victoria Street, at Dundas Street E (416
364 7517). Streetcar 505/subway Dundas.*
Open 5-10.30pm Tue-Thur; 5-11.30pm Fri-Sun.
Main courses $23-$32. **Credit** AmEx, DC, MC, V.
Map p277/p278 F7.

Bubble tea

Every US TV sitcom seems to have its
own coffeehouse, where pretty young things
gather to whine about life's injustices. A
Toronto version of *Friends* would require
an entirely different set. True, natives buzz
on latte from Lettieri, Second Cup and
Starbucks, but hundreds of thousands of
Chinese in the city have fuelled a craze for
a different sort of jet fuel. Bubble tea, which
first burst into shops and lounges about five
years ago, has rapidly made its way from the
Asian suburbs of Markham and Richmond Hill
to the city's trendiest neighbourhoods.
Introduced from the street stands of Taiwan,
where it became an obsession beyond Print
Club and Pokémon, the drink combines cold,
sweet liquid with black, pea-sized tapioca
'bubbles', called pearls or 'bobo'. (Bubble tea
has a confusing list of akas including pearl
shake, pearl tea, black pearl tea, big pearl,
Chinese cola and zhen zhu nai cha.)

Served in tall sundae glasses or
transparent plastic cups, 'BBT' is sipped
through straws fat enough to guide the
squishy balls. The fun is in the movement of
the gummy pearls as they ascend to the lips,
in the pastel brightness of the tea, and in
a list of flavours that can run longer than a
classroom register (think sesame, red bean,
mango, taro, peanut). Most bubble tea
houses have lively, pop art decor, pop music
and a youthful Asian clientele who will plunk
down $3 to $5 on a midday stimulant.

Which bubble venue to choose can be as
challenging to negotiate as the sometimes
baffling menu. Here's our selection:

Love & Scandal.

eZone

*170 Spadina Avenue, Chinatown (416
603 1700).*

Furama Cake and Dessert Garden

*248 Spadina Avenue, Chinatown (416
504 5709).*

Love & Scandal

*120 Cumberland Street, Yorkville (416
964 0302).*

Tea Shoppe 168

*419 College Street, Chinatown (416
603 9168); 377 Yonge Street, Dundas
Square (416 979 0168).*

Tiger Lily's

*257 Queen Street W, Entertainment
District (416 977 5499).*

In the shadow of the Eaton Centre, Torch is a good pre-theatre choice: its front windows look out on to the Canon Theatre's stage door and the Elgin and Winter Garden are just down the street. But the bistro-style food is good any time. Start with the crab cakes and move on to the steak frites, served with copious amounts of the latter. Booths along one wall are enclosed by dark wood panelling, with a curtain at each entrance for seclusion. On the opposite wall are enormous leather banquettes, and upstairs the Top 'o the Senator jazz club (*see p202*).

North American

Barberian's Steak House

7 Elm Street, at Yonge Street (416 597 0335). Streetcar 505/subway Dundas. **Open** noon-2.30pm, 5pm-midnight Mon-Fri; 5pm-midnight Sat, Sun. **Steaks** $22-$46. **Credit** AmEx, DC, MC, V. **Map** p277/p278 F6.

The golden years are waning for the Barberian family, which has been operating this deep-city cavern for four decades. The celebs, politicians and fat cats have come and gone: steak isn't for everyone these days, and only a few old boys hold 'regular' status. That said, there should be no other destination for those seeking slabs of red meat with the essential side of starch. Forgo the chain establishments and Bay Street hideaways for this throwback to the era of bellies and butter-soaked baked potatoes.

Chinatown/Kensington Market

Chinese & Vietnamese

Lee Garden

331 Spadina Avenue, at Baldwin Street (416 593 9524). Streetcar 505, 510. **Open** 4pm-midnight Mon-Thur, Sun; 4pm-1am Fri, Sat. **Main courses** $12-$16. **Credit** AmEx, MC, V. **Map** p277 D6.

Locals decided long ago that Sunday would be the night for Chinese. While the rest of the city grinds to a halt, Spadina gears up for its biggest evening of the week. Lee Garden is markedly more popular than its compatriots, and dishes are characterised by their freshness (fish is the main draw, crisp vegetables another) rather than by their fiery temperature – this is Cantonese, after all. Prepare to wait, and then to be whisked to a table by staff who deliver your order swiftly and with gusto.

Pho Hung Restaurant

350 Spadina Avenue, at St Andrews Street (416 593 4274). Streetcar 505, 510. **Open** 11.30am-10.30pm daily. **No credit cards. Map** p276 C6.

There's plenty of Cantonese and Szechuan in Chinatown but not much Vietnamese of merit. If you're looking for Asian but eschew all those thick, heavy sauces, try a warm and medicinal tureen of

Aunties and Uncles. See p114.

pho washed down with some of the cheapest beer south of College. Noodles aren't the only dishes on the menu – though, naturally, they're the speciality. Other delicacies are wrapped in shrimp rice paper or golden buns and you can also get a mean curry.
Branch: 200 Bloor Street W, University (416 963 5080).

Swatow

309 Spadina Avenue, at D'Arcy Street (416 977 0601). Streetcar 510, 505. **Open** 11am-2.30am daily. **Main courses** $5-$10. **No credit cards. Map** p277 D6.

Late-night eating is Asian territory in most cities and Toronto is no exception – Chinatown is one of the most reliable zones for hungry clubbers. Though it doesn't offer the most authentic Cantonese (soups and sauces are starchy and orange), Swatow will nonetheless fill you up for a song. Its $5 'Rice on Plate' meals offer heaped portions of sliced meats stir-fried with black beans, pineapple and garlic. The crispy duck is an ideal addition to the lazy Susan, enough for your entire posse.

Wah Sing Seafood

47 Baldwin Street, at Henry Street (416 599 8822). Streetcar 505, 506, 510. **Open** 11.30am-10.30pm daily. **Main courses** $8-$15. **Credit** MC, V. **Map** p277 D6.

Seafood junkies with a soft spot for Chinese cuisine are drawn to Wah Sing. Many of the Far East

Eat, Drink, Shop

operations in the area will claim to serve the best seafood in town (notice the profusion of fish tanks in windows), but none has the right to like Wah Sing, which draws you in with its two-for-one lobster deal and keeps you there with all manner of underpriced bottom-feeder specialities. You won't want to linger after the last claw or tail – atmosphere is apropos in this no-nonsense outfit – but there's lots else to enjoy on this endearing local drag.

Continental

Café La Gaffe

24 Baldwin Street, at McCaul Street (416 596 2397). Streetcar 505, 506, 510. **Open** 11.45am-11pm Mon-Sat; 11.45am-10pm Sun. **Main courses** $15-$19. **Credit** DC, MC, V. **Map** p277 D6.

Tucked into a discreet street between Chinatown and Downtown that's bursting with dining possibilities, this colourful bistro seduces with its candlelit ambience and cool jazz standards. If you can't find a seat in the Manhattan-style room, grab one at the bar. Staff are gracious and knowledgeable about the daily catch and the appropriate wine to serve. Old, painterly French posters are the mainstay of the decor; the rest is simple, particularly the covered back patio. Highlights are mussels and a selection of generously sized pizzas.

La Palette

256 Augusta Street, at Oxford Street (416 929 4900). Streetcar 506, 510. **Open** noon-4pm, 6-11pm Wed-Fri; noon-4pm, 6pm-midnight Sat; noon-4pm, 6-10pm Sun. **Set menus** $17-$31. **Credit** AmEx, DC, MC, V. **Map** p276 C6.

It was only a matter of time before Kensington Market gave us a reason – other than the purchase of used denim – to hang out. For residents of the market, this classic French boite for bohemians offers respite from Szechuan beef and the stench of fish. The fishy smell creeps in now and then, though happily in the form of moules soaked in tangy juice. La Palette's set menu has the most agreeable price tag in town – more to do with the culture of the clientele than with the quality of the three courses, which are of the highest order.

North American

Agora Restaurant

Art Gallery of Ontario, 317 Dundas Street W, at McCaul Street (416 979 6612/www.ago.net/www/ services/agora). Streetcar 505/subway St Patrick. **Open** noon-2.30pm Tue-Fri; 11am-3pm Sat, Sun. **Main courses** $15-$20. **Credit** AmEx, DC, MC, V. **Map** p277 D6.

This eatery in the Group of Seven arcade at the Art Gallery of Ontario produces artfully designed meals and particularly fine desserts. It opens its solarium-like space only in the day, though its lunches resemble dinners in their complexity: pork tenderloin might be wrapped in bacon, for instance; layers upon

layers of veg – aubergine, truffle, rhubarb, onion, watercress – are employed in lieu of serving up an actual painter's palette. If you happen to be in town while the AGO undergoes an exhibition change, try to visit more than once: menus rotate with the artwork, reflecting their themes and imagery. Lovely brunches at weekends mitigate the annoying foot traffic you'll endure in the gallery.

Thai

The Red Room

444 Spadina Avenue, at College Street (416 929 9964). Streetcar 506, 510. **Open** 11am-2am daily. **Main courses** $7-$8. **No credit cards.** **Map** p277 D6.

There's no end to a student's need for bargain restaurants. This one, on the southern edge of the University of Toronto campus, had the rotten luck of opening just before the neighbouring El Mocambo live music club shut its doors. Never mind: the Red Room packs the house to full, despite its vast size. The decor is unmistakably Thai, but the fare runs the gamut – from all-day breakfast to salads and burgers and, of course, the odd curry. That just one

Dim sum

While some cultures have their high tea and others their brunch, Toronto's Chinese – and, indeed, thousands of other keen eaters – love their lunchtime dim sum ('heart's delight' in Cantonese). Throughout the 1980s, when an economic boom attracted waves of Hong Kong expatriates, dim sum evolved into a refined and authentic luncheon experience, with the top chefs from the Far East moving in to help further the craft.

The practice of dim sum dining involves flagging down trolleys displaying exotic delicacies in bamboo steamers, such as crab claws, sticky rice in lotus leaves, pork dumplings, deep-fried shrimp rolls, taro cakes or octopus tentacles. Finding an English-speaking waiter is challenging, but no matter — patrons mark their choices by number on order pads left at the table, or simply grab them off the pushcart when it stops by the table. Recognising a dish's content isn't easy, so it's advisable to dine with an adventurous, non-allergic bunch who don't mind the hit-and-miss nature of the outing. If money's no object, head directly to smart Lai Wah Heen at the Metropolitan Hotel (108 Chestnut Street, 416 977 9899) for superlative dim sum.

genre does not hold court is the Red Room's down-fall. But the students don't seem to mind. The Drinks here are remarkably cheap, smoking is permitted and the French fries are a better bet than at Burger King across the street.

University

Continental

Courtyard Café

Windsor Arms Hotel, 18 St Thomas Street, at Bloor Street (416 921 2921/www.windsorarmshotel.com). Subway Bay, Bloor or Museum/bus 6. **Open** 7am-2.30pm Mon; 7am-2.30pm, 6-11pm Tue-Sat; 10.30am-3.30pm Sun. *High tea* 1.30-3pm, 3.30-5pm daily. **Main courses** $27-$39. **Credit** AmEx, DC, MC, V. **Map** p280 E4.

In early September the Toronto International Film Festival attracts the toast of Hollywood to the smart Windsor Arms Hotel. Courtyard Café is the ideal place for people-spotting: by night it's a fantastical, lofty pillared ballroom with a splendid domed ceiling, by day a milky white garden room full of intimate breakfast nooks. The food is by no means

It's an enormous departure from the often-greasy pedestrian fare offered at other Cantonese restaurants, with dishes that incorporate foie gras, minced lobster, Dungeness crab, papaya and calamari mousse noodles, in crystal wraps twisted into mystical shapes.

Other dim sum we love: **Dragon Dynasty** (2301 Brimley Road, North Side, 416 321 9000); **Dynasty** (131 Bloor Street W, University, 416 923 3323); **King's Garden** (214 King Street W, Entertainment District, 416 585 2221); **New Treasure** (150 Dundas Street W, Chinatown, 416 977 3778; pictured); **Pearl Harbourfront Chinese Restaurant** (207 Queens Quay W, Waterfront, 416 203 1233).

your average hotel fare. The menu is exciting, an ever-changing selection of sophisticated continental classics, and the outstanding dessert list cannot be ignored, even for the sake of a famous waistline.

JK at the ROM

Royal Ontario Museum, 100 Queen's Park, University (416 586 5578/jamiek@rom.on.ca). Subway Museum or St George. **Open** 11.30am-3pm daily. **Main courses** $13-$18. **Credit** AmEx, MC, V. **Map** p280 E4.

The cultured setting, at times a bit stuffy, in no way detracts from the pleasures of the plate to be had atop the Royal Ontario Museum. Jamie Kennedy's inventive take on Canadian specialities brings elk, venison and moose to the table. Inventive veggies and some of the best frites with mayo in town go with just about everything. Lunch only.

Senses

15 Bloor Street W, at Yonge Street (416 935 0400/www.sensesdc.com). Subway Bloor-Yonge. **Open** 11.30am-2.30pm, 6-10pm Mon-Sat. **Main courses** $27-$46. **Credit** AmEx, DC, Disc, MC, V. **Map** p280 E4.

Chef Claudio Aprile is one of those world travellers who manages to incorporate elements from sushi to salsa in his cooking without making things seem overly 'nouveau'. Senses also takes that rare step of offering a tasting menu with a vegetarian option. Fluffy desserts from the baker's below keep shoppers gossiping – banana cream pie and a kaffir lime tart stir all five senses. Check out the window seats overlooking Holt Renfrew.

North American

Patriot

Colonnade Plaza, 131 Bloor Street W, 2nd floor, at Bay Street, University (416 922 0025). Subway Bay or Museum. **Open** 11.30am-3pm, 5.30-9.30pm Mon-Wed, Sun; 11.30am-3pm, 5.30-10pm Thur-Sat. **Main courses** $18-$27. **Credit** AmEx, DC, MC, V. **Map** p280 E4.

The view is disappointing, when you consider that Patriot looms over the most affluent stretch of merchants in the city: a Chapters bookseller and a nondescript condo dominate the scene outside. Indeed, Colonnade Plaza is somewhat outdated in its faux-gilded glamour. Still, the ever-reliable Patriot emerges as one of the city's (nay, country's) finest purveyors of Canadian cuisine. It all starts with the service – always gentle and knowledgeable, offering pleasant commentary on locally pressed wines. All ingredients are Canadian grown, from the tender lamb and beef (Alberta) to the more adventurous game (rhea and ostrich from Ontario and Quebec quail). Canadian grown vegetables are added to the line-up according to what's in season. Perhaps the most amusing dish is the gourmet poutine, a Quebecois frites, curd and gravy standard sometimes mimicked by the odd traditional fast food joint but accorded grave attention by chefs here.

Harbord

Cafés & coffeehouses

Aunties and Uncles
74 Lippincott Street, at Bloor Street (416 324 1375).
Streetcar 506, 511. **Open** 9am-4pm Tue-Sun. **Main**
courses $5-$8. **No credit cards. Map** p280 C4.
Set up to resemble your granny's kitchen, with mismatched Arborite tables and vinyl seats, Aunties is
classic 'what you see is what you get' territory.
Grilled cheese sandwiches and French toast are
made from fresh, chubby challah bread. Club sandwiches are impossible to eat neatly for all their
chunky cuts of chicken breast and tomato. Potato
salad goes with everything. And, just as granny
would have it, prices are blissfully low.

Fresh by Juice for Life
521 Bloor Street W, at Croft Street, (416 537
4573/www.juiceforlife.com). Streetcar 511/
subway Bathurst. **Open** 11.30am-11pm Mon-Fri;
10.30am-11pm Sat, Sun. **Main courses** $8-$12.
Credit AmEx, DC, MC, V. **Map** p280 C4.
The whir of blenders is omnipresent in this juice
bar-cum-vegan paradise. If you can get past the
noise – and the queues by the entrance – you'll find
Fresh a refreshing departure from the usual bistros
and trattoria. The establishment that introduced
wheatgrass to Bloor Street (and then to Queen West)
has grown into much more than the 50 varieties on
its juice menu. Wraps, rice bowls and miso burgers
are mainstays; spicy Cajun fries are a calorie-laden
relief from the wholesome theme.

Future Bakery
483 Bloor Street W, at Brunswick Avenue (416 922
5875). Streetcar 510, 511/subway Bathurst or
Spadina. **Open** 7.30am-1am daily. **Main courses**
$7-$10. **Credit** AmEx, MC, V. **Map** p280 C4.
There's nothing futuristic about it. The food harks
back to granny's childhood in Poland; the desserts
are enormous; the beer is basic. Even the style is a
bit outdated: wobbly tables scattered about the vast
layout and patio, grungy, dusty floors, walls stained
with decades of cigarette smoke (though smoking is
no longer allowed). The one thing Future has going
for it is its location – on the main strip of the Annex,
one of the most eccentric pedestrian corners in the
city. And, if you happen to like mashed potatoes and
pierogis, there's an added bonus in it for you.
Branches: 2199 Bloor Street W, West End (416 769
5020); 95 Front Street E, St Lawrence (416 366 7259).

Continental

Rouge
467 Bloor Street W, at Spadina Avenue (416
413 0713). Streetcar 510/subway Spadina.
Open 5.30-11pm Mon, Tue; noon-3pm, 5.30-11pm
Wed-Sat. **Main courses** $11-$24. **Credit** AmEx,
DC, MC, V. **Map** p280 C4.

Possibly because a new chic city spot seems to open
its doors every week, Rouge got little attention when
it first made an appearance in 2001. But word got
around. Though the atmosphere is decidedly slick,
with a red lacquered bar as its centrepiece, food is
of the upscale comfort variety: think borscht, lobster
ravioli, Cornish hen.

Japanese

Sushi on Bloor
515 Bloor Street W, at Bathurst Street (416 516
3456). Streetcar 511/subway Bathurst. **Open** noon-
11pm Mon-Sat; noon-10pm Sun. **Main courses** $3-
$18. **Credit** AmEx, DC, MC, V. **Map** p280 C4.
First you have to get past the idea of cheap sushi
(it's not as dubious as it can be), then you have to
get past the queues. You'll be well fed here – if not
by the end of an appetiser and main, then after the
complimentary green tea ice-cream. Add two beers
to your bill and you'll emerge just $25 poorer.

Latin

The Boulevard Café
161 Harbord Street, at Borden Street, Harbord
(416 961 7676). Streetcar 510/bus 94. **Open**
11.30am-4pm, 5.30-11pm Mon-Sat; 11am-4pm, 5.30-
11pm Sun. **Main courses** $18-$27. **Credit** AmEx,
MC, V. **Map** p280 C4.
Many restaurateurs looking for grand, open spaces
to show off their talents have gathered in this modest thoroughfare, wedged between the University of
Toronto campus, the Annex and Little Italy. Our
favourite is the Latin-flavoured Boulevard Café. If
you're averse to the forceful taste of coriander, stop
reading here – it takes over the salsas, sauces and
salads that accompany most dishes. But if you're a
seafood fan, give it a chance. The culinary atmosphere here is decidedly Mediterranean, and the fish
and cornbread fantastic. It also boasts the jolliest
patio on the boulevard.

North American

Southern Accent
595 Markham Street, at Bloor Street W (416 536
3211). Streetcar 511/subway Bathurst. **Open** 6-10pm
Mon-Wed, Sun; 6-11pm Thur-Sat. **Main courses**
$12-$17. **Credit** AmEx, DC, MC, V.
A quick hop across Bathurst from the Annex, tucked
in behind Honest Eds (famous not only for its tacky
sign but for the number of lightbulbs in it), Southern
Accent looks a bit out of place. In fact, it would be
out of place anywhere but the Bayou, with its eccentric decoration, madcap staff and resident fortune
teller. Offerings are not for the weak of heart: black-
ened livers and spicy sausage will set your tongue
on fire, and 'heavy' isn't a word that worries the chef.
Side orders include fried green tomatoes, and the bar
does a renowned bourbon sour.

Wish for a calm, kindly place to eat.

Church & Wellesley

Cafés & coffeehouses

7 West
*7 Charles Street W, at Yonge Street (416 928 9041).
Subway Bloor-Yonge or Wellesley.* **Open** 24 hours
daily. **Main courses** $5-$15. **Credit** AmEx, MC, V.
Map p281 F4.
Happily for its neighbours in the umpteen condo
complexes nearby, 7 West is open late. It's also open
early. In fact, you can count on it being open when-
ever you pop round. Which is likely to be often given
its location near the crossroads of Bloor and Yonge,
in a three-storey Victorian. Interesting sandwiches,
a range of pastas, the usual salads, Moroccan platters and meaty mains share the bill.

Mediterranean

Byzantium
*499 Church Street, at Wellesley Street (416 922
3859). Subway Wellesley.* **Open** 5.30-11pm daily.
Main courses $14-$24. **Credit** AmEx, MC, V.
Map p281 F5.
Boystown is best known for its rainbow flags, outdoor mingling, late-night parties and traffic, but
Byzantium goes to show there are also some keen
eaters in the 'hood and a spot of serenity. It remains
true to its geography, serving up a sweet seafood

selection. Also home to a well-regarded martini bar,
Byzantium invites you to sip away before or after
your gastronomic adventures.

North American

Wish
*3 Charles Street E, at Yonge Street (416 935
0240). Subway Bloor-Yonge or Wellesley.*
Open 10am-midnight daily. **Main courses** $15-$30.
Credit AmEx, MC, V. **Map** p281 F4.
The location is curious – if convenient – for a cosy,
tranquil eaterie: it faces a particularly raucous portion of Yonge Street. But tranquil it remains. The
mood is reflected in the fountain at the courtyard
entrance, the white upholstered *chaises* that surround it and throws on the indoor seating. Mains are
ambitious: expect a large amount of lamb, prime rib
and duck, accompanied by substantial vegetable
sides of rapini and Chinese broccoli. Kindly staff.

Cabbagetown

Cafés & coffeehouses

Jet Fuel
*519 Parliament Street, at Carlton Street (416 968
9982/www.jetfuelcoffee.com). Streetcar 506/bus 65.*
Open 7am-8pm daily. **Cakes** $1. **Drinks** $2-$3.
No credit cards. Map p281/p278 G5.
For those who don't live in one of the remarkably
maintained Victorian residences here, Cabbagetown
seems a long way from the city's eating hubs. But if
there's a reason you're already here, there's no reason why you shouldn't visit Jet Fuel. A favoured
hangout meeting place for Don River cyclists, bike
couriers and architecture buffs doing a heritage tour,
Jet Fuel is one of the last remaining independent
cafés in the city. And there's a reason for that: the
coffee is the true gourmet equivalent of jet fuel.

St Lawrence

Continental

Esplanade Bier Markt
*58 The Esplanade, between Church & Yonge Streets,
St Lawrence (416 862 7575). Streetcar 504/
subway King.* **Open** 11am-midnight Mon-Wed, Sun;
11am-1am Thur-Sat. **Main courses** $12-$32.
Credit AmEx, DC, MC, V. **Map** p277/p278 F8.
A beer hall may not be everyone's ideal venue for a
romantic tête-a-tête. Still, the Bier Markt is not your
average Belgian beer hall. The decor is tasteful and
elegant with a brass rail bar, marble tabletops and
chequered tile floors. Mussels are served fresh from
an iced buffet in the back room. The chips are the
highlight, served in a playful display with mayo and
ketchup. Oh, and the beers number 150.

Eat, Drink, Shop

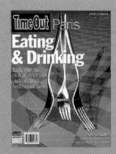

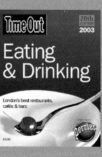

La Maquette

111 King Street E, at Church Street, St Lawrence
(416 366 8191/http://lamaquette.com). Streetcar
504/subway King. **Open** noon-2.30pm, 5-10.30pm
Mon-Fri; 5-10.30pm Sat. **Main courses** $17-$34.
Credit AmEx, DC, MC, V. **Map** p277/p278 F8.
Apart from the CN Tower or, perhaps, the Toronto
Island, you won't find a better location for a restaurant. For one, La Maquette faces St James Cathedral,
a grand, Gothic structure that fills even atheists with
awe; and its location in the heart of the old St
Lawrence neighbourhood, with its stellar architecture, makes for fine after-dinner strolling. La
Maquette's second-floor solarium also overlooks a
patch of green that is home to a rotating sculpture
and a tremendous three-storey wall of falling water.
The menu hails from the south of France, so bistro
standards are crossed with Italian flavour. An
inspired choice for early summer evening, when
golden sun splashes yellow brick.

Italian

Bravi

40 Wellington Street E, at Church Street, St Lawrence
(416 368 9030/www.bravi.ca). Streetcar 504/subway
King. **Open** noon-2pm, 5-10pm Mon-Wed; noon-2pm,
5-11pm Thur-Sat. **Main courses** $16-$30. **Credit**
AmEx, DC, MC, V. **Map** p277/p278 F8.
If you're feeling organised, call ahead to book the
best seat in the house: a table for two ensconced in
an old freight elevator that rises to the top of this
two-storey dining room at the push of a button. Sited
between the historic St Lawrence neighbourhood
and the financial district, across the street from the
Hummingbird Centre, Bravi couldn't be more convenient for post-walk, post-work or post-ballet nosh.
Prices are, predictably for the area, on the high side
for a quick bite, so you might want to save Bravi for
a special occasion. In any case, the venison osso
bucco here deserves to be savoured; it's best enjoyed
with the best bottle of Italian vino you can afford
and in the company of a very good friend.

Japanese

Nami

55 Adelaide Street E, at Church Street, St Lawrence
(416 362 7373). Subway King or Queen. **Open**
noon-2.30pm, 5.30-10.30pm Mon-Fri; 5.30-10.30pm
Sat. **Main courses** $15-$29. **Credit** AmEx, DC, MC,
V. **Map** p277/p278 F7.
A classic Japanese meeting place that tucks you into
sushi bars or discreet alcoves shielded by rice paper
or curtains. Long in the running for the freshest
sushi in town, at least until sushi became ubiquitous,
it's still up there. A 'sushi pizza' is an interesting,
some might say disturbing, choice. For the purists,
there's sashimi, makimono and sushe all present and
correct. Tender teriyaki off the menu is perfectly
matched by beautifully seasoned, grilled accompa-
niments from the robata bar.

Cafés & coffeehouses

Amore

2425 Yonge Street, at Eglinton Avenue, Davisville
(416 322 6184). Subway Eglinton. **Open** 11.30am-
10.30pm Mon-Fri; 10.30am-10.30pm Sat, Sun.
Main courses $7.50-$16. **Credit** AmEx, DC, MC, V.
Yonge & Eglinton tends to seem exclusive when it
comes to eating out: the finest restaurants are too
fine for a casual bite but the casual places are downright grungy. Locals love the fact that Amore lets
them pop in for a bowl of pasta on the way home.
The food is homely, as are the portions, bolognese
abounds and pizzas are a welcome change from
home-delivery fare. The service will make your day.

Bregman's

1560 Yonge Street, at St Clair Avenue, Davisville
(416 967 2750). Subway St Clair. **Open** 7am-10pm
Mon-Thur, Sun; 7am-11pm Fri, Sat. **Main courses**
$8-$15. **Credit** AmEx, MC, V.
An emporium with two faces – part bakery, part
restaurant – Bregman's can be hit and miss. Arrive
on a weekend morning and the queue extends down
the stairway from the raised dining room; enter any
later than 2pm and it's deserted. The consensus is
that Bregman's is best for brunch. Egg dishes and
lox and cream cheese platters are fresh, light and
ample, the *pièce de résistance* always being the bagel
or bread. Sandwiches are New York deli-style.

By the Way Café

400 Bloor Street W, at Spadina Avenue, the
Annex (416 967 4295). Streetcar 510/subway
Spadina. **Open** 10am-11pm Mon-Fri; 10am-midnight
Sat. **Main courses** $10-$17. **Credit** AmEx, DC, MC,
V. **Map** p280 C4.
The Annex may have been overrun lately by cheap
sushi and haughty bistros, but By the Way has managed to stay true to its roots, keeping prices low and
servings simple. Dinners are Moroccan in flavour,
though the falafel platter can be a bit bland. By the
Way is great for weekend brunch: eggs benedict is
topped with a supreme hollandaise and bagels are
fresh. And the patio can't be beat for sun and scene.

Café Nervosa

75 Yorkville Avenue, at Bellair Street, Yorkville
(416 961 4642). Bus 6/subway Bay or Bloor-Yonge.
Open 11.30am-11pm Mon-Sat; 11.30am-10pm Sun.
Main courses $20-$25. **Credit** AmEx, DC, MC, V.
Map p280 E4.
Celebs in town lounge at the Four Seasons or Windsor
Arms Hotels. Wannabe celebs loll here, at the gateway to tiny, tony Yorkville. If you're coiffed, bleached,
manicured and/or animal printed, you'll blend right
in – particularly with the leopard-accented upstairs
refuge (smoke to your heart's content up there).
There's nothing to be nervous about in terms of food:
pizza is terrifically thin and there are light dishes such
as spinach salad and angelhair pasta.

Grazie

2373 Yonge Street, at Eglinton Avenue,
Davisville (416 488 0822/www.grazie.ca).
Subway Eglinton. **Open** noon-11pm Mon-Thur,
Sun; noon-midnight Fri, Sat. **Main courses**
$9-$11. **Credit** AmEx, DC, MC, V.

This excellent pizzeria is what those ubiquitous
wood-oven pizza chains would be if they'd stop trying to expand so quickly. The atmosphere is strictly
Southern Italian, friendly and chipper with casual yet
brisk service (all the better for the preoccupied pre-
cinema crowd that comes here). Delicately crusted
pizzas nearly cave in under the weight of grease-free
meats and flavoursome cheeses. A favourite main is
salmon pasta in a vodka tomato sauce.

Marmalade Café

306 Davenport Road, at Bedford Road, the Annex
(416 921 5666). Subway St George. **Open** noon-2am
Mon-Sat; noon-4pm Sun. **Main courses** $10-$18.
No credit cards. Map p280 D3.

This modest corner resto was slow to catch on, perhaps partly because its predecessor was boarded up
following a fatal shooting. Nonetheless, the reliable
Marmalade has redeemed the location with its soothing atmosphere and savoury staples. Parisian 'plats'
include hearty cassoulet, coq au vin and a warming
French onion soup. Fruity Marmalade's sweetest
touch, however, is its house DJ, who jazzes up
evenings with trip hop and rare groove.

Patachou

1095 Yonge Street, at Price Street, Rosedale
(416 927 1105). Subway Rosedale or Summerhill.
Open 8.30am-7pm Mon-Fri; 8.30am-6pm Sat.
Main courses $6.50-$7. **Credit** V. **Map** p281 F2.

Few of the New World patrons had ever seen a
croissant when Patachou opened its doors a quar-
ter-century ago at the opposite end of Forest Hill.
They learned the easy way. Patachou's pastries are
fit for aristocracy – indeed their crumbs can be found
on the upholstery of many a well-to-do Range Rover.
Bistro tables, outside and in, encourage visitors to
enjoy a prepared salad or enchanting slice of gateau
on the premises; as long as the heavy street traffic
doesn't make you lose your appetite.

Vesta Lunch

474 Dupont Street, at Bathurst Street, the Annex
(416 537 4318). Bus 7, 26/subway Bathurst or
Dupont. **Open** 24 hours daily. **Main courses**
$5-$10. **No credit cards. Map** p280 C2.

The ancient neon sign says 'Reputable since 1955',
which begs the question: was it disreputable before
that? Possibly. The myth behind this 24-hour hamburger bar is that the owner left behind his family
in Greece to make his fortune in Canada – and never
called them over. Still, staff seem jolly enough flipping average meat, dusting salads with feta and
deep-frying potatoes for the after-hours set. Though
it's much maligned by locals, the house is nevertheless packed on most nights, with regulars chatting
up strangers and drunken students spilling ketchup.

Cakes to write home about at **Patachou**.

Continental

Amber

119 Yorkville Avenue, at Old York Lane, Yorkville
(416 926 9037). Subway Bay. **Open** 5-11pm Tue-
Thur; 5pm-midnight Fri, Sat. **Main courses** $14-
$24. **Credit** AmEx, DC, MC, V. **Map** p280 E4.

Yorkville is a place for high heels, coiffed hair, short
skirts, silk shirts and whitened teeth. If you have a
few of the above, you won't feel out of place at
Amber, a destination for Porsche-driving night
crawlers under the age (physically or mentally) of
40. The name is reflected in the glow of the lighting,
the cut roses on the tables and the hue on the walls.
The food leans to the continental, with tinges of

Eat, Drink, Shop

Middle Eastern flavour. But the food is not the focus. Most patrons head to the bar or the back patio after the meal for a look-see and a champagne cocktail or forgo the meal altogether.

Centro Grill & Wine Bar

2472 Yonge Street, at Eglinton Avenue, Davisville (416 483 2211/www.centrorestaurant.com). Subway Eglinton. **Open** 5-11.30pm Mon-Sat. **Main courses** $28-$42. **Credit** AmEx, DC, MC, V.
Long a destination for uptown A-listers, Centro has the feel of a Hollywood dining room. Enter, past the team of valets, into a multi-tiered playground for the well coiffed. Linger on the wine list – of which you'll find few rivals north of Eglinton – while the band plays on in the lounge below. If you fancy pasta, it's all home-made and fresh here, accented with smoked chicken and grilled Treviso cheese, or Taggiasche olives. Purists will opt for the steak, but disitnctive-ly-flavoured ostrich loin is also on offer. It'll be midnight before you have the spirit to leave.

Curiosity

430 Bloor Street W, at Brunswick Avenue, the Annex (416 968 0404). Streetcar 510/subway Bathurst or Spadina. **Open** 11am-11pm Tue-Fri; 10am-11pm Sat; 10am-10pm Sun. **Main courses** $14-$24. **Credit** AmEx, DC, MC, V. **Map** p280 C4.
Those for whom Bloor West is too crunchy, too per-ogies-and-ale for an evening out, seek out Curiosity for brunch. For at any time of day, you'll see bleary-eyed Annex types shuffling in for a latte and poached egg. When the sun sets, the mood becomes very Left Bank. Mirrors reflect candlelight, and the narrow, confined room starts to make sense. The style is rich to heavy French bistro, leaving little room for curiosity. Servers are as congenial and knowledgeable as they come.

Fat Cat Bar & Bistro

376 Eglinton Avenue W, at Avenue Road, Forest Hill (416 484 4228). Subway Eglinton West. **Open** 5.30-10.30pm Tue-Sat. **Main courses** $19-$28. **Credit** AmEx, DC, MC, V.
Fat Cat, as satisfying as the name implies, is not for the temperamental tongue: sweetbreads share the plate with veal tenderloin, after all. But the cat in you will love stir-fried calamari, if not all the other heavy-ish meats and treats. This is first and fore-most a neighbourhood joint, so expect conversation to compete with scores of affluent locals discussing their BMWs, bikini waxes or holidays in Aruba.

Goldfish

372 Bloor Street W, at Spadina Avenue, the Annex (416 513 0077). Streetcar 510/subway Spadina. **Open** 11.30am-3.30pm, 5.30-10.30pm Wed; 11.30am-3.30pm, 5.30-11pm Thur, Fri; 10am-3pm, 5.30-11pm Sat; 10am-3pm, 5.30-10.30pm Sun. **Main courses** $14-$28. **Credit** AmEx, DC, MC, V. **Map** p280 C4.
The Annex was decidedly lowbrow before Goldfish stepped in to take advantage of millennial affluence. The bubble has since burst, but Goldfish still holds appeal for local urban professionals. Decor is unchar-acteristically sterile for this neighbourhood, the food suitably modern in its preparation. Gnocchi is light despite a dousing of creamy pesto, foie gras cedes to an Asian dressing of ginger, tandoori seasoning and snap peas. The name implies the experience will be like that of a fish in a bowl, but don't fear: no one stares any more: the novelty is gone.

Diners

Once upon a time, Toronto's greatest culinary statement was the diner. Eggs were indulgent, hash was hip, bran muffins decadent. After the ethnic explosion of the second half of the 20th century, diners lost their allure. Chrome tarnished and bakelite cracked, and the city's psyche turned to more exotic fare. But urbanites can be a fickle bunch. Once the '40s were distant enough to inspire nostalgia, the lust for kitsch proved to be more durable than the bakelite. The most wistful entrepreneurs reopened the greasiest doors and fluffed those diners back to life.

The Senator (253 Victoria Street, Dundas Square, 416 364 7517) was the first to be rescued, in the '80s – giving the area around Yonge and Dundas something to boast about with its slick black vinyl and New York City fry-ups. Up in the nether regions of Dupont and Shaw, the **Universal Grill** (1071 Shaw Street, West End, 416 588 5928) was recently degreased and revived, kickstarting a widespread revitalisation of the area. Now it serves huevos rancheros and steak 'n' eggs by day, moules and lamb by night.

The Queen Street Mental Health Centre across the street did nothing to improve the image of the waning **Swan** diner in the '60s (892 Queen Street W, West End, 416 532 0452). Taking pity on the unloved joint was a band of investors who switched on the background jazz and iced the oyster bar. And it's been a quarter of a century since the **Rosedale Diner** (1164 Yonge Street, Rosedale, 416 923 3122) was transformed into a bistro-style grill where patrons sip red at the steel bar before delving into their sesame chicken.

Others we love:

Sunset Grill (2006 Queen Street E, the Beach, 416 690 9985); **Lakeview Lunch** (1132 Dundas Street W, West End, 416 530 0871); **Mars** (432 College Street, Harbord, 416 921 6332).

North 44

2537 Yonge Street, at Eglinton Avenue,
Davisville (416 487 4897). Subway Eglinton.
Open 5-10pm Mon-Sat. **Main courses** $31-$45.
Credit AmEx, DC, MC, V.

Its name refers to the line of latitude on which
Toronto sits, and the mod decor echoes that theme
(compass points embedded into flooring, and so on).
The menu balances cuisines of several continents
(no Canadian focus): pizzas and pastas are Cal-Ital,
seafood is Mediterranean inspired, and Asian and
Mexican influences inform the side dishes. The
grand wine list is what lures the locals.

Steakfrites

692 Mount Pleasant Road, at Soudan Avenue,
Davisville (416 486 0090/www.steakfrites.net).
Bus 34/subway Eglinton. **Open** 5.30-9.30pm daily.
Main courses $17-$23. **Credit** AmEx, DC, MC, V.

What uptown restaurant-goers want, uptown
restaurant-goers get, and this time they wanted a
bistro as magnificent as those in the heart of downtown. Vaulted ceilings give Steakfrites an open, airy
feel despite its cosy Parisian atmosphere. The spotlight is on the steak frites, as one might guess – here
they are served with delicious Roquefort butter.
Diversions might leave you disappointed (must anyone still serve sweetbreads?), though Steakfrites
makes up with brilliant desserts. Who could resist
the Smallest Chocolate Mousse Ever for that touch
of sweet that won't push the belly over the beltline?

Scaramouche & Scaramouche Pasta Bar

1 Benvenuto Place, off Edmond Avenue, at
Avenue Road, Casa Loma (416 961 8011).
Streetcar 512/subway Summerhill. **Open** 5.30-10pm
Mon-Sat (pasta bar usually closes 30mins later).
Main courses Dining room $36-$42. Pasta bar
$19-$26. **Credit** AmEx, DC, MC, V. **Map** p280 E1.

The old guard of the Toronto restaurant scene
stands overlooking the city from atop a midtown
hill. Scaramouche still has the look of a grandiose
'80s hotspot: furnishings – and clientele – are brassy.
Book ahead for a window seat and all the gloss will
be behind you and the view downtown unsurpassed.
The food is a stellar accompaniment, as decadent as
can be sourced in Toronto in the main dining room
(the menu sounds like a Cordon Bleu exam), and
slightly more modest at the Pasta Bar next door.

Fusion

JOV Bistro

1701 Bayview Avenue, at Eglinton Avenue,
Leaside (416 322 0530). Bus 11/subway Eglinton.
Open 5.30pm Wed-Sun, closing time varies.
Main courses $19-$35. **Credit** DC, MC, V.

Welcome to one of the most talked about restaurants
around, not only for its magical menu but also
for its location in unlikely Leaside. The philosophy
here is Asian fusion, but ingredients run the gamut
from truffles and chestnuts to ostrich and squab.

A four-course 'blind' menu ($50) is worth investing
in for entertainment value; don't let the risk factor
keep you away – it's guaranteed to appeal to even
grumpy gastronomes. Whimsical and warm decor
helps JOV to a place in Toronto's fine-dining canon.

Indian

Indian Rice Factory

414 Dupont Street, at Howland Avenue, the Annex
(416 961 3472). Bus 7, 26/subway Bathurst or
Dupont. **Open** noon-3pm, 5-10pm Mon-Fri; 5-10pm
Sat, Sun. **Main courses** $10-$15. **Credit** DC, MC, V.
Map p280 C2.

Head north along Howland Avenue through the
heart of the Annex and you'll hit on a small island
of gastronomy. On an otherwise uneventful residential stretch, the Indian Rice Factory is something
of a hub – at least to those who favour clean, classy
Indian cuisine over the more rugged, gritty kind you
get in Little India. Though some complain that such
sophistication comes at too high a price, a mere taste
of the butter chicken usually shuts them up. The
lamb is cooked just right, tender and carefully
spiced; the vegetables keep their individuality, they
don't drown in heavy sauces; the light, flaky
samosas won't sabotage the main course. Even early
in the week this restaurant can be busy, so best call
ahead if you don't want to wait.

Nataraj

394 Bloor Street W, at Brunswick Avenue, the
Annex (416 928 2925/www.nataraj.ca). Subway
Bathurst or Spadina. **Open** noon-2.30pm, 5-10pm
Mon-Fri; 5.30-10.30pm Sat. **Main courses** $8-$10.
Credit AmEx, DC, MC, V. **Map** p280 C4.

As Little India is so far off the subway line, there's
much debate over the best Indian cuisine in the city's
core. Though fancier spots may get a mention, those
in the know vote Nataraj. Show up any night of the
week and the door doesn't stop flapping. Grab a
Cobra and select fragrant saffron rice, piquante tandoori and palak paneer you won't forget in a hurry.

Italian

Gio's

2070 Yonge Street, at Lola Road, Davisville
(416 932 2306). Subway Davisville or Eglinton.
Open 5-11pm Mon-Sat. **Main courses** $8-$10.
Credit AmEx, DC.

Your memory of 'the Nose' (so dubbed for the giant
appendage standing in for a sign) will be hazy – as
much because of the atmosphere, thick with evening
cacophony and steam from the open kitchen as for
the feeling of having consumed rather too much
well-priced vino. Good-humoured servers will tease
you with pasta lore, then serve it lovingly stuffed
and surrounded with fresh tomato, ricotta and moist
bolognese. But the real story here is in the attitude.
Every night becomes a party, as much for parties of
two as for 17 – Gio's full capacity.

Lucky the diner who finds a table at **7 Numbers**.

Grano

2035 Yonge Street, at Lola Road, Davisville (416 440 1986). Subway Davisville or Eglinton. **Open** 10am-10pm Mon-Sat. **Main courses** $10-$25. **Credit** AmEx, MC, V.

At once elegant and casual – think antique posters, warm-hued walls and front deli counter – with the service veering between the two. Grano is something of a legend in North Toronto, nestled in a decidedly family-oriented neighbourhood but attracting Italophile foodies from across town. Choice is far from abundant, but you'll find something for everybody: lively pastas, rich risottos and chunky salads – with some hearty Mediterranean-style meats and sides to appeal to more traditional tastes. The revelling continues well past suitable family hours.

7 Numbers

343 Eglinton Avenue W, at Avenue Road, Forest Hill (416 322 5183). Subway Eglinton West. **Open** 5-11pm Tue-Sun. **Main courses** $20-$22. **Credit** AmEx, DC, MC, V.

The atmosphere is half the fun here: staff doubly blessed with good manners and good looks shoehorn you into a funky cast-off table (a terrace twice the size of the interior successfully risks some communal seating, a rare thing in this city) in full view of the open kitchen. Rosa Marinuzzi chefs up Old World specialities with a zeal and timing that only an Italian mama can muster. Dishes of grilled veggies, pastas and seafood are filled to overflowing.

Sotto Sotto

116A Avenue Road, at Davenport Road, Yorkville (416 962 0011). Bus 5, 6/subway Museum. **Open** 5.30-11.30pm daily. **Main courses** $15-$32. **Credit** AmEx, MC, V. **Map** p281 E3.

Observe the Polaroids of famous patrons in the foyer that betray Sotto Sotto's location between tony Rosedale, Forest Hill and the priciest hotels in town. But if you're on a mission to stargaze, forget it. The

subterranean collective of stucco-walled rooms is grotto-like and candlelit – not ideal conditions. Service is warm and the food trattoria fare: meat, fish and pasta in copious amounts, not the cheapest.

Japanese

EDO

484 Eglinton Avenue W, at Avenue Road, Forest Hill (416 322 3033). Bus 32/subway Eglinton. **Open** 5-11pm daily. **Main courses** $18-$25. **Credit** AmEx, DC, MC, V

Hardly the only of its kind in town to be operated by non-Japanese, this Forest Hill stalwart is helmed by a local restaurateur who nevertheless knows what his peers want: generous portions, relaxed, attentive service and none of the harsh lighting and dubious offerings of many fast food sushi joints. On the contrary, you'll want to spend the night picking away at plump sashimi and hand rolls, and tempura that won't wilt in your grasp. And you may learn a thing or two from the staff about the many sakes.

Mediterranean

Jerusalem

955 Eglinton Avenue W, at Rostrevor Road, Forest Hill (416 783 6494). Bus 32/subway Eglinton West. **Open** 11.30am-10.30pm Mon-Fri, Sun; 11.30am-midnight Sat. **Main courses** $11-$13. **Credit** AmEx, MC, V.

Before falafel became ubiquitous further downtown as a staple pub crawlers snack, there was Jerusalem, frequented mainly by the hundreds of Jewish families in the neighbourhood. Not quite as dowdy as its environs would suggest, Jerusalem's menu flows from meze to mains to fresh seafood. You won't find dips this tantalising on most of the finer Greek menus. There are more tasting platters than dishes, which appeals to the adventurous.

North American

Sassafraz
*100 Cumberland Street, at Bay Street, Yorkville
(416 964 2222/www.cafesassafraz.com). Subway
Bay or Bloor-Yonge.* **Open** 11am-11pm daily.
Main courses $19-$39. **Credit** AmEx, DC, MC,
V. **Map** p280 E4.

This site has changed hands several times in the
past few decades, but whatever its name, you can
bet there'll be a gleaming, dark windowed Mercedes
parked illegally out front. Or a Porsche, or a Beemer,
or a Ferrari. One of the best places in town to spot
those celebrities who want to be spotted, fashionable
Sassafraz is well known for its ubiquity in the city's
gossip columns. Food, however, is not really its forte.
If you need some sustenance while you're lurking
around the place with your autograph book, you'd
be better off ordering an appetiser and a few drinks.
A full three-course meal will easily absorb the
contents of your wallet.

West End

Cafés & coffeehouses

Bar Italia
*582 College Street, at Manning Avenue, Little
Italy (416 535 3621). Streetcar 506, 511.* **Open**
10.30am-10pm Mon-Thur, Sun; 10.30am-11pm Fri,
Sat. **Main courses** $10-$20. **Credit** AmEx, DC,
MC, V. **Map** p276 B6.

Before a visit to Little Italy meant dodging hordes
of pedestrians, prams and poodles – when all that
existed here were canoli bakeries, trattorias and old
men playing bocci – there was Bar Italia. Having
changed locations in the past decade, its new millennial incarnation is as slick as anything else on the
block. But it's become a symbol of all that this neighbourhood once was (authentic old world) and all that
it has become (so-so food, so-so service). Prepare to
be shoved aside by a passer-by trying to squeeze on
to a friend's table. It's very popular.

Local hero Susur Lee

The media tracks him like they would a
typhoon. Indeed, when Hong Kong-born chef
Susur Lee disappeared from Toronto in 1997
in order to consult for restaurants in the Far
East, there was widespread panic that he
wouldn't return. And the worry wasn't media
triggered. Popular opinion held that Lee was
a genius, the finest chef in the country, if not

the world. When he returned in 2000 to open
Susur, the metaphorical bar was raised in
Toronto. The name of the ponytailed prodigy
was on everyone's lips. Sharp-tongued
restaurant critics held their cynicism in check
for the time it took to write a review. Local
bohemians ate tinned ravioli for weeks in
order to save for a meal. Young *naïfs* blew
their savings on first dates, because the
restaurant was the only one about which
they had ever heard their parents gush.

People have fun at Susur because they
can taste the joy of the chef with each nibble.
His drive to discover new textures, new tastes
and new blends is manifest. (Even his tasting
menu is enlightened, served backwards, with
the appetisers following mains.) Susur has
been fundamental in making eating an event
in the city. Not a stodgy, black-tie affair, but
rather Vivienne Westwood, Betsey Johnson,
Alexander McQueen – thrilling, electrifying,
stimulating, while in excellent taste.
**Honourable mentions: Guy and Michael
Rubino**, owners of Rain (*see p105*) and
Zoom, a financial district dining mecca. Guy
is the chef at both. **Claudio Aprile**, the world-
wandering wonder from Uruguay who returned
to his adopted town to steam up the exotic
menu at Senses (*see p113*).
Previous contender: Greg Couillard, a
colourful chef who made a name for the
Parrot, Stelle and Oceans while propelling
himself to celebrity status.

Café Diplomatico

594 College Street, at Clinton Street, Little Italy (416 534 4637). Streetcar 506, 511. **Open** 10am-1.30am Mon-Fri; 10am-3.30am Sat, Sun. **Main courses** $5-$15. **Credit** AmEx, DC, MC, V. **Map** p276 B6.

It's a trade-off: the Dip wins hands-down for the best people-watching facilities in Little Italy, inside or on the vast patio. But you'll have to contend with poor service and mediocre food. The best thing about the menu is its comprehensiveness. All the Italian greats are there – the veal sandwich, the bruschetta, the pasta and pizza – but so is everything else, including some of the best French fries on the strip. But forget about the eats – the Dip is all about sitting back with a Stella and a cigarette and watching the world strut by.

Dipamo's Barbeque

838 College Street, at Ossington Avenue, Little Italy (416 532 8161). Streetcar 506/bus 63. **Open** noon-3pm, 5-9pm Mon-Sat. **Main courses** $11-$19. **Credit** V.

The division between Little Italy and Little Portugal is nebulous. But Dipamo's clearly occupies the latter. Though the plattered chicken and ribs reference the American South, the experience aligns itself with the churrasquerías of neighbouring Ossington, Dovercourt and Dundas. The dining room is decidedly no-frills but jazz over the stereo is a nice touch. Dishes are bursting with flavour, particularly the beef brisket, stewing in its own tangy juices and partnered with a generous serving of barbecued beans. Pulled pork sandwiches are a good lunchtime alternative to hot dogs and BLT.

Dufflet Pastries

787 Queen Street W, at Euclid Avenue (416 504 2870/www.dufflet.com). Streetcar 501, 511. **Open** 10am-7pm Mon-Sat; noon-6pm Sun. **Cake slices** $4-$5. **Credit** AmEx, DC, MC, V. **Map** p276 B7.

Her older brother was called Duff. Little sister came into her own in the '70s with a wholesale baking business. Today, she has a café of her own, perfectly positioned at the hub of the Queen West homestores. Weekend shoppers and pouty locals pull up a stool for a latte and a bite of heaven. Cakes sound more complex than they taste: cappuccino dacquoise is a simple pleasure.
Branch: 2638 Yonge Street, Midtown (416 484 9080).

Faema

672 Dupont Street, at Christie Street (416 535 1555/www.faema.ca). Bus 26, 126/subway Christie or Dupont. **Open** 8am-10pm Mon-Fri; 9am-10pm Sat; 10am-10pm Sun. **Main courses** $7-$10. **Credit** AmEx, DC, MC, V.

Faema is a manufacturer of commercial coffee-making equipment. The retail operation has moved into one of the refurbished lofts upstairs and just this sprawling café remains, widely considered the finest purveyor of coffee city-wide. What better way to taste-test Faema's stock-in-trade than at a bistro table, on the terrace or by the bar watching sports? A selection of dishes is served as well as the coffee.

Ferro. See p124.

The Fish Store

The curbside catch is fresh daily at this cubbyhole in the heart of Little Italy (around 651 College Street, but there's no number or phone), open from mid-morning until midnight. Leo, the gas grill maestro, serves up generous fillet cuts of salmon, swordfish, halibut, tuna and king fish, and nestles these marinated slabs into a dough bun. Basil, tomato and gorgeous;y caramelized red onions make these sandwiches ($5-$8) a street food treat. Lean on the counter or just pull up a chair at one of just three outdoor tables and take in the passing scene.

Mezzetta

681 St Clair Avenue W, at Christie Street (416 658 5687). Streetcar 512. **Open** noon-2.30pm, 5-10pm Tue-Sun. **All dishes** $2.95. **Credit** DC, MC, V.

Mezze are the name of the game in this little warren of exotic eats. Dozens of mixed salads, rice dishes, stews, skewers and dips have a place on the buffet. The minds behind Mezzetta know you won't eat just one, so they offer a deal if you buy in bulk, which just makes the process of choosing more fun. And it goes on: when you're finished with your falafel, fish or bean salad, move on to the yummy pastries, laced with sweet cheeses, almonds and apricots.

Terroni

720 Queen Street W, at Claremont Street (416 504 0320/www.terroni.ca). Streetcar 501. **Open** 9am-10pm Mon-Thur, Sun; 9am-11pm Fri, Sat. **Main courses** $8-$13. **No credit cards. Map** p276 B7.

Eat, Drink, Shop

Despite its pejorative name, Terroni (Italian for 'bloody southerners') manages to attract country-men in their droves. Waiting for a table (and wait you will at mealtimes) is a lesson in dialect: you'll hear it from the patrons and wait staff alike. Perhaps most appreciated here are the pizzas, 23 old-school configurations that average $10 but could feed a couple with scant room left for the famed canoli. Conspicuously absent from Little Italy, Terroni occupies equally trendy ground here on Queen West, in Rosedale, and on the cusp of the financial district, near some of the city's historic theatres.
Branches: 1 Balmoral Avenue, Rosedale (416 925 4020); 106 Victoria Street, Dundas Square (416 955 0258).

Utopia
586 College Street, at Clinton Street, Little Italy (416 534 7751/www.utopiacafe.ca). Streetcar 506, 511. **Open** 11.30am-1am Mon-Fri; noon-1am Sat, Sun. **Main courses** $8-$12. **Credit** AmEx, MC, V. **Map** p276 B6.
When the streets were punctuated with fast-ish burger joints bearing names like Fat Phil's and Fatsos, we craved an establishment that at least sounded healthy. Utopia entered the scene a few years back with the look of a West Coast juice bar and a fan base that preferred dreads and piercings to the trucker look. There's plenty to choose from here – as long as you fancy a burger or burrito – but there are enough options in the vegetarian department. Fries are freshly cut in an endearingly haphazard way, and salads abundant.

Vienna Home Bakery
626 Queen Street W, at Markham Street (416 703 7278). Streetcar 501, 511. **Open** 10am-7pm Wed-Sat. **Main courses** $7-$8. **No credit cards.** **Map** p276 B7.
Everything here is made from scratch and the menu is short and sweet, offering a few breakfast items like granola, yoghurt and fruit plus soups and sandwiches. For pud, there's fruit pies, muffins and maple treats. The signature phallic-shaped bread loaves add some sauce to the mumsy cooking. Just a few tables and counter, and a patio in summer.
Branches: 87 Avenue Road, Yorkville (416 922 8512); 79 Front Street E, St Lawrence (416 203 2134); 123 Queen Street W, Entertainment District (416 922 8512).

Continental

Brasserie Aix
584 College Street, at Clinton Street, Little Italy (416 588 7377). Streetcar 506, 511. **Open** 6-10pm Mon-Fri; noon-10pm Sat, Sun. **Main courses** $15-$25. **Credit** AmEx, DC, MC, V. **Map** p276 B6.
Brasserie Aix is the kind of place where only the most shameless hipsters feel comfortable. If you're too timid to attend the earsplitting front bar for a cocktail, head straight to the back dining room: a glorious hideaway with romantic velvet banquettes

and a ceiling to rival a cathedral dome. Output is at times disappointing for the price, but as French restos go, this is the one you'll want to save time and money for. And the steak frites is always reliable.

Café Societa
796 College Street, at Ossington Avenue, Little Italy (416 588 7490). Bus 63/streetcar 506. **Open** 6-11pm Tue-Sun. **Main courses** $15-$23. **Credit** AmEx, MC, V.
Those in the know reach beyond the well trodden pavements of Little Italy to this off-course nook. As chic bistros go, this is the genuine article – it's so intimate there are twice as many patio seats as there are in the restaurant proper. Smoked salmon and sirloin are the highlights, the former served with tropical vegetables, the latter with purple potatoes. Linguini comes dressed with artichoke hearts.

Gypsy
817 Queen Street W, at Bathurst Street (416 703 5069/www.bandofgypsies.com). Streetcar 501, 511. **Open** 6-10pm Mon; noon-midnight Tue-Sat. **Main courses** $10-$15. **Credit** AmEx, DC, MC, V. **Map** p276 B7.
Call it a one-stop venue for the club crowd. Patrons can dine first on bistro-esque delights up front in the small dining room. But the fun begins after dinner, when you can lounge by the fire in the back room or dance to the DJ's beats by the bar. The in-house psychic could even swing by to read your palm. When not hosting private parties, the Hooch upstairs will entertain overflow, or pump out its own tunes. On the way out, stop at the front counter for a pick at the shelves of retro candy, for which it set a a trend.

Italian

Bar One
924 Queen Street W, at Shaw Street (416 535 1655). Streetcar 501. **Open** 11.30am-4pm, 5-10pm Tue-Fri; 9am-4pm, 5-10pm Sat; 9am-4pm Sun. **Main courses** $9-$26. **Credit** AmEx, DC, MC, V. **Map** p276 A7.
Now that they've made their mark on Little Italy with Bar Italia (*see p122*), the owning Barone family are working on still trendier Queen West. This place is more intimate, with communal seating at the marble-topped counter and curved-wood booths. A friendly place for brunch; evenings are more harried. Dinners range from squash-stuffed ravioli to fillet of salmon. The hidden patio out back is a delight.

Ferro
769 St Clair Avenue W, at Arlington Avenue (416 654 9119). Streetcar 512. **Open** 11am-10pm Mon-Sat; 5-10pm Sun. **Main courses** $20-$30. **Credit** AmEx, MC, V.
The collegiate and yuppie patrons may not like being snubbed for the modelgenic crowd at the bar, but this is the coolest place in the neighbourhood. Not too cool to put on good food. Salads, pizzas and panini are a successful marriage of crisp leaf, imported cheese

and bread that won't slice the roof of your mouth; and risotto crops up most nights. There's a backroom pool table and a mini front patio.

Japanese

Sushi Kaji

860 The Queensway, at Plastics Avenue (416 252 2166). Bus 80. **Open** 6-9pm Tue-Sun; closed every 3rd Sun. **Set menus** $45-$120. **Credit** AmEx, MC, V.

Normally it wouldn't be worth coming to the Queensway, an extension of King Street that heads westward into the suburbs. But enough locals are raving about Sushi Kaji that it's probably worth alerting intrepid foodies. Still something of a secret, Kaji may yet have space at the intimate eight-seat sushi bar for your party. There, you'll watch masters at work slicing seafood in manners you may never see again. There are also plenty of vegetarian options and a couple for meat-and-potato types.

Tempo

596 College Street, at Clinton Street, Little Italy (416 531 2822/www.tempotoronto.com). Streetcar 506, 511. **Open** 6-11.30pm daily. **Main courses** $20-$24. **Credit** AmEx, MC, V. **Map** p276 B6.

Somehow, this über-trendy sushi joint managed to snap up some of the finest real estate in town, a corner property on this strip of high-density hipness. Despite the fashionable veneer, however, Tempo's nibblies don't dash high hopes. Portions are on the

An octopus gets prepared. **Sushi Kaji**.

large side (particularly the sushi), so there's scope for sharing, though we recommend you keep the seared tuna and hamachi tartare to yourself.

Korean

Korea House

666 Bloor Street W, at Manning Avenue, the Annex (416 536 8666). Subway Bathurst. **Open** 11am-midnight daily. **Main courses** $10-$15. **Credit** MC, V. **Map** p276 B6.

Restaurants in the Annex tend to be pretty mainstream. But if the occasion calls out for something more exotic than comfort food or continental, stray a few blocks west to Little Korea. Order a *soju* (Korea's answer to sake) and watch the dishes of kim chee and its cousins appear. Be Bim Bop gives you all your food groups – and all your calories – in one bowl; bulgogi beef surpasses your typical Chinese shredded kind. Queues aren't unusual.

San Korean Restaurant

676 Queen Street W, at Bathurst Street (416 214 9429). Streetcar 501, 511. **Open** 11.30am-10pm Tue-Thur; 11.30am-10.30pm Fri; noon-10.30pm Sat; 5-10pm Sun. **Main courses** $10-$17. **Credit** AmEx, DC, MC, V.

You don't normally find it outside the confines of Little Korea, but now there's San – damn good Korean fare in a Queen West style centre that packs customers in nightly, and spits them out satisfied every time. You'll spot the similarities with Japanese in bento boxes stuffed with dumplings, tempura, tuna rolls and teriyaki. But San also does shredded beef and barbecued ribs with distinctly Korean flavours. And here, you'll linger longer over beer, wine and complimentary goodbye tea.

Latin

El Bodegón

537 College Street, at Euclid Avenue, Little Italy (416 944 8297). Streetcar 506, 510. **Open** 11.30am-10pm Wed-Sun. **Main courses** $10-$15. **Credit** AmEx, MC, V. **Map** p276 B6.

We wouldn't blame you for thinking an evening of Peruvian would hold little promise, but think again. Even if you're annoyed after waiting by the entrance for a table (where tables are shoehorned in), you'll have forgotten about it after the first sangria. El Bodegón's extensive menu will be hard to navigate for novices of the culture, but staff will talk you through. Seafood eaters have the best of this menu.

Julie's Cuban Restaurant

202 Dovercourt Road, at Foxley Street (416 532 7397). Streetcar 505. **Open** 5.30-11pm Tue-Sun. **Main courses** $11-$17. **Credit** MC, V.

Word is getting around about this, one of the city's best-kept secrets. But by virtue of its location – on a residential stretch of Dovercourt, north of Queen – Julie's remains untarnished by tourists or cruisers

Eat, Drink, Shop

Julie's Cuban Restaurant. A Latino landmark. *See p125*.

of the main drags. If you can't squeeze on to the patio, squeeze into one of the old kitchen tables indoors. Cuba is not lauded for its culinary flair, but Julie's fried green plantains and corn fritters always please. Otherwise, expect the traditional Cuban rice dishes, fried with pork, chicken or beef, and spices culled from Caribbean climes.

Mediterranean

Sintra Wine Bar & Grill

588 College Street, at Clinton Street, Little Italy (416 533 1106). Streetcar 506, 511. **Open** noon-3pm, 5-10pm Tue, Wed, Sun; noon-3pm, 5pm-midnight Thur-Sat. **Main courses** $17-$28. **Credit** AmEx, DC, MC, V. **Map** p276 B6.
This Iberian beachhead in the heart of Little Italy reflects the times and the steadily encroaching Portuguese influence on La Strada Italiana. Grilled fish is the speciality, or try the cod cakes or spicy shrimp broth to start. Portuguese wines (many available by the glass) and ports are matched right through to the native desserts.

Teatro

505 College Street, at Palmerston Avenue, Little Italy (416 972 1475). Streetcar 506, 511. **Open** 6pm-midnight Tue-Sat. **Main courses** $17-$22. **Credit** AmEx, DC, MC, V. **Map** p276 B6.
Lean back and relax, you could be here a while. Service takes a while to warm up, though it befits this Little Italy upstart, which is worth a visit if only because it's the centre of the world these days. Thankfully, the food lives up to the attitude. Appetisers are of the stacked variety, layered with

veggies, pâtés, cheeses and savoury sauces. Mains are just as theatrical, and ample enough to intimidate the fashionistas who order them. When dinner's done, stick around – on weekends, DJs take to the turntables, playing until last call.

North American

Cities Bistro

859 Queen Street W, at Niagara Street (416 504 3762). Streetcar 501, 511. **Open** 5.30-9pm Mon, Sun; 5.30-10pm Tue-Thur; 5.30-11pm Fri, Sat. **Main courses** $11-$22. **Credit** AmEx, MC, V. **Map** p276 B7.
The bland interior doesn't live up to the calibre of the cooking. Still, the warmth of the service more than makes up for the cold surroundings. Though it's located on that wing of Queen West that's fast gentrifying, the food at Cities is far from trendy. Simple cuts of steak, breasts of chicken and fish are garnished with greens and corn on the cob. Potatoes are mashed with an extra punch of rosemary.

Lemon Meringue

2390 Bloor Street W, at Jane Street (416 769 5757/www.lemonmeringue.com). Bus 35/subway Jane. **Open** 10am-10pm Tue-Sat. **Main courses** $15-$30. **Credit** AmEx, MC, V.
New to the brunch scene in Bloor West village, this patisserie also works the night shift with a short list of engaging dinner dishes whose presentation matches the minimalist decor of the intimate candle-lit room. Seared calamari with lemon zest and miso-glazed salmon steer you to the eponymous dessert, and very good it is too.

Oyster Boy

872 Queen Street W, at Strachan Avenue (416 534 3432/www.oysterboy.com). Streetcar 501. **Open** 5-11pm Mon-Wed; 5pm-midnight Thur-Sun. **Main courses** $10-$15. **Credit** AmEx, DC, MC, V. **Map** p276 A7.

This narrow hideaway on the fringe of Queen West is a refreshing change from the raucous, guys'-night-out atmosphere of most oyster bars. The menu has few surprises, and few options for those averse to crustaceans, but Oyster Boy may be the best place to slurp your Malpeques outside of Prince Edward Island. At the very least it's the most amusing. The convivial atmosphere will certainly tempt you you to linger longer. And why not? There's nowhere else to have this much fun for blocks.

East Side

Cafés & coffeehouses

Bonjour Brioche

812 Queen Street E, at DeGrassi Street (416 406 1250). Streetcar 505, 506. **Open** 8am-5pm Tue-Fri; 8am-4pm Sat; 8am-3pm Sun. **Main courses** $5-$8. **No credit cards. Map** p279 K7.

You might not want to find yourself in this down-at-heel neighbourhood, but if you happen to be around, you'll probably spot Bonjour Brioche a mile off from the queues outside the door. Even on slushy winter mornings, supporters of this French-accented bakery-café wait in a huddle on the street outside, dreaming of brioche, buttery croissants and warm baguettes. For brunch, try baked French toast or croque madame with a bowl of café au lait.

Lick's

1962 Queen Street E, at Kenilworth Avenue, the Beach (416 362 5425/www.lickshomeburgers.com). Streetcar 501. **Open** 11am-11pm daily. **Main courses** $3-$8. **Credit** AmEx, MC, V.

Little boys with sandy feet have been urging their sunburnt saronged mothers into the queue at Lick's for dozens of years. And it's been argued that Lick's at the Beach (there are others, including one at Yonge and Eglinton) still flips the best hamburgers in the city. Indeed, the flipping is an integral part of the experience. Hosts take your order while you wait, and rush it to the counter, where the cooks compose odes and limericks around your name. Never out of the loop, customers can track the progress of their meal by following the sound of singing voices. Chilli dogs of astounding girth leave nothing to be desired and scarcely enough room for pudding, but you'd regret not going for the ice-cream course. The stock-in-trade at Lick's be had in the form of sundaes, shakes and cones in eccentric flavours with various toppings.

Branches: throughout the city.

Myth

417 Danforth Avenue, at Arundel Avenue, the Danforth (416 461 8383/www.myth.to). **Subway Chester.** **Open** 5-11pm Mon-Wed; noon-midnight Thur; noon-2am Fri, Sat; 2pm-midnight Sun. **Main courses** $14-$26. **Credit** AmEx, DC, MC, V.

Brawny East Siders with a penchant for the cue pool around for hours with a few beers while others hug the walls with trendy cocktails or dine alfresco. The food is a tasty mix of the Greek Isles (typical of a Danforth joint) and California (read: fish, fish and more fish). And the music is all over the map.

Get your laughing gear round the goodies at **Lick's**.

Donut lore

It was an American settler in Maine who invented the donut in 1847, knocking out the centres of his mother's doughy fried cakes upon hearing that the uncooked middles were spreading disease. Still, Canada claims the donut (from the archaic dough knot) as its legitimate son. The fast food classic began to rise in popularity in the '50s, when boomers dragged their mums to suburban plazas for a cheap treat and dads drove in for a sugar hit en route to work. Shift workers shmoozed, students skipped class, and soon Canada had more donut shops per capita than the United States. The decidedly lowbrow enterprise (the average price of a donut is 65 cents) survived economic downturns and the Starbucks explosion on the premise that you can while away hours at a donut shop and still only spend a buck.

In Toronto today, there's a donut shop for about every 5,000 people, where, along with the simple ring and coffee you can get bagels, subs and soups. And subtract smokers, in most establishments, at least.

The most prevalent are the **Tim Horton's** famous donut shops – the closest thing to McDonald's in the industry. Founded in 1964 by a Hamilton, Ontario, hockey legend, Horton's accounts for about half of the donut shops in the city, and is unofficially considered to have the best coffee in town. Its 56 varieties of donut (at 250 calories apiece) include Canadian Maple, and hockey lore shrouds the place in Canadiana even though, ironically enough, it is owned by US burger empire Wendy's.

Tim Horton's main rival, **Coffee Time**, has followed suit with slicker stores and product diversity (some double as internet cafés). **Country Style** is the runner up, though its popularity seems to be waning, judging by its shrinking market share. All are ubiquitous.

Continental

Café Brussel

124 Danforth Avenue, at Broadview Avenue, the Danforth (416 465 7363). Streetcar 504, 505/subway Broadview. **Open** 5-11pm Tue-Sat. **Main courses** $20-$30. **Credit** AmEx, DC, MC, V. **Map** p279 J4.

This ambassador of northern Europe specialises in mussels. A sniff upon entering will tell you that every table has indulged in the satisfyingly rattly mountains of of perfectly prepared *moules*. Steeped in tradition, the menu proffers all things Belgian – crisp, golden frites, endive, chocolate in many forms for an indulgent sweet course (but no waffles).

Indian

Madras Durbar

1435 Gerrard Street E, at Ashdale Avenue, Little India (416 465 4116). Streetcar 506/bus 22. **Open** 11am-11pm daily. **Main courses** $3-$7. **Credit** AmEx, DC, MC, V.

Most Torontonians will tell you they never knew a Little India existed in their city until curry came into vogue. Finding Madras Durbar is a treat in itself: the streetcar traverses a lowly stretch of Gerrard Street, approaches the grand-but-grimy Don Jail, then curves into the colourful madness of markets, bakeries and fabric shops. The restaurant itself is an even bigger treat, where plates are the size of platters and prices staggeringly reasonable. Samosas are some of the best in the neighbourhood.

Japanese

Akane-ya

2214 Queen Street E, at Fernwood Park Avenue, the Beach (416 699 0377). Streetcar 501. **Open** 5.30-10.30pm Tue-Sat; 5-10pm Sun. **Main courses** $15-$20. **Credit** AmEx, DC, MC, V.

Fresh faced and windswept from a day by the boardwalk, you might want something fresh and fast. Other haunts may do the former, but local legend Akane-ya serves both purposes. Sidle up to the sushi bar for the usual fare – so fresh you may forget you're in freshwater territory. Fixed dinners can save you money that would otherwise be spent on portion after portion from the à la carte.

Lily

786 Broadview Avenue, at Danforth Avenue, the Danforth (416 465 9991). Streetcar 504, 505/subway Broadview. **Open** 5-11pm Mon-Sat. **Main courses** $18-$30. **Credit** AmEx, MC, V.

The decor is as close to art deco as Japanese gets, maybe because this venue was previously a Belgian bistro and some of the accents have lingered, as has an artistry in the preparation. Every traditional item on the menu has a twist: lime is a favourite, adding a flourish to soups and mains. Ingredients are layered and layered again, and the result is delicious.

Verveine

1097 Queen Street E, at Pape Avenue, East Side (416 405 9906). Streetcar 501/bus 172. **Open** 6-10pm Mon-Thur; 6-10.30pm Fri; 10am-3pm, 6-10.30pm Sat; 10am-3pm Sun. **Main courses** $16-$23. **Credit** AmEx, DC, MC, V.

on this resto-heavy strip; meat and fish platters are generous to overflowing. Appetisers (moussaka, meze platters, salads) are less ambitious though, leaning to the conventional in nature and in flavour.

Mediterranean

Lolita's Lust

513 Danforth Avenue, at Logan Avenue, the Danforth (416 465 1751). Bus 72/subway Chester or Pape. **Open** 6-11pm Tue, Wed; 6pm-midnight Thur-Sat. **Average meal** $40-$60. **Credit** AmEx, MC, V.
You won't see or be seen through the opaque front window – but why worry when all local poseurs are already in the house? Snug Lolita's is less about eating than about sipping wine and complaining loudly about one's 'industry'. Though service isn't known for its warmth, it may help to sport fashionable gear. Smack in the core of Greektown, Lolita's fare toes the line, veering to substantial meaty mains. End with a cocktail at the Chinchilla Lounge upstairs (weekends only).

North American

Tulip Steak House

1606 Queen Street E, at Coxwell Avenue (416 469 5797). Streetcar 501/bus 22. **Open** 7am-midnight Mon-Sat; 7am-11pm Sun. **Main courses** $15-$18. **Credit** AmEx, DC, MC, V.
You won't happen by the Tulip while casing the beach: this dowdy diner is just off the beaten track, west of the action. Which is probably one reason it hasn't changed in all these years (50, to be exact). You can dine on anything your heart desires – from scrambled eggs to schnitzel – but the real joy is in the beef. For Tulip is actually a steakhouse, without the heavy drapery and white-shirted waiters. Don't leave without sharing a T-bone, or at least a brisket. And save room for the luscious chocolate cake.

Pub food

Allen's

143 Danforth Avenue, at Broadview Avenue (416 463 3086/www.allens.to). Streetcar 504, 505/subway Broadview. **Open** 11.30am-11pm Mon-Fri; 11am-11pm Sat, Sun. **Main courses** $10-$26. **Credit** AmEx, DC, MC, V. **Map** p279 J4.
Toronto has Irish pubs in spades. But this one, on the fringe of Greektown, curiously, has a classy, polished-oak Manhattan feel. Regulars crowd the brass rail bar, partaking in the 150-plus beer selection. At the front, tables are tucked into windows, corners and on to platforms; further back is the dining room, where larger parties congregate; the back patio seats dozens more. The menu is sophisticated, listing Irish favourites including Kerry lamb and bistro specialities such as Atlantic salmon. If you're feeling lowbrow, indulge in a burger – truly one of the best in town – and a side of sweet potato fries.

Verveine is a break in the clouds in an area that offers few high-quality dining possibilities – consistently scrumptious, consistently funky and bathed in calming neutral tones. The menu is modern, with a touch of trendy comfort food thrown into the mix. Pork tenderloin is a highlight.

Greek

Ouzeri

500A Danforth Avenue, at Logan Avenue, the Danforth (416 778 0500/www.ouzeri.com). Subway Chester. **Open** 11am-midnight daily. **Main courses** $12-$20. **Credit** AmEx, DC, MC, V.
Budget eaters prefer pseudo-Greco platters of souvlaki, fries and salad at generic eateries throughout Greektown. But for an ante of mere pocket change, you can enjoy the real thing. A clean scheme of white with coloured tiles makes a welcome change from checked tablecloths. Magnificent dips and oven-warmed pitta are the prelude to a seafood list of Aegean proportions. The odd flaming platter may come your way, but you won't hear too many 'opas'.

Pan

516 Danforth Avenue, at Ferrier Avenue, the Danforth (416 466 8158). Subway Pape. **Open** 5-11pm Mon-Thur, Sun; 5pm-midnight Fri, Sat. **Main courses** $13-$23. **Credit** AmEx, MC.
Fine dining of the white tablecloth variety is crossed with southern European attitude. Staff are genuinely glad to see you arrive, and attend to your every whim – though they may be dressed like they're just hanging out. Mains are generally superior to most

Eat, Drink, Shop

Bars

With beer you can taste, a cocktail culture and venues from divey to vibey, Toronto is a barcrawler's town.

For cruising, schmoozing and good old-fashioned boozing, Toronto is a drinker's playground. Whether it's sipping a $15 custom-designed martini or crying into a $2 glass of beer, you'll rarely have to look far to find a place to consume.

When planning a night on the town, it's best to choose an area and stick to it – many neighbourhoods have more than enough variety to keep imbibers occupied until the wee hours. The section of College Street that runs through Little Italy is crammed with more martini and wine bars than you can shake a stirstick at. The whole area positively glows with the warm light of candles, patios abound and you'd be forgiven for thinking there was a bylaw keeping all the non-attractive people at home after dark. Many people rate Little Italy as Toronto's best drinking region, but other strips, such as the grittier Queen Street West, the student-powered Annex and the Danforth – mixing the area's Greek heritage with a range of newer establishments – compete strongly.

Restrictive provincial laws mean that one area Toronto comes up short is in the brew-pub department. **The Granite Brewery** (*see p136*) in Eglinton is the best of a very small batch of pubs that sell their own beer. But that doesn't mean Toronto lacks a beer culture. The annual Festival of Beer in August features brews from around the world, and even run-of-the-mill pubs often have a good selection of imported beers on tap. Many foreign visitors hold on to the outdated idea that Canadian beer only involves products from the spigots of Molson and Labatt. But many smaller Ontario breweries produce a broad and interesting range of beers, with great variety of flavour and intensity. Particularly worth sampling are Creemore Springs' Premium Lager, Steam Whistle's Pilsner or Sleeman's Cream Ale.

Toronto is also near the Niagara wine region, and many bars carry a good selection of Ontario wines. Niagara has an ideal climate for icewine (*see p235*) – an extremely sweet dessert wine made from grapes that have been left on the

Bars

To hang on the patio
Black Bull Tavern. *See right.*

In winter
Dora Keogh. *See p138.*

For cocktails
Souz Dal. *See p138.*

For views
The Roof Lounge. *See p136.*

For posing
Red Drink Boutique. *See p132.*

vine to freeze in the winter. A glass of icewine from the Strewn or Peller winery is a pricey but delicious local treat and is highly recommended.

Entertainment District

The Bar at the Amsterdam
600 King Street W, at Portland Avenue (416 504 1040). Streetcar 504, 510/subway St Andrew or Spadina. **Open** noon-11pm Mon-Wed; noon-midnight Thur; noon-2am Fri, Sat; 1-8pm Sun. **Credit** AmEx, MC, V. **Map** p276 C8.

People come for the speciality beers made at the small Amsterdam brewery on the same site (ask about tours at the bar). Along with regulars like Nut Brown, Dutch Amber and the raspberry flavoured Framboise, the Amsterdam fills out its menu with seasonal speciality beers. The bar, like the area, is slowly being overrun with advertising types.

Black Bull Tavern
298 Queen Street W, at Spadina Avenue (416 593 2766). Streetcar 501, 510. **Open** noon-2am daily. **Credit** MC, V. **Map** p277 D7.
This British-style pub has one of the largest and best patios in the city: thanks to a parking lot across the street, it gets plenty of afternoon sunshine. The Bull used to be a serious biker bar (until the city cracked down on people parking their Harleys on the sidewalk), but these days it's filled with the regular Queen Street crowd.

Cameron House
408 Queen Street W, at Spadina Avenue (416 703 0811). Streetcar 501, 510/subway Osgoode. **Open** 10pm-2.30am daily. **Credit** V. **Map** p276 C7.
Old-cool and new-school Queen Street mix in this dark and friendly bar. Artists and musicians haunt the former flophouse, gaining inspiration from the faded murals on the ceiling, as well as from inexpensive drinks and free conversation. More murals cover the exterior, including Toronto artist John Marriott's cheery 'Art That Says Hello' on the east wall. The back room is a theatre for experimental art and music (*see p200*).

Red Drink Boutique. *See p132.*

Eat, Drink, Shop

Mint et Menthe

647 King Street W, at Bathurst Street (416 361 9111). Streetcar 504, 511. **Open** 9pm-3pm Tue-Sat. **Credit** AmEx, MC, V. **Map** p276 C8.

A mint green tile-and-glass exterior allows only a glimpse of the long, low, glamorous lounge within. The multi-level interior is icy white and severe in its minimalism. But its popularity with the high-cheekboned set hasn't deterred the owners from redefining cool to include Tuesday night karaoke. Call ahead to check door policy.

Monsoon

100 Simcoe Street, at Adelaide Street W (416 979 7172). Streetcar 504/subway St Andrew. **Open** 11.30am-2.30pm, 5pm-2am Mon-Fri; 5pm-2am Sat. **Credit** AmEx, MC, V. **Map** p277/278 E7.

Softly glowing yellow pillars, steam rising out of illuminated vases and couches with curved backs that practically force you to cuddle with your neighbour. This bar's award-winning design makes it a prime spot both to wind down from a hard day's work and to get wound up for a night of intense clubbing. Mystified by the stone sinks in the loos? Look for a pedal on the floor. Cocktails are cheaper if you're drinking before 7pm.

The Paddock

178 Bathurst Street, at Queen Street W (416 504 9997). Streetcar 501, 511. **Open** 5pm-2am daily. **Credit** AmEx, MC, V. **Map** p276 C7.

The Paddock's history as a local dive has been eradicated. The bar has hauled itself up and out of its seedy surroundings, and has all the hallmarks of an upscale pub: a beautiful curved bar, dim lights and cool jazz, plus the clientele of journalists, documentary makers and advertising people, who come to drink lavender cocktails and imported and local beer.

Red Drink Boutique

225 Richmond Street W, at Duncan Street (416 351 0408/www.reddrinkboutique.com). Streetcar 501. Call for further details. **Map** p277 D7.

A semi-private, aggressively glamorous lounge in the middle of Toronto's nightclub district, where entrance is primarily by guest list. Still, you can

Killing me softly with your song

Eat, Drink, Shop

In a city where the Asian population is half a million strong, the karaoke had better be great. Traditional bars, public and private, have popped up in most Far Eastern communities – from Little Korea to Kensington Market to the Japanese-style suburban übermalls. But the current vogue is for karaoke the North American way: country and western, rock 'n' roll and '80s nostalgia. At a host of trendy nightspots-cum-soundstages, you'll find barflies and hipsters sharing the stage on virtually any night of the week. And those conventional karaoke venues are still attracting the wannabe Streisand and Iglesias.

If it hadn't been for its karaoke, the live music venue **Healey's** (178 Bathurst Street, Entertainment District, 416 703 5882) might not have registered on the radar of the city's young and fabulous. The eponymous boite of blind rocker Jeff Healey is the smoky site of a Tuesday night singalong, featuring 30-something arty types doing the 'white man's overbite'. It's the best reason most people can give for going out on a Tuesday night, and guests spilling out on to the street after their curtain call tend to find themselves in front of the Paddock – an excuse to have one more nightcap for the road.

The most authentic karaoke in the downtown area comes courtesy of **XO** (693 Bloor Street W, West End, 416 535 3734),

accessed through an inconspicuous street-level entrance that leads to an upper-floor lair. More Korean den of self-indulgence than party bar, XO consists of a series of private rooms that charge by the hour. Inside, black 'leather' couches and big-screen TVs are the backdrop to your own personal concert stage. The poor-quality Asian videos and ridiculous song selection can often be more fun than the singing itself.

If all the vocal practice you got as a kid was to the Sex Pistols and Kraftwerk, pass a Wednesday evening at the **Bovine Sex Club** (542 Queen Street W, Entertainment District, 416 504 4239), a decade-old hole-in-the-wall that attracts those types you'd expect to eschew such naffness: goths, ravers and punk rockers. Staff invite the odd celebrity ringer to get the audience going, then open the floor to the public.

Imagine your grandmother's mah-jong buddies next to a bunch of truckstop flotsam and you're halfway to picturing the colourful crowd at the **Gladstone Hotel** (1214 Queen Street W, West End, 416 531 4635; pictured) in rough-around-the-edges Parkdale. Also present are rhinestone cowboys, welfare mums and a posse of stylish urbanites who queue up from Wednesday to Saturday to belt out mangled versions of hits by the likes of Tammy Wynette, Johnny Cash, Elton John and Dr John.

sometimes get in by hanging around the back-alley entrance in the hopes that you'll meet the bouncers' 'personality code' (midweek they seem happy enough to wave most people through). Once in, you'll see impossibly attractive waiting staff serve premium wines and liquors in sumptuous ruby and amber surroundings.

The Rivoli
332 Queen Street W, at Spadina Avenue (416 596 1908). Streetcar 501/subway Osgoode. **Open** 11.30am-1am daily. **Credit** AmEx, MC, V. **Map** p277 D7.
A classic Queen Street bar, the Riv has one of the best patios in the city, a popular restaurant and a long martini bar, which is often crowded with fashionable types. The pool hall upstairs has less attitude, and the back room is one of the city's great music venues (*see p199*).

Smokeless Joe's
125 John Street, at Richmond Street W (416 591 2221). Streetcar 501, 504/subway St Andrew. **Open** 4pm-2am daily. **Credit** AmEx, MC, V. **Map** p277 D7.

Others we love
Peel Pub (276 King Street W, Entertainment District, 416 977 0003, Monday); **Spirits Bar & Grill** (642 Church Street, Church & Wellesley, 416 967 0001, Saturday & Sunday); **Sushi Bistro** (204 Queen Street W, Entertainment District, 416 971 5315, Monday); **Winchester Tavern** (537 Parliament Street, Cabbagetown, 416 929 1875, Wednesday).

It's easy to miss this lovely little bar, which is overshadowed by the strip of massive meat-market joints that dominate this area. What makes it great is not the abundance of fresh air – even the patio is non-smoking – but the availability of more than 250 types of beer, many of which are not available anywhere else in Ontario.

Wheat Sheaf Tavern
667 King Street W, at Bathurst Street (416 504 9912). Streetcar 504, 511. **Open** 11am-2am daily. **Credit** AmEx, DC, MC, V. **Map** p276 C8.
Opened in 1849, the Wheat Sheaf proudly and loudly trumpets its status as Toronto's oldest bar. A beer-drinking tradition is palpable, especially in the historic neon signs advertising Molson Canadian, not to mention ye olde giant-screen TV.

YYZ Restaurant & Wine Bar
345 Adelaide Street W, at Spadina Avenue (416 599 3399/www.yyzrestaurant.com). Streetcar 510, 504. **Open** 4.30pm-2am daily. **Credit** AmEx, DC, MC, V. **Map** p277 D7.
Opened in 2001, YYZ hopes to ride the wave of new condo developments along nearby King Street. Stepping down from the street into this softly luminescent white-walled bar is like entering a *Star Trek* film set. YYZ specialises in wines from new world boutique vintners, such as August Briggs and Livingston/Moffett. *See also p105.*

Financial District

Canoe Bar
Toronto Dominion Bank Tower, 66 Wellington Street W, at Bay Street (416 364 0054/www. canoerestaurant.com). Streetcar 504/subway King. **Open** 11am-2am Mon-Fri. **Credit** AmEx, DC, MC, V. **Map** p277/p278 D8.
Bartender Jeff Sampson creates his own vodka infusions for a martini menu that changes monthly. Sip a lotus martini – flavoured with sour cherries and lychees – while enjoying a stunning view of the harbour from the 54th storey of the Toronto Dominion Centre. The bar is busiest between 5pm and 9pm, and is only open Monday to Friday. Dress nice.

Library Bar
The Fairmont Royal York, 100 Front Street W, at University Avenue (416 368 2511/www.fairmont. com). Subway St Andrew or Union. **Open** noon-1am daily. **Credit** AmEx, DC, MC, V. **Map** p277/p278 D8.
The Library Bar – all leather chairs and literature-laden shelves – is a place for the rich, or for those who want to feel rich for the length of time it takes to drink a cocktail.

Dundas Square

Imperial Pub & Library Tavern
54 Dundas Street E, at Victoria Street (416 977 4667). Streetcar 505/subway Dundas. **Open** 11.30am-3am daily. **Credit** AmEx, MC, V. **Map** p277/p278 F6.

Eat, Drink, Shop

Few visitors venture the short block west of Yonge Street to visit this slice of faded grandeur. Their loss. Behind its dull brick exterior, the tavern glows with soft colours, photos of James Dean and paintings of Parisian whores. Drinkers gather around a circular bar. A well-populated aquarium hangs above the bar – a subtle reminder to drink like a fish.

Chinatown/Kensington Market

The Last Temptation
12 Kensington Avenue, at Dundas Street W (416 599 2551). Streetcar 505, 510. **Open** 11am-2am daily. **Credit** AmEx, MC, V. **Map** p276 C6.
A shady oasis by day, a pool of light on a dark street by night, the Temp's welcoming patio is a favourite with Toronto's alternative media people, as well as with haggard old-timers who quietly sip their beer and stare into space. Inside, the clocks on the wall have stopped, but the pool table still sees some action from time to time.

The Red Room
444 Spadina Avenue, at College Street (416 929 9964). Streetcar 510, 506. **Open** 11am-2am daily. **No credit cards. Map** p276 C6.
From the people who brought you the Green Room (*see below*) comes a less overwhelming, but still student-friendly pub. Old-fashioned street lamps light the patio and inside the casually hip crowd around the booths and tables, or slouch in the couches at the back. If you don't feel like alcohol, try an avocado milkshake instead.

University/Harbord

The Green Room
296 Brunswick Avenue, at Bloor Street W (416 929 3253). Subway Bathurst or Spadina. **Open** 11am-2am daily. **No credit cards. Map** p280 C4.
The back alley entrance leads into a large room cluttered with mismatched chairs and couches, and wobbly tables covered in wax from candles jammed into Molson Dry bottles. There's more of the same upstairs, and in the courtyard. It looks like a garage-sale fetishist's secret storehouse. The Green Room is popular with the alt.student crowd.

Insomnia Internet Bar/Café
563 Bloor Street W, at Bathurst Street (416 588 3907/www.insomniacafe.com). Streetcar 511/subway Bathurst. **Open** 4pm-2am Mon-Thur; 4pm-4am Fri; 10am-4am Sat; 10am-2am Sun. **Credit** AmEx, MC, V. **Map** p280 C4.
It started a few years ago as an internet café, but the only remaining vestiges are a single computer and late hours. The lounge is busiest in the winter when students are around and all the neighbourhood patios are closed. Local DJs play each night between 10pm and 2am. Thursday is cheap martini night, and beer is cheaper on Mondays.

Panorama Restaurant and Lounge
Manulife Centre, 55 Bloor Street W, at Bay Street (416 967 0000). **Open** 5pm-2am daily. **Credit** AmEx, MC, V. **Map** p280 E4.
On the 51st storey of the Manulife Centre, Panorama lives up to its name, with expansive views looking both north and south over the city. Poseurs among the lounge's cocktail-drinking crowd often seem either to be showing off to their dates, or just showing off their dates. The Panorama is best in the summer when the large rooftop patio is open.

sPaHa
66 Harbord Street, at Spadina Avenue (416 260 6133/www.spaha.com). Streetcar 510. **Open** 11.30am-2am Mon-Fri; 10.30am-2am Sat, Sun. **Credit** AmEx, MC, V. **Map** p280 D4.
A New York bistro wannabe – sPaHa's name, modelled on the SoHo/TriBeCa template, comes from its cross streets, Spadina and Harbord. The wraparound patio provides access to an airy space on the ground floor of a University of Toronto graduate residence and a more intimate bar in the basement. Student-compatible menus mean the bar serves up all-day breakfasts.

Ye Olde Brunswick House
481 Bloor Street W, at Brunswick Avenue (416 964 2242). Subway Bathurst or Spadina. **Open** 11am-2am daily. **Credit** AmEx, MC, V. **Map** p280 C4.
If it's your first time away from home, and mum and dad are no longer around to forbid you from binge drinking, head over to the Brunny – you'll be in good company. This century-old collegiate drunk tank has cheap pitchers, queues and live music after 10pm on weekends.

St Lawrence

C'est What
67 Front Street E, at Church Street (416 867 9499/www.cestwhat.com). Streetcar 504/subway King or Union. **Open** noon-2am Mon-Fri; 11am-2am Sat; 11am-1am Sun. **Credit** AmEx, MC, V. **Map** p277/p278 C8.
While it's not quite a brewpub, several beers, including a hemp ale and a coffee porter, are brewed offsite specifically for this warm and welcoming basement bar. It's a place to stay for hours, drinking fancy beer and playing backgammon or Scrabble (there are no darts or pool). The bartenders bring in their own CDs, so the music can range from hip hop to Beethoven, and the crowd is every bit as mixed.

Down One Lounge and Billiards
49 Front Street E, at Church Street (416 363 7565). Streetcar 504/subway King. **Open** 4.30pm-2am Tue-Sat. **Credit** AmEx, MC, V. **Map** p277/p278 C8.
The former Downunder pool hall has changed its name and gotten all clubby. Lava lamps light the warm brick walls, low ceilings and exposed pipes. Six pool tables are still scattered discreetly around the basement bar, but the focus has now switched

Beer haul

● Canadian beer is much more interesting than the watery and tasteless beer served in America – and its alcohol content is higher, too, so one can actually get quite 'hosed' on it. However, the nation's most popular beer is probably also the nation's worst beer: Labatt Blue.

● Canada is the third heaviest taxer of beer in the world (after Finland and Norway).

● In 1996, Moosehead, Canada's oldest independent brewery, sent cease and desist letters to makers of Moose Drool, Stoopid Moose and Moose Juice.

● The 'stubby' beer bottle, familiar to those who know Jamaica's Red Stripe beer, was Canada's industry standard until 1985 and is sentimentally remembered as a design classic by designers and drinkers alike. The stubby's sturdy structure allows it to be re-used twice as many times as the longneck version. Help bring it back by ordering at least one round of Red Cap, a fine local brew that appeared in 2002 suavely bottled in stubbies.

● In Ontario, you can only buy take-home beer from an LCBO liquor outlet (*see p153* **LCBO: buying alcohol**) or a 'Beer Store', which used to be called 'Brewers Retail'. However the name changed after years of visiting Americans on 'beer vacations' – as they are

often called – complaining they could never find a place to buy a bottle or 24 of beer.

● A 24-pack of bottled beer is called a 'two-four' (pronounced 'two-fur').

● A beer can also be called 'a brew', 'a brewski', 'a cold one' and a 'wobbly pop' in the local lingo.

● Canada's most successful TV commercial of all time was the 1994 Molson Canadian ad featuring 'Joe Canadian' doing an 'I am Canadian' rant. It created an unparalleled fever of Canadian nationalism. Its legacy can still be seen at www.iam.ca where one can also peruse a gallery of Canadian themed tattoos. Be warned: it's kind of scary...

● In 1981, the classic Canadian comedy show SCTV was told it needed more 'distinctly Canadian content'. Annoyed (as a piss-take of pop culture, the show could not get any more Canadian), cast members Rick Moranis and Dave Thomas came up with the unscripted sketch 'The Great White North' featuring Bob and Doug McKenzie, who wore plaid, had toques on their head, quaffed beer and talked about back bacon. It proved to be the show's greatest success and resulted in a Hollywood movie called *Strange Brew*, and such affectionate drinking insults as 'hosed', 'hoser', 'hosehead' 'hose off eh' and 'take off eh' entering the vernacular.

to a semicircle of couches facing a couple of turntables. With that in mind, there are DJ nights on Thursday, Friday and Saturday.

Esplanade Bier Markt
58 The Esplanade, between Church & Yonge Streets (416 862 7575). Streetcar 504/subway King. **Open** 11am-1am Tue-Sun. **Credit** AmEx, DC, MC, V. **Map** p277/p278 C8.
This faux Belgian brasserie has more than 100 brands of beer and lots of space in which to drink them. On a strip of bars and restaurants that includes Fionn MacCool's (*see below*), it serves the surrounding condo community and is a popular spot for after-work drinking and flirting.

Fionn MacCool's
70 The Esplanade, at Church Street (416 362 2495). Streetcar 504/subway Union. **Open** 11am-1am Mon-Thur; 11am-2am Fri, Sat; 11am-midnight Sun. **Credit** AmEx, MC, V. **Map** p277/p278 C8.
It's as if the owners ordered the complete product line from 'The Authentic Irish Pub Catalogue' – Guinness posters, a snug, plenty of dark wood and corned beef and cabbage on the menu. Live Irish music is as likely to be U2 covers as a traditional reel.

Irish Embassy Pub and Grill
49 Yonge Street, at Wellington Street (416 866 8282). Streetcar 504/subway King or Union. **Open** 11.30am-2am Mon-Fri; 11am-2am Sat, Sun. **Credit** AmEx, MC, V. **Map** p277/p278 C8.
This historic British colonial building, built in 1873, was the first merchant bank in Toronto. Its financial past was not forgotten when it opened as an upscale Irish pub on St Patrick's Day, 2000. The vaulted ceiling and marble columns are original. At lunchtime, stockbrokers and corporate lawyers come here to drink Guinness and eat Irish stew, while watching stock tickers on TV.

Midtown

Yorkville

Avenue
Four Seasons, 21 Avenue Road, between Yorkville Avenue & Cumberland Street (416 928 7332/www.fourseasons.com/toronto). Subway Bay or Museum. **Open** 11.45am-1am daily. **Credit** AmEx, MC, V. **Map** p280 E4.

Yorkville's Four Seasons hotel is a tall building with great aerial views. And yet, in 2001, it opened an upmarket bar on the ground floor. It specialises in martinis, but also has 25 wines by the glass.

Hemingway's

142 Cumberland Street, at Bay Street (416 968 2828/www.hemingways.to). Bus 6/subway Bay. **Open** 11am-2am daily. **Credit** AmEx, MC, V. **Map** p280 E4.

New Zealander Martin McSkimming opened this restaurant and bar in 1980, and you'll still find him hanging around chatting with the regulars. Much Yorkville pedestrian traffic stops by here. The rooftop patio is open year-round (enclosed in the winter), and there's live music downstairs at weekends. On February 6 each year, Hemingway's celebrates Waitangi Day, the Kiwi national holiday.

The Roof Lounge

Park Hyatt Hotel, 4 Avenue Road, Bloor Street W (416 324 1568). Subway Bay or Museum. **Open** noon-1am daily. **Credit** AmEx, MC, V. **Map** p280 E4.

A mere 18 storeys off the ground, this is by no means the highest bar in the city. But it is still the most pleasing of Toronto's high-altitude drinking establishments. The stunning skyline is enhanced by a large fireplace, a leather-lined bar and deep green marble tables. In summer, the terrace is always crowded with patrons enjoying the view of the University of Toronto and the skyscrapers beyond.

The Annex

Bedford Academy

36 Prince Arthur Avenue, at Bedford Road (416 921 4600). Subway St George. **Open** 11am-2am daily. **Credit** AmEx, MC, V. **Map** p280 E4.

This old townhouse is one of the more civilised drinking establishments in the Annex. The bar gets plenty of the university trade, but its proximity to

Yorkville means that celebrities such as Harrison Ford and Mike Myers have been known to wander in as well. In addition to a good range of beers on tap and heady cocktails, the Academy also has a better than average pub menu.

The Duke of York

39 Prince Arthur Avenue, at Bedford Road (416 964 2441). Subway St George. **Open** 11am-2am daily. **Credit** AmEx, MC, V. **Map** p280 E4.

Red pseudo-tartan carpet covers one spacious room after another – upstairs, downstairs and in my lady's smoking and non-smoking chambers. A British-style pub, the Duke's quiet vibe attracts professors as well as students. Every Thursday, it has beer tasting sessions with free samples and information.

The Madison Avenue Pub

14 Madison Avenue, at Bloor Street W (416 927 1722/www.madisonavenuepub.com). Streetcar 510/subway Spadina. **Open** 11am-2am daily. **Credit** AmEx, MC, V. **Map** p280 E4.

The Frankenstein's monster of the frat scene, the Maddy is made up of three Victorian mansions grafted together into five patios, six rooms (each of which holds about 200 people), 137 beer taps, a kitchen, a scotch bar and, inevitably, a merchandise stand. Like Mary Shelley's creation, this beast isn't quite so scary as it at first seems and you can enjoy a drink and a meal in relative peace.

Davisville/Yonge & Eglinton

Granite Brewery

245 Eglinton Avenue E, at Mount Pleasant Road (416 322 0723/www.granitebrewery.ca). Subway Eglinton. **Open** 11.30am-1am daily. **Credit** AmEx, MC, V.

Dedicated beer aficionados travel great distances for a taste of Peculiar, the strongest of the Granite's many aggressive own-brewed ales. Unfortunately,

Bloody Caesar!

The makings of Canada's trademark cocktail.

The Bloody Caesar was invented in Alberta in 1969, far from Rome – or even the sea, for that matter. Nonetheless, restaurateur Walter Chell came up with his spin on the Bloody Mary by changing the juice from tomato to clamato. Why he called it a Caesar is a mystery that Chell took to his grave.

● Rim a highball glass with lemon juice and dip into celery salt
● Add ice
● Shake in a few drops of Tabasco sauce or other hot pepper sauce

● Add Worcestershire sauce (¼ teaspoon)
● Pour in 1½ ounces vodka
● Squeeze in 1½ teaspoon lemon juice
● Stir contents of glass and then add 4-6 ounces of Clamato juice
● Garnish with celery stick
● Top with a lemon wedge

When making more than one at a time, a cocktail shaker can be used to mix the ingredients in the same order, then strain over ice cubes in each glass.

Enjoy a spectacular skyline from the **The Roof Lounge**. *See p136.*

you can't stock up, as provincial law dictates that all beer must be sold and consumed on the premises. The restaurant often features food made with beer, served with complementary (sadly, not complimentary) beer.

West End

Little Italy

Bar Italia

582 College Street, at Manning Avenue (416 535 3621). Streetcar 506, 511. **Open** 10.30am-2am Thur-Sun. **Credit** AmEx, DC, MC, V. **Map** p276 B6.
The original Bar Italia was situated next door. It went upmarket a few years ago, and now the noisy chatter in the downstairs section can be attributed mostly to the clientele of film and television people hashing out their pitches. Upstairs, the bar makes more of an attempt at intimacy, with regular DJs to spin tracks and candlelight to cast seductive shadows, but it's fighting a losing battle – this is too large an operation to ever feel all that cosy. The upstairs bar is also sometimes used for performances and readings.

Cobalt

426 College Street, at Bathurst Street (416 923 4456). Streetcar 506, 511. **Open** 9pm-2am Mon-Wed, Sun; 8pm-2am Thur-Sat. **Credit** AmEx, MC, V. **Map** p276 B6.
In the wild borderlands on the eastern end of Little Italy, Cobalt's extensive martini list lets you choose

from four different chocolate martinis. Middle Eastern-inspired cubby-hole booths in the back are private and romantic. Soft lighting, deep blue walls, and dark corners make Cobalt a romantic option.

College Street Bar

574 College Street, at Manning Avenue (416 533 2417). Streetcar 506, 511. **Open** 5pm-2am daily. **Credit** AmEx, MC, V. **Map** p276 B6.
Exposed brick and dark wood set the tone for this old favourite. Less formal than some of its swanky neighbours, it's still a place where the young and fashionable come to see and be seen. The seafood-intensive menu has a good reputation.

Liquids Lounge

577 College Street, at Clinton Street (416 530 7990). Streetcar 506, 511. **Open** 10pm-2am Mon-Sat. **Credit** AmEx, MC, V. **Map** p276 B6.
This sylish hideaway lounge above Joya Restaurant lazily opens its unobtrusive door late in the evening, and the place slowly picks up speed. There's no cocktail menu, but the bar staff are willing to experiment on your behalf, if you're feeling brave enough.

South Side Louie's

583 College Street, at Clinton Street (416 532 1250). Streetcar 506, 511. **Open** 11.30am-1.45am daily. **Credit** AmEx, MC, V. **Map** p276 B6.
If you've overdosed on Little Italy's fashion-model scene, this casual pub is a good place to recover. A nice cold pint, some solid pub food and a hearty conversation over the pool table will have you feeling like a thousand bucks again in no time.

Souz Dal

636 College Street, at Grace Street (416 537 1883).
Streetcar 506. **Open** 8pm-2am daily. **Credit** AmEx,
MC, V. **Map** p276 B6.
This small cocktail bar holds only 50 people
(another 25 can squeeze on to the back patio) and
it gets very crowded on the weekends. When it's not
packed, it's dark and seductive, with red plush
chairs and candlelight reflecting off the burnished
copper wedges that decorate the bar. Down a couple of martinis from the long list and you can't help
but feel romantic, even if you're on your own.

Ted's Collision & Body Repair

*573 College Street W, at Bathurst Street (416 530
7569). Streetcar 506, 511.* **Open** 6pm-2am daily.
Credit DC, MC, V. **Map** p276 B6.
Imagine finding beer on martini-saturated College
Street! Just across the road from College Street Bar
(*see p137*), this is a Little Italy staple, a classic,
unpretentious spot to unwind after a sweaty day's
work. Drinks are cheap, and pitchers are served for
those who really have a thirst to quench.

Veni, Vidi, Vici

650 College Street, at Grace Street (416 536 8550).
Streetcar 506, 511. **Open** 5pm-2am Tue-Sun.
Credit AmEx, MC, V. **Map** p276 B6.
The award-winning Roman-themed interior design
tends to attract the darlings of fashion. You'll see a
lot of busts here (not to mention a few sculptures)
among high-backed booths, an arched, pressed-tin
ceiling, and softly glowing chandeliers. In the back,
a luxurious enclosed rotunda can hold up to 12
people for a private party.

Wild Indigo

607 College Street, at Clinton Street (416 536 8797).
Streetcar 506, 511. **Open** 8pm-2am daily. **Credit**
MC, V. **Map** p276 B6.
In the tranquil backyard patio, a Buddha, backlit
with blue light, sets the tone for this mellow, con-
versation-friendly martini bar. The martini menu is
mercifully short on double entendres (although you
can grit your teeth and ask for a Sex on the Couch
if you must). It also has a reasonable range of wines
and imported beers.

East Side

The Danforth

Chinchilla Lounge

*513 Danforth Avenue, at Logan Avenue (416 465
1751). Bus 72/subway Chester or Pape.* **Open** 8pm-
2am Fri, Sat. **Credit** AmEx, MC, V.
Upstairs from Lolita's Lust restaurant (*see p129*),
the Chinchilla Lounge is open only at weekends,
when the after-dinner crowd kicks back, relaxes
and listens to a DJ spin house and funk. Light
wood floors and beige walls help to create the feeling that the small lounge is larger than it actually

is. The design is always evolving, but usually features geometric paintings by well-regarded local
artist Malcolm Brown.

Dora Keogh Traditional Irish Pub

*141 Danforth Avenue, at Ellerbeck Street (416 778
1804). Streetcar 504, 505/subway Broadview or
Chester.* **Open** 4.30pm-2am daily. **Credit** AmEx,
MC, V.
The Irish aspect of the pub is kept pleasantly
low-key. It's a favourite for locals to meet for a pint
of Guinness or a glass of Jameson's. The bar has a
handsome wood and copper decor, a working
fireplace and a snug.

Myth

*417 Danforth Avenue, at Arundel Avenue (416 461
8383). Subway Chester.* **Open** 5-11pm Mon-Wed;
noon-midnight Thur; noon-2am Fri, Sat; 2pm-
midnight Sun. **Credit** AmEx, DC, MC, V.
The Danforth's nod to the College Street scene, this
restaurant and upscale cocktail bar attracts an after-
dinner, over-30 crowd, as well as some of the
Danforth's younger demographic. The dressy bar is
a good place to find a conversation and the pool
tables are a good place to continue it over a rack or
two. The bar also occasionally has live jazz music
to fill in the gaps between the chat.

The Beach

@2066 Lounge Bar

*2066 Queen Street E, at Hambly Avenue (416 698
2066). Streetcar 501.* **Open** 4pm-2am daily. **Credit**
AmEx, MC, V.
Like the Beach, but don't like pubs? This bar is a
cool candle-lit alternative to the area's more noisy
establishments. Soft yellow walls and wood highlights make it cosy and warm. There are bands on
Saturday afternoons but mostly it's just a good place
for a quiet conversation.

Lion on the Beach

*1958 Queen Street E, at Kenilworth Avenue (416
690 1984). Streetcar 501/bus 92.* **Open** 11.30am-
2am daily. **Credit** AmEx, MC, V.
This informal pub is many people's introduction to
the Beach, and it is a popular gathering spot for
larger groups. A somewhat generic throwback to
the area's historic status as a British enclave, the
pub has two quiet patios, and hosts live and lively
music at weekends.

Quigley's Pub & Bistro

*2232 Queen Street E, at Beach Avenue (416 699
9998/www.quigleysonthebeach.com). Streetcar 501.*
Open 11am-2am Mon-Fri; 9am-2am Sat, Sun. **Credit**
AmEx, MC, V.
Since it opened in 1987, locals and world travellers
have been drawn to this community pub by above
average food, a shady patio and low-key, live music.
The pub hosts special events for most major
holidays, from specials for Mother's Day to haggis
for Burns Night.

Shops & Services

In which the one-offs put up a good fight against the chain gang and the customer comes out on top.

It's a common sentiment in Toronto that there's nothing you can get elsewhere that you can't get here, so exotic is the selection of food, furnishings and fashion. And, luckily for fossickers, although multinational chains both discount and designer have found their way into once-quaint corners, Toronto is still a fan of the little guy: the market fishmonger, the Chinese grocer, the home outfitter who uses local woods or the designer who stitches away at the rear of her boutique.

How prices pan out depend on where you come from and how exchange rates are doing. If, as seems likely, the Canadian dollar remains weak against the US version and the UK pound, Brits and Americans will continue to find prices enticingly low. A lot of cars and trucks drive in across the US border empty and out full. And although you pay 15 per cent sales tax on most non-essentials (not included in the prices marked) the refund scheme (*see p254*) is flexible and easy to use. Canadians, however, find Toronto expensive.

SHOPPING AREAS

Depending on what you're after, shopping can be quite a manageable experience in Toronto largely because shops of a feather tend to flock together. So, conquering, say, the upscale antiques quarter can be done in a few hours, leaving ample time to hunt down a far-flung one-off. Classy antiques congregate along Davenport Road at Avenue Road; just a slight jog north-east will bring you to the Yonge and Summerhill corridor, where they become less exclusive and more eclectic. More pockets are at the furthest reaches of Queen Street, west at Roncesvalles Avenue and east at Pape Avenue, where there's a hotchpotch of as-is relics and mid-century booty, and on Queen Street west of Bathurst Street or – better still – on King Street East past Jarvis Street for modern European and innovative Canadian meubles.

Fashion shopping areas are less defined. The international names – from Gucci to Vuitton – are stationed, as if by mandate, along Bloor Street around Bay Street and Avenue Road (*see p146* **Gimme Bloor**). Several equally pricey but less traditional designers are based in Yorkville, the tiny collective of lanes just north of the stretch of

Bloor known as the mink mile (between Yonge Street and Avenue Road). The area around Queen Street West and Spadina Avenue, which earned the moniker SoHo back when safety pins and biker boots were typical attire, has now achieved high-street status, forcing the lower-rent boutiques that once defined it further west towards Ossington Avenue. The vintage hub remains Kensington Market (*see p150*), also a centre for food shopping, along with the indoor St Lawrence Market (*p154*).

One-stop

Department stores

Holt Renfrew

50 Bloor Street W, at Bay Street, Yorkville (416 922 2333/www.holtrenfrew.com). Subway Bay or Bloor-Yonge. **Open** 10am-6pm Mon-Wed, Sat; 10am-8pm Thur-Fri; noon-6pm Sun. **Credit** AmEx, DC, MC, V. **Map** p280 E4.

New York has Barney's and Toronto has Holt Renfrew, a multi-level temple for high-end attire and pampering products. Visiting celebs and local gentry have been known to send their chauffeurs inside to collect goods while they wait in the limo. Inside, however, you'll still find peroxide blondes carrying lapdogs in their Gucci handbags. If you're looking for Halston, Armani, Manolo or the latest European blue jeans, your gold card will lead you here.

Malls

Hazelton Lanes

55 Avenue Road, at Bloor Street, Yorkville (416 323 0615/www.hazeltonlanes.com). Bus 6/subway Bay or Museum. **Open** 10am-6pm Mon-Wed, Fri, Sat; 10am-7pm Thur; noon-5pm Sun. **Credit** varies. **Map** p280 E4.

A 1960s monstrosity on the outside, a quaint web of courtyards within, Hazelton Lanes was fashion central for the rich and glamorous until the lean 1990s, when flamboyance went the way of shoulder pads and half the mall lay vacant. Footsteps still echo in the halls and construction works make getting around difficult, but the Lanes have begun to attract some vital tenants, for example, the highly priced Whole Foods Market (*see p156*) in the basement. TNT – the très trendy men's and women's boutiques – have had a facelift, and Teatro Verde (*see p160*) has expanded its high-end home accessories centre.

Hazelton Lanes. *See p139.*

Toronto Eaton Centre

*1 Dundas Street W, at Yonge Street, Dundas Square
(416 598 8560/www.torontoeatoncentre.com).
Streetcar 501, 505/subway Dundas or Queen.*
Open 10am-9pm Mon-Fri; 9.30am-7pm Sat; noon-
6pm Sun. **Credit** varies. **Map** p277/p278 F6.
The landmark – though not terribly beautiful –
shopping centre retains its name even though the
Eaton heirs drove the eponymous department store
to its knees (Sears picked up the pieces in 1999).
The centre bridges the old Eaton's and another
department store, the Bay, still thriving under the
400-year-old Hudson's Bay Company. Between
them the two stores offer clothing running from
mid-range international to more pedestrian, home-
grown styles, plus basic kitchenware and appliances and mainstream beauty products. Spanning
the two, a multi-level 1970s mall of gargantuan proportions bustles in a greenhouse-style glass enclosure. Few shops stand out but all the basics are
here, including books at Indigo, a basic food court,
plus a ticket booth and tourist info stand, reflecting the Eaton Centre's inexplicable status as a top
tourist destination.

Yorkdale Shopping Centre

*3401 Dufferin Street, at Eglinton Avenue W, West
End (416 789 3261/www.yorkdale.com). Subway or
GO Yorkdale.* **Open** 10am-9pm Mon-Fri; 9.30am-9pm
Sat; 11am-6pm Sun. **Credit** varies.
You might have noticed Yorkdale, the first mall in
North America, on your drive into the city. This
sprawling neon behemoth – not unlike Vegas – has
been expanding since its inception in the mid 20th
century, leaving no retailer (local or foreign) unin-
vited. Once a hangout for teens from local working
class neighbourhoods, Yorkdale has scrubbed up its
image, now housing a Holt Renfrew, Harry Rosen,
Pottery Barn and 200 other shops.

Discount malls

Winners

*444 Yonge Street, at College Street, University
(416 598 8800). Streetcar 506/subway College.*
Open 9am-9pm Mon-Fri; 9.30am-6pm Sat; 11am-
6pm Sun. **Credit** MC, V. **Map** p277/p278/p281 F5.
After ruling in the suburbs – and drawing downtown denizens out to the sticks for knocked down
prices on fashions – Winners has arrived in the
heart of the city. Designer dresses, casual sportswear and men's and children's clothing can be
found with hefty discounts on a selection of samples and overruns.

Antiques

Butterfield 8

*235 Danforth Avenue, at Playter Boulevard,
East Side (416 406 5664). Subway Broadview or
Chester.* **Open** 10am-6pm Mon-Sat; noon-4pm Sun.
Credit AmEx, MC, V.

You can comb the Harbourfront Antique Market (*see
below*) or stake out the junk shops on Queen, but
you're unlikely to find the high-quality kitsch that
can be unearthed here. The true collectibles can be
found in cigarette paraphernalia (enamel cases and
lighters), and neo-kitsch appears in the form of cute
carryalls and home accessories.

Clutter's Art Deco/Modern Gallery

*692 Queen Street E, at Broadview Avenue,
East Side (416 461 3776). Streetcar 501, 504,
505.* **Open** 11am-6pm Mon-Fri; 11am-5pm Sat;
noon-5pm Sun. **Credit** AmEx, MC, V. **Map** p279 J7.
Chairs upon trunks upon tables, with funky lighting filling the spaces. If you're nostalgic for the
'50s – or just wish you could call them your own –
some meticulously maintained pieces will appeal
(ashtrays and crockery will please light travellers).

Harbourfront Antique Market

*390 Queens Quay W, at Spadina Avenue,
Waterfront (416 260 2626/www.hfam.com).
Streetcar 510.* **Open** 10am-6pm Tue-Sat.
Credit AmEx, MC, V. **Map** p276 C9.
Toronto's most non-European characteristic is its
dearth of markets, but this antiques arcade is enough
to sate any enthusiast. Two huge floors present the
usual china, silver and jewellery – worth sifting
through only if you're a collector. Twentieth-century
curios include silk-tasselled lamps from Vaudeville
days, magazines, old tin product advertisements,
wedding gowns and gloves. There's also a decent
selection of antique maps, and natural-fibre rugs for
the home decorator.

Passion for the Past

*1646 Queen Street W, at Wilson Park Road,
West End (416 535 3883). Streetcar 501, 504.*
Open noon-6pm Wed-Sun. **Credit** V.
The market atmosphere is pervasive at Passion,
where haggling is not the offensive practice it has
become elsewhere. The quality Victorian furnishings
on which this outlet was founded are becoming
scarce – but they do exist, and are fine representa-
tions of Toronto's beginnings.

Quean Antiques

*1716 Queen Street W, at Roncesvalles Avenue,
West End (416 588 6951). Streetcar 501, 504.*
Open 11am-5pm Tue-Fri; 10am-6pm Sat; noon-5pm
Sun. **Credit** AmEx, MC, V.
This cheerful, well-lit space on the furthest reaches
of Queen West belies the nature of its contents: dusty
artefacts from the attics and basements of Canada.
Quixotic Canadiana might include the old metal
apothecary cabinets that have become so trendy of
late, but also plenty of Quebecois pine and cottage
chic: tabletops resting on a severed tree stump, animal hides as rugs and even a buffalo head.

WA Casa

*192 Davenport Road, at Avenue Road, Casa Loma
(416 921 1326). Bus 6/subway Museum.* **Open** 10am-
5pm Mon-Fri. **Credit** AmEx, MC, V. **Map** p280 E3.

Eat, Drink, Shop

An off-beat 'zine dream: **The Beguiling**. *See p143.*

Who said kitsch had no place on haughty Davenport Road? If you've managed to maintain your a sense of humour yet can afford to shop at this upscale design strip, poke your nose into WA Casa, purveyor of Lucite, plaster busts, mod lighting and mid-century vanities, along with the odd serious piece from Louis XV France.

Books, newspapers & magazines

Book City

1430 Yonge Street, at St Clair Avenue, Casa Loma (416 961 1228). Subway St Clair. **Open** 9.30am-10pm daily. **Credit** MC, V. **Map** p281 F1.
Even with five locations citywide, Book City is still the ideal small book shop. Sophisticated, hard-to-find literary magazines and low-budget Canadian upstarts all feature, and there are few better places to pick up a Sunday *New York Times* (though copies sell quickly). The rough-around-the-edges decor is charming rather than dusty.
Branches: 348 Danforth Avenue, East Side (416 469 9997); 2350 Bloor Street W, West End (416 766 9412); 501 Bloor Street W, the Annex (416 961 4496).

Chapters

110 Bloor Street W, at Bay Street, the Annex (416 920 9299/www.chapters.indigo.ca). Bus 6/subway Bay. **Open** 9am-10pm Mon-Thur; 9am-11pm Fri, Sat; 10am-10pm Sun. **Credit** AmEx, MC, V. **Map** p280 E4.

The first mega-bookstore in Canada, Chapters caused controversy when – nearly a decade ago – it bought Coles and Smith Books and began to multiply, putting the quainter booksellers out of business. It got a taste of its own medicine when rival big-box Indigo set up shop two years later and in 2001 Indigo gobbled up Chapters whole, creating Chapters/Indigo Inc. Chapters does have one thing going for it, though: it allows you to browse, chat, thumb through magazines, pull up a chair, enjoy a coffee, then walk out without buying so much as a TV guide. It also offers a healthy discount on popular hardbacks.
Branches: 2225 Bloor Street W, West End (416 761 9773); 142 John Street, Entertainment District (416 595 7349); 2901 Bayview Avenue, North Side (416 222 6323).

Indigo Books & Music

55 Bloor Street W, at Bay Street, University (416 925 3536/www.chapters.indigo.ca). Bus 6/subway Bay. **Open** 9am-10pm Mon-Wed, Sun; 9am-11pm Thur-Sat. **Credit** AmEx, MC, V. **Map** p280 E4.
It's the better looking of the two mega-book rival outlets. Still, rummaging through Indigo is like shopping at IKEA: you're there because you have to be, and lingering is not a great option (even though most locations have their own cafés). Indigo's best asset is its lecture circuit. Celebrity authors often make pitstops for signings or promotions.
Branches: 2300 Yonge Street, North Side (416 544 0049); 3401 Dufferin Street, Yorkdale Shopping Centre, North Side (416 781 6660); 220 Yonge Street, Toronto Eaton Centre, Dundas Square (416 591 3622).

Nicholas Hoare

*45 Front Street E, at Church Street, St Lawrence
(416 777 2665). Streetcar 504/subway Union.*
Open 10am-6pm Mon-Wed; 10am-8pm Thur, Fri;
9am-6pm Sat; noon-6pm Sun. **Credit** AmEx, MC, V.
Map p277/p278 F8.
No magazines or newspapers are to be found here.
Hoare is all about books, stacked right up to the
ceilings and accessed by dark oak ladders on brass
rails. Classical music streams out from speakers,
while an erudite few peruse poetry, haul out coffee
table books and investigate the latest in home-
grown literature. Skylights illuminate a space that
otherwise resembles an old English study; plush
seating is strategically located in front of a stone
fireplace that crackles and scents the shop on cold
winter days. Hoare makes a refreshing change from
the chain stores.

Pages

*256 Queen Street W, at John Street, Entertainment
District (416 598 1447). Streetcar 501/subway
Osgoode.* **Open** 9.30am-10pm Mon-Wed; 9.30am-
11pm Thur, Fri; 10am-11pm Sat; 11am-8pm Sun.
Credit AmEx, MC, V. **Map** p277 D7.
It's no surprise that a Queen West bookstore should
assume a Queen West sensibility. Pages' forte is
heavy art tomes, obscure magazines and quirky
postcards. Staff are more interested in minding their
watches than in minding the customers, but don't
let that deter you from ducking in.

Comics

The Beguiling

*601 Markham Street, at Bloor Street, West End
(416 533 9168/www.beguiling.com). Streetcar
511/subway Bathurst.* **Open** 11am-7pm Mon-Thur;
11am-9pm Fri; noon-6pm Sat. **Credit** AmEx, MC, V.
The name does not lie. A trip to this Mirvish Village
boutique, tucked away in an unconventional corner
on the outskirts of the Annex, is an eye-opener.
Around since 1987, the feel at The Beguiling is
avant-garde and underground, and the interior dark
and clandestine. Young unknowns – particularly
new local comic talent – are featured, along with a
slew of female artists. On the ground floor, find
mini-comics, magazines and alternative gifts; more
mainstream mags occupy the first floor. The staff
know their stuff.

The Silver Snail

*367 Queen Street W, at Spadina Avenue,
Entertainment District (416 593 0889). Streetcar
501, 510.* **Open** 10am-6pm Mon, Tue, Sat; 10am-
8pm Wed-Fri; noon-6pm Sun. **Credit** AmEx, MC, V.
Map p276 C7.
Amidst the cool chaos of Queen West, the Silver
Snail is an appropriately hip comic book emporium:
the decor is modern and sales people are suitably
trendy. The Silver Snaeil stocks small-press reads,
graphic novels, Japanese toys and some back issues
for collectors.

Used books

The quaint thoroughfare of Harbord Street
has developed into something of a used-book
haven, most likely owing to its cheap rent and
proximity to the University of Toronto. The
highest concentration of booksellers runs west
from Spadina Avenue. Specialists in texts and
academic (Atticus Books, 84 Harbord Street,
416 922 6045; Caversham Booksellers, 98
Harbord Street, 416 944 0962), rare editions
(East West Books, 128 Harbord Street, 416 923
1725) and women's studies (Toronto Women's
Bookstore, 73 Harbord Street, 416 922 8744) can
be sniffed out among the stores selling new
books. Walk north on Spadina Avenue for one
or two more golden browsing opportunities.

Fashion

See also p150 **Kensington Market**.

Boutiques

Awkso

*675 Queen Street W, at Bathurst Street,
Entertainment District (416 703 6660). Streetcar
501, 511.* **Open** noon-6pm Mon, Tue; noon-7pm
Wed-Fri; 11am-7pm Sat; noon-5pm Sun. **Credit**
AmEx, DC, MC, V. **Map** p276 C7.
The content is alternative but wholly wearable. And
what's more, the sassy designs are largely local –
the ideal souvenir. Toronto designers Wolves and
Mabel, as well as Paris-based Canadian Tara
Jarman, feature in the repertoire. Styles veer from
the playfully ironic to conservative woolies.

Hoax Couture Boutique

*114 Cumberland Street, at Yonge Street, Yorkville
(416 929 4629/www.hoaxcouture.com). Bus
6/subway Bay.* **Open** 11am-6pm Mon-Wed; 11am-
9pm Thur, Fri; 10.30am-6pm Sat; noon-5pm Sun.
Credit AmEx, DC, V. **Map** p281 F4.
Men risk looking fey just by crossing the threshold. Hoax's approach is decidedly far-out: shirts
have cutouts and ribbon flourishes; favoured fabrics are silk and leather; skirts are de rigueur.
Women's styles are a bit rigid in form (taffeta is
employed to theatrical effect), but lively in colour
and pattern.

Kitsch Boutique

*325 Lonsdale Road, at Spadina Road, Forest Hill
(416 481 6712). Subway St Clair West.* **Open**
10am-9pm Mon-Fri; 10am-6pm Sat; noon-5pm Sun.
Credit AmEx, MC, V.
It's worth a jog to this neighbourhood shop for
eleventh-hour cocktail attire by mostly US labels. A
few minutes here will net all you require for an
impromptu soirée, including wrap, shoes and faux
jewels. A 'bargain' basement houses designer duds
at a significant discount.

Eat, Drink, Shop

Planning a
trip to New York?

(A) For a day.

(B) For a weekend.

(C) For a week.

For answers to what to do for all of the above, log on to timeoutny.com and click on ITINERARIES. You'll find ready-made travel plans that take the guesswork out of Gotham.

Lilith

541 Queen Street W, at Augusta Avenue,
Entertainment District (416 504 5353). Streetcar
501, 511. **Open** noon-7pm Mon; 11am-7pm Tue,
Wed; 11am-8pm Thur-Sat; noon-6pm Sun.
Credit AmEx, MC, V. **Map** p276 C7.
Few local designs make it out of the country, but the
funkiest find their way to Lilith, the authority on
urban frocks and accessories to set them off. If basic
black is your thing, you might want to miss out this
lively den of mauve, turquoise, orange and all tones
in between. The Yummy Mummy line of maternity
wear defies the norm.

Mendocino

294 Queen Street W, at Peter Street, Entertainment
District (416 593 1011). Streetcar 501, 510.
Open 10am-7pm Mon-Wed, Sat; 10am-9pm Thur,
Fri; 10am-6pm Sun. **Credit** AmEx, MC, V.
Map p277 D7.
There are designer creations from the catwalks of
Milan and then there is Mendocino, house of knock-
offs. Of-the-moment fashions can be spotted in here
within a week of their appearance in *Vogue* (think
corsets, peasant tops and dirty denim). Still, there's
the odd garment from notable names like William B
and Diane von Furstenberg.

Risqué

404 Bloor Street W, at Brunswick Avenue, the
Annex (416 960 3325). Subway Bathurst or
Spadina. **Open** 11am-7pm Mon-Fri; 11am-6pm Sat;
noon-6pm Sun. **Credit** AmEx, MC, V. **Map** p280 C4.
The Annex is better known for patchouli and batik
than the cleavage-enhancing blouses and hip-hugging
trousers that are Risqué's stock in trade, so the boutique has become a welcome addition. Prices are a
bit higher than one would expect for the quality, but
the clothes are so pretty, you're unlikely to resist.

San Remo

23 St Thomas Street, at Sultan Street, University
(416 920 3195). Bus 6/subway Bay or Museum.
Open 10am-6pm Mon-Wed, Sat; 10am-8pm Thur, Fri;
1-5pm Sun. **Credit** AmEx, MC, V. **Map** p280 E4.
When there's a new trend on the catwalk, you'll see
it here writ large. When ruffles and lace were the
thing, no item went without; ditto for ribbon trim on
hipster flares and asphyxiating corsets.

Wenches & Rogues

610 Queen Street W, at Bathurst Street,
Entertainment District (416 536 2172). Streetcar
501, 511. **Open** 11am-7pm Mon-Wed; 11am-8pm
Thur, Fri; 10am-6pm Sat; noon-6pm Sun. **Credit** MC,
V. **Map** p276 C7.
A Newfoundland import, Wenches made its first
appearance in Little Italy, working its way via
Yorkville to Queen West hawking Canada's finest
and most talked about designs for men and women.
It's still the city's foremost supporter of home-grown
labels – Mimi Bizjak, Dubuc, Olena Zylak and
Misura among them – though it's added other for-
eigners to the collection in recent years.

Hoax Couture Boutique. *See p143.*

Children

Chocky's

327 Spadina Avenue, at St Andrews Street,
Chinatown (416 977 1831). Streetcar 510, 505, 506.
Open 9am-5pm Mon-Fri; 10am-5pm Sat; 11am-5pm
Sun. **Credit** AmEx, MC, V. **Map** p276 C6.
Chocky's is an insitution for kids stocking up on
underwear, T-shirts, pyjamas and rain gear. Once a
wholesaler, Chocky's has maintained its cut-rate
pricing system, and now offers trendier clothing too.
Branch: 2584 Yonge Street, North Side (416 483 8227).

Jacadi

87 Avenue Road, at Elgin Avenue, Yorkville
(416 923 1717). Bus 6/subway Bay or Museum.
Open 10am-6pm Mon-Wed, Fri, Sat; 10am-7pm
Thur. **Credit** AmEx, MC, V. **Map** p280 E3.
Shopping here is remarkably simple, with everything
mixing and matching. If that spells relief for you, soak
it up – because the prices will make your heart pal-
pitate. This is more Sunday best than sandpit gear.

Misdemeanours

322-½ Queen Street W, at Spadina Avenue,
Entertainment District (416 351 8758). Streetcar 501,
510. **Open** 10am-7pm Mon-Wed, Sat; 10am-9pm
Thur, Fri; 11am-6pm Sun. **Credit** AmEx, MC, V.
Map p276 C7.

Eat, Drink, Shop

Gimme Bloor

Known to locals as the mink mile, the strip of Bloor Street West from Yonge Street to Avenue Road (subway stops Bay or Museum) has become even more luxurious in the last decade, as an inflated market and significant immigration from Hong Kong have propelled demand for upmarket indulgences. Designers are expanding and renovating, so there's little you can't find on Bloor Street that you'd otherwise seek at emporia of luxury like Harvey Nichols or Saks Fifth Avenue.

Chanel Boutique

131 Bloor Street W, at Queens Park (416 925 2577). **Open** 10am-6pm Mon-Sat.

Gucci

130 Bloor Street W, at Queens Park (416 963 5127). **Open** 10am-7pm Mon-Fri; 10am-6pm Sat; noon-5pm Sun.

Hermès

131 Bloor Street W, at Queens Park (416 968 8626). **Open** 10am-6pm Mon-Sat; noon-5pm Sun.

Louis Vuitton

110 Bloor Street W, at St Thomas Street (416 944 8725). **Open** 10am-6pm Mon-Wed, Sat; 10am-8pm Thur, Fri.

Max Mara

131 Bloor Street W, at Queens Park (416 928 1884). **Open** 10am-6pm Mon-Wed, Fri, Sat; 10am-7pm Thur.

Plaza Escada

110 Bloor Street W, at St Thomas Street (416 964 2265). **Open** 10am-6pm Mon-Sat; noon-5pm Sun.

Prada

131 Bloor Street W, at Queens Park (416 513 0400). **Open** 10am-6pm Mon-Wed, Fri, Sat; 10am-7pm Thur.

Tiffany & Co

85 Bloor Street W, at St Thomas Street (416 921 3900). **Open** 10am-6pm Mon-Sat.

Walter Steiger

38 Avenue Road, at Prince Arthur Avenue (416 515 7666). **Open** 10am-6pm Mon-Sat; noon-5pm Sun.

The spawn of theatrical Fashion Crimes across the street, Misdemeanours has all its mother's histrionics and none of the puerile fabrics so common in children's boutiques. Expect to see a feather boa paired with these outfits, trimmed with marabou, faux fur or other amusing synthetics. Saturated colours turn their noses up at run-of-the-mill pastels.

General

Club Monaco

157 Bloor Street W, at Avenue Road, University (416 591 8837). Subway Bay or Museum. **Open** 10am-8pm Mon-Wed, Sat; 10am-9pm Thur, Fri; 11am-7pm Sun. **Credit** AmEx, MC, V. **Map** p280 E4.
CM was one of the first fashion chains to recognise the elegance of Japanese lines and simple, patternless colour. What then made it an international star was its outstanding pricing. Designs are wearable and affordable: buy a pair of jeans and a ribbed turtleneck and you'll have them for life – and neither will you suffer embarrassing out-of-fashion stigma. Sale items are ubiquitous, as are locations – in every mall and shopping district in the city. **Branches**: throughout the city.

Over the Rainbow

101 Yorkville Avenue, at Hazelton Avenue, Yorkville (416 967 7448). Subway Bay or Museum. **Open** 10am-6pm Mon-Wed, Sat; 10am-8pm Thur, Fri; noon-5pm Sun. **Credit** AmEx, MC, V. **Map** p280 E4.
Push past bratty teens with their mums in tow to discover the latest in denim (the fact that the kids actually want to shop here proves the jeans are up-to-date at least). Styles are stacked with precision from floor to ceiling. Also available are fun and sporty T-shirts, sweats and accessories from Paul Frank, Triple Five Soul, Miss Sixty and Diesel.

Roots

Toronto Eaton Centre, 220 Yonge Street, at Dundas Street (416 593 9640/www.roots.ca). Streetcar 505/subway Dundas. **Open** 10am-9pm Mon-Fri; 10am-7pm Sat; 11am-6pm Sun. **Credit** AmEx, DC, MC, V. **Map** p277/p278 F6.
You won't meet anyone in the city who doesn't remember a favourite Roots possession, whether it's a sweatshirt, a fleece or a pair of clunky boots. The Canadian icon started cobbling reverse-heel shoes in the '70s, then branched out into leisurewear – to the joy of outdoors people everywhere. Today, styles are spicier, but you can still find the basics. Roots dresses the Canadian and US Olympic teams, which irritatingly allows them to promote their red and white gear at every turn.
Branches: throughout the city.

Menswear

Boomer

309 Queen Street W, at John Street, Entertainment District (416 598 0013). Streetcar 501/subway Osgoode. **Open** 10.30am-7pm Mon-Wed, Fri;

10.30am-8pm Thur; 10.30am-6pm Sat; 1-5pm Sun.
Credit AmEx, DC, MC, V. **Map** p277 D7.
Boutique in size only, Boomer quietly offers the best
of what you'd find at the finer department stores.
You'll uncover a share of Boss and trendy Ted Baker
(stock is chosen with the Queen Street crowd in
mind); original output is restricted to Boomer's own
French-cut dress shirts.

Great Stuff
*870 Queen Street W, at Massey Street, West End
(416 533 7680). Streetcar 501.* **Open** 11am-7pm
Tue, Wed, Fri; 11am-8pm Thur; 10am-6pm Sat;
noon-5pm Sun. **Credit** DC, MC, V.
The offerings look like a vintage clothes store but
the retro feel comes from the choice of designer
samples and line ends from Kenneth Cole,
Marzotto, Mexx, Tony Bahama and others. Fitted
shirts, silk sweaters and Swedish suits are part of
a constantly changing inventory at Great Stuff
priced well below the norm.

Harry Rosen
*82 Bloor Street W, at Bellair Street, Yorkville
(416 972 0556/www.harryrosen.com). Subway Bloor-
Yonge.* **Open** 10am-7pm Mon-Wed; 10am-9pm Thur,
Fri; 10am-6pm Sat; noon-5pm Sun. **Credit** AmEx,
DC, MC, V. **Map** p280 E4.
Some might snub Harry for being on the conserv-
ative side of the spectrum, yet there was a time
when he was the only game in town for respectable
styling – one brogue-shod step from Savile Row.
Service is also top-notch.
Branches: throughout the city.

Street/clubwear

Châteauworks
*340 Queen Street W, at Spadina Avenue,
Entertainment District (416 971 9314). Streetcar
501, 510.* **Open** 10am-9pm Mon-Fri; 9.30am-8pm
Sat; noon-6pm Sun. **Credit** AmEx, MC, V.
Map p276 C7.
The Montreal-based trend machine Le Château
claimed this as its Toronto flagship years ago.
Anything the clothier offers can be had here: men's
polyester club shirts with collars that could cut
bread, floor-length faux-suede coats with faux-fur
trim, wear-once-and-blister shoes and neon fishnets,
kid's hipsters… If you don't mind the patchy quality, you can get away with buying a season's
wardrobe for under $300.

Delphic
*706 Queen Street W, at Manning Avenue,
West End (416 603 3334). Streetcar 501, 511.*
Open 11am-7pm Mon-Wed, Sat; 11am-8pm Thur,
Fri; noon-6pm Sun. **Credit** AmEx, DC, MC, V.
Map p276 B7.
If your idea of lounging around involves a cocktail,
a French cigarette and your mildly scuffed
Campers up on a Lucite coffee table, happening
across Delphic might make your day. The look is
Euroboy, the atmosphere hip without trying too

hard. Furnishings and homewear mingle with
clothing, with a little for-sale art thrown in. The fit
at Delphic is slim and crisp – no slouches allowed.

Vintage/second-hand

Courage My Love
*14 Kensington Avenue, at Dundas Street W,
Kensington Market (416 979 1992). Streetcar 505,
510.* **Open** 11.30am-6pm Mon-Fri; 11am-6pm Sat;
2-5pm Sun. **Credit** AmEx, MC, V. **Map** p276 C6.
Kensington Market was never about fashion until
Courage came along, decades ago, and made
Kensington Market a centre for vintage chic. It still
the cheapest ticket in town for generations-old
eveningwear, leather, crafts, exotic costume jewellery and retailored threads from charity shop
sweats and T-shirts.

Magder Furs
*202 Spadina Avenue, at Phoebe Street,
Chinatown (416 504 6077). Streetcar 501, 505, 510.*
Open 9.30am-6pm Mon-Wed, Sat; 9.30am-7pm Thur,
Fri; 11am-5pm Sun. **Credit** AmEx, DC, MC, V.
Map p277 D7.
Rockers and grannies alike appreciate Magder's
vintage skins, recrafted with a edgy, modern feel or
20th-century aura. It's not very PC, but at least buy-
ing second-hand keeps down demand for new.

Courage My Love: racks of retro.

Londoners take when they go out.

Time Out
London

EVERY WEEK

Preloved

613 Queen Street W, at Bathurst Street,
Entertainment District (416 504 8704). Streetcar
501, 511. **Open** 10am-7pm Mon, Tue, Sat;
10am-8pm Wed-Fri; noon-6pm Sun. **Credit** AmEx,
MC, V. **Map** p276 C7.
Though Preloved's prices have shot up in recent
years, they're still reasonable considering the high
fashionability factor. Perhaps this is down to the raw
materials used: the signature collection is creative-
ly cut and pasted from clothing discards. The T-
shirts are the most fun, bearing now-extinct logos
and embellishments from defunct nighties.

Print Vintage

834A College Street, at Ossington Avenue,
West End (416 504 2267). Bus 63/streetcar 506.
Open noon-4pm Thur; noon-7pm Fri; 1-6pm Sat.
No credit cards.
A closet-sized outpost for ancient Dior, Pucci and
Versace. Some of the best labels are to be found in
handbags, shawls, muffs, sunglasses and dresses.
The cute A-line is the thing at Print Vintage.

Value Village

2119 Danforth Avenue, at Woodbine Avenue, East
Side (416 698 0621). Bus 92/subway Woodbine. **Open**
9am-9pm Mon-Sat; 10am-6pm Sun. **Credit** MC, V.
Some prefer Goodwill, Canada's Oxfam, for its
boot-sale goodies (you'll find locations all over the
city), but more honed stock can be found at this
bargain extravaganza of leather trenches, well-
worn denim, retro (and often scuffed) shoes and
dandy *chapeaux.*

Fashion accessories

Hats

Lilliput Hats

462 College Street, at Bathurst Street, Harbord
(416 536 5933). Streetcar 506, 511. **Open** 10am-
6pm Mon-Fri; 11am-6pm Sat; by appointment Sun.
Credit MC, V. **Map** p276/p280 C5.
Milliners are an endangered breed in Toronto, but
the lust for vintage has brought hats back. Lilliput
makes the classic cloche and the mohair fedora
redux, along with other hip headwear.

Jewellery

Experimental Jewellery

588 Markham Street, at Bloor Street, West End
(416 538 3313). Streetcar 511/subway Bathurst.
Open 11am-6pm Wed-Fri; 10am-6pm Sat; noon-5pm
Sun. **Credit** AmEx, MC, V.
Even if organic shapes and unusual settings aren't
your thing, this light-saturated boutique may still
be worth a peek for its wearable art. The jewellery
reflects the quirky location – Mirvish Village – noted
for its offbeat restaurants, wacky clothiers and dark,
dusty collectibles outlets.

Global bazaar

The name refers to the origin of the
stock, though the mall is almost as
vast as the ocean itself. Pacific Mall is
America's largest shopping centre selling
Asian goods, a sea-blue monstrosity on
Toronto's northern fringes, in an area that
otherwise sees only overheated cars and
industrial parks. It could take a day to
explore this mini-village of toys, togs
and treats. On the ground floor, wares
are housed in a streetscape of 150
fishbowl-like, glass-enclosed kiosks
containing shelf upon shelf of candy-
coloured mobile phones, sneakers, T-
shirts, school supplies and piles of Hello
Kitty products. As payback for the effort
you've made to get here, goods are offered
at discount prices, and the excitement is
almost palpable. A second level is devoted
to Far Eastern edibles – pastries, dim sum,
noodles – and counters of sticky candy,
which ravenous consumers attack with
gluttonous glee. The climax, at least
for the Asian expats who congregate at
weekends, is the mock-up of Hong Kong's
Temple Street Night Market, offering more
of what Westerners would identify as junk.
Blasphemy, the die-hards say.

Pacific Mall

4300 Steeles Avenue E, at Kennedy Road,
Markham (905 470 8785/www.pacificmall
toronto.com). Bus 43, 53. **Open** noon-8pm
Mon-Thur, Sun; noon-9pm Fri, Sat. **Getting**
there Take the Don Valley Parkway north to
provincial route 404 north, take exit 22 at
RR-8, Woodbine Avenue/Steeles Avenue,
turn right on to Steeles Avenue.

Mark Lash Designs

938 Eglinton Avenue W, at Rostrevor Road,
West End (416 256 5229/www.marklash.com).
Bus 32/subway Eglinton West. **Open** 10am-5pm Tue-
Sat. **Credit** AmEx, MC, V.
On the edge of exclusive Forest Hill, Mark Lash is a
true neighbourhood boutique, catering to the tastes
of the upper classes – who see Mark as a master.
Diamonds and platinum are the focus here: no one
would dare ask for yellow gold in this day and age.

Mink

550 College Street, at Euclid Avenue, Little Italy (416
929 9214). Streetcar 506, 511. **Open** 11am-7pm
Tue-Fri; 11am-6pm Sat. **Credit** MC, V. **Map** p276 B5.
The lust for gangster style has brought to vogue
chunky, diamond-encrusted jewels. Because most

Eat, Drink, Shop

Kensington Market

The hybrid nature of Kensington means that, depending on your viewpoint, it could offer a little of everything or a hell of a lot of nothing. Only the open-minded need embark on a journey through this cluster of narrow, shop-lined streets, past the bike mechanics, racks of rags and kiosks of cheap luggage to the area's real gems. Begin with brunch at the **Bellevue Diner** (61 Bellevue Avenue, 416 597 6912) or at the lovely **La Palette** (*see p112*), then find your way to the top of Augusta Avenue for a logical entry point. Knitwear specialist **Fresh Baked Goods** (274 Augusta Avenue, 416 966 0123) is a punchy start with its shocking-hued angora. Styles are funky by nature, sleeves fashionably long and hems flared. The oddest corner shop in town is **Casa Acoreana** (235 Augusta Avenue, 416 593 9717), a general store stocked with innumerable glass jars of candy, nuts, grains and baking goods on one side, the other side, called **Louie's Coffee Stop** (pictured), is an open coffee hut, inviting shoppers to pull up a stool for a quick espresso. A holdover from the market's days as a Jewish textile centre, **Tom's Place** (190 Baldwin Street, 416 596 0297) is a famed no-frills discount fashion outlet. Women's clothing – from Donna Karan and Anne Klein collections past – holds court on the ground floor, but the upstairs men's department is the real draw, offering suits by Zegna, Boss and Armani at prices lower than the department stores' summer sales. If you haven't already enjoyed the pungent odour the market exudes, you'll find an interesting mix of aromas at neighbouring **My Market Bakery** (172 Baldwin Street, 416 593 6772), **European Quality Meats & Sausages** (176 Baldwin Street, 416 596 8691) and **Cheese Magic** (182 Baldwin Street, 416 593 9531).

Down Kensington proper is where the sartorial grit begins, with a string of vintage boutiques almost indistinguishable from one another for all the racks of denim and leather on the sidewalk (**Asylum**, 42 Kensington Avenue, 416 595 7199, is the prime offender). One of the best is **Exile** (20 Kensington Avenue, 416 596 0827), a forum for outlandish retro and brand new fetish wear, with its own press for iron-on T-shirts. The legendary **Courage My Love** (*see p147*) is at the end of the row.

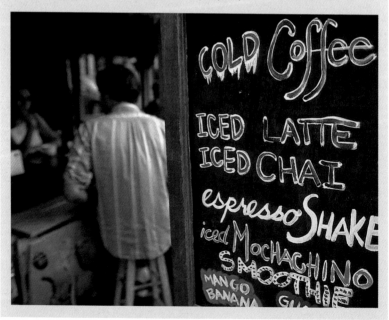

of us can't afford the real thing, Mink brings us faux flash in the form of rhinestone rings and monogram necklaces on a grand scale. Daintier pieces can be found too.

Leather

Augustina
138 Cumberland Street, at Avenue Road, orkville (416 922 4248). Bus 6/subway Bay.
Open 10am-6pm Mon-Wed, Sat; 10am-7pm Thur, Fri; noon-5pm Sun. **Credit** AmEx, MC, V. **Map** p280 E4.
Most designer handbags have a knock-off twin somewhere in the world. But few pirates could mimic Augustina's imports – gasp-worthy bags that are rarely spotted elsewhere from the most under-rated designers worldwide. There's also costume jewellery, belts and underwear.

Lingerie

Avec Plaisir
124 Cumberland Street, at York Lane, Yorkville (416 922 7702). Bus 6/subway Bay. **Open** 10am-6pm Mon-Wed, Sat; 10am-7pm Thur, Fri.
Credit AmEx, DC, MC, V. **Map** p280 E4.
The stuff that lines the trousseaus of the rich and famous can be tracked down to this house of delicate European understyle. Espousing the philosophy that luxury begins at the core, Avec Plaisir dedicates itself to intricate laces and precious silks – if it can be tumble-dried, it won't be found here. Invest in the finest fishnets on the planet.

Body Body Wear
500 Church Street, at Alexander Street, Church & Wellesley (416 929 2639/www.bodybodywear.com). Streetcar 506/subway Wellesley. **Open** 11am-7pm Mon-Thur; 11am-8pm Fri; 10am-8pm Sat; 11am-6pm Sun. **Credit** AmEx, MC, V. **Map** p281 F5.
The alluring mannequins in the window look out on to locals who convene on the front steps when weather permits. It's in the heart of Church & Wellesley – burly Boystown – yet (nearly) every-one can wear the skin-hugging tanks, tees and thongs on display at Body Body Wear. You won't find droopy boxer shorts inside, but instead an encyclopaedic set of tighty whities (also available in a range of other colours).

Secrets From Your Sister...
476 Bloor Street W, at Bathurst Street, the Annex (416 538 1234). Streetcar 511/subway Bathurst.
Open 11am-7pm Mon-Sat; noon-6pm Sun.
Credit AmEx, MC, V. **Map** p280 C4.
Neighbourhood gals with a thirst for the exotic shun department store underwear in favour of this shoe-box's goodies. Its styles, fabrics and outlandish colours are unlike anything your mother ever recommended, though the attitude is appropriately no-nonsense: pyjamas come in flannel and bras can accommodate a voluptuous D cup.

Bags of style at **Augustina**.

Shoes

B2
399 Queen Street W, at Spadina Avenue, Entertainment District (416 595 9281). Streetcar 501, 510. **Open** 10am-7pm Mon-Wed, Sat, Sun; 10am-9pm Thur, Fri. **Credit** AmEx, MC, V. **Map** p276 C7.
You might have come across this boutique's parent company, Browns, at one of the swisher department stores. But B2 is more fun – if only for gawking at eccentric four-inchers you know you can't afford. It carries the international – Costume National, Miu Miu, Hush Puppy, Camper – along with its own Euro-looking brands at more reasonable prices.

Davids
66 Bloor Street W, at Yonge Street, Yorkville (416 920 1000). Subway Bloor-Yonge. **Open** 9am-6pm Mon-Wed, Sat; 9am-8pm Thur, Fri; noon-5pm Sun. **Credit** AmEx, MC, V. **Map** p281 F4.
If the currency exchange is working in your favour, you'll find Davids more rewarding than the average foot fetishist shoe shops. The spotlight is on high Italian designs in buttery leathers and four-inch stilettos. Loafers befit boardroom dwellers and the more active ladies-who-lunch.

Eat, Drink, Shop

Get Out Side

437 Queen Street W, at Spadina Avenue,
Entertainment District (416 593 5598). Streetcar
501, 510. **Open** 11am-8pm Mon-Fri; 10am-8pm Sat;
noon-7pm Sun. **Credit** AmEx, MC, V. **Map** p276 C7.
Carnaby Street and deepest Tokyo have nothing on
this selection of disco boots, wedges and sparkly
sneakers. Prices are right for pubescent ravers who
ambush it on Saturdays but adults like the youthful
designs (many imported from Japan) too for the same
level of comfort that allows the kids to dance all night.

John Fluevog Shoes

242 Queen Street W, at John Street, Entertainment
District (416 581 1420/www.fluevog.com). Streetcar
501/subway Osgoode. **Open** 11am-7pm Mon-Wed,
Sat; 11am-8pm Thur, Fri; noon-6pm Sun. **Credit**
AmEx, MC, V. **Map** p277 D7.
The Vancouver-based cobbler has become something
of an icon with his chunky, western-style creations.
They may look severe in this era of dainty, slender
footwear, but Fluevogs are surprisingly comfortable.

Jumas Shoe & Clothing Boutique

655 College Street, at Grace Street, Little Italy
(416 530 0207). Streetcar 506, 511. **Open** noon-
7pm Mon-Sat; noon-6pm Sun. **Credit** AmEx, MC, V.
Map p276 B5.
Considering the number of fashionistas walking
about, Little Italy used to be noticeably short on clothing – until Jumas moved in. The New York and LA
imports are some of the most innovative Toronto has
seen. And, while the men's shoes are your basic clod-
hoppers, the women's are really something to dance
about: cutouts, ostrich, python and patent leather are
not alien to Jumas boots, and heels inspire vertigo.

Fashion services

Dove Cleaners

1560 Yonge Street, at Heath Street, Forest Hill (416
413 7900/www.dovecleaners.com). Subway St Clair.
Open 7am-6pm Mon-Fri. **Credit** AmEx, MC, V.
With home and office pick-up and delivery (an easy
net-based system is in place), Dove's high-end service is ideal for the moneyed customer.
Branch: 40 King Street W, Financial District
(416 869 3000).

Splish Splash

590 College Street, at Clinton Street, Little Italy (416
532 6499). Streetcar 506. **Open** 8am-10pm Mon-Fri;
9am-8pm Sat, Sun. **No credit cards**. **Map** p276 B5.
This launderette/convenience store is a friendly
meeting place for young urban types.

Shoe repair

Nick's Shoes & Custom Footwear

169 Dupont Street, at St George Street, the Annex
(416 924 5930/www.nickscustomboots.com). Subway
Dupont. **Open** 8am-6.30pm Mon-Fri; 9am-6pm Sat.
No credit cards. **Map** p280 D2.

A quick walk from Dupont station, Nick is known for
his reliability and magical skill: you're unlikely to lose
a heel twice if he's in your little black book. His aux-
iliary talent is for imitation – footwear can be crafted
in the likeness of coveted $500 Stuart Weitzmans.

Novelty Shoe Rebuilders

119 Yonge Street, at Adelaide Street, St Lawrence
(416 364 8878). Streetcar 501, 504/subway King or
Queen. **Open** 8.30am-5.30pm Mon-Fri; 8.30am-5pm
Sat. **Credit** MC, V. **Map** p277/p278 F7.
Shoe styles come and go but this institution has been
taking care of wayward soles for 70 years at the
same location in the Financial District. Repairs are
done while you wait or slip into one of the funky
wooden booths for a quick polish.

Tuxedo rental

Tuxedo Royale

Toronto Eaton Centre, 220 Yonge Street, at Dundas
Street, Dundas Square (416 591 7200/www.tuxedo
royale.com). Streetcar 505/subway Dundas. **Open**
10am-9pm Mon-Fri; 9.30am-7pm Sat; noon-6pm Sun.
Credit AmEx, MC, V. **Map** p277/p278 F6.
That there are 17 locations across the city is a good
indicator that prom-goers from Scarborough to
Mississauga frequent Royale. If you're stepping out
and need to rent a penguin suit, this is the place. The
assumption here is that you're not looking for up-to-
the-minute Boss looks. But you won't be risking a
polyester rash either. Rental prices from $99.

Electronics

Bay Bloor Radio

55 Bloor Street W, at Bay Street, University (416 967
1122/www.baybloorradio.com). Bus 6/subway Bay.
Open 10am-7pm Mon-Wed; 10am-9pm Thur, Fri;
10am-6pm Sat. **Credit** AmEx, MC, V. **Map** p280 E4.
One of those shops that puts out ads on rock radio
that are so annoying you can't help but remember
them, Bay Bloor is probably the best-known purveyor of audio and visual equipment in the city.
You'll rarely hit a weekend without a sale.

Brack Electronics

44 Wellington Street E, at Church Street, St
Lawrence (416 366 3636). Streetcar 504/subway
King. **Open** 10am-7pm Mon-Fri; 10am-6pm Sat.
Credit AmEx, MC, V. **Map** p277/p278 F8.
Housed in a heritage building in St Lawrence, Brack
is no budget shop but it draws in customers with
good sales throughout the year. Those for whom
sound quality is sacred will appreciate Brack's attention to the latest models and elite foreign brands.

Future Shop

355 Yonge Street, at Elm Street, Dundas Square
(416 971 5377/www.futureshop.ca). Bus 6/streetcar
505, 506/subway College or Dundas. **Open** 10am-
9pm Mon-Fri; 10am-6pm Sat, Sun. **Credit** AmEx,
MC, V. **Map** p277/p278 F6.

First time renters are Future's desired customer base, and B-rated models its stock in trade. If you just need a functional VCR or a boom box for the beach, Future is the place. But, as with any budget shop, ask about any extra costs before laying down plastic.
Branch: 2529 Yonge Street, North Side (416 489 4726).

PCUsed & CPUsed

488 Dupont Street, at Bathurst Street, the Annex (416 537 2001/533 2001/www.pcused.com/www.cpused. com). Subway Bathurst or Dupont. **Open** 9am-6pm Mon-Wed; 9am-8pm Thur, Fri; 10am-6pm Sat; noon-5pm Sun. **Credit** AmEx, MC, V. **Map** p280 C2.

CPUsed is a Mac specialist while, down the hall, PCUsed is for IBM users. There's new stuff to be had, but the best deals are on used goods. Notebooks go for a song. Technicians speak in layman's terms, and can do repairs.

Food & drink

Bakeries

Harbord Bakery

115 Harbord Street, at Major Street, Harbord (416 922 5767). Bus 94/streetcar 510. **Open** 8am-7pm Mon-Thur; 8am-6pm Fri, Sat; 8am-4pm Sun. **Credit** V. **Map** p280 C4.

This Jewish bakery has been here since the middle of the last century, when Eastern Europeans began to immigrate into the neighbourhood. You can still find some of the city's freshest challah, rye bread and bagels (with some huge, twisted variations), and a selection of pastries, strudels and tarts.

Confectioners

Nostalgia is a sweet thing, and throughout the past decade, several testaments to sweet times past have cropped up around town. Today, you can get Wacky Taffy, Rain-blo gumballs, frozen Lolas and pink popcorn along with trolleys of Pez and any other treat Willy Wonka is spitting out. The first **Sugar Mountain** opened in clubland (320 Richmond Street W, Entertainment District, 416 204 9544), but soon expanded into the Yonge Street, St Clair and Queen West areas. The copycat **Suckers** (450 Danforth Avenue, East Side, 416 405 8946) tends to be patronised by Greektown yuppies. **Laura Secord** (3401 Dufferin Street, Yorkdale Shopping Dale, 416 789 5697) has become a local institution as makers of bite-sized candy bars. The **Nutty Chocolatier** (2179 Queen Street E, the Beach, 416 698 5548) taunts chocolate and fudge nuts in the Beach.

LCBO: buying alcohol

Whereas in most other parts of the world – indeed in other provinces of Canada – picking up a bottle en route to a party is a simple matter of ducking into the corner store, here it means making a special trip to a government-run outlet with limited operating hours. At least stocks aren't too bad when you get there. The 600 **LCBO** (Liquor Control Board of Ontario) stores across the province offer a full range of spirits, along with wines from every producing nation, plus some domestic and imported beers. The larger outlets boast a vintage room, too.

The LCBO is a hangover from the demise of Prohibition. It emerged in 1927 as a means of regulating the safe consumption of booze; the fact that it's a substantial source of state income makes a moot point of whether such nannying is still necessary. The LCBO is a cash cow, with profits of about $900 million a year. It likes to boast that it is the largest single purchaser of wine and spirits in the world. This buying muscle should be reflected in the prices, but the government can't resist taxing booze to the hilt, and with a monopoly in place there's nothing to stop it. The only competition comes from the **Wine Rack** (560 Queen Street W, Entertainment District, 416 504 3647; and other locations), a small chain licensed to sell burgeoning Ontario wines; you'll find them at various outposts in Loblaws and Dominion stores, and on the street.

If beer is your fancy, hit the simply named **Beer Store**, home to brews from Brussels to BC. Like the LCBO, it was also started post-Prohibition, albeit by a consortium of private brewers (Labatt, Molson and Sleeman own it today) working in conjunction with provincial regulators. The practice here is akin to picking up your medication from the pharmacy: place your order with the agent at the counter, who relays it by microphone to a colleague out back; your case will come out on a conveyor belt (no prescription needed). In some outlets, you're free to roam the chilly warehouse and lug your purchases to the checkout.

While hours vary for both the Beer Store and the LCBO, most close at 8pm, with the odd straggler open until 10 or 11pm (stores open at 10am Monday to Saturday and noon on Sundays). There are several around town, including 87 Front Street (368 0521), 337 Spadina (597 0145) and 545 Yonge Street (923 8498).

Eat, Drink, Shop

St Lawrence Market

'Market' used to mean cheap eats. But vendors at St Lawrence Market have cottoned on to the going rates (and food zeitgeist), and now prices match the mainstream. Even so, nothing could mar its atmosphere: it's as rich with local products as it must have been 150 years ago, when lakes were full of fish and farm vegetables grew a short stroll from these iron gates, plus international and deli items.

It can be hard for an outsider to evaluate the mass of similar stalls, so tour the premises before making your choices. On the ground floor, sample from the wheels and wedges of international cheeses from **Alex Farms** or **Chris Cheesemonger**, a specialist in Quebecois provisions who, incidentally, dishes out fantastic Middle Eastern dips. Seafood is everywhere; if you're here for a quick bite, pick up a slice or two of freshly smoked salmon or Arctic char at **Seafront**, then queue up for a bagel at **St Urbain**, one of the few bakers in the city offering the Montreal style: dense, chewy and salty. **Churrasco St Clair**, a satellite of the famed uptown take-out churrasquería, makes a killer chicken sandwich on a kaiser roll.

The traditional fast food offering here is a peameal sandwich – thick slices of cornmeal-crusted bacon on a doughy kaiser, best smothered in mustard. You can't miss the queues at **Carousel** bakery along the west wall, though they are served at other stands, too.

Fruit and veg are downstairs, and some stalls present exotic picks. But the top-notch nosh can be found in the furthest reaches of the basement, where barrels of bulk food – nuts, chocolate, confectionery – beg to be bagged at **Domino's**.

Across the street, in a building characterised by the cheerful mural painted along its side, a farmer's market takes place on Saturdays (until 5pm), hosted by a motley crew of overalled and aproned visitors from small towns in the area. On Sundays the space is taken over by a weekly antiques fair.

St Lawrence Market

93 Front Street E, at Jarvis Street, St Lawrence (416 392 7219). Subway Union Station. **Open** *8am-6pm Tue-Thur; 8am-7pm Fri; 5am-5pm Sat.* **Map** *p277/278 F8.*

Gourmet grocers

Bruno's Fine Foods

*1560 Yonge Street, at St Clair Avenue, Forest Hill
(416 923 1311/www.brunosfinefoods.com). Subway
St Clair.* **Open** 8am-9pm daily. **Credit** AmEx, MC, V.
Map p281 F1.

Once just a glorified butcher, Bruno's has grown into
a neighbourhood standby for fine foods, late-night
pick-up and home delivery. Expect to pay more for
your cornflakes here than at the local Loblaws but
the veg will probably look healthier.
Branches: throughout the city.

Pusateri's

*1539 Avenue Road, at Lawrence Avenue, North Side
(416 785 9100/www.pusateris.com). Bus 52/subway
Lawrence.* **Open** 8am-8pm Mon-Fri; 8am-9pm Sat;
9am-9pm Sun. **Credit** AmEx, MC, V.

Uptown matrons send their nannies here for groceries or stop by for gourmet takeaway. A pricey
one-stop for folk who value time over money.

Groceries

Dominion

*89 Gould Street, at Church Street, Dundas Square
(416 862 7171). Streetcar 505/subway Dundas.*
Open 24 hours daily. **Credit** AmEx, MC, V.
Map p277/p278 F6.

Dominion hasn't kept up with rival Loblaw's: you'll
queue for a cashier pretty much any time of the day
or night, and be baffled by the shelf organisation. But
its flexible hours (several outlets are open 24 hours)
make it a favourite among students, shift workers and
partiers who crave late-night butterscotch ripple.
Branches: throughout the city.

Loblaws

*650 Dupont Street, at Christie Street, West End
(416 588 4481/www.loblaws.ca). Bus 26/subway
Christie or Dupont.* **Open** 8am-10pm Mon-Sat;
9am-8pm Sun. **Credit** AmEx, MC, V.

It's been around for 85 years and is now in the hands
of Holt Renfrew owner George Weston Ltd but until
recently Loblaws was your average grocer. Less than
a decade ago, the stores began a clean-up process and
expanded into veritable mini-malls: well lit, with
in-house cafés, wine depots, sushi chefs and dry-
cleaners. The in-house brand – President's Choice –
undercuts name brands on many products. Service is
swift and, despite its gilded appearance, Loblaws
manages to keep prices competitive.
Branches: throughout the city.

Health food

The Big Carrot

*348 Danforth Avenue, at Hampton Avenue, East
Side (416 466 2129). Subway Chester.* **Open** 9.30am-
7pm Mon-Wed; 9.30am-9pm Thur, Fri; 9am-8pm Sat;
11am-6pm Sun. **Credit** AmEx, MC, V.

Harbord Bakery. *See 153.*

Social consciousness and groceries didn't mix back
when this worker-owned cooperative opened 20
years ago. Today, even though prices are what
you'd expect in a niche market, it's near impossible
to squeeze in here – especially at weekends. Come
to the biggest natural food store in the city for free-
range chicken and eggs, sustainably harvested fish,
supplements, additive-free meat and wholewheat
just about everything you can imagine.

Noah's Natural Foods

*322 Bloor Street W, at Spadina Avenue, the Annex
(416 968 7930). Streetcar 510/subway Spadina.*
Open 10am-8pm Mon-Wed; 10am-9pm Thur, Fri;
10am-7pm Sat; 11.30am-6pm Sun. **Credit** AmEx,
MC, V. **Map** p280 C4.

A favourite pitstop for Annex dwellers on their way
home from yoga, Noah's has been around these parts
for decades. The growing obsession with organic
and all-natural foods has no doubt brought about its
recent growth, and now you can find your sprouts,
carob chips and oatmeal cleansers at several handy
points in the city. There's also a vegan café for those
who can't wait to tuck in.
Branches: 667 Yonge Street, the Annex
(416 969 0220); 2395 Yonge Street, North Side
(416 488 0904).

Had it with boring old A4? Let **The Japanese Paper Place** guide you. *See p157.*

Whole Foods Market

87 Avenue Road, Hazelton Lanes, Yorkville (416 944 0500/www.wholefoods.com/toronto). Bus 6/subway Bay. **Open** 9am-10pm Mon-Fri; 8am-9pm Sat; 9am-8pm Sun. **Credit** AmEx, MC, V. **Map** p280 E4.

This Texas-based healthy-foods conglomerate has more than 130 stores in North America. This is the only Canadian outpost, and it's big, offering a rainbow of produce, striking seafood displays, a sushi bar, preservative-free baked goods and irresistible gourmet deli.

Speciality

Greg's Ice Cream

200 Bloor Street W, at Avenue Road, the Annex (416 961 4734). Subway Museum or St George. **Open** noon-11pm daily. **No credit cards**. **Map** p280 E4.

This old standby at the northern border of U of T is a zoo come summertime, packing in pints of the chunkiest, most authentic flavours this side of Martha Stewart's kitchen.

Kristapsons

1095 Queen Street E, at Winnifred Avenue, East End (416 466 5152). Bus 72/streetcar 501. **Open** 9am-2pm Mon; 9am-4pm Tue-Thur; 9am-noon Sat. **Credit** V.

In this age of diversification, you'll be hard-pressed to find another Kristapsons. The skinny, sterile space offers nothing but BC salmon. Order ahead and your catch will be smoked on the premises.

Sanko Trading Co

730 Queen Street W, at Niagara Street, West End (416 703 4550). Streetcar 501, 511. **Open** 10am-7pm Mon, Wed-Sun. **Credit** MC, V.

It keeps a veritable library of Japanese mags and suspicious-looking videotapes, but you're more likely to leave Sanko with a jar of miso soup, vacuum-packed kim chee or a wad of seaweed. Kids are kept enthralled by confectionery, cookies and drinks imported from the Far East.

Flowers

The strip of sidewalk along Avenue Road just south of Davenport Road is known for its buckets of fresh and flamboyant cut flowers. Also doubling as mini grocers, the Chinese shops that line the west side of the street teem with inexpensive stems and bunches.

Gifts & specialist

Art Interiors

446 Spadina Road, at Thelma Avenue, Forest Hill (416 488 3157). Subway St Clair West. **Open** 10am-5pm Mon-Sat. **Credit** MC, V.

It takes an experienced eye to spot quality artwork, but the owners of Art Interiors make it their business to scout around. They celebrate the finest new and unknown artists in town, then push their pieces at this loft boutique in Forest Hill Village. Prices are remarkably low for originals this appealing – and you may end up with a treasure on your hands.

F Correnti Cigars Ltd

606 King Street W, at Portland Street,
Entertainment District (416 504 4108).
Open 7.30am-8pm Mon-Sat. **Credit** AmEx, MC, V.
Map p276 C8.
Stepping inside this cigar factory is akin to walking
on to the set of *Carmen*. Hand-rolled cigars are fash-
ioned from Cuban raw leaf (Correnti is the exclusive
importer for Canada). Clientele includes an array of
movie stars, politicians and sport heroes and some
request their own custom-made cigars. The casual
puffer can walk in and pick up a box or a single cigar.

Ice

163 Cumberland Street, at Avenue Road,
Yorkville (416 964 6751). Bus 6/subway Bay.
Open 10am-7pm Mon-Sat; 11.30am-6pm Sun.
Credit AmEx, MC, V. **Map** p280 E4.
Try not to knock over a display of flashy lip gloss,
fun jewellery, slogan tees or kitschy throw cushions:
this emporium of the overpriced is crammed with the
latest in trendy 'stuff' beloved by Yorkville types. For
gift-giving, Ice is over-equipped with decorative high-
balls, party games and humour handbooks.

The Japanese Paper Place

887 Queen Street W, at Walnut Avenue, West End
(416 703 0089/www.japanesepaperplace.com).
Streetcar 501. **Open** 10am-6pm Mon-Wed, Sat;
10am-8pm Thur, Fri. **Credit** AmEx, MC, V.
Map p276 B7.
For those who take paper seriously, there are origami
classes, invitation workshops and lectures at weekends. But this is really just a pretty place to wander
around, feeling paper samples, filling Christmas
stockings and getting whiffs of inspiration.

Health & beauty

Beauty shops

PIR Cosmetics

25 Bellair Street, at Cumberland Avenue,
Yorkville (416 513 1603/www.pircosmetics.com).
Bus 6/subway Bay. **Open** 11am-6pm Mon; 10.30am-
6pm Tue; 10.30am-6.30pm Wed; 10.30am-7pm Thur,
Fri; 10am-6pm Sat; 1-5pm Sun. **Credit** AmEx, MC,
V. **Map** p280 E4.
More BelAir, California, than Bellair, Yorkville, this
boutique is a hub for talked-about and hard-to-find
Japanese, Italian and French brands. Also on offer
are make-up application lessons, eyebrow shaping,
nail 'adventures' (during which customers enjoy an
essential oil treatment with an exotic theme) and the
requisite coif.
Branch: 71 Front Street E, St Lawrence
(416 513 1603).

Rubies Beauty Bar

715 Queen Street W, at Bathurst Street,
Entertainment District (416 601 6789). Streetcar
501, 511. **Open** noon-6pm Mon-Sat; noon-5pm Sun.
Credit AmEx, DC, MC, V. **Map** p276 C7.

Rubies Beauty Bar is *the* place for one-stop beauty
shopping. A cheeky underwear boutique introduces
a bar where fragrance shots are served and make-
up samples can be devoured like free peanuts. A
back-room massage is the perfect antidote to the
post-shopping hangover.

Complementary medicine

One of the more enlightened cities you'll visit,
Toronto is a haven of safe alternative medicine.
The **Toronto Healing Arts Centre** (717
Bloor Street W, West End, 416 806 7378) enlists
licensed homeopaths, hypnotists and other
holistic professionals for a range of therapies.
Or you can regroup, rebalance and rejuvenate
at the **Centre for Life Essentials** (755
Avenue Road, Suite 111, Forest Hill, 416 932
9028, www.life-essentials.com), specialising
in stress-, pain- and fatigue-management
through a variety of therapies, including
reflexology, aromatherapy, chakra balancing
and meditation.

Find you way to the **Yellow Brick Road**
on Dupont Street (*see p159*) to cleanse your
system, and for aromatherapy, reflexology,
ear candling and other therapies.

The best Shops for...

... bargains

Art Interiors (*see p156*) for original
artwork, without the zeros; **Chocky's** (*see
p145*) for popular childrenswear at a snip;
Châteauworks (*see p147*) for the stylish
but skint fashionista; **PCUsed & CPUsed**
(*see p153*) for used (but not abused)
computers and accessories.

... browsing

Caban (*see p159*), the place for dream-
home hankering; **Courage My Love** (*see
p147*), Kensington's haven of vintage
fashion; **Ice** (*see p157*) for trendy trinkets;
Nicholas Hoare (*see p143*) for bookish
browsing; **Sanko Trading Co** (*see p156*) for
a miscellany of Japanese goodies.

... souvenirs

Book City (*see p142*) to pick up a
Canadian literary classic-to-be; **Butterfield
8** (*see p141*) for the cream of vintage
kitsch collectibles; **Harbourfront Antique
Market** (*see p141*) to sift through the
rubble of times past; **Roots** (*see p146*) for
All-Canadian leisurewear; **Sugar Mountain**
(*see p153*) because retro sweets rule, OK.

Eat, Drink, Shop

Hairdressers

Coupe Bizarre

704 Queen Street W, at Manning Avenue, West End (416 504 0783). Streetcar 501, 511. **Open** 10am-8pm Mon-Fri; 10am-6pm Sat; noon-6pm Sun. **Credit** MC, V. **Map** p276 B7.

Your best bet for a Mohawk, shag, manufactured dreads or David Beckham hair-do. Stylists are as wild looking as the glossy vinyl furnishings – indeed recognising them from one week to the next is quite a challenge. Coupe is so common a haunt for the urban contingent, the name is almost cliché.

First Choice Haircutters

1730 Bloor Street W, at Indian Grove, West End (416 766 7222). Subway Keele. **Open** 9am-9pm Mon-Fri; 8am-6pm Sat; 11am-5pm Sun. **No credit cards**.

The $11 snip may not be ideal for some of the girls who brush through town but to others it means a competent cut that leaves you enough cash for a night out to celebrate it afterwards. And the first-come, first-served policy at First Choice will suit those on the fly.

Branches: throughout the city.

John Steinberg & Associates

585 King Street W, at Portland Street, Entertainment District (416 506 0268/www.john steinberghair.com). Streetcar 501, 504, 510. **Open** 10am-8pm Mon; 10am-6pm Wed; 10am-9pm Thur, Fri; 10am-4pm Sun. **Credit** V. **Map** p276 C8.

A fixture on King Street W before the area became trendy – the cutters at this salon, including its namesake, have a loyal following among actors and media types. While you're getting a new, stylish look, check out the art exhibits that change every six weeks – almost as frequently as hair trends.

Opticians

Josephson Opticians

60 Bloor Street W, at Bay Street, Yorkville (416 964 7070/www.josephsonopt.ca). Bus 6/subway Bay. **Open** 9.30am-6pm Mon-Wed, Fri, Sat; 9.30am-8pm Thur. **Credit** AmEx, MC, V. **Map** p280 E4.

This family operation has been around since the '30s. Never a stodgy mom-and-pop outfit, it stocks the cream of Lacroix, Chanel, Mikli and Prada, along with the more common specs from LA Eyeworks et al. Turnaround on glasses is about between two and four days, but emergency lenses are available in less than a day.

Branches: throughout the city.

Pharmacies

Shoppers Drug Mart (360 Bloor Street W, the Annex, 416 961 2121; and other locations) is the most prevalent of Toronto's pharmacies,

PIR Cosmetics. *See p157.*

with many locations open until midnight. You can also find them in malls and underground paths. **PharmaPlus** (concourse level, 55 Bloor Street W, University, 416 923 0570; and other locations), formerly Boots, is slightly less ubiquitous, and hours are less flexible. The same can be said for **IDA** (66 Avenue Road, the Annex, 416 922 5555; and other locations). More more information *see p256*.

Spas

Estée Lauder

Holt Renfrew, 50 Bloor Street W, at Bay Street, Yorkville (416 960 2909). Bus 6/subway Bay or Bloor-Yonge. **Open** 10am-6pm Mon-Wed, Sat; 10am-8pm Thur, Fri; noon-6pm Sun. **Credit** AmEx, MC, V. **Map** p280 E4.

Comfort incarnate, right down to the highest quality terry robe you'll be idling in. Staff run a tight ship, getting their hands to the problem area in record time, though they can be strict about your usual 'routine'. Treatments run from single manicures via facials and make-up to elaborate whole-body day packages. If the condescending attitude doesn't get the better of you, you should emerge feeling as light as a powder puff.

Mira Linder Spa in the City

*108 Avenue Road, at Tranby Avenue, the Annex
(416 961 6900). Bus 6/subway Bay.* **Open** 9am-7pm
Tue-Thur; 9am-5pm Fri, Sat. **Credit** AmEx, MC, V.
Map p280 E3.

The destination for the uptown girl who craves cel-
lulite reduction and body 'polish' (application of fake
tan), along with the usual seaweed wraps and deep-
tissue massages. Manicures at Mira Linder include
a sojourn in a vibrating chair.

Yellow Brick Road

*258 Dupont Street, at Spadina Avenue, the Annex
(416 926 1101). Subway Dupont.* **Open** 10am-7pm
Mon-Sat. **Credit** MC, V. **Map** p280 D2.

A modest juice bar occupies the storefront;
upstairs, earthy Annex folk flush your system – be
it your ears or your colon – to a calming soundtrack
of Enya or Sarah McLachlan. There's a neurother-
apist in residence.

Tattooing & piercing

The obvious direction to head is west along
Queen Street (the stretch from University
Avenue to Dufferin Street will net you a dozen
shops), though with the current demand you
can find studios pretty much anywhere. **Way
Cool Tattoos** (679 Queen Street W, West
End, 416 603 0145, www.waycool-queen.com;
5203 Yonge Street, North Side, 416 226 4142,
www.waycool-uptown.com) has garnered
word of mouth praise as much for the beauty
of its artists as for the beauty of its art. It gets
points, though, for enterprise – one location
is north of the Highway 401, where bored teens
roam in herds. **Stainless Studios Body Art**
(609 Queen Street W, Entertainment District,
416 504 1433), is run by a team of funky
women. If you want your body art to carry
spiritual or religious significance, try **Urban
Primitive Body Design** (216 Carlton Street,
Cabbagetown, 416 966 9155), specialising
in symbols that mark spiritual growth and
personal transformation.

Home

L'Atelier

*1224 Yonge Street, at Alcorn Avenue, Casa Loma
(416 966 0200). Subway St Clair or Summerhill.*
Open 10am-6pm Mon-Sat. **Credit** AmEx, MC, V.
Map p281 F2.

Part bachelor pad, part French château, part garden
of delights, L'Atelier has plenty of gems in store,
whether gilded Italian birdcages, Lucite loungers or
thick marble mantels. Dramatic dressers and lighting set the scene, and lesser knick-knacks are on
hand for the weak of budget. Explore this stretch of
Yonge – between Rosedale and Summerhill subway
stations – for a slew of French antiques and contemporary look-alikes.

Du Verre

*188 Strachan Avenue, at Queen Street W, West End
(416 593 4784). Subway 501.* **Open** 11am-6pm Tue-
Sat; 1-5pm Sun. **Credit** AmEx, MC, V. **Map** p276 A7.

Du Verre, in an old coach house off an unremarkable
stretch of Queen West, stocks tribal imports characterised by clean, contemporary lines. Japanese
screens shield tables from Tibet and accessories
from India. Brand new metal hardware from home-
grown artists offers some mod sheen.

LA Design

*788 King Street W, at Tecumseth Street, West End
(416 363 4470). Subway 504.* **Open** 10.30am-6pm
Mon-Fri; 10.30am-5pm Sat; noon-5pm Sun. **Credit**
AmEx, MC, V. **Map** p276 B8.

The initials stand for Living Arts, but the feel is
luxury. Los Angeles furnishings jive with a
Californian home-on-the-ocean aesthetic. Colour
reigns supreme, with alternative materials such as
Mongolian lambswool (throws, cushions) and ham-
mered silk (upholstery). Most of the content is
designed by the owner.

Roots Home

*195 Avenue Road, at Davenport Road, Yorkville
(416 927 8585/www.roots.ca). Bus 6/subway Bay or
Museum.* **Open** 10am-6pm Mon-Wed, Fri, Sat; 10am-
8pm Thur; noon-5pm Sun. **Credit** AmEx, DC, MC, V.
Map p280 E3.

The home decor arm of this Canadian über-retailer
expands on the down-home theme. Blankets are
modelled after the woolly Roots camping sock. The
twist is in the colour: leather appears in turquoise,
fuchsia and yellow. And some items are flashier than
their rustic counterparts.

UpCountry

*214 King Street E, at Frederick Street, St Lawrence
(416 777 1700/www.upcountry.ca). Streetcar 504.*
Open 10am-6pm Mon-Wed, Sat; 10am-7pm Thur, Fri;
noon-5pm Sun. **Credit** AmEx, MC, V. **Map** p278 G8.

The anchor of the King Street East design corridor,
UpCountry moved in before the avant-garde Italian
set moved in. But it's still a big draw with sleek
Canadian designs in sumptuous fabrics and rich
woods. There's a smattering of vintage downstairs.

Accessories

Caban

*262-268 Queen Street W, at Beverley Street,
Entertainment District (416 596 0386/
www.caban.ca). Streetcar 501/subway Osgoode.* **Open**
10am-7pm Mon-Wed, Sat; 10am-8pm Thur, Fri; 11am-
6pm Sun. **Credit** AmEx, DC, MC, V. **Map** p276 D7.

There's something for everyone here – from the
home-office freelancer to the hostess-with-the-
mostest. Caban doesn't sell the stuff of heirlooms,
but rather functional, of-the-moment homeware in
the likes of chrome and suede. An extension of the
Club Monaco brand, it also hawks clothing that's
priced more reasonably than that of its parent.

Beautiful breakables at **William Ashley**.

Teatro Verde

55 Avenue Road, Hazelton Lanes, Yorkville (416 966 2227/www.teatroverde.com). Bus 6/subway Bay. **Open** 10am-6pm Mon-Sat; noon-5pm Sun. **Credit** AmEx, MC, V. **Map** p280 E3.

Once a fashionable florist, this dealer has expanded to embrace the cocooning craze. Everything 'home' is represented, from sari-covered cushions and throws to kitchen gear and cookbooks to boudoir accessories. And, naturally, you'll still find the odd vase, planter and recliner for the garden.

William Ashley

55 Bloor Street W, at Bay Street, University (416 964 2900/www.williamashley.com). Bus 6/subway Bay. **Open** 10am-6pm Mon-Wed, Sat; 10am-7.30pm Thur, Fri. **Credit** AmEx, MC, V. **Map** p280 E4.

Local hero Greg Davis

Music geeks were never a particularly appealing breed, but after *High Fidelity* hit cinemas a few years back, they at least earned our understanding. Not that those in the know didn't have the good sense to appreciate Greg Davis right from his humble start. A former accountant who has spent the best part of the past 20 years under his headphones, Davis decided to put his knack for numbers to more gratifying use: stocking his sterile white boutique – **Soundscape** (*see p161*; pictured), in hipper-than-thou Little Italy – with a digestible and tasteful agglomeration of alt.country, guitar rock, electronic beats, jazz and world music, arranged in aficionado-friendly categories, such as the *MOJO* Top 100. Though selective, Davis' retailing technique has nonetheless drawn in a broad fan base, with most customers scanning the weekly staff picks (far beyond the league of those at the local video store) or chatting with the lads at the counter before buying. Unassuming as he seems, Davis is cast as a celebrity when out and about. Spotting him at Lee's Palace or the Horseshoe Tavern is quite moving for some – it reconfirms your sentiment that you're at the hottest gig in town.

Honourable mentions

Rotate This (*see p161*); **Play de Record** (*see p161*).

Previous contenders

Eastern Bloc Records, formerly of Adelaide Street W, was the destination for rave anthems previously unheard. Now it occupies an annexed corner of **Sunrise Records** (336 Yonge Street, Dundas Square).

Don't be intimidated by the *haute* look: everyone in Toronto visits Ashley's, whether for gifts or entertaining necessities – and it's the first name on anyone's lips for wedding lists (stressed-out couples wander the maze of china in their dozens). Staff are notably well informed at Ashley's and seem to enjoy discussing the finer points of pie cutters and crystal goblets.

Music

HMV
333 Yonge Street, at Gould Street, Dundas Square (416 586 9668/www.hmv.ca). Streetcar 505/subway Dundas. **Open** 10am-10pm Mon-Thur; 10am-midnight Fri; 9am-midnight Sat; 11am-6pm Sun. **Credit** AmEx, MC, V. **Map** p277/p278 F6.
HMV can afford to offer the best deals, and its flagship at Yonge and Dundas carries everything you could possibly want in the way of audio entertainment. Staff are generous with listening posts. **Branches**: throughout the city.

Play de Record
357A Yonge Street, at Dundas Street, Dundas Square (416 586 0380). Streetcar 505/subway Dundas. **Open** noon-8pm Mon-Sat; noon-6pm Sun. **Credit** MC, V. **Map** p277/p278 F6.
Squeeze past shelves of video tack to the vinyl haven at the back, where local DJs and hooded club kids come to spin rare editions and the latest releases from the worlds of hip hop, rap, Latin, electronica and jazz. Prices aren't cheap, but you're paying for records unavailable anywhere else in town. Turntables are on hand for those who like to know exactly what they're buying. Tickets to small-venue shows are available at the counter.

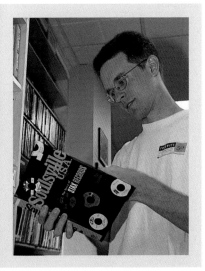

Rotate This
620 Queen Street W, at Markham Street, Entertainment District (416 504 8447). Streetcar 501. **Open** 11am-7pm Mon-Thur, Sat; 11am-8pm Fri; noon-6pm Sun. **Credit** MC, V. **Map** p276 B7.
Aesthetics are of little interest, the staff have attitude, vinyl is in abundance and we dare you to find the latest Geri Halliwell. Obscure comic books at the front offer reading to those awaiting the headphones at the counter for a record preview. The CD selection is good, divided into a few digestible bins. Prices tend to be higher than average, even for used stuff.

Sam the Record Man
347 Yonge Street, at Gould Street, Dundas Square (416 646 2775). **Open** 9am-10pm Mon-Thur; 9am-midnight Fri, Sat; 11am-7pm Sun. **Credit** AmEx, MC, V. **Map** p277/p278 F6.
The giant spinning neon platters above the legendary record (and video) store bask in the glow of better days – Sam went bust in 2002 and the national chain closed up shop. But the flagship store survived on a bail-out from Sam's sons, who now run the place. Known for the encyclopaedic staff, the high-quality classical and jazz sections and for promoting Canadian artists, Sam's keeps the competitors on their toes in this music-heavy block of Yonge Street, where prices are the lowest in the city.

Soundscapes
572 College Street, at Manning Avenue, Little Italy (416 537 1620). Streetcar 506, 511. **Open** 10.30am-11pm Mon-Thur, Sun; 10.30-1am Fri, Sat. **Credit** AmEx, MC, V. **Map** p276 B5.
The speciality here is not a particular genre, but rather 'good' music. A former accountant and passionate listener, Greg Davis (*see also* **Local hero** *p160*) started this Little Italy venture to promote new local talent, classic rock, electronica and international beats that aren't getting satisfactory recognition elsewhere. The sparse shop is about the size of a bistro restroom, but there's enough space at the entrance to post lists of employee favourites.

Second-hand

Second Spin
386 Bloor Street W, at Spadina Avenue, the Annex (416 961 7746). Streetcar 510/subway Spadina. **Open** 11am-11pm Mon-Fri; 10am-11pm Sat; 11am-9pm Sun. **Credit** MC, V. **Map** p280 C4.
If you're selling, you stand to make a decent sum at Second Spin: it offers as much as $7 for a well-kept CD. Then again, you're sure to spend your winnings on something from the remarkably extensive dance collection or a rock classic.

Photography

For developing holiday snaps on the quick and cheap, the best deals are at the supermarkets. But if you're fussy about the finer points, it's probably best to stick with the specialists, the most prominent of which are **Black's** (130 King Street W, Financial Disctrict, 416 363 5563; and other locations), **Henry's** (119 Church Street, St Lawrence, 416 868 0872) and **Japan Camera** (48 Front Street W, St Lawrence, 416 363 7476; and other locations). They can be pricey, but offer alternatives to the basic matt and gloss with border options and custom alterations (along with the machines that print zoom images of your pics). Professionals or aspiring photographers tend toward **West Camera** (514 Queen Street W, Entertainment District, 416 504 9432) and **Vistek** (496 Queen Street E, Moss Park, 416 365 1777), where you can also pick up new or used replacement equipment.

Sex shops

In the '60s, when Toronto was young, inexperienced and bursting with potential there was only one sex shop to satisfy its impulses. **Lovecraft** (27 Yorkville Avenue, Yorkville, 416 923 7331) was disconcertingly open-concept, with romantic rose-coloured walls and brazen dildo displays. Now the city has grown up, and it's easy to acquire a butt plug when required. The **Condom Shack** (729 Yonge Street, Rosedale, 416 966 4226; 231 Queen Street W, Entertainment Disctrict, 416 596 7515) is the McDonald's of pleasure and protection, with a bright, scrubbed feel; **Come As You Are** (701 Queen Street W, Entertainment District, 416 504 7934) is more modern in its sensibility, with 'get-to-know-yourself' manuals, oils and toys geared toward same-sex partners. Across the street, get your bondage gear and trampy undergarments at **Miss Behav'n** (650 Queen Street W, Entertainment District, 416 866 7979), featuring live window models at weekends.

Sport & outdoor

Mountain Equipment Co-op (MEC)
400 King Street W, at Peter Street, Entertainment District (416 340 2667/www.mec.ca). Streetcar 504, 510/subway St Andrew. **Open** 10am-7pm Mon-Wed; 10am-9pm Thur, Fri; 9am-6pm Sat; 11am-5pm Sun. **Credit** MC, V. **Map** p276 D8.
This Canadian company is world-renowned for the quality and scope of its outdoor gear. A co-op (so you have to pay a nominal joining fee), it has motivated staff and a family feel. Prices on outdoor equipment (tents, sleeping bags, even canoes) and hiking wear (fleeces galore) go down to bargain levels off-season.

Sporting Life
2665 Yonge Street, at Lytton Boulevard, North Side (416 485 1611). Subway Eglinton or Lawrence. **Open** 9.30am-9pm Mon-Fri; 9am-6pm Sat; 10am-6pm Sun. **Credit** AmEx, MC, V.

Top-of-the-range kit for a broad range of sports, and also a necessary destination for trendy sportswear. Range Rovers line up on weekends to enter the small parking lot and inside it's madness – shoes, jackets and bathing suits piled everywhere. Great sales.

Travellers' needs

Luggage

Evex
465 Eglinton Avenue W, at Avenue Road, Forest Hill (416 966 1422). Bus 32/subway Eglinton. **Open** 9am-6pm Mon-Wed, Fri; 9am-8pm Thur; 9am-5pm Sat. **Credit** AmEx, MC, V.
If your luggage need only last until the next destination, it would suffice to wander the streets of Chinatown and Kensington. But for bags to last, Evex is the source. Prices are as low as wholesale and, though it won't win points for decor, all the notable names are represented.

Photocopying

With all the expat neighbourhoods in the city, it's likely you'll come across the odd corner store with a mini-office in back for phoning, faxing and copying. Going this route might prove more adventuresome than necessary though, so you could opt for **Kinkos**, which has branches in the Annex (459 Bloor Street W, Harbord, 416 928 0110), the Financial District and Yonge Street (at several junctions).

Shipping

It's convenient and relatively cheap. Shippers will pick up your purchases, pack them, crate them and haul them overseas – right to your door – quicker than you'd think. **A Alliance Services International** (416 469 5252) and **Worldwide Shipping & Forwarding** (905 673 9244) are both tried and tested.

Travel agents

Flight Centre
55 Yonge Street, at King Street, St Lawrence (416 304 6170/www.flightcentre.ca). Streetcar 504/subway King. **Open** 9am-6pm Mon-Fri; 10am-4pm Sat. **Credit** AmEx, MC, V. **Map** p277/p278 F8.
There's a reason the Flight Centre is expanding to Starbucks proportions. It will undercut any price on any flight you've been quoted – with a smile and a free lollipop. As close to a bucket shop as you'll find in Canada, Flight Centre always finds a way, even if you have to go through Atlanta on your route. Both international and internal flights are available.
Branches: throughout the city.

Arts & Entertainment

Features

Festivals & Events

From highbrow to low-key, Toronto's cultural calendar keeps visitors entertained come rain or shine (or ice).

Well-heeled Torontonians traditionally hunker down in the winter and flee the city to a cottage in the summer. And it's still true that Toronto on a summer long weekend can feel like a ghost town. Established arts groups like the opera, ballet and symphony orchestra programme their subscription series from September to June, leaving locals gasping for culture in the summer. But innovative arts programmers have worked hard to fill the gap and now Toronto's hot, humid summer boasts some of the funkiest festivals of the year. Almost every weekend in summer, it seems, something is happening. Many events are aimed at niche markets, but others are big enough to affect the whole city. So if you're coming into town for **Pride**, **Caribana** (now officially known as **Toronto International Carnival** but rarely referred to as such) or any of the other big festivals, you'll want to plan well ahead, as hotels invariably fill up. Check out the listings in the monthly city magazine *Toronto Life*, or the alternative weeklies *eye* and *NOW*, or, online, consult www.toronto.com.

Spring

Canada Blooms
Metro Toronto Convention Centre, 222 Bremner Boulevard, at Simcoe Street, Entertainment District (416 447 8655/www.canadablooms.com). Subway St Andrew or Union. **Map** p277 D8. **Date** Mar.
A massive flower and garden show running from Wednesday to Sunday, this floral wonderland attracts hordes of homeowners desperate for a first glimpse of spring. The main attractions are the display gardens and prize-winning floral arrangements.

Good Friday Parade
College Street/Little Italy. **Map** p276 B6. **Date** Good Friday.
A re-enactment of the procession of Jesus Christ bearing his cross to crucifixion in a sombre Good Friday spectacle that is broadcast to many countries. Roman centurions, candle-bearing worshippers, the odd donkey even, take to the streets of Little Italy.

Cinéfranco
Various venues (416 928 6595/ www.cinefranco.com). **Date** weekend in Apr.
Cinéfranco offers an eclectic mix of arty and mainstream French-language flicks. All of the films have English subtitles.

iMAGES Festival of Independent Film & Video
Various venues (416 971 8405/ www.imagesfestival.com). **Date** 1 week in Apr.
The flicks at iMAGES tend to be terribly imaginative, of the sort that are long on art and short on story. But fun. Sometimes.

NHL Hockey Play-offs
Date mid Apr-mid June.
Though mostly taken in on the telly (tickets to hockey games are near impossible to score except through scalpers), this rite of spring whips a good portion of the city into a frenzy. Bars and cafés do brisk business as long as local team the Maple Leafs are still in the running. They haven't won the Stanley Cup since 1967, a drought that's sated each year by plenty of draught beer and consternation.

Hot Docs Canadian International Documentary Festival
Royal Cinema, 608 College Street, at Clinton Street, Little Italy (416 203 2155/www.hotdocs.ca). Streetcar 506. **Map** p276 B6. **Date** 10 days late Apr-early May.

Cabbagetown Festival. *See p168.*

North America's largest documentary festival features more than 100 films from around the world, from classics to the best of the current scene. Workshops and masterclasses are available but not all are open to the public.

Sprockets

Downtown/midtown cinemas (416 967 7371/ www.e.bell.ca/filmfest. **Date** 10 days late April-early May.

The fragmentation of film festival themes and audiences knows no bounds in Toronto. Most fall under the long shadow cast by the biggest of them all, the Toronto International Film Festival, the same group that is responsible for unspooling this niche fest for children aged 4-14 with international titles and animation workshops for budding cineastes. *See chapter* **Film** for cinemas.

CONTACT

Various locations (416 539 9595/ www.contactphoto.com). **Date** May.

A month-long festival of Canadian and international photography exhibited in galleries, bars and restaurants across the city. Photographers discuss their craft in workshops and seminars.

Inside Out Toronto Lesbian & Gay Film & Video Festival

Various venues (416 977 6847/www.insideout.on.ca). **Date** 10 days in May.

Canada's largest gay and lesbian film festival and a magnet for arty gays.

Toronto Jewish Film Festival

Bloor Cinema, 506 Bloor Street W, at Bathurst Street, the Annex (416 324 9121/www.tjff.com). **Map** p280 C4. **Date** 1 week in May.

The largest festival of its kind in North America outside San Francisco, this event features Jewish-themed films, shorts and documentaries from all over the world.

Victoria Day Weekend

Throughout the city. **Date** 24 May long weekend.

Victoria Day weekend is the unofficial launch of summer. Gardeners get busy, cottages are opened up and fireworks are displayed. All in honour of a dead queen whose birthday the British don't even recognise. It is widely known as the 'May Two-Four' weekend, as in a 24-box of beer (the largest you can buy), though it was traditionally named thus for the queen's actual birthday. Queen Victoria probably wouldn't be amused. Check local papers for events.

Doors Open Toronto

Various locations (416 338 3888/ www.doorsopen.org). **Date** weekend in late May.

This two-day celebration lets you tour 100-odd sites of architectural or historical interest, many of them normally closed to the public. There is no formal tour. Participating landmarks simply hang out a welcoming blue banner. Watch local papers for a map. And, best of all, it's free.

Summer

North by Northeast Music & Film Festival

Various locations (416 863 6963/www.nxne.com). **Date** early June.

The sounds of independent music, the kind unfettered by those big record label contract obligations, tear up the downtown core during this popular three-day event. Tens of thousands of music fans prowl dozens of clubs, catching the hot talent from Canada, the US and around the world. You can bet the musicians treat the whole thing as an audition for the ears of all those record company executives who trawl the festival in search of the next big sound.

Rhythms of the World

Harbourfront Centre, 235 Queens Quay Boulevard W, Waterfront (416 973 3000/www.harbourfront. on.ca/rhythms). Streetcar 509, 510. **Map** p277/ p278 E9. **Date** June-Sept.

This summer-long series of weekend festivals spotlights different cultures through food, dance, art, film and, most importantly, music. The (mainly free) concerts are surprising, intriguing, offbeat and of an amazingly high quality, often featuring internationally known stars, while the open-air, lakeside venue makes this one of the best places in town to hear music on a summer's evening. The noise of passing cruise ships and tour boats can be annoying, but then again it's also part of its charm. Start with the JVC Jazz Festival in June and dance your way through to autumn.

BuskerFest

Various locations (416 964 9095/ www.torontobuskerfest.com). **Date** June.

Living statues and other street performers – jugglers, mime acts, magicians, fire dancers, acrobats and so on – do their thing for the benefit of Epilepsy Toronto. Entertainingly bizarre.

Fashion Cares

Metro Toronto Convention Centre, 255 Front Street W, at Simcoe Street, Entertainment District (416 340 2437/www.fashioncares.com). Streetcar 504/subway St Andrew or Union. **Map** p277 D8. **Date** June.

Toronto fashionistas turn out in droves for this enormous AIDS fundraiser, an outrageous fashion show that doubles as an alternative society ball. The after-party goes on until very late.

Festival Caravan

Various locations (416 977 0466/ www.festivalcaravan.com). **Date** June.

Toronto's many cultures offer food and entertainment at pavilions – Tokyo, Waikiki, Manila and so on – throughout the city. For such a multi-culti event, though, it never quite manages to capture the spirit of the city, and feels like culture in a vacuum on display for gawking. The festival runs from Wednesday to Sunday.

Arts & Entertainment

Stand up and be counted at **Pride Week**.

Worldwide Short Film Festival

Various venues (416 445 1446 ext 815/www.
worldwideshortfilmfest.com). **Date** 1 week in June.
This festival features films so short you can cram
seven or eight of them into a single session. Expect
several hundred films from around 40 countries.

CHIN International Picnic

Exhibition Place, Lake Shore Boulevard W, between
Strachan Avenue & Dufferin Street, West End
(416 531 9991/www.chinradio.com). Bus 29/
GO Exhibition/streetcar 509, 511/subway Union.
Map p276 A9. **Date** late June-early July.
Best known for its his-and-hers bikini contests, this
massive event features entertainment from a raft
of Toronto communities – Chinese, Italian, South
Asian, Portuguese, Greek and more. There are head-
liners from Europe and Asia but the crowd's the real
show. About 250,000 people attend.

Pride Week

Various venues, Church & Wellesley (416 927 7433/
www.pridetoronto.com). **Date** late June.
Toronto's gay and lesbian community turns partying into an art with beer gardens, arts events, circuit
parties and parades. Not for the shy or the prudish.
Still, up to a million people flock to the parade, and
not just to see the nudists strut their stuff. *See also*
p190 **Proud & clear**.

The Queen's Plate

Woodbine Race Track, 555 Rexdale Boulevard,
at Highway 427, West End (416 675 7223/
www.woodbineentertainment.com). Bus 37A,
191. **Date** late June.
Three-year-old Canadian-bred thoroughbreds compete in one of the country's most famous horse races,
the first leg of the triple crown. It's the oldest continuously run horse race in North America, and
royalty – or their representatives, at least – are usually in attendance.

Toronto Downtown Jazz Festival

Various venues, Downtown (416 928 2033/
www.torontojazz.com). **Date** late June.
During this fest, hundreds of artists perform all
styles of jazz at dozens of clubs, theatres and outdoor stages throughout downtown.

Toronto International Dragon Boat Race Festival

Centre Island, Toronto Islands (416 595 1739/
www.dragonboats.com). Ferry terminal at Bay Street
& Queens Quay W (call 416 392 8193 for ferry
schedule). **Date** weekend in late June.
The colourful dragon boats are the centrepiece of
this Chinese festival – with food, games, music and
dance – attracting more than 100,000 people to the
verdant shores of the Toronto Islands.

Canada Day

Nathan Phillips Square
100 Queen Street W, at Bay Street, Downtown (416 338 0338/www.city.toronto.on.ca/special_events).
Streetcar 506/subway Queen. **Map** p277/p278 E7.

Mel Lastman Square
5100 Yonge Street, at Sheppard Avenue, North Side (416 338 0338/www.city.toronto.on.ca/special_events). Subway North York Centre.

York Quay Centre
235 Queens Quay W, Waterfront (416 973 3000/www.harbourfront.on.ca). Streetcar 509, 510.
Map p277/p278 E9.

Downsview Park
John Drury Drive, at Sheppard Avenue, North Side (416 952 2222/www.pdp.ca). Subway Downsview.
Date July 1 long weekend.

Torontonians celebrate Canada's birthday (1 July 1867) with a very Canadian mixture of deference and pride, usually by leaving town for the long weekend. Best bets for some fun-filled patriotic activity are Nathan Phillips Square, Mel Lastman Square, Harbourfront Centre and Downsview Park. Most of them feature top-drawer Canadian entertainers and night-time fireworks displays.

Toronto Fringe Theatre Festival

Various venues (416 966 1062/
www.fringetoronto.com). **Date** 12 days early July.

Here the trick is seeing the hit shows before they close. Venues are tiny and the grapevine quick, so getting in can be tricky, but with more than 100 troupes on hand, from both Canada and abroad, there's plenty of choice, and a very good chance of high quality. Some of Toronto's leading theatrical lights – including Sky Gilbert, Daniel Brooks and Daniel MacIvor – have passed this way before. The Annex home base for the festival has a beer tent where you can pick up the buzz on the hits and misses. This is not a juried festival – productions are selected by lottery to give certain quotas of local, national and international acts. You've been warned.

Beaches International Jazz Festival

Various locations, East Side (416 698 2152/
www.beachesjazz.com). **Date** 3rd weekend in July.

Musicians perform on street corners and parks close to the lake, beach and boardwalk.

Britpics

Bloor Cinema, 506 Bloor Street W, at Bathurst Street, the Annex (416 604 2506/www.toronto britpics.com). Streetcar 511/subway Bathurst.
Map p280 C4. **Date** 1 week in July.

Another boutique fest: the best of current British cinema comes to town.

Celebrate Toronto Street Festival

Various venues along Yonge Street (416 338 0338/www.city.toronto.on.ca/special_events).
Date weekend in July.

Toronto's main drag turns into a giant amusement park with different intersections (Dundas Street, Bloor Street, St Clair Avenue, Eglinton Avenue and

Lawrence Avenue) featuring different kinds of music – everything from world to baroque opera to the latest pop sensation. There are carnival rides for the kids and drinks for the adults.

Molson Indy

Exhibition Place, Lake Shore Boulevard W, between Strachan Avenue & Dufferin Street (416 872 4639/www.molsonindy.com). Bus 29/GO Exhibition/streetcar 509, 511/subway Union. **Map** p276 A9.
Date weekend in July.

Drivers burn rubber on the streets near Exhibition Place and the hoop-la surrounding the five key races (CART Atlantic, Skip Barber Dodge, CASCAR Super, Formula F-1600, and the big one, the FedEx Championship) is just as stoked. Lots of testosterone-driven music and street parties.

Toronto Outdoor Art Exhibition

Nathan Phillips Square, 100 Queen Street W, at Bay Street, Downtown (416 408 2754/www.torontoout doorart.org). Streetcar 501/subway Queen. **Map** p277/p278 E7. **Date** weekend in July.

Once dismissed as kitsch, the largest outdoor art exhibition in North America is now bargain central for interesting art, with more than 550 juried artists showing everything from painting to jewellery and ceramics. Artists range from established to students.

Fringe Festival of Independent Dance Artists

Various venues (416 410 4291/www.ffida.org).
Date July-Aug.

Short works by experienced and emerging choreographers with some site-specific works. A gamble, but usually worth it.

Tennis Masters Canada & the Rogers AT&T Cup

York University, 3111 Steeles Avenue W, North Side (416 665 9777/www.tenniscanada.com). Subway Downsview, then bus 106 or subway Keele, then bus 41. **Date** late July-early Aug.

The name changes to suit the event: one year it's the Canadian men's tennis championships, the next it's the women's. Lots of top-seeded play either way.

Toronto International Carnival (formerly Caribana)

Various venues (416 285 1609/www.toronto internationalcarnival.info). **Date** Simcoe Day long weekend, late July/early Aug.

North America's largest Caribbean festival attracts a million-plus tourists and sends what little remains of Toronto's stodgy Anglo past into a happy tailspin. Thousands of colourfully costumed revellers participate in events like the King and Queen of the Bands competition, usually at Lamport Stadium (1155 King Street W, West End) and the climactic parade that sees dozens of 'mas' (masquerade) bands floating west on Lake Shore Boulevard. A two-day cool-down cum arts festival follows the parade and takes place on Olympic Island, a short ferry ride across the harbour. You can't miss the parade (or the thumping car stereos on Yonge Street at night) but the many associated events are sometimes hard to find. Check the local weeklies for last-minute details.

Taste of the Danforth

Various locations along Danforth Avenue, East Side (416 469 5634/www.tasteofthedanforth.com). Subway Broadview, Chester, Jones or Pape. **Date** 1 week in early Aug.

Hundreds of thousands of people sample all kinds of food in a nominally Greek neighbourhood that actually houses all kinds of restaurants. Top entertainers perform on three stages. All in all, a big, bustling people-friendly event.

SummerWorks Theatre Festival

Various venues (416 410 1048/ www.summerworks.ca). **Date** 10 days Aug.

Somewhere between a fringe and a mainstream theatre festival, SummerWorks encourages new work with juried productions.

Toronto's Festival of Beer

Historic Fort York, 100 Garrison Road, West End (1 888 948 2337/www.thebeerstore.ca/festivals/festivals-toronto.html). Streetcar 511. **Date** weekend in Aug.

A chance to sample more than 150 beers, including the best of the local microbreweries – Amsterdam, Steamwhistle, Sleeman's et al – on the site of one of the bloodiest battles of the War of 1812.

Canadian National Exhibition

Lake Shore Boulevard W, between Strachan Avenue & Dufferin Street, Waterfront (416 263 3800/www.TheEx.com). Bus 29/GO Exhibition/ streetcar 509, 511/subway Union. **Map** p276 A9. **Date** 2 weeks mid Aug-early Sept.

A cross between an old-fashioned agricultural fair and a modern-day expo, the CNE or the Ex, as it's known locally, mixes sheep shearing and milking demonstrations with pop entertainment and theme days devoted to Toronto's various ethnic communities. Some folks come just for the sideshows, but the real thrill is the nostalgia. They just don't make 'em like this anymore. Stick around for the last three days of the fair on Labour Day Weekend when high-flying acrobats take to the skies for the Canadian International Air Show. It's a blue-sky wonder. Canada's own performing poodles of the sky, the Snowbirds aeronautic squad, is a perennial favourite.

Autumn

Cabbagetown Festival

Various locations near Carlton & Parliament Streets, Cabbagetown (416 921 0857/www.old cabbagetown.com). Streetcar 506. **Map** p278 G6. **Date** weekend in early Sept.

A tribute to a working-class neighbourhood turned affluent enclave, this fest offers corn roasts, street dances, pancake breakfasts, an arts and crafts fair, a parade and tours of some of the neighbourhood's unique bay 'n' gable houses.

Toronto International Film Festival

Various venues (416 967 7371/www.bell.ca/filmfest). **Date** 10 days early Sept.

The glam public event of the year, it features hundreds of films and just as many celebrities. Even work-obsessed Torontonians take time off for this one. The giddiness is pervasive. Celeb-spotting is all the rage as the city basks in the glow of the biggest media event of the year. Public screenings run through the day, starting at 9am, and go well past midnight at various venues. *See also p24* **The Toronto International Film Festival**.

Planet in Focus Toronto International Environmental Film & Video Festival

Innis College, 2 Sussex Avenue, at St George Street and Bloor Street W, University (416 531 1769/ www.planetinfocus.org). Subway Museum or St George. **Map** p280 D4. **Date** 1 week in late Sept.

Small but focused, Canada's only environmental film and video festival offers a few dozen films and videos from around the world.

The Word on the Street

Various locations along Queen Street W, Entertainment District (416 504 7241/www. thewordonthestreet.ca). Streetcar 501/subway Osgoode. **Map** p274 C7/D7. **Date** late Sept.

More than 100,000 people clog a pedestrianised section of Queen West during a street-savvy celebration of literacy that sees publishers and writers promoting their wares with readings and signings. Kids get their own special tent.

University of Toronto Book Sales

Victoria College, 71 Queen's Park Crescent E; University College, 15 King's College Circle; Trinity College, 6 Hoskin Avenue. Bus 94/subway Museum. **Date** late Sept-late Oct.

A must for bibliophiles, the autumn U of T book sales offer great used books – everything from classic Penguins to yesterday's bestsellers to out-of-print rarities for as little as $1 – in settings that evoke learned colloquies and ancient manuscripts. Each of the three colleges – Victoria, University and Trinity – offer upwards of 50,000 books and organisers often complain about the lack of space, but it's the academic setting that makes the events. Get there early to beat the dealers. Opening night queues are huge. Watch the local papers for exact dates and times.

Royal Agricultural Winter Fair

Exhibition Place, National Trade Centre, Lake Shore Boulevard W between Strachan Avenue & Dufferin Street, West End (416 263 3400/www.royalfair.org). Bus 29/GO Exhibition/streetcar 509, 511/subway Union. **Map** p276 A9. **Date** 10 days early Nov.

A mix of down-home and high-class, the Royal showcases both hokey agricultural exhibits (butter sculptures, giant vegetables and so on) and elegant equestrian events like the Nations Cup Challenge. Sheep, cows and other animals compete for prizes and the attention of schoolchildren.

Nathan Phillips Square gets the neon treatment at the **Cavalcade of Lights**.

Santa Claus Parade

Various locations along Bloor Street and University Avenue, Entertainment & Financial Districts (416 599 9090 ext 500). Streetcar 501, 504, 505/subway King, Museum, Osgoode, Queen's Park, St Andrew, St Patrick or Union. **Date** Sat in Nov.

Santa and his friends relieve November's greyness with a storybook parade featuring plenty of bands, clowns and costumed paraders. Thousands of local small fry watch from their parents' shoulders. Very Toronto indeed.

Canadian Aboriginal Festival

SkyDome, 1 Blue Jays Way, Entertainment District (1-519 751 0040/www.canab.com). Streetcar 504/ subway Union. **Map** p277 D8. **Date** late Nov-early Dec.

North America's largest multi-disciplinary aboriginal arts event features fashion, films, lacrosse, a giant music awards show and a powwow with up to 1,000 dancers and drum singing groups.

Winter

Cavalcade of Lights

Nathan Phillips Square, 100 Queen Street W, Downtown (416 338 0338/www.city.toronto.on.ca/ special_events). Streetcar 506/subway Queen. **Map** p277/p278 E7. **Date** late Dec.

A hundred thousand lights illuminate the city's central square, kicking off a month of skating parties and other events that culminate in a televised New Year's Eve party with top Canadian acts.

First Night

SkyDome, 1 Blue Jays Way, Entertainment District (416 362 3692). Streetcar 504/subway Union. **Map** p277 D8. **Date** late Dec.

A booze-free, family-friendly New Year's Eve celebration, First Night started as an arty streetfair and has morphed into a three-day indoor celebration of the arts with hundreds of artists performing on multiple stages. There's a kid-friendly 'mini-midnight' at 9pm and the real thing, complete with indoor fireworks and 'Auld Lang Syne', a few hours later.

Toronto Winterfest

(416 338 0338/www.city.toronto.on.ca/winterfest). Mel Lastman Square, 5100 Yonge Street, at Sheppard Avenue, North Side (subway North York Centre); Nathan Phillips Square, 100 Queen Street W, at Bay Street, Dundas Square (streetcar 501/subway Queen). **Map** p277/p278 E7. **Date** weekend in early Feb.

An attempt to prove that Toronto in February is fun, Ontario's second largest winter festival is, well, a good try. Top-notch ice skaters and other entertainers do their thing, much of it family-oriented, all of it outdoors. Best enjoyed with mittens and scarves.

Arts & Entertainment

Children

Major fun for minors.

Toronto is celebrated for its cleanliness and safety and indeed sightseeing *en famille* is easy and pleasant here. But indoors and out, there are also all kinds of places for kids to cut loose and enjoy each other's company while parents chill out and keep an eye on their progeny. The **Toronto Eaton Centre** (*see p141*) is the most concentrated shopping haven downtown. **The Beach** (*see p98*), with its aromas of hot dogs and sun-kissed water, and **Harbourfront** (*see p51*), a playground of trapeze lessons, art classes and musical distraction, particularly in summer, also please little outdoorsy types.

Babysitting & daycare

Any number of websites (www.e-kidstoronto.com is one of the best) will provide a database of daycare centres in the Toronto area, but few will open their doors to drop-ins, and even fewer to visitors disinclined to register with the agency. Visit the above site for information about supervised playgrounds, community centres that cater for single parents and emergency services. For a directory of downtown drop-ins and times, call **Community Information Toronto** (416 397 4636). Otherwise, the **YMCA** (Family Development Centre 416 928 9622) runs centres throughout the city, is open from dawn till dusk and will take kids from 18 months to 12 years.

Major hotels will be able to arrange babysitting, or call a reputable agency such as **Christopher Robin** (416 483 4744, after midnight and emergencies 416 439 1883, $50 for first three hours, then $12 per hour thereafter).

Attractions & activities

Art Gallery of Ontario

For full listings, *see p68*. **Admission** $12; $9 concession; $6 6-15s; free under-6s; $25 family.
Weekends here see any number of restless kids descend to the basement for hands-on art instruction. It's rather like spending an extended period in art class that resources teachers can only dream about. Sundays after 1pm are for family drop-ins.

CBC Broadcasting Centre

250 Front Street W, at John Street, Entertainment District (museum 416 205 5574/tours 416 205 8605/www.cbc.ca/museum/www.cbc.ca/aboutcbc/ discover). Streetcar 504/subway Union or St Andrew.
Open *Museum* 9am-5pm Mon-Fri; noon-4pm Sat. *Tours* 9am-5pm Tue-Fri. **Admission** *Museum* free. *Tour* $7; $5 children; free under-4s. **Credit** MC, V. **Map** p277 D8.
Tots likely won't recognise the characters of TV past on show at the network's main-floor museum, but there are also interactive stations featuring newsreels, children's shows and sports trivia. Guided tours to the upper floors reveal acres of soundstage and the chaotic home of the evening news.

Hockey Hall of Fame

For full listings, *see p63*. **Admission** $12; $8 4-13s; $8 concessions; free under-4s.
How many museums have their own ice rink where you can test your slapshot skills? This impressive building houses the world's greatest hockey memories and lets you record your own broadcast.

Lorraine Kimsa Theatre for Young People

165 Front Street E, at Frederick Street, St Lawrence (416 862 2222/www.lktyp.ca). Streetcar 504.
Open *Box office* 9am-5pm Mon-Fri. **Shows** 10am Sat, Sun. **Tickets** $18-$28. **Credit** AmEx, MC, V. **Map** p277/p278 F8.
Toronto's premier venue for children's theatre offers productions that are aimed at kids but will appeal to their adult companions. Its visual vocabulary is a triumph of the imagination and it plays an important cultural role in promoting theatre for young people.

Ontario Science Centre

For full listings, *see p63*. **Admission** $13; $9 concessions; $8 13-17s; $7 5-12s; free under-5s.
At this hangar-like gallery exiled to the concrete jungle of Don Mills, kids can digest all the physics, biology and chemistry they've been sleeping through at school. The Science Centre makes it attractive, roping visitors into demonstrations on aerospace, gravity, electricity, astronomy and the body.

Paramount Canada's Wonderland

9580 Jane Street, at MacKenzie Drive, Vaughan (905 832 7000/www.canadas-wonderland.com). Yorkdale or York Mills subway, then GO bus/ Highway 400, exit Rutherford Road (just north of Highway 401). **Open** *Late May-mid June* 10am-6pm daily. *Mid June-Aug* 10am-10pm daily; *Sept-mid Oct* 10am-8pm Sat, Sun. Closed mid Oct-late May. **Admission** $47; $29 concessions; $23.50 3-6s. **Credit** AmEx, MC, V.
Catch a bus from Yorkdale or drive up Highway 400 to this Six Flags-style amusement park a short drive north of town. Rollercoasters are smooth and modern, and parents can sigh in relative relief in

Animal magic at **Toronto Zoo**.

Hanna-Barbera Land, a scream-free children's playground. The city's grittier midway, the Canadian National Exhibition (*see p168*), operates for two weeks leading into Labour Day (first Monday in September) at Exhibition Place, and goes down well with kids.

Paramount Toronto
For full listings, *see p179*. **Admission** $8.50-$13.50; $8.50 concessions; $7.50 children.
More than a dozen screens on site, and a healthy share of them devoted to G- (general viewing) rated films. Gone are the days of queuing for a flick. Here, the 'waiting lounge' is a rather noisy video arcade surrounded by kiosks of junk food, sweet and savoury. This all spells nightmare for adults, and the kids will have to be bribed to leave.

Playdium
99 Rathburn Road W, opposite Square One Shopping Centre, Mississauga (905 273 4810/www.playdium. com). Subway Islington, then any Mississauga Transit bus to Square One. **Open** noon-midnight Mon-Thur; 10am-2am Fri, Sat; 10am-midnight Sun. **Admission** call for details. **Credit** AmEx, MC, V.
Arcades aren't the nickel-and-dime funfairs they were when we were young. Today, a half-day of virtual motorcross, table hockey pinball or other

frantic, child-friendly diversions can cost more than your hotel room, and Playdium is no exception. It's a way out of town, but vast enough to please.

Royal Ontario Museum
For full listings, *see p73*. **Admission** $18; $14 concessions; $10 5-14s; free under-5s; free for all 1hr before closing daily.
Parents accompany children under ten, but the rest can feel their own way through the Discovery Gallery, packed with fancy dress, make-believe caves, dinosaurs and artefacts. The permanent collection offers 'Hands-on Biodiversity' rooms with interactive plant and animal displays. Grab a schedule to track down upcoming ROM bus excursions.

Speakers Corner
ChumCity Building, 299 Queen Street W, at John Street, Entertainment District (416 591 5757/www. citytv.com). Streetcar 501/subway Osgoode. **Open** 24hrs daily. **Fee** $1. **No credit cards. Map** p277 D7.
A good one for the older kids, this. Named after the ranters at London's Hyde Park, a soapbox ensconced in one corner of the Citytv building encourages passers-by of all ages to speak their minds. Depositing a loonie will trigger the video camera; pull back the curtain and you're a pundit. The network airs the best comments in a weekly timeslot.

Toronto Hippo Tours
416 703 4476/www.torontohippotours.com. Tours leave from 151 Front Street W, at Simcoe Street, Entertainment District. **Tours** May-Nov hourly 11am-6pm daily. Closed Dec-Apr. **Rates** $35; $30 students 13-17; $23 3-12s; free under-3s; $100 family. **Credit** MC, V. **Map** p277/p278 E8.
Even residents are tempted to ride this amphibious tour bus, which morphs into a raft at the Toronto harbour. Meet the crew at the south-east corner of Front and Simcoe Streets for a guided scoot around downtown and a panoramic view from the harbour.

Toronto Zoo
361A Old Finch Avenue, Meadowvale Road, north of Highway 401, North Side (416 392 5900/www.torontozoo.com). Bus 85/GO Rouge Hill Station. **Open** Mar-Apr, Sept-Oct 9am-6pm daily. May-Aug 9am-7.30pm daily. Oct-Dec, Jan-Mar 9.30am-4.30pm daily. **Admission** $17; $9 4-12s; $11 concessions; free under-4s. **Credit** AmEx, MC, V.
That it's located on the edge of the city is a bonus for roaming elephants, tigers, lions and wolves. But on humid days, you'll see little but their overheated bodies sleeping in slivers of shade. The gorilla rainforest is a highlight. Hop on to the Zoomobile to see the sights when the little ones tucker out.

Outdoor

Vast tracts of grass are usually enough to keep energetic children busy for hours, but if they need any further entertainment, there's always **Riverdale Park** (*see p77*), with its farm,

Arts & Entertainment

petting zoo and milking, shearing and butter-churning demonstrations. In the West End, **Centennial Park** (56 Centennial Park Road) has an Olympic-sized swimming pool, baseball diamond, mini-golf course, tennis courts, go-karts and, in winter, ski hill (*see p213*).

Ontario Place

For full listings, *see p56*. **Admission** $10-$25.50; $12-$15 concessions; $4-$15 children; free under-4s. *IMAX* $6. **Credit** AmEx, MC, V.

This is the sort of mega-playground kids dream about. Water activities include slides and bumper boats, and a huge concrete field where massive features spray water and serve as jungle gyms. Dry delight can be had with the funhouse, fast food and various amphitheatres (including an IMAX).

Skating in Nathan Phillips Square

For full listings, *see p212*. **Admission** free.

Innocent though it may sound, this vast rink at New City Hall attracts riff-raff late on winter evenings, making it impossible to stabilise oneself for fear of being rammed by a hostile teenager. On weekdays, the coast is clear. Rentals and sharpening services are positioned by the snack bar. It's open from December to February, weather depending.

Eating out

The overpriced emporium-style restaurant is a fixture in most tourist districts and Toronto's are no exception. In most cases they lack imagination, and you'll rarely find lobster bisque on the menu – but that's the whole point. Fussy little eaters will be silenced for that hour's respite between the museum and shopping spree. Most visitors will know the **Planet Hollywood** drill (277 Front Street W, 416 596 7827); here, it has a handy location between the CN Tower and SkyDome. The Entertainment District is lined with bustling eateries catering to large groups. **Wayne Gretzky's** (99 Blue Jays Way, 416 979 7825) and **Alice Fazooli** (294 Adelaide Street W, 416 979 1910) are both in the John–Adelaide–Peter Street corridor and serve the requisite wings, burgers and bottomless Cokes. Down on King Street W, things get spicier. Try **Kit Kat Italian Bar & Grill** (297 King Street W, 416 977 4461) for down-home southern Italian or **N'Awlins Jazz Bar & Grill** (299 King Street W, 416 595 1958) for down-home cajun. Few restaurants in Chinatown will turn away rambunctious patrons and the more adventuresome kids might delight in their first moo shoo pork; if nothing else, they'll be glued to the tanks of live eel, lobster and carp.

Keg Steakhouse & Bar

12 Church Street, at Front Street, St Lawrence (416 367 0685/www.kegsteakhouse.com). Streetcar 504/subway Union. **Open** 4pm-1am Mon-Sat;

4-11pm Sun. **Main courses** $12-$32. **Credit** AmEx, DC, MC, V. **Map** p277/p278 F8.

Steak and chicken, steak and ribs, steak and lobster. All the combinations for the little carnivore are at your saucy fingertips, with burgers for the pickiest. Quality is high, and service smiley, American style.

Mövenpick Yorkville

133 Yorkville Avenue, at Avenue Road, Yorkville (416 926 9545/www.movenpickcanada.com). Subway Bay. **Open** *Oct-Apr* 11.30am-midnight Mon-Fri; 7.30am-midnight Sat, Sun. *May-Sept* 7.30am-midnight daily. **Main courses** $12-$22. **Credit** AmEx, DC, MC, V. **Map** p280 E4.

A maze of buffets, sweet tables and gastro tableaux to keep children distracted (or lost) for hours.

Old Spaghetti Factory

54 The Esplanade, at Front Street, St Lawrence (416 864 9761/www.oldspaghettifactory.ca). Streetcar 504/subway Union. **Open** 11.30am-11pm Mon-Thur; 11.30am-midnight Fri, Sat; 11.30am-11pm Sun. **Main courses** $11-$18. **Credit** AmEx, DC, MC, V. **Map** p277/p278 G8.

Toronto's answer to Chuck-E-Cheez has been filling kids with 'pasghetti and meat bulbs' for more than three decades. Good for fuelling families en route to the nearby St Lawrence Centre for the Arts (*see p80*).

Shopping

At **Roots** (*see p146*) send them off to choose their own hats, T-shirts or sports kit. **Ice** (*see p157*) will keep anyone busy for an hour picking through the gaudy gifts, candy-coloured make-up and cool casuals. For children's clothes, *see p145*.

Kidding Awound

91 Cumberland Street, at Bay Street, Yorkville (416 926 8996). Subway Bay. **Open** 10.30am-6pm Mon-Wed; 10.30am-8pm Thur-Sat; noon-5pm Sun. **Credit** AmEx, MC, V. **Map** p280 E4.

Set a child loose to pick out their own toy, or search for a trinket to bring back to those at home. You'll find things to be wound, spun, coloured and laughed at, and a selection of antique toys for big kids.

Mastermind

3350 Yonge Street, at Lawrence Avenue, Midtown (416 487 7177/www.mastermindtoys.com). Subway Lawrence. **Open** 9.30am-6pm Mon-Wed; 9.30am-9pm Thur, Fri; 9am-6pm Sat; 11am-5pm Sun. **Credit** AmEx, MC, V.

This one's for the budding scientist, or the child who's forever asking why. Learning toys and brain-teasers are the forte, but there are also train sets and musical gifts.

The Sassy Bead Co

2076 Yonge Street, at Eglinton Avenue, Forest Hill (416 488 7400). Subway Eglinton. **Open** 10am-6pm Mon, Tue, Sat; 10am-9pm Wed-Fri; noon-5pm Sun. **Credit** MC, V.

String your own from plentiful beads and baubles, or buy a ready-made piece of costume jewellery.

Arts & Entertainment

Comedy

Get your laughing gear around Toronto's top-notch comedy haunts.

Second City. *See p174.*

Although the stereotypical Torontonian is a humourless Bay Street lawyer who wouldn't know a good joke if it walked up and bit his assets report, the city has supported a world-famous comedy scene for decades. From **Second City**'s rise to fame, to the 1980s boom that produced Jim Carrey and Howie Mandel, to the current comedy renaissance, Toronto has always had a laughable reputation.

The current boom is thanks largely to the Comedy Network, a new-ish Canadian TV channel that over the past few years has given many local comics new prominence. At a fistful of comedy clubs around the city, you can catch the famous, the soon-to-be-famous, and, let's be honest, the soon-to-be-in-a-different-profession. Much of Toronto's funny business happens within a small area in the Entertainment District, but a few venues, such as the **Comedywood Restaurant & Comedy Club**, are worth travelling further afield for.

Toronto's comedy scene is a mix of stand-up, sketch and improv. It's also an incubation system, which feeds and nurtures Canadian comedians until they reach maturity. As soon as they are ripe and ready, Canadian jokers are shipped off to the big markets in New York and Los Angeles. Most Canadians keep a long list in their heads of US comedic superstars who cut their teeth north of the border (*see p175* **Borderline funny**) – this has as much to do with obsessive compulsion as with national pride. Interestingly, Canadians pay much less attention to those comedians who choose to stay in Canada. While that's bad news for the comedians, it's good news for club-goers. The lack of a celebrity system means that you can often get an evening of seasoned, professional-quality laughs for peanuts.

The inevitable caveat is that comedy is less consistent than most forms of entertainment. The older troupes place heavy stock in their illustrious alumni, but, as anyone who watches *Saturday Night Live* – a TV show produced by a Canadian – can tell you, just because a group produces funny stuff one year, doesn't mean they'll do it again the next.

Venues

Alt.COMedy Lounge
The Rivoli, 332 Queen Street W, at Spadina Avenue, Entertainment District (416 596 1908). Streetcar 501/subway Osgoode. **Show** 8.30pm Mon. **Admission** pay what you can. **Credit** AmEx, MC, V. **Map** p274 D7.
Once a week, the versatile back room at the Rivoli is transformed into a cabaret, where Toronto's self-declared alternative comedians come out to play. On

some nights, it seems 'alternative' is a metaphor for 'poorly rehearsed' but it's cheap to get in, which means the dollar-per-laugh ratio is usually pretty good. If you're lucky, you'll catch a visiting celebrity dropping in to blow off some mainstream steam. Scott Thompson, Janeane Garofalo, Will Ferrell and Tom Green have all made appearances.

Comedywood Restaurant & Comedy Club
800 Steeles Avenue W, at Bathurst Street, North Side (905 761 0543). Bus 60, 160. **Shows** 8pm Wed, Thur; 8.30pm & 10.45pm Fri, Sat. **Tickets** $8-$15. **Credit** AmEx, MC, V.

It's a little out of the way, but you'll see things here you can't get elsewhere. The most popular act at Comedywood is Incredible Boris, a hypnotist who also happens to be Boris Cherniak, part owner of the club. The stable of regulars also includes comedic musical acts alongside more traditional stand-up comics. They also bring in eclectic guest performers, including Michael Winslow (better known as Larvell Jones, the sound effects guy from the *Police Academy* movies), Howie Mandell and Tommy Chong (of Cheech and Chong). If you get bored, the 350-seat theatre also has pool tables and a TV.

The Laugh Resort
370 King Street W, at Peter Street, Entertainment District (416 364 5233). Streetcar 504/subway St Andrew. **Shows** 8.30pm Tue-Thur; 8.15pm & 10.30pm Fri, Sat. **Tickets** $7-$15. **Credit** AmEx, MC, V. **Map** p277 D8.

This cosy 100-seat theatre is in the basement of a Holiday Inn, but it feels like the basement of someone's house. The 12-year-old club moved to this smaller theatre a few years ago, and now it's a great place to get within spitting distance of some of comedy's finest. The intimate setting means the heckling can be fast and furious, and there's no place to hide if a performer sets their satirical sights on you. In addition to hosting local stars, the venue has traditionally been a good spot to see international acts just before they hit the big time. Adam Sandler, David Spade and Ellen Degeneres all performed here shortly before they became household names.

Second City
56 Blue Jays Way, at King Street W, Entertainment District (416 343 0011). Streetcar 504/subway St Andrew. **Shows** 8pm Mon-Fri, Sun; 8pm &10pm Sat. **Tickets** $21-$27; $12-$16 concessions; $54-$56 incl dinner. **Credit** AmEx, DC, MC, V. **Map** p277 D8.

Founded in 1973 this is actually the second Second City, an offshoot of the famous club in Chicago. Toronto's oldest and best known comedy venue is still the best place in town to take in an evening of sketch comedy. The main productions at the theatre are loosely interlocked sketches with at least some attempt made at narrative continuity. After the show, members of the audience can stick around to watch the same performers hone their improvisation skills. The resident comedians use these improv

nights to develop material for the next big show. Lists of alumni are etched on the theatre's main doors, and include Dan Aykroyd, Eugene Levy, Dave Thomas, Martin Short, Gilda Radner and John Candy. The building also houses the Tim Sims Playhouse, Second City's second theatre. Named after a much-loved Second City alumnus who died in 1995, this cabaret-style theatre is a showcase for less established performers, often with an edgier bent than the main stage.

Tom Foolery's Comedy Club
194 Bloor Street W, at Avenue Road, The Annex (416 967 5005/www.tomfoolerys.ca). Subway Museum or St George. **Shows** call for details. **Tickets** $15. **Credit** AmEx, MC, V. **Map** p280 D4.

This is the new kid on the block, a recently opened 160-seat theatre that mostly features stand-up but also presents some sketch and improv. 'Fresh Meat Night', as its name suggests, showcases up-and-coming amateurs, but also features professional comics who want to try out new material.

Yuk Yuk's
224 Richmond Street W, at Duncan Street, Entertainment District (416 967 6425). Streetcar 501/subway Osgoode. **Shows** 8.30pm Mon-Thur, Sun; 8.30pm & 11pm Fri, Sat. **Tickets** $2-$15; $24-$35 incl dinner. **Credit** AmEx, MC, V. **Map** p274 D7.

This national chain recently invested $2.5 million in an upscale, 3,700-sq-ft (344-sq-m), 350-seat cabaret in the heart of Toronto's nightclub district. Its new flagship venue showcases mainly Canadian stand-up artists, though international stars also appear here from time to time. Yuk Yuk's also has regular amateur nights, which feature the comedic stylings of students from Toronto's Humber School of Comedy, the only degree-granting institution of its kind in the world. These nights are cheap and often worth it.

Improv

Theatresports Toronto
Various venues (416 491 3115). **Shows** 8pm Sun (Poor Alex Theatre Cabaret Space, 296 Brunswick Avenue, at Bloor Street W, the Annex, tickets $10).

Although it's been established as one of the city's best improv groups for more than 20 years, Theatresports Toronto isn't tied down to a particular venue. The only regular event they do is at the Poor Alex Theatre Cabaret Space on Sundays but you can always find them performing somewhere, and they're worth tracking down. For an established improv group – their alumni include the Kids in the Hall, Kevin Frank and Colin Mochrie – the group is surprisingly welcoming to ordinary people. Comics are happy to share their wealth of improvisation experience and knowledge. While many of their classes are heavy-duty, and are aimed at creating the next generation of Toronto Theatresports performers, they also hold casual drop-in workshops where anyone can try their hand at improvisation.

Borderline funny

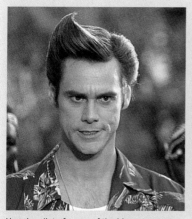

Here is a list of some of the biggest names in American comedy of recent years: Jim Carrey, Mike Myers, Tom Green, Michael J Fox, Catherine O'Hara, Martin Short, John Candy, Leslie Nielson, Phil Hartman, Matthew Perry and Dan Ackroyd.

However there is something that sets them apart: they are as Canadian as dead red leaves and fat flat-tailed water rats. And many of them – including perhaps the two biggest names, Jim Carrey and Mike Myers – originate from the ultimate butt of Toronto jokes: Toronto suburbia. However the stature of the Canadian comic in America isn't as funny as it sounds. Excepting Leslie 'Naked Gun' Nielson, who is a unique case since he began as a dramatic actor long before evolving to personify all that is good and slapstick in this world, all of these comedians were brought up in an era when the Canadian government spent millions on hyping a concept of 'Canadianness' in a country that has too many televisions picking up broadcast signals from south of the border. And since puberty's greatest form of expression is taking the piss – and Canadians have neighbours as ripe for piss-taking as the Americans (and in particular, their television output) – the situation then starts to make perfect sense. Put simply: Canadian comedians are outsider satirists looking in, who happily come pre-programmed to be 'a little different', while still being remarkably easy to disguise as bona fide Americans. An example: the satirist and illustrator for the *New Yorker*, Bruce

McCall, has built his career on the ironic detachment he brings to his adopted city.

Another contributing factor is that there has been a long-standing tradition of sucking talent from north to south ever since DW Griffith picked a nice young Toronto gal called Gladys Smith to be renamed Mary Pickford and become 'America's Sweetheart' and the world's first movie star. Fact: Los Angeles has a higher Canuck population than the Canada's capital Ottawa. For the past couple of decades, the Canadian Chuckle Conduit has been overseen by *Saturday Night Live* producer Lorne Michaels – yes, also a Canadian – who generally does an annual cull of the Toronto stand-up club scene if there isn't any culling to be done from such classic home-grown comedy shows as *SCTV* or *Kids in the Hall*.

Visiting comedy fans to Toronto should rightly visit the city's legendary stand-up clubs, but we also recommend a much more cultural – or rather Canadian – experience: make some Canadian friends and berate them (they are an easily berateable folk after all...) until they take you home with them to show you their stash of videos with prime episodes of *SCTV*, *Kids in the Hall*, *CODCO* and *This Hour has 22 Minutes*.

And if one wants an extra immersion into the classics of Canadian comedy, look no further than William Shatner's attempts at singing, Keanu Reeves' attempts at acting and Celine Dion's attempts to avoid her face being photographed at an angle...

Film

First dibs on the new releases, first to have an IMAX, this is silver screen city.

Sceptics claim Toronto movie-goers are undiscerning – they'll see anything, anywhere. Others take a different approach, holding up local audiences as passionate, discerning cineastes. Either way, it's true that this city is movie mad; full of fans who haul themselves off to cinemas weekly – come rain, sleet, or snow.

Torontonians see the latest Hollywood hits before most Americans do. The big studios launch most of their offerings in New York, Toronto and Los Angeles. This city is also home to a few significant firsts in film-going, including the original multiplex shoebox – Toronto has the dubious honour of having multiplex originator Garth Drabinsky as one of its own – and a new concept that allows for that 'in-with-the-in-crowd' sensation: the Varsity's VIP screening rooms, which mimic the mogul's private screening room.

Movie-goers here are up for just about anything. There are a hundred or so film festivals of every rank, including the world's second most important (*see p24* **Toronto International Film Festival**). There's an excellent cinematheque, a healthy chain of rep houses, the Festival Group (with screenings from midday to midnight), a new drive-in on the

waterfront, outdoor screenings, a glut of multi and monsterplexes, and a guy with two rooms and a projector who has become a local legend.

Pick any week, and you can see Shanghai Samurai, retro romances, art cinema, dirty cartoons, documentaries, Bollywood's latest hits (in original language), and kids' classics – on top of the latest releases. One thing you probably won't see is a Canadian movie: in 2001, home-grown fare racked up just 0.02% of screen time. If you're determined to see something local, check out Cinematheque Ontario or the rep houses – the city usually finds a way to satisfy most movie urges.

Too bad that the best cinemas are gone. Even in the heart of the city, it's usually a choice between going to a multiplex or a monsterplex – places where people with limited attention spans and unlimited cellphone time struggle with pizza and other viscous foods not meant to be eaten in the dark. They may have gathered for the latest Hollywood franchise movie, but, with the dedicated cinephiles across town and the crowds of Bollywood fans in the suburbs, they're keeping the city's reputation as a buzzing movie hive alive and well.

TICKETS AND INFORMATION

The cost of going to the pictures keeps climbing. Tickets for a first-run cinema range from $8 to $13.50; best deals are 'Half-Price Tuesdays' and matinees. The rep circuit and the Cinematheque Ontario tickets range from $7 to $9.60. Check listings in the summer for free outdoor screenings in Nathan Philips Square, at the CHUM/Citytv parking lot and in various neighbourhood venues (mostly parks).

The daily papers publish movie sections on Fridays and the two free weeklies – *eye* and *NOW* – have reviews and listings.

Arts & Entertainment

The best Cinemas

To take a date
The Docks Drive-In (*see p179*).

For cinephiles
Cinematheque Ontario (*see p177*).

If you can't sleep
The midnight screenings **at Bloor Cinema** (*see right*).

For movie mogul wannabes
Varsity VIP Screening Rooms (*see p179*).

For raucous popcorn-fuelled pzazz
Paramount Toronto (*see p179*).

For a new domension in film-making
Cinesphere (*see p178* **Local hero**).

Arthouse & rep

Bloor Cinema

506 Bloor Street W, at Bathurst Street, The Annex (416 516 2330/www.bloorcinema.com). Streetcar 511/subway Bathurst. **Admission** $7; $3-$5 concessions. For 4.30pm show Mon-Fri $5. **No credit cards. Map** p280 C4.
The flagship cinema of the Festival Group rep chain is a little ragged round the edges, but it has a lot of heart. It shows a mix of first-run releases on their last stop before video/DVD, classics and foreign titles.

Royal Cinema. *See p178.*

Carlton

20 Carlton Street, at Yonge Street, Church & Wellesley (416 598 2309/www.cineplex.com). Streetcar 506/subway College. **Admission** $10; $5.75 concessions; $6 before 4pm, all day Tue. **Credit** AmEx, MC, V. **Map** p281 F5.

This arthouse multiplex, owned by Cineplex Odeon, shows the latest foreign flicks, commercial-free. The nine theatres are small, the walls are thin, but if you want to catch the latest Godard, this might be your only choice in the city.

CineForum

463 Bathurst Street, at College Street, Kensington Market (416 603 6643). Streetcar 506, 511. **Admission** $10. **No credit cards. Map** p276 C6.

Owner Reg Hartt claims he was the first to screen the porn classic, *Deep Throat*: admission was free if you showed up naked. His 'theatre' is in his modest home near modish College Street, where he revels in the weird. He was once called 'a perv with a projector' but others hail him as a local hero. Cartoons are his speciality. His Animation Symposium – highlighting more than 20 animators including Tex Avery, Bob Clampett and Friz Freleng – is available to tour.

Cinematheque Ontario

Advance ticket box office: 2 Carlton Street, Suite 1600, at Yonge Street, Church & Wellesley (416 968 3456/www.e.bell.ca/filmfest/cinematheque). Streetcar 506/subway College. **Open** noon-5pm Mon-Fri. **Map** p281 F5.

Screenings: *Art Gallery of Ontario, Jackman Hall, 317 Dundas Street W, at McCaul Street, Chinatown.*

Streetcar 505/subway St Patrick. **Admission** $9.60-$11; $5.25-$7 concessions. **Credit** AmEx, MC, V. **Map** p277 D6.

Housed in the Art Gallery of Ontario's renovated theatre, this year-round cinematheque is one of the best anywhere. Programmers offer movie classics, children's classics, foreign rarities – Kon Ichikawa, anyone? – and new discoveries from some of the world's finest film-makers.

Fox Theatre

2236 Queen Street E, at Beech Avenue, East Side (416 691 7330). Streetcar 501. **Admission** $7; $4 concessions. **No credit cards.**

An old cinema, which has seen better days, but for the Beaches crowd, this Festival Group single-screen theatre is a reliable and familiar place to see recent releases and foreign films.

Paradise Cinema

1006 Bloor Street W, at Ossington Avenue, West End (416 537 7040). Bus 63/subway Ossington. **Admission** $8; $4 concessions. **No credit cards.**

Situated in a nondescript part of town – between the Annex and Bloor West Village – this single-screen movie house has little character but is comfortable and benefits from Festival Cinemas programming.

Regent Theatre

551 Mount Pleasant Road, at Davisville Avenue, Midtown (416 480 9884). Subway Davisville, then bus 28. **Admission** $9; $5 concessions. **No credit cards.**

One of Toronto's few independent theatres, the Regent has a long and distinguished career as a one-time theatre palace. Today, it's a modest cinema with dim lights and a warm atmosphere, and much loved by its loyal band of neighbourhood supporters. It screens beyond-first-run releases for those who are playing catch up on their film-watching.

Revue Cinema

400 Roncesvalles Avenue, at Dundas Street W, West End (416 531 9959). Subway Dundas West. **Admission** $8; $4 concessions. **No credit cards.**
The Revue is a long-standing favourite among arthouse fans and neighbourhood movie-goers. Tucked in the heart of Roncesvalles Village, this classic local cinema, owned by the Festival Group, still retains some characteristics of its 1920s origins.

Royal Cinema

606 College Street W, at Bathurst Street, Little Italy (416 516 4845). Streetcar 506, 511. **Admission** $8; concessions $4. **No credit cards. Map** p276 B6.
This single-screen cinema, owned by the Festival Group, has a terrific location slap bang in the heart of trendy College Street. Unadventurous programming may miss the opportunity to reflect the identity of the Italian neighbourhood, but at least there are plenty of places to sip a decent espresso while chatting about the film afterwards.

Mainstream & first-run

Canada Square

2190 Yonge Street, at Eglinton Avenue, Midtown (416 646 0444/www.famousplayers.ca). Subway Eglinton. **Admission** $11; $6.75 concessions; $7 before 6pm Mon-Fri, all day Tue; $8.25 before 6pm Sat, Sun. **Credit** AmEx, MC, V.
This compact 13-screen theatre, operated by Famous Players, is conveniently located on the subway and offers a sensible mix of foreign films and first-run mainstream pictures. It's a classic example of the 1980s cookie-cutter multiplex, but somehow everything fits – no one feels cramped.

Colossus

Westin Road and Highway 7, North Side (905 851 1001/www.famousplayers.ca). **Admission** $13.50; $7.50 concessions; free under-3s; $8.50 before 6pm Mon-Fri, all day Tue; $10.50 before 6pm Sat, Sun. **Credit** AmEx, MC, V.
During the 1990s movie exhibitors kept on building them larger and larger, until they finally hit their max. For Famous Players, this is it. How many screens of entertainment, rows of concession stands,

Local hero IMAX

This giant-screen movie format was developed and launched in Toronto in the early 1970s by a group of engineers and film-makers. They wanted to make movies on a grander scale – literally. IMAX's first film was the documentary *North of Superior,* a wonderfully nostalgic bit of Canadiana that sails from one aerial shot to another, taking its viewers on a thrilling trip across vast stretches of autumnal wilderness, dancing around the dazzling cascades of Niagara Falls, and down into the heat of a forest fire where rescuers struggle to control the blaze. Today, IMAX still makes nature films while tackling new territory, such as *At the Max,* the popular documentary about the Rolling Stones on tour in the '90s, and historical dramas (largely panned by the critics).

Cinesphere, the first IMAX theatre anywhere, opened in 1971 in the grounds of Ontario Place, the waterfront park. Its glittering geodesic dome still stands out as a modern architectural classic. Occasionally, you can catch a screening of *North of Superior* here. Giant-format films run daily in addition to the latest Hollywood offerings in 35mm or 70mm. The screen is the largest in the city and the theatre resonates with 24,000 watts of digital sound. Truly an impressive experience all round.

Honourable mentions

You can catch IMAX movies at the Paramount (*see p179*), the Colossus (*see above*) and the Ontario Science Centre (*see p189*).

Cinesphere

955 Lake Shore Boulevard W, Harbourfront (416 314 9900/www.ontarioplace.com). Streetcar 509, 511/subway Union/bus 29/GO Exhibition. **Admission**: $8-$10; $6 concessions. **Credit** AmEx, MC, V.

Driving range and movie theatre, **The Docks Drive-in** is for those who like films with balls.

games and other distractions can you handle? The answer lies across the street where rival exhibitor AMC went one bigger with something called Interchange 30 (at Highways 400 and 7). The name refers to the number of pounding screens it delivers.

Alliance Atlantis Cumberland 4 Cinemas
159 Cumberland Street, at Avenue Road, Yorkville (416 646 0444/www.allianceatlantiscinemas.com). Subway Bay. **Admission** $12.75; $6.75 concessions; $7.50 all day Tue; $8.50 before 6pm Mon-Fri; $9.75 before 6pm Sat, Sun. **Credit** MC, V. **Map** p280 E4.
Once this was the only theatre in Canada with reserved seating, but that gimmick has died out. Today the comfortable multiplex shows a mix of foreign and independent movies with the occasional mainstream hit. Similar theatres, all operated by Alliance Atlantis, are the Beach Cinemas (1651 Queen Street E, 416 646 0444) and Bayview Village (Bayview and Sheppard, 416 646 0444).

The Docks Drive-In
11 Polson Street, at Cherry Street, East Side (416 461 3625/www.thedocks.com). Bus 72. **Open** May-Sept; call for details. **Admission** $12 per car, incl entrance to the nightclub. **Credit** AmEx, MC, V.
This nightclub/theme park on the waterfront runs double bills of mainstream flicks three times a week (Tue, Fri and Sat) in the summer to approximately 500 cars. The same lot is used as a golf driving range when movies aren't running.

Humber Cinemas
2442 Bloor Street W, at Jane Street, West End (416 769 1177/www.cineplex.com). Subway Jane. **Admission** $10; $5.75 concessions; $6 before 4pm and all day Tue. **Credit** AmEx, MC, V.
This old theatre in the heart of Bloor West Village remains one of the few that offers first-run releases in ample surroundings. Time has not been kind to this somewhat neglected cinema, but it's solidly comfortable, if a bit dowdy and lacking in glitz. Its days may be numbered.

Paramount Toronto
259 Richmond Street W, at John Street, Entertainment District (416 368 5600/www. famousplayers.ca). Streetcar 501, 504. **Admission** $13.50; $7.50 concessions; free under-3s; $8.50 before 6pm Mon-Fri, all day Tue; $10.50 before 6pm Sat, Sun. **Credit** MC, V. **Map** p274 D7.
This gambling/theatre complex owned by Famous Players delivers a bruising assault on the senses. It has 13 screens, as well as an IMAX 3D theatre.

Silver City Yonge & Eglinton
2300 Yonge Street, at Eglinton Avenue, Midtown (416 544 1236/www.famousplayers.ca). Subway Eglinton. **Admission** $13.50; $7.50 concessions; free under-3s; $8.50 before 6pm Mon-Fri, all day Tue; $10.50 before 6pm Sat, Sun. **Credit** MC, V.
There are a collection of Silver City cinemas around town. They're multiplexes with all the noise, bright lights, games and junk food you'll (n)ever want.

Varsity Cinemas
55 Bloor Street W, Manulife Centre, at Bay Street, University (416 961 6303/www.cineplex.com). Subway Bay, Bloor-Yonge. **Admission** *Main theatre* $13.50; $7.50 concessions; $8.50 before 6pm Mon-Fri, all day Tue; $10.50 before 6pm Sat, Sun. *VIP theatres* $15.50; $11.50 before 6pm Mon-Fri; $13.50 before 6pm Sat, Sun. **Credit** AmEx, MC, V. **Map** p280 E4.
This eight-screen mutiplex on the mink mile boasts top facilities and a good mix of mainstream, independent and foreign fare. In addition, the four VIP screening rooms, with concession service delivered to your seat, offers some of the most intimate viewing experiences outside a home theatre system. The VIP theatres range from 28 to 36 seats.

> ▶ For more on Toronto's film industry and Toronto International Film Festival *see p21* **Hollywood North**; for listings of Toronto's other film festivals, *see p164* **Festivals & Events**.

Galleries

In the wake of a millennial renaissance, Toronto's art scene is flourishing.

There has been a remarkable resurgence in the art scene in Toronto recently and an enthusiasm that hasn't been seen since the boom years of the 1980s. Since the millennium, more than 30 new galleries have opened up and an ever-increasing number of artists are jumping into the fray.

A high proportion of the art seen in Toronto – whatever the neighbourhood – is by young emerging artists. This is a global phenomenon for artists working in new digital- and time-based media, but a couple of other factors are also at play here. The art market in Toronto was one of the casualties of the recession of the early 1990s, so for a good ten years it wasn't much fun being an artist or running a gallery. And if you are an established Canadian art star you are probably going to be based in either New York or Los Angeles.

Most of the new galleries that have sprung up are in the **Queen Street West** neighbourhood, where the young and hip choose to be. West of Bathurst Street, it seems like someone is blowing the paint dry on a brand new gallery every week. **Monte Clark** from Vancouver has opened up a space here and **DeLeon White** has recently relocated. Most of the galleries are small converted

Massive attack

Forget huddling in cosy galleries on QSW. Toronto has a squad of artists whose work comes right out to find you – and is as likely to *be* a wall than to hang on one. Bigger (and weirder) is better for:

Tiff Isza makes anti-decoration interventions in people's houses that are violent, beautiful and subversive. This often involves eviscerating a wall to expose the cavity or the soft pink insulation inside. At the moment she is running the project space ne plus ultra (*see p184*).

Janet Morton is an artist who has made a practice out of knitting. She has knitted the

storefronts and on a warm evening of exhibition openings you will see crowds of trendies spilling out on to the streets and whole posses of artists hopping from one gallery to the next. Several specialise in photography, including the **Stephen Bulger Gallery** (700 Queen Street W, 416 504 0575), **Tatar Alexander Gallery** (183 Bathurst Street, 416 360 3822) and **LEE fotogallery** (Unit 116, 993 Queen Street W, 416 504 9387). To find out about what's on in the area visit www.artwestqueenwest.com.

Artists and galleries have often led the way in revitalising neighbourhoods – they essentially transformed Queen Street West, west of Bathurst. To see a work in progress that hopes to do for the East Side what Queen West has already achieved, visit the Gooderham and Worts Distillery district east of St Lawrence. This neglected part of town has been used for many movie shoots because of its intact 19th-century industrial settings. Developers are quickly moving in, providing space for artists,

as are several high-end galleries. As part of the plan to introduce Torontonians to this once-decrepit corner of the city, weekly arts festivals are to be staged in summer; visit www.thedistillerydistrict.com for details.

Until recently the gallery scene was focused in and around the **Yorkville** area at Bloor Street and Avenue Road. Once upon a time this neighbourhood was a hippie hangout where art and love were free, until the flower children discovered the virtues of employment and designer suits and it became more upscale. Yorkville's art market heyday was in the 1980s but there are still a number of galleries on and around Hazelton Avenue. Many of them, however, are beginning to show the conservatism and inertia that can come with age. The exceptions are **Sable-Castelli**, which has managed to maintain a strong stable of artists, and **Artcore**, a relative newcomer.

The listings in this chapter are a broad sample of the fare to be found around the city.

news and knitted a tree, but without a doubt her *House Cozy* (pictured left) made of old sweaters and knitted bits, which completely enveloped someone's residence on Toronto Island, took the prize for charm and ambition. **Noel Harding**'s monumental sculpture (pictured below) has been focusing on the

interface between organic and synthetic systems of life. His *Elevated Wetlands* south of Don Mills on the Don Valley Parkway is a series of walking planters made of waste plastic in which trees and grasses grow, and through which the very polluted Don River is filtered.

Arts & Entertainment

There are also a number of galleries in the warehouse building at 401 Richmond Avenue, and still more across the road at 80 Spadina Road. For comprehensive listings of current exhibitions, read *Now* (www.nowtoronto.com; out on Thursdays) and the monthly *Slate Art Guide*, free in most galleries or read online at www.slateartguide.com. For reviews check out the 'Gallery Going' section of the *Globe and Mail* newspaper (www.globeandmail.com).

Downtown Toronto

Angell Gallery

890 Queen Street W, at Crawford Street, Entertainment District (416 530 0444/ www.angellgallery.com). Streetcar 501, 510. **Open** noon-6pm Wed-Sat. **Credit** V. **Map** p276 A7.
Though you do see photography here once in a while, Angell is one of the few galleries to continue to survive on a steady diet of canvas paintings.

Jamie Angell opened his gallery on Queen Street West in 1996, making him something of an elder statesman on the scene.

Jane Corkin Gallery

Suite 302, 179 John Street, at Queen Street W, Entertainment District (416 979 1980/www. janecorkin.com). Streetcar 501/subway Osgoode. **Open** 9.30am-5.30pm Tue-Fri; 10am-5pm Sat. **Credit** V. **Map** p274 D7.
Jane Corkin's coloured walls show mainly photographs but sculpture and drawing occasionally find their way here. It is a well established gallery with a presence abroad and represents photographers Robert Bourdeau, Lori Newdick and Barbara Astman, among others.

Robert Birch Gallery

241 King Street E, at Sherbourne Street, St Lawrence (416 955 9410/www.robertbirch gallery.com). Bus 75/streetcar 504/subway King. **Open** 11am-6pm Wed-Sat. **Credit** V. **Map** p278 G8.

Local hero Euan Macdonald

At first glance, Euan Macdonald's short video loops look like the shots that you would edit out of your home movie, but he has an uncanny ability to hone in on details that turn it into a freak epiphany that transports you from your reality into a witty, charming and sometimes menacing one. His *Three Trucks* (pictured) was showing recently at the Art Gallery of Ontario: in it an old ice-cream truck playing a tinging rendition of *It's a Small World After All* pulls in at a nondescript intersection. Before long another ice-cream truck of the same description and playing the same cloying tune – but in a different key and at a different speed – pulls into the same intersection and stops in apparent confrontation. Then a third ice-cream truck pulls up playing a different tune and befuddles the cacophony. They nudge towards each other menacingly. You are mesmerised.

Euan Macdonald has a magical gift for making dramatic tension out of almost nothing – and making it funny. In *Hammock Sleep*, shown at the Robert Birch Gallery in 2001, someone swings drowsily in a hammock on a summer's day. The wind is playing in the leaves and just when you're beginning to identify with the lounger's lassitude the hammock suddenly and inexplicably swings faster and higher and finally does a complete 360-degree spin.

Euan has recently moved Los Angeles, but Torontonians still call him their own.

Honorable mentions: David Acheson (at Christopher Cutts) is one of the best sculptors around, making heroes out of exit-sign figures and superheroes into real people. **Jubal Brown** used to be a very bad boy but is now showing signs of growing into a smart and tightly controlled video artist. **Max Dean** (at Susan Hobbs) made a table at the Venice Biennale in 2001 that would choose a gallery-goer and follow them around. **John Dickson** (at Archive) is an intervention artist, who has embedded crying eyes in the walls of public places and bubble machines that spell out ephemeral messages. **Eric Glavin** (at Robert Birch) makes beautiful bright graphic paintings like advertisements without words. **Germaine Koh** has begun to receive attention for her quiet little interventions. She puts commonplace objects in a meditative context, like a turnstile in a public place that spins according to the force of the wind or an office computer that blows smoke signals in Morse code. **Badanna Zack** (at DeLeon White) sculpts beautiful things out of old newspapers; **Janieta Eyre** (at Christopher Cutts) takes deadpan funny photos of herself.

Previous contenders
General Idea was the corporate title that a trio of artists took for their collective in the late 1960s. Immediate heirs to Fluxus,

An unassuming-looking gallery, it still has the sign from a previous occupant, Clyde Fans, on the window. Robert Birch has an excellent band of artists, including Lee Goreas, Eric Glavin and Euan Macdonald, for whom it often seems an easy step into big museum collections. Like the gallery itself, works here are often deceptively simple.

S.P.I.N. Gallery

156-158 Bathurst Street, at Richmond Street W, Entertainment District (416 530 7656/www.spin gallery.ca). Streetcar 501, 511. **Open** noon-6pm Wed-Sat; 1-4pm Sun. **No credit cards.** **Map** p276 C7.

One of the new galleries that has sprung up in the Queen Street area, S.P.I.N. is dedicated to showing work by emerging local artists like Catherine Heard, John Scott and Fiona Smyth, plus the occasional well-known name like Floria Sigismondi.

YYZ Artists' Outlet

401 Richmond Street W, Suite 140, at Spadina Avenue, Entertainment District (416 598 4546/

cousins in spirit to Gilbert and George, and born in the age of Marshal McLuhan when the medium was the message, they were the witty admen of the art world here to reveal the truths espoused and obscured by the messages of popular media. Among many provocative AIDS-related works, they designed a logo for the disease, borrowing Robert Indiana's well-known LOVE design. In the mid 1990s two of the three members died of the disease. Survivor AA Bronson (http://users.rcn.com/aamark/), recently seen at the Whitney Biennale, is now working in a deeper, more ruminative tone.

www.yyzartistsoutlet.org). Streetcar 504, 510/subway Osgoode. **Open** 11am-5pm Tue-Sat. **Credit** MC, V. **Map** p274 D7.

An artist-run centre that aims to show work not being shown by commercial galleries and institutions. Like Mercer Union (*see p184*), it's a forum for smart artists, like Germaine Koh, to exhibit works that you can't hang above your couch.

Yorkville

Artcore Gallery

33 Hazelton Avenue, at Scollard Street (416 920 3820/www.artcoregallery.com). Subway Bay. **Open** 10am-6pm Tue-Sat. **No credit cards.** **Map** p280 E3.

With two floors, and two exhibitions running concurrently, this is one of the more progressive spaces in the otherwise relatively staid atmosphere of Yorkville. It is also one of the few galleries in Toronto with international pretensions, showing both Canadian and international artists.

Edward Day Gallery

33 Hazelton Avenue, at Scollard Street (416 921 6540/www.edwarddaygallery.com). Subway Bay. **Open** 10am-6pm Mon-Thur, Sat; 10am-9pm Fri; noon-5pm Sun. **Credit** AmEx, MC, V. **Map** p280 E3.

This is a buffet-style gallery – a whole lot of different tastes in close proximity. There are styles and artistic temperaments ranging from the high to the low and everything in between. It usually leaves you feeling full, and sometimes satisfied.

Sable-Castelli Gallery

33 Hazelton Avenue, at Scollard Street (416 961 0011/www.artnet.com/sable-castelli.html). Subway Bay. **Open** 10am-5pm Tue-Sat. **No credit cards.** **Map** p280 E3.

In a small basement gallery, Sable-Castelli is one of the venerable grandaddy galleries on the scene, showing some enduringly popular Canadian artists such as Betty Goodwin, Tony Scherman and the poetic Spring Hurlbut.

West End

Queen Street West & around

Archive

883 Queen Street W, at Strachan Avenue (416 703 6564/www.archivegallery.com). Streetcar 501. **Open** noon-6pm Tue-Fri; noon-5pm Sat. **No credit cards.** **Map** p276 B7.

This little space was designed by architect Johnson Chou and, as its name might suggest, it has a sizeable computer database of artists, mostly from Toronto and Montreal. It also holds exhibitions compiled from the works of artists in the archive by guest curators. Oddly enough, its website does not link to the artist database but it does show pictures of their current exhibition.

Olga Korper Gallery (*see p185*), where Tim Whiten makes a sweeping statement (right).

BUSgallery, 1080BUS & Katharine Mulherin Gallery

1040, 1080 & 1086 Queen Street W, at Brookfield Street (416 537 8827/www.busgallery.com). Bus 63/streetcar 501. **Open** *BUSgallery & 1080BUS* noon-5pm Fri-Sun. *Katharine Mulherin Gallery* noon-5pm Wed-Sun. **Credit** V.

Katharine Mulherin works with a large number of young artists and the work she shows is often humble and personal, despite owning three galleries on Queen Street.

DeLeon White Gallery

1096 Queen Street W, at Dovercourt Road (416 597 9466/www.eco-art.com/deleon). Bus 29, 63/streetcar 501. **Open** noon-6pm Wed-Sun. **No credit cards.**

DeLeon White Gallery's new digs are spacious and elegant in a neighbourhood on Queen Street that is going upscale faster than the fresh paint can dry. This gallery's mandate is to resist the purblind commodification of art by keeping in mind its relationship to nature and the environment. With artists like Aganetha Dyck, Noel Harding and Badanna Zack, it manages nevertheless to resist sentimentality. Check out the roof deck in good weather.

Mercer Union

37 Lisgar Street, at Queen Street W (416 536 1519/www.mercerunion.org). Streetcar 501, 510. **Open** 11am-6pm Tue-Sat. **No credit cards.**

A long-standing ideologically and theoretically driven artist-run space, Mercer Union is actually more fun than it sounds. It has seen many of Canada's best artists pass through. The exhibition space is divided into three distinct areas, allowing for concurrent exhibitions, lectures, video screenings and performance.

Monte Clark Gallery

752 Queen Street W, between Walnut Street & Niagara Avenue (416 703 1700/www.monte clarkgallery.com). Streetcar 501, 511. **Open** 11am-7pm Wed-Sat; noon-5pm Sun. **Credit** V. **Map** p276 B7.

This new gallery has become one of the most watched spaces in the city, with a style that is cool, wry and luscious to the eye. The artists it represents are mainly drawn from the original Monte Clark Gallery in Vancouver, including Roy Arden, Graham Gillmore and the author-artist Douglas Coupland. Monte Clark is the flavour of the moment, attracting the cultural elite, the criminally beautiful and the hordes of hip freeloaders in the area.

ne plus ultra

1080 Queen Street W, at Dovercourt Road (416 451 9802/www.ne-plus-ultra.com). Bus 63/streetcar 501. **Open** noon-5pm Thur-Sun. **No credit cards.**

One of the most recent additions to the Queen West gallery family, ne plus ultra puts on installations, performances, video and internet-based projects. Rob Hengeveld's 2002 installation *Residue* – layers of evidence of previous inhabitants of Hengeveld's fictitious empty apartment – was one of the highlights of the year.

Paul Petro Contemporary Art

980 Queen Street W, at Ossington Avenue (416 979 7874/www.interlog.com/~petro). Bus 63/streetcar 501. **Open** 11am-5pm Wed-Sat. **No credit cards.** **Map** p276 A7.

There is a tiny, easy-to-miss sign outside the gallery; there may be art in the window to help you find your way in, but if there isn't, this place is inscrutable

from the street. Inside, artwork centres on personal identity and identity politics by the likes of Paul P, Julie Voyce and Jay Isaac.

Susan Hobbs Gallery

137 Tecumseth Street, at Richmond Street W (416 504 3699/www.susanhobbs.com). Streetcar 501, 504, 511. **Open** *1-5pm Thur-Sat and by appointment.* **No credit cards. Map** p276 B7.

On a side-street off the main Queen Street strip, Susan Hobbs hosts mainly sculpture and installation by some of the more established Canadian artists such as Ian Carr-Harris, Robin Collyer, Max Dean, Robert Wiens and Shirley Wiitasalo, many of whom are very well known in Canada but not necessarily elsewhere.

Elsewhere

Art Metropole

2nd floor, 788 King Street W, at Bathurst Street (416 703 4400/www.artmetropole.com). Streetcar 504, 511. **Credit** MC, V. **Map** p276 A7.

This gallery and art bookstore was created in 1974 by a team of artists called General Idea. There is usually an installation with a conceptual bent here and always a lot of clever little multiples and publications. Exhibitions also delve into video, audio and electronic media.

Christopher Cutts Gallery

21 Morrow Avenue, at Dundas Street W (416 532 5566/www.cuttsgallery.com). Streetcar 505/subway Dundas West or Lansdowne. **Open** *10.30am-5.30pm Tue-Fri; 11am-6pm Sat.* **No credit cards.**

This immaculate gallery is well worth the time it will take you to find it. It's off the beaten track in a small complex of galleries, which also includes the Olga Korper Gallery (*see below*). It exhibits work by pioneers of modern Canadian painting like Kazuo Nakamura and Ray Mead, founding members of Painters Eleven from the 1950s, and an excellent bunch of younger artists such as Janieta Eyre, Richard Stipl and David Acheson.

Olga Korper Gallery

17 Morrow Avenue, at Dundas Street W (416 538 8220/www.olgakorpergallery.com). Streetcar 505/subway Dundas West or Lansdowne. **Open** *10am-6pm Tue-Sat.* **Credit** AmEx, V.

Established in 1973, this is probably the most beautiful gallery in the city – a cavernous and nicely lit space that was once a foundry then a garbage repository for a mattress factory. Olga Korper has become something of an institution on the art scene in Toronto and has a strong group of artists including Angela Grauerholz, Marcel Dzama, Paterson Ewen and Tim Whiten.

Ydessa Hendeles Art Foundation

778 King Street W, between Niagara & Tecumseth Streets (416 413 9400). Streetcar 504, 511. **Open** *noon-5pm Sat or by appointment.* **Admission** $5. **No credit cards. Map** p276 B8.

When Ydessa was an art dealer, representing artists like Jeff Wall and Jana Sterback, she began collecting art herself. And when the line between curating and collecting blurred, she opened up her remarkable and ever-developing collection to the public. Her collection is an art in its own right, with Maurizio Cattelan's sculpture of a praying Hitler residing beside a room covered from top to bottom in thousands of black and white photographs of people with their teddy bears.

Gay & Lesbian

Toronto's gay scene is highly civilised – unless you prefer it otherwise.

From a visitor's point of view, the Toronto gay scene is pretty much ideal. It's heavily concentrated in one small area that is close to the subway (both College and Wellesley stations on the Yonge Street line) and easily toured on foot. Most of the bars are either on Church Street, one block east of Yonge Street, or on the sidestreets in between. So if you don't like one bar, you can easily walk to another. Only one major bar, the **The Toolbox** (*see p189*), lies far outside the so-called 'gay ghetto'.

Like Toronto itself, local gays may seem a bit standoffish, but they usually respond well to subtle and not-so-subtle hints. The frostiest queen may melt for a smile, or an outstretched hand, at the baths. Unlike most American cities, Toronto never closed its bathhouses, even at the height of the AIDS epidemic, and somewhat to the natives' surprise the city has gradually developed a vaguely sexy reputation. There are now nine bathhouses, not to mention a strip joint where the boys bare all.

Not everyone enjoys the bar and bath scene, of course, and many local gays organise their social lives around volunteer organisations or the city's many active sports leagues – baseball and volleyball for the men, hockey and soccer for the women. A couple of these leagues are among the largest gay organisations in the city.

Lesbians have been more visible on Church Street in recent years but the scene is still hard to find. There are only a couple of dedicated lesbian bars in the city and many women prefer to socialise elsewhere, either through sports leagues or in some of the city's trendier, gay-friendly neighbourhoods. Both the studenty Annex and Queen Street West west of Bathurst Street, including Parkdale, are popular. For further information, check out the **Lesbian Social and Business Network** (www.lsbn toronto.com) or the bulletin board at the **Good For Her** sex shop (*see p193*).

In terms of inter-orientation attitudes, the thing to remember is that Toronto is not the US and Canadian attitudes towards gays are considerably more liberal (not to say blasé) than those in the US. (There aren't nearly as many members of the religious right for starters.) Gays serve in the armed forces, gay couples have pretty much the same rights and responsibilities as common-law straight couples and gay marriage is all but here. Locally, it's

much the same story, but more so. Ever since the legendary bath raids of the early 1980s, the local community has enjoyed a sure sense of self. The bath raids were Toronto's Stonewall and the community came of age in that struggle and the subsequent one against AIDS.

While there's still some friction with the police, the local community has political clout and a very visible presence. An openly gay councillor represents the local ghetto at City Hall, the mayor sometimes joins the **Pride Week** parade (*see p190* **Proud and clear**) and the public library keeps a collection of gay and lesbian books (available in the Yorkville branch, 22 Yorkville Avenue, 416 393 7660).

This is not to say that attitudes don't differ widely within the city. Gay couples hold hands quite openly downtown, particularly in the 'gay village' around Church and Wellesley, but are more circumspect in the 'old suburbs' of Etobicoke or Scarborough, or even in the straight part of the Entertainment District – Richmond–Adelaide – only a few subway stops away, where testosterone can sometimes get in the way of tolerance.

MEDIA

The key local paper is *Xtra!*, 'Toronto's Lesbian & Gay Biweekly' (www.xtra.ca). A direct descendant of an influential activist paper called *The Body Politic* that flourished in the 1970s, *Xtra!* has a political pedigree that makes it the local paper of record. It focuses on art, entertainment and politics and maintains a guide to local community groups that is listed in the back of the newspaper and accessible by phone at 416 925 9872. For a lighter, more ironic guide to the local scene, try *fab* (www.fab magazine.com). It's the one with cute boys on the cover and loads of party dish inside. Both papers are distributed free in bars, shops and restaurants within the ghetto and further afield. *Xtra!* has its own pink newspaper boxes on street corners throughout the city.

Siren serves the lesbian community but only appears every two months and can be hard to find. Try the 519 Church Street Community Centre (416 392 6874/www.the519.org) or *Siren* magazine (www.siren.ca).

Online, Gay Guide Toronto (www.gayguide toronto.com) offers comprehensive listings as well as tips on upcoming events. Features are updated monthly.

Arts & Entertainment

Bars & clubs

Local bars have grown increasingly specialised over the past few years. Gone are the days of one size fits all. Now's there's something for everyone, but keeping track of who's going where can be a full-time job, especially the one-night-a-week events that are increasingly popular with the young dance set. They change too often to be listed with any confidence, but promising venues include **Government** (132 Queens Quay E, Harbourfront, 416 869 0045, www.theguvernment.com); **IT** nightclub (167 Church Street, 416 410 1902, www.itsaboys life.com) and **Lee's Palace/The Dance Cave** (529 Bloor Street W, the Annex, 416 532 1598, www.leespalace.com). Check the local gay media for further information, or stand around Church Street and wait for a young 'un to give you a promotional flyer.

Licensing laws dictate that bars officially close at 2am and all alcohol must be 'off the tables' within half an hour. Therefore after-hours partying tends to be limited except at weekends, when places like **5ive**, **Fly** and the **Barn** stay open late.

The unmissable **Woody's**. *See p188.*

Church & Wellesley

Bar 501
501 Church Street, at Wellesley Street (416 944 3272). Bus 94/subway Wellesley. **Open** 11am-2am daily. **Credit** AmEx, MC, V. **Map** p281 F5.
Friendly, down-home bar known for its Sunday afternoon drag shows.

The Barn/The Stables
418 Church Street, at Granby Street E (416 977 4702). Streetcar 506/subway College. **Open** 9pm-3am Mon-Thur; 9pm-4am Fri, Sat; 4pm-4am Sun. **Credit** AmEx, MC, V. **Map** p277/p288 F6.
Recent renovations haven't changed the flavour of this Toronto favourite. Its brief stint as a backroom bar ended some years ago but the down and dirty atmosphere still lingers. This is where people come to shed their inhibitions and do some serious dancing. Open late and very popular even among people who claim to hate it. The Sunday afternoon underwear party is a big draw.

The Black Eagle
457 Church Street, at Alexander Street (416 413 1219/www.blackeagletoronto.com). Bus 94/subway Wellesley. **Open** noon-2am daily. **Credit** AmEx, MC, V. **Map** p281 F5.
A leather and denim cruise bar with dress codes (and porn) to match, this two-storey bar varies from casual to intense depending on the day of the week. Watch the signs at the door. It can be disconcerting to walk in on a watersports night when you just wanted some boot lickin'. The second-floor deck is a pleasant oasis of quiet on a summer night.

Crews & Tango
508-510 Church Street, at Alexander Street (416 972 1662/www.crews-tango.com). Streetcar 506/subway Wellesley. **Open** noon-2am daily. **Credit** AmEx, MC, V. **Map** p281 F5.
Technically Crews is for gay men and Tango is for women, but the two bars (in two connecting Victorian houses) flow into each other and everyone mingles.

Byzantium
499 Church Street, at Wellesley Street E (416 922 3859). Subway Wellesley. **Open** 5.30-11pm daily. **Credit** AmEx, MC, V. **Map** p281 F5.
The well-toned trade quips and drink martinis in a narrow designer space. *See also p192.*

Fly
8 Gloucester Street, at Yonge Street, Church & Wellesley (416 925 6222/www.flynightclub.com). Bus 94/subway Wellesley. **Open** 9pm-3am Sat. **Credit** AmEx, MC, V. **Map** p281 F4.
Celebrity DJs attract the circuit boy set and hold them until early the next morning. Saturdays only.

Hair of the Dog
425 Church Street, at Grenville Street (416 964 2708). Streetcar 506/subway Wellesley. **Open** 11.30am-2am daily. **Credit** MC, V. **Map** p281 F5.

Arts & Entertainment

Call in at **Remington's** for maximum exposure. *See p189.*

Cosy upscale pub with a quiet patio (in summer) and a good selection of draught. Good for chats, lousy for cruising. Men and women, gay and straight.

Pegasus Bar
489B Church Street, at Wellesley Street E (416 927 8832/www.pegasusonchurch.com). Bus 94/streetcar 506/subway Wellesley. **Open** noon-2am daily. **Credit** AmEx, MC, V. **Map** p281 F5.
Comfortable, well-lit, second-floor pool hall attracting both men and women.

Pope Joan
547 Parliament Street, at Wellesley Street E (416 925 6662/www.popejoan.ca). Bus 94/streetcar 506. **Open** 8pm-2.30am Fri, Sat; noon-2.30am Sun. **Credit** AmEx, MC, V. **Map** p281 H5.
Out to the east of the Church & Wellesley drag is the oldest lesbian bar in town, which also has the most diverse crowd.

Slack Alice
562 Church Street, at Wellesley Street E (416 969 8742/www.slackalice.ca). Subway Wellesley. **Open** 4pm-2am Mon-Fri; 11am-2am Sat, Sun. **Credit** AmEx, MC, V. **Map** p281 F5.
Older, upscale lesbians dominate this bar-restaurant on weekends, but the rest of the time it's a real mix, not to mention a hoot. Patrons have been known to dance on the bar.

Tallulah's Cabaret
12 Alexander Street, at Yonge Street (416 975 8555/www.buddiesinbadtimestheatre.com/tallulahs.php). Streetcar 506/subway Wellesley. **Open** 10.30pm-2am Fri, Sat. **Credit** MC, V. **Map** p281 F5.

A dance club on Friday and Saturday nights, this intimate space attracts a young, hip, media-savvy crowd, the sort of people who treat Britney Spears with both irony and respect. Both men and women, in a 70/30 split.

Trax V
529 Yonge Street, at Maitland Street (416 963 5196). Bus 94/streetcar 506/subway Wellesley. **Open** 11am-2am daily. **Credit** AmEx, MC, V. **Map** p281 F5.
Multi-level bar that rambles every which way, apparently determined to provide something for everybody: a piano bar at the front, a deck on the upper floors and a stage that supplies entertainment seven nights a week. Old, established and rumoured to sell more beer than any other bar in town.

Wett Bar
7 Maitland Street, at Homewood Avenue (416 966 9388). Bus 94/streetcar 506/subway Wellesley. **Open** 9pm-2.30am Thur-Sun. **Credit** AmEx, MC, V. **Map** p281 F5.
Tiny trendy niche bar for men with an eye for the right tank top.

Woody's/Sailor
465-7 Church Street, at Maitland Street (416 972 0887/www.woodystoronto.com). Bus 94/subway Wellesley. **Open** 2pm-2am daily. **Credit** AmEx, MC, V. **Map** p281 F5.
One of the most popular bars in the city, Woody's has had a lock on the mainstream market for more than a decade. Don't let the name fool you. Everyone calls it Woody's and everyone goes there sooner or later. The bar was famous long before it became a recurring character on the American

Queer As Folk and, in a market known for fickleness, has demonstrated an astonishing longevity. It's a little too respectable for some tastes and lots of folks prefer to do their cruising elsewhere. But still they come, especially at weekends, and Thursday and Sunday nights when drag shows and 'best chest' contests hold the stage. Straight-owned, it's one of the biggest local boosters of community events and institutions.

Zipperz

72 Carlton Street, at Church Street (416 921 0066). Streetcar 506/subway College. **Open** noon-2am daily. **Credit** AmEx, MC, V. **Map** p281 F5.
The piano bar in the front wrestles with the dancefloor in the back for aural domination, but the high noise levels are offset by the easy atmosphere. Zipperz is an old-style gay bar where men of all ages and classes mingle.

Yonge Street & around

Before the scene shifted to Church Street in the late 1980s, Yonge Street was the centre of the gay action. All that remains of that heady time is the tottering Victorian clock tower atop 488 Yonge Street, former home of the legendary St Charles Tavern until 1987. But some gay bars and clubs still cling to Toronto's main drag and its sidestreets.

5ive LifeLounge & DanceClub

5 St Joseph Street, at Yonge Street, University (416 964 8685/www.5ivenightclub.com). Bus 94/subway Wellesley. **Open** 9pm-3.30am Wed-Sun. **Credit** AmEx, MC, V. **Map** p280 E5.
This slick, design-conscious dance club attracts everyone from twinks to leathermen.

Remington's

379 Yonge Street, at Gerrard Street, Dundas Square (416 979 0943/www.remingtons.com). Streetcar 505/subway Dundas. **Open** 3pm-2am daily. **Credit** AmEx, MC, V. **Map** p277/278 F6.
The infamous 'Sperm Attack' Monday is no more, but numerous hunky strippers continue to bare all on two stages and in private sessions.

Sneakers

502A Yonge Street, at Alexander Street, University (416 961 5808/www.gaytoronto.com/sneakers). Subway Wellesley. **Open** 11am-2am daily. **Credit** AmEx, MC, V. **Map** p281 F5.
Skinny young guys, hefty older men. Need we say more?

Further afield

Ciao Edie

489 College Street, at Bathurst Street, Little Italy (416 927 7774). Streetcar 506, 511. **Open** 8pm-2am Mon-Sat; 9pm-2am Sun. **Credit** AmEx, MC, V. **Map** p276 B6.

A retro-funky bar in the newly hip College Street strip, this hot-spot hosts a long-running women's night on Sunday, which is popular with a hip, arty crowd.

The Toolbox

508 Eastern Avenue, at Morse Street, East Side (416 466 8616/www.toolboxtoronto.com). Streetcar 501. **Open** 5pm-2am Mon-Fri; noon-2am Sat, Sun. **Credit** MC, V. **Map** p279 J8.
Leather and uniforms abound in a bar not far from lower Riverdale, home to innumerable gay couples.

Bathhouses

The Barracks

56 Widmer Street, at Richmond Street W, Entertainment District (416 593 0499/www.barracks.com). Streetcar 504/subway St Andrew. **Open** 24 hours daily. **Credit** AmEx, MC, V. **Map** p277 D7.
Edgier sex with leather accessories in a small townhouse not so far from the establishment arts palace, Roy Thomson Hall.

The Bijou

370 Church Street, at McGill Street, Church & Wellesley (416 971 9985). Bus 94/subway Wellesley. **Open** 9pm-4am Wed, Thur, Sun; 9pm-5am Fri, Sat. **No credit cards.** **Map** p277/p278 F6.
Once home to the infamous 'slurp ramp' (don't ask), this former backroom bar-cum-porno palace is now officially a bathhouse, or as they like to say, a 'porno palace (with showers)'.

Cellar

78 Wellesley Street E, at Church Street, Church & Wellesley (416 975 1799). Bus 94/subway Wellesley. **Open** 24 hours daily. **No credit cards.** **Map** p281 F5.
This 24-hour bathouse is widely known as the darkest bathhouse in town. This joint doesn't even have a sign, just a black door.

Club Toronto

231 Mutual Street, at Granby Street, Church & Wellesley (416 977 4629/www.clubtoronto.com). Subway Wellesley. **Open** 24 hours daily. **Credit** AmEx, MC, V. **Map** p277/278 F6.
Old and rambling, this Victorian mansion has a whirlpool and a tiny outdoor pool, sometimes hosting a women's night known as Pussy Palace.

St Marc Spa

543 Yonge Street, 4th floor, at Wellesley Street, Church & Wellesley (416 927 0210). Subway Wellesley. **Open** 24 hours daily. **Credit** MC. **Map** p281 F5.
Big and popular with a pleasantly labyrinthine layout and a near-perfect location, close to the Yonge Street subway and late-night bus. Hop on, hop off.

Spa Excess

105 Carlton Street, at Jarvis Street, Church & Wellesley (416 260 2363/www.spaexcess.com). Streetcar 506. **Open** 24 hours daily. **Credit** AmEx, MC, V. **Map** p277/278 F6.

Arts & Entertainment

Large and licensed, this four-floor wonder exudes a boy-next-door wholesomeness that's offset by the dark, maze-like area on the top floor.

The Spa on Maitland

66 Maitland Street, at Church Street, Church & Wellesley (416 925 1571/www.thespaonmait land.com). Bus 94/subway Wellesley. **Open** 24 hours daily. **No credit cards. Map** p277/p278 F5.
Busy licensed bath with a very indiscreet entrance, directly opposite the busiest patio in town.

Cafés

'The Steps' in front of the **Second Cup** started the Church Street revolution back in 1984 and coffeeshops have played a crucial role ever since. Each has its distinct clientele; all are popular with folks looking for an alternative to the bars.

Second Cup

546 Church Street, at Maitland Street, Church & Wellesley (416 964 2457/www.secondcup.com). Subway Wellesley. **Open** 24 hours daily. **Credit** MC, V. **Map** p281 F5.
Open 24/7, this Toronto institution attracts a decidedly mixed clientele, many of them young.

Starbucks

485 Church Street, at Maitland Street, Church & Wellesley (416 922 2440/www.starbucks.com). Bus 94/subway Wellesley. **Open** 6am-midnight Mon-Thur, Sun; 6am-1am Fri, Sat. **Credit** AmEx, MC, V. **Map** p281 F5.
Students study on the airy second floor while boulvardiers hog the two tiny, but well-placed, tables on the front patio.

Timothy's World Coffee

500 Church Street, at Alexander Street, Church & Wellesley (416 925 8550/www.timothys.ca). Bus 94/ streetcar 506/subway Wellesley. **Open** 7pm-12.30am daily. **Credit** MC, V. **Map** p281 F5.
An older, affluent crowd mingles comfortably both inside and outside what has become known as the Steps II. Popular with the local deaf community.

Cruising

Cruising is in the eye of the beholder, of course, and in a large gay centre like Toronto, it can happen anywhere, but a few spots retain their hold on the popular imagination, notably Hanlan's Point on the Toronto Islands, where there's a 'clothing optional' beach; the wooded ravines of David Balfour Park, near tony Yonge

Proud and clear

One of the largest Pride events in the world, alongside Sydney, San Francisco and New York, Toronto's Pride in June attracts about 800,000 people and generates more than $40 million for the city. But those are just the stats. Let's talk atmosphere.

The excitement starts to build up early, usually at the beginning of the week's events, and hits the roof on Friday night when Church Street closes to traffic and the locals start to sniff the air for action. Women take to the street Saturday afternoon for the Dyke March and all fun breaks loose on Sunday as the big parade makes its way down Yonge Street.

What started out as a small political picnic in 1970 has turned into a brash commercial success that's more celebration than march. There are beer gardens and tons of entertainment on several stages in and around Church Street throughout the weekend – everything from disco to alterna-queer to lesbian folk.

Off site, local promoters offer a series of massive circuit parties focused on leather, military, skirt-gun and other themes, culminating in the **Unity** party at Exhibition Place (www.unitytoronto.com).

Finding a quieter form of culture can be difficult but not impossible. There's a 5km (3 mile) charity run called the **Pride & Remembrance Run** on the Saturday morning and the local queer theatre company, **Buddies in Bad Times** (*see p191*), usually holds a week of plays, staged readings, dances and drag shows. And for something really different try Cheap Queers, several nights of casual cabaret featuring local theatre and comedy stars. The locale varies but it's worth a peak.

As for the big parade itself: bring lots of water, hang on to your friends and don't even think of trying to meet anyone at a specific time or place. It's not that the parade itself is anything special: the usual drag queens and muscle boys dress up for the delight of giddy onlookers. But the atmosphere is heady and, this side of Caribana, it's as close to a Latin carnival as Anglo Toronto is ever likely to get.

For more information call 416 927 7433 (www.pridetoronto.com), or check local publications closer to the event. *Xtra!* usually publishes a stand-alone guide to the festivities in early June. *See also p166.*

Buddies in Bad Times Theatre – the ghetto's cultural heart.

Street and St Clair Avenue; Riverdale Park on the eastern edge of the Don Valley, where there's a spectacular view of the city, not to mention an outdoor pool favoured by homos in the summer; the bike trails around Cherry Beach on the Toronto waterfront; and High Park in the west end of the city. All at your own risk, of course; visits from the police are always a possibility.

Culture

Queer culture is found in many mainstream venues, from established alternative theatres like the **Factory** and the **Tarragon** (for both, *see p219*) to the local arthouse multiplex, the **Carlton** cinemas (20 Carlton Street, at Yonge Street, Church & Wellesley, 416 598 2309; *see p177*), venue for many a first date. But it's the queer-run venues that set the pace for cutting-edge culture.

Buddies in Bad Times Theatre

12 Alexander Street, at Yonge Street, Church & Wellesley (416 975 8555/www.buddiesinbadtimes theatre.com). Streetcar 506/subway Wellesley.
Box office noon-5pm Tue-Sat. **Tickets** $15-$25.
Credit MC, V. **Map** p281 F5..
The largest lesbian and gay theatre in North America, Buddies moved to its present location, just off Church Street, in 1994, and has almost single-handedly made the ghetto into something more than a non-stop cruise fest. Not everyone goes to the theatre, of course, but Buddies offers everything from

a serious subscription season to a popular lesbian cabaret night (Strange Sisters) to regular dance nights like **Tallulah's Cabaret** (*see p188*). Its something-for-everybody approach, plus its location beside a tiny but welcoming urban park, give it a real local presence. Not to be missed.

Canadian Lesbian & Gay Archives

56 Temperance Street, at Bay Street, Entertainment District (416 777 2755/www.clga.ca). Streetcar 501.
Open 7.30-10pm Tue-Thur or by appointment.
Admission free. **Map** pp277/p278 E7.
The second largest lesbian and gay archive in the world, the CLGA houses the world's largest collection of lesbian and gay periodicals – amounting to more than 6,100 titles – not to mention books, buttons and T-shirts. Call before you turn up as hours are limited.

Inside Out Toronto Lesbian & Gay Film & Video Festival

Various venues (416 977 6847/www.insideout.on.ca).
Date May. Call for details.
Valued as much for the looks in the line-up as the sights on screen, this popular festival – now in its 13th year – brings out the community's arty elite. Now the second largest film festival in the city, Inside Out plays everything from commercial product to obscure documentaries.

We're Funny That Way

Buddies in Bad Times Theatre, 12 Alexander Street, at Yonge Street, Church & Wellesley (416 975 8555/ http://members.aol.com/werefunny). **Date** May.
Map p281 F5.

Wilde Oscar's: if only he knew. *See p193*.

Queer comedy so good it's been filmed for TV, producing at least two specials. Everyone from Maggie Cassella to Lea DeLaria performs here.

Gyms

Bally Total Fitness
80 Bloor Street W, at Bay Street, Yorkville (416 960 2434/www.ballyfitness.com). Subway Bay. **Open** 6am-11pm Mon-Fri; 8am-7pm Sat, Sun. **Credit** AmEx, MC, V. **Map** p280 E4.
Brutal lighting doesn't dissuade a very gay clientele at Bally. Maybe 'cause the entrance is next to Banana Republic.
Branches: throughout the city.

Epic Fitness
9 St Joseph Street, at St Nicholas Street, University (416 961 1705). Subway Wellesley. **Open** 6am-midnight Mon-Thur; 6am-11pm Fri; 7.30am-8pm Sat; 7.30am-7pm Sun. **Credit** AmEx, MC, V. **Map** p280 E5.
The closest thing in the city to an all-gay gym, this minimalist wonder caters to the circuit boy crowd.

Metro-Central YMCA
20 Grosvenor Street, at Bay Street, University (416 975 9622/www.ymcatoronto.org). Streetcar 506/subway Wellesley. **Open** 6am-11pm Mon-Fri; 7am-8pm Sat, Sun. **Credit** AmEx, MC, V. **Map** p280 E5.
Even with 11,000-plus mostly heterosexual members, the gay presence here is immediately noticeable. A range of facilities is on offer, including a beautiful pool and spacious indoor track.

Restaurants

With few exceptions, it's safe to say that nobody goes to Church Street for the food. The food is the price you pay for dining in a gay environment. So if you're looking for something beyond burgers, pasta and other culinary mainstays, you may want to look elsewhere. That said, a few recent arrivals have tried to buck the trend and raise standards.

Byzantium
499 Church Street, at Wellesley Street E, Church & Wellesley (416 922 3859). Subway Wellesley. **Open** 5.30-11pm daily. **Main courses** $14-$24. **Credit** AmEx, MC, V. **Map** p281 F5.
Solid bistro-style food like steak and frites and fish in an upscale, very designer environment.

The Garage Sandwich Co
504 Church Street, at Grosvenor Street, Church & Wellesley (416 929 7575). Bus 94/subway Wellesley. **Open** 11am-8pm Mon-Sat; noon-7pm Sun. **Main courses** $5-$10. **Credit** MC, V. **Map** p281 F5.
Tiny, funky sandwich place known for its vegetarian and meat-based chilli con carne.

Inspire
491 Church Street, at Wellesley Street E, Church & Wellesley (416 963 0044). Bus 94/subway Wellesley. **Open** 5pm-midnight Mon, Sun; 5pm-2am Tue-Sat. **Main courses** $10-$28. **Credit** AmEx, DC, MC, V. **Map** p281 F5.
Inspire serves Asian fusion food in a minimalist white room with a sensual groove and good-looking

servers. The bar in the middle of the room is a great place to chat, but not to stand alone. Try it and you're going to feel very self-conscious.

Mitzi's Café
100 Sorauren Avenue, at Pearson Avenue, West End (416 588 1234). Streetcar 501. **Open** 7.30am-5pm Mon-Fri; 9am-4pm Sat, Sun. **Main courses** $7-$10. **No credit cards.**
Situated in newly trendy Parkdale in the West End of the old city of Toronto near High Park, Mitzi's Café is a retro '50s diner with a gay-friendly atmosphere and a strong female following.

Mitzi's Sister
1600 Queen Street W, at Beaty Avenue, West End (416 588 1100). Streetcar 501. **Open** 4-10pm Mon-Fri; 11am-4pm Sat, Sun. **Main courses** $7-$12. **No credit cards.**
Mitzi's Sister, just around the corner from Mitzy's Café, holds a women's night twice a month. Though both venues are popular brunch spots, only the Sister is licensed.

PJ Mellon's
489 Church Street, at Wellesley Street E, Church & Wellesley (416 966 3241). Bus 94/subway Wellesley. **Open** 11.30am-10.30pm Mon-Thur; 11.30am-midnight Fri, Sat; 11am-10pm Fri-Sun. **Main courses** $9-$18. **Credit** AmEx, DC, MC, V. **Map** p281 F5.
Tries to cater to all tastes with everything from burgers to pasta to French onion soup and, judging from its longevity, it usually succeeds. Tchotchke-riddled brick walls give it the feel of a family restaurant with an all-gay clientele. Relaxed.

Trattoria Al Forno
459 Church Street, at Grosvenor Street, Church & Wellesley (416 944 8852). Bus 94/subway Wellesley. **Open** 5-10pm Mon-Thur; 5-11pm Fri-Sun. **Main courses** $9-$18. **Credit** AmEx, DC, MC, V. **Map** p281 F5.
Pizza and pasta place with a family atmosphere and a gay clientele.

Wilde Oscar's
518 Church Street, at Maitland Street, Church & Wellesley (416 921 8142). Bus 94/streetcar 506/subway Wellesley. **Open** 11am-2am daily. **Main courses** $11-$20. **Credit** AmEx, DC, MC, V. **Map** p281 F5.
The best patio on the strip. It's a great spot for people watching, especially if you want to see who's going into the bathhouse across the street.

Zelda's Restaurant Bar Patio
542 Church Street, at Maitland Street, Church & Wellesley (416 922 2526/www.zeldas.ca). Subway Wellesley. **Open** 11am-2am Mon-Fri; 10am-2am Sat, Sun. **Main courses** $7-$14. **Credit** AmEx, MC, V. **Map** p281 F5.
Reviewers have dissed the food, but Zelda's rocks on, loaded with zany gay atmosphere. The servers are cute, the Sunday brunch is a mass of eye contact and there are pink flamingos in the fake foliage on the roof. What more do you want? There are huge queues for the summer patio, but under no circumstances let them stick you near the alley at the back of the building. That way smelly dumpsters lie.

Shopping

See also p151 **Body Body Wear**.

Glad Day Bookshop
598A Yonge Street, at Dundonald Street, Church & Wellesley (416 961 4161/www.gladday bookshop.com). Bus 94/subway Wellesley. **Open** 10am-7pm Mon-Wed, Sat; 10am-9pm Thur, Fri; noon-7pm Sun. **Credit** AmEx, MC, V. **Map** p281 F5.
The second oldest gay and lesbian bookstore in the world (est 1970), Glad Day has an astonishing range of hard-to-find titles. It stocks current bestsellers and maintains a popular 'adult section' but the majority of its 14,000 titles are out of print. Everything from fiction to parenting to transgender issues can be found, plus a good selection of queer videos and DVDs, both arty and mainstream.

Good For Her
175 Harbord Street, at Spadina Avenue, Harbord (416 588 0900/www.goodforher.com). Bus 94/streetcar 510. **Open** 11am-7pm Mon-Thur; 11am-8pm Fri; 11am-6pm Sat; noon-5pm Sun. *Women-only* 11am-2pm Thur; noon-5pm Sun. **Credit** AmEx, MC, V. **Map** p280/p276 C5.
Known for educational workshops on everything from lesbian love to better orgasms, this women-centred sex shop is also a good source of information on lesbian events. It's open to everyone but some times of the week are for women only.

Out on the Street
551 Church Street, at Monteith Street, Church & Wellesley (416 967 2759). Bus 94/subway Wellesley. **Open** 10am-8pm Mon-Wed, Sun; 10am-9pm Thur-Sat. **Credit** AmEx, MC, V. **Map** p281 F5.
Aimed squarely at gay men, Out on the Street is a three-level shop carrying casual men's clothing, plus a broad selection (over 100) of T-shirts with catchy queer slogans.

Priape
465 Church Street, at Maitland Street, Church & Wellesley (416 586 9914/www.priape.com). Bus 94/subway Wellesley. **Open** 10am-9pm Mon-Sat; noon-6pm Sun. **Credit** AmEx, DC, MC, V. **Map** p281 F5.
Dildos and porn and everything leather, but some folks come just for the sexy swimsuits. Not to mention tickets for events and community information.

> ▶ For gay accommodation and help and information contacts, *see p255* **Resources A-Z: Gay & Lesbian**.

Arts & Entertainment

Music

From high operatics to lounge-lizardry, Toronto knows the score.

Classical

If it were in the United States, Toronto would be considered a mid-sized city, and would likely have a middling cultural scene to match. But as it is, the city is the biggest fish in the small pond known as Canada, and that has helped its classical ensembles gain international stature. Most of the big performing groups have been around for decades, and most have gone through hard times at some point. But in a way, that's a good thing. It's given groups such as the **Toronto Mendelssohn Choir** and the **Toronto Symphony Orchestra** a chance to demonstrate their staying power. In addition to presenting prime quality music, these groups have been around long enough now to bring a sense of history and tradition to the stage.

In 2002, the Ontario and national governments finalised one of the largest ever investments in Canadian arts: more than $200 million to fund a decade-long project of building and rebuilding many structures that house Torontonian cultural institutions. The plans include the construction of a long-delayed opera house (to be called **Four Seasons Centre for the Performing Arts**) and dramatic improvements to **Roy Thomson Hall**. Heady with this rare recognition of their value to the city, many ensembles are planning ambitious projects to coincide with their new digs. In other words, there has never been a better time to take in Toronto's classical offerings.

Performing groups

Canadian Opera Company
416 363 8231/www.coc.ca.
Buoyed by plans for an expensive new opera house in the heart of Toronto's theatre district, the COC's general director Richard Bradshaw announced that the company will mount Richard Wagner's massive tetralogy, *Der Ring des Nibelungen*. The complete cycle of four operas, more than 16 hours of music, is the largest work in the history of Western music. The first performance is scheduled for 2004. The half-century-old company has long been touring and selling CDs internationally, but the Ring Cycle is its shot at the biggest of the big time. Canada's top guns will be hauled in for the project. Film-maker Atom Egoyan will direct *Die Walkure* (*The*

George Weston Recital Hall: world-class acoustics worth the trip. *See p196.*

Valkyrie), while François Girard, Michael Levine and Tim Albery will each direct one of the other three operas. Bradshaw will conduct for all.

Meanwhile, the COC remains in its Hummingbird Centre base, where it takes pains to keep opera relevant to the modern world. You see this in such calculatedly crowd-pleasing performances as *Oedipus Rex* and *The Turn of the Screw*, in experimental adaptations of shows such as Tchaikovsky's *Queen of Spades*, and in regular lectures, primers, and glossaries for opera newbies. The COC also promotes itself as a company of the people by staging charity concerts, and shows on the waterfont, meaning you can get often your operatic toes wet for cheap.

Tafelmusik Baroque Orchestra & Chamber Choir

416 964 6337/www.tafelmusik.org.

Somehow this choir and ensemble manages to make baroque chamber music sexy. Its shows are witty, entertaining and technically superb, winning it popular and critical acclaim at home and abroad. When it's not touring Canada and the world, Tafelmusik presents more than 40 concerts a year at Trinity-St Paul's Centre. The ensemble's rise to prominence is largely down to its musical director Jeanne Lamon, an award-winning violinist and baroque specialist.

Toronto Mendelssohn Choir

416 598 0422/www.tmchoir.org.

This mostly amateur ensemble, with a core of about 20 professional singers, has been a Toronto mainstay for over a century. Some critics have accused the 180-voice choir of being in a slump of late, but under artistic director Noel Edison, who has led the group since 1998, it continues to seek out innovative ways to present choral music. The ensemble is a regular companion of the TSO, Les Grands Ballets Canadiens and the National Arts Centre Orchestra, and its performances have taken in such quirky gems as *Music Meets Canvas*, in which artist Joseph Drapell created a painting on stage to the tune of the *Kaddish Symphony* by Leonard Bernstein.

Toronto Symphony Orchestra

416 598 3375/www.tso.on.ca.

The city almost lost its most prominent philharmonic ensemble in 2002, or so the TSO's fundraisers would have us believe. Big debt and small audiences prompted its chairman, former Ontario premier Bob Rae, to warn that the orchestra was on the 'precipice of complete collapse'. The alarm came just in the nick of time. Private donors ponied up more than $1 million in donations, a figure matched by the federal government. The TSO's finances are back on track, ticket sales are up and Rae is no longer mixing his metaphors. It looks like the city will keep its world-class symphony.

The TSO was founded in 1922 as the New Symphony Orchestra, featuring local musicians performing under the baton of Viennese-born conductor Luigi von Kunits. In its 60 years at Massey Hall and more than two decades at Roy Thomson

The best Venues

To don a beret and scribble Beat poetry

Rex Hotel Jazz & Blues Bar (*see p202*) – if you're lucky, the band might let you up on stage to read.

To go when you've hit bottom

The blues at the **Silver Dollar Room** (*see p202*) will sink down to your depths, and then raise you up to new heights.

To see big names looking small

SkyDome (*see p199*) – the stadium that caters to all your megastar needs.

For contemporary jazz in a retro setting

Enjoy top-notch jazz with 1920s elegance at **Top o'the Senator** (*see p202*).

For a spot of alt.everything

Swerve off the mainstream at **The Rivoli** (*see p199*).

To maximise chances of having sex on a first date (for a man)

A Tafelmusik concert at **Trinity-St Paul's Centre** (*see p197*) is the perfect chance to demonstrate your appreciation of art and architecture, your sophistication and sensitivity: if she doesn't fall for that, she's not falling for anything.

To maximise chances of having sex on a first date (for a woman)

Maybe it's the smart music at **Nia** (*see p199*), or perhaps the warm lighting, but whatever it is, you'll become instantaneously more sexy the moment you walk through the door.

Hall, the orchestra has earned a reputation for diversity and accessibility. Instrumentalists Yo-Yo Ma and Yehudi Menuin, dancer Karen Kain and the Magic Circle Mime Company have been among the guest performers, and Igor Stravinsky once guest-conducted his own work with the orchestra. Recent seasons have included old favourites from Mozard and Beethoven, interspersed with more contemporary composers such as R Murray Schafer and Jean Sibelius. The orchestra also does pop concerts and special youth performances. At press time, the TSO was searching for a new artistic director, with Brit Daniel Harding being touted as a front-runner.

Arts & Entertainment

Smaller performing groups

The **Royal Conservatory of Music** (416 408 2824/www.rcmusic.ca) organises symphonic and small ensemble recitals at various venues around town. Founded in 1974, the **Toronto Symphony Youth Orchestra** (416 598 3375) has alumni performing all over the world. The members of 50-year-old **Orchestra Toronto** (416 467 7142/www.orchestratoronto.org), the artists formerly known as the East York Symphony in pre-amalgamation days, have an ongoing mission to make orchestral music accessible to a broad audience. The 80-voice **Orpheus Choir of Toronto** (416 530 4428/www.orpheus.on.ca), under the direction of Trinidadian import Brainerd Blyden-Taylor, performs excellent but infrequent concerts. **Toronto Chamber Choir** (416 968 1338/ www.geocities.com/torontochamberchoir) is a 40-voice ensemble with a repertoire that ranges from medieval to modern, with an emphasis on Renaissance and baroque.

Venues

The Carlu

College Park, 444 Yonge Street, at College Street, University (416 410 8727/www.thecarlu.com). Streetcar 506/subway College. **Open** call for details. **Map** p281 F5.

Torontonians remember it as the Eaton Auditorium, a 1930s deco dream that had sat empty for the last 30 years. Citizens' groups fought hard to protect it from the wrecking ball and now, after a loving restoration, it is set to open in the spring of 2003. The new name recalls its French architect, Jacques Carlu, who also worked on the Rockefeller Center. The 1,000-seat venue on the seventh floor has such good acoustics that the notoriously fickle Glenn Gould insisted on recording here. Billie Holiday and other jazz legends also performed. The adjoining round-room restaurant is back in service.

George Weston Recital Hall

5040 Yonge Street, at Hillcrest Avenue, North Side (416 733 9388/www.tocentre.com). Subway North York Centre or Sheppard. **Open** Box office 11am-6pm Mon-Sat; noon-4pm Sun. **Tickets** $40-$60. **Credit** AmEx, MC, V.

Loved by performers and concert-goers alike, this hall is one of Canada's (and the world's) finest. Located far from the city centre in the Toronto Centre for the Arts in North York, the elegant 1,032-seat theatre is modelled on European concert halls such as Amsterdam's Concertgebouw, and has outstanding acoustics and sightlines. In addition to many quality international performers, the Canadian Opera Company and Tafelmusik perform concert series here.

Glenn Gould Studio

Canadian Broadcasting Centre, 250 Front Street W, at John Street, Entertainment District (ticketline 416 205 5555/http://glenngouldstudio.cbc.ca). Streetcar 504/subway St Andrew. **Open** Box office 11am-6pm Mon-Fri. **Credit** AmEx, MC, V. **Map** p277 D8.

This theatre doubles as a recording studio for the Canadian Broadcasting Corporation. CBC radio's 'On Stage' concert series (September-May) is recorded here with performances from classics to jazz. The 340-seat venue makes for an intimate evening of Canadian and international artists.

Harbourfront Centre Concert Stage

235 Queen's Quay Boulevard W, at Lower Simcoe Street, Waterfront (416 973 3000/www.harbourfront.on.ca). Streetcar 509, 510/subway Union. **Open** Box office 1-8pm Tue-Sat. **Tickets** $20-$60. **Credit** AmEx, MC, V. **Map** p277/p278 E9.

The fan-shaped outdoor stage looks out on to Lake Ontario and the Toronto Islands. It usually hosts folk or pop music from remote parts of the world, but you can sometimes see the Canadian Opera Company or other classical ensembles here. The view makes this a memorable place to catch a show, although noise laws mean that the fun must end by 11pm so the condo-dwellers can get some shut-eye.

Hummingbird Centre for the Performing Arts

1 Front Street E, at Yonge Street, St Lawrence (416 393 7469/www.hummingbirdcentre.com). Streetcar 504/subway King or Union. **Open** Box office 11am-6pm Mon-Sat. **Tickets** $20-$150. **Credit** AmEx, MC, V. **Map** p277/p278 F8.

This is where the Canadian Opera Company has hung its helmet since 1961 (though it was known as the O'Keefe Centre then). But change has been in the air for some time. Everyone agrees that the 3,000-seat theatre lacks the intimacy needed for operatic performance. The Canadian Opera Company will stick around until the new opera house is ready (probably in 2005), and then they'll fly the coop. Will the Hummingbird develop empty-nest syndrome? Not a chance. The stage in this multi-purpose theatre has been trodden by such diverse stars as The Clash, Charles Aznavour, Robin Williams and Björk.

Massey Hall

178 Victoria Street, at Shuter Street, Dundas Square (416 872 4255/www.masseyhall.com). Streetcar 501, 505/subway Dundas or Queen. **Open** Ticketline 9am-8pm Mon-Fri; noon-5pm Sat. **Tickets** $20-$100. **Credit** AmEx, MC, V. **Map** p277/p278 F7.

The first concert at this historic auditorium took place in 1894 and featured Handel's *Messiah*, performed by a 500-member choir and 70-piece orchestra. Today, the 2,765-seat hall is still one of the most rewarding places in the city to hear classical music. Sightlines vary, and the upper seats are hard and cramped, but the acoustics and intimacy more than make up for any shortcomings. Before Roy Thomson Hall was opened, this was the home of the TSO. The orchestra returned here temporarily in 2002 while Roy

Roy Thomson Hall keeps beating its drum (now with new warmer tones).

Thomson was being renovated and many symphony subscribers were very happy that they did. With the TSO back at RTH, classical concerts are rare now at Massey Hall. But you can still see the best of folk, blues and jazz. There is simply no better place to catch acts such as Bruce Cockburn, Wynton Marsalis, Alison Krauss and BB King.

Roy Thomson Hall

60 Simcoe Street, at King Street W, Entertainment District (416 872 4255/www.roythomson.com). Streetcar 504/subway St Andrew. **Open** *Ticketline 9am-8pm Mon-Fri; noon-5pm Sat. Box office (in person) 10am-6pm Mon-Fri; noon-5pm Sat.* **Tickets** *$29-$135.* **Credit** *AmEx, MC, V.* **Map** *p277 D8.*
This big snare-drum shaped building is best known as the place to catch the Toronto Symphony Orchestra, but the 2,812-seat theatre also hosts many other classical ensembles, along with occasional visits from pop music performers such as Bonnie Raitt and Nelly Furtado. Opened in 1982, the hall was supposed to be acoustically perfect, but it didn't live up to expectations. Major renovations completed in 2002 replaced the austere concrete interior with warm wood tones that have given it the high-quality acoustics it was always intended to have.

Trinity-St Paul's Centre

427 Bloor Street W, at Robert Street, Harbord (416 922 4954/www.tspucc.org). Streetcar 510/subway Spadina. **Tickets** *call for details.* **Map** *p280 C4.*
Intimate, sacred and mellow. With those qualities, it's no surprise that this has been Tafelmusik's main stage for almost 25 years. Musicians say the acoustics are good, but audiences say they're great,

and the deep horseshoe layout means that everyone gets close to the stage. The church is also used by many other chamber music ensembles, as well as by quiet pop artists such as Rufus Wainwright.

Rock, Roots & Jazz

Chicago has the blues. Seattle has grunge. New Orleans has jazz. Kentwood, Louisiana has Britney Spears. But it's not so easy to pin down the Toronto sound: the city's music scene remains steadfastly independent and diverse. Part of the reason for this is that it's filled with people who come from somewhere else. Canadians from every region move to Toronto to find work, and the city is also the natural place for immigrants to make a start in Canada.

More important still to the city's eclecticism, though, is the difficulty of a Toronto-based musician ever becoming truly famous. If a band is a hit in Los Angeles, they've already made it big. If they're a hit in Toronto, they're merely preparing to make it big. But that, in turn, means there are no megalithic recording companies pressuring bands to instantaneously go multi-platinum. And that means Toronto musicians are not beholden to the lowest common denominator. They have the freedom to experiment and refine their music. As a result, the city produces bands such as the Barenaked Ladies and Moxy Früvous, whose slow-cooked, folk-influenced pop music is

Orbit Room: for when you want to scale things down. *See p200.*

characterised by clever lyrics, complex melodies and harmonies, and self-deprecating humour. And the live scene benefits.

Toronto has historically pushed more than its share of jazz, folk, heavy metal, new wave and blues musicians on to the world stage, almost always with a strong emphasis on singer-songwriters. Masterful songwriters such as the legendary **Ron Sexsmith** and **Kyp Harness** often play around town and are always worth hearing. It's also worth catching the anarchic music collective known as **Wayne Omaha** as they experiment with improvisational grooves. Also notable is the two-man band **Elliot Brood**, if only to see vocalist Mark Sasso pull off the astounding trick of making a banjo sound mournful.

Of course, being the largest city in Canada, Toronto does get its share of superstars passing through. If, as often happens, a Backstreet Boys or a U2 tour has only one stop in Canada, it's likely to be here. But the most exciting music continues to happen in the back rooms of bars along Queen Street W and College Street, and in small performance spaces such as **Nia**, the **TRANZAC Club** and **Hugh's Room**.

Since 1995, Toronto's music scene has been greatly enhanced by the **North by Northeast** festival, inspired by the influential American media and arts festival, South by Southwest. Every June, hundreds of musicians,

thousands of music and media executives and tens of thousands of fans descend on the city, and for a few days, Toronto's clubs are jammed with the cream of the musical crop. *See also p165.*

TICKETS AND INFORMATION

The free entertainment weeklies *eye* and *NOW* have extensive listings sections. For people who are unfamiliar with particular venues or acts, *NOW*'s listings are marginally easier to use, but in the end, both tabloids carry pretty much the same information. *Toronto Life* magazine has very good upmarket listings, and its website (www.torontolife.com) has a handy 'What's on today?' feature.

Even on a school night, many club shows have a scheduled start time of 10pm or 10.30pm, and often don't really get going until later. Most club shows are pay-at-the-door, but some larger clubs take reservations. Many gigs sell out quickly, so it's prudent to book ahead, or at least show up early. Most stadium shows, as well as some events at smaller halls, are handled through **Ticketmaster** (416 870 8000/www.ticketmaster.ca), which has outlets at **Sunrise** record stores (336 Yonge Street, Dundas Square, www.sunriserecords.com; call 416 498 6601 for branches throughout the city) and at the **SkyDome Box Office** (*see p199*), among other locations.

Venues

Stadiums/arenas

Air Canada Centre

40 Bay Street, near Front Street W, Entertainment District (416 815 5500/www.theaircanadacentre. com). Subway Union. **Open** *Box office* 9.30am-5pm Mon-Fri; 9.30am-4pm Sat, Sun. **Tickets** $50-$350. **Credit** AmEx, MC, V. **Map** p277/p278 E8.

This modern 21,000-seat arena tends to pull in head-liners like the Backstreet Boys or Neil Diamond. The centre can be reconfigured (by pulling a giant curtain across the auditorium) into a 5,200-seat venue called the Sears Theatre. Don't worry, though: this smaller stage has all the acoustic quality you expect from a stadium show.

Molson Amphitheatre

909 Lakeshore Boulevard W, West End (416 260 5600). Bus 29/streetcar 509, 511. **Open** *Box office* 11am-8pm daily. *Concerts* 8pm-1am. **Tickets** $10-$90. **Credit** AmEx, MC, V.

Of Toronto's three major rock venues, the Molson Amphitheatre is by far the best place to see big names. Situated inside the Ontario Place amusement park, the amphitheatre has 9,000 seats, plus room for another 7,000 people to sit on the grass. In good weather, there's nothing nicer than watching the sunset as you listen to the sounds of Paul Simon or Lenny Kravitz.

SkyDome

1 Blue Jays Way, at Front Street W, Entertainment District (416 341 3663/ticketline 416 870 8000/ www.skydome.com). Streetcar 504/subway Union. **Open** for details. **Open** *Box office* (in person at Gate 7) 10am-6pm Mon-Sat. **Tickets** $20-$300. **Credit** AmEx, DC, MC, V. **Map** p277 D8.

If you like stadium shows, you got 'em. It's the biggest place in town, so when it's not being used for baseball, football or monster truck rallies, SkyDome rocks to big-name sounds such as the Rolling Stones, Rod Stewart and the Three Tenors.

Mid-sized venues & clubs

Hugh's Room

2261 Dundas Street W, near Bloor Street W, West End (416 531 6604/www.hughsroom.com). Streetcar 504, 505/subway Dundas West. **Open** 8.30pm-2am Tue-Sat. **Admission** $10-$20. **Credit** AmEx, MC, V.

Brothers Richard and Hugh Carson always talked about opening a classy folk club. Hugh died before the dream was realised but his name and spirit live on at this fine venue in the West End. Hugh's Room attracts attentive audiences who come for dinner and a show. Richard uses the broadest possible definition of folk, including worldbeat, blues and singer-songwriters, in addition to more traditional artists. Book in advance for major concerts.

Lee's Palace & the Dance Cave

529 Bloor Street W, at Bathurst Street, Harbord (416 532 1598/www.leespalace.com). Streetcar 511/subway Bathurst. **Open** 9pm-2am Mon-Sat. **Tickets** free-$20. **Credit** MC, V. **Map** p280 C4.

The high, wide stage, the low cover charges and the proximity to the University of Toronto have ensured Lee's an enduring place in the hearts of the poor, the disenfranchised and the unwashed fans of alternative rock. The Dance Cave on the second floor is a popular spot for alternative dance music DJs.

Nia

19 Church Street, at Front Street E, St Lawrence (416 867 1573/www.cestwhat.com/music.html). Streetcar 504/subway King. **Open** 9pm-1.30am daily. **Admission** free-$8. **Credit** AmEx, MC, V. **Map** p277/p278 F8.

Housed in a century-old building in the historic St Lawrence neighbourhood, the cosy Nia attracts a handsome young crowd of indie pop fans. The well-appointed basement regularly features ambient music, alternative country and established musicians experimenting with new genres. The speciality beers are very good.

Opera House

735 Queen Street E, at Broadview Avenue, East Side (416 466 0313/www.theoperahousetoronto.com). Streetcar 501, 504, 505. **Open** call for details. **Admission** $8-23. **No credit cards**. **Map** p279 J7.

This former vaudeville theatre, built in the early 1900s, was converted into a multi-level, multi-purpose venue in 1990. On a run-down section of Queen Street in the East Side, it has had to work hard to compete with more central venues. Work hard it has, and the hall has become a favourite destination for many major touring groups, from Radiohead to Björk.

Phoenix Concert Theatre

410 Sherbourne Street, near Carlton Street, Church & Wellesley (416 323 1251). Streetcar 506/subway Wellesley. **Open** 8pm-2.30am Thur-Sun. **Admission** $5-$50. **Credit** MC, V. **Map** p281 G5.

Part nightclub, part concert venue, the 1,858-square-metre (20,000-square-foot). Phoenix keeps set builders on hand to redesign the theatre to suit incoming acts. Opened in 1991, it has given exposure to many Canadian acts. It books a wide mix of pop and rock, with an emphasis on R&B and hip hop at weekends. Occasional all ages shows.

The Rivoli

334 Queen Street W, near Spadina Avenue, Entertainment District (416 596 1908/http://rivoli. ca). Streetcar 501/subway Osgoode. **Open** 10pm-1am Thur-Sun. **Admission** $5-$10. **Credit** AmEx, MC, V. **Map** p277 D7.

Past the front terrace, behind the long, narrow bar where Queen Street's hipsters quench their thirst, the back room at the Rivoli is an old favourite for all things alternative. Whether it's rock music, riverboat jazz, funk or punk, it is encouraged at the Riv.

Arts & Entertainment

You will be delighted or horrified to learn that smoking is no longer allowed in the back room.

Toronto Australia/ New Zealand Club

292 Brunswick Avenue, at Bloor Street W, Harbord (416 923 8137/www.tranzac.org). Streetcar 511/subway Spadina. **Open** *Lounge* 9pm-1.30am Mon-Fri. **Admission** free. **No credit cards.** **Map** p280 C4.

Bluegrass on Tuesdays is just one of the good weekly events at the smaller of two rooms at the TRANZAC. There's also Monday's Celtic jam night, Wednesday's gypsy swing music and Thursday's acoustic blues. The larger hall, with a capacity of about 200, generally has at least one major folk concert each week. From September to May the ultra-trad **Flying Cloud Folk Club** (416 410 3655) organises many of these shows.

Bars

Café May

396 Roncesvalles Avenue, at Lynd Avenue, West End (416 532 9218). Streetcar 504/subway Dundas West. **Open** 8pm-midnight Thur-Sun. **Admission** free. **No credit cards.**

The informal and friendly acts are chosen by the informal and friendly Yawd Sylvester, who might also be behind the bar serving you an inexpensive brew. He first started booking local musicians in an effort to help the café's ancient Japanese owner, who had broken several of her bones in a nasty spill. Old wooden beams and walls lined with booths big enough for six make this the perfect place to hear small experimental folk groups.

Cameron House

408 Queen Street W, at Cameron Street, Entertainment District (416 703 0811). Streetcar 501, 510/subway Osgoode. **Open** 10pm-2.30am daily, plus performances 6-8pm Sat, Sun. **Admission** *Front room* free. *Back room* $5-$10. **Credit** V. **Map** p276 C7.

Even after two decades of live music, it's still hard to pin the Cameron down. In the bar's front room, you can see regular favourites like the surreal Kevin Quain and the Mad Bastards (accordion, trumpet and musical saw), the Cameron House Singers (straight-up classic country), or swing, blues or gospel. In the back room, you're more likely to catch an up-and-coming singer-songwriter, or even experimental theatre, poetry or spoken word.

Country Music Store

2889 Danforth Avenue, at Luttrell Avenue, East Side (416 690 5564). Subway Victoria Park. **Music sessions** 3-6pm Sat. **Admission** free.

This obscure CD store in the East Side has acoustic jam sessions every Saturday afternoon, where anyone is welcome to listen, and just about anyone is welcome to play. Country Music Store Saturdays are a rare gem for folk traditionalists.

Dora Keogh Traditional Irish Pub

141 Danforth Avenue, at Broadview Avenue, East Side (416 778 1804/www.allens.to/dora). Streetcar 504, 505/subway Broadview. **Music sessions** 9pm-1am Thur; 5-8pm Sun. **Admission** free. **Credit** AmEx, MC, V.

No stage here, but a couple of times a week, a changing group of musicians crowd into one corner to play. Usually, it's low-key, with the performers and punters barely noticing each other. Occasionally, though, the Chieftains or Natalie MacMaster will join in and things get decidedly more intense.

Duke of Argyle

86 John Street, at Pearl Street, Entertainment District (416 340 9700). Streetcar 504, 510/subway St Andrew. **Open** 9pm-1am Thur-Sat. **Admission** free. **Credit** AmEx, DC, MC, V. **Map** p277 D7/8.

This pub features East Coast beer and East Coast Celtic music, often with a modern edge. It can be as dark and gloomy as a Nova Scotia fogbank if you're forced to sit inside, but summer concerts on the patio can make you forget you're even in a city.

Horseshoe Tavern

370 Queen Street W, at Spadina Avenue, Entertainment District (416 598 4753/www.horse shoetavern.com). Streetcar 501, 510. **Open** 9pm-1am Mon-Thur; 9pm-2.30am Fri-Sun. **Admission** free-$25. **No credit cards.** **Map** p277 D7.

The rough-and-ready Horseshoe has been serving up pints and kick-ass tunes for as long as anybody can remember (well, since 1947 anyway). Smack in the middle of Queen Street's fancy pants district, the former country bar keeps its jeans firmly on. It can hold 500 people, an audience large enough to prompt regular appearances from major acts like the Tragically Hip and Wilco, but on Tuesdays it also has no-cover 'Development nights' to give exposure to up-and-coming Toronto bands.

Orbit Room

580 College Street, at Manning Avenue, Little Italy (416 535 0613). Streetcar 506, 511. **Open** 10.30pm-1.30am daily. **Admission** $5. **Credit** AmEx, MC, V. **Map** p276 B5.

This small, second-floor bar in the heart of Little Italy is a happy place to hear upbeat Hammond organ funk and jazz. It has a small dancefloor but it gets crowded even on Sunday nights, so be prepared to wriggle into place. You want intimate? This place is so cosy you have to walk through the band to get to the small terrace out back. Retro decor and friendly staff keep the place pleasingly unpretentious.

Jazz & blues

Toronto's jazz clubs, most notably the **Top o' the Senator**, are known and respected across North America. In the summer, major annual events such as the **Toronto Downtown Jazz Festival** (416 928 2033; *see also p166*) and the **Beaches International Jazz Festival**

Local hero Hawksley Workman

Once seen, he's not easily forgotten. Which is, you suspect, just how he likes it. Why else would he dress with such eye-catching insouciance (safety pins on the flies of his too-tight trews, outlandish sunglasses, red tiger-print fake-fur jacket)? And why else would Huntsville, Ontario, native Ryan Corrigan have decided to rename himself Hawksley Workman?

Perhaps surprisingly, it was not Toronto that 'got' him first, but London. And not London, Ontario, but London, England. The 1999 release of outrageously ambitious debut *For Him And The Girls* on teensy British indie label Loose had critics falling over

themselves to offer praise for Workman's captivating mix of grandiloquent power pop and intimate, beautifully underplayed balladry. Its success led to him signing with the by-no-means-teensy Universal Music in time for 2001's *(Last Night We Were) The Delicious Wolves*, which offered a shinier version of the formula. That both records – and Workman's charming Christmas record, *Almost a Full Moon* – were written, played and produced almost entirely by the still-twentysomething Workman in his home studio is a fact almost as impressive as the records themselves, and confirms his choice of surname is no ironic boast.

After periods spent living in Toronto and Paris, where his extravagant theatrics went down a treat, Workman's now back in Huntsville, ensconced in his home studio and – as of early 2003 – working on his third album. Hopes are high for it, after Workman won two Junos at the 2002 awards. A born performer, his shows veer wildly from high-camp vaudeville to freeform stand-up to spine-tingling torch song. You'd do well to see him.

Honourable mentions: Hayden returned from several years in the wilderness in 2001 with his third album, *Skyscraper National Park*; it's also his best. Appearing on it is **Howie Beck**, author himself of two beautiful albums. **Sarah Harmer**'s first record, *You Were Here* (2001), drew praise from Toronto stalwart **Ron Sexsmith**, whose *Cobblestone Runway* (2002) was his most high-profile release to date.

Previous contenders: Both **Neil Young** and **Joni Mitchell** only found fame and acclaim after leaving Toronto (Young for California, Mitchell for Detroit).

(416 698 2152; *see also p167*) raise the profile of local musicians, which helps keep the clubs packed and lively throughout the rest of the year. That's where you'll hear the likes of **Laura Hubert**, who has a terrific voice for old jazz standards and puts on an entertaining show. For swing music with a hint of rock 'n' roll, you can't beat the Danny B Band, who play regularly at the **Reservoir Lounge**. Toronto's blues community is small but very enthusiastic. If you want to hear something that goes beyond your basic 12-bar, track down **Paul Reddick and the Sidemen**, whose raw, harmonica-led blues complements highly poetic, cerebral lyrics. Among the noteworthy venues are:

Blues on Bellair

25 Bellair Street, at Yorkville Avenue, Yorkville (416 944 2095/www.bluesonbellair.com). Subway Bay. **Open** 9.30pm-1am Tue-Sun. **Admission** free-$10. **Credit** AmEx, MC, V. **Map** p280 E4.
For those who like their blues fancy, this dressy Yorkville bar-restaurant has fine dining, served with electric blues, acoustic soul, blues jams and occasional jazz. Blues recently received some buzz when Prince sat in with a regular bands for an impromptu jam.

Grossman's Tavern

379 Spadina Avenue, at Cecil Street, Chinatown (416 977 7000/www.grossmanstavern.com). Streetcar 506, 510. **Open** 8pm-1am Mon-Sat; 4-8pm Sun. **Admission** free. **Map** p276 C6.

Silver Dollar Room: get your blues in the dark.

On the northern edge of Chinatown, this tavern was opened in 1949 and some of the seasoned regulars look as though they came with the original furniture. Beery, smoky and a little grimy, the bar often has loud blues played by locals and visiting dignitaries. It can also be a good place for jazz and Dixie.

Reservoir Lounge

52 Wellington Street E, at Church Street, St Lawrence (416 955 0887). Streetcar 504/subway King. **Open** 10pm-2am Mon-Thur; 9.30pm-2am Fri, Sat. **Admission** free-$10. **Credit** AmEx, DC, MC, V. **Map** p277/p278 F8.

Close to St Lawrence Centre for the Performing Arts and the Hummingbird Centre, this basement lounge is an ideal place to kick back with a post-theatre martini and listen to Toronto's best swing bands. Low ceilings and brick pillars, high tables and long red velvet couches set the scene. The food is pricey, but very good. It gets packed at weekends, but there's always a couple or two who find space to dance.

Rex Hotel Jazz & Blues Bar

194 Queen Street W, at St Patrick Street, Entertainment District (416 598 2475). Streetcar 501/subway Osgoode. **Open** 6.30-8pm, 9.30pm-1.30am Mon-Fri; 3.30-5pm, 9.30pm-1.30am Sat, Sun. **Admission** free-$7. **No credit cards. Map** p277 D7.

The casual atmosphere, friendly regulars and a wide range of beers on tap make this a social place to hear the best local jazz artists (stars such as Harry Connick Jr have also been known to jam on its stage). The Rex keeps things cheap, with cover charges rarely over $10, so it's good for those on a budget.

Silver Dollar Room

486 Spadina Avenue, at College Street, Chinatown (416 763 9139/www.silverdollar room.com). Streetcar 506, 510. **Open** 10pm-1.30am daily. **Admission** free-$15. **No credit cards. Map** p276/p280 C5.

It doesn't look like much from the outside, and it doesn't look like much on the inside. Which is kind of part of this long, dark bar's charm. And it gets in top-notch swamp and electric blues. Another plus: this is one of the larger venues in town, so if it's not full, there's room to dance. On Mondays, ordinary people can get on stage and jam with local bluesman Danny Marks. High Lonesome Wednesdays feature bluegrass musicians who are so virtuosic they don't seem to care whether the audience pays attention.

Top o'the Senator

253 Victoria Street, at Dundas Square, Dundas Square (416 364 7517/www.thesenator.com). Streetcar 505/subway Dundas. **Open** 8.30pm-1am Tue-Sat; 8pm-midnight Sun. **Admission** $8-$25. **Credit** AmEx, MC, V. **Map** p277/p278 F7.

Deco lights and long leather seats give the club a touch of 1920s elegance that enhances the emphasis on contemporary jazz. The Senator doesn't get going until late, but then it really gets going. The bar is heavy on bebop, though you can also catch A-list vocalists like Diana Krall and Holly Cole. Covers are often high but students get in for half price on Wednesdays. Top o'the Senator also does dinner-and-show specials in conjunction with the Torch Bistro (*see p109*) downstairs.

Nightlife

The clubs stack up long and strong in this top-deck DJ city.

Torontonians have bitter words for their city when it comes to location: for a cultural epicentre, it is remarkably isolated, expensive to leave and, well, in Canada. But where nightlife is concerned, Toronto wins the geographical lottery. It finds itself on a flightpath between Chicago, home of house, and New York, the city that never sleeps, with techo-centre Detroit a four-hour drive away. To the joy of underage ravers from the suburbs, urban poseurs and pleasure-seekers from Buffalo, NY (who take advantage of the friendly drinking age and the friendlier currency exchange), Toronto hosts a constant influx of A-list DJs (Alton Miller, Little Louie Vega, Mark Farina), and also finds itself on the North American tour routes of many Britishers (Carl Cox, Paul Oakenfold, John Digweed). The multicultural patchwork that is Downtown makes for a funky variety of sounds: where one venue might reverberate with trance, its neighbour might pulse with a disco beat or sway to reggae.

There's never a shortage of late-night entertainment in Toronto, particularly in the summertime, when promoters rent out outdoor and waterfront venues and keep parties steaming till dawn. To find out what's on, grab a copy of giveaways *NOW* or *eye* from one of the ubiquitous sidewalk boxes.

An overwhelming percentage of clubbing activity takes place in the Entertainment District. The area roughly bordered by Queen Street, Spadina Avenue, King Street and University Avenue particulary is subjected at weekends to heavy traffic, outlandish parking fees, promotional litter, public drunkenness, fighting hooligans and a relentless thumping from clubs licensed to stay open long past the 2am last call. Despite such general extroversion, individual venues are coy about announcing their whereabouts: most have ambiguous signs – if any at all – and you'll likely find your destination by the burly guards standing in the doorway. Treat them nicely: Toronto bouncers are a power-tripping lot and don't take well to whining schemers.

If you're paying moret than $10 to enter, you can expect an evening of revelry that carries on until morning joggers take to the streets; otherwise, expect to be shown the door after 4am. Toronto has always been a fairly egalitarian city and it couldn't tolerate too many velvet-rope venues, so attitudes, guest lists and dress codes are laxer than in other cities. Most clubs – save for chi-chi This Is London and the like – will forgive trainers and denim, though you might want to pay your wardrobe some special attention to be safe.

Entertainment District

Element Bar

553 Queen Street W, at Denison Avenue (416 359 1919/www.elementbar.com). Streetcar 501.
Open 10pm-3am Thur-Sun. **Admission** $5-$10.
Credit MC, V. **Map** p276 C7.
Not everyone is in their element here. Baggy trousers are de rigueur, shoes are chunky, girls show skin where they can. Yet the mood is easy despite the frenetic house beats engulfing two dancefloors, one in a clammy basement. It might be the diminutive size that dictates the cosy atmosphere, or the deep-lounging chaises. The toilet situation is poor.

Fluid Lounge

217 Richmond Street W, at Duncan Street (416 593 6116/www.fluidlounge.com). Streetcar 501.
Open 10pm-3am Wed-Sun. **Admission** call for details. **Credit** AmEx, MC, V. **Map** p274 D7.

The best Nightlife

Excuse to pull up in cowboy boots at 3am
Matador Club Country Music (*see p207*).

Chance of spotting a minor local celeb
Shmooze (*see p205*).

Place to witness a Cuban defection
La Cervejaria (*see p207*).

Bet for billiards and beer
The Mockingbird (*see p204*).

Way to keep the party going till Monday
The Comfort Zone (*see p206*).

For good-looking bartenders
Tonic (*see p205*).

Arts & Entertainment

Groove, booze and check the loos at Toronto's nightlife bright light **Shmooze**. *See p205.*

Nice place… shame about the crowd. That's the consensus of downtowners, who appreciate the postmod environment and sleek, contoured bars but resent the influx of the S&M crowd (sububanites from Scarborough and Mississauga) at weekends.

Hotel Boutique Bar

77 Peter Street, at Richmond Street (416 345 8585). Open 10pm-3am Mon, Thur-Sat. **Admission** call for details. **Credit** AmEx, MC, V. **Map** p277 D7.
As the name suggests, it acts like the lounge of an upscale boutique hotel, then spirals into a funked-out club after the midnight hour. Resident DJs take few chances, and the results are less frenetic than typical dancefloors might produce. A modern walnut and smoky glass decor stops the maze of cosy coves from feeling uncomfortably claustrophobic.

Joker

318 Richmond Street W, at Widmer Street (416 598 1313/www.libertygroup.com). Streetcar 501. Open 9pm-3am Thur-Sat. **Admission** $10. **Credit** AmEx, MC, V. **Map** p274 D7.
One of the founding fathers of clubland continues to attract crowds of debauched kids. It's well past its peak of credible popularity, but still knows how to put on a show when it wants to: there are four floors with music ranging from Top 40 chart hits to progressive house; the lights are entrancing; and a rooftop patio is a sweat reducer. Alas, the queues can be ridiculously long.

The Living Room

330 Adelaide Street W, at Peter Street (416 979 3168/www.theroom.ca). Streetcar 504. **Open** 10pm-3am Fri, Sat. **Admission** call for details. **Credit** AmEx, MC, V. **Map** p277 D7.
Other than the pumping house it plays, the Living Room lives up to its name nicely: more comfortable put-your-feet-up lounge than frantic put-your-arms-in-the-air club, it has fabric-swathed alcoves and a decor that bleeds baroque.

Mad Bar

230 Richmond Street W, at Duncan Street (416 340 0089/www.mad-bar.com). Streetcar 501. Open 10pm-3am Fri, Sat. **Admission** $10. **Credit** MC, V. **Map** p274 D7.
Hip hop and old school have always been the way at this miniscule veteran. Recent renos have added cool, illuminated tabletops to the futuristic decor.

The Mockingbird

580 King Street W, at Morrison Street (416 504 3081). Streetcar 504, 510, 511. **Open** 6pm-1am Wed,Thur; 6pm-2am Fri; 8pm-2am Sat. **Admission** free. **Credit** AmEx, DC, MC, V. **Map** p276 C7.
This second-floor loft can be as unpredictable as its namesake. It's usually open Wednesday through Saturday, but sometimes… it's not. Or perhaps there's a private party. At times, it's as empty and echoing as a defunct warehouse. If you happen to catch the place open and raging, it's a pelvis-rocking affair, with local media and film types strutting away on the makeshift dancefloor (anywhere the pool tables, bar or DJ booth are not). Friendly service.

Money Night Club/Wallpaper Room

199 Richmond Street W, at Duncan Street (416 591 9000/www.moneynightclub.ca). Streetcar 501. Open 10pm-2am Fri, Sat. **Admission** call for details. **Credit** AmEx, MC, V. **Map** p274 D7.
The first step to marrying a millionaire (or a man who wants you to think he is) is a trip here, where looking rich, drinking rich and acting rich is almost a religion. AMoney is still cashing in '90s style, luring DJs away from neighbouring clubs for its fabled Friday nights. The music, like the attitude, is a '90s relic. Less hardcore is the subterranean Wallpaper Room.

NASA Dance Pub

609 Queen Street W, at Bathurst Street (416 504 8356/www.nasadancepub.ca). Streetcar 501. Open 11pm-3am daily. **Admission** free. **Credit** MC, V. **Map** p276 C7.

The recent installation of a tiny front patio allows NASA to capitalise on early-to-bed loungers and dinner-hour walk-ins. But at midnight expect the foundations to shake with UK house and garage. Sundays are crowd-pleasing nights, though the front-window lounge (furnished with airplane-issue seating) satisfies beat lovers week-long.

RoxyBlu

12 Brant Street, at King Street (416 504 3222/www.roxyblu.com). Streetcar 504, 510. **Open** 10pm-3am Fri, Sat. **Admission** $10-$15. **Credit** MC, V. **Map** p276 C7.

Back when baggy trousers and glowsticks were the clubbing dress code, the 'urban' ('black' in Toronto trade parlance) music contingent pined for somewhere like this. Finally, they got it: an unpretentious, velvet-swathed mecca for slaves to rare grooves, hip hop, funk and soul. Fridays trump Saturdays, when suburbanites make the pilgrimage.

Shmooze

15 Mercer Street, at King Street W (416 341 8777). Streetcar 504. **Open** *Dinner* 4-9pm Fri; 5-9pm Sat. *Club* 9pm-3am Fri, Sat. **Admission** call for details. **Credit** AmEx, MC, V. **Map** p277 D8.

An over-30 crowd means a little dancing and a lot of schmoozing. The rooftop patio makes a delightful escape from the dancefloor (if the funky sounds release you); the loos are all Hollywood hyperbole.

Cue up for **The Comfort Zone**. *See p206.*

System SoundBar

117 Peter Street, at Richmond Street (416 408 3996/www.systemsoundbar.com). Streetcar 501, 504. **Open** *Sept-May* 10pm-2am Wed-Sun. *June-Aug* 10pm-2am Tue-Sun. **Admission** $5-$15. **Credit** AmEx, MC, V. **Map** p277 D7.

A seemingly permanent queue confers a perceived desirablity on System, which however is less remarkable than one might expect. The subterranean space is simply a decent place to dance.

This is London

364 Richmond Street W, at Peter Street (416 351 1100/www.thisislondonclub.com). Streetcar 501. **Open** 10pm-3am Sat. **Admission** $20. **Credit** AmEx, MC, V. **Map** p274 D7.

You get a more refined kind of hedonism at This Is London, styled after a velvet-roped Soho palace. Sophisticates sip Veuve or premium vodka in the upstairs lounge while bouncers oversee the lower-level party with military tenacity. In the loos beauticians await with scissors and styling gels, and racks of magazines provide distraction from the courtship dance outside. Free bottled water compensates for the hefty cover – another London byproduct.

Tonic

117 Peter Street, at Richmond Street W (416 204 9200/www.tonicnightclub.com). Streetcar 501. **Open** 10pm-3am Wed-Sat. **Admission** $10. **Credit** AmEx, MC, V. **Map** p274 D7.

Surlyburly bouncers keep the gate at Tonic, where you should anticipate an impenetrable velvet rope. If you do manage to gain entrance, you'll have access to spinners of utmost repute, even if the dancefloor can be too jammed for maximum enjoyment. There are always the bathrooms for relief from the tumult, some of the most decadent on the scene.

Turbo

360 Adelaide Street W, at Peter Street (416 408 2646/www.turboniteclub.com). Streetcar 504. **Open** 10pm-3am Tue-Sun. **Admission** call for details. **Credit** AmEx, MC, V. **Map** p274 D7.

The place recently fell from grace at turbo-driven speed, thanks to the departure of one of the best bookers in the neighbourhood. But it's still a hotspot for superior drum 'n' bass on the lower level; an upper level is disco-a-go-go with mini mirror balls hanging from the ceiling.

Una Mas

422 Adelaide Street W, at Spadina Avenue (416 703 4862/www.unamas.net). Streetcar 504, 510. **Open** 10pm-3am Wed-Sat. **Admission** free-$5. **Credit** AmEx, MC, V. **Map** p276 C7.

Located on the fringes of clubland as if to turn a shoulder against the vulgar frenzy of the core, Una Mas has innate cool, a scarce quality among Toronto clubs. Booths along one wall are ample enough for eight, while low lounges at the back are more intimate. A long, lean bar is perfect for a lean while bobbing your head to rare grooves, funk and hip hop. The basement serves as a sweaty dance pit.

Other downtown areas

The Comfort Zone
486 Spadina Avenue, at College Street, Harbord
(416 763 9139/www.comfortzone.to.com). Streetcar
501, 510. **Open** 9pm-3am Wed-Fri; 9pm Sat-3am
Mon. **Admission** call for details. **Credit** MC, V.
The party after the after-party. Ravers trip in around
10am on Sunday and emerge squinting at the sun-
light hours later (unless they push on till early
Monday morning). The Comfort Zone won't score
points for form over function – it's a bit dingy, but
that doesn't stop it being a favourite of DJs local and
imported, who save their best sets for the Zone. Chill.

The Guvernment
132 Queens Quay E, at Lower Jarvis Street,
Waterfront (416 869 0045/www.theguvern
ment.com). Streetcar 509. **Open** 10pm-3am
Thur, Fri; 10pm-6am Sat. **Admission** $10-$15.
Credit AmEx, MC, V. **Map** p277/p278 F9.
While its current clientele were still crawling, this
venue – as the celebrated RPM – held marathon parties for mods, Goths, classic rockers, whatever the
scene du jour. It eventually met its end, and now an
equally enduring clubbing complex enjoys the lakefront venue. The Guvernment attracts Toronto's top
house DJs (Mark Oliver et al) along with international spinning royalty. Bouncers won't turn away
the shabbily dressed, but they will make you wait:
it's a rare night that doesn't see a queue wrapped
around the building. The hangar-like space is also
home to concert venue Kool Haus, which attracts top
international DJs and eclectic acts (Kruder and
Dorfmeister, Tenacious D); the lounges Orange
Room, the Drink and Acid; and the rooftop Sky Bar.

Midtown

Babaluu
136 Yorkville Avenue, at Avenue Road, Yorkville
(416 515 0587/www.babaluu.com). Bus 6/subway
Bay. **Open** 9pm-3am Tue-Sun. **Admission** call for
details. **Credit** AmEx, MC, V. **Map** p280 E4.
Rappers and Latin pop stars have grown out of the
projects and into furs and diamonds and the Cristal
lifestyle, so it's only natural that their fans and fol-
lowers might lust after a similarly decadent lifestyle.
Babaluu brings the barrio to hedonistic Yorkville,
playing hot Latin beats for a sweaty crowd of still-
soulful grown-ups, who put down their platinum
cards for top-rate libations before the conga line
sweeps them away.

West End

El Convento Rico
750 College Street, at Crawford Street, Little Italy
(416 588 7800/www.elconventorico.com). Streetcar
506, 511. **Open** 10pm-3am Thur; 8pm-4am Fri, Sat.
Admission $5. **Credit** AmEx, MC, V.
At weekends you'll find several types here: Latin singles dancing in pairs, rowdy women on a girls' night
out, gay revellers, bachelor party participants.
They've all come here for one thing: the midnight
drag show that takes lip synching to a new (and not
necessarily higher) level. Transvestites strut about
in falsies and too-tight trousers, miming to the banal
lyrics of mainstream pop and R&B (gone are the
days of Diana Ross and Tina Turner). Euro dance
tunes kick in later. It's all extremely kitsch, of course,
but that doesn't stop the crowd from having a ball.

Local hero DJ AMtrak

There's a reason Element (see p203)
has garnered a reputation as the city's
Saturday-night stalwart – it's benefited
from the nimble fingers of resident DJ AMtrak
[sic]. The initials are those of one Ann Marie
McCullough, a former Vancouverite who first
turned to the tables in the late '90s and
shipped her vinyl over to Canada's club
central for the Millennium.

By all accounts AMtrak's sound moves a
little smoother than her railroad namesake.
She keeps her listeners in perpetual motion,
bumping and grinding and sweating out all
those bottles of Evian. Her deep, progressive
house – crossed with tribal beats, funk and
rare instrumental jazz (she's classically
trained on the clarinet and saxophone) – is
just the lift you need after an evening of slow
but sure lubrication and acceleration. When

AMtrak takes to the floor at Element or Mad
Bar, groovers make the trip.

Nobody bothers to label AMtrak a 'chick',
even though her tame blonde locks and milky
complexion lend her the appearance of a
soccer mom. That said, she's headlined at
many a 'Chicks Dig It' night. And she's
shared centre stage with some of the leaders
in oestrogen entertainment: UK's Ann Savage
and Queen Maxine, Chicago's Heather and
LA's Dazy. With a week in the city, you should
be able to catch her somewhere, though her
international dance card is filling up, and we
hear she has designs on the South Pacific.
And who knows what territory she'll be
shaking up from there.

Honourable mentions: Mark Oliver, Jason
Palma, Kenny Glasgow.

Previous contenders: Denise Benson.

Arts & Entertainment

Night owls at **Matador Club Country Music** are more Johnny Cash than John Digweed.

La Cervejaria

Downtown Bar & Grill, 842 College Street, at Ossington Avenue, Little Italy (416 588 0162). Streetcar 506. **Open** *Restaurant* 11am-2am daily. *Club/music* 10pm-2am Fri, Sat. **Admission** $5. **Credit** MC, V.

Timing is key at this hybrid beer hall/salsa haven. If you're lucky, the weekend will bring live Brazilian beats, care of a charismatic several-piece orchestra, and the house will be on its feet spinning and twisting two by two. Otherwise, it's Euro disco mixed with overplayed Latin pop, an unattractive alternative to the football highlights and pitchers o' beer featured out front.

Matador Club Country Music

466 Dovercourt Road, at College Street, West End (416 533 9311). Streetcar 506, 511. **Open** 2am-5.30am Fri, Sat. **Admission** call for details. **Credit** call for details.

While the rest of the city is running out of gas, the Matador – a barn-like arena on an obscure residential block north of College Street – is revving up for a marathon night of reckless dancing. Music is appropriate barnyard rock, proffered by amateur musicians quick with a Stones cover. Sounds naff, but its late hours have made it clubbing's cult institution for all-night types of various stripes.

Revival

783 College Street, at Shaw Street, West End (416 535 7888). Streetcar 506. **Open** 5pm-2am daily. **Admission** $5. **Credit** AmEx, MC, V.

The building (the former Polish Leisure Hall) was rescued from uncertain fate by entrepreneurs betting on its value as a club. Therein lies the origin of

the name – and the theme behind the mini-club's musical output. DJs tend toward soul, funk and newly mixed Brazilian beats. Live acts appear on Wednesday nights and Saturday night is Mod Night, featuring a couple of veteran rockers spinning old standards by the Jam and Who, and 'vintage' Blur for the neophyte.

Shallow Groove

559 College Street, at Manning Avenue, Little Italy (416 944 8998). Streetcar 506. **Open** 9pm-3am Thur-Sat. **Admission** free. **Credit** MC, V. **Map** p276 B6.

One of few dancehalls on loungey College Street, the Shallow Groove (the name referencing its setting in the basement of an unremarkable office complex) may as well be on a college campus. The hit parade is uninspired and the patrons collegiate. Still, it manages to fill to capacity at weekends, and its friendly atmosphere has likely spawned more than a few bleary-eyed romances. Then again, who wouldn't bond after a half hour languishing in line?

East Side

The Docks

11 Polson Street, at Cherry Street, East Side (416 469 5655/www.thedocks.com). Bus 72. **Open** *Sept-May* 9pm-3am Sat. *June-Aug* 9pm-3am *Fri, Sat.* **Admission** call for details. **Credit** AmEx, MC, V.

This 'Waterfront Entertainment Complex' also includes a drive-in and driving range: its contribution to Toronto's nightlife is a veritable theme park of waterslides, Jell-O-wrestling rings and bungee towers. That it's the only place in town where you can dance under the stars is a quality worth mentioning.

Sport & Fitness

This major league sports town also takes good care of its amateurs.

When it comes to sport and fitness, Toronto is a city of enthusiasts. Those less kind (and Canadians from anywhere else) would find 'fad-addicts' and 'bandwagon-jumpers' more apt. Everyone seemed to be climbing rocks when rock-climbing was cool – or they dressed for it at least. Queen Street was overrun with trendy scooters when they popped up a couple of years back, though a case could fairly be argued that each one was ridden only once. Whether it's spinning or pilates, whatever's new is best in Toronto.

Locals always seem willing to fork out the dough to buttress the city's much sought-after major league image and the city is jam-packed with first-class facilities, excellent access to top-notch equipment (new, used, rentals), and a truly mind-boggling number of free public playing fields, rinks, pools and courts.

Fan support, however, tends to run a mile wide but an inch deep. Professional baseball and basketball teams, staffed almost exclusively by foreign-born athletes, broke attendance records in their initial seasons as Torontonians embraced them as though they were home-grown. But once the win-loss numbers teeter towards the latter, the boosterism dries up faster than a Mats Sundin slapshot. The glaring exception to this is, of course, hockey.

Spectator sports

American football

Football, as it is played in Canada, is nowhere near the high-priced glamour sport seen south of the border. With three downs (instead of four in the US game) and fields that are both wider and longer, the Canadian game is allegedly faster and more dramatic than its American counterpart. But salaries skew closer to that of a supply teacher than a CEO and player ranks are studded with has- and never-beens from the NFL – this hasn't won the hearts and minds of the status-conscious locals. The **Toronto Argonauts**, though often contenders at season's end, have long suffered from the apathy of their home town. Attendance seems only to spike when a rock band or a sports celebrity is scheduled to appear as half-time entertainment. This, in spite of the fact that,

when they're winning, the Argos can provide excellent bang for the buck. The league's head office nixed plans for pre-game wet T-shirt contests because no one knew what would be worse – if the gimmick failed or if it actually succeeded in seducing a larger crowd.

Toronto Argonauts

SkyDome, 1 Blue Jays Way, at Front Street, Entertainment District (information 416 489 2746/tickets 416 872 5000/www.argonauts.on.ca). Subway King or Union. **Season** June-Nov. **Tickets** $7-$35. **Credit** AmEx, DC, MC, V. **Map** p277 D8.

Baseball

Toronto has joyously embraced America's pastime since the first snow-blanketed game, played at (now demolished) Exhibition Stadium back in 1977. Fan fervour grew through the late 1980s and exploded during the World Series-winning seasons of '92 and '93, but since the strike-shortened season of 1994 attendance has steadily declined (as it has throughout the sport). Even so, there's no more relaxing way to spend a sunny afternoon in mid June or a steamy summer night in August than at an open-roof game at the SkyDome.

Toronto Blue Jays

SkyDome, 1 Blue Jays Way, at Front Street W, Entertainment District (information 416 341 1000/tickets 416 341 3000/www.bluejays.com). Streetcar 504/subway St Andrew or Union. **Season** May-Sept. **Tickets** $16-$180. **Credit** AmEx, DC, MC, V. **Map** p277 D8.

Basketball

The city is proving to have something of a love-hate relationship with its NBA **Raptors**. The question is how long can fans wait for the team to realise the potential it shows at the beginning of every season, only to watch it waste away by the end. Every other year some new hero, from pint-sized Damon Stoudamire to legendary giant Hakeem 'the Dream' Olajuwon, seems to be deposited in the line-up, hailed as the team's future, only to be ignominiously shunted aside a disappointing season or two later. The team's one undisputed superstar, Vince Carter, has been plagued with season-shortening injuries, though he can consistently provide thrills when he's healthy. What's truly amazing to witness

Blue Jay Josh Phelps hits back. *See p208.*

is the absolutely un-Canadian behaviour of the spectators. While most too-polite-for-words Torontonians grew up shushing each other to silence during foul shots, the raucous, mind-numbing, buzzer-to-buzzer cacophony that constitutes an NBA game requires them to frequently, if uncharacteristically, scream at the top of their lungs. Shocking… simply shocking.

Toronto Raptors

Air Canada Centre, 40 Bay Street, at Front Street, Entertainment District (info 416 815 5600/tickets 416 872 5000/www.nba.com/raptors). Subway King or Union. **Season** Oct-June. **Tickets** $10.50-$625. **Credit** AmEx, DC, MC, V. **Map** p277 D8.

Horse-racing

These days **Woodbine Racetrack** (out by the airport) is the only game in town. But if ou love all manner of horse-racing you won't need to go anywhere else. It is the only racetrack in North America that can offer both thoroughbred and standard-bred horse-racing on the same day, as well as providing video links to several other major racetracks, including Churchill Downs and Aqueduct. The track is home to a number of $1 million-plus races, including North America's oldest stakes race, the **Queen's Plate** (which has been run without interruption since 1860), the **ATTO Mile** and harness racing's **North America Cup**. More recently slot machines have been added to the mix so you can really work on your gambling. There are a couple of out-of-

town alternatives at **Mohawk** (a 45-minute drive away in Campbellville, near Guelph, for harness racing) and **Fort Erie** (just over an hour's drive, in Fort Erie, thoroughbreds).

Fort Erie Race Track

230 Catherine Street, Fort Erie (905 871 3200 or 1-800 295 3770/www.forterieracetrack.ca). **Open** 9am-3am Mon-Thur; 9am Fri-3am Sun. **Admission** free. **Credit** AmEx, MC, V.

Mohawk Racetrack

9430 Guelph Line, Campbellville (1-888 675 7223/www.woodbineentertainment.com). **Open** 9am-3am daily. **Admission** free. **Credit** AmEx, MC, V.

Woodbine Racetrack

555 Rexdale Boulevard, at Highway 427, Rexdale (1-888 675 7223/www.woodbineentertainment.com). Subway Islington. **Open** 9am-3am daily. **Admission** free. **Credit** AmEx, MC, V.

Ice-hockey

Win or lose, Toronto loves its **Maple Leafs**. Almost as much as everyone else in the country hates them. They are the most watched, most analysed, most adored and most reviled team in NHL history. They have won more league championships than any team save their long-standing rivals the Montreal Canadiens, but sadly all the wins were prior to 1967, the last time the Lord Stanley's Cup was hoisted by a Leaf in victory. Oddly enough, the decades-long absence of a championship team is about equal to the length of time you'd have to wait to get a decent season ticket – the Leaf's legendary waiting list is more accurately measured in generations than in years. Virtually every game is sold out. Attendance remains constant even after the team moved from the venerable nostalgia of grotty, old Maple Leaf Gardens to the sanitised confines of the high-tech, antiseptic Air Canada Centre in 1999. The best tickets for games are generally only attainable through ticket agencies and scalpers at inflated prices – sometimes they're even worth it.

Toronto Maple Leafs

Air Canada Centre, 40 Bay Street, at Front Street, Entertainment District (information 416 815 5700/tickets 416 703 5323/www.torontomapleleafs. com). **Subway** King or Union. **Season** Oct-Apr. **Tickets** $24-$390. **Credit** AmEx, DC, MC, V. **Map** p277/p278 E8.

Lacrosse

For a city that adores champions, Toronto has inexplicably ignored its winning pro Lacrosse team, **The Rock**. Since its inception in 1998 the team has won three league titles, yet their triumphs have gone largely unnoticed by the masses. Perhaps it's the difficulty of the game. A centuries-old sport created by native North Americans, at one time it was played by hundreds of contestants over several days and often took the place of lethal combat in settling scores between tribes. It's an extremely rough-and-tumble sport with little glamour, but also one of the most exciting and physically challenging contests a human can endure. The Rock can be found at the Air Canada Centre from January to April. Lacrosse is the official national sport of Canada, protestations from hockey enthusiasts aside.

Toronto Rock

Air Canada Centre, 40 Bay Street, at Front Street W, Entertainment District (information 416 596 3075/tickets 416 872 5000/www.torontorock.com). **Subway** King or Union. **Season** Jan-Apr. **Tickets** $19-$48. **Credit** AmEx, DC, MC, V. **Map** p277/p278 E8.

Local hero Trish Stratus

The obvious jokes about free-standing structures aside, the once and no doubt future pro wrestling champion, Trish Stratus, is a fitting symbol for sports in her home town.

Like many of the city's professional teams, buff, blonde, hazel-eyed Stratus (pictured) is perhaps better looking than she is physically intimidating. The comparisons don't stop there. Like the Blue Jays she has taken the top prize and shown world-class flair. Like the Raptors she came out of nowhere and earned respect on both sides of the US/Canadian border. Like the Maple Leafs she has broken innumerable hearts. And, like the Argonauts, she has demonstrated she can take a beating.

Born Trisha Stratigias in December 1975, Stratus can blame her unexpected career on being in the right place at the right time. Not that long ago she was taking pre-med courses at a local university when the staff there went on strike. To fill her time she found a job as a receptionist in a gym, where her eyes were opened to the world of physical fitness. In no time the always-active 21-year-old had the chiselled abs and fully loaded guns of a veteran bodybuilder and was turning more than a few heads. One of them belonged to someone with links at *MuscleMag International* and a new pumping iron poster girl was born.

At the same time a mini-revolution was taking place in the soap opera world of professional wrestling. Women had been relegated to peripheral roles in the WWF (now WWE) circus of the late '90s, but that was about to change. Usually confined to eye-candy roles of 'manager' or 'escort', now the women were duking it out with both men and their rival sisters before, during and after regularly scheduled bouts. Soon they were challenging each other and in no time a new stable of female wrestlers was established. In March, 2000, Trish Stratus joined their ranks.

Initially Stratus appeared as the 'manager' for the tag team of Test and Albert, better known as T&A, and developed a weasly rep for sneaking up behind people and pummelling them with her boots. But in no time she was taking matters into her own hands and entering the ring on her own terms. By 2001 Trish had won the league's distaff championship and held it through several face-bashing, body-slamming defences, often employing her trademark move, the 'StratusFaction Bulldog'.

Stratus' status as a champ isn't confined to theatrical antics in the ring. Innumerable TV and radio appearances have proven her to be intelligent, articulate and funny. Her popularity was confirmed when she was voted the WWE's 'Babe of the Year' in both 2001 and

Soccer

Soccer is the fastest-growing team sport in Canada in terms of individual participation, but observing the game locally seems to be confined to those who play it (and their relatives). Over the years, leagues have swiftly blown in and out of town. Street celebrations ensue during every World Cup, bringing out the city's rich multi-culturalism) but the TV-viewing fans have yet to materialise into support for Toronto's pro team, **The Lynx**. Affiliated with the US-based United Soccer Leagues, the Lynx has fielded a competitive team since its inception in 1997, but the demolition of central Varsity Stadium in 2002, relegating them to Centennial Park Stadium in the West End, hasn't helped their profile.

Toronto Lynx

Centennial Park Stadium, Renforth Drive, at Eglinton, West End (416 251 4625/ www.lynxsoccer.com). Subway Royal York, then bus 48. **Tickets** $7.50-$15. **Credit** V.

2002. After being blasted by a fire extinguisher and levelled by a Snap Suplex, Trish lost her grappling title to Victoria at the close of 2002 but there's no way that's the end of the story. After all, Fabulous Moulah won her first championship belt in 1956 and captured it for the ninth time in 1999.

Active sports & fitness

Cycling

Toronto is a great city for cycling. Most major thoroughfares have bike lanes and, for the most part, drivers respect them. While you might win an occasional door prize (local jargon for being hit by an opening car door) and, as anywhere, accidents do happen, generally speaking you can traverse the entire city by bike with nary a scratch. Travel east–west (most spectacularly along the scenic lakeshore) and the ride is mostly flat. Head north and things start getting hilly, but at least that means the ride back is mostly downhill. For route maps check out www.city.toronto.on.ca/parks/maps.htm or visit a bikeshops. Try the **Martin Goodman Trail** along the lakeshore or pedal across to the **Toronto Islands** for spectacular views. If you think you'll want a bike for more than the day, you might want to check out **Bikeshare**, the yellow bike lending programme that has sprouted up all over the world. You can pick up or leave your bike (which comes with a lock, bell and basket) at one of several hubs around the city and the one-year membership of $25 is comparable to multi-day rentals anywhere else.

Bikeshare

761 Queen Street W, at Palmerston Street, West End (416 504 2918/www.bikeshare.org). Streetcar 501. **Open** noon-6pm Mon; 9am-6pm Tue-Fri. **Cost** $25 1-yr membership. **No credit cards**.

Toronto Island Bicycle Rental

Centre Island, 1 Island Airport, Harbourfront (416 203 0009). **Open** May-Sept. Call for more details.

Wheel Excitement

5 Rees Street, next to SkyDome, Entertainment District (416 260 9000/www.wheelexcitement.com). Streetcar 510/subway Union. **Open** 10am-6pm daily. **Rates** in-line skate & mountain bike rentals $14 per 2hrs. **Credit** MC, V. **Map** p277 D9.

Golf

See *p214* **Putt it right there**.

Gyms

Daily rates of about $15 are available at several excellent gyms in the heart of downtown. The **YMCA** and **Bally Total Fitness** both have locations within easy walking distance of many centrally located hotels, and the University of Toronto's massive **Athletic & Physical Education Centre** also has a day rate. Known as the AC, it has several gyms, pools, a strength and conditioning centre and an indoor running

Air Canada Centre (*see p209*): home to the Raptors, the Leafs and The Rock.

track. From pilates to spinning, yoga to stretching, you can choose pretty much any form of sweat extraction in Toronto. Bally also has personal trainers available.

Bally Total Fitness
80 Bloor Street W, at Bay Street, the Annex (416 960 2434/www.ballyfitness.com). Subway Bay. **Open** 6am-11pm Mon-Fri; 8am-7pm Sat, Sun. **Cost** $15 per day. **Credit** AmEx, MC, V. **Map** p280 E4.

Metro-Central YMCA
20 Grosvenor Street, at Yonge Street, Church & Wellesley (416 975 9622/www.ymcatoronto.org). Streetcar 506 /subway Wellesley. **Cost** $15 per day. **Open** 6am-11pm Mon-Fri 7am-8pm Sat, Sun. **Credit** AmEx, MC, V. **Map** p281 F5.

University of Toronto Athletic & Physical Education Centre
55 Harbord Street, at Spadina Avenue, University (416 978 3437/www.utoronto.ca/physical). Streetcar 510. **Open** 7am-11pm Mon-Fri; 10am-5pm Sat, Sun. **Cost** $15 per day. **Credit** AmEx, MC, V. **Map** p280 D5.

Ice-skating/'shinny'

While most of the city's many indoor rinks have designated skating hours at affordable prices (and there are more than two dozen well-maintained free outdoor rinks dotting the landscape),there are two outdoor rinks in particular that people flock to. You can tool around with your sweetie 'til your heart's content in the dramatic shadow of City Hall

at Nathan Phillips Square, or down by the lake at the Harbourfront Centre. Skate rental is available at both. The outdoor skating season runs from roughly December through to the beginning of March.

Hockey enthusiasts don't have to look far to find a great game of 'shinny' (the informal, non-contact, 'be nice' version of the game) at any public rink, particularly at weekends. Just bring a stick and your skates and the locals will make you feel welcome.

Harbourfront Centre
235 Queens Quay W, at York Street, Harbourfront (416 973 4866/www.harbourfront.on.ca). Streetcar 509, 510. **Open** 10am-10pm daily. **Rentals** $5-$7. **No credit cards. Map** p277 D9.

Nathan Phillips Square
100 Queen Street W, at Bay Street, Chinatown (416 338 7465/www.city.toronto.on.ca/parks/ recreation_facilities/skating/skating.htm). Streetcar 501/subway Osgoode or Queen. **Open** 10am-10pm daily. **Rental** $7.50; $6.50 concessions/2hrs (deposit ID or $40). **Map** p277/p278 E7.

In-line skating

In a hockey-mad town like Toronto, it's no surprise that in-line skating is hugely popular. During rush-hour cyclists have to share their bike lanes with all manner of skaters gliding to and from work. The city's many hiking and bike trails are perfect for the sport, and rental skates are available at many bike hire outfits, including **Wheel Excitement** (*see p211*).

Arts & Entertainment

Pool/billiards

Pool playing, in all its myriad forms, is well-loved and readily available throughout Toronto. The number of bars *without* a table would be easier to count than those with, and an array of specialised pool halls have sprouted up for the more practised player. The most exotic establishment is the luxurious **Academy of Spherical Arts**, located in the former Brunswick Billiards factory in the factory district. The Academy boasts 15 sumptuous antique billiard tables, several valued at over $100,000 (and one formerly owned by the Prince of Wales). With high ceilings, art-covered walls and several rooms to choose from, this place is a throwback to the days of Rudyard Kipling and Phineas Fogg. Fast-forward a century or so and you'll find the Academy's modern counterpart at **The Rivoli Pool Hall**, upstairs from one of Queen Street's trendiest night spots. It's stocked with 13 vintage pool tables (smaller for faster games). There's also a bar and DJ lounge plus live jazz on Sundays (*see p199*).

Academy of Spherical Arts

38 Hanna Avenue, at King Street W, West End (416 532 2782/www.sphericalarts.com). Streetcar 504. **Open** noon-2am Mon-Fri; 5pm-2am Sat. **Credit** AmEx, DC, MC, V.

The Rivoli Pool Hall

334 Queen Street W, at Spadina Avenue, Entertainment District (416 596 1501/http:// rivoli.ca). Streetcar 501. **Open** 4pm-1am Thur-Sun. **Credit** AmEx, MC, V.

Rock climbing

Joe Rockhead's, Canada's largest indoor climbing facility with over 50 ropes and 3,000 square feet of bouldering, is deep in the heart of Toronto. **Toronto Climbing Academy** in the East Side has ten different climbing areas, which include caves and overhangs, and can provide instruction. For the real thing, travel west of town to the Niagara Escarpment. **Mountain Equipment Co-op** is the city's best resource for both climbing equipment and information .

Joe Rockhead's Indoor Rock Climbing

29 Fraser Avenue, at Liberty Street, West End (416 538 7670/www.joerockheads.com). Streetcar 504. **Open** noon-11pm Mon-Fri; 10am-7pm Sat; 10am-6pm Sun. **Admission** $8-$14. **Credit** MC, V.

Mountain Equipment Co-op

400 King Street W, at Peter Street, Entertainment District (416 340 2667/www.mec.ca). Streetcar

504, 510. **Open** 10am-7pm Mon-Wed; 10am-9pm Thur, Fri; 9am-6pm Sat; 11am-5pm Sun. **Credit** AmEx, MC, V. **Map** p277 D8.

Toronto Climbing Academy

100A Broadview Avenue, at Queen Street, East Side (416 406 5900/www.climbingacademy. com). Streetcar 501, 504. **Open** noon-11pm Mon-Fri; 10am-10pm Sat, Sun. **Admission** $10-$12. **Credit** V.

Skiing

Ontario doesn't have the Alps or the Rockies but it does have lots of hills and plenty of snow in winter. Skiing inside Toronto's borders is pretty much confined to the cross-country variety on bike trails and in city parks, although families and learners can pick up the basics (downhill, cross-country and snowboarding) at two parks – **Earl Bales** (4169 Bathurst Street, 416 395 7934) and **Centennial** (256 Centennial Park Road, 416 394 8750) – in Toronto's northern reaches. Call 416 338 6754 for information on public skiing or visit www.city.toronto.on.ca/parks/ recreation_facilities/skiing/skiing.htm.

If you want a run that takes longer than a sneeze, there are many downhill resorts to choose from once you leave town and head north. Less than an hour's drive from the city core, near Barrie, is **Horseshoe Resorts** – a well-maintained year-round facility with seven lifts and 22 runs. It also has 35 kilometres (22 miles) of cross-country trails, as well as snowboarding areas and lessons. It would be worth it, though, to drive an hour further, to Collingwood, to hit Ontario's largest resort, **Blue Mountain**. There you'll find 34 trails and 12 lifts that accommodate all manner of skiing for beginners, as well as challenging double black diamond runs for experts, three half-pipes for snowboarding and a snowtubing park.

Blue Mountain

RR3, Collingwood, ON L9Y 3Z2 (705 445 0231/416 869 3799 from Toronto only/ www.bluemountain.ca).

Horseshoe Resort

Box 10, Horseshoe Valley, RR1, Barrie, ON L4M 4Y8 (1-800 461 5627/416 283 2988 from Toronto only/www.horseshoeresort.com).

Swimming

The City of Toronto operates more than 30 public pools in just the central core alone, and more than half of those are indoors and open all year round. Of the many outdoor pools, the most significant one is the **Gus Ryder**

Sunnyside Pool (1755 Lakeshore W, 416 392 6696) next to Budapest Park on the Lakeshore. Originally built as part of a vast amusement complex in the 1920s, Sunnyside was the city's most popular destination for outdoor summer fun for decades. At one time it boasted the largest heated swimming pool in the world. If you'd rather not deal with the general public, both the **YMCA** and U of T **Athletic Centre** have pools (for both, *see p212*). For more information on public pools call 416 392 8189 or visit www.city.toronto.on.ca/parks/recreation_facilities/swimming/swim_index.htm.

Tennis

While there are many private tennis clubs in Toronto that require a member to get you in, there are also over 30 courts in public parks, some of them covered in the winter (for example, **Eglinton Flats Park** in the West End), which have slots available to one and all. Generally from 9am to 5pm on weekdays you can use these courts at will, while at weekends and in the evenings they become semi-private – which means if a club member shows up, you have to relinquish your court. As for the free courts, the best maintained ones are in the more upmarket neighbourhoods, like Rosedale and Forest Hill. Moore Park, at Bayview and St Clair Avenues, also has particularly nice courts. If the club life is what you desire, then among the best are the **Toronto Lawn Tennis Club** (44 Price Street, 416 922 1105/www.torontolawn.com) and the **Boulevard Club** (1491 Lakeshore Boulevard W, 416 532 3341/www.boulevardclub.com). For a list of public courts, call 416 392 1111 or visit www.city.toronto.on.ca/parks/recreation_facilities/tennis.

Watersports

You don't ever really want to swim in Lake Ontario (sure, there are times when the pollution dissipates to a non-toxic level, but, do bear in

Putt it right there

Golf is often seen as an elitist, prohibitively expensive sport, but here in Toronto it is widely accessible to one and all. There are all manner of courses and driving ranges both inside the city limits and within easy driving distance though, of course, they vary widely in quality. The most famous is **Glen Abbey**, which was designed by Jack Nicklaus and was the home of the Canadian Open when Tiger Woods made a dramatic winning shot to take the title in 2000. It's a short drive west out of town (in Oakville) and a bit pricey, but open to all.

ScoreGolf magazine, Canada's golf bible, rates the much more affordable **St George's Golf & Country Club** in the West End as the country's No.1 (Glen Abbey rated No.13). You'll need a letter of reference from your home club but non-members are welcome by advance arrangement.

Public courses can be found throughout the city with prices ranging from $12 for nine holes on a weekday to a high of $49 for 18-holes at the weekend – a far cry from the couple of hundred bucks the private clubs charge. Dentonia, Don Valley, Humber Valley, Scarlett Woods and Tam O'Shanter, all handsomely wooded, are listed below. For more information call Toronto Parks & Recreation on 416 392 8186 or visit www.city.toronto.on.ca/parks/recreation_facilities/golfing/golf_index.htm.

If checking out the occasional celebrity duffer is to your liking, the coolest course in the neighbourhood is **Wooden Sticks**, just outside of town in Uxbridge. Purportedly owned by several hockey players, this is where sport freaks go to see and be seen. Wooden Sticks has been hailed as the best new course in Canada, in part because it has several holes inspired by classic courses like Augusta National and the Old Course at St Andrews. Your $200 green fee includes 18 holes, lunch, a cart and refreshments along the way.

Recently the number of local driving ranges has increased so if you absolutely, positively have to hit a bucket of balls or two, you can easily get your fix. Right downtown, in the shadow of the CN Tower, lies the **Citycore Golf Course & Driving Range**. Unless your short game needs serious work forget about the nine-hole, par 3 course. Instead you can slam away at unlimited balls by the hour or half-hour from the three-tiered driving range that is open all year round. The huge entertainment complex at The Docks includes several golf activities, such as sand traps, a chipping green and an 18-hole Pro Putt course as well as 75 hitting stations at the driving range (which doubles as a drive-in cinema; *see p179*).

The golf season runs from mid April to mid November.

mind that every day's a good day for the lamprey eels), but that doesn't mean you can't enjoy some fun on the water. Marinas dot the entire lakeshore and there are several places where visitors can enjoy all manner of wet recreation from canoes, kayaks and sailboards to round-the-lake tours. For family fun head over to Centreville on the Toronto Islands for rowing and pedal boats (*see p53*). For a good list of local windsurfing sites consult www.toronto windsurfingclub.com. **Harbourfront Canoe & Kayak Centre** provides rentals and lessons. It probably goes without saying that watersports are a highly seasonal activity.

Harbourfront Canoe & Kayak Centre

283 Queens Quay W, 416 203 2277/www.paddletoronto.com). Streetcar 509, 510. Call for more details. **Map** p277 D9.

Queens Quay Yachting

275 Queens Quay W (416 203 3000). Streetcar 509, 510. Call for more details. **Map** p277 D9.

City-side sailing.

Citycore Golf Course & Driving Range

2 Spadina Avenue, at Front Street W, Entertainment District (416 640 9888/citycore@centtel.com). Streetcar 510. **Fees** $20-$22. **Credit** AmEx, MC, V. **Map** p276 C8.

Dentonia Park Golf Course

Victoria Park Avenue, at Danforth Avenue, East Side (416 392 2558). Subway Victoria Park. **Fees** $7.50-$20 Mon-Fri; $9.50-$22 Sat, Sun. **Credit** AmEx, MC, V.

The Docks

11 Polson Street, at Cherry Street, East Side (416 469 5655/www.thedocks.com). Bus 72. **Open** Sept-May 9am-9pm daily. May-Aug 8am-dusk daily. **Fees** Mini-putt $6. Putting range $10. **Credit** AmEx, MC, V.

Don Valley Gold Course

Yonge Street, just south of Highway 401, North Side (416 392 2465). Subway York Mills. **Fees** $15-$45 Mon-Fri; $18-$49 Sat, Sun. **Credit** AmEx, MC, V.

Glen Abbey Golf Club

1333 Dorval Drive, Oakville (1-800 288 0388/905 844 1811/www. glenabbey.com). **Fees** $100-$235. **Credit** AmEx, MC, V.

Humber Valley Golf Course

Beattie Avenue at Albion Road, West End (416 392 2488). Subway Royal York, then bus 73. **Fees** $13-$36 Mon-Fri; $16-$42 Sat, Sun. **Credit** AmEx, MC, V.

St George's Golf & Country Club

1668 Islington Avenue, at Eglinton Avenue W, Etobicoke, West End (416 231 9350/www.stgeorges.org). Streetcar 505/subway Islington. **Fees** $100-$240. **Credit** AmEx, MC, V.

Scarlett Woods Golf Course

Eglinton Avenue W, at Jane Street, West End (416 392 2484). Bus 32, 35, 79. **Fees** $10-$26 Mon-Fri; $13-$31 Sat, Sun. **Credit** AmEx, MC, V.

Tam O'Shanter Golf Course

Birchmount Road at Sheppard Avenue E, North Side (416 392 2547). Bus 17, 85. **Fees** $14-$37 Mon-Fri; $16-$43 Sat, Sun. **Credit** AmEx, MC, V.

Wooden Sticks

Elgin Park Drive, between Main & Toronto Streets, Uxbridge, East Side (905 853 4379/www.woodensticks. com). **Fee** $200 plus tax. **Credit** AmEx, MC, V.

Theatre & Dance

Hype aside, Toronto's scene is set for a bit of Broadway and a lot of off.

Theatre

Since the early 1980s, Toronto has been billing itself as the third-largest theatre centre in the English-speaking world, after London and New York. This fact holds true in terms of the sheer volume of venues and the larger number of independent theatre companies in the city, but is debatable in terms of quality or government support – compared to, say, the standard of work and public funding that Chicago theatres receive. Toronto is not a theatre city and its residents are not known for their love of the stage. In fact, the third-place status often comes as a surprise to average Torontonians who couldn't name a single Canadian playwright or stage actor (unless they made a transition to US film or TV; local boy Eric McCormack of *Will & Grace* fame is a case in point). And sure, there are always a good few big-budget global-franchise shows drawing solid local audiences from a deep Canadian and US hinterland, as well as the tourist trade, but that's true of a good clutch of cities worldwide.

So how come there's such a sizeable theatre scene in Toronto? One reason is the concentration of Canadian cultural production here. Like New York and London, the city is an artist-magnet. There are five theatre schools in the Greater Toronto Area churning out hundreds of wannabe actors, playwrights, directors and designers. Many new theatre companies have been started over the past two decades by such graduates.

Indigenous theatre is a relatively new phenomenon that can be traced back to the late 1960s. Until then, Toronto played host to touring companies from the UK and the US. A repertoire of musicals, variety shows and mid-brow fair was the norm. The establishment of **Theatre Passe Muraille** in 1967, the oldest alternative theatre in Canada, marked a turning point in what can be safely termed Canadian-themed theatre. The 1970s saw an explosion of other local companies (**Tarragon Theatre**, **Factory Theatre**); the busy scene today is a direct result of those formative years.

It all translates to a very lively, sometimes groundbreaking, sometimes insufferably sophomoric efforts. When theatre in Toronto is good, it's thrillingly so. But quality varies wildly so check local newspapers for reviews.

Bigger theatres do not mean better plays and the best of Toronto theatre is found in smaller venues dotted around town, where creativity abounds even if money is in short supply.

TICKETS AND INFORMATION

Most performances are at 8pm Tuesday to Saturday, with Sunday matinees at 2.30pm, for which many small and mid-size theatres run a Pay-What-You-Can (PWYC) policy. Larger theatres also have shows on Monday and Saturday matinées. Prices range from $9.99 in the independent sector to up to $100 for such crowd-pleasers as *The Lion King* or *Mamma Mia!* (which the exchange rate usually makes a relatively good deal for non-Canadians). For tickets to big shows call TicketKing (416 872 1212/www.ticketking.com) or Ticketmaster (416 870 8000/www.ticketmaster.ca). Tickets for most mid-size theatres average $30. Call the box office directly to reserve seats and arrive early (they don't tend to have numbered seating).

TO Tix, located on Level Two of the Eaton Centre (416 536 6468 ext 40), sells discounted (usually by 50 per cent) tickets on the day of the performance. There are no online or telephone reservations – although a recorded phone message changes every day, so you can call ahead to see what's on offer.

As well as the free listings magazines *eye* and *Now* (*see p259*), another excellent source of information is the website torontoperforms. com, with constantly updated listings of live performances in the city.

Toronto's theatre scene is supplemented by serious contributions from the classical repertoires of the **Shaw Festival** in Niagara-on-the-Lake (*see chapter* **Niagara & Around: Niagara-on-the-Lake**) and the **Stratford Festival** (*see chapter* **Quick Trips: Stratford**), both of which have a wider appeal than their names may suggest.

If you're in Toronto in July, check out the ever-expanding Toronto Fringe Festival. The smaller but more consistently rewarding festival, Summerworks, is held in the first week of August. Check local listings for details.

Theatres & other venues

None of Toronto's theatres has a resident company. Every season (September to May), each venue offers a selection of plays, some of

The decoratively dramatic **Elgin** and **Winter Garden** theatres (*see p218*).

which are co-productions with local or regional theatre companies, some produced individually in-house, and some touring. Quality therefore varies, so choices should be made on the basis of individual productions.

Alumnae Theatre

70 Berkeley Street, at Adelaide Street, St Lawrence (416 364 4170/www.alumnaetheatre.com). Streetcar 504. **Open** *Box office* 10am-4pm Mon-Fri. **Tickets** $10-$15. **Credit** MC, V. **Map** p278 G7.

Founded in 1919 by women graduates of the University of Toronto, this is the closest Toronto came to avant-garde theatre in the 1940s and '50s. It's no longer affiliated with the university but its knack for presenting critically acclaimed local and international productions has not diminished.

Artword Theatre

75 Portland Street, at King Street W, Entertainment District (416 408 2783/www.artword.net). Streetcar 504, 511. **Tickets** $10-$30. Call for box office and ticket details. **Map** p276 C8.

An independently run space with a hit-and-miss programme of plays and dance performances. The main theatre seats 150. A smaller space, Artword Alternative, seats about 60 and is a favourite for young, upcoming theatre companies.

Berkeley Street Theatre

26 Berkeley Street, at Front Street E, St Lawrence (416 368 3110/www.canstage.com). Streetcar 504.
Open *Box office* 10am-6pm Mon-Sat. **Tickets** $25-$49. **Credit** AmEx, MC, V. **Map** p278 G8.

CanStage sends its edgier work to this recently renovated 240-seater. Its industrial warehouse look often complements the raw onstage fare.

Bluma Appel Theatre

St Lawrence Centre, 27 Front Street E, St Lawrence (416 366 7723/www.stlc.com). Streetcar 504/subway King or Union. **Open** *Box office* 10am-6pm Mon-Sat. **Tickets** $40-$75. **Credit** AmEx, MC, V. **Map** p277/p278 F8.

This 875-seater is where CanStage's flashier productions are staged (*Wit, How I Learned to Drive, Proof*). It's a relatively large space, but its good sightlines make it feel quite intimate.

Buddies In Bad Times Theatre

12 Alexander Street, Church & Wellesley (416 975 8555/www.buddiesinbadtimestheatre.com). Streetcar 506/subway Wellesley. **Open** *Box office* noon-5pm Tue-Sat. **Tickets** $18-$25. **Credit** MC, V. **Map** p281 F5.

North America's largest queer theatre (call it gay and lesbian at your peril) dates back to 1979 and is a focal point for the gay community, at whose heart it resides. Its heyday was the 1980s when its then artistic director Sky Gilbert made it home to grungy, postmodern gay-themed plays that had edge but not enough audiences. Today, its reputation for gutsy work is a thing of the past but it continues to produce decent work that appeals to gay and straight audiences. There's a small cabaret theatre, too.

Local hero David Mirvish

Depending on whom you ask, nobody has done as much or as little for Toronto theatre as David Mirvish. His Mirvish Productions, Canada's largest commercial theatre producer, is responsible for bringing shows like *Les Misérables, Miss Saigon, The Lion King* and *Mamma Mia!* to Toronto. Good news for the hundreds of actors and stagehands this brand of musical theatre employs but little comfort to Canadian playwrights or composers whose work rarely make it to his subscription seasons. With the demise of Garth Drabinsky's Livent Theatre in 1998 – once Mirvish's only serious rival – the scene was set for his domination of the commercial theatre sector. No other producer can compete: he owns the three largest theatre venues in town; has the largest subscription base in the country; and operates at an international level that reflects the company's 40-year history. (The company was established by his father Ed in 1962, on the left in the picture.)

You'd expect a theatre impresario of this magnitude to be a ruthless SOB. Far from it. Mirvish's nice-guy reputation travels further than the shows he brings to town and his generosity (donating rehearsal space or services) to the theatre community is well documented. What could be more appropriate: a crowd pleaser who produces crowd pleasers.

Honourable mentions: Bill Glasco (director, co-founder Tarragon Theatre); Paul Thompson (playwright/director, founding member Theatre Passe Muraille); Ken Gass (playwright/director, founder Factory Theatre).

Canon Theatre

263 Yonge Street, at Dundas Street, Dundas Square (416 872 1212/www.onstagenow.com). Streetcar 505/subway Dundas. **Open** *Box office* 10.30am-6pm Tue-Sat (box office located at 244 Victoria Street, at the back of the theatre). **Tickets** $44-$94. **Credit** AmEx, DC, MC, V. **Map** p277/p278 F7.

This exquisitely restored theatre (which was previously known as the Pantages) is now owned by Mirvish Productions. When the venue is not used as part of the Mirvish subscription season – the local production of *The Producers* opened there in spring 2003 – it becomes the location of choice for box-and-truck touring musicals.

Elgin & Winter Garden Theatre Centre

189 Yonge Street, at Dundas Street, Dundas Square (416 314 2884/www.ticketmaster.ca). Streetcar

505/subway Dundas or Queen. **Open** *Box office* 11am-6pm Mon-Sat. **Tickets** $38-$55. **Credit** AmEx, DC, MC, V. **Map** p277/p278 F7.

The only remaining double-decker theatre complex – a popular design in the early 1900s – in North America, the Elgin and the Winter Garden were restored after decades of neglect in the 1980s. The larger Elgin is richly appointed, with ornate fabrics and gilt cherubs. The Winter Garden sits above, festooned with Arcadian watercolour scenes. The theatres are now home to productions that vary from Baroque opera in the grand Elgin to one-woman shows in the Winter Garden. It draws international touring productions and well-to-do north Toronto crowds for whom theatre is a diversion after dinner and before nightcaps. The Elgin doubles as a cinema during the Toronto International Film Festival. Mirvish Productions uses both venues for its subscription season.

Factory Theatre

125 Bathurst Street, at King Street W,
Entertainment District (416 505 9971/www.factory
theatre.ca). Streetcar 501, 511. **Open** *Box office*
noon-8pm Tue-Sat. **Tickets** $18-$25. **Credit** AmEx,
MC, V. **Map** p276 C7.
The quintessential Canadian theatre. Established in
1970 by Ken Gass, who returned in 1997 as artistic
director, it was the first in Canada to be dedicated to
works by indigenous playwrights. Artists have a
soft spot for the venue since many of them got their
first break here. A Victorian building on the edge of
the 'Garment District', it defines shabby genteel.
Historical significance aside, approach with care:
each season the Factory plays host to a clunker or
two in the name of national pride.

Harbourfront Centre

235 Queen's Quay Boulevard W, Waterfront
(416 973 4000/www.harbourfront.on.ca). Streetcar
509, 510/subway Union. **Open** *Box office* 1-8pm
Tue-Sat. **Tickets** $20-$60. **Credit** AmEx, Disc,
MC, V. **Map** p277/p278 E9.
The Centre is known as a producer of major festivals (jazz, authors', children's). Its month-long World
Stage Festival in April is to local theatre aficionados
what the Toronto International Film Festival is to
film buffs: a chance to experience more global theatre. Harbourfront also rents out the du Maurier
Theatre Centre and Premiere Dance Theatre.

Hummingbird Centre for the Performing Arts

1 Front Street E, at Yonge Street, St Lawrence
(416 393 7469/www.hummingbirdcentre.com).
Streetcar 504/subway King or Union. **Open** *Box*
office 11am-6pm Mon-Sat. **Tickets** $20-$150.
Credit AmEx, MC, V. **Map** p277/p278 F8.
Named after a sponsoring Toronto software firm,
this barn-like home of Canadian Opera Company
and the National Ballet of Canada theatre seating
over 3,000 has an uncertain future, because its prestigious tenants are planning a move to the new Four
Seasons Centre for the Performing Arts in a few
years' time. Until then, the theatre will no doubt
continue to mount a mishmash of variety shows:
everything from magicians to Abba extravaganzas.

Princess of Wales Theatre

300 King Street W, at John Street, Entertainment
District (416 872 1212/www.onstagenow.com).
Streetcar 504/subway St Andrew. **Open** *Box office*
10.30am-6pm Mon; 11am-8.30pm Tue-Sat; 11am-7pm
Sun. **Tickets** $26-$94. **Credit** AmEx, DC, MC, V.
Map p277 D8.
This venue in the heart of the Entertainment District
is the first privately owned theatre built in Canada
since 1907. With Peter Smith as its architect, Yabu-
Pushelberg as its interior design firm and Frank
Stella responsible for its murals, this place is noted
as much for its design as its productions. It opened
in 1993 with *Miss Saigon* and continues to bring in
the coachloads for long-running Broadway shows.
It's presently occupied by Disney's *The Lion King*.

Royal Alexandra Theatre

260 King Street W, at University Avenue,
Entertainment District (416 872 1212/www.
onstagenow.com). Streetcar 504/subway St
Andrew. **Open** *Box office* 10.30am-6pm Mon;
10.30am-8.30pm Tue-Sat; 11am-3pm Sun.
Tickets $44-$86. **Credit** AmEx, DC, MC, V.
Map p277/p278 E8.
Once described as an 'Edwardian jewel box', this
1907 theatre encapsulates grand chapters of Toronto
theatre history. In its environs John Gielgud and
Ralph Richardson played; Piaf belted and Fred
Astaire put on the Ritz. In 1962 it was bought by Ed
Mirvish and served as the premier venue of his sub-
scription season until *Mamma Mia!* came along.
This smash-hit musical should keep them dancing
in the aisles for years to come.

Tarragon Theatre

30 Bridgman Avenue, at Howland Avenue,
Casa Loma (416 531 1827/www.tarragontheatre.
com). Bus 7/subway Dupont. **Open** *Box office*
10am-5pm Mon; 10am-8pm Tue-Sat; 1-2.30pm
Sun. **Tickets** $15-$31. **Credit** AmEx, MC, V.
Map p280 C2.
By far the most reliable, artistically and financially,
theatre in Toronto and, probably, Canada. Here
you're likely to see Canadian theatre at its best as
well as some fine productions of, say, David Hare,
David Mamet or Tony Kushner. English transla-
tions of major works from Quebec are a house
speciality. The programming emphasis remains on
well-established Canadian playwrights. Tarragon
has two auditoria: the main theatre, a 205-seater for
works of wider appeal, and the Extra Space, one
of the best small venues in town, where edgier or
small-scale plays are staged.

Theatre Passe Muraille

16 Ryerson Avenue, at Carr Street, Entertainment
District (416 504 7529/www.passemuraille.on.ca).
Streetcar 501, 511. **Open** *Box office* noon-5pm
Mon; noon-8.30pm Tue-Sat; noon-4pm Sun. **Tickets**
$16-$38. **Credit** AmEx, MC, V. **Map** p276 C7.
The who's who of Canadian theatre started here.
Some, like Ann-Marie MacDonald and Michael
Ondaatje, have since became internationally
renowned novelists. Of late however hits have
been the exception rather than the rule, though
The Drawer Boy by Michael Healey (*see p221* **The**
write stuff) in 1999 made up for a dearth of popular or critical successes. The main stage has a
jazz-bar feel with an open balcony and well-
stocked bar; the small Backspace is notoriously
uncomfortable (patrons are provided with cushions as they enter) but has seen some important
independent productions.

Companies

There were an estimated 200 theatre companies
in Toronto in 2002. Below is a select list of those
that have stood the test of time and critics.

Arts & Entertainment

Alianak Theatre Productions

416 535 5956.
Since its inception in 1996, this company's work has been both intense and intensely political. Artistic director Hrant Alianak's *Walls of Africa* (2002) won a deserved Dora Mavor Moore Award (Toronto's equivalent of the Oliviers or Tonys) and future productions at time of writing will cover such subjects as the Holocaust and the Armenian genocide.

Canadian Stage Company

416 368 3110/www.canstage.com.
With an annual operating budget of $8 million, CanStage (as it likes to be known) is the envy of every theatre company in town. Recent seasons have included an overwhelming number of US, British and Irish plays that make light of the fact that this is the nearest Canada has to a national theatre. Still, productions are always polished, and cast and directors are the crème de la crème of Toronto theatre. CanStage operates a number of theatres, with its main roster in the Bluma Appel and edgier stuff in the Berkeley Street (for both, *see p217*).

Crow's Theatre

416 504 5962.
In the late 1980s and early 1990s, Crow's Theatre's name was associated with the best of alternative, in-your-face work and its artistic director Jim Millan was the hottest young thing in Toronto. Recent productions have been either tamer or shocking for shock's sake, but traces of the old magic persist.

Da Da Kamera

416 586 1503.
One of the best, most original and consistently superior theatre companies in Canada is a showcase for its artistic director's writing and acting talent. Daniel MacIvor (also a filmmaker) creates plays with a heightened sense of theatricality and deceptive simplicity. The work ranges from multi-character dramas to MacIvor's own brand of one-man performance-art-meets-theatre.

DNA Theatre

416 504 5099/www.dnatheatre.com.
Few theatre directors have been described as both a 'genius' and an 'asshole' in one sentence (in the famous words of a local scribe) but such is the reputation of Hillar Liitoja, DNA's mastermind. Staging works in living rooms and other unorthodox spaces creates performances with a voyeuristic, claustrophobic quality. It's something to be experienced and examined rather than enjoyed.

Modern Times Stage Company

416 790 1016.
Artistic director Soheil Parsa's company fuses Middle Eastern theatrical traditions with Western ones to create a uniquely bi-cultural experience. Emphasis on movement and imagistic theatre result in an evocative experience – even if the work suffers from over-stylisation. Still, expect to be dazzled.

The **Tarragon Theatre**. *See p219.*

Native Earth Performing Arts

416 531 1402/www.go.to/nativeearth.com.
The first theatre company dedicated to developing and creating works that express the aboriginal experience in Canada. Its most famous alumni is Tomson Highway, whose *The Rez Sisters* and *Dry Lips Oughta Move to Kapuskasing* are Canadian (not just Native) classics. The company continues to handhold a number of playwrights and performers with various degrees of success.

Necessary Angel Theatre

416 703 0406/www.necessaryangel.com.
A company whose name is associated with serious and intellectually stimulating theatre – a reputation it has lived up to since its inaugural production in 1981. Artistic director Richard Rose has taken over the helm at Tarragon Theatre but promises to continue his association with Necessary Angel. Playwrights whose works it has presented include Jason Sherman, Colleen Murphy and David Young, all Toronto theatre A-listers.

Nightwood Theatre

416 944 1740/www.nightwoodtheatre.net.
Nightwood focuses on work by women writers and has a strong feminist bent but has emerged over the last 20 years as a home of good theatre, period.

Soulpepper Theatre Company

416 203 6264/www.soulpepper.ca.
Before Soulpepper set up in 1998, fans of classical theatre had to travel to the Stratford or Shaw festivals for performances of this level of craft and attention to emotional and physical detail. Now they get them from Soulpepper. Savvy marketing has something to do with its phenomenal success: a typical season runs from June to October, when most Toronto theatres are on their summer hiatus. In productions of Anton Chekhov's *Uncle Vanya* (2001) and Jean Genet's *The Maids* (2002), the company proved a match to anything produced in London or New York. Youth training and mentoring programmes ensure a long-lasting legacy.

Theatre Columbus

416 504 0019/www.go7.ca/theatrecolumbus.html.
One of the few theatre companies in Toronto whose work is a collaborative, improvisational process, Theatre Columbus explores comedy (particularly the art of clowning) and pathos. The results vary but their plays are a performance delight. Columbus has a strong association with the Factory Theatre (*see p219*) where its recent projects premièred.

Theatre Smith-Gilmour

416 504 1277/www.go7.ca/ theatresmithgilmour.html.
Since 1980, artistic directors Dean Gilmour and Michele Smith have been creating original, improvisational theatre inspired by sources as various as clown theatre and Dante. But only since they let their imagination loose on the fiction of Anton Chekhov have they become local heroes, collecting eight Dora Awards for productions in 2000 and 2002 based on the Russian master's fiction. A European influence pervades but the talent is 100 per cent Canadian.

Volcano

416 535 1932/www.go7.ca/volcano.html.
Arguably the only theatre company to have successfully integrated text, movement and dance in its productions, thanks to Ross Manson's attentive artistic direction. For theatre with built-in appeal to heart, mind and body, this is a company to watch.

Dance

In terms of size and cultural significance, Toronto's contemporary dance scene is small fry compared to Montreal's, the dance capital of Canada. The biggest event to hit the dance scene was Mikhail Baryshnikov's defection from the USSR while performing in Toronto in 1974. The National Ballet of Canada may have their headquarters in Toronto, but dance in general (and contemporary dance in

The write stuff

On Toronto's theatre scene, it's the writers rather than the actors who are the true stars and driving forces. The association of a big writing name with a new play is a guarantee of attention from both audience and press. Of playwrights currently working, Jason Sherman and Michael Healey are virtually royalty.

During the 1990s, Sherman wrote a string of works that are already part of the Canadian drama canon. These include *The League of Nathans* (1992); *Three in the back, Two in the Head* (1994) *Patience* (1998) and *It's All True* (1999). His work is a combination of political philosophy and carefully planted schtick, infused with a deep sense of humanity. He is closely associated with the Tarragon Theatre – where he was playwright-in-residence for seven years – and with Necessary Angel, where his work with director Richard Rose was a landmark in playwright-director collaboration. Sherman also writes for Canadian and American TV.

Michael Healey (who is also a terrific comic actor) made his writing debut at

Toronto Fringe Festival with a one-act play called *Kicked* (1996). But it wasn't until March of 1999 when *The Drawer Boy* opened at Theatre Passe Muraille that his promise as a playwright was realised beyond all expectations. The play (which is a tribute to the transformational powers of theatre) went on to sweep the Dora Mavor Moore Awards and has since been picked up by Chicago's prestigious Steppenwolf Theatre in a production co-starring John Mahoney (of *Frasier* fame). *The Drawer Boy* remains the most successful play to come out of Toronto in the past 20 years. Healey's follow up solo play – he co-authored two one-act plays with partner Kate Lynch later in 1999 – was *Plan B* in 2002. Ostensibly a political thriller, it used the thorny issue of Quebec separation from Canada as a backdrop to discuss relationship anxieties. It wasn't as big a hit as *The Drawer Boy* but still won a Dora for best new Canadian play.

Other writers to watch out for are George F Walker, Linda Griffith and Judith Thompson.

particular) is an ostracised art form here. Those who remain active are working on the edge of creative and financial anxieties, which lends a rough, compelling edge to the scene. This, combined with visits from touring groups, means there is enough here for the dance-loving traveller. *See p216* for ticket information; www.danceumbrella.net is a great resource for Ontario's dance devotees.

Theatres & other venues

Toronto's queer stage, **Buddies in Bad Times Theatre** (*see p217*), is a major dance venue. It often features Danny Grossman Theatre Company as part of its subscription season, and every August hosts fFida, fringe Festival of Independent Dance Artists.

Betty Oliphant Theatre

404 Jarvis Street, at Wellesley Street, Church & Wellesley (416 964 5140/www.nbs-enb. on.ca). Subway Wellesley. **Open** *Box office* 10am-4pm Mon-Fri. **Tickets** $18-$25. **Credit** MC, V. **Map** p281 F5.

Part of National Ballet School of Canada, this 300-seat space was designed with dance performance in mind in general and ballet in particular – which explains why local and touring dance companies return to it year after year. Its huge stage can overwhelm more minimalist choreography.

Premiere Dance Theatre

Harbourfront Centre, 235 Queens Quay W, Waterfront (416 973 4000/www.harbourfront. on.ca). Streetcar 509, 510. **Open** *Box office* 1-8pm Tue-Sat. **Tickets** $20-$50. **Credit** AmEx, MC, V. **Map** p277/p278 E9.

Home to World Moves Dance series, which features the best in contemporary dance from around the world. The curated series runs from October to May and always has spots showcasing Canadian companies as well as international ones. It remains the only place where you can see dancing troupes from Finland and Japan on the same bill.

Theatre Centre

1087 Queen Street W, at Dovercourt Road, West Side (416 538 0988/www.theatrecentre.org). Streetcar 501. **Open** *Box office* noon-5pm Mon-Fri. **Tickets** $10-$20. **Credit** MC, V.

As part of its experimental mandate, the Theatre Centre launched the annual Body Geometry dance-theatre festival in 1998. The sky may be the limit when it comes to the creative energies flowing around this venue but a low ceiling and a cramped performance space are sorely limiting.

Winchester Street Theatre

80 Winchester Street, at Parliament Street, Cabbagetown (416 967 1365/www.tdt.org). Bus 65/streetcar 506. **Open** *Box office* 10am-5pm Mon-Fri. **Tickets** $10-$25. **Credit** MC, V. **Map** p281 H5.

This Cabbagetown theatre is operated jointly by Toronto Dance Theatre (TDT) and the School of Toronto Dance Theatre. With 115 seats it may be a small venue but its medium-sized stage is ideal for a mixture of choreographic styles.

Companies

Dancemakers

416 535 8880/www.dancemakers.org.

Toronto's most challenging dance company, physically and intellectually, has had French émigré and poet Serge Bennathan as artistic director since 1990. The company's work reflects his poetic vision. Dancemakers' most recent project was based on the work of French composer Erik Satie, who is a personal idol for Bennathan.

Danny Grossman Dance Company

416 408 4543/www.dgdance.org.

Grossman single-handedly defined the landscape of contemporary dance in Toronto. A living legend, he choreographs and presents at least two shows a year here. Physical storytelling is the best description of his work. Recent shows have also included work by other Canadian choreographers, part of his mission to preserve dance history in Canada.

Toronto Dance Theatre

416 967 1365/www.tdt.org.

Formed in 1968, TDT has been part of the evolution of dance culture in Toronto. Current artistic director Christopher House adds visual and dramatic appeal to a controversial company that has as many hardcore fans around town as it has detractors.

National Ballet of Canada

416 345 9595/www.national.ballet.ca.

The standards may be international but artistic director James Kudelka has been infusing his programming with works by local choreographers. Yes, expect to see the standard (but lavish) interpretations of *Swan Lake* or *Giselle* but keep an eye open for the groundbreaking choreography he sneaks up on his blue-rinse audiences.

Kaeja d'Dance

416 516 6030/www.kaeja.org.

Husband and wife team Allen and Karen Kaeja are the Nick and Nora of modern dance – except that their playing field is contact- and improv-based. Their work for the past decade has been focused on a series of trilogies on the theme of the Holocaust – which may explain the reverence with which their projects are usually discussed in the media.

Peggy Baker Dance Projects

416 504 6429.

The grande dame of contemporary dance has worked with the Lar Lubovitch Dance Company and Mikhail Baryshnikov's White Oak Dance Projects in New York in 1970s and continues to be a role model for young dancers and choreographers. Recent work has focused on women's bodies and ageing.

Arts & Entertainment

Trips Out of Town

Getting Started

Big country, small curiosities and the mother-in-law of all waterfalls.

Map pp272-273

Ontario is the most populous province in Canada. It is also both the geographical and the political centre (separating the constant and often fractious 'east–west' national positions), the country's main base for industry and trade and home of two capital cities: Toronto is the capital of Ontario while Ottawa is the capital of the Canada (though the 'Capital City Region' does extend into Quebec to appease the never-ending English-French rivalries).

Populous though the state might be, about 85 per cent of Ontario's 12 million inhabitants live within 100 miles of the US border, which leaves a lot of space for uninhabited wilderness, rugged campgrounds, provincial parks, luxury tennis retreats, family resorts, fly-in fishing camps, winter ski hills, miles of quiet cross-country trails and an unending supply of Great Outdoors including about half a million lakes and rivers (give or take a couple of thousand).

In fact, it looks like a reference to water gave Ontario its original name by the Native tribes. The word either comes from the Huron ('beautiful or sparkling water') or from an Iroquois term meaning 'rocks standing near the water' that referred to the now-famous Falls of the Niagara Escarpment. Either way, the word describes Ontario's original transport system.

The province is a little too big to experience in one weekend, with an area of approximately a million square kilometres, or 412,582 square miles. To put that in perspective, you could fit all of France, Germany and Italy within its borders. If you decided to spend the weekend driving north from Toronto to Thunder Bay, on the north shore of Lake Superior, it would take you, well, all weekend, just to get there. And then if you really wanted to drive north to the provinces furthest border – forget it, there are no roads. Destinations in this section, then, are a manageable distance away from town, covering the nearby Niagara area, the choicest day trips and samplings of the most easily accessed country and wilderness areas .

Visitors should keep in mind that half the urban population seems to have a summer cottage, while the other half cultivates friends who do, so there's a mass exodus from the city on summer Fridays and major roads can get

Rock of ages: the **McMichael Canadian Art Collection**. *See p237.*

Niagara-on-the-Lake. *See p233.*

Niagara Falls. *See p226.*

clogged, especially out towards the Muskokas and Haliburton Cottage Country. Niagara Falls is heaving from Friday to Sunday. So if you can, plan your getaways during the week.

GETTING AROUND

Public transport is patchy, and car is the only option for many trips out of town. For rental offices, *see p252*. However **VIA Rail** (65 Front Street W, 1-888 842 7245/ www.viarail.ca) provides an excellent service along the well-travelled 'corridor' route from Windsor through Toronto, Kingston, Ottawa, Montreal and Quebec City. A new service called 'the Renaissance' was brought in in 2002, and while it may not go as fast as its European counterparts, it gets you from Windsor to Quebec City in style. The main departure point is Union Station on Front Street (*see p250*).

Greyhound buses (1-800 661 8747/416 594 1010/www.greyhound.ca) are more likely to serve the smaller places on the map, and will be cheaper as well. They are the fastest public transport to Niagara Falls, though the station is less than convenient. Greyhound's main Toronto terminal is centrally located at 610 Bay Street, at Edward Street (*see p250*).

Camper vans are a good way of exploring the Ontarian vastness. **CanaDream Campers** rent out all kinds of moving accommodation.

The office is near Pearson International Airport at 1065B Martingrove Road, Etobicoke (416 243 3232/1-800 909 7631/www.canadream.com).

If you're on a limited time and budget and prepared to sacrifice the independence of the open road, contact **CanaBUS Tours** (74 Gerrard Street E, 416 977 8311, www.canabus. com), for various tours of the highlights of the province lasting between one and eight days.

TOURIST INFORMATION

The best place to gather information on the province is the **Tourism Ontario** (*see p252*). Particularly useful are its 'Day Tours from Toronto' brochure and the accommodation guide 'Experience it in Ontario'.

For information on parks and camping, contact the **Ministry of Natural Resources** on 1-800 667 1940 or **Ontario Parks** on 1-888 668 7275/www.ontarioparks.com; for information on Ontarios' many heritage sites, contact the **Ontario Heritage Foundation** (416 325 5000/www.heritagefdn.on.ca).

TELEPHONE CODES

All numbers given are long-distance calls from Toronto, so you will need to dial '1' before the area code unless you're calling locally. This goes for the Niagara region's 905 code, even though some Toronto numbers have the same prefix.

Trips Out of Town

Niagara Falls & Around

The unmissable yet exploited Falls and their culturally compensatory surrounds:
Wine Country and the charming Niagara-on-the-Lake.

Niagara Falls

Compare and contrast North America's two greatest natural wonders, the Grand Canyon and Niagara Falls. The former in the heart of a wilderness national park dedicated to preservation, the latter manicured, exploited and commercialised to within a rainbow of its life. Torontonians disdain the Falls, seeing them primarily as an easy way of getting rid of houseguests for the day. But watching half a billion gallons of water a second slide off a cliff right in front of you is pretty damned impressive by any standards: if you're in Toronto, you should make the trip. And cynical though the surrounding town's exploitation might be, hell, some people like viewing towers, sightseeing 'experiences' and tourist attractions of an entirely unashamed nature. Millions certainly come; over 12 million a year, in fact, to the Canadian side alone (and 35,000 people a day to Casino Niagara). If you're not expecting to commune with nature, it can be, well, fun.

The first European to witness the spectacle in 1678 was Jesuit Louis Hennepin who was introduced to the then-sacred site by local native tribes. The missionary was awestruck by what he saw and immediately sent word of this wonder back to Europe, effectively launching a form of eco-tourism. But it wasn't long before the tacky trappings that have long been associated with the Falls first kicked in. The first record of a couple spending their honeymoon at this site was in 1801; in 1803 Jerome Bonaparte, Napoleon's little brother, brought his bride here, sparking off something of a fad: the city of Niagara Falls now issues 13,000 honeymoon certificates a year. Oscar Wilde famously summarised the visit by newlyweds to Niagara as 'the second biggest disappointment of the honeymoon'. Border skirmishes in the early part of the 19th century inconveniently deterred visitors, but by 1827, when the three hotels of the time combined to float a boatful of animals over the Horseshoe Falls, 10,000 peple turned up to watch. When the railway arrived in 1840, tourists swarmed in and the sideshow culture started to properly evolve. In 1859 Blondin made the first of his nine tightrope crossings; ever since then a rash of the rash have jumped, plunged and barrelled over, across or into the Falls and rapids, including Annie Taylor, the first barreller, who went over in 1901 as a 63-year-old teacher hoping to seal her financial future (and died in poverty) and the multiple stunter Bobby Leach (who died some years later after a wound became infected after he slipped on a piece of orange peel). Visit http://www.iaw.com/~falls/devil_frame.html for a full list, including the many who died.

With 'experiences' rather than stunts taking over in the later 20th century (the Maid of the Mist, Journey Behind the Falls, IMAX, cable cars, etc) and death-defying plunges firmly outlawed (though not altogether knocked on the head), Niagara has became increasingly sanitised. Recently the region has undergone a transformation, expanding from purely Falls-oriented attractions into more general tourist activity – shopping, golf, gambling, miscellaneous mainstream attractions – in an attempt to keep visitors overnight and fill those thousands of hotel rooms, with and without heart-shaped tubs. Niagara Falls is Canada's number one tourist attraction. You can take that to the bank.

THE FALLS

The Niagara river is the border between Canada and the US. It is effectively a drainage channel between Lake Erie and Lake Ontario, tranporting 200,000 cubic feet of water per second for 34 miles (55 kilometres), with a total drop of 108 metres (350 feet). It runs over the Niagara Escarpment, in which sedimentary layers of hard and soft rock from the ancient Michigan Sea are tilted at an angle. The Niagara Falls are at a bend in the river about halfway along its length, where its total width is about a mile. Goat Island sits just closer to the US side, with the American Falls (56 metres/184 feet high) and the smaller Bridal Veil Falls on that side of the stream; the more impressive Canadian Falls (Horseshoe Falls; 54 metres/177 feet) link the island to the Canadian bank in 675-metre 2,125-foot arc. The geology here is in a continual state of flux: turbulence at the foot of the Falls erodes the soft rock layer, digging out a deeper drop; periodically, the increasingly unsupported upper, heavier layer breaks off, with the result that the Falls retreat

Niagara Falls (rainbow not guaranteed).

very gradually upstream, at a rate of about
a foot every ten years. At the end of the last
ice age, 10,000 years ago, the Niagara Falls
were 11 kilometres (seven miles) closer
to Lake Ontario, as high cliffs testify.

Falls views are marred by the hydroelectric
harware visible, though the main facililties
of the Niagara Power Project are a few miles
downstream. This joint Canadian/US project
generates 2.4 million kilwatts by diverting part
of the flow through its turbines. A hard-argued
1950 pact limits it to leaving at least 100,000
cubic feet per second in the original river
during daylight hours in the visitor season,
a mere half of the average total flow (helping
to limit erosion). Take time to imagine how
the Falls would be naturally: twice as much
crashing water in a world with 24 million
fewer lightbulbs.

ORIENTATION
Falls activity is centred on two spots on the
river, the Falls area itself and the Whirlpool
Basin area three miles north. A road and a strip
of parkland with a railed walkway and viewing
platforms built along the cliffs link the two. The
town of Niagara Falls and its tourist attractions
are set on a rise above the river with a hotel
hinterland stretching west; you could walk
between the two but people seldom do. There's
a funicular (the Falls Incline Railway) near the
Horseshoe Falls; hotels run shuttle buses and
most tours take you straight to the Falls. In

summer, the city wheels out its 'people movers',
frequent shuttle buses run between the Falls
and various points in town; out of season
you'll have to manage on normal city buses.
The train and Greyhound stations are a five-
minute walk from the nearest bus stop, which
is at the corner of Bridge and Erie Streets.

The Niagara Parkway runs the whole
length of the river on the Canadian side. North
and south of the Falls are, yes, more attractions,
plus parks, picnic areas and viewpoints. It's
pretty, in a regulated sort of a way.

You can cross over to the US side of the
river on foot or by car on either the Rainbow
Bridge (near the Falls) or the Whirlpool Rapids
Bridge. If you do, take your passport and
any visa documentation and be prepared for
security checks and body searches. Queues
are inevitably longer since 9.11. Given that the
views are less impressive, it's not really worth it.

WHAT TO SEE
First – and quite possibly only – the Falls
themselves. There are always crowds, often
dozens deep, at the main **Table Rock** site,
where you can stand (behind a strong stone and
metal railing) a mere metre away from the edge
of the Horseshoe Falls. There is a spot where
you are literally at the peak of the cascade
as it rushes by your toes, plummeting 54 metres
(177 feet) down into the foaming, misty gorge.
You may have to jostle a while to get into
position by the railing but it's worth the wait.

Tack attack

As if to offset the spectacular natural beauty of the area, the City of Niagara Falls is, let's face it, pretty tacky. And the tackiest, most endearing tack, has pooled in its own little area along the steep street called Clifton Hill (www.cliftonhill.com), which runs up into town from the Maid of the Mist departure point. It's filled with garish but appealingly traditional attractions such as the Haunted House, the Mystery Maze, the Movieland Wax Museum of Stars, Ripley's Believe It or Not, the Great Canadian Midway and the House of Frankenstein and Dinosaur Park, a fun putting course. Most Canadians imagine they'd have to cross the border for so much corn, yet here it all is, on the one cob. You can even stay in the middle of this carnival atmosphere at the Travelodge Clifton Hill (see p230). Just don't plan on going to bed early.

The Table Rock Complex has a restaurant, snack bar and souvenir shops filled with weird and tacky trinkets and is also the entry point for the **Journey Behind the Falls**. Visitors take a lift down 125 feet (38 metres) through solid rock, suit up in bright yellow rain suits and then walk through a tunnel directly behind the curtain of water plunging over the Horseshoe Falls. There is also an outdoor observation deck at the side where you can watch the thundering waters hit the gorge and turn into white mist.

Half a mile north is the departure point for the **Maid of the Mist**, at the bottom of Clifton Hill, opposite the American Falls. There's a direct road from town, or you can take the crowded, scenic and invariably damp riverside walk through Queen Victoria Park, where special events are often held. You can't book in advance so prepare for a lengthy queue or get there early – the first cruise leaves at 9.45am – but this is one water ride that is well worth the wait. A funicular takes you to the bottom of the cliffs, where you get suited up in bright yellow slickers. The little ship chugs past the American Falls and Cave of the Winds before it charges straight into the horseshoe of water. Passengers aboard the bucking boat will find the world turns totally white as they disappear into the mists of Niagara. Make no mistake, you will get wet. But it's worth it for the thrill.

Three move river-centric attractions are based in the Whirlpool Basin area, a couple of miles further north. **The Great Gorge Adventure** (905 371 0254, closed Nov-late April) takes you down in a lift to a boardwalk beside the seething rapids; the **Niagara Spanish Aero (cable) Car**, built in 1913, spans the dramatic whirlpool (subject to weather conditions) and **Niagara Helicopters Limited** (905 357 5672), where you can take a swooping flight over the Falls and through the Niagara Gorge in a six-seater Bell 407 helicopter.

Many people prefer to visit Niagara during the frigid, white winters. For one thing, there are no crowds. But the main reason is that the entire area around the Horseshoe Falls turns into a stunning winter tableau of ice and snow. The mist covers buildings, trees, railings and coats everything with layers of ice. It is a beautiful spectacle, especially at night, when the Niagara Light Show (year round after dusk) bathes the water, mist and ice in colours of startling white, red and blue. Note that many attractions (and restaurants) will be closed, though, or operating on reduced opening hours.

In the town itself, you can pretty much take your pick of international tourist franchises, viewing towers and general assorted attractions. The **Skylon Tower** is by nature not hard to find. Take one of the little 'yellow bug' exterior lifts for a ride to the indoor or outdoor Observation Deck. This will give you another view of the Falls – and it is breathtaking – from some 236 metres (775 feet) above ground level. You can see the perfect horseshoe shape of the Canadian Falls and the plume of mist spilling up hundreds of metres from the rolling waters of the Niagara river. It's also fun to watch the toytown-tiny **Maid of the Mist** fight its way toward the Horseshoe Falls and completely disappear into their white swirls.

The **IMAX Theatre Niagara Falls & Daredevil Gallery** showcases the largest collection of barrels and home-made contraptions used to challenge the Falls, succesfully and otherwise. To save you making the leap yourself, there is some incredible video footage filmed by a daredevil through the reinforced window of his barrel. Don't miss the photos of Blondin as he crossed the gorge on the highwire. The stunning IMAX film entitled *Niagara: Miracles, Myths and Magic* plays every hour on the hour on the six-storey screen.

MarineLand is one of the town's most popular attractions. The show features killer whales, sea lions and leaping dolphins; there's also a zoo with elk, buffalo and bears.

When Niagara's city fathers looked for ways to boost tourism in the area, gambling was the obvious – and natural – way to go. The town has always had the ersatz ambience of an Atlantic City or Las Vegas and slot machines certainly put those places on the map. Gambling is now as much a part of the Niagara culture as fudge factories and snow domes.

Casino Niagara has 9,000 square metres (96,000 square feet) of gaming space, 2,700 very busy slot machines and 144 tables. It's open 24 hours a day, every day, and since there is no gambling yet in the US border town of Niagara Falls or nearby Buffalo there is a steady stream of high rollers driving across the bridges. Admission is free but you must be 19 years of age to step on the floor. A still larger casino is due to open in the spring of 2004.

At the opposite end of the tourist spectrum is **Niagara Parks Butterfly Conservatory**, about eight kilometres (five miles) north along the Niagara Parkway and just south of the Floral Clock (a free attraction which is exactly what it sounds like). This living museum features more than 2,000 live butterflies from around the globe. It's an explosion of colours in a lush, climate-controlled rainforest setting. Wear colourful clothing and the butterflies will land on you for the perfect photo op. The Butterfly Conservatory is part of the **Niagara Parks Botanical Gardens** (905 371 0254), tours of which are available.

Casino Niagara

5705 Falls Avenue, Niagara Falls (1-888 946 3255/905 374 3598/www.casinoniagara.com). **Open** 24hrs daily. **Admission** free. **Credit** AmEx, MC, V.

IMAX Theatre Niagara Falls & Daredevil Gallery

6170 Fallsview Boulevard, Niagara Falls (905 374 4629/www.imaxniagara.com). **Open** 11am-8pm daily; call for show times. **Admission** $12; $6.50-$8.50 concessions. **Credit** MC, V.

Journey Behind the Falls

Niagara Falls (1-877 642 7275/905 371 0254/ www.niagaraparks.com). **Open** year round, limited winter viewing. Call for details. **Admission** $7; $3.50 concessions; free under-6s. **Credit** AmEx, MC, V.

Maid of the Mist

5920 River Road, Niagara Falls (905 358 5781/ www.maidofthemist.com). **Departures** Apr-Oct call for times. Closed Nov-Mar. **Admission** $12.25; $7.50 concessions; free under-6s. **Credit** AmEx, MC, V.

MarineLand

7657 Portage Road, Niagara Falls (905 356 9565/www.marinelandcanada.com). **Open** *May-Oct* 10am-5pm Mon-Fri; 10am-6pm Sat, Sun. *July-Sept* 10am-5pm daily. Closed mid Oct-early May. **Admission** $16.95-$24.95; $12.95-$21.95 concessions; free under-4s. **Credit** AmEx, MC, V.

Niagara Parks Butterfly Conservatory

Niagara Parkway, Niagara Falls (905 358 0025/ www.niagaraparks.com). **Open** daily year-round; times vary. **Admission** $8.50; $4 concesssions; free under-6s. **Credit** AmEx, MC, V.

Skylon Tower

5200 Robinson Street, Niagara Falls (1-877 475 9566/905 356 2651/www.skylon.com). **Open** *Observation* deck May-Sept 8am-midnight daily. *Sept-Apr* 10am-10pm daily. **Admission** $9.50; $5.50-$8.50 concessions. **Credit** AmEx, MC, V.

Where to eat

As you can imagine with its pervasive tourism, Niagara Falls is not known for its fine dining. This is not the place to visit for a deluxe five-star meal. Fast and theme food is the order for the day (the Hard Rock and other usual suspects are all there). However there are two places that are always busy, if not for the food, then for the view. The **Table Rock Restaurant** serves good casual meals and snacks at fair prices, but it has a constant queue because it is only 100 metres from the Horseshoe Falls (hence you are not encouraged to linger over coffee). You can reserve a table but not a window seat.

The Skylon Tower has two restaurants, the revolving **Skylon Tower Restaurant** and the static **Summit Suite Dining Room**, both with spectacular 775-foot (236-metre) views. The food at the former is of the rich, international type that aims to impress, and farily pricey; the latter serves buffets, breakfast included in high season.

Skylon Tower Restaurant

Skylon Tower, 5200 Robinson Street, Niagara Falls (1-877 475 9566/905 356 2651/www.skylon.com). **Meal served** *May-Sept* 11.30am-2pm, 4.30-10pm daily. *Oct-Apr* 11.30am-2pm, 4.30-10pm Mon-Sat; 4.30-10pm Sun. **Main courses** $36.50-$63.75. **Credit** AmEx, DC, MC, V.

Summit Suite Dining Room

Skylon Tower, 5200 Robinson Street, Niagara Falls (1-877 475 9566/905 356 2651/www.skylon.com). **Meals served** seasonal hours year-round; call for details. **Credit** AmEx, DC, MC, V.

Table Rock Restaurant

6650 Niagara Parkawy, Niagara Falls (905 354 3631/www.niagaraparks.com). **Open** seasonal hours year-round; call for details. **Main courses** $7-$15. **Credit** AmEx, MC.

Where to stay

If you're here to see the Falls themselves, you will not need or likely want to stay in Niagara. Either you'll be carless and on a day trip or driving, with the option therefore of staying downriver in the far more pleasant Niagara-on-the-Lake. However, if you're going along with the whole pleasure-cruise ethos and here for a few days, you have a choice between one of the the the many uniform chain hotels, the down and dirty 'no tell motel' strip above Clifton Hill or the opulence of a palatial suite overlooking the Falls (with, perhaps, a fireplace and heart-shaped jacuzzi. Such things are almost de rigeuer in the honeymoon suites). Contact **Niagara Falls Tourism** (*see below*) for comprehensive suggestions. Hotel rates vary hugely according to season, time of week, view and level of luxury. Off-season particularly, always ask about deals and packages.

The two most prominent hotels in the city, the **Brock Plaza Hotel** and the adjacent **Sheraton on the Falls**, stand side by side a block from the Niagara Parkway in the giant Falls Avenue complex (along with the casino and various theme restaurants), with views of the American Falls. For a room in the shadow of the Skylon Tower, check out the **Holiday Inn by the Falls**, or if you want a less anonymous location, try the **Travelodge Clifton Hill** in the

colourful carnival atmosphere of Clifton Hill, a stone's throw away from the House of Frankenstein.

Brock Plaza Hotel

5685 Falls Avenue, Niagara Falls, ON L2E 6W7 (905 374 4444/1-800 263 7135/fax 905 371 8349/www.niagarafallshotels.com). Rates $50-$259 single/double Oct-Mar; $179-$360 single/double Apr-Sept. **Credit** AmEx, DC, MC, V.

Holiday Inn by the Falls

5339 Murray Street, Niagara Falls, ON L2G 2J3 (905 356 1333/1-800 263 9393/fax 905 356 7128/www.holidayinn.com). **Rates** $69-$265. **Credit** AmEx, DC, Disc, MC, V.

Sheraton on the Falls

5875 Falls Avenue, Niagara Falls, ON L2G 3K7 (905 374 4444/1-888 229 9961/fax 905 371 8349/ www.niagarafallshotels.com). **Rates** $99-$529. **Credit** AmEx, DC, Disc, MC, V.

Travelodge Clifton Hill

4943 Clifton Hill, Niagara Falls, ON L2G 3N5 (905 357 4330/1-800 668 8840/fax 905 357 0423/www.niagara.com/falls). **Rates** $59-$299 single/double Sept-June; $199-$299 single/double July, Aug. **Credit** AmEx, DC, MC, V.

Tourist information

Niagara Economic & Tourism Corporation

2201 St David's Road, PO Box 1042, Thorold, ON L2V 4T7 (905 984 3626/1-800 263 2988/www.tourismniagara.com).

Niagara Falls Tourism

5515 Stanley Avenue, Niagara Falls, ON L2G 3X4 (1-800 563 2557/905 356 6061/ 905 356 5567/www.discoverniagara.com). **Open** *mid May-end Aug* 8am-8pm daily. *Sept-mid May* 8am-6pm Mon-Fri; 10am-6pm Sat; 10am-4pm Sun.

Niagara Parks Commission

905 371 0254/1-877 642 7275/fax 905 356 8448/www.niagaraparks.com. **Open** Information Centre at Table Rock Complex open year-round, but hours vary, so call for details.

Getting there

By car

Niagara is a simple 90-minute drive on one highway, the Queen Elizabeth Way from the city, rounding Lake Ontario. Take the well-signed Highway 420 to drive the last few miles into town.

By public bus

Greyhound buses (1-800 661 8747/416 594 1010) run throughout the day from Toronto. But at $54 return, they're not an awful lot cheaper than a tour bus, and less convenient at both ends.

Bus tours/day trips

Several companies run scheduled tours from
Toronto to Niagara. Their literature is ubiquitous,
their attraction packages manifold (from transport
only to the full excursion/attraction monty) and
their differences negligible. Your best bet is to
ask at your hotel; staff should know which are
the most convenient and may have deals going.
Standard operators include **Gray Line** (416 594
0343/www.grayline.ca) and **Niagara & Toronto
Tours** (416 868 0400/www.torontotours.com).
The **Magic Bus Company** (416 516 7433/
www.magic buscompany.com) sends out a funky,

brightly coloured bus round the hostels before
trundling down to Niagara where it stops at a
winery for a free tasting, gives the trippers three
to five hours at the Falls and stops at the whirlpool
and other attractions before heading back for a
bottom-dollar $35.

Casino Niagara (*see p229*) has contracts with
several companies, including Tripmate (416 599
8892/www.itripmate.com), to bus in the punters
for a minimal fare (it's $18 with Tripmate).
Snags: over-18s only are allowed, and they don't
make a stop at the Falls, though they're only about
10 minutes' walk away.

Getting into Gehry

Niagara's newest winery has already
guaranteed its place on the international scene
even though it isn't scheduled to produce its
first bottle of Chardonnay until 2006. Le Clos
Jordan, near the tiny town of Lincoln, is
currently on the drawing board of world-
renowned architect Frank Gehry (pictured on
screen below). And even there it looks radical.

The Toronto-born, Los Angeles-based Gehry
is probably best known to the general public
for his award-winning Guggenheim Museum in
Bilbao, Spain. Combined with his forthcoming
extension to the Art Gallery of Ontario (*see
p68*), Le Clos Jordan is destined to further
enhance Gehry's international reputation
both inside and out of Canada.

The design – 'a cathedral to wine' –
complements the Niagara landscape with its
gently flowing structure with softly curving

white plaster walls and undulating metal
roof (model pictured below). Visitors entering
Gehry's Great Hall will be greeted with floor-
to-ceiling columns soaring dramatically from
underground cellars to disappear seemingly
into the heavens. As well as production
facilities, the grand space will include
a tasting lounge and wine shop for the
company's various VQA brands.

The multi-million dollar 1,900 square-
metre (20,000 square-foot) building will
be situated in the middle of Le Clos Jordan's
principal vineyard, which was planted in
2000. The joint project of Niagara's Vincor
International and Boisset, La Famille des
Grand Vins of Nuits-St-Georges, France,
Le Clos Jordan promises to become one
of Niagara's main tourist attractions – even
for beer lovers and teetotallers.

By air

If road transport is too mundane for you, you could take a helicopter tour out of Pearson with **Niagara Airbus** (905 374 8111/1 800 268 8111/www.niagara airbus.com); prices are lower than you might expect, but you do have to get to Pearson.

By water

Seaflight (416504 8825/www.seaflight.com), Canada's only hydrofoil service, takes you across the lake and along the Niagara river to Queenston in an hour and 10 minutes. Ticket prices include road transfers to the nearby Falls and Niagara-by-the-Lake. It's a summer-only service, running from mid May to mid September; tickets are $80.

Wine country

The southern part of the Golden Horseshoe that wraps around Lake Ontario from Toronto to Niagara has always been known for its fertile farmlands. This is where the bulk of the province's fruit grows. It's also home to the largest part of Canada's wine industry. Until 20 years ago that would be reason enough to stay away. Just thinking about Canadian wine made many quaffers turn to beer. Niagara excelled at producing a syrupy sweet concoction called 'Baby Duck' and other fizzy abominations that bore little resemblance to anything that should have come from grapes.

Thankfully, that has all changed. Niagara is well on its way to thinking of itself as Napa of the North. The climate, moderated by the lake and protected by the Niagara Escarpment, is comparable to Burgundy, the Loire Valley and parts of New Zealand. Wine making has been practised here for 200 years but was hampered by government regulations forcing the wine makers to use the very harsh and acidic local Lambrusca grape. In the late 1970s wine growers were finally allowed to blend classic varietal grapes from Europe and around the world. The vines found a happy home in the Niagara soil. Perhaps the most successful transplant to date is the Riesling , which does well in northern climes. Wines made from Pinot Noir and Chardonnay are also worth seeking out.

The Vintners Quality Alliance, or VQA, was established in 1989 to control standards of wine production in the province in much the same way as the AOC and DOC appellation guarantees origin and content of French and Italian wines. In a burgeoning sector in which quality was inconsistent, this standard for public recognition has gone a long way to put some distance between Ontario's wine making past and present.

The first to experiment and the first to achieve global recognition for its blends was **Inniskillin** wines. Inniskillin is also one of

a handful of wineries to produce icewine (*see p235* **Ice, ice bab**y), which you can sample at the historic Brae Burn Barn on the Inniskillin estate and at local restaurants. The **Henry of Pelham Family Estate Winery** also features some excellent VQA products in its cellars. The highlight of its winery and vineyard tours is wine tasting on its patio, next to Short Hills Provincial Park. The **Cave Spring Cellars** begs not just for a tour but a weekend visit. The winery has its own sumptuous 26-room inn, Inn on the Twenty, with jacuzzis and fireplaces in each suite, as well as one of the Niagara area's best dining spots, On The Twenty. The winery is just across the street in the village of Jordan.

Other names to look out for when ordering a bottle of local wine with your meal include Reif Estate Winery, Jackson-Triggs, Peller Estates, Daniel Lenko and Stoney Ridge.

Best time to go wine touring is from May to October; bar a little pruning not a lot goes on in winter or spring. The major event of the year is the annual late September celebration of the harvest, the **Niagara Grape & Wine Festival** (905 688 0212/www.grapeandwine.com). Over 100 events include tours, tastings, concerts and seminars and food samplings, set off by the brightly coloured fall foliage.

Cave Spring Cellars

3836 Main Street, Jordan (905 562 3581/ www.cavespringcellars.com). **Tours** *July-Oct* 3pm Mon-Fri; 11am, 3pm Sat, Sun. *Nov-June* 3pm Sat, Sun. **Shop open** *May-Oct* 10am-6pm Mon-Sat; 11am-6pm Sun. *Nov-Apr* 10am-5pm Mon-Sat; 11am-5pm Sun. **Admission** $2 redeemable with wine purchase. **Credit** AmEx, MC, V.

Henry of Pelham Family Estate Winery

1469 Pelham Road, St Catharines (905 684 8423/ www.henryofpelham.com). **Tours** *May-Oct* 1.30pm daily. Call for details and prices of winter tours. **Shop open** (one complimentary tasting) May-Oct 10am-6pm daily. *Nov-May* 10am-5pm Mon-Fri; 11am-5pm Sat, Sun. **Admission** free May-Oct. **Credit** AmEx, MC, V.

Inniskillin

RR 1, Niagara Parkway, just outside Niagara-on-the-Lake (1-888 466 4754/905 468 3554/ www.inniskillin.com). **Tours** *Nov-Apr* 10.30am, 2.30pm Sat, Sun. *May-Oct* 10.30am, 2.30pm daily. **Shop open** *May-Oct* 10am-6pm daily. *Nov-Apr* 10am-5pm daily. **Tasting bar open** *Nov-Apr* 11am-4.30pm. *May-Oct* 11am-5.30pm daily. **Tours** free-$20; call for details. **Credit** AmEx, MC, V.

Wine tours

Wine tourism has come of age with many wineries now proud to show off their liquid assets and many punters happy to leave their

Inniskillin winery.
See p232.

cars behind and indulge in a spot of risk-free
tasting. Both scheduled and custom tours
are available; they usually include a meal
as well as several winery visits and a
knowledgeable guide. You will usually need
to arrange a pick-up in the Wine Country or
Niagara-on-the-Lake area, though sometimes
transport from Toronto or elsewhere can be
arraged. Tour companies include **Crush on
Niagara Wine Tours**; **Wine Country
Tours** and **Niagara Nature Tours**, which
has an eco-slant and can also cover regional
cooking, history, agriculture and gardens.
For something a little more challenging,
sign up for the bike tours of Niagara wineries
with **Steve Bauer**.

Crush on Niagara Wine Tours

905 562 3373/1-888 408 9463/www.crushtours.com.
Tours year round; call for details. **Credit** MC, V.

Niagara Nature Tours

*RR 1, Vineland Station, ON L0R 2E0 (1-888 889
8296/905 562 3746/www.niagaranaturetours.com).*
Tours year round; call for details. **Credit** AmEx,
MC, V.

Steve Bauer Bike Tours

*PO Box 428, Vineland, ON L0R 2C0 (905 562
0788/www.stevebauer.com).* **Tours** call for details.
Credit V.

Wine Country Tours

*2755 Hurricane Road, Welland (905 892 9770/
www.winecountrytours.ca).* **Tours** year round;
call for details. **Credit** AmEx, MC, V.

Tourist information

The tourist offices in Niagara Falls and
particularly Niagara-on-the-Lake also have
information on Wine Country.

Wine Council of Ontario

*110 Hanover Drive, St Catharines (905 684 8070/
1-888 594 6379/www.wineroute.com).*

Getting there

You can't properly experience Wine Country
without your own transport, though several
Niagara tours (*see p231*) include a winery stop.

Niagara-on-the-Lake

The drive from Niagara Falls along the
precipice of the Niagara Gorge is one of the
most scenic routes in the country. The towering
cliff faces reveal the extent of the erosion that
has seen the Falls steadily carve their way
backwards through this dramatic setting.
The Niagara Parks Commission has controlled
development and growth along the Canadian
side of the river since 1885. The result is the
Niagara Parkway, a verdant green belt through
which a leisurely winding drive brings you
to the perfectly preserved 19th-century village
of Niagara-on-the-Lake.

In 1792, Niagara-on-the-Lake became
the first capital of Upper Canada, later the
Province of Ontario, and was a major site in

the occasional wars against the American forces just across the river. The **Historic Fort George** national park just south of the town is a restored version of the original fort (1797) where costumed staff provide the history lessons.

When you leave the Fort, you will find yourself in the village itself. The first major building you pass, set back on the left, is the **Shaw Festival** theatre, one of the province's most important professional theatres (the season runs from April to November). The company's mandate is to present plays written by George Bernard Shaw 'and his contemporaries' – although that has been stretched somewhat to include plays set in the Shaw era. The company has performed such varied fare as GBS' *Caesar and Cleopatra*, Noel Coward's *Hay Fever* and a revival of Stephen Sondheim's musical *Merrily We Roll Along*. The Shaw Festival has turned this sleepy hamlet, formerly a retirement community, into one of the province's most popular and thriving tourist and theatre communities.

After you have picked up your tickets (best to order some months in advance; *see p236*) park your car anywhere you can find a space and then stroll around town. It isn't very big and you can't really get lost. The **Clock Tower**, in the middle of the road, marks the centre of town.

On the corner opposite the clock is the **Niagara Apothecary Museum** (5 Queen

Wine country is Ontario's fruit basket.

Ice, ice baby

In addition to producing numerous award-winning VQA wines, Ontario has rapidly achieved a reputation for creating some of the world's best icewines. This is due partially to the soil and climate but mainly because Ontario is the only wine-producing region in the world with a winter cold enough to guarantee a consistent icewine crop every year. It was icewine – first produced by **Inniskillin** winery (*see p232*) – that shocked international critics into recognising Ontario as a potential producer of international-standard wine, by winning numerous international gold awards. Other Ontario wineries have since focused on icewine production and consumers should also look for bottles from Reif Estate Winery, Henry of Pelham and Château Des Charmes.

The uninitiated should think of icewine as a unique dessert wine produced from naturally frozen grapes. These grapes, which are left

on the vines long after the September harvest, freeze at minus 8˚C (17˚F) and must be picked before 10am each day – a dreary, cold and wet job. While the grapes are still frozen they are pressed and squeezed. This leaves a highly concentrated sweet juice – high in acids, sugars and aromatics. Icewine is very sweet (a four-ounce glass with dessert will be plenty) and quite expensive – a half-bottle may cost as much as $50. But even a neophyte will realise the sweet, thick nectar with a subtle intensity merits its pricetag.

All Ontario icewines are subject to the rules and regulations of the VQA control board and must pass rigorous scrutiny before released for public consumption.

Every January, a series of events is organised for **Niagara Grape & Wine Festival Icewine Celebrations**. For more information, visit www.grapeandwine.com or call 905 688 0212.

Trips Out of Town

Street, 905 468 3845), a perfectly preserved 'drug store' from 1866, operated and maintained by the Ontario College of Pharmacists. Note the original walnut and butternut fixtures and rare collection of apothecary glass.

There's lots of shopping here, the majority of it of an indulgent, browseable nature: you can buy fudge, chocolate, wine, candles, deli goods, antiques and paintings. Or, at **Greaves Jams & Marmalades** (55 Queen Street, 905 468 7831) flavoured spreads made using the full range of products of the local fruit harvest.

The area's lengthy history is explained in detail at the **Niagara Historical Society Museum** (43 Castlereagh Street, 905 468 3912), one of Ontario's oldest local history museums. Founded in 1907, it contains over 20,000 artefacts from the periods of the Loyalists, the War of 1812 and the Victorian age.

Historic Fort George

Queen's Parade, Niagara-on-the-Lake (905 468 4257/www.niagara.com/~parkscan). **Open** Apr-Oct 10am-5pm daily. *Nov-March* by appointment. **Admission** $6; $4-$5 concessions; free under-6s. **Credit** MC, V.

Where to eat

This little town is a diner's delight – a sort of culinary antithesis to Niagara Falls. Forget the conventional wisdom that the restaurant in your hotel is just there as a promotional exercise; the

inns of this community are known nationally for their cuisine and service. Some of the best places to eat are also the best places to stay. Prime examples, and fairly expensive ones, include the **Oban Inn**, which serves hearty continental fare in a 19th-century style dining room and sunny atrium. You can have dinner in the gorgeous **Escabèche** in the Prince of Wales Hotel or lunch in its Churchill Bar. For more casual fare, try the **Buttery Theatre Restaurant**, though you'll have to like a bit of pageantry: serving wenches in period costume bring out bowls of home-made soup and hearty sandwiches. The Buttery stages the Henry VIII Feast and Buttery Theatre Cabaret on Friday and Saturday nights. Pub fare is served all day in the bar of the the **Olde Angel Inn**, which features plenty of draught beer and local wines. If there's no time for a leisurely lunch before the theatre, you can grab a sandwich or salad at the **Shaw Café & Wine Bar**, directly across from the Royal George Theatre.

Buttery Theatre Restaurant

19 Queen Street (905 468 2564/www.thebuttery restaurant.com). **Meals served** 11am-11pm daily; dinner theatre 8.30pm Fri, Sat. **Main courses** $8-$16; dinner theatre $55. **Credit** AmEx, MC, V.

Escabèche

6 Picton Street (905 468 3246/1-888 669 5566/ www.vintageinns.com). **Meals served** noon-2pm, 5-9pm Mon-Fri; noon-2pm, 5-10pm Sat, Sun. **Main courses** $16-$36. **Credit** AmEx, DC, MC, V.

Inniskillin: one of the few producers of icewine. *See p232.*

ICE WINE GRAPES

Inniskillin

Niagara-on-the-Lake. *See p233.*

Oban Inn
*160 Front Street (905 468 2165/1-888 669 5566/
www.vintageinns.com).* **Meals served** 11.30am-
2.30pm, 5-8.30pm daily. **Main courses** $11.95-$30.
Credit AmEx, DC, MC, V.

Olde Angel Inn
*224 Regent Street (905 468 3411/www.angel-
inn.com).* **Meals served** *Oct-Apr* 5.30-9pm daily.
May-Sept 5.30-11pm daily. **Main courses** $26.95-
$35.95. **Credit** AmEx, MC, V.

Shaw Café & Wine Bar
*92 Queen Street (905 468 4772/www.vintageinns.
com).* **Meals served** 10am-9pm Sun-Thur; 10am-
10pm Fri; 10am-11pm Sun. **Credit** AmEx, MC, V.

Where to stay

The quaintness of this little 18th-century
community has earmarked it as a favorite
weekend getaway. Billed as one of the world's
finest heritage hotels, the **Prince of Wales
Hotel** with new spectacular spa facilities
is everyone's first choice for deluxe
accommodation right in the middle of
town. The **Oban Inn** is a charming 25-room
country inn right beside the golf course with a
magnificent view of the lake. The **Olde Angel
Inn** is the town's oldest inn, with cosy colonial-
style guest rooms and two rental cottages.
The cottages are lovely but if you wish to

catch a glimpse of the Olde Angel's famous
wandering ghost, you should stay in the main
inn. The **Moffat Inn** is an affordable 22-room,
two-storey historic inn just off the main street
with an elegant penthouse suite.

Niagara-on-the-Lake likely has more B&Bs
and private lodgings than any other village
its size in Ontario. Check with the local tourism
office and the Shaw Festival office (for both,
see below) for more information.

Moffat Inn
*60 Picton Street, PO Box 578, Niagara-on-the-Lake,
ON L0S 1J0 (905 468 4116/www.moffatinn.com).*
Rates *Nov-May* $69-$149. *Apr-Oct* $89-$169.
All year $325-$575 penthouse apartment.
Credit AmEx, DC, MC, V.

Oban Inn
*160 Front Street, Niagara-on-the-Lake,
ON L0S 1J0 (905 468 2165/1-888 669 5566/
fax 905 468 4165/www.vintageinns.com).*
Rates *Nov-Mar* $150-$275 single/double. *Apr-Oct*
$230-$355 single/double. *All year* $330-$455 suites.
Credit AmEx, DC, MC, V.

Olde Angel Inn
*224 Regent Street, PO Box 1603, Niagara-on-
the-Lake, ON L0S 1J0 (905 468 3411/www.angel-
inn.com).* **Rates** *Nov-Apr* $79-$169 single/double.
May-Oct $119-$229 single/double. **Credit** AmEx,
DC, MC, V.

Prince of Wales Hotel
*6 Picton Street, Niagara-on-the-Lake,
ON L0S 1J0 (905 468 3246/905 468 5521/
1-888 669 5566/www.vintageinns.com).*
Rates *Nov-Mar* $225-$395 single/double.
Apr-Oct $290-$460 single/double. *All year* $475-
$610 suites. **Credit** AmEx, DC, MC, V.

Tourist information

Niagara-on-the-Lake Chamber of Commerce and Visitor & Convention Bureau
*26 Queen Street, PO Box 1043, ON L0S 1J0
(905 468 4263/fax 905 468 4930/www.niagaraon
thelake.com).* **Open** *Nov-Mar* 10am-5pm daily.
Apr-Oct 10am-7.30pm daily.

Shaw Festival
*10 Queen's Parade (905 468 2172/1-800 511 7429/
www.shawfest.com).* **Box office open** 9am-5pm
Mon-Sat. *Apr-Sept* 9am-8pm daily. **Tickets** $26-$75.
Credit AmEx, MC, V.

Getting there

By car
This drive is 80 miles (129 kilometres) from
Toronto. Same directions as Niagara Falls except
turn off the QEW onto Highway 55, just past the
St Catharines turn-off.

Quick Trips

The best days (and nights) out: festivals both cultural and bacchanal, and some time for religious reflection.

McMichael Canadian Art Collection.

For theme park fun at **Paramount Canada's Wonderland**, *see p170*, and for local skiing hills at **Barrie** and **Collingwood**, *see p213*. These destinations are recommended as the best local day trips so no accommodation listings are given, but if you want to spend the night, the tourist offices listed will be able to recommend a variety of places to stay.

Kleinburg

Founded in 1848, the small farming town of Kleinburg used to be famous to Torontonians for one thing only: the **Binder Twine Festival**, held each September, during which farmers would tie their sheaves of wheat and then enjoy a lavish feast. The festival continues to this day; so does catering to city folk who hanker for a whiff of country living on Toronto's doorstep. That means plenty of tea shops and cafés and knick-knack stores selling books, candles and crafts.

But Kleinburg is better known for its rich artistic patrimony. It's home to the **McMichael Canadian Art Collection**, an impressive

gallery situated amid a forest on the edge of a valley, a setting that blends perfectly with the principal theme of its permanent collection: the Canadian landscape. Philanthropists Robert and Signe McMichael built an immense building of rough stone and raw timber to showcase their collection of paintings by **Tom Thomson** and the **Group of Seven**. These early 20th-century artists spent years in the wilderness capturing the majestic scenery and brilliant colours of a country few of their contemporaries had ever experienced (*see p244* **The Magnificent Seven**).

The gallery's design is in keeping with the artists' wilderness landscapes: after staring at a sublime Lawren Harris painting on an October day, you can gaze out of one of the full-length windows at a forest of changing autumn leaves. There are also Inuit and Native Canadian artworks, including paintings and soapstone sculptures; most notable are the bold designs of Morriseau, who captured the ancient legends of warriors and gods on canvas. Join in a guided tour, then take a hike down into the woods to

Trips Out of Town

refresh the senses for a slice of real Canadiana. And before you leave, pay homage to six members of this famed group of painters at their burial sites, which are marked by jagged grey and pink boulders.

McMichael Canadian Art Collection

10365 Islington Avenue, Kleinburg (905 893 1121/www.mcmichael.com). **Open** *Nov-Apr* 10am-4pm daily. *May-Oct* 10am-5pm daily. **Admission** $12; $9 concessions. **Credit** AmEx, MC, V.

Where to eat & drink

The Doctor's House is Kleinburg's most historic building, dating from 1867, the year Canada achieved independent confederation status from Britain. It's now a classy venue for banquets and weddings, with a restaurant that's open to the public (Sunday brunch is a speciality). If teatime with country cuisine and fresh desserts is in order, drop into Mr McGregor's House.

The Doctor's House

21 Nashville Road, Kleinburg (905 893 1615/ 416 234 8080/www.thedoctorshouse.ca). **Meals served** noon-3pm, 5.30-11pm Mon-Sat; 10.30am-3.30pm, 5.30-11pm Sun. **Main courses** $18-$36. **Credit** AmEx, MC, V.

Mr McGregor's House

10503 Islington Avenue, Kleinburg (905 893 2508). **Meals served** 10am-5pm Mon-Fri; 10am-6pm Sat, Sun. **Credit** MC, V.

Getting there

Drive north from the city on Highway 400, exit west at Major MacKenzie Drive and continue to Islington Avenue. Public transport is not an option.

So spa, so good

Getting primed, pampered and plucked is all part of the spa experience, a trend that has taken southern Ontario by storm. You can justify indulging in the soft touch by first tackling nature head-on at some of the more rustic settings, or blithely head out of town for a sybaritic experience in the clean country air.

Closest to Toronto, a 45-minute drive north will take you to the spectacular scenery of the Forks of the Credit River parklands and the **Hockley Valley Resort**, which has a spa facility offering body wraps, hydrotherapies and something called 'the Throne'. Don't ask. Just outside Cambridge, to the west of Toronto (not far from Kitchener–Waterloo), is the very august **Langdon Hall Country House Hotel & Spa**, once a summer home for New York's Astor family. The Federalist Revival manse is set restful country grounds, and its full-service spa piles on the tranquility. Try the hot stone therapy for the ultimate in stress relief. You'll probably need help getting back to your cosy room to veg in front of the wood-burning fireplace.

In Niagara-on-the-Lake, the **Secret Garden Spa** is part of the Prince of Wales, an elegantly restored 1860s Victorian hotel that's usually booked solid during the Shaw Festival theatre season.

Cottage Country has some top-end resort properties with spa facilities to match. At **Deerhurst Resort** in Huntsville, you can swim, play tennis or golf, even climb mountainous terrain in 4-WD before hitting the massage beds and saunas.

Our suggestions are merely a tasting: for a complete guide to spa facilities throughout the province, contact **Spas Ontario** (176 Napier Street, Barrie, ON L4M 1W8, 705 721 9969/ 1-800 990 7702/www.spasontario.com).

Deerhurst Resort

1235 Deerhurst Drive, Huntsville, ON P1H 2E8 (1-800 461 4393/705 789 6411/fax 705 789 2431/www.deerhurstresort.com). **Rates** $99-$319 single/double; $189-$859 suite. **Credit** AmEx, DC, MC, V.

Hockley Valley Resort

RR 1, Orangeville, ON L9W 2Y8 (519 942 0754/416 363 5490/fax 519 942 0833/ www.hockley.com). **Rates** $175-$455 single/ double. **Credit** AmEx, MC, V.

Langdon Hall Country House Hotel & Spa

1 Langdon Drive (519 740 2100/1-800 268 1898/fax 519 740 8161). **Rates** $259-$609 single/double. **Credit** AmEx, DC, MC, V.

Secret Garden Spa

Prince of Wales Hotel, 6 Picton Street, Niagara-on-the-Lake (1-888 669 5566/ 905 468 3246/fax 905 468 5521/ www.vintageinns.com). **Rates** $225-$460 single/double; $475-$610 suite. **Credit** AmEx, DC, MC, V.

Elora & St Jacobs

Elora and **St Jacob's**, two villages directly west of Toronto, are time-warp destinations. They're about 90 minutes' drive from Toronto, but really they're several worlds away.

Elora is a former mill town that has transformed itself into a small arts and crafts community. Most of the stately stone 19th-century buildings have been renovated with period sensitivity and the little shops in town sell everything from antiques and home-made candles to hand-knit sweaters and cappuccinos. The most prominent building is the original 1859 gristmill, **Elora Mill** (77 Mill Street W, 519 846 5356/1-866 713 5672), now a combination inn and restaurant.

The best time to visit is during the second and third weeks of July, during the **Elora Festival** (1-519 846 0331/1-800 265 8977), a musical extravaganza of choral and classical music performed in some rather creative venues, ranging from a floating raft in the middle of the Elora Quarry to a barn used to store road salt in the winter.

In **St Jacobs**, a Mennonite Community where the basic mode of transport is horse and buggy and the only bustle to be found is in the ladies' undergarment section of the **General Store**, horse-drawn buggies fill the streets with clip-clopping sounds and lots of manure; leave the car parked and watch where you walk; this, after all, is a Mennonite community of farmers who still maintain the traditions of their German ancestors. It's also a great place to shop, both for old-fashioned and contemporary goods: the **St Jacobs Farmers Market & Flea Market** (47 King Street, 519 747 1830), open on Thursdays and Saturdays plus Tuesdays during the summer, is a vast and crowded old-time farmers' market filled with hundreds of stalls of fresh produce, arts and crafts and a huge flea market. For a dose of modern merchandising, head over to the nearby **St Jacobs Outlet Mall** (25 Benjamin Road, 519 888 0138/1-800 265 3353) for discount designer jeans and dresses.

Make sure you visit the **Mennonite Story**, a multimedia museum in St Jacobs visitor centre, which recounts the history of the Ontario Mennonites. Less spiritually, the **Maple Syrup Museum of Ontario** spins the sticky tale of turning maple sap into sweets, naturally offering samples along the way.

If you're in the mood for a romantic photo-op, head for the **Kissing Bridge**, the last remaining covered wooden bridge in the province. It's situated in the hamlet of West Montrose, just north of town along Regional Road 86 (watch the signs, which can be tricky).

Maple Syrup Museum of Ontario

8 Spring Street, St Jacobs (519 664 3626). **Open** 10am-5pm Mon-Fri; noon-5pm Sat, Sun. **Admission** free.

The Mennonite Story

St Jacobs Visitor Centre, 1408 King Street N, St Jacobs (519 664 3518/www.stjacobs.com/ html/museum.html). **Open** call for details. **Admission** $3. **No credit cards**.

Where to eat

You'll find great home cooking at the two main restaurants in St Jacobs. **Benjamin's Restaurant & Inn** and the **Stone Country Bakery & Bakery Café** both serve hearty portions fit for hard-working farmers, using recipes created by their Mennonite ancestors.

Benjamin's Restaurant & Inn

1430 King Street N, St Jacobs (519 664 3731/ www.stjacobs.com/benjamins). **Meals served** 11.30am-9pm daily. **Main courses** $16.95-$21.95. **Credit** AmEx, DC, MC, V.

Stone Country Bakery & Bakery Café

1402 King Street N, S. Jacobs (519 664 3612/ www.stjacobs.com/html/dining.html). **Meals served** 6.30am-6pm Mon-Sat; 12.30-5pm Sun. **Credit** AmEx, MC, V.

Tourist information

Village of Elora

519 846 9841/fax 519 846 2058/www.eic.elora.on.ca.

St Jacobs Country Tourism Office

1-800 265 3353/519 664 1133/www.stjacobs.com. **Open** *Answering machine* 24hrs daily.

St Jacobs Visitor Centre

1408 King Street N, St Jacobs (519 664 3518/ www.stjacobs.com).

Getting there

By car

Elora and St Jacobs are about 90 minutes west of Toronto by car (the only option). Take Highway 401 for about 96km (60 miles), turn north on to Highway 6, then take Wellington County Road 7 right to Elora. St Jacobs is a lovely meandering 24km (15 mile) country drive away, south on County Road 18, which turns into CR 22, then west on CR 17. Just follow the signs.

Kitchener-Waterloo

The twin city of **Kitchener-Waterloo**, due west of Toronto along Highway 401, is known primarily for its annual **Oktoberfest**

Trips Out of Town

celebrations – said to be the largest celebration of this Bavarian Festival outside Munich. This farming area was settled by 19th-century German immigrants who originally called the settlement Berlin, a name they changed to Kitchener during the First World War.

Some residents cringe at the fact that their city is primarily known for **Oktoberfest**, because the city does have other attractions, such as the **Centre in the Square** (101 Queen Street N, 1-800 265 8977/519 578 1570, www.centre-square.com), a 2,000-seat performing arts centre, home of the **Waterloo Symphony** and the **Kitchener-Waterloo Art Gallery**. There's also a water park, **Bingemans**. But it is the one million-plus partygoers who pile into the twin cities during the ten-day festival of 'suds, sausage and schnitzel' that make up the vast majority of visitors to K-W. Mind you, the beer halls already have a ready supply of customers among the student population of the huge University of Waterloo. During the festival, every German social club, beer hall, pub and restaurant – as well as numerous beer tents that sprout up throughout the town – pay homage to the autumn harvest with a liquid celebration of malt, barley, hops and wheat. Heady stuff.

Bingemans

1380 Victoria Street N, Kitchener (519 774 1555/www.bingemans.com). **Camping** *Open* year-round. *Rates* $26-$132; call for details. **Water park** *Open* Jun-Sept. *Admission* $12.25; $3.36-$8.18 concessions; free under-2s. **Credit** AmEx, MC, V.

Kitchener-Waterloo Art Gallery

101 Queen Street N, Kitchener (519 579 5860). **Open** 10am-5pm Tue, Wed, Fri, Sat; 10am-9pm Thur; 1-5pm Sun. **Admission** free.

Where to eat

If you like heavy, hearty old-style German cooking, Kitchener-Waterloo will not disappoint. Schnitzel and sausage are everywhere: just look for any restaurant whose name ends in 'haus'. However, there are other choices, such as **artbar**, where the waiting staff recommend a selection of sampling portions for the table. If you really want to mix up your cuisine, check out the **Rude Native Bistro**, which blends global cooking from the East Indies, Thai, India and Japan.

Art Bar

101 Queen Street N, Kitchener (519 568 8660/ www.artbar.ca). **Meals served** 11.30am-midnight Tue-Sun. **Main courses** $13-$30. **Credit** AmEx, MC, V.

Rhythm and booze at **Oktoberfest**.

Rude Native Bistro

2-4 King Street N, Waterloo (519 886 3600/ www.rudenative.com). **Meals served** 11.30am-10pm Mon-Thur; 11.30am-11pm Fri; noon-11pm Sat; 10am-3pm, 5-10pm Sun. **Main courses** $9.95-$14.95. **Credit** AmEx, MC, V.

Tourist information

Kitchener-Waterloo Oktoberfest

17 Benton Street, PO Box 1053, Kitchener, ON N2G 4G1 (1-888 294 4267/519 576 4267/fax 519 742 3072/www.oktoberfest.ca).

Kitchener-Waterloo Tourism

80 Queen Street N, Kitchener (1-800 265 6959/ 519 745 3536/www.kw-visitor.on.ca). **Open** 9am-5pm daily.

Getting there

By car

K-W is about 75 minutes west of Toronto. Take Highway 401 about 96km (60 miles), then turn north on Highway 8.

By rail

VIA Rail trains (1 888 842 7245/www.viarail.ca) operate from Union Station.

By bus

Greyhound bus service runs throughout the day from Toronto (610 Bay Street, 1-800 661 8747/416 594 1010/www.greyhound.ca).

Stratford

One of Toronto's main attractions is its diverse and flourishing theatre scene. Rural Ontario also has its own network of summer-stock theatre, but it is the small town of Stratford that put the province on the world map for theatre-goers. The internationally acclaimed **Stratford Festival** celebrated its golden anniversary season in 2002, featuring Shakespeare (Christopher Plummer as King Lear), contemporary pieces (Brian Bedford's one man show *The Lunatic, the Lover and the Poet*) and classic musicals (Lerner & Loew's *My Fair Lady*). The festival has grown from its inauspicious debut in 1952, when Sir Michael Langham's production of *Richard III* starring Alec Guinness and Irene Worth was performed in sweltering conditions in a canvas tent. Little did they know then that Stratford would become the largest classical repertory theatre in North America.

The festival now presents 19 plays and musicals (performed in four major venues) during the six-month season. The four stages include the world-famous proscenium stage of the **Festival Theatre**, the **Avon**, the **Tom Patterson Theatre** (named after the local founder of the festival) and the new **Studio Theatre** for more experimental projects and original Canadian drama.

As the festival grew, the demand for upscale tourist facilities grew right along with it. Now, Stratford boasts some of the country's finest restaurants; its culinary reputation received a further boost with the advent of the **Stratford Chef School**, which has produced some of the country's finest culinary wizards.

The town itself is a picturesque portrait of small-town Ontario with the added bonus of five-star restaurants, excellent accommodation and more than 1,000 groomed acres of parkland lining the swan-dotted Avon river. Many restaurants provide takeaway picnic lunches, allowing for a leisurely alfresco picnic before the curtain rises. While wandering east through the park, stop at the little **Gallery Stratford**: it offers changing displays of contemporary and traditional art, with an emphasis on the art and costumes from the past 50 years of the Stratford Festival.

Gallery Stratford

54 Romeo Street (519 271 5271/www.gallery stratford.on.ca). **Open** *Jan-Apr* 1-4pm Tue-Fri, Sun; 10am-4pm Sat. *Apr-May* 10am-5pm Tue-Sat; 1-4pm Sun. *June & July* 10am-5pm Tue-Sat; 1-5pm Sun. *Sept-Nov* 9am-5pm Tue-Sun. *Dec* 1-4pm Tue-Fri, Sun; 10am-4pm Sat. **Admission** *Sept-Apr* $5; $4 concessions; free under-12s; *May-Aug* $10; $7-$8 concessions; free under-12s. **Credit** MC, V.

Where to eat

With half a million hungry theatre-goers to feed each year, Stratford has an embarrassment of culinary riches. **Rundles** restaurant always makes top ten lists of the best restaurants in Canada. It overlooks the park and river but you may not notice the scenery when the food reaches the table. **The Church** serves up divine dishes in a deconsecrated church with seating under the vaulted ceiling – tables and chairs have replaced the pews – or upstairs in the more casual Belfry. The cosy **Old Prune** is a favourite with theatre fans, while **Bistro 104** is a more casual dining spot and drinking hole.

If you aren't attending a matinee, take a drive east on Highway 7/8 to the **Waterlot** for a leisurely lunch in this old mill.

Bistro 104

104 Downie Street, Stratford (519 275 2929/ www.bistro104.com). **Meals served** 11am-2pm, 5-9pm daily. **Main courses** $10-$21.95. **Credit** AmEx, DC, MC, V.

The Church

70 Brunswick Street, Stratford (519 273 3424/ www.churchrestaurant.com). **Meals served** 5-11pm Tue-Fri; 11.30am-1.30pm, 5-11pm Sat, Sun. Closed Nov-mid Apr. **Main courses** $29-$44. **Credit** AmEx, DC, MC, V.

The Old Prune

151 Albert Street, Stratford (519 271 5052/ www.oldprune.on.ca). **Meals served** 5-11pm Tue; 11.30am-1.30pm, 5-11pm Wed-Sun. **Set dinner** $62.75. **Credit** AmEx, MC, V.

Rundles

9 Cobourg Street, Stratford (519 271 6442/ www.rundlesrestaurant.com). **Meals served** 5-10pm Tue; 11.15am-1.15pm, 5-10pm Wed; 5-10pm Thur, Fri; 11.30am-1.15pm, 5-10pm Sat, Sun. **Set dinner** $63.50-$73.50. **Credit** AmEx, DC, MC, V.

The Waterlot

17 Huron Street, New Hamburg (519 662 2020/ www.waterlot.com). **Open** 11.30am-2pm, 5-11pm Tue-Sun. **Main courses** $19-$28. **Credit** AmEx, MC, V.

Tourist information

Stratford Festival

PO Box 520, Stratford, ON N5A 6V2 (1-800 567 1600/519 271 4040/fax 519 273 6173/ www.stratfordfestival.ca). **Season** late Apr-early Nov. **Tours** year-round; call for details. **Tickets** $32-$100; $28-$61 concessions. **Credit** AmEx, MC, V.

Tourism Stratford

47 Downie Street, Stratford, ON N5A 1W7 (1-800 561 7926/519 271 5140/fax 519 273 1818/www.city.stratford.on.ca/tourism). **Open** 8.30am-4.30pm daily.

Getting there

By car

From Toronto, drive west along Highway 401, turn north on Highway 8 to Kitchener-Waterloo, then follow signs west to Stratford along Highway 7/8.

By rail

VIA Rail trains (1 888 842 7245, www.viarail.ca) operate from Union Station.

By bus

Greyhound bus service runs throughout the day from Toronto (610 Bay Street, 1-800 661 8747/416 594 1010, www.greyhound.ca).

Trips Out of Town

Further Afield

The Great Outdoors. And then some more of it.

Cottage Country

The beautiful wilderness region north of Toronto – actually, north of Barrie – is known as Cottage Country. However, the term is most often applied to the combined holiday area of the **Muskokas** and **Haliburton** that stretches to **Algonquin Provincial Park**, a gentrified playground of villages, lakeside resorts, boats and beaches set on countless lakes and rivers. Cottages both palatial and plain are traditionally opened up on the long weekend in May and keep lucky Torontonians in the swim through to Labour Day at the start of September. As the city grows and more cottages crowd the shoreline, those embarking on a great weekend escape must first endure the battling SUVs on the choked highways. If you can, visit the area during the week.

MIDLAND AND PENETANGUISHENE

Midland's **Sainte-Marie-Among-the-Hurons** is a mission fort built by Jesuit missionaries in the 17th century, their most westerly European outpost and the largest European inland settlement north of New Orleans. It became home to the local Huron Indian tribe, who converted to Christianity, and was the site of Ontario's first church, hospital, blacksmith shop and farm. Here, guides clad in 17th-century costumes will be able to answer your questions about the pioneer era.

Next door is the appealing **Mye Marsh Wildfife Centre**, offering lots of bird-, frog- and animal-watching. Across the road, the **Martyrs' Shrine** is a church dedicated to eight Catholic missionaries killed 350 years ago. Pilgrims make the trip, and healings and small miracles have been reported.

Just a few miles away in **Penetanguishene**, you can wander along the boardwalks of a restored 19th-century British naval base at **Discovery Harbour**. Replicas of the **HMS Tecumseth** and **HMS Bee** are docked here and set sail in Georgian Bay on selected days in summer; stop here for lunch or a snack at one of the dockside pubs. For another kind of watery adventure, climb aboard the **MS Georgian Queen** downtown for the lush, scenic **Penetanguishene 30,000 Islands Cruise**. The service operates from early May to October; call for a complete schedule.

GRAVENHURST

This pretty Muskoka town is best known as the birthplace of Dr Norman Bethune, whose 1890s home, the **Bethune Memorial House National Historic Site** charts his career as a pioneer of innovative surgical techniques: he developed a mobile blood transfusion procedure during the Spanish Civil War. Bethune also became a hero to the Chinese people when he laboured on their battlefields; indeed, he is buried in China and is commemorated as a hero of the Communist Revolution.

A must for anyone visiting the area is a watery ride through the Muskoka lakes aboard the spectacular 1887 **RMS Seguin**, a restored 99-passenger vessel and the oldest operating coal-fired steamship in North America. There are a variety of cruises from which to choose, lasting anywhere from one to seven hours; among the most popular are the Dinner and Twilight cruises. Back on shore, the **Gravenhurst Opera House** is a landmark heritage building from 1901 restored to its original splendour and with perfect acoustics. It hosts musical productions, touring shows and local theatre groups.

ALGONQUIN PROVINCIAL PARK

There are many provincial campgrounds throughout Cottage Country where you can pitch a tent and commune with nature or the people in the campsite next to you. But to really get away from it all, nothing comes close to the wilderness of **Algonquin Provincial Park**: its 7,725 square kilometres (3,000 square miles) of forests, lakes and rivers make it the biggest in southern Ontario.

For early settlers, Algonquin meant a constant battle against the elements, whether black bears, voracious bugs or the bitter cold of long winter days. Those hardships remain today but the terrain is breathtaking and beautiful, one of rugged outcroppings, pristine lakes and pure stillness. Canoeists can spend weeks traversing and portaging the waterways, and the fishing is superb. But if anything embodies the spirit of the north, it's the wild call of the loons reverberating across the water and the dazzling display of Northern Lights.

The park is located about 275 kilometres (175 miles) north of Toronto: take Highway 400 north, picking up the northbound 11 at Barrie to

4pm daily. *Oct-May* 1-4pm Mon-Fri. **Admission** $3.50; no concessions. **Credit** V.

Discovery Harbour
93 Jury Drive, Penetanguishene (705 549 8064/
www.discoveryharbour.on.ca). **Open** *May-June*
10am-5pm Mon-Fri. *July-Sept* 10am-5pm daily. Closed
Oct-Apr. **Admission** $3.50; $5.50 with guided tour;
free under-6s. **Credit** AmEx, MC, V.

Gravenhurst Opera House & Arts Centre
295 Muskoka Road S, Gravenhurst (1-888 495
8888/705 687 5550/www.gravenhurst.net/theop).
Box office *July, Aug* 10am-4pm Mon, Tue, Sun;
10am-9pm Wed-Sat. *Sept-June* 10am-4pm Mon-Fri.
Admission call for details. **Credit** MC, V.

Martyrs' Shrine
Midland (705 526 3788/www.jesuits.ca/martyrs-
shrine/default.htm). **Open** call for details.
Admission $3; free under-11s. **No credit cards**.

Penetanguishene 30,000 Islands Cruises
Main Street Harbour (1-800 363 7447/705 549
7795/www.georgianbaycruises.com). **Open** *May-Sept.*
Rates $18; concessions $8-$15; free under-5s.
Credit MC, V.

RMS Segwun
Muskoka Fleet, 820 Bay Street, Gravenhurst (705
687 6667/www.segwun.com). **Cruises** mid May-mid
Oct. **Rates** $23-$63.

Sainte-Marie Among the Hurons
Highway 12 E, Midland (705 526 7838/
www.saintemarieamongthehurons.on.ca). **Open**
Mid May-mid Oct 10am-5pm daily. *Mid Oct-early*
Nov 1-3pm daily. **Admission** $9.75; $5.25-$6.25
concessions; free under-5s. **Credit** AmEx, MC, V.

Wye Marsh Wildlife Centre
Highway 12, across from Martyrs' Shrine, Midland
(705 526 7809/www.wyemarsh.com/home.html).
Open 9am-5pm daily. **Admission** $6.50; $5.50
concessions; free under-4s. **Credit** MC, V.

Where to eat

Despite the best efforts of the cooks at
Deerhurst Resort and the **Delta
Grandview Resort**, there aren't really
any don't-miss gourmet joints in Cottage
Country, though you do get plenty of comfort
and luxury. Most people eat at their resort
or find good home cooking in the many
restaurants along the highways or small
towns. However, every motorist should stop at
Weber's along Highway 11. This legendary
hamburger pitstop has become so popular the
restaurant built a bridge across the highway
to service customers heading to and from
their cottage weekends.

Cabin in **Algonquin Provincial Park**.

Huntsville, and then heading east on 60 to
the park entrance. There are eight official
campgrounds with 1,248 sites and countless
wilderness sites for those paddling through the
canoe routes. A less demanding journey will
take a motorist along 56 kilometres (35 miles) of
Highway 60, from the West Gate at Oxtongue
Lake to the town of Whitney in the east. Along
this route, you'll find campgrounds, beaches,
picnic areas and interpretative hiking trails, as
well as the **Algonquin Interpretative
Centre**, **Logging Museum** and wildlife-heavy
Algonquin Museum. The prettiest time of
year here is late September, when the maples
turn brilliant shades of red, gold and yellow.

Algonquin Provincial Park
Box 219, Whitney, ON K0J 2M0 (reservations
1-888 668 7275/information 705 633 5572/
www.algonquinpark.on.ca). **Open** *Reservations*
7am-11pm daily. *Information* 8am-4.30pm daily.

Bethune Memorial House National Historic Site
235 John Street N, Gravenhurst (705 687 4261/
www.friendsofbethune.on.ca). **Open** *June-Oct* 10am-

The Magnificent Seven

They were led by Tom Thomson. Among his original comrades were JEH MacDonald, Arthur Lismer, Frederick Varley, Frank Johnston, Franklin Carmichael and AY Jackson. In later years the initial group expanded to include such luminaries as Lawren Harris and Emily Carr. But irrespective of numerical accuracy, the Group of Seven forever changed the focus and direction of painting in this country by celebrating the natural rugged beauty of the Canadian wilderness.

Thomson and his pals spent their lives capturing the distinct yet elusive light of northern landscapes, the intense colours of autumn and the shimmering surface of undiscovered northern lakes. They were bold explorers, trekking through the province and living in wilderness undiscovered by the public in an attempt to perfect their art.

As well as exploring Algonquin Park, the artists made forays into the remote and rugged Algoma region of northern Ontario. Hitching rides on freight trains, the Group would disembark at deserted lumber camps. There, they would often set up home in a boxcar on a siding, and make their way into the great unknown, on foot or by canoe. Inside their boxcar bases they would set up bunks, wood stoves, benches and tables.

'We worked from early morning until dark, in sun, grey weather, or rain,' wrote Lawren Harris. 'In the evening by lamp or candlelight each showed the others his day's work. This was a time for criticism, encouragement, and discussion, for accounts ... for our thoughts about the character of the country.'

Thomson's determination to immerse himself in the wilderness was legendary. While the other artists would huddle inside during fierce storms, Thomson would grab his sketch box, run out into the gale and paint furiously in a bid to capture the drama. At night, he would get into his canoe and paddle out into the middle of the lake, curl up in a blanket and go to sleep. However, his adventurous spirit may have cost him his life: Thomson drowned in mysterious circumstances in 1917 while exploring Canoe Lake in Algonquin Park.

As a lasting tribute to these artists and their belief in this country's natural beauty, the McMichael Canadian Art Collection in Kleinburg (*see p237*), offers a year-round 'Arts in the Wild' creative programme. Students can choose their own artistic expressions from sketching and painting to woodcarving and Aboriginal arts, from a one-day seminar in the woods of Kleinburg to several weeks in the northern wilderness.

Deerhurst Resort

1235 Deerhurst Drive, Huntsville (1-800 441 1414/705 789 6411/www.deerhurst.on.ca). **Open** 8am-11pm daily. **Main courses** $22-$31. **Credit** AmEx, DC, MC, V.

Delta Grandview Resort

939 Highway 60, Huntsville (1-800 461 4454/705 789 4417/www.deltahotels.com). **Open** 7am-9pm Mon-Thur, Sun; 7am-10pm Fri, Sat. **Main courses** $14-$30. **Credit** AmEx, DC, MC, V.

Paul Weber Drive-In

Highway 11 N, near Orillia (705 325 3696/www.webersrestaurants.com). **Open** May-Nov call for details. Closed Dec-Apr. **Main courses** $2.39-$4.59. **Credit** MC, V.

Where to stay

One of the great pleasures of Cottage Country is the variety of resorts, lodges, country inns, hotels, motels and family lakeside cabins for rent. The choice ranges from five-star accommodation with culinary aspirations to a

basic getaway bunkhouse, with beer and burgers at the local pub. For a full list, check with **Resorts Ontario** (*see p245*).

Deerhurst Resort, just north of Huntsville on Peninsula Lake, has long been known as Ontario's premier resort. It's vast: there are golf courses, tennis courts, saunas, spas and swimming pools, plus waterskiing, five-star dining and accommodation ranging from chalets to timeshare condos. For something more rustic, call **Pow Wow Point Lodge** for one of its five lakefront cottages on Pen Lake.

The stunning **Arowhon Pines** resort, in Algonquin Provincial Park, has huge log cabins with cathedral ceilings and a gorgeous wilderness setting on Little Joe Lake. Campers will need to contact Algonquin Park to reserve one of the 1,248 sites in eight public campgrounds, or obtain maps on wilderness canoe routes.

Algonquin Provincial Park

Box 219, Whitney, ON K0J 2M0 (reservations 1-888 668 7275/information 705 633 5572/

Spruce and Snow by Group of Seven painter **Lawren Harris**.

www.algonquinpark.on.ca). **Open** *Reservations* 7am-11pm daily. *Information* 8am-4.30pm daily.

Arowhon Pines Summer Resort & Restaurant

Summer address: Box 10001, Algonquin Park, Huntsville, ON P1H 2G5 (705 633 5661/705 633 5795/www.arowhonpines.ca). Winter address: 297 Balliol Street, Toronto, ON M4S 1C7 (416 483 4393/fax 416 483 4429/www.arowhonpines.ca). **Open** Apr-mid-Oct. **Rates** $190-$340 per person incl 3 meals daily & recreational facilities. **Credit** MC, V.

Deerhurst Resort

1235 Deerhurst Drive, Huntsville, ON P1H 2E8 (1-800 461 4393/705 789 6411/fax 705 789 2431/ www.deerhurstresort.com). **Rates** $99-$319 single/double; $189-$859 suite. **Credit** AmEx, DC, MC, V.

Pow-Wow Point Lodge

RR. # 4, Huntsville, ON (1-800 461 4263/705 789 4951/fax 705 789 7123/www.powwowpointlodge. com). **Rates** call for details. **Credit** MC, V.

Tourist information

Gravenhurst Chamber of Commerce

685-2 Muskoka Road N, Gravenhurst, ON P1P 1N5 (705 687 4432/fax 705 687 4382/ www.gravenhurstchamber.com). **Open** 9am-5pm Mon-Fri.

Huntsville-Lake of Bays Chamber of Commerce

8 West Street N, Unit 1, Huntsville, ON P1H 2B6 (705 789 4771/www.huntsvillelakeofbays.on.ca). **Open** 9am-5pm Mon-Fri.

Penetanguishene Tourist Information Centre

2 Main Street, Penetanguishene, ON L9M 1T1 (705 549 2232/fax 705 549 6640/www.southerngeorgian bay.on.ca). **Open** *May-Sept* call for details.

Resorts Ontario

29 Albert Street N, Orillia, ON L3V 5J9 (1-800 363 7227/705 325 9115/fax 705 325 7999/www.resorts-ontario.com). **Open** 8.30am-4.30pm Mon-Fri.

208 King Street, Midland, ON L4R 3L9 (705 526 7884/fax 705 526 1744/www.southerngeorgianbay. on.ca). **Open** 9am-5pm Mon-Fri.

Getting there

By car

For the **Penetanguishene** area, drive north from Toronto on Highway 400, then continue north on Highway 93. For **Gravenhurst** and **Huntsville**, drive north on Highway 400 past Barrie, then Highway 11 north. Continue past Huntsville for **Algonquin Park**, then take Highway 60 W straight through the park.

By bus

For **Penetanguishene**, take the Penetang-Midland Coach Lines from Toronto, connecting through Barrie (1-800 461 1767/www.greyhoundtravel.com/charter/ pmcl). For **Gravenhurst** and **Huntsville**,there is a Greyhound Canada bus daily from Toronto (1-800 661 8747, 416 594 1010, www.greyhound.ca).

By rail

For **Gravenhurst** and **Huntsville**, take the Ontario Northland (Northlander) from Toronto (1-800 461 8558/www.ontc.on.ca).

South-western Ontario & Lake Erie

Put off by the perhaps excessive popularity of Cottage Country, many locals and visitors have in recent years been discovering the more rustic joys of south-western Ontario. It's a land of small, pleasant towns, rich farmlands, summer resort villages and miles of white sand beaches that rival those of much more southerly climes. The drive from Toronto to the north shores of Lake Erie takes less than two hours.

Long-time residents refer to the area as the North Shore. However, tourism officials have dubbed it Ontario's South Coast in a sly attempt to conjure up images of South Beach-style warmth. Certainly, the weather is Floridian in summer, when temperatures regularly hit 30°C (85°F), but winter is another story: ski boats give way to snowmobiles and main streets begin to resemble frozen ghost towns.

Long Point is a 30-kilometre (19-mile) finger of sand that juts out into Lake Erie, and is filled with row upon row of cottages along its white

Northern desires

There's a case to be made that the populated part of Canada is but a thin line sandwiched between Disneyland America to the south and a vast endless expanse of white, wild nothingness to the north. When Torontonians grow tired of television and traffic jams, they pack up their cars and join the traffic jams heading north to Cottage Country to do The Nature Thing, which is usually accompanied by The Beer And Jetskiing Thing. Some of the more ambitious go even further north to places like Algonquin Park to do The Hardcore Nature Thing, although, truth be told, this is more about battling black flies than black bears.

In either case, the pure and unadulterated 'Idea of North' still has a stranglehold on the Canadian imagination. And the recent creation of Nunavut, a self-ruled native province that has been carved out of the Northwest Territories, has only increased the national interest in Canada's great white north. Every Torontonian – for whom the north begins once the last strand of Toronto suburb is no long visible – has a small part of their brain that repeats: 'If I totally fuck things up in the city, I can always go and live off the land in a shack in the middle of nowhere'.

Certainly, there have been endless dissertations written about how the north plays a distinctive role in defining the nebulous concept of Canadian identity.

The north also explains why the most popular theme in Canadian arts and letters – besides ranting about Disneyland America – is loneliness. Ever since the Group of Seven (*see p244* **The Magnificent Seven**) made their mark, the typical career trajectory for a Toronto artist or writer is to make a splash with some savvy insights into urban living before spending the rest of their oeuvre contemplating nature and the Canadian relationship with it. A prime example of this process is pianist Glenn Gould, who gave up global acclaim as a concert pianist to spend much of his time making fugue-like radio documentaries; among these was the aptly named *Solitude Trilogies*, which wove together the sounds of the north and the observations of its inhabitants.

For the complete Canadian experience, then, try to get a taste of the north, even if it's just for the time-tested joys of 'hubcap camping'; best appreciated when the car trunk is packed with lawn chairs and a beer-filled cooler.

Lake Erie: feel sand between your toes.

sands. A number of people live here year round, but it's chiefly a summer vacation spot with few full-time amenities bar a few restaurants and a couple of general stores. That said, it is a terrific beach resort for families, and **Long Point Provincial Park** (519 586 2133) is always full of campers.

You can't drive to the end of Long Point – the road ends at the provincial park – or even hike there. In fact, only official park rangers and the lighthouse keeper can walk to the tip of the peninsula, as the park is a protected World Biosphere Preserve. For ordinary mortals, the best way to see the stunning tip is to rent a boat or become friends with someone who has one.

If Long Point is more suitable for family holidays, then **Turkey Point** (take Highway 24, then head south on 10) is a swinging beach town for the younger set. The focal point for evening entertainment is the **Turkey Point Hotel** (93 Cedar Drive, 519 426 6236), where live bands play on a large outdoor patio. A diversion: while approaching Turkey Point along Highway 24, jog north off the highway toward Vittoria for a stop at **Kernal Peanuts** for fresh-roasted peanuts, sweets, fudge and their own addictive Honey Peanut spread. Since the area's main cash crop – tobacco – has pretty much gone up in smoke, many farmers have planted alternatives, among them peanuts and ginseng.

The central community for the area is **Port Dover**. Unlike the two resorts mentioned above, this is an actual town with a host of amenities: grocery and video stores, bars and restaurants, hotels and inns, summer theatre (the **Lighthouse Festival Theatre**) and tourist attractions (among them the **Harbour Princess** cruise ship, which offers regular dinner and party cruises on the lake, and the **Port Dover Harbour Museum**, whose nautical treasures include artefacts from the *Titanic*). There are even theme weekends here: among them are **Fish Fest** in July and **Art & Crafts in the Park** in August. For a more surreal celebration, check out Port Dover on any Friday 13, when some 50,000 motorcycle enthusiasts descend upon the little town. Incredibly, there hasn't been any trouble in the past 20 years. If you want to see 'the hidden Dover', take the **RiverRider**, a 40-passenger pontoon boat that sails past fishing tugs, yacht clubs, million-dollar homes and nature reserves. Tickets can be purchased at the pier.

Harbour Princess Cruises
Harbour Street, Port Dover (519 583 0202/ www.harbourprincesscruises.com). **Open** call for details. **Rates** $15-$85. **Credit** AmEx, MC, V.

Lighthouse Festival Theatre
Corner of Main and Market Streets, Port Dover (519 583 2221/www.lighthousetheatre.com). **Open** early June-mid-Sept. **Rates** $17-$22; concessions $7.

Port Dover Harbour Museum
44 Harbor Street, Port Dover (519 583 2660). **Open** 10am-4.30pm Mon-Fri; 11am-4pm Sat, Sun. **Admission** free.

Where to eat

Fish lovers tend to head for the **Erie Beach Hotel** for platters of perch and jugs of draught, or **Knechtels**, where perch is accompanied by a salad bar and diners can eat outside. For basic pub grub, try **Callahan's Beach Restaurant**, with its beachfront patio. The **Arbor**, meanwhile, is famous for foot-long hot dogs, fries and unique Golden Glow fruit drinks.

The most popular watering hole in town is the **Norfolk Tavern**, which has a steady clientele of regulars and always resembles a big friendly house party. Students of history should note that the bar, erected in 1812, was among those used by William Lyon Mackenzie and his ill-fated band of rebels who marched through the Muddy York in 1837.

The Arbor
17 Main Street, Port Dover (519 583 0611/ www.eriebeachhotel.com). **Open** *Apr-Oct* 9am-10pm daily. **Main courses** $4-$10. **Credit** MC, V.

Trips Out of Town

Callahan's Beach House Restaurant
2 Walker Street, Port Dover (519 583 0880).
Open 11.30am-11pm daily. **Main courses** $6-$15.
Credit MC, V.

Erie Beach Hotel
Walker Street, Port Dover (519 583 1391/
www.eriebeachhotel.com). **Open** call for details.
Main courses $7-$15. **Credit** AmEx, MC, V.

Knechtel's
Walker Street, Port Dover (519 583 1908).
Open 11am-11pm daily. **Main courses** $6-$10.
Credit MC, V.

Norfolk Tavern
200 Main Street, Port Dover (519 583 0048).
Open 11am-2am daily. **Credit** AmEx, MC, V.

Where to stay

If you want to stay in something other than
a tent, Port Dover has the biggest selection
of overnight accommodation, though every
little beach community has rental cottages for
longer stays. In Dover, check out the 12-room
Brant Hill Inn & Spa, situated at the top of a
hill overlooking the harbour; the 22-room **Erie
Beach Hotel**, just a short block to the beach,
or **Buck's Cottages** for a larger, family
holiday. However, note that rooms are at a
premium in the area: people often book a year
in advance. Contact the local tourist office for
a complete list of B&Bs.

If you can't find room at the inn,
the best place to book is the attractive
town of **Simcoe**. You'll find good basic
accommodation at the **Comfort Inn** or the
Travelodge Simcoe, with indoor pool, sauna
and fitness centre.

Accommodation on Turkey Point consists of
the aforementioned **Turkey Point Hotel** (*see
below*), little cabins, such as the **Whispering
Pines**, cottage rentals, or camping at the better-
reserve-early 235-campsite in **Turkey Point
Provincial Park** (519 426 3239). If you need
to dock your boat or rent one for the day, try the
Turkey Point Marina Basin.

All information and bookings at provincial
park campgrounds throughout the province –
such as **Turkey Point** and **Long Point** – are
handled through one website, **www.ontario
parks.com**, and one central telephone number,
1-888 688 7275. Reservations can be made
in person, but sites often fill up well in advance:
you can book up to four months ahead.

Brant Hill Inn & Spa
*30 John Street, Port Dover, ON N0A 1N7 (519 583
1501/fax 519 583 9975/www.branthillinnandspa.
com).* **Rates** $69-$109. **Credit** AmEx, MC, V.

Buck's Cottages
*206 St George Street, PO Box 299, Port Dover,
ON N0A 1N0 (519 583 2263/fax 519 583 2875/
buckscottages@sympatico.ca).* **Rates** $650-$700 per
week. **Credit** MC, V.

Comfort Inn
*85 Queensway E, Simcoe, ON N3Y 4M5 (1-877
424 6423/519 426 2611/fax 519 426 0053/
www.comfortinn.com).* **Rates** $89-$120.
Credit AmEx, DC, MC, V.

Erie Beach Hotel
*Walker Street, Port Dover, ON N0A 1N0 (519 583
1391/fax 519 583 3250/www.eriebeachhotel.com).*
Rates $65-$100. **Credit** AmEx, MC, V.

Turkey Point Marina Basin
*92 Club House Road, Turkey Point (519 426 6795/
www.tpmarina.com).* **Rates** call for details.

Whispering Pines Cottages
*230 Cedar Drive, Turkey Point, ON N0E 1T0 (519
426 0959/whisperingpines@turkeypointbeach.com).*
Rates $375-$850 weekly. **Credit** MC, V.

Travelodge Simcoe
*385 Queensway W, Simcoe, ON N3Y 2M9
(1-888 515 6375/519 426 4751/fax 519 426 2222/
www.the.travelodge.com/simcoe11723).* **Rates** $90-
$120. **Credit** AmEx, DC, MC, V.

Tourist information

Long Point World Biosphere Reserve Foundation
*General Delivery, Port Rowan, ON N0E 1M0 (519
586 2444 answering machine only/www.kwic.com/
~longpointbio).*

Port Dover Board of Trade
*19 Market Street W, P.O. Box 239, Port Dover, ON
N0A 1N0 (519 583 1314/fax 519 583 3275/www.
portdover.ca).* **Open** 9am-5pm Mon-Fri.

South Coast Tourism
*395 Queensway W, Suite 31, Simcoe, ON N3Y
2M9 (1-800 699 9038/519 426 1693/fax 519
428 0074/www.ontariossouthcoast.com).*
Open 9am-5pm Mon-Fri.

Getting there

By car
The North Shore of Lake Erie is approximately
140 kilometres (90 miles) from Toronto. Take the
Queen Elizabeth Way (QEW) west for about 64
kilometres (40 miles). The highway forks: take
the right turn which becomes Highway 403. Keep
driving for 40 kilometres (25 miles) to Brantford;
turn south on to Highway 24; and then drive about
40 kilometres (25 miles) through Simcoe and follow
the signs to the beach community of your choice.

Directory

Directory

Getting Around

By air

Lester B Pearson International Airport

Terminal 1 & 2 416 247 7678; Terminal 3 416 776 5100; www.torontoairport.ca.
Pearson, in the north-western suburbs, is in the middle of a ten-year reconstruction and, as work progresses, airlines are shifted from one terminal to the next. As of June 2001, all passengers have been charged an airport improvement fee. The fee – $10 for passengers departing from the airport, $4 for passengers making connecting flights – is included in your ticket price.

The best way to get to Pearson by bus is Pacific Western Airport Express (1-800 387 6787/www. torontoairportexpress.com). Buses and vans pick up/drop off passengers at many downtown hotels and the Greyhound bus terminal every 30 minutes from 3am to 1am daily. The trip takes 20-40 minutes, depending on where you get on and the time of day, and costs $14-$18 one-way or $25-$30 return.

City buses also serve the airport, but the routes are long and circuitous and there's nowhere to put your luggage. If that excites the masochist or the penny-pincher in you, yes, it is possible to get to the airport for the baseline TTC fare of $2.25: take the 192, 58 or 307to Islington subway station, and transfer.

If you want to connect with the subway, take express GO bus no.427 from Terminal 2 to Yorkdale orYork Mills subway station ($3.40 one way).

Most taxi companies offer a flat rate to the airport of around $40. Confirm the price before you set off.

Toronto City Centre Airport

416 203 6942/www.torontoport. com/TCAA.htm. **Map** p276 B10.
Air Ontario commuter flights serve this airport, on the Toronto Islands. Shuttle buses from the Fairmont Royal York Hotel are available for Air Ontario passengers, and there's a ferry service to and from the foot of Bathurst Street.

Airlines

Air Canada 1-888 247 2262/www.aircanada.ca
Air Canada Jazz 1-800 315 1390/www.flyjazz.com
Air Ontario www.airontario.com
Air Canada Tango 1-800 315 1390/www.flytango.com
Air France 416 922 5024/ www.airfrance.com
Air Jamaica 416 229 6024/ www.airjamaica.com
American Airlines 416 283 2243/www.aa.com
America West Airlines 1-800 235 9292/www.americawest.com
British Airways 416 250 0880/www.britishairways.com
CanJet Airlines 1-800 809 7777/www.canjet.com
Continental Airlines 1-800 784 4444/www.continental.com
Cubana Airlines 416 967 2822/www.cubana.cu
Delta Air Lines 1-800 221 1212/www.delta.com
Northwest Airlines 1-800 441 1818/www.nwa.com
United Airlines 1-800 241 6522/www.united.com
US Airways 1-800 943 5436/www.usairways.com

By bus

Greyhound Canada (416 594 1010/1-800 661 8747/www. greyhound.ca) runs many routes to Toronto from other parts of Canada and the US. The main terminal is located very centrally at 610 Bay Street, at Edward Street, Downtown, open from 5am to 1am daily. Note that arrivals come in to the smaller terminal directly across Elizabeth Street from the main terminal.

By rail

VIA Rail trains (1 888 842 7245/www.viarail.ca) operate from Union Station (65 Front Street W, at University Avenue, 416 366 8411). If you're coming in from the States your AMTRAK train will be given VIA Rail regalia and staff and bring you in at Union. You can buy tickets at most travel agents in Canada or the US. In the UK, contact Leisurail (0870 750 0222/ www.leisurail.co.uk).

Union Station is centrally located between the Financial District and the Waterfront and on the Yonge-University-Spadina subway line. Long- and short-term parking is available; call 416 366 9314.

By boat

For details of docking facilities call the harbour commission (416 863 2000).

Toronto has an efficient and easy-to-use public transport service run by the Toronto Transit Commission (TTC). In the central city frequent subway services, buses and streetcars ply the major arteries in complementary fashion (so University Avenue and Yonge Street don't have regular buses as the subway runs beneath).

Subway services generally start around 6am Mon-Sat, and the last train runs at around 1:.30am. On Sundays, service starts at around 9am and ends at around 1am. Buses and streetcars generally run from 6am to midnight or 1am daily. The Blue Night Network of buses, identified by a blue stripe on the curbside sign, takes over at night.

If you need to transfer from one mode of transport to another, be sure to obtain a transfer/proof of purchase when you start your trip. They're available from the red machines in subway stations or from the streetcar or bus driver. If you leave it too long before starting the second stage of your journey, TTC staff may not accept the transfer ticket, though it's a rather ad hoc system. Still, most passengers play fair.

The TTC takes safety seriously. Subway trains have alarms in every car, and there is a Designated Waiting Area on each platform that is brightly lit and has a 'push for help' button. It's also the spot where the conductor's car always stops. Women using buses between 9pm and 5am can ask to get off between stops to minimise the walk to their final destination.

TTC INFORMATION

Call 416 393 4636 or log on to www.city.toronto.on.ca/ttc. Network maps are free from all subway station offices.

FARES AND TICKETS

Cash fare for adults is $2.25. Seniors 65 and older and students pay $1.50 (with photo ID), and children 12 and under pay 50¢ for a one-way trip. (Kids two and under are free.) Subway fare collectors can give change, but it's exact fare only on streetcars and buses.

Fares are nominally cheaper if you buy tickets or tokens in bulk. Adults can buy five for $9 or ten for $18. Five senior or student tickets are $6 and ten $12 (again, take photo ID), and ten children's tickets are $4. Tokens are available only at subway stations, while tickets are sold at convenience and other stores.

If you're going to be covering a lot of ground, best bet is a day pass for $7.50, allowing unlimited travel from 9.30am Mon-Fri and all day long on Sat and Sun. The same pass, for the same price, can be used for groups of six, with no more than two adults, for unlimited travel on Sundays and public holidays.

A monthly pass gives you unlimited travel at any time of day. It's $93.50 for adults or $80 for seniors and students, but only available on the last three and first three days of the month.

Subway

There are four main subway lines. The Bloor-Yonge line runs from Kipling Station in the west, in the former city of Etobicoke, to Kennedy Station in the east, in the former city of Scarborough. The north–south line is divided into two parallel arms – the Yonge line, which runs from Union Station to Finch Station, and the University-Spadina line, which runs from Union Station to Downsview Station. The new fourth line (opened in November 2002) runs along Sheppard Avenue, from Yonge-Sheppard Station to Don Mills Station on the North Side. (Don't be fooled into thinking there is something to see up there just because there's a subway – aside from a nearby IKEA and a hospital, it's mostly suburban housing.)

The major transfer points between these east–west and north–south lines are Bloor-Yonge, St George and Yonge-Sheppard stations, where the lines run over each other, with platforms linked by stairs. You don't need a transfer to change subway trains.

Bus

Bus stops are marked by red and white poles or bus shelters and are often just before an intersection. Many – but not all – shelters have posted route timetables. Generally, buses arrive every 8-10 minutes during the day and every 20-30 minutes after 1am. Most of Toronto's current fleet are so-called kneeling buses, which allow for easier access for the elderly and disabled.

Streetcars

Toronto's streetcars are the best way to get around the city. Because they run on rail tracks in dedicated central lanes, they usually run to schedule. And they retain a feeling of nostalgia, romance, even. Conveniently for visitors, many of the main central arteries – Queen, College, Queen, Dundas, King and Spadina – are served by streetcars (whose numbers start with a 5) well into the suburbs.

To take the streetcar, wait at the stop (they look the same as bus stops) and cross in front of stopped cars to board by the front door. Sometimes you'll need to look for a shelter in the middle of the road, especially along the 509 Spadina route. (Passengers who have a transfer or pass may board by the back door along the busy 501 Queen line only – you must use the front door on all other lines). To disembark, step down into the stairwell and push open the doors using the bars. Cars are supposed to stop well behind streetcar doors but it's always a good idea to look right before getting out. Streetcars are not wheelchair accessible.

Rail

The Scarborough Rapid Transit line is a suburban above-ground extension of the Bloor-Yonge subway line that most visitors only see en route to the Toronto Zoo. GO Transit, the suburban transport company, runs a commuter rail network, but it's of little use to visitors.

Water transport

The city operates ferries from Harbourfront to Centre Island (summer only), Hanlan's Point and Wards Island. Call 416 392 8193 for schedule information or log on to www.city.toronto.on.ca/parks/to_islands/ferry.htm. Return fares are $5 for adults; $3 for seniors 65 and older and students 19 and younger; $2 for kids 14 and younger; kids 2 and younger are free. The ferry terminal is at the foot of Bay Street, at Queens Quay W, by the Westin Harbour Castle. Ferries generally run from 6.30am to midnight daily at 30-minute to 2.5 hours intervals but services change depending on the season and the weather: always call ahead, and be careful not to miss the last boat back.

Taxis

Toronto taxis operate under a standard system of fees and rights as set out by the city. The meter starts at $2.50 and increases by 25¢ for every 0.235km driven or 30 seconds of waiting. As usual, check it's been reset when you get into the cab.

Drivers are not allowed to recommend restaurants or hotels unless you make a

Directory

request, and they must follow any route you suggest or otherwise take the most direct route. Drivers must comply if you want to ride in silence.
Beck Taxi 416 751 5555/www.becktaxi.com
CO-OP Cabs 416 504 2667/www.co-opcabs.com
Crown Taxi 416 750 7878
Diamond Taxicab 416 366 6868/http://diamondtaxi.on.ca
Yellow Cab 416 504 4141

The taxi complaints line is 1-877 868 2937, 24 hours daily.

Driving

As with most big North American cities, you should avoid having to drive in Toronto if you can help it. During morning and afternoon rush hours especially, jams are long and tedious, and public transport or your own two feet will always get you where you're going quicker.

You need to be at least 16 years old and have a valid licence from your home country to drive in Toronto. The city speed limit is generally 50kmph (about 31mph) while the major highways are 100kmph (62mph). While you can drive close to 120kmph (75mph) on the major 400-series highways to keep up with the pace of traffic without getting a speeding ticket, don't try that on city streets. Police enforce speed limits strictly, especially in marked school zones where the limit is reduced to 40kmph. In Toronto, it's legal to make a right turn on a red light if you first come to a full stop.

As in most cities, drivers are required to stop for school buses picking up passengers. You must stop for a school bus on either side of the road unless you're on a divided highway, and for streetcars picking up passengers. It's illegal to drive around one, and you'll not only get a ticket but also risk getting an earful from disgruntled commuters.

Pedestrians have the right of way at crosswalks, which have painted markings and a string of lights, and can be tricky to spot in congested areas.

Breakdown services

Canadian Automobile Association

461 Yonge Street, at Carlton Street, Church & Wellesley (416 221 4300; emergencies 416 222 5222/www.caa.ca). **Open** 9am-6pm Mon-Fri; 9.30am-4pm Sat; emergency line 24hrs daily. **Map** p281 F5.
Breakdown services for members and members of reciprocal organisations, depending on their level of cover. Great free maps for members.
Branches: throughout the city.

Fuel stations

Esso

581 Parliament Street, at Amelia Street, Cabbagetown (416 925 5448 or 1-800 567 3776/www.imperial oil.ca). **Open** 6am-midnight daily. **Credit** AmEx, MC, V. **Map** p281 H5.
Branches: throughout the city.

Petro-Canada

55 Spadina Avenue, at King Street W, Entertainment District (416 977 3653/1-800 668 0220/www.petro-canada.ca). **Open** 24 hrs daily.
Credit AmEx, MC, V. **Map** p277 D7.
Branches: throughout the city.

Parking

Steep: you'll pay as much as $4 for half an hour or $20 for a day of parking in a privately run downtown lot. City-operated lots are a little less expensive at $2 or $3 an hour (look for the green 'P' emblem).

Parking on most city streets is illegal without feeding a nearby meter, and parking enforcement officers are ever vigilant. Street parking privileges are withdrawn during rush hour on busy roads, usually between 7-9am and 3.30-6.30pm.

Vehicle hire

You must be 21 to rent a car in Ontario. Rental companies will offer you accident and collision insurance and although it may seem expensive, you'd be wise to take it if not covered by your own policy.

Alamo

920 Yonge Street, Casa Loma (416 935 1533/1-800 462 5266/www.alamo.com). *Subway Bay.* **Open** 7am-7pm Mon-Fri; 7am-6pm Sat; 9am-5pm Sun. **Credit** AmEx, MC, V. **Credit** AmEx, DC, V. **Map** p280 E3.

Budget

556 St Clair Avenue W, at Bathurst Street, Forest Hill (416 651 0020/1-800 561 5212/www.budgettoronto.com). *Subway St Clair.* **Open** 8am-6pm Mon-Fri; 8am-5pm Sat. **Credit** AmEx, MC, V.
Branches: throughout the city.

Discount Car & Truck Rentals

243 Danforth Avenue, at Broadview Avenue, East Side (416 465 8776 or 1 866 310 2277/www.discountcar.com). *Streetcar 504, 505/subway Broadview.* **Open** 8am-6pm Mon-Fri; 8am-4pm Sat. **Credit** AmEx, MC, V.
Branches: throughout the city.

Enterprise Rent-a-Car

700 Bay Street, between College & Dundas Streets, Chinatown (416 599 1375/1-800 7368 2227www.enterprise.com). *Subway College/streetcar 506/bus 6.* **Open** 7.30am-6pm Mon-Fri; 9am-noon Sat. **Credit** AmEx, MC, V. **Map** p277/p278 E6.
Branches: throughout the city.

Cycling

Experienced city cyclists will find Toronto a doddle, with easy navigation and about 35km (22 miles) of bike lanes. But don't start your career here – you need street smarts, and accidents are a regular occurrence. For info about city bike programmes, call 416 392 9253 or see www.city.toronto.on.ca/cycling/cycling.htm.

Walking

Toronto is a city made for walking, with lots of ample sidewalks. For off-street strolls, take a self-guided Discovery Walks through parks and points of interest – contact the city's Parks and Recreation department (www.city.toronto.on.ca/parks/.

Resources A-Z

To drink and purchase alcohol in Ontario, and to buy tobacco products, you must be 19. Note that fines for buying tobacco for minors are steep. To drive a car or truck, you must be 16 or over.

The age of consent for heterosexual sex, according to Canada's Criminal Code, is 14, or 18 if one party is in a position of legal authority over the other. The age of consent for gay sex in Ontario is also 14 (18 in most other parts of the country).

Attitude & etiquette

Toronto is a casual, relaxed city, and while Torontonians more than other Canadians may bristle at the idea that Canadians are polite to a fault, it's mostly true. Unless you're meeting with the CEO of a major corporation, casual dress is de rigueur for most business situations, especially on Fridays. While wearing jeans to a business function may be pushing your luck, men are rarely required to wear suits (khakis or dress pants are fine) and women wear pretty much what they please.

Greeting friends, women kiss once on the cheek. Guys tend to go for as little contact as possible – a stiff handshake is usual.

Business

Conventions & conferences

International Centre
6900 Airport Road, at Derry Road, North End (905 677 6131/www.internationalcentre. com). Subway Lawrence West, then bus 58B.

Metro Toronto Convention Centre
255 Front Street W, at John Street, Entertainment District (416 585 5000/www.mtccc.com). Streetcar 504/subway Union or St Andrew. Map p277 D8.

Couriers & shippers

FedEx
215 Lakeshore Boulevard E, at Sherbourne Street, Waterfront (1-800 463 3339/www.fedex.com). **Open** 24hrs daily. **Credit** AmEx, MC, V. **Map** p278 G9.

Purolator Courier
335 Bay Street, at Adelaide Street, Financial District (1-888 744 7123/ www.purolator.com). Subway King/ streetcar 501. **Open** 24hrs daily. **Credit** AmEx, MC, V. **Map** p277/p278 E7.

Quick Messenger Service
296 Richmond Street W, at John Street, Entertainment District (416 368 1623/www. qms-tor.com). Streetcar 501, 504. **Open** 24 hrs daily. **No credit cards.** Map 277 D7.

Office hire/services

Alicos Digital Copy Centre
66 Gerrard Street E, at Church Street, Dundas Square (416 977 6868/www.alicos.com). Subway Dundas/streetcar 505. **Open** 8.30am-7.30pm Mon-Fri; 10am-4pm Sat. **Credit** AmEx, MC, V. **Map** p277/p278 F6.
A range of services: copying, print, binding, self-serve computers, graphic design, resumé/CV service and more.
Branches: 346 Bloor Street W, The Annex (416 962 6618); 233 College Street, University (416 598 1818); 203A College Street, University (416 599 2342).

Kinko's
459 Bloor Street W, at Spadina Avenue, The Annex (416 928 0110/ www.kinkos.com). Subway Spadina/ streetcar 510. **Open** 24 hrs daily. **Credit** AmEx, MC, V. **Map** p280 D4. **Branches**: throughout the city.

Secretarial services

BBW International
2336 Bloor Street W, at Windermere Avenue, West End (416 767 3036/ www.bbwinternational.com). Subway Jane. **Open** 9am-5pm Mon-Fri. **Credit** AmEx, MC, V.

Translators & interpreters

ABCO International Translators & Interpreters
330 Bay Street, at Adelaide Street W, Entertainment District (416 359 0873). Streetcar 504. **Open** 9am-5pm Mon-Fri. **Credit** AmEx, MC, V. **Map** p277/p278 E7.

Travel advice

For up-to-date information for travelling to a specific country – including the latest news on safety and security, health issues, local laws and customs – contact your home country government's department of foreign affairs. Most have websites packed with useful advice.

Australia
www.dfat.gov.au/travel

New Zealand
www.mft.govt.nz/travel

Republic of Ireland
www.irlgov.ie/iveagh

UK
www.fco.gov.uk/travel

USA
http://travel.state.gov/travel

South Africa
www.dfa.gov.za/

Directory

Berlitz GlobalNET

1-888 802 5494/info@mtl.berlitz.com
Based at Berlitz's Montreal office,
translators and interpreters are
available across the country.

Useful organisations

Business Information Centre, Toronto Reference Library

*789 Yonge Street, just north of
Bloor Street, Yorkville (416 395
5577/www.tpl.toronto.on.ca).
Subway Bloor-Yonge.* **Open**
10am-8pm Mon-Thur; 10am-5pm
Fri, Sat. **Map** p281 F4.
Helpful librarians help find a range of
information on Canadian industry,
business practices and stocks.

Toronto Board of Trade

*1 First Canadian Place, at King and
Bay Streets, Financial District (416
366 6811/www.bot.com). Subway
King/streetcar 504.* **Open** 9am-5pm
Mon-Fri. **Map** p277/p278 E8.
Canada's largest chamber of
commerce.

TSX Group

*130 King Street W, at Bay Street,
Financial District (416 947 4670/
www.tse.com). Streetcar 504/subway
King, St Andrew.* **Open** 8.30am-5pm
Mon-Fri. **Map** p277/p278 E8.
Home of the Toronto Stock Exchange
and TSX Venture Exchange, Canada's
foremost stock market.

Consulates

American Consulate General

*360 University Avenue, University
(416 595 1700). Subway Osgoode/St
Patrick.* **Open** 8.30am-1pm Mon-Fri.

Australian Consulate General

*175 Bloor Street E, at Jarvis Street,
Church & Wellesley (416 323 1155).
Subway Sherbourne.* **Open** 9am-1pm,
2-4.30pm Mon-Fri. **Map** p281 F4.

British Consulate-General

*777 Bay Street, at College
Street, Chinatown (416 593
1290). Subway College/streetcar
506.* **Open** 9am-4.30pm Mon-Fri.
Map p277/p278 E6.

Consulate General of Ireland

*20 Toronto Street, St Lawrence
(416 366 9300). Streetcar 501.*
Open 10am-4pm Mon-Fri.
Map p277/p278 F7.

New Zealand Consulate

*67 Yonge Street, Financial District
(416 947 0000). Subway King or
Union/streetcar 504.* **Open** 9am-4pm
Mon-Fri. **Map** p277/p278 E8.

South African Consulate

*2 Bloor Street W, at Yonge Street,
Yorkville (416 944 8825). Subway
Bloor-Yonge.* **Open** 8.30am-4.30pm
Mon-Fri. **Map** p280 E4.

Consumer

Ontario has strong consumer
protection laws. Currently,
consumers may cancel any
contract for any reason within
five days and get all their
money back if they give written
notice of cancellation. To lodge
a complaint against a business
or obtain further information,
contact the Ontario Ministry of
Consumer & Business Services,
General Inquiry Unit (416 326
8555/www.cbs.gov.on.ca).

Customs

Canada customs regulations
allow you to bring the
following into the country
without paying tax: 200
cigarettes or 50 cigars plus
1.5 litres of wine, 1.14 litres of
liquor or 24 cans of beer. You
may also bring gifts worth less
than $60 each.

You are prohibited from
carrying firearms, weapons
(including knives of any sort),
drugs, endangered species
(plant or animal) and cultural
property (as in antiquities, not
released-in-Australia-only Kylie
Minogue albums). Canada
Customs and Immigration can
provide more information (1-
204 983 3500 outsideCanada; 1-
800 461 9999 in Canada/www.
ccra-adrc.gc.ca).

UK Customs & Excise
(www.hmce.gov.uk) allows
returning travellers to bring
home £145 worth of gifts and
goods and any sum of money
they can prove is theirs. As of
November 2002, US Customs

(www.customs.ustreas.gov)
allows Americans to return
home from Canada with
US$800 worth of gifts and
goods duty-free.

Disabled

Toronto is fairly well set up
for people with disabilities in
terms of having accessible
buses and public buildings.
Many restaurants and shops
are also accessible, but it's
always best to call ahead.

Tourism Toronto has a
useful guide for disabled
visitors, available via the
website www.toronto
tourism.com, (click on the
wheelchair symbol).

Ontarians With Disabilities Act Committee

*(416 480 7012/www.oda
committee.net).*
A good reference for services and
issues related to disabilities.

Drugs

Although you may have read
that Canada's Senate supports
the idea of decriminalising the
use of marijuana, Toronto is
not the Amsterdam of North
America. Drug offences
are taken very seriously in
Canada, so it's best to avoid
the use of narcotics while in
the country.

Electricity

Just like the US, Canada uses
110-volt electric power with
two- or three-pin plugs.
Visitors from the UK and
Europe will need adaptors,
available at most hotels and
department stores, to use their
appliances from home.

Emergencies

If you require emergency
assistance from police,
firefighters or medical
technicians, call 911. It's a
free call from all phones.

Directory

For hospitals, *see below* **Health**. For other emergency numbers, *see* **Helplines** and **Police**.

Poison Information Centre
1-800 268 9017.

Gay & lesbian

Toronto is a very gay-friendly city, all things considered. You can freely hold hands with your partner in the Church & Wellesley neighbourhood and make out to your heart's content. You may even get away with it along some parts of Queen Street W, but otherwise, it's best to play it cool. Toronto is, by and large, an accepting city, but gay bashings are not unheard of.

Accommodation

There's no need to worry about a frosty reception at local hotels. The major ones are fully aware of the value of the pink dollar and many advertise in Tourism Toronto's official gay guide (1-877 848 3888 or www.torontotourism.com for a copy). But for a specifically queer ambience, try the many gay-friendly B&Bs within striking distance of the ghetto.

Dundonald House
35 Dundonald Street, at Church Street, Church & Wellesley (416 961 9888/www.dundonaldhouse. com). Subway Wellesley. **Rates** single/double $85-$185. **Credit** AmEx, V. **Map** p281 F5.
One of the oldest gay-owned and operated B&Bs in the city, Dundonald has seven rooms, sauna, hot tub, workout area and bikes.

Immaculate Reception Bed & Breakfast
34 Monteith Street, off Church Street, Church & Wellesley (416 925 4202). Subway Wellesley. **Rates** single/double $85-$150. **Credit** MC, V. **Map** p281 F5.
Located in an 1885 townhouse, this quiet four-room B&B faces Cawthra Park, home to summer sunbathers and an AIDS memorial. One room has period furniture, another has a private terrace on the third floor.

Lavender Rose Bed & Breakfast
15 Rose Avenue, at Lancaster Avenue, Cabbagetown (416 962 8591/www.lavenderrosebb.com). Streetcar 506. **Rates** double $95-$125. **Credit** MC, V. **Map** p281 G5.
Lesbian-owned and operated, this small B&B is located in a renovated Victorian home just around the corner from Pope Joan (*see p188*) and a 15-minute walk from Church Street.

Mike's on Mutual
325 & 333 Mutual Street, at Maitland Street, Church & Wellesley (416 944 2611/www.mikesonmutual. com). Streetcar 506/subway Wellesley. **Rates** $65-$75. **Credit** AmEx, MC, V. **Map** 281 F5.
Great location right behind Woody's (*see p188*). Some of the rooms have private baths, some have shared; many have decks or balconies. Situated in two houses, one more than a century old, Mike's caters to both gay men and lesbians.

Help & information

For HIV/AIDS information, *see below* **Health**.

519 Church Street Community Centre
519 Church Street, at Dundonald Street, Church & Wellesley (416 392 6874/www.the519.org). Subway Wellesley. **Open** 9am-10pm Mon-Fri; 9am-5.30pm Sat; 10am-5pm Sun. **Map** p281 F5.

Gay Bashing Reporting Line
416 392 6878 ext 337.

Lesbian Gay Bi Youth Line
416 962 9688. **Open** 4.30-9pm Mon-Fri; Sun.
Trained youth volunteers provide support for callers under the age of 27 with problems associated with sexual orientation and are a wealth of information on related social services and social groups.

Health

Accident & emergency

If you need immediate medical attention, dial 911 from any phone.

If you need medical information but it's not a life-or-death situation, call **Telehealth Ontario** on 1-866 797 0000. Registered nurses take calls 24 hours a day, seven days a week, and can help diagnose your problem over the phone. They can't send out prescriptions but can refer you to a pharmacy and help decide if you need hospital attention. The service is free to everyone, including visitors, and provides help in English and French, with translation support for 110 other languages.

To contact the police in a non-emergency situation, telephone 416 808 2222.

Contraception & abortion

Hassle Free Clinic
556 Church Street, at Wellesley Street, Church & Wellesley (416 922 0566 women/www.hasslefreeclinic. org). Streetcar 506/subway Wellesley. **Open** call for hours. **Map** p281 F5.

Planned Parenthood of Toronto
36B Prince Arthur Avenue, Yorkville (416 961 0113/www.ppt.on.ca). Subway Bay or Museum. **Open** 9am-5pm Mon, Tue, Thur, Fri; 9am-noon Wed. **Map** p280 D4.

Dentists

Ontario Dental Association
416 922 3900/www.dental.oda.on.ca.
For references to local dentists.

Doctors

The College of Physicians & Surgeons of Ontario
416 967 2603/www.cpso.on.ca
For references to local doctors.

Hospitals

The hospitals listed below all have emergency wards open 24 hours daily.

Hospital for Sick Children
555 University Avenue, at Gerrard Street E, Chinatown (416 813 5807). Subway St Patrick/streetcar 506. **Map** p277/p278 E6.

Mount Sinai Hospital
600 University Avenue, at College Street, University (416 586 5054). Subway Queen's Park/streetcar 506. **Map** p280 E5.

Directory

North York General Hospital
4001 Leslie Street, at Sheppard Avenue E, North Side (416 756 6001). Subway Leslie.

St Joseph's Health Centre
30 The Queensway, at Roncesvalles Avenue, West End (416 530 6003). Streetcar 504.

St Michael's Hospital
30 Bond Street, at Queen Street E, Dundas Square (416 864 5094). Streetcar 501/Subway Dundas or Queen. **Map** p277/p278 F7.

Toronto East General Hospital
825 Coxwell Avenue, at Mortimer Avenue, East Side (416 469 6435). Subway Coxwell.

Toronto General Hospital
200 Elizabeth Street, at University Avenue, Chinatown (416 340 3649). Subway Queen's Park. **Map** p277 E6.

Toronto Western Hospital
399 Bathurst Street, at Dundas Street W, Chinatown (416 603 5757). Streetcar 505, 511. **Map** p276 C6.

Opticians
See p158 for optician and optometrist contact information.

Pharmacies & prescriptions
Pharmacies are allowed to set their own dispensing fee, which can range from $6 to $14 on top of your drug cost. The cheapest drugs are available from department stores such as Zellers (www.hbc.com/zellers) or Wal-Mart (1-800 328 0402).

Pharmacies are ubiquitous in Toronto. Most open between 9am and 10am and close between 10pm and midnight. Some open later in the evening and others are open 24 hours a day. For locations and hours, contact Shoppers Drug Mart (1-800 746 7737/www.shoppersdrugmart.ca); *see p158* for our recommendations.

STDs, HIV & AIDS

AIDS Committee of Toronto
339 Church Street, at Gerrard Street, Church & Wellesley (416 340 2437/www.actoronto.org). Streetcar

506/subway College. **Open** 10am-9pm Mon-Thur; 10am-5pm Fri. **Map** p277/p278 F6.

Hassle Free Clinic
556 Church Street, at Wellesley Street, Church & Wellesley (416 922 0566 women; 416 922 0603 men/www.hasslefreeclinic.org). Subway Wellesley/streetcar 506. **Open** call for hours. **Map** p281 F5.

Helplines

Alcoholics Anonymous
416 487 5591/www.aa.toronto.org

Assaulted Women's Helpline
416 863 0511/www.awhl.org. Crisis counselling, shelter referrals, legal advice.

Distress Centres of Toronto
416 408 4357. Trained volunteers are available 24 hours daily for people who need to talk to someone or are feeling suicidal.

Kids Help Phone
800 668 6868/http://kidshelp. sympatico.ca.

Narcotics Anonymous
416 236 8956/www.torontona.ca.

Toronto Rape Crisis Centre
416 597 8808.

Victim Support Line
416 325 3265. Advice from the provincial attorney general's office on what to do if you're caught in the criminal justice system.

ID
You must be 19 or older to buy tobacco products, and most corner stores will ask for photo ID if you look 25 or younger.

Getting carded in a Toronto bar is unusual, but it does happen, so carrying photo ID is a good idea. It's rare in gay bars; straight dance clubs tend to card more often.

Insurance
Canada does not provide health or medical services to visitors for free, so travel and health insurance is a must.

Hospitals and walk-in clinics will want the name of your insurer and policy number, so be sure to keep them handy.

Internet
Toronto hotels are very switched on to internet access, and usually provide sockets in rooms for laptop users (though speed and reliablility vary), sometimes via ethernet, and/or lobby consoles. Public access is available at most public library branches and many cafés. For library locations, contact the Toronto Public Library (416 393 7131/www.tpl.toronto.on.ca).

For useful Toronto websites, *see p264* **Further Reference**.

Bell Sympatico
416 310 7873/www.sympatico.ca. A reliable, reasonably priced internet service provider that offers dial-up or DSL connections.

Insomnia Internet Bar/Café
563 Bloor Street W, at Bathurst Street, The Annex (416 588 3907/www.insomniacafe. com). Subway Bathurst/streetcar 511. **Open** 4pm-2am Mon-Thur; 4pm-4am Fri; 10am-4am Sat; 10am-2am Sun. **Credit** AmEx, MC, V. **Map** p280 C3.

Kinko's
459 Bloor Street W, at Spadina, The Annex (416 928 0110/www. kinkos.com). Subway Spadina/ streetcar 510. **Open** 24hrs daily. **Credit** AmEx, MC, V. **Map** p280 D4. **Branches**: throughout the city.

Language
English is the main language used in Toronto, although with such a vast multicultural population, you're likely to hear everything from Mandarin to Punjabi on the streets. Business is conducted largely in Canadian English, which is only subtly different from US and British English. Although Canada is officially bilingual, French-speaking travellers will have trouble getting good service in French.

Some common expressions vary from US and UK English, or use one over the other. You'd get in the **line-up** to order food **to go** (put the wrapper in the **garbage**), or eat in and ask for the **bill** (though '**check**' is creeping in). You may need to visit the **washroom**. If you bump into someone on the **sidewalk**, say '**sorry**'. You fill your car with **gas** at a **gas station**, put your luggage in the **trunk** and may need to look under the **hood**.

Left luggage

There are lockers at Terminals 1 and 2 at Lester B Pearson International Airport, and at the downtown Greyhound terminal, but none at City Centre Airport or Union Station (though if you're travelling with VIA Rail you can check bags in for same-day pick up).

Legal help

If you run into legal trouble, contact your insurers or your national consulate (*see p249*).

Libraries

Toronto Public Library
789 Yonge Street, just north of Bloor Street, Yorkville (416 393 7131/www. tpl.toronto.on.ca). Subway Bloor-Yonge. **Open** 10am-8pm Mon-Thur; 10am-5pm Fri, Sat. **Map** p281 F4. **Branches**: throughout the city.

Lost property

Airports

Report lost luggage claims to your airline immediately. If you've lost property in the airport itself, call 416 776 7750 (Terminals 1 & 2) or 416 776 4816 (Terminal 3). Call City Centre Airport on 416 203 6942.

Public transport

All lost property found on subways, buses and streetcars ends up at Bay Station, at

Bloor Street W and Bay Street. You may visit the Lost & Found office in person from 8am-5pm Mon-Fri or call 416 393 4100 (noon-5pm Mon-Fri).

Taxis

If you leave something in a taxi, call the company directly.

Media

Toronto is the centre of virtually all media for Canada's English-speaking majority, a fact that contributes to the country's resentment towards the city. The Toronto-centric tone and attitude on the airwaves and in print is frequently ridiculed as the bluster of a self-important city that barely looks beyond its own polluted horizons to explain Canada to Canadians. This leaves plenty of earnest journalists on the national beat feigning real concern for events in Saskatoon or St John's and fighting for the column inches to tell their stories. Do Torontonians care? Try asking them.

Still, Torontonians love their media. They're permanently plugged in, switched on or buried in newsprint. The largest media market in the country is thriving. Where many big cities in North America have been reduced to one-newspaper towns, Toronto boasts four big dailies: the *Toronto Star*, the *Globe and Mail*, the *Toronto Sun* and the *National Post*. Old-fashioned newspaper wars rage on with free copies handed out liberally.

Newspapers & magazines

The Toronto Star

The Star is Canada's biggest daily paper yet unlike two of its cross-town rivals (the *Globe* and the *Post*) it doesn't have national distribution. It's small 'l' liberal in outlook, claims to defend the working stiff and covers city news like no one else.

The 'What's On' section on Thursdays is a good heads-up for weekend attractions.

The Globe and Mail

The *Globe and Mail* is considered the paper of record for the country. Smart columnists and strong international coverage make it *The New York Times*-light. Business is its strength.

The Toronto Sun

'The little paper that could' is a feisty tabloid rag with knee-jerk conservatism as its guiding light. Cheesecake and beefcake photos are part of the daily diet.

The National Post

Who knows what will become of this struggling upstart launched by Conrad Black before he bailed out on Canada? It's obsessed with celebrity coverage, gossip and how much things cost.

Metro

Strap-hangers have an even cheaper way to absorb the day's headlines. Toronto has its own edition of this internationally syndicated freebie that offers news in pre-digested, bite-sized bits. Find it in the subway or in garbage bins.

Alternative papers

They're called alternatives but *Now* and *eye* have established themselves squarely in the mainstream. Both are free weeklies that come out on Thursday. *Now* is more Granola and *eye* hipper to the downtown music scene. Both have extensive entertainment listings. You'll find them in street boxes or on the floor of many pubs, cafés and stores.
Xtra! and *Fab* compete on the gay scene. At least they've co-ordinated their publication dates, coming out every two weeks on alternating Thursdays.

Foreign-language press

Pick a country and there's probably a Toronto-based publication that caters to its expat community. Weekly papers can be had in French, German, Greek, Spanish, Ukrainian, Hindi and Malaysian, to name a few. The Portuguese community is served by a bi-weekly and papers appear daily in Italian and Korean; there are three daily newspapers in Chinese.
Newsstands carry lots of UK and US press, or try Book City (*see p142*).

Toronto Life

A monthly glossy with upscale attitude reflecting Toronto's expanding bourgeoisie. Its listings are useful for planning ahead.

Directory

Local hero Ted Rogers

The Rogers have long been major players in Canada's media and telecommunications sector as major cable and mobile phone providers, experts in seeing a gap in the market and levering it wide open.

Ted Rogers Junior began his foray into the family business in 1960 by buying a small Toronto radio station, CHFI. He pioneered FM radio at a time when only five per cent of Toronto's households had FM receivers, and was the first to broadcast in stereo. Similarly, he got into cable TV on the ground floor and for a brief period in the early 1980s operated the biggest cable company in the world. Always looking for the next wave of technology, he slimmed down on cable holdings, moved into cellular phone technology and then took on Ma Bell in the long-distance phone market. Rogers has compared his corporate philosophy to the likes of Rupert

Murdoch's News Corp with a credo that only by playing with the big boys can Canada hope to retain control of its media (although laws limit foreign ownership).

Rogers is still the biggest cable operator in Canada, runs a chain of video stores, owns a stable of magazines including *Maclean's* and *Chatelaine*, has 43 AM and FM radio stations and launched the country's first multi-lingual TV station, now called Omni. The community channel, Rogers Cable 10, has evolved into a fairly decent source of programming about events in and around Toronto.

Coulda been a contender: Conrad Black. A newspaper baron Canada-wide, Black chose to leave the country in order to secure a peerage in Britain, where he owns the *Telegraph* and *Spectator*. This despite having to abandon his fledgling, and struggling, Toronto paper, the **National Post**.

Radio

The competitive radio field means that formats change as often as station managers' underwear on ratings day. The battle to win the ear of Toronto listeners keeps things interesting, if rarely innovative. There are 33 stations (AM frequencies are difficult to tune to downtown because of interference from office towers – the CN Tower notwithstanding). Talk rules – in many tongues – on AM with all sports (**The Fan 590**), all news (**CFTR 680**), more talk (**CFRB 1010**) and oldies (**AM 0, 1050 CHUM** and **CKOC 1150**). **MOJO Radio 640** pioneered a new format for guys only. You've been warned.

Flick over to FM where you'll find adult contemporary dominates on barely distinguishable services: **EASY ROCK 97.3**, **CHFI 98.1**, **CKFM 99.9** and **CHUM FM 104.5**. Classic rock blares on **Q107** while **THE EDGE 102.1** tries to find just that from the morass of contemporary pop and rock music.

The CBC, the taxpayer-funded national service, doesn't draw the numbers in Toronto that it commands elsewhere. **Stereo One** (99.1) is predominantly talk, with national shows that go in search of the Canadian identity blended with local and regional programmes. It's about the only place you'll hear new radio drama. The flagship current affairs programme, *As it Happens*, is a much-loved national institution.

Stereo 2 (94.1) plays light classics mixed with Cape Breton fiddlers and weekend jazz and opera. **CJBC** (90.3) is CBC's French service with superb classical, jazz and contemporary music content. More classics are on the commercial **CFMX** (96.3), which has a penchant for waltzes. **JAZZ FM** (91.1) is finding its way now that it runs commercials (it was previously funded by donations).

After years of having to turn the rabbit ears south to pick up hip hop and R&B from Buffalo, New York, **Flow** (93.5) brought a black voice to mainstream radio in Toronto in 2001. Now it has competition for the urban sound from **CISS FM** (92.5).

As is often the case, it is left to campus radio to push the frontiers of programming. Their wildly eclectic tastes make them unlistenable over long stretches, but dropping in on **CKLN** (88.1), **CIUT** (89.5) and **CHRY** (105.5) is certain to refresh.

Television

Torontonians like to watch, and they've developed their thumbs into lean, mean channel-flipping machines. There has always been an embarrassment of channels, even in pre-cable days when US signals were beamed in. Now things may have gone too far. The 500-channel universe was a nice metaphor for the wired future, but when you're confronted with such a staggering selection, a kind of video paralysis sets in.

Specialty channels cater to niche tastes and generalised topics – history, speed, golf, hockey, news, more news, just local news, food, the home and the great outdoors, which most viewers aren't seeing much of. A rash of digital channels launched in 2001 break down the market even further and in some cases spawned entire channels from an existing TV show (Fashion Television – the Channel). Whether anyone is watching is rather beside the point as broadcasters grasp to control their corner of the TV band.

So, when you flick on the set and want a dose of Canadian TV, here are some of the better options: **CBC** (Channel 5) keeps Canadian content up front along with strong news and sports coverage. **CTV** (Channel 9) is the largest private broadcaster and relies heavily on US programming, as does **Global TV** (Channel 6,41). Citytv (Channel 57; see *pXXX* Citytv) has shaped cultural coverage with intelligent shows on film, media, fashion and music.

All US channels are available, and the main private broadcasters, CTC, Global and City, often simulcast prime-time US viewing.

Money

Each dollar is made up of 100 cents. Coin denominations include the one-cent penny (copper in colour), the 10-cent dime (silver, with the Bluenose schooner depicted), the 25-cent quarter (which usually features a caribou), the one-dollar loonie (gold-bronze in colour) and the two-dollar twoonie (two-tone nickel and aluminum with a polar bear depicted). Notes, or bills, come in denominations of $5 (blue), $10 (purple), $20 (green), $50 (pink) and $100 (brown). Lately, shops have begun refusing $50 and $100 bills because of counterfeit worries. The Bank of Canada recently changed the design of it $5 and $10 bills, and it's still common to use both designs.

ATMs

Known in Canada as ABMs (automatic bank machines), bank machines are ubiquitous. Your best bet is to use one operated by a major bank. Privately owned and operated machines are starting to pop up in bars and shops and while they may be handy, most charge an additional user fee of between $1-$2 (though Brits sometimes escape this).

Most ABMs are part of either the Interac, Plus or Cirrus network, so non-Canadians shouldn't have any trouble accessing their home account. But it's best to check in advance with your home bank to find out what the charge bands are.

For ABM locations, call one of the major banks (*see below* **Banks**).

Banks

CIBC
2 Bloor Street W, at Yonge Street, Church & Wellesley (416 231 5441/ www.cibc.com). Subway Bloor-Yonge. **Open** 8am-4pm Mon-Wed; 8am-5pm Thur, Fri; 10am-3pm Sat. **Map** p281 F4.
Branches: throughout the city.

Metro Credit Union
800 Bay Street, at College Street, University (416 252 5621/www. metrocu.com). Subway College/ streetcar 506. **Open** 9.30am-4pm Mon-Wed; 9.30am-6pm Thur, Fri.
Map p280 E5.
Branches: throughout the city.

Royal Bank
200 Bay Street, at King Street, Financial District (416 974 3940/www.royal bank.ca). Subway King/streetcar 504. **Open** 9am-5pm Mon-Fri.
Map p277/p278 E8.
Branches: throughout the city.

Scotiabank
222 Queen Street W, at McCaul Street, Entertainment District (416 866 6591/www.scotiabank.ca). Streetcar 501/subway Osgoode. **Open** 10am-4pm Mon-Thur; 10am-5pm Fri. **Map** p277 D7.
Branches: throughout the city.

TD Canada Trust
65 Wellesley Street E, at Church Street, Church & Wellesley (416 944 4135/www.tdcanadatrust.com). Subway Wellesley/streetcar 506. **Open** 9.30am-4pm Mon-Thur; 9.30am-5pm Fri. **Map** p281 F5.
Branches: throughout the city.

Bureaux de change

American Express
100 Front Street West, Fairmont Royal York, at University Avenue, Financial District (416 363 3883/www.americanexpress.ca). Subway St Andrew or Union. **Open** 8.30am-5.30pm Mon-Fri; 9am-4pm Sat. **Map** p277/p278 E8.
Branches: throughout the city.

Thomas Cook
2300 Yonge Street, at Eglinton Avenue, Davisville (416 486 7055/ www.thomascook.ca). Subway Eglinton. **Open** 9.30am-7pm Mon-Thur; 9.30am-5.30pm Fri; 9.30am-5pm Sat.
Branches: throughout the city.

Credit cards

Most businesses in Toronto take Visa, MasterCard and American Express. High-end shops and restaurants also accept Diners Club. You can make toll-free calls to report lost or stolen cards at the numbers below 24 hours a day, seven days a week:

American Express
1-800 668 2639.

Diner's Club
1-800 663 0284 standard card; 1-800 563 4653 Gold card; 1-800 363 3333 Silver card.

Discover
1-801 902 3100 (long-distance call).

MasterCard
1-800 307 7309.

Visa
1-800 847 2911.

Tax

Most goods and services bought in Ontario are subject to two taxes – the seven per cent federal Goods and Services Tax and the eight per cent Provincial Sales Tax. Both taxes are levied on just about everything you can imagine, other than books and most groceries, and even those are PST exempt only.

The good news is visitors are eligible for a GST refund on goods and short-term accommodations. Generally, you must have spent at least $200 to qualify. For more information, contact the Visitor Rebate Program at 1-800 668 4748 (within Canada) or 1-902 432 5608 (outside Canada), or visit the Canada Customs and Revenue Agency web site at www.ccra-adrc.gc.ca/visitors. Major shops will have information and claim forms on hand.

Natural hazards

Although it's no Los Angeles, Toronto's summertime smog will be a concern to elderly travellers or those with respiratory problems. Call the public health department at 416 392 0808 or log on to www. airquality ontario.com for current conditions. On heat alert days, which often coincide with smog alerts, when the mercury can hit 40°C (105°F), the elderly and people with respiratory problems are advised to stay somewhere cool and drink lots of water.

Opening hours

Opening hours vary depending on the business and time of year. Shops tend to open at around 10am and close around 6pm. Many stay open till 9pm from June to August. Banks generally open 9am to 5pm during the week. Many offer evening and weekend hours. Post offices generally open between 10am and 5pm.

Police stations

To report an emergency, dial 911. If it's not an emergency, call the police at 416 808 222. Toronto Police Service headquarters is at 40 College Street, at Bay. For more information consult www. torontopolice.on.ca.

Directory

Postal services

Mailing a standard-sized letter within Canada costs 48 cents for anything up to 30 grammes. Standard letters and postcards to the US cost 65¢ up to 30 grammes and standard letters anywhere outside Canada and the US $1.25 up to 30 grammes and $1.75 for between 30 and 50 grammes. For couriers, *see p248*.

Post offices

Canada Post
260 Adelaide Street E, at George Street, M5A 1N1, St Lawrence (416 865 1833/www.canadapost.ca). Streetcar 504. **Open** 9am-4pm Mon-Fri; 10am-4pm Sat. **Credit** AmEx, MC, V. **Map** p278 G7.
Toronto's first post office – and one of its last. The days of the stand-alone post office are numbered here, so check pharmacies and general stores for post office counters (use the website to find addresses). Stamps, however, are available in most general stores and pharmacies. **Branches**: throughout the city.

Poste restante/general delivery

If you want to receive mail while in Toronto but lack a permanent address, you can have mail sent to you 'care of General Delivery' to any post office with a postal code. You must retrieve it within 15 days of it being received and show at least one piece of photo identification.

Religion

Anglican

Church of the Holy Trinity
10 Trinity Square, beside Toronto Eaton Centre, Dundas Square (416 598 4521/www.holytrinitytoronto. org). Subway Dundas/streetcar 505. **Services** 9am, 10.30am Sun; 12.15pm Wed. **Map** p277/p278 E7.

Baptist

Walmer Road Baptist Church
188 Lowther Avenue, at Spadina Avenue, The Annex (416 924

1121/www.walmer.ca). Subway Spadina/streetcar 510. **Service** 11am Sun. **Map** p280 C3.

Catholic

St Michael's Cathedral
65 Bond Street, at Shuter Street, Dundas Square (416 364 0234). Subway Dundas/streetcar 505. **Services** 7.30am, 8.30am, 12.10pm, 5.30pm Mon-Fri; 7am, 8.30am, 12.10pm, 5pm Sat; 8am, 9am, 10.30am, noon, 5pm, 9pm Sun. **Map** p277/p278 F7.

Jewish

Adath Israel Congregation
37 Southbourne Avenue, at Bathurst Street, North Side (416 635 5340/www.adathisrael.com). Bus 7/subway Wilson. **Services** generally 7am, 8pm daily; call for details.

Lutheran

Redeemer Lutheran Church
1691 Bloor Street W, at Keele Street, West End (416 766 1424). Subway Keele. **Service** 9.30am Sun.

Metropolitan

Metropolitan Community Church of Toronto
115 Simpson Avenue, at Howland Avenue, East Side (416 406 6228/www.mcctoronto.com). Streetcar 504, 505. **Services** 9am, 11am Sun. **Map** p279 K6.
A key player in the fight for gay marriage, MCC goes downtown for Pride Day services and a big Xmas Eve service at Roy Thomson Hall.

Muslim

Madina Masjid
1015 Danforth Avenue, at Donlands Avenue, East Side (416 465 7833). Subway Donlands. **Services** Prayers 5 times daily; call for details.

Pentecostal

Queensway Cathedral
1536 The Queensway, at Kipling Avenue, West End (416 255 0141/www.queenswaycathedral.com). Subway Kipling, then bus 44. **Services** 10.45am, 6pm Sun.

Presbyterian

Knox Presbyterian Church
630 Spadina Avenue, at Harbord Street, Harbord (416 921 8993/www.knoxtoronto.com). Streetcar 510/bus 94. **Services** 11am, 7pm Sun. **Map** p276/p280 C5.

United

Metropolitan United Church
56 Queen Street East, at Church Street, Dundas Square (416 363 0331/www.metunited.org). Subway Queen/streetcar 501. **Service** 11am Sun. **Map** p277/p278 F7.

Safety & security

Toronto is a safe city but common sense should always prevail.
● Don't walk around with valuables. Leave them in a hotel safe, and get a receipt.
● Pulling out a map on a street corner is an invitation to trouble, so don't do it.
● The homeless people collecting change on the streets are mostly harmless. Most sit on the street and never move. Still, it pays to be cautious, so stay away from anyone who gives you a bad vibe.
● Don't carry all your cash or cards with you at one time. Travellers' cheques are accepted almost everywhere.

Smoking

Smoking is prohibited just about everywhere but in the open air in Toronto. That includes all offices, malls, shops and, since 2001, restaurants. Some restaurants have designated smoking sections, which now must be enclosed and ventilated, but that's the only place you can light up. Patios are still by and large open to smokers. Adult-only bars are still open to smoking (although that's expected to change some time in the near future).

Study

Universities

To study in Canada, foreign students need a study permit. Depending on which country you come from, a temporary visa may also be required. Applications are through your local Canadian embassy or high consulate (*see p262*).

Ryerson University

University *350 Victoria Street, at Gould Street, Dundas Square (416 979 5000/www.ryerson.ca). Subway Dundas/streetcar 505.* **Map** p277/p278 F7.
Students union *RyeSac, 380 Victoria Street, Room A62, at Gould Street, Dundas Square (416 507 0723/www.ryesac.ca). Subway Dundas/streetcar 505.* **Map** p277/p278 E7.
Although it is often sneered at by those at the city's older and stuffier universities (it only became an official, degree-granting school in the 1990s), Ryerson draws on its background as a polytechnic institute to deliver first-rate hands-on learning in the heart of city. The school is best-known for its journalism, fashion and computer programmes.

University of Toronto

University *416 978 2011/www.utoronto.ca. Subway St George, Spadina/streetcar 506.*
Students' union *Students' Administrative Council, 12 Hart House Circle, University (416 978 4911/www.sac.utoronto.ca). Subway St George.* **Map** p280/p274 D5.
The closest thing Canada has to an Ivy League institution, U of T consistently ranks among the country's top schools. It's also one of the best-funded schools around, thanks to an incredible fundraising department, so it has the best facilities for every kind of programme you can think of, from medicine to law to Celtic studies.

York University

University *4700 Keele Street, North Side (416 736 2100/www.yorku.ca).*
Students' union *York Federation of Students, 336 Student Centre, North Side (416 736 5324/www.yfs.on.ca).* **Both** *Subway Downsview then bus 106.*
York would have a better reputation if it weren't so far from downtown and if it didn't have such an ugly, bleak campus, which is what people talk about most often when they talk

about York. That said, it is well-regarded and is as known as much for its lefty women's and environmental studies programmes as its more conservative business and law schools.

Telephones

Dialling & codes

Greater Toronto has three area codes: 416, 905 and 647. Generally, businesses and residences in the city have 416 numbers, while those outside the city proper (Mississauga, Richmond Hill, Markham, Pickering) have 905 numbers. The 647 code was introduced in 2001, so it's still unusual, and isn't location-specific.

Keep in mind that as well as being a local code, 905 is also a long-distance code for southern Ontario cities such as Oshawa and Hamilton. Dialling numbers in those cities means dialling a 1 before the code and paying a long-distance charge.

The following codes are all toll-free: 800, 888, 877, 866.

Making a call

All calls within Toronto must be dialled by using a 10-digit number (the first three are the area code; dial it even if you share it). To make a long-distance call in Canada or to North America, dial 1, the area code, and then the seven-digit phone number. To call overseas, dial 011, the country code, then the number (in some cases dropping the initial zero). The country code for the **UK** is 44, for **Australia** it's 61, **New Zealand** 64, **Republic of Ireland** 353 and **South Africa** 27.

Public phones

If you can find one, payphones cost 25¢ per local call. Bell and the private sector are fighting over the loose-change business. A Bell pre-paid phonecard available from most phone shops, grocery stores and pharmacies works only in Bell phones. Dial-in phonecards, Bell's included, are widely available and your best bet for long-distance and international calls.

Operator services

Dial 0 from any phone to speak to an operator (free from payphones). Dial 00 for the international operator.

Telephone directories

To find a number, dial 411 for information from any phone. It will cost 25¢ from a pay phone or 75¢ from

a private phone (unless your listing can't be found, then it's free). Don't be surprised if you end up talking to a computer. If the speech-recognition technology fails, a human operator is patched through to you.

Mobile phones

As in the US, Canada's mobile phone (cellphone) network operates on 1900 megahertz. This means that depending on their billing plan US travellers should be able to use their usual handset (though should check their tariffs for costs). Few UK mobiles will work in North America – you'll need a tri-band or 'world phone' – but even if you don't have one, contact your service providers to find out if they have a way around it. Some will arrange for you to have a temporary phone while away.

If none of this works for you, you have three options. If you're a frequent visitor, you could consider setting up your own local account, though this is unlikely to be worthwhile. A better option would probably be to buy a pay-as-you-go-phone, starting at around $150-$175. One of the local carriers, **Fido**, **Bell Mobility**, **Rogers AT&T** or **Telus Mobility** will be able to help you with either of these options. Their outlets are ubiquitous. Alternatively, you could rent a phone via your hotel or from a private company such as **Hello, Anywhere** (416 367 4355 or 1-888 729 4355/www.helloanywhere.com; credit card required) or **Cell Express** (905 812 1307 or 1-877 626 0216/www.cell-express.com; credit card or $500 deposit required), which deliver phones to your hotel for $35-$50 a week ($60-$80 a month).

Faxes

Fax services are available in most corner stores, but you'll get a better price at a copy shop. See p162.

Telegrams

American Telegram

1-800 824 7363/www.american telegram.com. **Open** 24hrs daily.

Time

Toronto is in the Eastern Time Zone – just like New York – which is five hours behind Greenwich Mean Time. Daylight Saving begins at 2am on the first Sunday in April and ends at 2am on the last Sunday in October.

Tipping

Tipping is expected and, for the most part, deserved in by Toronto workers. Restaurant and bar staff have a lower minimum wage than most Canadians because they're expected to make up for it in tips. Generally, tip 15 per cent on meals (add the Provincial Sales Tax and Goods and Services Tax on your bill) and a buck or two on drinks at a bar. Hotel cleaning staff and bellhops also deserve a buck or two. Hairdressers expect tips of between 10 and 20 per cent.

Toilets

Public toilets are scarce in Toronto, so your best bet is to use one in a restaurant or coffee shop, though note that most are reserved for customers.

Tourist information

While both the city and state tourist boards have excellent websites (visit them to have copious info sent), their offices are a bit basic.

Tourism Ontario
Level 1, Toronto Eaton Centre, 1 Dundas Street W, at Yonge Street, Dundas Square (905 282 1721/1-800 668 2746/http://ontariotravel. net). Streetcar 501, 505/subway Dundas or Queen. **Open** 10am-9pm Mon-Fri; 9.30am-7pm Sat; noon-6pm Sun. **Map** p277/p278 F6.

Tourism Toronto
Queen's Quay Terminal, 207 Queen's Quay West, at York Street (416 203 2600/1-800 363 1990/www.toronto

tourism.com). Subway Union/ Streetcar 509, 510. **Open** 10am-4pm Mon-Sat; noon-4pm Sun. **Map** p277/p278 E9.

Visas & immigration

Visitors to Canada may stay here for six months at a time. Residents of Britain, the US, Australia, New Zealand and Ireland do not need visas to visit Canada, though conditions can change without warning. For up-to-date information, see www. cic.gc.ca/english/visit/visas. html or contact the Canadian embassy or high commission in your country. For a list, log on to www.dfait-maeci.gc.ca/ world/embassies/menu-en.asp.

Weights & measures

Canada uses the metric system. 1 centimetre = 0.394 inches
1 metre = 3.28 feet
1 sq metre = 1.196 sq yards
1 kilometre = 0.62 miles
1 kilogramme = 2.2 pounds
1 litre = 1.76 UK pints, 2.113 US pints

When to go

Climate

Toronto has one of the mildest climates in the country, thanks to the moderating effects of Lake Ontario. And winter is never as bad as you've heard: the city gets less snow than it used to – usually in the 10 centimetre

(4 inch) range – and has seen more slush than snowbanks in recent years. Toronto gets plenty of sunshine year-round and is generally temperate.

Public holidays

New Year's Day (1 Jan; if a Sun, then holiday is the following Mon); **Victoria Day** (24 May if a Mon, otherwise preceding Mon); **Canada Day** (1 Jul); **Simcoe Day** (1st Mon Aug); **Labour Day** (1st Mon Sept); **Thanksgiving** (2nd Mon Oct); **Christmas** (25 Dec); **Boxing Day** (26 Dec). **Good Friday** and **Easter Monday** are also holidays. While government offices and most banks close on **Remembrance Day** (11 Nov), most businesses remain open.

Women

Toronto is as safe a city for women as most other cities its size in North America. Women travelling alone are unlikely to have any trouble, but it's still a good idea to use common sense and avoid deserted streets after dark. It's also a good idea to keep an eye on your drink while at the bar – use of Rohypnol (the 'date-rape drug') isn't as widespread here as in some major US cities, but it's not unheard of.

For helplines, *see p.156*.

National Action Committee on the Status of Women
234 Eglinton Avenue E, Forest Hill (416 932 1718/www.nac-cca.ca) Subway Eglinton. **Open** 9am-5pm Mon-Fri.

Working in Toronto

To work legally in Canada, non-nationals need a temporary work permit from Citizenship and Immigration Canada. Regulations are very stringent; among other criteria you have to convince the authoritiesthat the job you have lined up could not be done by a Canadian. For more information, contact Citizenship and Immigration Canada (www.cig.ca) or your local embassy of high Commission (*see above*).

Average temperatures

	High (C/F)	Low (C/F)			
Jan	-1°/30°	-7°/19°	June	23°/73°	15°/59°
Feb	0°/32°	-6°/21°	July	26°/78°	18°/64°
Mar	5°/41°	-2°/28°	Aug	25°/77°	17°/62°
Apr	11°/51°	4°/39°	Sept	20°/68°	13°/55°
May	19°/66°	10°/50°	Oct	14°/57°	7°/44°
			Nov	7°/44°	2°/35°
			Dec	2°/35°	-4°/24°

Directory

Further Reference

See also p26 Literary Toronto.

Books

Fiction

Margaret Atwood *Alias Grace; Cat's Eye; The Edible Woman; The Robber Bride.* See p27.

Robertson Davies *The Fifth Business; The Rebel Angels; What's Bred in the Bone; The Manticore.* See p28.

Timothy Findley *The Wars* See p28. *Headhunter*, an updated take on Joseph Conrad's Heart of Darkness is set – where else? – Toronto.

Anne Michaels
Fugitive Pieces
This multiple-award winning debut novel starts in Poland during the World War II and moves to Toronto, to explore memory, loss and landscape. Movie on the way.

Michael Ondaatje *In the Skin of a Lion.* See p28.

Jane Urquhart *Away*
This haunting tale by the master of what some have called 'southern Ontario gothic', tells a story that begins in Ireland and ends in early-days Toronto.

Gwendolyn MacEwen
Selected Poetry
One of the city's better-known poets, MacEwen evokes Toronto in the 1960s and 1970s. Edited by Margaret Atwood.

Non-fiction

Max Allen (ed) *Ideas that Matter: The Worlds of Jane Jacobs*
Based on a radio documentary about the life of this influential critic of the urban landscape.

Eric Arthur *Toronto: No Mean City*
Still the definitive history of Toronto's architectural history 40 years after it was published. An updated edition places the city's growth in context.

Marc Baraness and Larry Richards (eds) *Toronto Places: A Context for Urban Design*
An omnibus account of the mistakes and milestones of Toronto's rapid growth.

Pierre Burton *Niagara: A History of the Falls*
An absorbing confection of geological and human history.

Nancy Byrtus, et al *East/ West: A Guide to Where People Live in Downtown Toronto*
An appreciation of architecture from the perspective of the places people choose to live.

William Dendy *Lost Toronto*
This nostalgic look at the Toronto lost to the wrecking ball – food for thought for what might have been.

Robert Fulford *Accidental City: The Transformation of Toronto*
A personal look at the city's coming of age which begins, the writer argues, with the international competition to design the new City Hall.

Mike Filey *Mount Pleasant Cemetery*
This prolific Toronto historian digs dirt in one the city's best-known cemeteries.

Edith G Firth *Toronto in Art*
150 years in the city through the eyes of artists.

Greg Gatenby *Toronto: A Literary Guide*
Discover the haunts of home-grown scribes and landmarks noted by visiting writers through the 20th century.

Richard Harris *Unplanned Suburbs: Toronto's American Tragedy 1900-1950*
A urban sociologist smashes myths about Toronto's idealised suburbs and concludes they're no better than the typical North American, developer-driven nightmare.

Tony Ruprecht *Toronto's Many Faces*
A guide to the history of 60 cultural communities.

Rudy Cristle/David Crombie
Toronto the Celebration
Today's city lovingly photographed with text by former mayor Crombie.

Brian D Johnson
Brave Films, Wild Nights: 25 Years of Festival Fever
A paparazzi-laden tribute to a quarter century of the Toronto International Film Festival.

Geoff Pevere and Greig Dymond *Mondo Canuck*
Didn't know they were Canadian? This cheeky, exhaustive tell-all puts Canuck celebs in the spotlight.

Ron Brown *Toronto's Lost Villages*
Illustrated history of Toronto before the sprawl.

John Sewell *Doors Open Toronto: Illuminating the City's Great Spaces*
A former city mayor provides architectural insights into the buildings that are part of the popular annual tour of the city's hidden treasures.

Lenny Wise & Allan Gould *Toronto Street Names: An Illustrated Guide to their Origins*
Ever wonder how the streets got their names (and why Spadina is hard to pronounce?). It's all in here.

Murray Seymour
Toronto's Ravines
Thirty-four walks in Toronto's leafy arteries.

Films

Ararat
(dir. Atom Egoyan 2002)
The acclaimed Toronto director (*The Sweet Hereafter*, *Exotica*) reaches back to his Armenian roots in a film within a film made in contemporary Toronto.

Eclipse
(dir. Jeremy Podeswa 1994)
Tale of sexual liaisons leading up to a solar eclipse.

Directory

Face-Off
(dir. George McCowan 1971)
Dated tale of romance between
a hockey pro and a hippy.
Some nice vintage street
scenes and hockey action.
Goin' Down the Road
(dir Don Shebib 1970)
Two drifters come to Yonge
Street in search of a better life.
A Canadian classic.
Hollywood Bollywood
(dir. Deeptha Metha 2002)
This cheesy musical comedy
celebrates the vibrant East
Indian culture in Toronto.
**I've Heard the
Mermaids Singing**
(dir. Patricia Rozema, 1987)
Tale of self-deprecating
secretary who lands a job in a
Toronto art gallery and must
deal with real self-delusion – a
favourite Canadian theme.
Last Night
(dir. Don McKellar 1998)
The apocalypse comes to
Toronto, sending a multi-culti
cast in all directions ruminating
on the meaning of it all.
Niagara
(dir. Henry Hathaway 1953)
The Falls are upstaged by the
presence of Marilyn Monroe in
this noirish murder tale with
great location shooting.
The Silent Partner
(dir. Daryl Duke 1978)
The Eaton Centre stars in
this offbeat thriller.
**Thirty-two Short Films
About Glenn Gould**
(dir. Francois Girard 1993)
An innovative bio-pic about
the legendary Toronto pianist.
Zero Patience
(dir. 1993 John Greyson)
The ghost of 'patient zero',
the air steward fingered for
bringing AIDS to North
America, stalks the city while
Victorian explorer Sir Richard
Burton tries to hold down a job
as a taxidermist.

Music

Songs
Bare Naked Ladies
'The Old Apartment'

Bruce Cockburn
'Coldest Night of the Year'
Larry Coryell 'Toronto
Under the Sign of Capricorn'.
Randy Coven 'Toronto Blues'
Murray McLaughlin
'Down By the Henry Moore'
Groucho Marx
'The Toronto Song'
Jackie Mittoo
'Toronto Express'
Mighty Sparrow
'Toronto Mas'
Max Webster
'Toronto Tontos'

Albums
Bruce Cockburn *Stealing
Fire* (1984)
The most successful album
from the onetime Yorkvillian
features 'If I Had a Rocket
Launcher' and 'Lovers in a
Dangerous Time'.
Jazz at Massey Hall (1953)
A legendary concert featuring
Charlie Parker, Dizzy Gillespie,
Art Powell, Charles Mingus and
Max Roach on the only night
they ever played together.
Holly Cole Trio *Girl Talk*
(1990)
A pleasing set from this
acclaimed local jazz singer.
Later album *Temptation* was a
set of songs by Tom Waits.
Cowboy Junkies *The Trinity
Session* (1988)
Easily the finest album from
the Timmins clan, *The Trinity
Sessions* was recorded live
to one microphone at the
Church of the Holy Trinity in
downtown Toronto.
Glenn Gould *A Sense of
Wonder* (2002)
A long overdue set that collects
Gould's two miraculous
recordings of Bach's *Goldberg
Variations* from 1955 and 1981.
Gordon Lightfoot
Songbook (1999)
More of the Yorkville folker
than you could ever need –
nearly 90 tracks over four CDs.
Martha & the Muffins
Far Away in Time (1988)
The apogee of the never-quite-
made it foursome, containing
the immortal 'EchoBeach'.

The Quintet *Jazz at Massey
Hall* (1953)
Charlie Parker and Dizzy
Gillespie together for the last
time on record.
Rolling Stones *Love You
Live* (1977)
Mick, Keef et al captured in
mid-1970s form live in Toronto.
Ron Sexsmith
Cobblestone Runway (2002)
The Toronto singer-
songwriter's fifth album (his
best remains his second, *Other
Songs*), and includes 'Dragonfly
on Bay Street', a disco song
about his pre-fame experiences
working as a messenger in
downtown Toronto.
The Tragically Hip *Up to
Here* (1989)
Start at the beginning or,
because the beginning wasn't
much cop, with the second
album from Ontario's finest,
still together after two decades.

Websites

www.city.toronto.on.ca
A comprehensive guide to all
kinds of attractions along with
an exhaustive history and
archive photos, put together by
the City of Toronto.
www.martiniboys.com
Decent nightlife reviews by a
group of nonprofessionals plus
good recipes for their
namesake cocktail.
**www.toronto-
underground.com**
A directory of shops, services
and entertainment resources
focusing on unique and
overlooked small businesses in
downtown Toronto.
www.jazz.fm
Tune into Canada's only all-
jazz radio station.
www.infiltration.org/
The website of the Toronto-
based underground infiltration
organisation goes down and
dirty underneath the city's
clean and not so mean streets.
www.cbc.ca
Explore the length and breath
of the country as it is covered
by the public broadcaster CBC.

Directory

Index

Index

Advertisers' Index

Place of interest and/or entertainment	
Railway & bus stations	
Parks	
Hospitals/universities	
Neighbourhood	MOSS PARK
Subway station	Ⓢ
Bus route	—75—
Streetcar route	—501—
Subway route	——

Maps

Toronto Overview

Ross Lord Park

FINCH AVE-W
Finch

NORTH YORK

Gibson House

North York Centre

York Cemetery

North York Civic Center

Seneca College-Finch Campus

FINCH AVE-E

VAN HORNE AVE

Fairview Mall

SHEPPARD AVE-W

Yonge-Sheppard

Earl Bales Park

Bayview
Bessarion
Leslie

North York General Hospital

Don Mills

MACDONALD-CARTIER EXPWY

SHEPPARD AVE-E

NORTH SIDE

Don Valley G.C.

YORK MILLS

401

Wilson

WILSON AVE
York Mills

YORK MILLS RD

West Don River

Donalds G.C.

Yorkdale Shopping Center

Yorkdale

FAIRLAWN AVE

Lawrence

LAWRENCE AVE-E

York University-Glendon Campus

DON MILLS

LAWRENCE AVE-E

LAWRENCE AVE-W

Lawrence West

Sunnybrook Hospital

Sunnybrook Park

Wigmore Park

EAST SIDE

Eglinton West

FOREST HILL

Eglinton

EGLINTON AVE-E

DAVISVILLE

Ontario Science Centre

LEASIDE

Flemingdon Park

EGLINTON AVE-E

O'CONNOR DR

Upper Canada College

Davisville

MILLWOOD RD

Ernest Thompson Seton Park

404

Mount Pleasant Cemetery

MOORE AVE

OVERLEA BL

Taylor Creek Park

Warder Woods

p280-281

ST CLAIR AVE-W

ST CLAIR AVE-E

Casa Loma

DAVENPORT RD

MIDTOWN

O'CONNOR DR

Riverdale Park

THE DANFORTH

Ossington

BLOOR ST-W

DANFORTH AVE

EAST SIDE

University of Toronto

p276-277

RIVERDALE

GERRARD ST-E

KINGSTON RD

COLLEGE ST

LITTLE INDIA

GERRARD ST-E

Toronto Western Hospital

DOWNTOWN TORONTO

DUNDAS ST-E

THE BEACH

RC Harris Filtration Plant

QUEEN ST-W

QUEEN ST-E

KING ST-W

Historic Fort York

SkyDome

KING ST-E

Union Station

CN Tower

LAKE SHORE BL-E

Ashbridge's Bay Park

hibition Park

Ontario Place

PORT OF TORONTO

p278-279

Toronto City Centre Airport

Toronto Inner Harbour

Centre Island

Clark Beach Park

Centreville Amusement Park

Toronto Outer Harbour

Tommy Thompson Park

0   2 miles

0   3 km

© Copyright Time Out Group 2003

Time Out Toronto Guide **275**

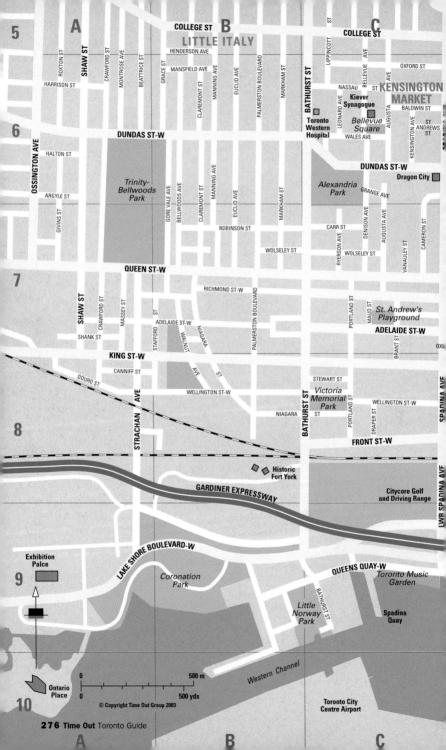

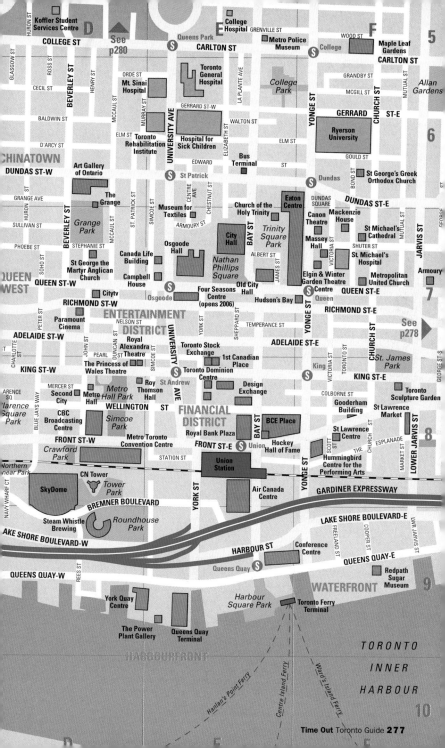

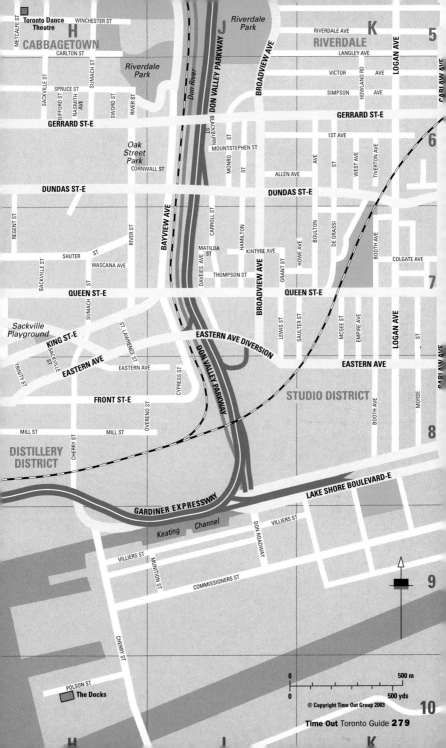

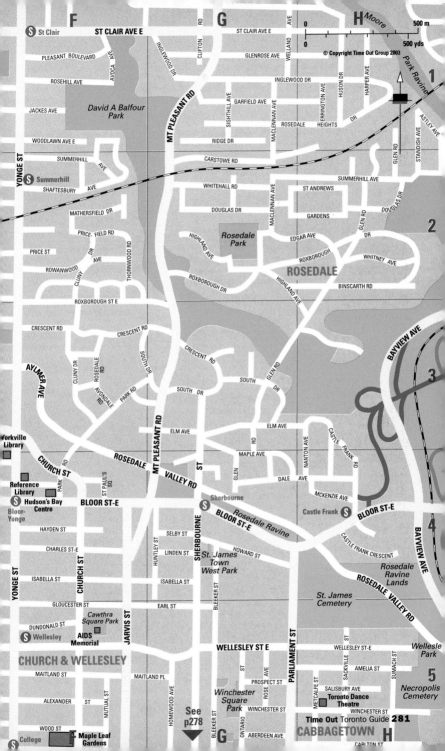

Street Index .